11th International Workshop on Tree Adjoining Grammars and Related Formalisms 2012 (TAG+11)

Paris, France
26 – 28 September 2012

ISBN: 978-1-5108-2682-3

Printed from e-media with permission by:

Curran Associates, Inc.
57 Morehouse Lane
Red Hook, NY 12571

Some format issues inherent in the e-media version may also appear in this print version.

Copyright© (2012) by the Association for Computational Linguistics
All rights reserved.

Printed by Curran Associates, Inc. (2016)

For permission requests, please contact the Association for Computational Linguistics
at the address below.

Association for Computational Linguistics
209 N. Eighth Street
Stroudsburg, Pennsylvania 18360

Phone: 1-570-476-8006
Fax: 1-570-476-0860

acl@aclweb.org

Additional copies of this publication are available from:

Curran Associates, Inc.
57 Morehouse Lane
Red Hook, NY 12571 USA
Phone: 845-758-0400
Fax: 845-758-2633
Email: curran@proceedings.com
Web: www.proceedings.com

Proceedings of the 11th International Workshop on

Tree Adjoining Grammars and Related Formalisms

26-28 September 2012
Paris, France

Production and Manufacturing by
INRIA, France

Eleventh International Workshop on Tree Adjoining Grammars and Related Formalisms
(TAG+11)
URL: `http://alpage.inria.fr/tagplus11`

Endorsed by

Sponsored by

Association
pour le Traitement
Automatique
des Langues

Preface

This volume contains papers accepted for presentation at the Eleventh International Workshop on Tree Adjoining Grammar and Related Formalisms, TAG+11 for short, to be held on September 26–28, 2012 in Paris. TAG+ is a biennial workshop series that fosters exchange of ideas among linguists, psycho-linguists and computer scientists interested in modeling natural language using formal grammars. The workshop series, since 1990, has demonstrated productive interactions among researchers and practitioners interested in various aspects of the tree adjoining grammar formalism and its relationship to other grammar formalisms, such as combinatory categorial grammar, dependency grammars, linear context-free rewriting systems, minimalist grammars, head-driven phrase structure grammars, and lexical functional grammars; hence the + in the name of the workshop.

We would like to thank the members of the program committee for their careful and timely work, especially those who participated in discussions on diverging reviews. This meeting would not have been possible without the hard work of all these people. We would also like to thank our invited speakers, Kevin Knight and Bonnie Webber, and the speakers at the tutorial program, David Chiang, Vera Demberg, Laura Kallmeyer and Andreas Maletti. We acknowledge the effort of these speakers in fostering new interest in TAG and more generally in formal research into natural language. Last but not least, we would like to thank the local organizers, Éric de la Clergerie, Djamé Seddah, Laurence Danlos and Chantal Girodon, for their invaluable contribution to the organization of the TAG+11 workshop in Paris, and for securing the necessary funding that made it possible to realize this workshop. We would also like to acknowledge the support staff at INRIA Paris Rocquencourt and at University Paris-Diderot. Funding for TAG+11 was provided by Google, the Association pour le Traitement Automatique des Langues (ATALA), INRIA Paris Rocquencourt, and University Paris-Diderot.

TAG+11 received 36 long abstract submissions from all over the world, and we were able to accept 28 papers out of these 36. This volume contains the 27 research papers to be presented at TAG+11 (one paper had been later withdrawn from the program). 19 papers are to be delivered in oral presentations and eight are to be presented as posters. As at previous TAG+ workshops, the topics addressed by the presentations belong to diverse areas of research, including mathematics of grammar formalisms, parsing algorithms for mildly context-sensitive grammars, language learnability, syntax and semantics of natural languages, and relation between TAG and other grammar formalisms. The oral presentations were thus organized into several different sessions: syntax/semantics, formalisms, derivation trees and applications, grammar extraction and grammar induction, and parsing. By bringing together these different topics under the common theme of Tree Adjoining Grammars, the workshop promises to be a venue for interesting discussion of the latest research in this area.

Chung-hye Han
Giorgio Satta
Program co-Chairs for TAG+11

Organizers

Program Chair:

Chung-Hye Han (Simon Fraser University, Canada)
Giorgio Satta (University of Padova, Italy)

Logistic Arrangements:

Éric Villemonte de la Clergerie (INRIA Paris Rocquencourt, France)
Djamé Seddah (University Paris Sorbonne Paris 4, France)
Laurence Danlos (University Paris Diderot, France)
Chantal Girodon (INRIA Paris Rocquencourt, France)

Programme Committee:

Srinivas Bangalore (AT&T Research, USA)
Rajesh Bhatt (University of Massachusetts at Amherst, USA)
David Chiang (USC Information Sciences Institute, USA)
Benoit Crabbé (University Paris-Diderot, France)
Robert Frank (Yale University, USA)
Claire Gardent (CNRS/LORIA, Nancy, France)
Daniel Gildea (University of Rochester, USA)
Julia Hockenmaier (University of Illinois at Urbana-Champaign, USA)
Liang Huang (USC Information Sciences Institute, USA)
Aravind Joshi (University of Pennsylvania, USA)
Laura Kallmeyer (University of Düsseldorf, Germany)
Makoto Kanazawa (National Institute of Informatics, Japan)
Alexander Koller (University of Potsdam, Germany)
Marco Kuhlmann (Uppsala University, Sweden)
Andreas Maletti (University of Stuttgart, Germany)
Yusuke Miyao (University of Tokyo, Japan)
Mark-Jan Nederhof (University of St Andrews, Scotland)
Steve DeNeefe (SDL Language Weaver, USA)
Owen Rambow (Columbia University, USA)
Maribel Romero (University of Konstanz, Germany)
Tatjana Scheffler (DFKI, Germany)
Anoop Sarkar (Simon Fraser University, Canada)
William Schuler (The Ohio State University, USA)
Stuart Shieber (Harvard University, USA)
Mark Steedman (University of Edinburgh, UK)
Matthew Stone (Rutgers University, USA)
Sylvain Salvati (INRIA Bordeaux Sud-Ouest, France)
Bonnie Webber (University of Edinburgh, Scotland)
Fei Xia (University of Washington, USA)

Invited Speakers:

Kevin Knight (University of Southern California, USA)
Bonnie Webber (University of Edinburgh, Scotland)

Tutorials:

David Chiang (USC Information Sciences Institute, USA)
Vera Demberg (Saarland University, Germany)
Laura Kallmeyer (University of Düsseldorf, Germany)
Andreas Maletti (University of Stuttgart, Germany)

Table of Contents

Conference Program

Wednesday, September 26th

9:15–9:30   Opening remarks

9:30–11:00   **Tutorial by David Chiang**
Synchronous Grammars

11:00–11:30   Coffee

11:30–13:00   **Tutorial by Vera Demberg**
Tree-Adjoining Grammars from a psycholinguistic perspective

13:00–14:30   Lunch

14:30–16:00   **Tutorial by Laura Kallmeyer**
LCFRS+: Linear Context-Free Rewriting Systems and Related Formalisms

16:00–16:30   Coffee

16:30–18:00   **Tutorial by Andreas Maletti**
Trees abound: A primer on tree automata and tree transducers

Thursday, September 27th

9:00–10:00   **Invited Talk by Bonnie Webber**
Alternatives, Discourse Semantics and Discourse Structure

10:00–10:20   Coffee

10:20–12:20   **Talk Session on Syntax/Semantics**

Delayed Tree-Locality, Set-locality, and Clitic Climbing
Joan Chen-Main, Tonia Bleam and Aravind Joshi

Deriving syntax-semantics mappings: node linking, type shifting and scope ambiguity
Dennis Ryan Storoshenko and Robert Frank

Tree Adjunction as Minimalist Lowering
Thomas Graf

A Frame-Based Semantics of Locative Alternation in LTAG
Yulia Zinova and Laura Kallmeyer

12:20–13:50   Lunch

Thursday, September 27th (continued)

13:50–15:20   **Talk Session on Formalisms**

A Logical Characterization of Extended TAGs
Uwe Mönnich

Synchronous Tree Unification Grammar
Timm Lichte

Synchronous Context-Free Tree Grammars
Mark-Jan Nederhof and Heiko Vogler

15:20–15:40   **Poster Quickfire Session**

Incremental Neo-Davidsonian semantic construction for TAG
Asad Sayeed and Vera Demberg

Representing Focus in LTAG
Kata Balogh

Describing São Tomense Using a Tree-Adjoining Meta-Grammar
Emmanuel Schang, Denys Duchier, Brunelle Magnana Ekoukou, Yannick Parmentier and
Simon Petitjean

*An Attempt Towards Learning Semantics: Distributional Learning of IO Context-Free Tree
Grammars*
Ryo Yoshinaka

15:40–16:30   Poster session and Coffee

16:30–18:00   **Talk Session on Derivation Trees and Applications**

Delayed Tree Locality and the Status of Derivation Structure
Joan Chen-Main

A Formal Model for Plausible Dependencies in Lexicalized Tree Adjoining Grammar
Laura Kallmeyer and Marco Kuhlmann

Using FB-LTAG Derivation Trees to Generate Transformation-Based Grammar Exercises
Claire Gardent and Laura Perez-Beltrachini

Friday, September 28th

9:00–10:00   **Invited Talk by Kevin Knight**
Transformation Frameworks for Machine Translation: Strings, Trees, and Graphs

10:00–10:30   Coffee

Friday, September 28th (continued)

10:30–12:30 **Talk Session on Parsing**

PLCFRS Parsing Revisited: Restricting the Fan-Out to Two
Wolfgang Maier, Miriam Kaeshammer and Laura Kallmeyer

Decomposing TAG Algorithms Using Simple Algebraizations
Alexander Koller and Marco Kuhlmann

Practical Parsing of Parallel Multiple Context-Free Grammars
Peter Ljunglöf

Idioms and extended transducers
Gregory M. Kobele

12:30–14:00 Lunch

14:00–15:30 **Talk Session on Grammar Extraction, Grammar Induction**

Creating a Tree Adjoining Grammar from a Multilayer Treebank
Rajesh Bhatt, Owen Rambow and Fei Xia

Search Space Properties for Learning a Class of Constraint-based Grammars
Smaranda Muresan

State-Split for Hypergraphs with an Application to Tree Adjoining Grammars
Johannes Osterholzer and Torsten Stüber

15:30–15:50 **Poster Quickfire Session**

Is Syntactic Binding Rational?
Thomas Graf and Natasha Abner

Incremental Derivations in CCG
Vera Demberg

On the Form-Meaning Relations Definable by CoTAGs
Gregory M. Kobele and Jens Michaelis

A linguistically-motivated 2-stage Tree to Graph Transformation
Corentin Ribeyre, Djamé Seddah and Éric Villemonte de la Clergerie

15:50–16:30 Poster session and Coffee

16:30–17:30 **Talk Session on Syntax/Semantics**

Scope Economy and TAG Locality
Michael Freedman

The Shape of Elementary Trees and Scope Possibilities in STAG
Robert Frank and Dennis Ryan Storoshenko

17:30–17:45 Closing remarks

Invited Talks

Transformation Frameworks for Machine Translation: Strings, Trees, and Graphs

Kevin Knight
University of Southern California, USA

Accurate machine translation (MT) of human languages is a longstanding challenge for computer science. Probabilistic string, tree, and graph automata provide nice formal frameworks for large-scale statistical MT systems. This talk addresses the power of these frameworks and how well they fit observed human translation data.

Alternatives, Discourse Semantics and Discourse Structure

Bonnie Webber
University of Edinburgh, Scotland

Sentence-level modality and negation give rise to "alternative" events and/or situations that contribute to discourse semantics in interesting ways. But they are not the only linguistic elements that do this. In this talk, I will try to characterise the range of elements that give rise to alternatives and the nature of these events and situations. I will then show how these alternatives are distinct from the coherence relations that provide a low-level of discourse structure.

Tutorials

Synchronous Grammars

David Chiang
USC Information Sciences Institute, USA

Synchronous context-free grammars (CFGs), first proposed in the 1960s, have become a popular and powerful tool in machine translation, semantic parsing, and other areas of natural language processing. Synchronous tree-adjoining grammars (TAGs) were first proposed in the 1990s and are starting to see interesting applications. The theory behind synchronous grammars, and the algorithms that power their applications, are sometimes natural extensions of those of conventional grammars, but there are also some surprising twists and turns. I will give an introduction to synchronous CFGs and TAGs, present some of their key formal properties, and describe the main algorithms that use them. I will also describe some synchronous grammar formalisms beyond synchronous TAG, like synchronous hyperedge replacement grammars.

Tree-Adjoining Grammars from a psycholinguistic perspective

Vera Demberg
Saarland University, Germany

We will first review some psycholinguistic experiments that are revealing about certain properties of human language comprehension, such as to what degree sentence processing is incremental and possibly even connected, as well as studies that indicate that humans actively predict upcoming input. We will thereby cover syntactic as well as semantic and discourse-level effects.

In the second part of the tutorial, I will discuss how these effects can be modelled using Tree-Adjoining Grammars.

LCFRS+: Linear Context-Free Rewriting Systems and Related Formalisms

Laura Kallmeyer
University of Düsseldorf, Germany

Recently, there has been an increased interest in Linear Context-Free Rewriting Systems (LCFRSs), due to their mild context-sensitivitiy and their capacity to describe discontinuous constituents and non-projective dependencies. LCFRS research has particularly intensified in the area of parsing.

In this tutorial, LCFRSs will be motivated and introduced. Furthermore, closely related formalisms such as Multiple Context-Free Grammars (MCFG) and simple Range Concatenation Grammars (RCG) will be defined and related to LCFRS. The link between LCFRS and the notion of mild context-sensitivity will be discussed and, in this context, the question whether one might even want to go beyond LCFRS will be raised. The more powerful formalisms of (unrestricted) RCG and Literal Movement Grammars (LMG) will be introduced that both are natural extensions of LCFRS, depending on whether the LCFRS rules are understood as manipulating strings or manipulating concrete occurrences of substrings of some input string. The former leads to LMG while the latter leads to RCG.

The aim of the tutorial is to give an overview of the formal grammar landscape ranging from CFG to LCFRS, RCG and LMG, relating the different types of rewriting rules and the different language classes defined by these formalisms. The expressive power and the limitations of these grammars are illustrated by numerous examples.

Trees abound: A primer on tree automata and tree transducers

Andreas Maletti
University of Stuttgart, Germany

We introduce tree automata and tree transducers formally and on examples. We also link them to the (synchronous) grammar notions that are better known in NLP. We then proceed to review most of the basic tree automata and tree transducer results with tie-ins into current results obtained in the NLP community. Finally, we cover some interesting advanced results that so far received little interest from the NLP community.

Delayed Tree-Locality, Set-locality, and Clitic Climbing

Joan Chen-Main*, Tonia Bleam+, and Aravind K. Joshi*

*Institute for Research in Cognitive Science
University of Pennsylvania
Philadelphia, PA 19104, USA
{chenmain, joshi)@seas.upenn.edu

+Department of Linguistics
University of Maryland
College Park, MD 20742, USA
tbleam@umd.edu

Abstract

Since Bleam's (2000) initial claim that capturing clitic climbing patterns in Romance requires the descriptive power of set-local MCTAG (Weir, 1988), alternative approaches to relaxing tree-locality restrictions have been developed, including delayed tree-local MCTAG (Chiang and Scheffler, 2008), which, unlike set-local MCTAG, is weakly equivalent to standard TAG. This paper compares 2-delayed tree-local MCTAG with set-local MCTAG in terms of how well the two formalisms can account for the clitic climbing data. We confirm that 2-delay tree-local MCTAG has the formal expressivity to cover the data by proposing an explicit grammar to do so. However, we also find that the constraint on set locality is particularly well-suited for capturing these clitic climbing patterns. I.e., though globally less restrictive, set-local MCTAG appears to be restrictive in just the right way in this specific case.

1 Introduction

Bleam (2000) argues that capturing patterns of clitic climbing in Spanish requires the descriptive power of set-local multi-component TAG (MCTAG) (Weir, 1988); the more restrictive tree-local MCTAG is not sufficient. Since Bleam's initial claim, alternative approaches to relaxing locality restrictions have been developed. Delayed tree local MCTAG, introduced by Chiang and Scheffler (2008), [1] is

one such proposal, but unlike set-local MCTAG, it is weakly equivalent to standard TAG. Each use of a multicomponent set introduces a *delay* into the derivation. A delay is the union of the paths in the derivation structure from each component of an MC-set S to the lowest node that dominates all members of S. A k-delayed tree-local MCTAG permits each node in the derivation structure to be a member of at most k delays. Fig. 1 replicates the example of a 2-delayed tree-local derivation given in Chiang and Scheffler (2008). The dashed boxes mark the delays. Thus, a valid k-delayed tree local MCTAG derivation permits members of the same MC set to compose into different trees, so long as all members of the MC set eventually compose into the same tree without exceeding k delays. Delayed tree-locality permits a limited amount of set-local composition, as illustrated in Fig.1, but it also permits some non-set-local derivational steps. 1-delayed and 2-delayed tree-local MCTAG have already been employed in linguistic analyses of anaphor binding (Chiang and Scheffler, 2008), non-local right node raising (Han et al., 2010), and binding variables (Storoshenko and Han, 2010).

This paper explores how well the additional descriptive power of 2-delayed tree-local MCTAG accommodates the available clitic climbing data and compares the new approach with the set-local MCTAG approach. In section 2, we review the data Bleam (2000) sought to account for. In section 3, we review why such data is problematic for tree-local MCTAG and

---

[1] As part of Chiang and Scheffler's proof showing the weak equivalence of delayed tree-local MCTAG to standard TAG, they show that any tree-local MC-TAG with flexible composition G can be converted into a 2-delayed tree-local MCTAG G' that is weakly equivalent to G and has exactly the same elementary structures as G. Described informally as *reverse adjoining* (Joshi et al. 2003), it recasts some previously non-tree-local derivations as abiding by tree-locality.

Proceedings of the 11th International Workshop on Tree Adjoining Grammars and Related Formalisms (TAG+11), pages 1–9,
Paris, September 2012.

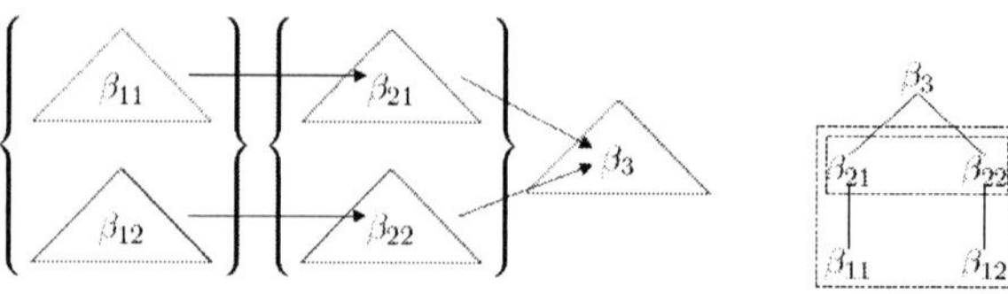

Figure 1: A 2-delayed tree-local MCTAG derivation. Delays are marked with dashed boxes. *(Figure taken from Chiang and Scheffler (2008).)*

present a set-local solution, slightly modified from Bleam (2000). In section 4, we provide and discuss a 2-delayed tree local MCTAG solution based on a small modification to our set-local MCTAG solution. In section 5, we show how the differences between the two MCTAG variants yield different predictions with respect to the number of clitics that can climb. However, the predictions turn out to be untestable given independent constraints on clitic clusters. In section 6, we conclude that though set-local MCTAG is particularly well-suited for modeling clitic climbing, we cannot escape the result that 2-delayed tree-local MCTAG eliminates the necessity of using set-local MCTAG.

2   Clitic Climbing in Romance

Spanish exhibits a phenomenon known as clitic climbing, whereby (one or more) pronominal clitics that are thematically dependent on a verb in an embedded clause can optionally appear in a higher clause. The phenomenon is illustrated in (1) and (2) where the clitic *lo* ("it") is thematically dependent on the verb *leer* (to read), but it can optionally "climb" or appear in the higher clause as in (2).

(1) Mari quiere leer-lo
     Mari wants to.read-it

(2) Mari lo quiere leer
     Mari it wants to.read

Clitic climbing is one consequence of the more general phenomenon often referred to as *restructuring* (Rizzi, 1982) or *clause reduction/union* (Aissen and Perlmutter, 1983). These are cases where two or more clauses act as a single clause for purposes of clitic placement, NP movement (as in reflexive passive or tough-movement), or scrambling (in German, eg.). Thus, dependencies (or "movements") that are usually clause-bounded are possible across clauses just in case the intervening predicates are all in the class of "trigger" predicates (Aissen and Perlmutter, 1983). Trigger predicates are those that select a "defective" or "reduced"

clausal complement, one that is tenseless, subjectless and that does not contain (intervening) functional elements such as sentential negation. In Bleam (2000), trigger verbs are analyzed as those that optionally select a VP complement (vs. a higher functional projection of the verb such as TP or CP).

As noted in Bleam (2000) and in other work, clitic climbing is unbounded. There appears to be no grammatical limit on the number of clauses that can be crossed by a clitic, as long as all of the intervening verbs are trigger verbs.[2]

(3) Juan quería dejar-**te** terminar de leer-**lo**
     Juan wanted to.let-you to.finish of to.read-it
     "Juan wanted to let you finish reading it"

(4) Juan **te lo** quería dejar terminar de leer.

Clitic clusters can involve two clitics that are thematically dependent in a single clause or they can be formed by clitics originating in different clauses, climbing into a single higher clause, as shown in (3)-(4) and (5)-(7).

(5) Mari quiere permitir-**te** ver-**lo**
     Mari wants to.permit-you to.see-it
     'Mari wants to permit you to see it.'

(6) Mari **te lo** quiere permitir ver

(7) Mari quiere permitir-**te-lo** ver

When there are multiple clitics originating in different clauses, the clitic originating in the lower clause can move up one clause to join the other clitic, as shown in (7), but cannot "move past" the clitic in the higher clause, as shown in (8), unless it carries the second clitic along.

(8)   *Mari lo quiere permitir-**te** ver

(9)   Mari **te** quiere permitir ver-**lo**

(10) *Mari **te** quiere permitir-**lo** ver

---

[2] Of course processing becomes more difficult as the number of clauses increases, but speakers appear to be able to handle up to at least four clauses without much difficulty. Examples in text are adapted from Bleam (2000).

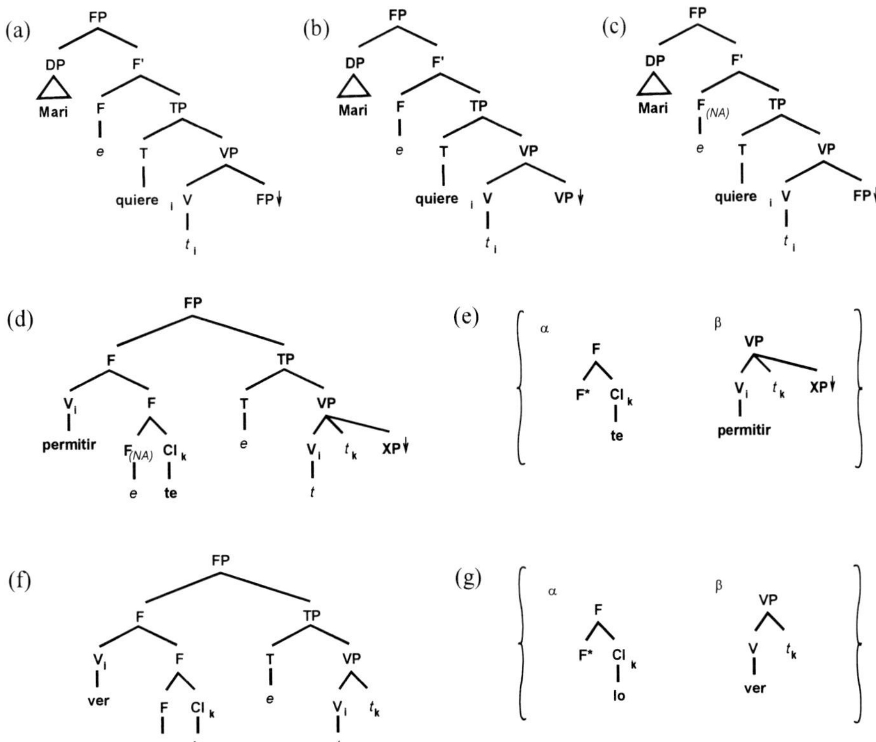

Figure 2: Grammar fragment for deriving patterns in (5) – (10). Three versions of *quiere* (a) used in the set-local account only, (b) used in both accounts, (c) used in the 2-delay tree-local account only; two versions of *permitir* (d) used when clitic remains low, (e) used when clitic climbs; two versions of *ver* (f) used when clitic remains low, (g) used when clitic climbs.

Further, while the higher clitic can move into the matrix clause leaving the lower clitic in situ, as in (9), it cannot do so if the lower clitic has moved into its clause, as shown in (10). These constraints on clitic clustering, or "bandwagon effects" (Bleam 2000)[3], suggest that there is a single position in the clause for clitics and that clitic clusters form a constituent.

3 Set-local MCTAG and Clitic Climbing in Romance

To account for the clitic climbing facts in Spanish (and for restructuring more generally), Bleam (2000) adopts a defective-complement analysis. In the MCTAG analysis, every non-finite clause with clitic arguments has two versions, illustrated for *permitir* ("to permit") in Figs. 2(d) and (e). 2(d) is a singleton set containing a contiguous tree containing the verb and its full extended projection[4], which also (necessarily) includes the dependent clitic(s) in a functional head which is agnostically labeled F. This version is the one utilized in cases where the clitic stays in the embedded clause in which it is thematically dependent. In the second version, Fig. 2(e), the tree set contains two components: one tree containing the verb in a VP projection, lacking its functional structure, and the other tree containing the dependent clitic (attached to a "higher" functional head). This version is used to derive cases of clitic climbing. Because the clitic is "loose," it is free to attach to the functional structure of a higher clause in the final derived tree. The linguistic intuition is that in the first case, the presence of higher functional structure in the same single tree with the verb provides a host site for the clitic and would entail a contiguous tree that included both verb and clitic.

---

[3] These phenomena were observed by Aissen and Perlmutter (1983) and fell out from their clause reduction analysis.

[4] I.e., in the sense of Grimshaw (1991), the functional projections that accompany a verb.

In the second case, the lack of higher functional structure necessitates a "loose" clitic in a separate component.

Trigger verbs (such as *querer* "to want") are clausal complement taking verbs that are flexible in the type of complement they take. They can either take a VP complement, in which case clitic climbing occurs due to the selection of the defective complement tree set (e.g. Fig. 2 (e) or (g)); or they can take a full FP complement (e.g. Fig. 2 (d) or (f)), in which case there will be no clitic climbing, due to the selection of the non-defective complement tree which necessarily contains the clitic. Note that the trees for the tensed trigger verb, *quiere*, in Figs. 2 (a) and (b), are exactly alike except that one takes an FP complement while the other takes a VP complement. [5,6] Non-trigger verbs (that do not trigger restructuring) will only have the option of taking a non-defective complement (FP or CP).

The set-local derivation of (6), where both clitics originate in separate clauses but end up clustering together in a single clause, is given in Fig. 3. The derivation involves the tree sets in Fig. 2 (b), (e), and (g). The VP tree for the most embedded verb, *ver*, substitutes into the VP node of the *permitir* tree, while the component with the clitic *lo* adjoins into the component with the clitic *te*. This creates a derived multi-component set, one component with the embedded verbs and the other with the clitics. The former substitutes into the VP verb complement position of the matrix tree and the latter adjoins into the F node of the same tree.

As should be clear from the derivation in Fig. 3, multi-component TAG is necessary to account for clitic climbing if we want to maintain the idea that a verb and its dependent clitic need to be represented in the same elementary object. Furthermore, as shown in Bleam (2000), set-local MCTAG permits an account for cases such as (6) that preserves the linguistic intuition that the clitics combine with one another to form a cluster, while tree-local MCTAG cannot. Although the more powerful set-local MCTAG must be adopted, requiring set-locality still constrains the possible derivations in ways that are linguistically relevant. Note that traditional

---

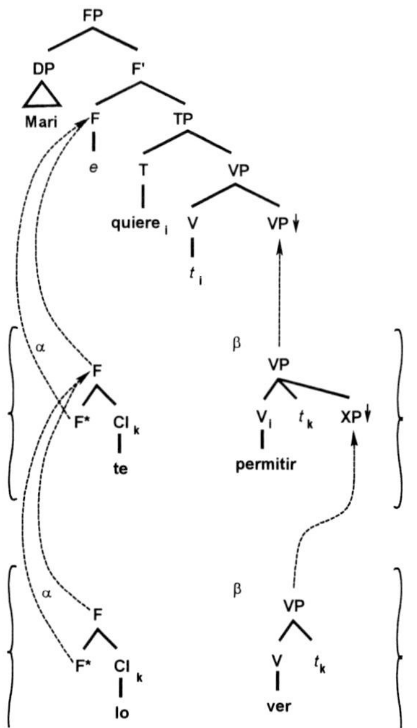

Figure 3: MCTAG derivation (set-local and also 2-delay tree-local) for climbed clitic clusters

set-local MCTAG does not allow for the *ver* component of Fig. 2(g) to substitute into the *permitir* tree in (d) while the component for the clitic *lo* remains unattached. The clitic may not "jump over" the *permitir* clause and adjoin directly into the matrix *quiere* tree. This non-set-local derivation is shown schematically in Fig. 4. Hence, clitics cannot climb past a clause without combining with other clitics in the intermediate clause, forcing them to all move together. Against a backdrop of reasonable linguistic assumptions, we see that the Bandwagon Effects are derived by the formal properties of set-local MCTAG.

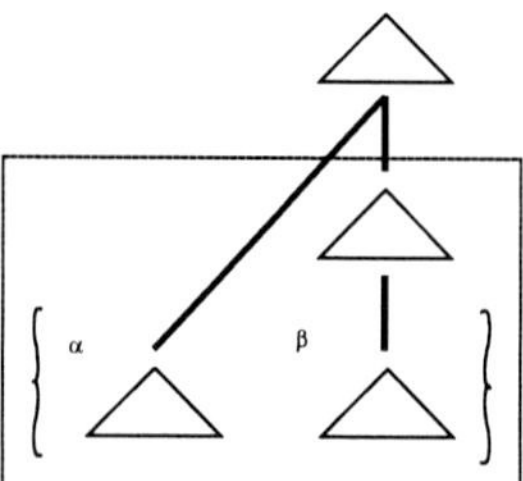

Figure 4: Derivation that is illegal in set-local MCTAG but legal in 2-delay tree-local MCTAG

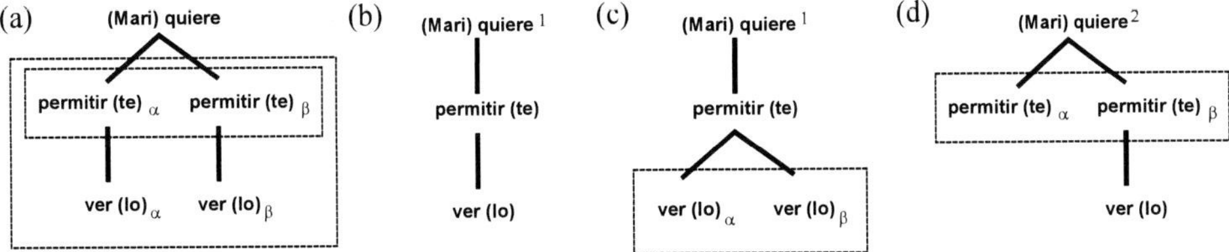

Figure 5. Derivation structures for examples (6), (5), (7), and (9), respectively, with delays marked

One final note is in order. Kulick (2000) identifies two types of constructions which he claims remain incorrectly prohibited by the Bleam analysis: constructions where clitic climbing co-occurs with raising or with long distance wh-movement. We show in Appendix A that set-local MCTAG actually is able to handle this data.

4 2-Delayed Tree-Local MCTAG and Clitic Climbing in Romance

Recall that in Bleam's set-local account, a sentence with two climbed clitics is formed by combining the two clitics and combining the two embedded predicates. This derivation is permitted in 2-delayed tree-local MCTAG. Fig.5(a) is the derivation tree for the derivation in Fig. 3 with delays marked. Note that the shape of Fig. 5(a) is exactly that of the example 2-delayed MCTAG derivation given in Fig.1. By considering the shapes of the derivations permitted by 2-delayed tree-local MCTAG, we can conclude that some account must be possible for the clitic climbing data presented here.

Recall also that it is the prohibition against the kind of derivation depicted in Fig. 4 in set-local MCTAG that ruled out the patterns exemplified by (8) and (10) where clitics ungrammatically do not cluster. Since the derivation in Fig. 4 is permitted by delayed tree-local MCTAG, the challenge for providing a 2-delayed MCTAG analysis of available clitic climbing data is how to avoid overgeneration.

It turns out that only a minor modification to the grammar fragment used for our set-local MCTAG account is needed to provide a 2-delayed tree-local MCTAG account of the data at hand. By adding a null adjoining constraint to the tree in Fig. 2(a), we obtain the tree in Fig. 2(c). Using the tree in Fig. 2(c) instead allows for the derivation of the grammatical patterns of clitic climbing in (5)-(7), and (9) while blocking the ungrammatical patterns in (8) and (10). Crucially, we assume clitics have a single position in the clause, which we represent here as an F node. (Thus, clitics adjoin to F but not V or T.) We maintain the general analysis of the two patterns of clitic placement utilized in the set local MCTAG account: When the clitic does not climb, the derivation involves a singleton tree set for the embedded verb which includes an F node for hosting a clitic. For examples (6), (7), and (9), when a clitic does climb, the derivation involves a set where the projection of the verb tree is too low to include an F node and the clitic is represented in a separate elementary tree. As in the set-local account, this captures the intuition that restructuring phenomena, such as clitic climbing, involves the selection of some type of reduced clause. Fig. 5 shows the derivation structures for the grammatical patterns in (5)-(7) and (9). The shapes of the derivations are, in fact, the same as those for set-local MCTAG, which the reader can verify.

Where the two accounts differ, however, is clearer when we consider how the unattested patterns in (8) and (10) are blocked. Let us consider the necessary tree sets for each example in turn. In (8), the clitic associated with the most embedded clause, *lo*, has climbed into the matrix clause while the clitic associated with the next highest clause, *te*, remains in its unclimbed post-verbal position. Since a successful derivation of (8) would require a host site for the climbed clitic *lo* in the matrix clause, the derivation would necessarily involve the tree set in Fig. 2(b). The quiere tree in 2(c) cannot host a clitic due to the null adjoining constraint on its F node. The postverbal position of *te* implies that the singleton set 2(d), whose root is labeled FP, should be used in deriving (8). However, Fig. 2(b) takes only a VP as *quiere*'s complement, not an FP, so the two sets cannot combine. Using the set in Fig. 2(e) instead will allow the component with *permitir* to substitute into *quiere*'s tree, but the component with the clitic will not have a position following *permitir* to adjoin into. Thus, neither available option for *permitir* and *te* will successfully yield (8).

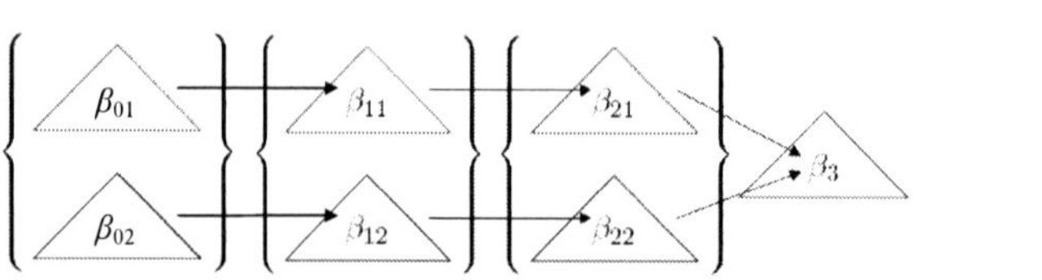 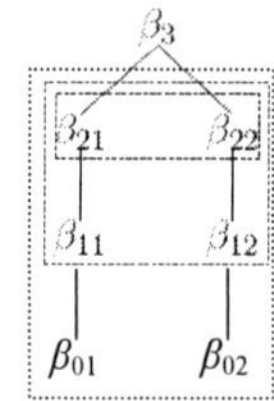

Figure 6. A 3-delayed tree-local MCTAG derivation. Delays are marked with dashed boxes.

In (10), the clitic associated with the most embedded clause, *lo*, has climbed into the next highest clause while the clitic associated with that clause, *te*, has climbed up to the matrix clause. As with (8), a successful derivation of (10) would require a host site for the climbed clitic in the matrix clause. Thus, the derivation would necessarily involve the tree in Fig. 2(b). Since both clitics climb, the derivation must involve the sets in Figs. 2(e) and (g), where the clitic is a separate component. This is unproblematic for deriving the positions for *permitir* and *te*: the *permitir* component substitutes into the VP node in the *quiere* tree while the *te* component adjoins into the F node. The *lo* component of Fig. 2(g), however, has no F node following *permitir* into which to adjoin. It can only adjoin into the F node of the *te* component or the F node of the matrix clause, which would yield the attested (6), not the unattested (10).

We see that our 2-delayed tree-local account depends on Fig. 2(b) having only VP (and not FP) as its verbal complement. That is, in this account, the possibility of taking an FP complement is linked to the presence of a null adjoining constraint, as instantiated in Fig. 2(c). It is the null adjoining constraint on the F node that blocks clitic climbing into the matrix clause, not the formal properties of 2-delayed tree-local MCAG. This machinery is available, but the use is not linguistically motivated beyond the goal of deriving the observed clitic climbing patterns.[7]

5 Clitic Clusters and a 2-Delayed Tree-Local MCTAG Prediction

As we have seen above, the set-local MCTAG account for climbed clusters of two clitics can be straightforwardly recast as a 2-delayed tree local MCTAG derivation. This does not, however, hold for the derivations of the two MCTAG variants in general. Consider, for example, the derivation in Figure 6. This is a straightforward set-local MCTAG derivation, but it is not a 2-delayed tree-local MCTAG derivation. Here, β_{21} and β_{22} are members of three delays, making it a 3-delayed tree-local MCTAG derivation.

In the context of clitic climbing, this translates into different predictions regarding the number of clitics that can originate in different clauses and form a climbed clitic cluster. The set-local account permits an unbounded number of multi-component clitic-verb sets to combine with each other, thus predicting that an unbounded number of clitics may form a climbed clitic cluster (in principle). In contrast, the 2-delayed MCTAG allows only two multi-component clitic-verb sets to combine with each other before combining into the same tree. This restriction predicts that it should not be possible to create a clitic cluster containing three clitics that originate in three different clauses and then climb into a fourth clause. More generally, a *k*-delayed tree-local MCTAG permits at most *k* clitics, each of which originates from a different clause, to form a climbed cluster. In testing this prediction, we find that speakers do not accept climbed clusters of greater than two, which appears at first to rule in favor of 2-delayed TL-MCTAG. However, this would only distinguish between the two variants if we could establish that clusters of three clitics are acceptable when they do not each originate from a separate clause. This turns out not to be the case: 3-clitic combinations are ruled out in cases where two of the clitics originate in one clause and the third clitic originates in a different clause, as shown in (11).

---

[7] Another option is to propose a *quiere* tree without an F node, i.e. we could posit that the matrix tree involved in clitic climbing is larger than the tree involved in non-climbing cases. However, the null adjoining account adopted above can also correctly rule out the the possibility of a clitic originating in clause 3 and moving to clause 1,crossing over an intermediate clitic from clause 2, when clause 1 itself contains a clitic.

    i)   Juan **te** permitió hacer**le** leer**lo**
    ii) *Juan **te lo** permitió hacer**le** leer.

(11) a. Juan no   quiere   permitir-**le**
     Juan neg   wants   to.permit 3p.dat
     escribir-**te-la**
     to.write- 2p-3p.fem.acc
     'Juan doesn't want to permit him/her to
     write it to you.'
   b. *Juan no quiere permitir-**se**[8]-**te-la** escribir
   c. *Juan no **se te la** quiere permitir escribir

The picture that emerges is that clusters of three clitics are difficult for speakers to accept for reasons that are independent of the combinatory operations that combine multiple clauses. Thus, Romance does not allow us to test the prediction due to restrictions on clitic clusters in general.[9] Although the data given here is inconclusive, the section serves to illustrate how the two MCTAG variants differ and identify the kind of data pattern that would distinguish between the two.

6 Conclusions

This paper demonstrates that although clitic climbing originally appeared to require formal power beyond that of tree-local MCTAG, the introduction of the weakly equivalent delayed tree-local MCTAG can account for the same body of data. Our set-local MCTAG account can, in fact, be translated into a 2-delayed tree-local MCTAG account with the addition of a null adjoining constraint to one of the trees in the set-local grammar: the *quiere* tree in Fig. 2(a) is replaced with the tree in Fig. 2(c). The 2-delayed account also retains the set-local account's reliance on the absence/presence of a functional node to host a clitic within the complement clause.

Where the two differ, however, is how the work of capturing the Bandwagon Effect is accomplished. In the set-local account, the Bandwagon Effects follow as a consequence of the permissible combinatory operations. Unattested patterns would require non-set-local derivations. In contrast, these non-set-local derivations are legal 2-delayed tree-local MCTAG derivations. The work of ruling these out to capture the Bandwagon Effects relies instead on the use of node labels and the null adjoining constraint. Both of these are legitimate,

computationally "safe" parts of TAG variants. However, as there is no obvious linguistic motivation for this particular use of a null adjoining constraint, from a linguist's standpoint, there is preference for the set-local analysis. It is interesting to note that despite its increased power in general, set-locality, in conjunction with linguistic facts, has just the right kind of restrictiveness to capture clitic climbing patterns, making the formalism a particularly good fit in this specific domain. This also suggests that we may wish to investigate other ways to modify tree-locality to permit a limited amount of set-local derivational steps with the goal of capturing the clitic climbing data more succinctly than the delayed tree-locality account given here.

The elegance of the set-local MCTAG account, however, should not obscure the conclusion that delayed tree-locality makes it possible to avoid the increased generative power of set-local MCTAG. We are aware of only two cases for which it has been argued that permitting set-local composition is necessary: clitic climbing in Romance, which we have discussed here, and double causatives in Japanese (Heycock, 1986). The shape of the set-local MCTAG derivation for the double causatives is the same as that given for a two-clitic cluster which has climbed. Just as the set-local analysis for the two-clitic cluster is also a legal 2-delayed tree-local analysis, so too is Heycock's set-local analysis for Japanese causatives a legal 2-delayed tree-local analysis. We are led to conclude that 2-delayed tree-local MCTAG eliminates the necessity of using set-local MCTAG not only for clitic climbing, but for all cases in which set-local composition was previously argued to be required.

Acknowledgments

We would like to thank the anonymous reviewers, Dave Kush, and Jeff Lidz for their helpful feedback, and Juan Uriagereka, Raffaella Zanuttini, Christina Tortora, Dave Kush, Ivana Mitrovec, Carmen Rio Rey and Leticia Pablos for their assistance with data.

Appendix A: Set-local Solutions for Clitic Climbing and Adjoined Predicates

Despite the increased derivational power of set-local MCTAG, Kulick (2000) identifies two types of constructions which he claims remain incorrectly prohibited by the Bleam (2000) analysis: constructions where clitic climbing

---

[8] This *le* is converted to *se* by a morphological rule known as the "Spurious se rule."

[9] The prediction also appears to be untestable in Serbian and Italian due to independent constraints. Thanks to Dave Kush, Ivana Mitrovic, Christina Tortora, and Raffaella Zanuttini (pc).

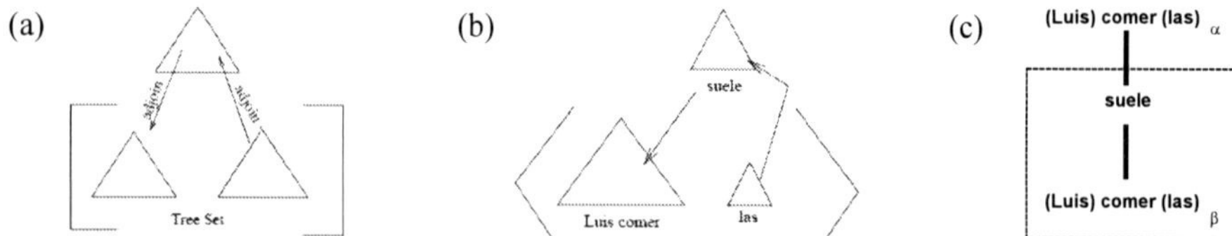

Figure 7: 1-delay tree-local MCTAG derivations which are not set-local. (a) schematic of derivation (b) schematic of derivation of clitic climbing with a raising verb (c) derivation structure with delay marked. *((a) and (b) taken from Kulick (2000))*

co-occurs with raising, as in (12), or with long distance *wh*-movement, as in (13).

(12) a. Luis suele comer-**las**
    b. Luis **las** suele comer
       Luis them tends to eat
       'Luis tends to eat them'

(13) a. Que quiere mostrar-**te** Juan
       What wants to-show-to-you Juan
       'What did Juan want to show to you?'
    b. Que **te** quiere mostrar Juan

The difficulty lies in combining the classic TAG accounts for raising and for *wh*-movement with the account developed for clitic climbing. In the former, both accounts involve adjoining of the matrix verb into the complement clause, thus "stretching apart" material in the lower clause. In the latter, clitic climbing is handled by positing an MC-set in which the clitic is its own component that adjoins into its host verbal element. A sentence like (12), then, would appear to require a derivation where the component for the clitic adjoins into the raising verb, which subsequently adjoins into the infinitival verb, the set-mate of the clitic. This is shown schematically in Fig. 7, taken from Kulick (2000). Such a derivation, where the clitic first combines into a tree while its set-mate remains uncombined, is not set-local.

However, as we show here, the tree set for "comer" assumed by Kulick is ruled out under Bleam's analysis. One of the key aspects of Bleam's (2000) analysis was that the size of the verb's tree determined whether the clitic was "loose" (instantiated as a separate tree in the tree set), and thus free to climb. Since the canonical position of the subject is above the position of the clitic, a tree anchored by comer and also having a position for a canonical subject must also contain a dependent clitic, as shown in Fig. 8(a). Thus, example (12), which combines raising and clitic climbing, will require trees as in

Fig. 8, where the raising verb suele adjoins in above the verb but below the clitic.[10]

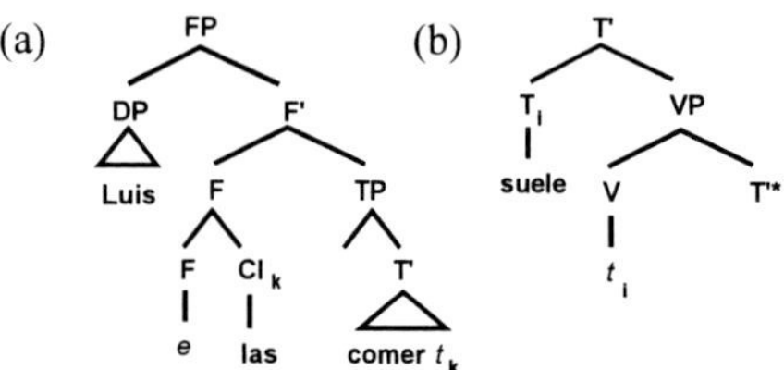

Figure 8: Trees for deriving example (12): cliting climbing co-occurs with raising.

The second type of example, (13), can be handled in a similar way, preserving the traditional TAG analysis of long distance *wh*-movement in which the verb and its dependent *wh*-expression (argument) are stretched apart through adjoining. Assuming that the *wh*-expression is in the specifier of CP (of the *mostrar* tree) and that the clitic is in a projection below CP, we posit a contiguous tree for the *mostrar* clause, and its *wh*-expression and clitic dependents, as in Fig. 9(a).

The matrix clause (*quiere*) must then adjoin in below the clitic. This requires us to adopt some crucial assumptions about the position of the post-verbal subject in *wh*-questions in Spanish.[11] We assume the canonical pre-verbal position of the subject to be the specifier of FP. However, the (non-canonical) post-verbal subject in *wh*-questions in Spanish (and Italian) has been argued to be in a lower position than that of canonical subjects (see Rizzi 1982, Torrego 1984, Suñer 1994). Following these standard sources, we posit the auxiliary tree in Fig. 9(b) for the matrix *quiere Juan* clause. In this tree the verb

---

[10] Note that *suele* is tensed and that tensed verbs are standardly assumed to move to T in Spanish; thus, we assume that root and foot nodes for the auxiliary tree for *suele* are TP (or T').

[11] Note that the position for the post-verbal subject "Juan" is assumed to originate in the elementary tree for "quiere" that becomes the matrix clause in this example.

(a)

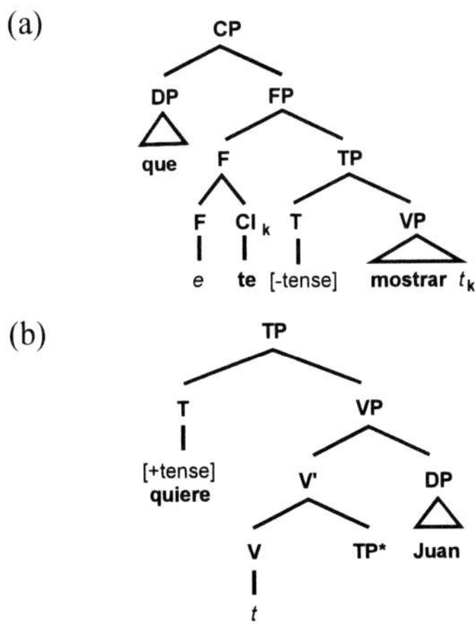

(b)

Figure 9: Trees for deriving example (13): cliting climbing co-occurs with *wh*-movement.

has moved past the subject, and the subject is a right-branching specifier of VP.[12]

Consequences of adopting this analysis to account for Kulick's data are (contra Blcam, 2000), (1) that not all cases of clitic climbing are a result of a "loose" clitic in a tree set; and (2) that not all infinitival verbs are in a pre-clitic position in the elementary tree.[13] But note that by adopting these relatively minor changes to the original analysis, the set-local analysis can handle these (apparent counter-) examples. In fact, for the particular examples mentioned here, tree-local MCTAG would be sufficient, but considering similar cases but with clitic climbing from multiple clauses would again require set-locality rather than tree-locality. It should be

---

[12] Alternatively, Ordoñez 1998 argues that, in general, VOS sentences in Spanish are derived via (a) movement of the verb to T, (b) the subject remaining in its base position, specifier of VP (left-branching), and (c) scrambling of the object (in this case a TP) to a position below T but above the in situ subject. This is illustrated below:

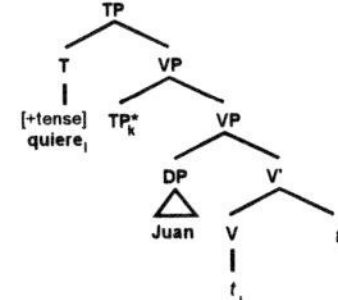

[13] Trees such as Fig. 8(a) will necessarily require adjoining of a tensed verb at TP in order to ensure appropriate case-licensing of the nominative subject and to ensure that the clitic has an appropriate verbal host. (In Spanish, clitics precede tensed verbs, but follow untensed verbs.) This can be accomplished via an obligatory adjoining constraint, plausibly as a top and bottom feature mismatch in a TAG system with features.

clear from the main text of the paper that these particular set-local MCTAG derivations are also legal 2-delayed tree-local MCTAG derivations.

References

Judith Aissen and David Perlmutter. 1983. Clause Reduction in Spanish. In D. Perlmutter (ed) *Studies in Relational Grammar.* (1976)

Tonia Bleam. 2000. Clitic climbing and the power of Tree Adjoining Grammer, In Anne Abeillé and Owen Rambow, eds., *Tree adjoining grammars: Formalisms, linguistic analysis, and processing,* 193-220. CSLI Publications, Stanford. (*1994*)

David Chiang and Tatjana Scheffler. 2008. Flexible Composition and Delayed Tree-Locality. In *Proceedings of TAG+9*, Tübingen, Germany.

Jane Grimshaw. 1991. *Extended projection.* Ms., Brandeis University, Waltham, Massachusetts.

Chung-Hye Han, David Potter, and Dennis Ryan Storoshenko. 2010. Non-local Right Node Raising: an Analysis Using Delayed Tree-Local MC-TAG. In *Proceedings of TAG+10*, New Haven, USA.

Caroline Heycock. 1986. *The structure of the Japanese causative.* Technical Report MS-CIS-87-55, University of Pennsylvania.

Aravind K. Joshi, Laura Kallmeyer, and Maribel Romero. 2003. Flexible composition in LTAG: quantifier scope and inverse linking. In H. Bunt and R. Muskens (eds.), *Computing Meaning* 3. Kluwer.

Seth Kulick. 2000. *Constraining Non-Local Dependencies in Tree Adjoining Grammar: Computational and Linguistic Perspectives.* PhD dissertation, University of Pennsylvania, Philadelphia, USA.

Francisco Ordoñez. 1998. Post-verbal Asymmetries in Spanish. *Natural Language and Linguistic Theory* 16, 313-346.

Luigi Rizzi. 1982. *Issues in Italian Syntax.* Foris.

Dennis Ryan Storoshenko and Chung-Hye Han. 2010. Binding Variables in English: An Analysis using Delayed Tree Locality. In *Proceedings of TAG+10*, New Haven, USA.

Margarita Suñer. 1994. V-Movement and the Licensing of Argumental Wh-Phrases in Spanish. *Natural Language and Linguistic Theory* 12, 335-372.

Esther Torrego. 1984. On Inversion in Spanish and Some of its Effects. *Linguistic Inquiry* 15, 103-129.

David Weir. 1988. *Characterizing mildly context-sensitive grammar formalisms.* PhD dissertation, University of Pennsylvania, Philadelphia, USA.

Deriving syntax-semantics mappings: node linking, type shifting and scope ambiguity

Dennis Ryan Storoshenko
Yale University
Department of Linguistics
370 Temple Street
New Haven, CT 06511
`dennis.storshenko@yale.edu`

Robert Frank
Yale University
Department of Linguistics
370 Temple Street
New Haven, CT 06511
`robert.frank@yale.edu`

Abstract

In this paper, we introduce a type-shifting operation which provides a principled means of describing the derivational links required in Synchronous TAG accounts of quantification. No longer do links appear on root nodes of predicates on an *ad hoc* basis, rather they are generated as a part of a type-shifting mechanism over arguments of the predicate. By introducing to the system a set of temporal variables, we show how this operation can also be used to account for the scope interactions of clausal embedding. We then move on to consider additional cases of multiple clausal embedding and coordination.

1 The Issue

Investigations of the syntax-semantics interface in Tree Adjoining Grammar, particularly those making use of Synchronous TAG, grapple with the limitations imposed by the restrictiveness of tree- or set-local MCTAG. To the degree that they successfully treat the mapping between syntax and semantics in this restricted setting, this provides evidence in favor of Joshi's hypothesis that the mild context-sensitivity of TAG is a fundamental property of grammar. Nonetheless, the analyses that have been put forward are at times ad hoc. One wonders why a certain semantic object is associated with some piece of syntax, and why certain nodes of the syntactic representations are linked to the semantics in one manner as opposed to another. In this paper, we report on our first efforts to formulate principles governing STAG pairings, in an effort to provide a more restrictive framework for characterizing STAG-derivable syntax-semantics mappings.

2 Tree Shapes and Type Shifting

We adopt a traditional view of syntactic elementary trees as the realization of a single lexical predicate and its grammatical "associates" (cf. the Condition on Elementary Tree Minimality and Theta Criterion of Frank (2002)). The corresponding semantic objects are composed from the meaning assignments for the lexical anchor together with the meanings associated with non-projected non-terminals. Substitution nodes are interpreted as typed variables (with types determined by a bijection from syntactic categories to semantic types: DP to type e, NP to type $\langle e, t \rangle$, CP, TP and VP to type t, etc. We follow Pogodalla (2004) in assuming that such variables are bound by (linear) lambda operators, and take syntactic substitution of S into T to correspond to (semantic) function application of T to S. For a syntactic node N targeted for adjoining, we assume that the corresponding node in the semantic representation is embedded beneath an abstracted function variable (with type $\langle \alpha, \alpha \rangle$ where α is the type determined by the category bijection for N). Adjoining of auxiliary tree A to tree T corresponds to application of T to A. We assume that adjoining always applies at nodes to which it may; when no content is added, a semantic identity function is applied. Some linkages between the syntactic and semantic trees are straightforward: non-projected non-terminals are linked to the lambda operators binding their associated variables, while projected nodes in the syntax are linked to lambda operators binding variables of the appropriate $\langle \alpha, \alpha \rangle$ type. This gives rise to a pairing of the sort in Figure 1 for the transitive verb *love*.

What is less clear is how to establish the non-bijective linkages between sites for syntactic at-

Proceedings of the 11th International Workshop on Tree Adjoining Grammars and Related Formalisms (TAG+11), pages 10–18,
Paris, September 2012.

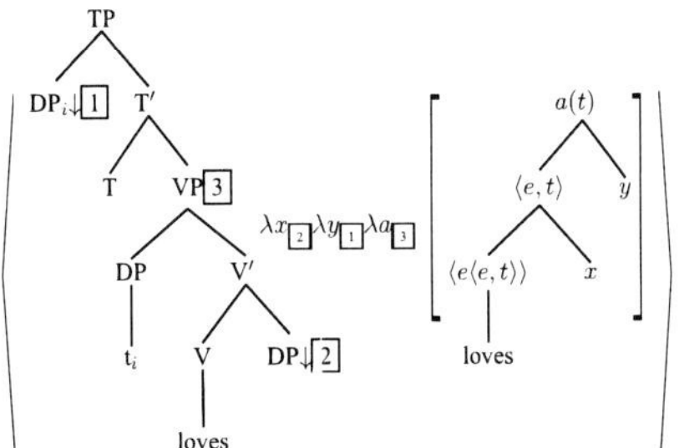

Figure 1: Syntactic and Semantic Tree Pair for *loves*

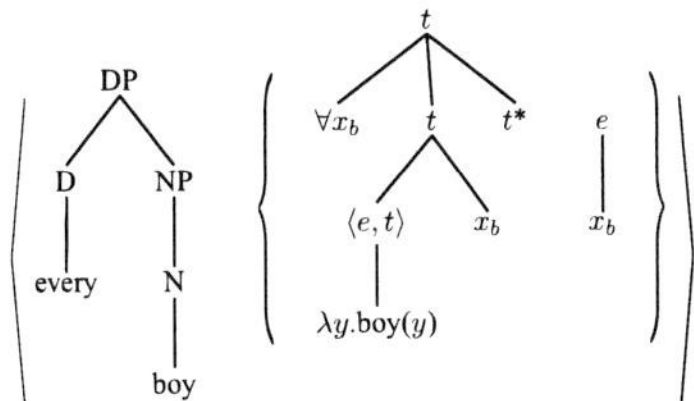

Figure 2: Tree Set for *every boy* (Schema for all Generalized Quantifiers)

tachment and semantic composition. Originating in Shieber and Schabes (1990), and continuing in all of the subsequent STAG-based work on scope we are aware of, it is assumed that the DP position in, say, the subject of a transitive verb-headed elementary tree is linked to both the e-type external argument of the predicate and the t-type root of the tree. This dual-linkage is mirrored in non-STAG accounts of quantification, such as the Hole Semantics-based account in Kallmeyer and Joshi (2003), and subsequent works in that tradition. No matter which type of semantic account the analyst prefers, it is widely accepted that quantification requires this simultaneous access to both an argument position and the root of a tree. Derivationally, this is of course simply a matter of tree-local MCS combination, but in STAG, there is the additional wrinkle of derivational links. Such multiple linkages are crucial for the establishment of scope for quantificational DPs, represented as multi-component sets (MCSs) in the semantics, but not the syntax, as in Figure 2. The variable component of this MCS substitutes into the e-type argument slot, while the t-recursive scope auxiliary tree adjoins at the semantic predicate's t root. It is difficult to see what within the verbal predicate itself directly motivates a link between the DP syntactic position and the t adjoining site in the semantics. We will assume that only the link-

age between the syntactic position and the semantic argument slot is basic, as given in Figure 1. Once these are established, semantic trees can undergo an operation that creates multiple linkages in a systematic fashion. Specifically, we make use of an operation similar to argument raising from Hendriks (1988). In Hendriks' operation, the type of an argument is lifted (Partee and Roth, 1983) from its basic e type to the generalized quantifier $\langle\langle e, t\rangle, t\rangle$ type, allowing a raised argument to effectively take scope over the predicate. Application of this operation to the internal argument of a two-place predicate is shown in (1).

(1) $\langle e, \langle e, t\rangle\rangle : f \Rightarrow$
$\langle e, \langle\langle\langle e, t\rangle, t\rangle, t\rangle :$
$\lambda x_e.\lambda T_{\langle\langle e, t\rangle, t\rangle}.T(\lambda y_e.f(y)(x))$

The lambda gymnastics involved here are substantial. We can accomplish a similar effect with the paired STAG structure in Figure 1 in a simpler way, if we allow one of the e-type arguments to be linked to a new functional $\langle\alpha, \alpha\rangle$ variable. We represent this linkage as the combination of two variables under the scope of a single lambda operator, as shown in Figure 3. We take such set-valued lambda operators to encode the fact that the arguments must be introduced in a single derivational step, via combination with a MCS. In order to ensure that the newly introduced functional variable Q does not disturb the surrounding semantic combinations, it is crucial that Q be type-preserving (i.e., of type $\langle\alpha, \alpha\rangle$ for some α).

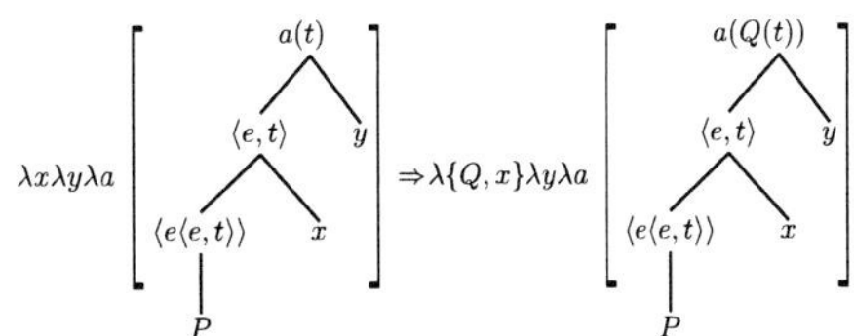

Figure 3: Schematic Example of Type Lifting in Trees (Shown for Internal Argument)

The linkage that has been widely exploited to handle quantifier interpretation fits this pattern: the e-type argument is linked with a $\langle t, t\rangle$ function variable, which will host its scope, shown in Figure 4. Whereas earlier accounts derived quantifier scope ambiguity through underspecified ordering of multiple adjoining at the root t-node of a verbal predicate's semantics, we derive the same ambiguity through underspecified ordering of type

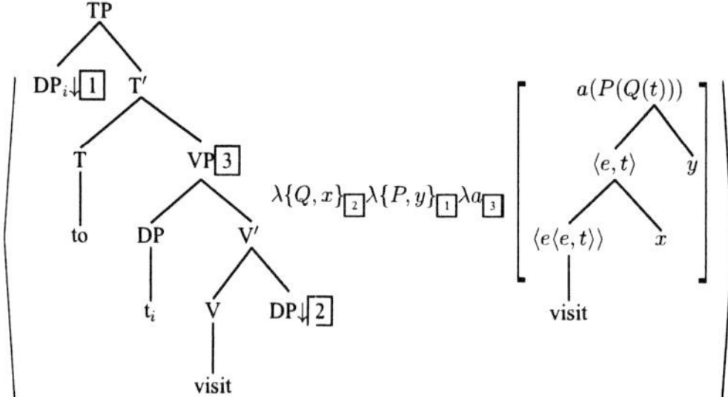

Figure 4: Syntactic and Semantic Tree Pair for *loves* (Type-lifted Internal Argument)

lifting operations, one for each of the predicate's arguments. These iterations of type-shifting take place after the construction of an elementary tree, but before the tree enters into any TAG combinatory operations. That is, the links (and their relative scopes) are all in place before any substitution or adjoining operations take place. What we have gained is that the additional non-bijective link which normally appears by stipulation now has a principled origin in the type-shifting operation which makes it possible for a semantic MCS to combine in a single derivational step.

3 Extending Beyond Quantifiers

Type lifting is not limited to linking e-type variables to quantificational scope. In principle, any argument slot can be linked to an arbitrary type-preserving function, so long as there is a MCS that can satisfy these two positions simultaneously. One case involves infinitival complements to control predicates. Under the analysis of control of Nesson and Shieber (2008), the control predicate's semantic representation is a MCS with an e-type variable to fill the embedded subject argument slot as well as a t-recursive auxiliary bearing the predicate's lexical content. Just as with quantifiers, we link the semantic slot for the e-type subject argument with the root t node, at which the embedding control predicate adjoins. Because this linkage is analogous to the one established in the case of quantifiers, we predict its interaction with other linkages to behave similarly. Specifically, we are led to expect that object quantifiers in the infinitival complement clause should be able to scope out of that clause, past the embedding control predicate (as well as quantifiers in the higher clause). This prediction is correct, as shown in (2).

(2) Someone wants to visit every European city. (want > ∀, ∀ > want)

The example is derivable using the tree set for the control predicate in Figure 6, along with trees for the embedded clause and for the quantifiers, all lexical variants of the trees in Figures 1 and 2. The embedded predicate is shown in Figure 5, with type-shifting having applied in the order which yields surface scope. Recall though that inverse scope is equally possible, as we place no restriction on the order of the applications of type-shifting. The derivation proceeds as in Figure 7, with the order of the two instances of type lifting over the arguments of *to visit* left unspecified.

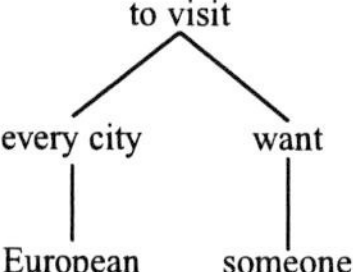

Figure 5: Non-finite predicate *to visit*, type-shifted for surface scope

Figure 7: Derivation Tree for (2)

The same scope facts are present in other examples of non-finite clausal embedding, such as raising and ECM, as in (3).

(3) a. Some member seems to like every amendment. (seems > ∀, ∀ > seems)

  b. Some member wants every minister to leave. (wants > ∀, ∀ > wants)

Stowell (1982) notes that unlike control, raising and ECM predicates temporally restrict the embedded clause. Matrix predicates routinely specify the embedded clause's temporal interpretation relative to the time of the higher clause, as in

(4) below: depending on the choice of the matrix predicate, the embedded event is understood to take place at a different relative time. For finite clausal complements as in (5), the temporal relation must be conveyed through tense marking in the embedded clause.

(4) a. John regrets missing your talk.
       (τ(missing-talk) $<$ now)

    b. John anticipates missing your talk.
       (τ(missing-talk) $>$ now)

(5) a. John regrets that he miss**ed** your talk.

    b. John anticipates that he **will** miss your talk.

It is straightforward to assume that the dependency in (3) results from the matrix predicate providing a temporal variable to the non-finite embedded clause. We implement this temporal variable using a simplified version of the presentation in Kusumoto (2005); most notably, we omit from our analysis additional situation variables also present in Kusumoto's analysis. This is done purely in the interest of keeping the semantics as clear as possible, and is not intended as an explicit claim that these variables are incompatible with the analysis.

We take the temporal dependency between clauses as in (3) and (4) to indicate multicomponent semantics in the matrix predicate, the use of which must be licensed by type lifting in the embedded clause. Once again, we should expect that this instance of type lifting can be interleaved with those for embedded quantificational arguments, predicting the observed scope facts. We illustrate using the ECM case (3b), beginning in Figure 8 with the elementary trees for the two predicates. ECM *want* is a MCS providing a temporal variable i of type τ, similar to a control predicate providing an argument of type e. The matrix predicate's temporal variable can be saturated by a temporal indexical, whose interpretation varies with the tense of the matrix clause. Crucial to our system is the notion that there is only one such indexical available per derivation. The embedded clause has a similar variable slot, but as just stated, it cannot be similarly filled by an indexical. By type lifting over this position, the ECM predicate may combine in exactly the same way as a quantifier. The derivation in Figure 9 yields the reported scope ambiguity through underspecification of the

order of type lifting in the embedded clause. A similar process yields (3a), using the trees in Figure 10, following the derivation in Figure 11.

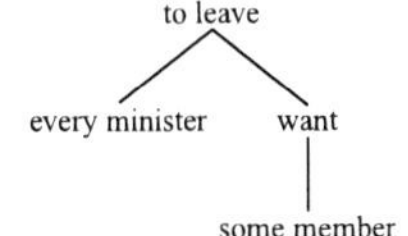

Figure 9: Derivation Tree for (3b)

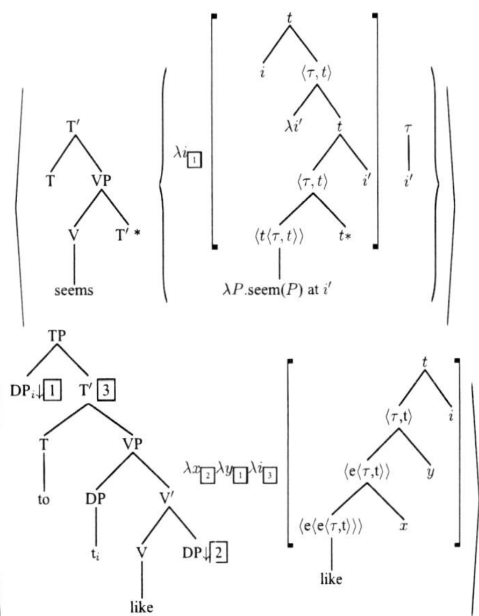

Figure 10: Elementary Trees for (3a)

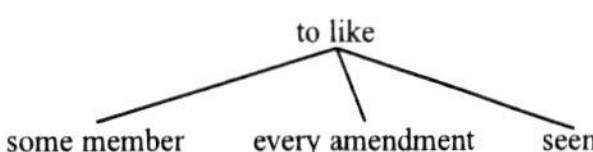

Figure 11: Derivation Tree for (3a)

4 Multiple Predicates

Thus far, we have limited our discussion to simple cases of single clause embedding; in this section we illustrate how the proposed system will interact with multiple embedding, and with coordination.

An example of multiple embedding is given in (6):

(6)   John wants Mary to be likely to win.

This is ECM *want*, which will, along with *to win*, use an elementary tree set essentially as in Figure

8. The raising predicate, for the moment, we assume will have the standard TAG syntax of recursion on T$'$, meaning that it is syntactically possible for both *wants* and *to be likely* to adjoin at different nodes in the *to win* tree. This raises two issues. Firstly, both the ECM and raising predicates would be adjoining at the same node in the semantics, predicting ambiguity between *wants* and *likely*. However, this ambiguity is not found, and only the surface scope of *wants* > *likely* is available. Secondly, there is an issue concerning the interval variables. The embedded predicate *to win* will have one open substitution site for an interval variable in its semantic elementary tree. However, both *likely* and *wants* have such a variable to pass on. It thus seems that under the proposed syntactic analysis, not only do we predict an unobserved ambiguity, but an interval variable will go unused.

To resolve this issue, we propose a tree set for the raising predicate as in Figure 12. Looking first at the semantics, as a clause which will adjoin into a non-finite clause, this passes down an interval variable, as described. However, this predicate itself also requires an interval argument of some sort to saturate its own type τ argument slot, and we assume that only one temporal indexical is available per derivation. If this indexical is to be substituted into the matrix ECM predicate, then that predicate's own interval variable must be the one which substitutes into the raising predicate. That is, *wants* must combine directly with *likely*, not *to win*. This is a welcome finding, as it also predicts the observed scope facts. This then leads us to discuss the syntax of this raising predicate; with an additional degenerate CP node which can serve as the destination of the ECM predicate, direct combination of *wants* into *likely* is now possible, with the CP-recursive *wants* auxiliary tree adjoining to the degenerate CP tree in the set associated with the raising predicate. Type-shifting over the interval variable position in *likely* allows the *wants* MCS to adjoin, and type-shifting over the interval variable in *to win* allows *likely* to adjoin, bringing the ECM predicate along, with both the T$'$- and CP-recursive adjoinings coming from one elementary tree set.

A slightly different problem arises when combining control with a raising predicate as in the similar (7):

(7)   John wants to be likely to win.

First, let us consider the scope facts. As in the previous case, there is only one possible reading here, the surface scope where *want* scopes over *likely*; it is not the case that John is likely to want to win, rather he wants to be likely to win. Thus, the same type of chained derivation would seem to be in order. However, there is an additional complication: we have already made the claim that control predicates pass down a type e argument to the clauses in which they adjoin, not type τ. As a raising predicate, *likely* should never take a type e argument unless an experiencer phrase is added. Further complicating matters is the fact that the type e variable provided by the control predicate is clearly an argument of *win*; this suggests that the derivation which we worked so hard to obviate in the previous case must be the only one available. Both *want* and *likely* should combine directly with the embedded predicate.

However, two new problems present themselves: firstly, given that these predicates will each combine via a type-shift, we predict again there to be a scope ambiguity, contrary to fact. Furthermore, there is the additional question of the open interval variable in the raising predicate. Assuming that *to be likely* here is of the same form as in Figure 12, then what will fill that argument position? We have already claimed that there is only one indexical available, and Stowell's observations make it clear that there is no temporal connection between a control predicate and the clause it embeds. In fact, this second question extends beyond this particular example. The elementary tree for the embedded clause in Figure 5 should likewise require an interval variable which is not provided by the matrix predicate.

To resolve this issue, we propose that non-finite predicates embedded under a control predicate contain a function INF from type $\langle \tau, t \rangle$ to t, given in (8):

(8) $\text{INF} = \lambda P.\Diamond \exists i_{Inf}.P(i_{Inf})$

This provides the necessary binding for the interval variable while remaining as non-committal as possible with regards to the actual existence of such an interval. We thus propose a revised version of the non-finite raising predicate as in Figure 13. Only to be used under a control predicate, this gives (local) wide scope to the INF operator. This bears on the second problem, the question of the relative scopes of the two predicates. Earlier, we had stated that because both *want* and *likely* would combine with *win* via a type-shift, their scopes should be permutable, but that only the surface scope is available. We speculate that it is the effect of this INF operator which serves to rule out the reading where *likely* outscopes *want*. This is because such a scope would also give the INF function wide scope over the whole expression, yielding a situation where the widest temporal operator carries this contingent existential, essentially making it possible for there to be no interval at which the described events took place, which is an undesirable result. Nothing in the derivation *per se* blocks this reading, rather a well-formedness constraint on semantic outputs would do so.

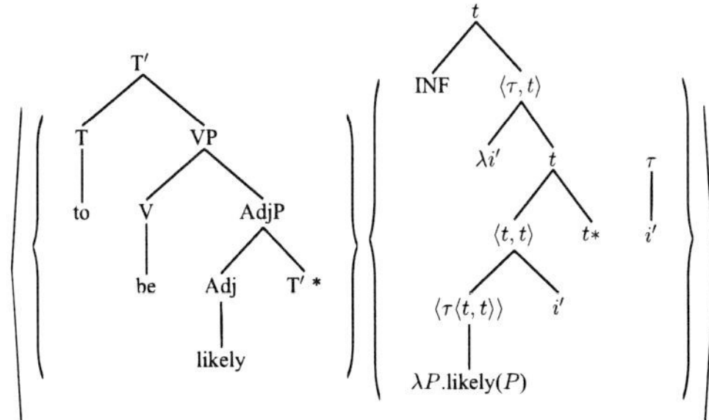

Figure 13: Non Finite Raising Predicate under Control

A reviewer notes that certain cases of Right Node Raising may present a particular challenge for our approach, with an example as in (9):

(9)   Every boy supported and every girl protested some amendment.

Specifically, the concern is in deriving the reading in which the shared argument's existential quantifier has narrow scope relative to the universals, since the right-node-raised existential object would appear to be derivationally higher than the subject quantifiers within the conjoined sentences. In fact, such cases can be treated if we adopt the approach to coordination presented in Sarkar and Joshi (1996), and further developed in Han et al. (2008), where examples like (9) are discussed. Under this approach, we allow elementary trees to contain nodes that are marked as shared arguments. When two predicate trees with nodes targeted for sharing (indicated by a circle) are combined, a node-contraction operation applies, such that the relevant shared nodes combine into a single node that is multiply-dominated

in both the derived syntax and semantics trees.[1] In Figure 14, we update the relevant Han et al. elementary trees with our new semantic notation, dispensing for the moment with interval variables.

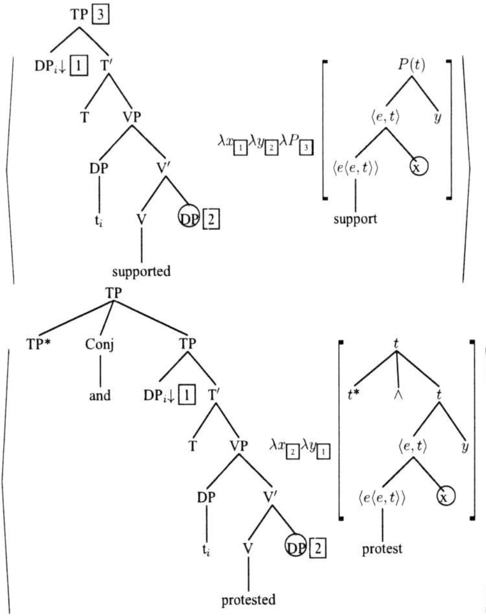

Figure 14: Elementary trees for Coordination

The *support* elementary tree contains three linked nodes: one for the subject, which is a standard type e substitution site, one for the object, which is marked for contraction, and one at the root, which corresponds to λP, which binds a function of type $\langle t, t \rangle$. The coordinator is treated as a functional element in the *protest* tree, projected in accordance with the CETM. The second elementary tree contains two links, one each for the arguments of the verb. These elementary trees however provide two new questions regarding the application of our type-shifting operation. The first concerns the status of the object in the *support* tree. A crucial feature of the Han et al. analysis is that the shared object, *some amendment* in this case, is not duplicated, but rather shared through multiple dominance. As such, its scope part can only combine with one of the two elementary trees. Thus, we do not apply the type-shifting operation at all to the *support* tree, as the only component of the quantificational MCS that is relevant here will be the type e variable. Type

---

[1] See Han et al. for a formal definition of semantic combination with multiple dominance.

shifting the *support* tree would force the quantifier's scope part into a position that does not dominate both of the contracted nodes after *protest* adjoins at the root of *support*, leaving an unbound variable.

The second question concerns the application of type-shifting in the *protest* elementary tree. This is the first time we have explicitly dealt with the question of how to apply the type shifting operation in an elementary tree with more than one available t node. Here, we suppose that the type-shifting operation targets only the root of the elementary tree. That is, both the shared and non-shared arguments of *protest* can take scope over the coordinator. In the case of the shared argument, this is treated as a necessity for proper variable binding in the original Han et al. presentation, an observation which we echo here. However, they treat it as equally necessary for the non-shared argument to take a low scope relative to the coordinator, and here our analyses diverge. We believe it should be possible to derive the reading in which the non-shared argument takes widest scope. Thus, type-shifting will link both arguments to the root of the *protest* tree.

Finally, it is just a matter of determining whether or not there is a possible derivational order which yields the narrow scope of the shared argument. First, we must examine the orderings of type-shifting. By first type-shifting the object position and then the subject position in the *protest* tree, *every girl* will take a wider scope than *some amendment* at the root of that tree. Similarly, the subject position in *support* will also undergo a type-shift, allowing the subject to outscope the coordinating predicate, which does not require a type-shift to combine. Once the predicates are combined, the universals will both outscope the existential, and the coordinator.

5 Type-Shifting and Scope Interleaving

Finally, a reviewer brings the question of whether or not the type-shifting operation will allow for the derivation of quantificational scopes not readily derivable by conventional set-local means. Specifically, an example such as that in (10):

(10)   John refused to want to visit every candidate.

The reading of interest here is the one where John refused, for every candidate, to want to visit that candidate. That is, *refuse* $> \forall >$ *want*. Again, because this involves a chain of control predicates, we can dispense with the interval variables for the time being and concentrate on the type e variables. The reviewer is quite correct in suspecting that there is nothing inherent in the type-shifting operation which will allow us to derive this reading. With the tools presently available, *refuse* will combine with *want*, and the embedded quantifier is predicted to scope over or under that compound predicate, yielding either $\forall >$ *refuse* $>$ *want* or *refuse* $>$ *want* $> \forall$.

However, we call readers' attention to Frank and Storoshenko (2012) in this volume. There, we motivate the breaking of predicate elementary trees in the semantics into "scope" and "variable" parts, along the same lines as the generalized quantifiers seen here. Following a suggestion in Nesson and Shieber (2008), a control predicate becomes a 3-member MCS consisting of this scope part containing the substitution site for the external argument, the predicate part, and the type e variable to be passed down. The type-shifting operation described here is not incompatible with that analysis, though its domain of application will naturally be limited to the scope parts of those elementary tree sets which contain substitution sites for type e (or type τ) variables. Again, our account of unspecified ordering of type-shifting applies only to this component of the larger MCS, rather than to the predicate tree.

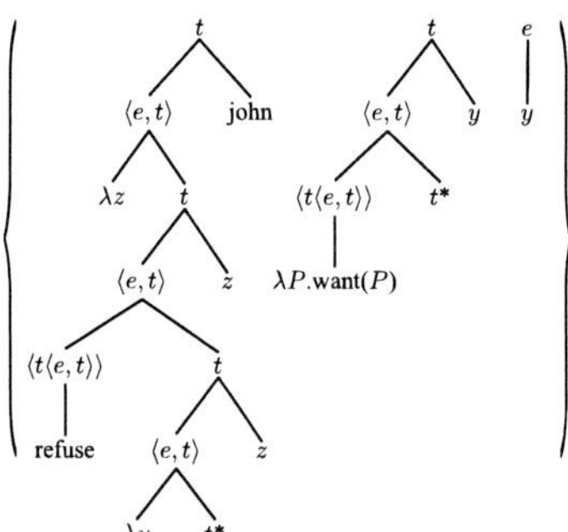

Figure 15: Partial Semantic Derived Tree Set for (10)

To illustrate the example in question, we present the partial derived structure in Figure 15, showing the stage at which *John* has combined with *refuse*, which has in turn combined with *want* after a type-shift over that predicate's open subject position. At this stage, *want* has the described

3-component structure. This will combine with *visit* via type-shifting. One wrinkle at this point is that our type-shifting operation has to this point only dealt with 2-member MCSs. Either the type-shifting operation can be re-defined to allow this triplet, or our preferred interpretation at this point is to maintain that a single link is going to be created, and we rely upon the constraints of the MCS such that the components will eventually collapse into a single tree structure, needing only one link.

As argued in the paper where these structures are introduced, we believe that, with some derivational flexibility, they make certain scopes available which are not otherwise derivable. In this case, as both *want* and *every candidate* will combine via a type-shift targeting the same node (the root of the scope part of *visit*), full freedom for multiple adjoining is possible, so long as all variables are properly bound. Thus, the tree component carrying the universal quantifier should be able to intervene between the two t-recursive components of *want*, deriving the desired reading. For more details on these scope possibilities, we refer readers to the cited paper.

6 Conclusion

In this paper, we have sought a more restrictive framework for linking syntactic and semantic trees in STAG. Combining our modified semantic representations with the type lifting operation provides us a principled account for the creation of the derivational links which captured the simultaneous substitution and adjoining of quantificational MCSs. Extending this operation to type-τ temporal variables, we have shown how embedded quantifiers can scope over raising and ECM predicates. It remains for future work to develop a fully fleshed-out account of the temporal system sketched here, including the links between open type-τ variables and multiple possible syntactic positions where different clauses may adjoin.

Acknowledgments

The authors would like to thank the reviewers for their many helpful comments and questions which have improved the quality of this paper, particularly forcing us to reconcile both our submissions to this volume. All errors remain our own. This work is partially-funded by SSHRC Postdoc Fellowship 756-2010-0677 to Storoshenko.

References

Robert Frank and Dennis Ryan Storoshenko. 2012. The shape of elementary trees and scope possibilities in stag. In *Proceedings of the 11th International Workshop on Tree Adjoining Grammars and Related Formalisms*.

Robert Frank. 2002. *Phrase Structure Composition and Syntactic Dependencies*. Cambridge, MA: MIT Press.

Chung-hye Han, David Potter, and Dennis Ryan Storoshenko. 2008. Compositional semantics of coordination using Synchronous Tree Adjoining Grammar. In Claire Gardent and Anoop Sarkar, editors, *Proceedings of the 9th International Workshop on Tree Adjoining Grammars and Related Formalisms*, pages 33–41.

Herman Hendriks. 1988. Type change semantics: The scope of quantification and coordination. In E. Klein and van Benthem J., editors, *Categories, Polymorphism and Unification*, pages 96–119. Centre for Cognitive Science, Edinburgh.

Laura Kallmeyer and Aravind K. Joshi. 2003. Factoring predicate argument and scope semantics: Underspecified semantics with LTAG. *Research on Language and Computation*, 1:3–58.

Kiyomi Kusumoto. 2005. On the quantification over times in natural language. *Natural Language Semantics*, 13:317–357.

Rebecca Nesson and Stuart M. Shieber. 2008. Synchronous vector TAG for syntax and semantics: Control verbs, relative clauses, and inverse linking. In Claire Gardent and Anoop Sarkar, editors, *Proceedings of the 9th International Workshop on Tree Adjoining Grammars and Related Formalisms*.

Barbara Partee and Mats Rooth. 1983. Generalized conjunction and type ambiguity. In Rainer Bäuerle, Christoph Schwaze, and Arnim von Stechow, editors, *Meaning, Use, and Interpretation of Language*, pages 361–383. Berlin: Mouton de Gruyter.

Sylvain Pogodalla. 2004. Computing semantic representation: Toward ACG abstract terms as derivation trees. In *Proceedings of the 7th International Workshop on Tree Adjoining Grammars and Related Formalisms*.

Anoop Sarkar and Aravind Joshi. 1996. Coordination in Tree Adjoining Grammars: formalization and implementation. In *Proceedings of COLING'96*, pages 610–615, Copenhagen.

Stuart M. Shieber and Yves Schabes. 1990. Synchronous tree adjoining grammars. In *Papers Presented to the 13th International Conference on Computational Linguistics*, volume 3, pages 253–258.

Tim Stowell. 1982. The tense of infinitives. *Linguistic Inquiry*, 13(3):561–570.

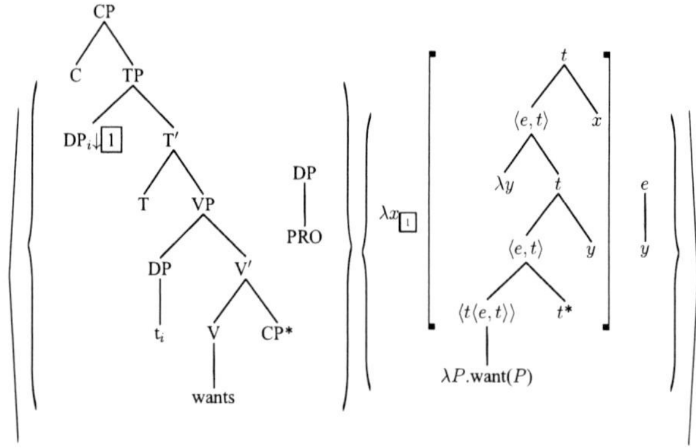

Figure 6: Control Predicate for (2)

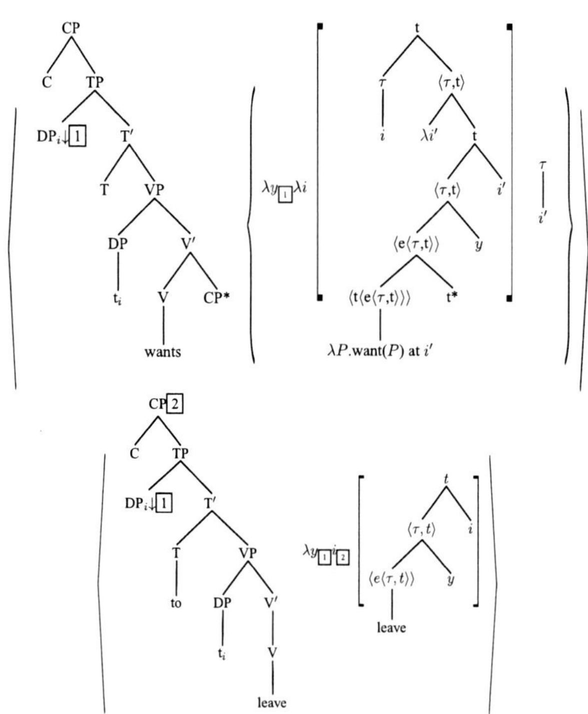

Figure 8: Elementary Trees for (3b)

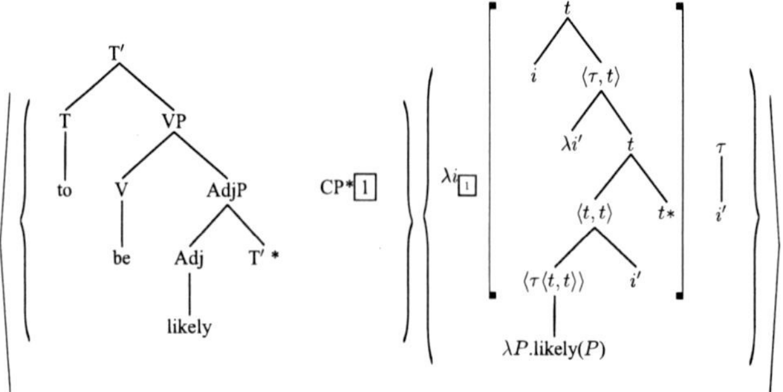

Figure 12: Embedded Raising Predicate for (6)

Tree Adjunction as Minimalist Lowering

Thomas Graf
Department of Linguistics
University of California, Los Angeles
3125 Campbell Hall
Los Angeles, CA 90095-1543, USA
tgraf@ucla.edu

Abstract

Even though Minimalist grammars are more powerful than TAG on the string level, the classes of tree languages the two define are incomparable. I give a constructive proof that if the standard Move operation in Minimalist grammars is replaced by *Reset Lowering*, every TAG tree language can be generated. The opposite does not hold, so the strong generative capacity of Minimalist grammars with Reset Lowering exceeds that of TAG.

1 Introduction

The comparison of grammar formalisms with respect to their expressive power has been essential to furthering our understanding of their inner workings (Weir, 1988; Joshi et al., 1991; Vijay-Shanker and Weir, 1994). Considering a formalism in isolation only takes us so far, it is by connecting it to other proposals that we see which parts are indispensable, why this is the case, and how they grant the grammar its power.

In recent years, significant attention has been devoted to the comparison of TAG and Minimalist grammars (MGs; Stabler, 2011). These two formalisms are interrelated in peculiar ways. MGs are weakly equivalent to MCFGs (Michaelis, 1998; Michaelis, 2001; Harkema, 2001) and thus subsume TAG on the string level. But with respect to the tree languages they generate, the two are in fact incomparable (Fujiyoshi and Kasai, 2000; Mönnich, 1999; Mönnich, 2006; Mönnich, 2007; Kobele et al., 2007), due a profound difference in how trees are cut up and reassembled in the respective formalisms.

What gives TAGs an edge over MGs is the limited kind of context-free tree manipulation granted by tree adjunction. Tree adjunction slices a tree in half and "glues" it back together with new material inserted in the middle, similar to how context-free string languages insert new substrings inside an existing string. This allows TAGs to generate tree languages that satisfy certain context-free path conditions, e.g. that a branch must be of the form $a^n b^n$ when read from the root towards the leaf.

In this paper, I show that the chasm between MGs and TAGs can be overcome by replacing the standard Move operation with *Reset Lowering*. The idea builds on earlier work of mine in Graf (2012), where I present a general schema for enriching MGs with new variants of Move without increasing their weak generative capacity. Using Reset Lowering, it is straight-forward to translate (suitably preprocessed) TAG derivation trees into Minimalist derivation trees that encode the same derived trees (*modulo* empty nodes left behind by movement).

Organization. I first introduce MGs with Reset Lowering in Sec. 2. The presentation is slightly informal, but all technical details can be deduced from Graf (2012). The remainder of the paper is devoted to the translation from TAG to MGs (Sec. 3). After a few remarks on how a given TAG's elementary trees can be brought in line with the kind of X'-like phrase structure template used by MGs (Sec. 3.2), I describe the actual translation in Sec. 3.3. I also discuss how the output of the translation can be guaranteed to be a well-formed Minimalist derivation tree language (Sec. 3.4). Some familiarity with TAG and MGs is presupposed on the reader's part.

Proceedings of the 11th International Workshop on Tree Adjoining Grammars and Related Formalisms (TAG+11), pages 19–27,
Paris, September 2012.

2 Minimalist Grammars with Reset Lowering

MGs are a highly lexicalized framework using two basic operations, *Merge* and *Move*. Merge combines two distinct trees and projects a label in an X′-style fashion, whereas Move applies to a single tree t, takes some subtree s of t and puts it into the specifier of the currently highest phrase of t. Every lexical item (LI) is associated with a sequence of Merge and Move features that need to be checked by these operations in the order that they occur in. Both types of features come in two polarities, positive and negative. By convention, every LI l has exactly one negative Merge feature (its *category feature*), which all of l's positive polarity features must precede and all other negative polarity features must follow. If two LIs have matching features of opposite polarities as their first unchecked feature, the corresponding operation is triggered. By the end of the derivation, all features must have been checked off except for the category feature of the LI that projects the root of the tree, which must be a specifically designated *final category*.

The MG apparatus can be viewed as a combination of well-formedness conditions on derivation trees combined with a mapping from derivation trees to derived trees. Graf (2012) uses this perspective to generalize both components along several dimensions while keeping MGs within the bounds of MCFLs. Three parameters are of interest here. First, every positive feature f is also specified for directionality, indicating whether the subtree headed by the LI with the matching feature for f is the left or the right daughter of the root of the newly constructed tree. Second, the size of the constituent carried along by an LI l that undergoes movement is no longer fixed to the entire phrase headed by l but can be specified explicitly for each feature. Third, the target site of Move is no longer restricted to a c-commanding position; any position that can be picked out by a formula of monadic second-order logic is sufficient.

The expanded feature system and the Minimalist lexicons one can build from them are defined as follows:

Definition 1. Let BASE be a non-empty finite set of *feature names*. Furthermore, OP := $\{merge, move\}$, POL := $\{+, -\}$, SIZE $\subset \mathbb{N}$ finite, and DIR := $\{\lambda, \rho\}$ are the sets of *operations, polarities, sizes,* and *directionality parameters*, respectively. A *feature system* is a non-empty set $Feat \subseteq$ BASE $\times$ OP $\times$ POL $\times$ SIZE $\times$ DIR.

Definition 2. Given a string alphabet Σ and feature system *Feat*, a *Minimalist lexicon* is a finite subset of $\Sigma \times \{::\} \times Feat$.

Note that the double colon serves only cosmetic purposes, and that features must still appear in the specific order described at the beginning of the section. Moreover, not all components are always meaningful: SIZE is irrelevant for all Merge features, DIR for all negative polarity features.

Derivation trees play a central role in this paper. Their leaves are labeled by LIs, while binary branching nodes are labeled Merge and unary branching ones Move. The crucial difference between derivation trees and derived trees is that movement is only indicated by the presence of a Move node marking its target site, while the subtree to be displaced remains *in situ* (skip ahead to Fig. 1 for an example).

The main duty of derivation trees is to encode the operations of the Minimalist feature calculus. Counting from an LI l towards the root, the i-th node is *associated* to the i-th positive polarity feature of l (if it exists). Every interior node mode must be associated to exactly one feature of exactly one LI — its *feature associate* — and every positive polarity feature of every LI must be a feature associate of exactly one node. The LI carrying an interior's node feature associate is also called its *lexical associate*. Furthermore, there must be a matching feature for every interior node's feature associate, where two features *match* iff they agree on their name, operation, and size, but have opposite polarities.

In general, there will be many matching features, but only one of them can be involved in checking off an interior node's feature associate. How this feature is determined varies between Merge and Move. For a Merge node n with lexical associate l, it is the category feature of the unique LI $l' \neq l$ that is the lexical associate of a node immediately dominated by n in the derivation tree. For n a Move node, on the other hand, the feature is determined via *occurrences*, where the definition of occurrences depends on the type of movement to be modeled.

I only present the definition for the type of

movement used throughout this paper, *Reset Lowering*. First, the k-root of l is the unique node n such that the shortest descending path from n to l has length k. The 0-root of l is l itself.

Definition 3. A Move node m associated to a feature f of size k is a *potential i-occurrence of l* iff the i-th negative Move feature of l matches f and the k-root of l c-commands m in the derivation tree. It is a potential occurrence of l iff it is a potential i-occurrence of l for some $i > 0$. It is an *i-occurrence of l* iff it is a potential i-occurrence of l and there is no $l' \neq l$ such that the k-root of l c-commands l' and n is a potential occurrence of l.

Intuitively, Move node n is an i-occurrence of l iff I) l has the right kind of feature, and II) the root of the subtree to be displaced c-commands n (i.e. the target site), and III) no other LI that is closer to n satisfies requirements I) and II).

Now the distribution of Move nodes can be regulated by two conditions.

Move. For every LI l with negative Move features $f_1, \ldots, f_n$, there exist distinct nodes $m_1, \ldots, m_n$ such that m_i (and no other node) is the i-th occurrence of l, $1 \leq i \leq n$.

SMC. Every Move node is an occurrence of exactly one LI.

This ensures in a purely tree-geometric fashion that all movement features in the derivation get checked.[1] Given a grammar G with lexicon L, its *Minimalist derivation tree language* is the set of all derivations that can be assembled from items in L and satisfy the conditions above.

Once the occurrences of all LIs l are known, the mapping from derivation trees to derived trees is straightforward. First, a branch is drawn from o to the respective k-root of l, where o is the i-occurrence of l with the highest value for i. Afterwards, the branch from the k-root to its mother is removed, so that o is the only mother of the k-root now. When this has been done for all LIs, any remaining unary branching nodes are given the empty string ε as their second daughter. The proper linearization of the derivation tree is controlled by the directionality of the positive fea-

---

[1]For *Reset Lowering*, it also implies that every LI has at most one negative movement feature of size k (otherwise every Move node c-commanded by its k-root would count as an occurrence, in violation of **Move**).

tures. Finally, it only remains to relabel the interior nodes by the distinguished symbols $<$ and $>$, which point in the direction of the projecting head — an interior node is labeled $<$ iff its feature associate has directionality ρ.

Let us finish with an example grammar for the language $a^n b^n$, $n \geq 2$. An easy way of generating it is to create multiple instances of ab and then lower each $\sigma \in \{a, b\}$ into the specifier of the next lowest σ. The grammar in Fig. 1, with f as its only final category, does just that. For the sake of succinctness, Merge features are given in lower case, Move features in upper case, polarities as superscripts, directionality as subscripts, and size in square brackets.

It should be easy to see that this grammar can be extended to $a_1^n \ldots a_k^n$ for any choice of k, proving that MGs with Reset Lowering trump TAG in terms of weak generative capacity (possible restrictions will be hinted at in Sec. 3.3.6). The same holds for the weakly equivalent standard MGs, though, yet they cannot generate all TAG tree languages. The translation presented in the next section proves that MGs with Reset Lowering can.

3 The Translation Procedure

3.1 Overview

The mapping from TAGs to MGs proceeds in three stages. First, the TAG grammar must be preprocessed to accommodate MGs' restriction to binary branching, X$'$-like tree structures. Afterwards, the translation proper is defined over derivation trees in a piece-wise by case fashion. This is done via three three functions ϕ, μ and τ. The role ϕ is to determine which features are needed for which nodes, and μ uses this information to transfer elementary trees in fragments of Minimalist derivations, which are then pieced together by τ. The specifics of μ vary depending on what kind of TAG operation needs to be emulated. While substitution is easily handled by standard Merge, reigning in adjunction via Reset Lowering depends on a trick: instead of adjoining tree u at node n, one can Merge it as a sister of n and subsequently lower the subtree rooted in n to where the foot node would be in u. The procedure is sketched in Fig. 2. After the derivation tree transduction from TAGs to MGs is put in place, it only remains to ensure that the resulting MG does

21

a1) $a :: A_\rho^+[0]\ a\text{-}lo^-$

a2) $a :: A_\rho^+[1]\ a\text{-}lo^-$

a3) $a :: A_\rho^+[0]\ b\text{-}lo_\lambda^+\ a\text{-}mid^-\ A^-[1]$

a4) $a :: A_\rho^+[1]\ b\text{-}lo_\lambda^+\ a\text{-}mid^-\ A^-[1]$

a5) $a :: A_\rho^+[0]\ b\text{-}mid_\lambda^+\ a\text{-}mid^-\ A^-[1]$

a6) $a :: A_\rho^+[1]\ b\text{-}mid_\lambda^+\ a\text{-}mid^-\ A^-[1]$

a7) $a :: b\text{-}lo_\lambda^+\ a\text{-}hi^-\ A^-[0]$

a8) $a :: b\text{-}mid_\lambda^+\ a\text{-}hi^-\ A^-[0]$

b1) $b :: B_\rho^+[0]\ a\text{-}lo_\lambda^+\ b\text{-}lo^-$

b2) $b :: B_\rho^+[1]\ a\text{-}lo_\lambda^+\ b\text{-}lo^-$

b3) $b :: B_\rho^+[0]\ a\text{-}mid_\lambda^+\ b\text{-}mid^-\ B^-[1]$

b4) $b :: B_\rho^+[1]\ a\text{-}mid_\lambda^+\ b\text{-}mid^-\ B^-[1]$

b5) $b :: a\text{-}hi_\lambda^+\ b\text{-}hi^-\ B^-[0]$

e) $\varepsilon :: b\text{-}hi_\lambda^+\ f^-$

Figure 1: Top: Reset Lowering grammar for $a^n b^n$, $n \geq 2$; Bottom: derivation and derived tree for $a^3 b^3$

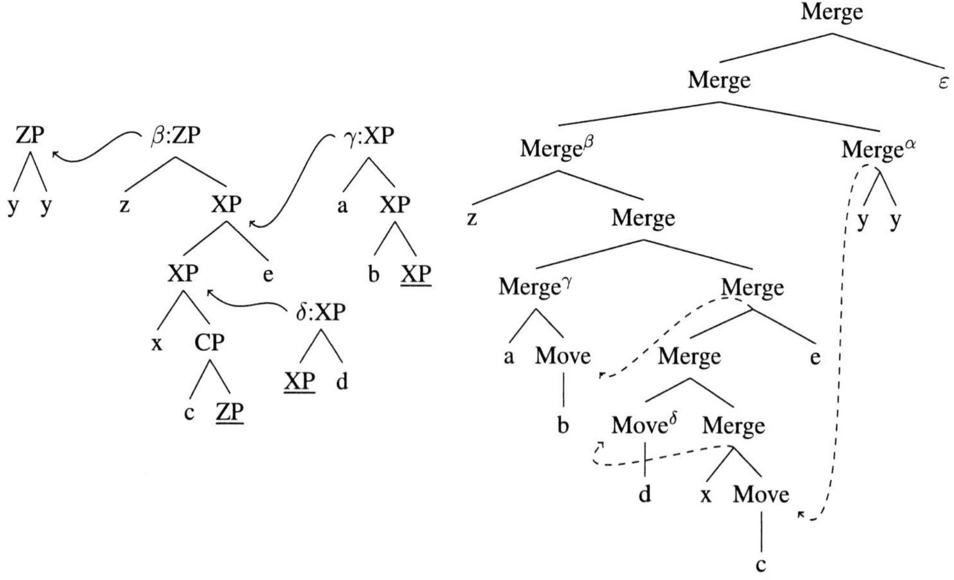

Figure 2: Tree Adjunction as Reset Lowering; solid arrows represent adjunction, dashed arrows movement, and the roots of the elementary trees are indicated by superscripts.

not overgenerate. This is a simple task, though, thanks to the attractive closure properties of MGs (Graf, 2011; Kobele, 2011).

3.2 Step 1: Preprocessing

We already saw in Sec. 2 that the tree languages derived by MGs are somewhat peculiar in that they are strictly binary branching and follow a projection scheme inspired by X'-theory. While the usual binarization strategies can easily be applied to TAG and need not be discussed here, imposing projection on an arbitrary TAG is slightly more tricky. Since not all elementary trees of a given TAG may necessarily contain any LIs, there might be no upper bound on the length of the shortest descending path in a derived tree from some interior node to some LI. This is impossible in MGs and thus needs to be prevented. A simple, albeit not particulary elegant solution is to insert empty LIs where necessary. How exactly one goes about this has no bearing on the translation procedure as long as every interior node with a non-terminal symbol is a projection of some LI.

Since every TAG is required to obey projection, it makes sense to introduce some extra notation to talk about trees more efficiently. The label of a node n is given by $\ell(n)$. For every node n, its head $\hbar(n)$ is the leaf l that n is a projection of. If t is a tree with root r, then $\hbar(t) := \hbar(r)$. In the other direction, $\pi(l) := p_1 \cdots p_n$ is the string of all projections of l such that each p_1 is the parent of l and each p_i is immediately dominated by p_{i+1}, $1 \leq i < n$. A node n is a *maximal projection* of l iff $l = n$ or n the last symbol of $\pi(l)$. Note that l can be its own maximal projection even though it is never included in $\pi(l)$. Parts of trees will sometimes be specified via functional notation such that $f(a, b)$ is a tree in which f immediately dominates a and b.

The following terminology will be adopted to avoid confusion brought about the fact that TAG allows for terminal nodes to be decorated with non-terminal symbols: leafs labeled with terminal symbols will be referred to as LIs, while non-terminal is used exclusively for interior nodes. Keep in mind that thanks to the projection requirement the only nodes with non-terminal symbols that aren't part of some LI's projection are foot nodes and substitution nodes.

3.3 Step 2: Translating TAG Derivations

3.3.1 Derivation Trees

The translation τ from TAGs to MGs operates at the level of derivation trees, which for TAG are defined as follows. Let E be some finite set of elementary trees and ν some function that assigns each $e \in E$ a unique name. A *derivation tree over* E is an ordered tree over the (unranked) alphabet $\Sigma := \{\nu(e) \mid e \in E\} \times (\{\varepsilon\} \cup A)$, where A is the smallest set containing an address for every node in every $e \in E$ (as a notational shorthand, e is often used instead of $\nu(e)$ where convenient). Since every $e \in E$ is finite in size and E has finite cardinality, A is finite, too, wherefore Σ is indeed an alphabet. If node n in derivation tree t is immediately dominated by node m such that m and n have labels $\langle u, a \rangle$ and $\langle v, b \rangle$, respectively, that is to be interpreted as tree v adjoining in tree u at the node p with address b (we require that this node exists in u). Often p will simply be referred to as b. The second component of a label is ε iff it is the label of the root of the derivation tree. Furthermore, if nodes m and n are siblings, their labels must differ in their second component. That is to say, no two trees ever adjoin to the same node, which guarantees that the branching factor of derivation trees is bounded and that there is a unique derived tree language. Note that elementary trees containing foot nodes and substitution nodes must have at least two nodes total. For every TAG G with set E of elementary trees, it holds that its derivation tree language is a subset of the set of all derivations over E.

3.3.2 Single Elementary Tree

We start with the simplest case, a derivation tree t that consists of only one node u. Note that u cannot contain a foot node or substitution node, for then t would not be well-formed. Hence every node in u is either an LI or part of the projection of some LI. We convert u into an MG derivation in two steps.

For every LI n in u, $\phi(n) := \langle \ell(n), merge, - \rangle$. If n is a non-terminal and its left daughter d is a maximal projection, $\phi(n) := \langle \ell(\hbar(d)), merge, +, \lambda \rangle$. Substitute ρ for λ if d is the right daughter of n. Since u is binary branching and every non-terminal in u must be a projection of some LI, ϕ is well-defined for all nodes in u.

Now for every LI n with $\pi(n) := p_1 \cdots p_n$,

let $\mu(n) := \ell(n) :: \phi(p_1) \cdots \phi(p_n) \, \phi(n)$. For all non-terminals n, $\mu(n)$ is the second component of $\phi(n)$, which so far is restricted to Merge. As ϕ before, μ is well-defined for all of u. This carries over to the standard extension of μ from nodes to trees, which is denoted by $\hat{\mu}$. It is easy to see that $\hat{\mu}$ maps u to its corresponding MG derivation. The required feature values are determined by ϕ — including values for the linear order of nodes — and then instantiated on the heads of the respective projections. Interior nodes are universally labeled Merge. Therefore the derived tree encoded by the Minimalist derivation $\hat{\mu}$ is identical to u (under a deterministic relabeling of interior node labels); we may safely set $\tau(t) := \hat{\mu}(u)$.

3.3.3 Substitution

Now consider a derivation t in which trees $v_1, \ldots, v_n$ substitute into tree u at addresses $a_1, \ldots, a_n$ (and there is no $v_j \neq v_i$, $1 \leq i \leq n$ that is dominated by u in t). Then u contains n distinct substitution nodes $s_1, \ldots, s_n$, where n is bounded by the size of u. By assumption (cf. Sec. 3.2) there are at least two nodes in u. Because substitution nodes must be leaves, this entails that each s_i has a parent p_i, which is the projection of some LI.

Let $\phi(p_i) := \langle \ell(\hbar(v_i)), merge, +, \lambda/\rho \rangle$ if s_i is the left/right daughter of p_i. In addition, $\mu(s_i) := \square_i$. Then $\tau(\langle u, a \rangle \, (\langle v_1, a_1 \rangle, \ldots, \langle v_n, a_n \rangle))$ is the result of replacing each $\square_i$ in $\hat{\mu}(u)$ by $\tau(\langle v_i, a_i \rangle \, (t_1, \ldots, t_k))$, where $t_1, \ldots, t_k$ are all the subtrees immediately dominated by v_i in t, $k \geq 0$. This yields once again a well-formed Minimalist derivation, as the feature instantiation of p_i and $\hbar(v_i)$ via ϕ ensures for all $1 \leq i \leq n$ that $\hbar(v_i)$ is selected by $\hbar(p_i)$.

3.3.4 Adjunction

Finally, suppose that trees $v_1, \ldots, v_n$ adjoin into tree u at $a_1, \ldots, a_n$. Each v_i contains a (unique) foot node f_i, which has a mother m_i that is the projection of some LI. This holds because v_i consists of at least two nodes and we preprocessed all elementary trees in order to make them projective. Note that for every TAG, adjoining v at the foot node of u is equivalent to adjoining u at the root of v, so we do not consider the case where a_i is a foot node. Adjunction at substitution nodes is superfluous for the same reason and usually forbidden. The only remaining cases, then, are for a_i

to be an LI or some projection thereof.

The translation of v_i is less involved than that of u, so it makes sense to discuss it first. For $\diamond$ some distinguished symbol, $\mu(f_i) := \diamond$. The $\diamond$ is used to mark the foot node f_i for deletion by τ. As for m_i, we set $\phi(m_i) := \langle \circ, move, +, connection(v_i) - 1 \rangle$, where $\circ$ is some arbitrary feature name. This turns m_i into a Move node that will serve as the landing site for a subtree in u as sketched in Fig. 2. The function $connection(v_i)$ determines the size of the movement feature and returns integer n iff the Merge node immediately dominating $\square_i$ in $\hat{\mu}(u)$ is the n-th projection of some node. In order to understand why this is the desired value, we need to look at the translation of u next.

For each a_i in u, a Merge node must be added immediately above it that serves in selecting v_i. These Merge nodes require new features on $\hbar(a_i)$. Moreover, $\hbar(a_i)$ must also carry the requisite number of Move features to undergo lowering, and all of them must have the correct size value. This requires special definitions for $\mu(a_i)$, $\phi(a_i)$, and $\mu(\hbar(a_i))$, respectively. I only discuss the case where a_i is an interior node. The procedure for a_i an LI is almost the same (see Fig. 3).

The value of $\phi(a_i)$ is the feature string $[\phi] \, \langle \ell(\hbar(v_i)), merge, +, \lambda \rangle$, where $[\phi]$ is what ϕ would return at a_i if it was a normal non-terminal (see Sec. 3.3.2). The corresponding part of the Minimalist derivation is $\mu(a_i) := \text{Merge}(\square_i, [\mu])$, where $[\mu]$ is what μ would return at a_i if it was a normal non-terminal. These notational contortions emulate the effect of treating a_i as usual except that a Merge node is added above it that v_i can be attached to.

Due to the complexities of the movement mechanism in the specification of $\hbar(a_i)$, this part is best split out into a separate component. Let $\xi(x, n) := \langle \circ, move, -, \delta_n \rangle$ if some a_i is the n-th projection of x, and ε otherwise. The integer δ_n is given by $|\, \{1 \leq j < n \mid \xi(x, j) \neq \varepsilon\} \,|$. As a more compact notation, let $\xi_i^n(x) := \xi(x, n) \, \xi(x, n - 1) \cdots \xi(x, i + 1) \, \xi(x, i)$ be the string concatenation of the outputs of $\xi(x, i), \ldots, \xi(x, n)$ listed in reverse. Now for $\pi(\hbar(a_i)) := p_1 \cdots p_z$, we define $\mu(\hbar(a_i)) := \ell(\hbar(a_i)) :: \phi(p_1) \cdots \phi(p_z) \, \phi(\hbar(a_i)) \, \xi_1^z(\hbar(a_i))$.

The peculiar formula for δ_n stems from a complication in how projections should be counted. Recall from the discussion in Sec. 2 that a fea-

24

ture's size plays an essential role in the mapping from derivation trees to derived trees by virtue of picking out the root of the moved subtree. For our purposes, a size value j should refer to the j-th projection of $\hbar(a_i)$ in u. But the mapping to derived trees operates over Minimalist derivation trees, and since μ adds new projections for $\hbar(a_i)$, that node's j-th projection in u might be its k-th projection in the corresponding Minimalist derivation tree fragment $\hat{\mu}(u)$, $k > j$ (see also Fig. 2). In order to correctly compute j, though, it suffices to know how many of the lower projections have been expanded into two Merge nodes rather one, which can be deduced from the number of values that aren't mapped to the empty string by ξ.

There is still one minor problem pertaining to adjunction at the root node of u when u is also the root of the derivation tree t. In this case, $\hbar(u)$ won't get its category feature $\langle l, merge, - \rangle$ checked, so it cannot undergo movement. This can be fixed by adding another LI on top of the derivation, as was done for the example grammar in Fig. 1: For a_i the root of u, u the root of t, and f some feature name, $\mu(a_i) := \mathrm{Merge}(\mathrm{Merge}, \varepsilon ::$ $\langle \ell(\hbar(a_i)), merge, +, \lambda \rangle \langle f, merge, - \rangle)$.

With these pitfalls out of the way, it only remains for us to assemble the individual outputs of μ into a coherent derivation: $\tau(\langle u, a \rangle (\langle v_1, a_1 \rangle, \ldots, \langle v_n, a_n \rangle))$ is the result of deleting every node labeled $\diamond$ in $\mu(u)$ and replacing each $\square_i$ as before.

3.3.5　Putting it All Together

The full specification of the translation procedure is given in Fig. 3. For a little bit of extra rigor, ϕ has been split into two functions, while space restrictions forced the use of additional notational shorthands. The result of removing all instances of $\diamond$ from tree u is denoted by $u \setminus \diamond$, and $u \leftarrow [t_1, \ldots, t_n]$ is the tree obtained from u by replacing each $\square_i$ by t_i. Given a feature f, $\omega(f)$ is the second component of f, i.e. the type of operation f regulates.

Several parameters must be kept track of in order for the functions to be well-defined. They are the current tree u, and its derivational daughters $v_1, \ldots, v_i$ with their respective addresses $a_1, \ldots, a_n$. In addition, computing $connection(v_i)$ requires access to the derivational mother o of u, or alternatively, storage of the

value during the computation of o. The (locally bounded) passing around of these parameters is not made explicit in the definitions in order to minimize notational clutter.

3.3.6　Correctness

The correctness of the translation for single node derivations as well as instances of substitution has already been established. It should also be clear that all cases of adjunction yield an output, so τ is at least well-defined. Moreover, these outputs are definitely Minimalist derivation trees. It still needs to be shown, though, that they are well-formed and that the intended derived tree can be obtained from them. The former depends on whether **Move** and **SMC** are satisfied. The latter follows rather straight-forwardly if this is the case.

The definition of Reset Lowering entails that every Move node m is an occurrence for at most one LI. Otherwise, there would be two LIs $l \neq l'$ whose k-th projections both c-command m without at least one c-commanding the other, which is impossible (k is the size value of the feature associate of m). That there is at least one LI l for every m follows from the definition of μ, which inserts the tree containing m as the sister of the k-root of l. The corresponding negative movement is also instantiated on l at the right position of the feature string. Thus **SMC** always holds.

Move is satisfied, too, because LI l contains a negative movement feature iff it selects a tree containing the required Move node m. Said tree cannot contain another LI l' that m is a potential occurrence for, because then there would also be another Move node m'. This argument can be continued until eventually there must be a Move node that isn't an occurrence for any LI, or for more than one. Either case violates **SMC**, yielding a contradiction.

As a result of all this, the Move node in tree $\hat{\mu}(v_i)$ is an occurrence of $\hbar(a_i)$, and for every negative Move feature on an LI there is an occurrence m such that lowering to m yields the same derived tree as adjunction. That this ensures the generation of the correct derived tree (*modulo* empty nodes left behind by movement) only requires a short proof by induction.

As a quick side remark, the use of only one feature name for movement features in the translation might provoke the conjecture that Reset Lowering

$$\varphi(x) := \begin{cases} \varphi(x_1) \cdots \varphi(x_n) & \text{if } x \text{ is a string of nodes } x_1, \ldots, x_n, \\ \langle \circ, move, +, connection(v_i) - 1, \lambda/\rho \rangle & \text{if foot node } f_i \text{ is the left/right daughter of } x, \\ \langle \ell(h(v_i)), merge, +, \lambda/\rho \rangle & \text{if } a_i \text{ is a substitution node and the left/right daughter of } x, \\ \langle \ell(h(y)), merge, +, \lambda/\rho \rangle & \text{if the daughter } y \text{ of } x \text{ is not part of the same projection,} \\ \langle \ell(x), merge, - \rangle & \text{if } x \text{ is an LI.} \end{cases}$$

$$\phi(x) := \begin{cases} \varphi(x) \langle h(v_i), merge, +, \lambda \rangle & \text{if } x = a_i \text{ and } x \text{ is an interior node,} \\ \langle h(v_i), merge, +, \lambda \rangle \varphi(x) & \text{if } x = a_i \text{ and } x \text{ is an LI,} \\ \varphi(x) & \text{otherwise.} \end{cases}$$

$$\xi(x, n) := \begin{cases} \langle \circ, move, -, n + | \{ 1 \le j < n \mid \xi(x, j) \ne \varepsilon \} | \rangle & \text{if some } a_i \text{ is the } n\text{-th projection of } x, \\ \varepsilon & \text{otherwise.} \end{cases}$$

$$\mu(x) := \begin{cases} \text{Merge}(\text{Merge}, \varepsilon :: \langle \ell(h(x)), merge, +, \lambda \rangle \langle f, merge, - \rangle) & \text{if } x = a_i \text{ is the root of } u \text{ \& } u \text{ the root of } t, \\ \ell(x) :: \phi(\pi(x)) \, \phi(x) \, \xi(x, n) \cdots \xi(x, 1) & \text{if some } a_i \text{ equals } x \text{ or is a projection of } x, \\ \text{Merge}(\Box_i, \omega(\phi(x))) & \text{if } x = a_i \text{ and } x \text{ is an interior node,} \\ \text{Merge}(\Box_i, \phi(x)) & \text{if } x = a_i \text{ and } x \text{ is an LI,} \\ \Box_i & \text{if } x \text{ is a substitution node,} \\ \diamond & \text{if } x \text{ is a foot node,} \\ \omega(\phi(x)) & \text{if } x \text{ is an interior node,} \\ \ell(x) :: \phi(\pi(x)) \, \phi(x) & \text{if } x \text{ is an LI.} \end{cases}$$

$$\hat{\mu}(x(x_1, \ldots, x_n)) := \begin{cases} \mu(x) & \text{if } n = 0, \\ \mu(x)(\mu(x_1), \ldots, \mu(x_n)) & \text{otherwise.} \end{cases}$$

$$\tau(\langle \nu(e), a \rangle (t_1, \ldots, t_n)) := \begin{cases} \hat{\mu}(e) \setminus \diamond & \text{if } n = 0, \\ (\hat{\mu}(e) \setminus \diamond) \leftarrow [\tau(t_1), \ldots, \tau(t_n)] & \text{otherwise.} \end{cases}$$

Figure 3: Definition of the translation from a TAG derivation t to the corresponding Minimalist derivation; where multiple conditions are satisfied at once, only the highest one applies; see Sec. 3.3.5 for an explanation of notation.

MGs satisfying this condition are weakly equivalent to TAGs (as Graf, 2012 erroneously does). However, even with just one feature name Reset Lowering MGs can still generate $a_1^n, \ldots, a_k^n$ for arbitrary k. This is so because features with different size values are considered distinct by **SMC** despite their identical feature name. For example, the grammar in Fig. 1 can be made to use only one feature name by having b merge with an empty head before selecting a so that the size value of its movement feature can always be one bigger than that of a's. If this loop-hole can be patched, though, a weak equivalence proof seems feasible.

3.4 Step 3: Intersection

The correctness of the translation only entails that the output of τ applied to a TAG derivation is a Minimalist derivation that can be mapped to the intended derived tree. Nothing so far guar-

antees that translating the TAG derivation tree language actually yields a Minimalist derivation tree language (MDTL), as not every set of well-formed Minimalist derivations is a well-formed MDTL. The closure of MDTLs under intersection with regular tree languages (Graf, 2011; Kobele, 2011), however, makes it straight-forward to construct an MDTL from the output of the translation.

It is a well-known fact that the image of a regular tree language under a linear transduction is also regular (Gécseg and Steinby, 1984), and τ is exactly such a (non-deterministic) transduction.[2] As TAG derivation tree languages are regular, so is the tree language produced by τ applied to a given TAG G_T. Now let G_M be the MG whose lexicon contains every LI that occurs in some tree

---

[2] Given a look-ahead of 1, it is even deterministic.

in $\tau(G_T)$. The intersection of G_M's derivation tree language with $\tau(G_T)$ yields the MDTL of some MG that generates the same derived trees as G_T.

4 Conclusion

I have given a productive proof via a translation procedure that MGs with Reset Lowering instead of standard Move can generate all TAG tree languages. I also showed that they are more powerful than TAGs on a string level, but a stronger version of **SMC** might actually be sufficient to make the two formalisms equivalent in this respect. For future work, it will be interesting to see if the translation can be extended to generalizations of TAG such as the one in Rogers (2003). If so, this would be an indication that the relation between adjunction and Reset Lowering isn't merely accidental but provides a fresh perspective on TAG.

Acknowledgments

My sincerest thanks go to Ed Stabler and Michael Freedman for earlier discussions of the material, as well as the three anonymous reviewers for their helpful comments that lead to several improvements in the presentation of the material.

References

A. Fujiyoshi and T. Kasai. 2000. Spinal-formed context-free tree grammars. *Theory of Computing Systems*, 33:59–83.

Thomas Graf. 2011. Closure properties of minimalist derivation tree languages. In Sylvain Pogodalla and Jean-Philippe Prost, editors, *LACL 2011*, volume 6736 of *Lecture Notes in Artificial Intelligence*, pages 96–111.

Thomas Graf. 2012. Movement-generalized minimalist grammars. In Denis Béchet and Alexander J. Dikovsky, editors, *LACL 2012*, volume 7351 of *Lecture Notes in Computer Science*, pages 58–73.

Ferenc Gécseg and Magnus Steinby. 1984. *Tree Automata*. Academei Kaido, Budapest.

Henk Harkema. 2001. A characterization of minimalist languages. In Philippe de Groote, Glyn Morrill, and Christian Retoré, editors, *Logical Aspects of Computational Linguistics (LACL'01)*, volume 2099 of *Lecture Notes in Artificial Intelligence*, pages 193–211. Springer, Berlin.

Aravind Joshi, K. Vijay-Shanker, and David Weir. 1991. The convergence of mildly context-sensitive grammar formalisms. In P. Sells, Shieber S. M., and T. Warsow, editors, *Foundational Issues in Natural Language Processing*, pages 31–81. MIT Press, Cambridge, MA, USA.

Gregory M. Kobele, Christian Retoré, and Sylvain Salvati. 2007. An automata-theoretic approach to minimalism. In James Rogers and Stephan Kepser, editors, *Model Theoretic Syntax at 10*, pages 71–80.

Gregory M. Kobele. 2011. Minimalist tree languages are closed under intersection with recognizable tree languages. In Sylvain Pogodalla and Jean-Philippe Prost, editors, *LACL 2011*, volume 6736 of *Lecture Notes in Artificial Intelligence*, pages 129–144.

Jens Michaelis. 1998. Derivational minimalism is mildly context-sensitive. *Lecture Notes in Artificial Intelligence*, 2014:179–198.

Jens Michaelis. 2001. Transforming linear context-free rewriting systems into minimalist grammars. *Lecture Notes in Artificial Intelligence*, 2099:228–244.

Uwe Mönnich. 1999. On cloning context-freeness. In Hans-Peter Kolb and Uwe Mönnich, editors, *Mathematics of Syntactic Structure*, pages 195–231. Walter de Gruyter, Berlin.

Uwe Mönnich. 2006. Grammar morphisms. Ms. University of Tübingen.

Uwe Mönnich. 2007. Minimalist syntax, multiple regular tree grammars and direction preserving tree transductions. In James Rogers and Stephan Kepser, editors, *Model Theoretic Syntax at 10*, pages 83–87.

James Rogers. 2003. Syntactic structures as multi-dimensional trees. *Research on Language and Computation*, 1(1):265–305.

Edward P. Stabler. 2011. Computational perspectives on minimalism. In Cedric Boeckx, editor, *Oxford Handbook of Linguistic Minimalism*, pages 617–643. Oxford University Press, Oxford.

K. Vijay-Shanker and David J. Weir. 1994. The equivalence of four extensions of context-free grammars. *Mathematical Systems Theory*, 27:511–545.

David Weir. 1988. *Characterizing Mildly Context-Sensitive Grammar Formalisms*. Ph.D. thesis, University of Pennsylvania. Available as Technical Report MS-CIS-88-74 of the Department of Computer and Information Sciences, University of Pennsylvania.

A Frame-Based Semantics of Locative Alternation in LTAG

Yulia Zinova
Heinrich Heine University Düsseldorf
Germany
zinova@phil.uni-duesseldorf.de

Laura Kallmeyer
Heinrich Heine University Düsseldorf
Germany
kallmeyer@phil.uni-duesseldorf.de

Abstract

In this paper we present an analysis of
locative alternation phenomena in Russian
and English within a frame-based LTAG
syntax-semantics interface. The combination of a syntactic theory with an extended
domain of locality and frames provides a
powerful mechanism for argument linking.
Furthermore, the concept of tree families
and unanchored trees in LTAG allows for a
decomposition of meaning into lexical and
constructional components.

Figure 1: Derivation for *John loves Mary*

1 Introduction

There is a number of formalisms that capture the
idea that the meaning of a verb-based construction
depends both on the lexical meaning of the verb
and on the construction in which the verb is used
(Goldberg, 1995; Van Valin and LaPolla, 1997).
The question is how exactly the meaning components are distributed and how they combine.

In (Kallmeyer and Osswald, 2012a) a combination of Lexicalized Tree Adjoining Grammars
(Joshi and Schabes, 1997) and Frame Semantics
is introduced. Since LTAG displays an extended
domain of locality and, related to this, elementary
trees contain slots for all arguments of their lexical anchor, LTAG is particularly well-suited for
combining it with a frame-based compositional
semantics. When coupling an elementary tree
with a semantic frame, as proposed in (Kallmeyer
and Osswald, 2012a), syntactic arguments can be
directly linked to their counterpart in the semantics. Semantic composition is then modeled by
unification which is a result of performing adjunctions and substitutions. Figure 1 provides a simple illustration of syntactic and semantic composition.

Linguistic generalizations in LTAG are captured a) by the distinction between lexical anchor and unanchored elementary tree, b) by the
concept of tree families (representing subcategorization frames) and c) by the factorization in the
metagrammar. Parallel to this syntactic factorization, a factorization of meaning is possible as
well. The resulting framework is very flexible
with respect to the decomposition and composition of lexical and constructional units on the syntax and semantics level.

In the following, we present an analysis of locative alternation that benefits from the flexibility
of this framework. The structure of the paper is
as follows. The next section presents the English
and Russian data we are dealing with in this paper. Then, in section 3, we briefly introduce the
framework of frame semantics in LTAG that we
are using. Section 4 proposes an analysis of the
locative alternation in English and Russian within
this framework. In section 5, we further decom-
pose the meaning of some Russian verbs, analyzing the semantics of certain prefixes that change
the verb meaning such that a locative alternation
becomes possible. Finally, section 6 concludes.

Proceedings of the 11th International Workshop on Tree Adjoining Grammars and Related Formalisms (TAG+11), pages 28–36,
Paris, September 2012.

2 The Data

(1) - (4) show basic examples of locative alternation in English and Russian. As there is no standard name for this constructions in the literature, let us call the first variant ((1), (3)) *prepositional phrase construction,* or *PPC,* and the second variant ((2), (4)) - *instrumental case construction,* or *ICC,* for convenience of referring to them.

(1)   John$_1$ loaded the hay$_2$ into the wagon$_3$.

(2)   John$_1$ loaded the wagon$_3$ with hay$_2$.

(3)   Ivan$_1$ zagruzil   seno$_2$ v vagon$_3$.
Ivan   loaded$_{perf}$ hay$_{acc}$ in wagon$_{gen}$.
Ivan loaded the hay into a/the wagon.

(4)   Ivan$_1$ zagruzil   vagon$_3$ senom$_2$.
Ivan   loaded$_{perf}$ wagon$_{acc}$ hay$_{instr}$.
Ivan loaded the wagon with hay.

PPCs are traditionally analyzed as having a change of location meaning and ICCs as having a change of state meaning (Kageyama, 1997; Levin and Rappaport Hovav, 1998; Goldberg, 1995). An analysis for (1) and (2) following (Kageyama, 1997) is provided in (5). It demonstrates that there is a difference between the two constructions, but only the difference in the perspective is shown.

(5)   a.   X CAUSE [BECOME [hay
BE ON truck]]

        b.   X CAUSE [BECOME [truck$_z$
BE [WITH [hay BE ON z]]]]

(6)   a.   [[x ACT] CAUSE [y
BECOME P$_{loc}$ z] [LOAD]$_{MANNER}$]

        b.   [[x ACT] CAUSE [z BECOME
[]$_{STATE}$ WITH-RESPECT-TO y]
[LOAD]$_{MANNER}$]

The analysis proposed in (Levin and Rappaport Hovav, 1998), which can be found under (6), provides more detailed information about the difference between PPCs and ICCs. (6-a) tells us that the hay changes its location as a result of the loading event, while (6-b) describes that the result is a change in the state of the wagon. One can notice that in (5) there is no explicit reference to the verb itself and the only component that is taken from the verb meaning is that the result of the loading is that the THEME is on the LOCATION in the end.

The question that arises if one looks carefully at what the sentences in (1) - (4) mean is whether it is really the case that there is no change of state in PPC examples? In fact, any loading activity leads to both a change of location of the content and some change of state of the container (if it is specified), just different components of the effect become more salient. As there is actually only one action, we propose the following formalization: the verb describes a change of location and the result state depends on the end amount of PATIENT at the GOAL. If this amount is equal to the capacity of the container, we get the change of state effect. If it is equal to the total amount of content, we have a holistic change of location effect.

Although at first Russian examples look similar to the English ones, there are a number of differences. While (4) has the same meaning as (2), (3) means that all the hay was loaded. On the other hand, if we consider imperfective examples (7) and (8), we find no holistic effect in either ICC and PPC case. Verbs *gruzit'* 'to load' and *mazat'* 'to spread', 'to cover' (examples (9) and (10)) are the only non-prefixed verbs that allow locative alternation in written language[1]. Other verbs allow only one construction in their non-prefixed variant (see (11) and (12)) and both constructions, when a prefix *za-* is added (see (13) and (14)). A prefix *na-* makes the verb perfective but does not change the set of constructions it can participate in, like in (15) and (16).

(7)   Ivan$_1$ gruzil   seno$_2$ v vagon$_3$.
Ivan   loaded$_{imp}$ hay$_{acc}$ in wagon$_{gen}$.
Ivan was loading the hay into a/the wagon.

(8)   Ivan$_1$ gruzil   vagon$_3$ senom$_2$.
Ivan   loaded$_{imp}$ w$_{acc}$ hay$_{instr}$.
Ivan was loading the wagon with hay.

(9)   On namazal   maslo na hleb.
He distributed$_{perf}$ butter$_{acc}$ on bread$_{acc}$
He distributed butter over a piece of bread.

(10)   On namazal   hleb   maslom.
He covered$_{perf}$ bread$_{acc}$ butter$_{instr}$
He covered a piece of bread with butter.

(11)   On sypal sahar   v banku.
He put$_{imp}$ suggar$_{acc}$ in can$_{acc}$
He was putting sugar in a/the tin.

(12)   *On sypal   banku saharom.
He covered/filled$_{imp}$ tin$_{acc}$ sugar$_{instr}$

---

[1] A couple more can be found in spoken language, for example *stelit'* 'to cover'

He covered/filled the tin with sugar.

(13) On zasypal sahar   v banku.
      He put$_{perf}$ suggar$_{acc}$ in can$_{acc}$
      He put sugar in a/the tin.

(14) On zasypal   banku saharom.
      He covered/filled$_{perf}$ tin$_{acc}$ sugar$_{instr}$
      He covered/filled the tin with sugar.

(15) On nasypal sahar   v banku.
      He put$_{perf}$ suggar$_{acc}$ in can$_{acc}$
      He put sugar in a/the tin.

(16) *On nasypal   banku saharom.
      He covered/filled$_{perf}$ tin$_{acc}$ sugar$_{instr}$
      He covered/filled the tin with sugar.

The aim of this work is to provide an analysis that correctly models the following: a) holistic effects for English ICC constructions, b) holistic effects for Russian PPC and ICC constructions with perfective verb, and c) no holistic effect in other cases. We also aim at providing an explanation of why some verbs allow locative alternation and some do not and how the addition of a prefix to a Russian verb changes the set of constructions it can participate in.

3 LTAG and Frame Semantics

Following (Kallmeyer and Osswald, 2012a), we adopt a syntax-semantics interface that links a single semantic representation (in our case, a semantic frame) to an entire elementary tree and that models semantic composition by unifications triggered by substitution and adjunction. In this we partly follow (Gardent and Kallmeyer, 2003; Kallmeyer and Romero, 2008), except that our focus is on event semantics and the decomposition of lexical meaning and we therefore use frames.

Formally, frames are taken to be typed feature structures. Each elementary tree is linked to a feature structure and unification is triggerd via the feature unifications in the syntax. For this purpose, some of the nodes in the elementary trees have semantic features such as I (for inidividual) and E (for event). Their unifications cause equations between metavariables. As a result, the corresponding semantic feature structures are unified as well. A simplified example was given in Fig. 1 where the substitutions trigger unifications between ① and ③ and between ② and ④, which leads to an insertion of the corresponding argument frames into the frame of *loves*.

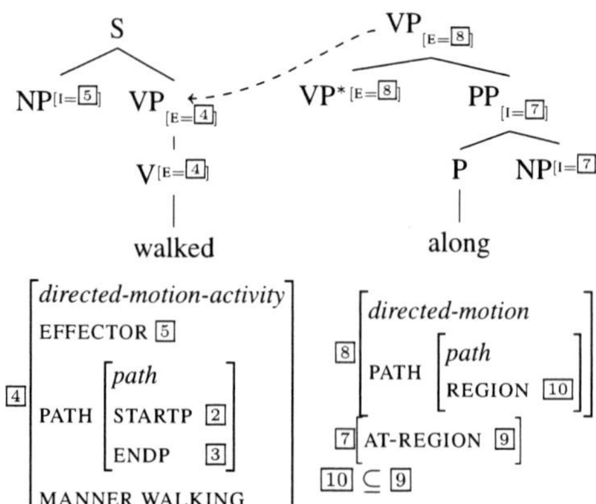

Figure 2: Path modification

An example taken from (Kallmeyer and Osswald, 2012a) involving an adjunction is given in Fig. 2 where the path of a walking activity is further restricted by an *along* ... PP modifier. The frames express that the AT-REGION of the NP embedded under the PP (for instance *the brook* in *John walked along the brook*) contains the REGION of the path. This containment is expressed as an additional relation between feature values.

Note that the feature structures used for semantics are more complex than the syntactic feature structures used in LTAG. However, this complexity is limited to the semantic part, the complexity of syntactic parsing remains unchanged.

As detailed in (Kallmeyer and Osswald, 2012a), LTAG's decomposition of elementary trees into a) unanchored trees and lexical anchor and b) tree fragments of unanchored trees in the metagrammar can be paired with a corresponding decomposition of meaning, in particular into contributions of constructions and of lexical elements. In this paper, we will exploit this for a distinction of the meaning contributions of ICC and PPC constructions and of their lexical anchors.

4 Locative Alternation: The Analysis

In this section, we will examine the possible unanchored trees involved in our examples of locative alternations, relating the elementary tree templates to the semantics of the construction. Furthermore, we will detail the semantics contributed by lexical anchors and we will show how syntactic composition triggers semantic frame unification.

In the case of the PPC in English, the semantics of the whole phrase can be compositionaly

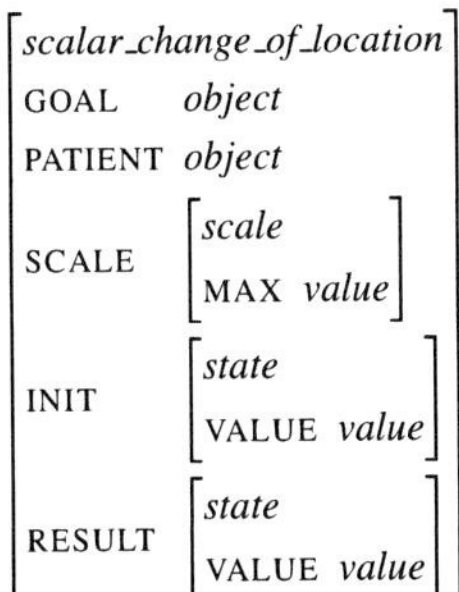

Figure 3: Signature for *scalar change of location*

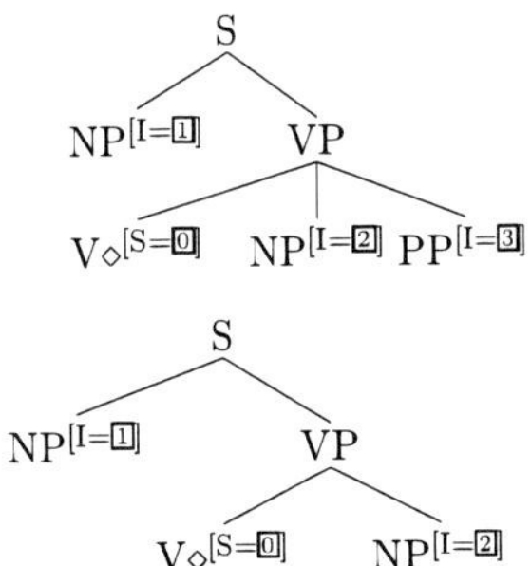

Figure 4: Unanchored trees for the PPC

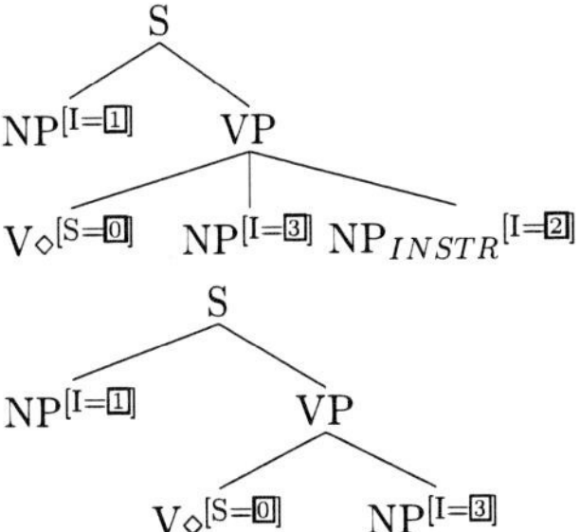

Figure 5: Unanchored trees for the ICC

derived from the semantics of the verb and its arguments, while in the case of the ICC there is a part of the meaning, that comes from the construction itself. The goal now is to provide the meaning of the ICC and of the verbs allowing locative alternation such that in combination they form the desired frame representation of the semantics of a sentence.

4.1 Feature Geometry

Following ideas in (Osswald and Van Valin, Jr., 2012) where one can find a discussion of the representation of events and results using Fillmores Frame Semantics (Fillmore, 1982) we introduce attributes of initial and result states and a scale which is determined by its type, maximum and minumum value. The change of state is either a decrease or an increase of a value on an ordered scale (a discussion of an analysis of scalar change can be found in (Kennedy and Levin, 2008)). The type of change of state determines the way the change happens. For example, change of location requires a patient and a goal and the patient is then moved to the goal according to the scale (for example, covered area or amount). Inside the scale attribute the maximum value (feature MAX) is specified, the minimum value is assumed to be 0. Some of the verbs specify a concrete initial or result state (INIT and RESULT respectively), but *load* does not have any initial or result state specified within its semantics, so it just determines the scale with its maximum. Summarizing the ideas, one obtains the following for our analysis of locative alternation:

- change of location and change of state are just different interpretations of the result state of the scalar change of location;
- a scalar change of location is described by

PATIENT, GOAL, SCALE and initial and result values on it, which means that there is a change of location of PATIENT to GOAL, such that the amount of PATIENT at the GOAL changes from the initial to the end value (cf. Fig. 3);

- the value of SCALE is of type *scale* with possible subtypes such as *volume*, or *area*, which can also have subtypes such as *capacity* and *amount* for *volume* or *coverage* for *area*.

4.2 The Construction

So far, we were looking only at examples where both container and content are realized. However, the constructions that are being discussed can also be used when only the direct object of the verb is present; in this case, they will have the same difference in semantics. Therefore, for the PPC and ICC construction, we obtain the unanchored elementary trees shown in Fig. 4 and Fig. 5.[2] In the ICC trees, the second NP_{INSTR} stands for both NP in instrumental case in Russian and PP with

---

[2] For this paper, we restrict ourselves to the base trees; other trees (for extraction and passivization, for instance) are of course in the tree family as well.

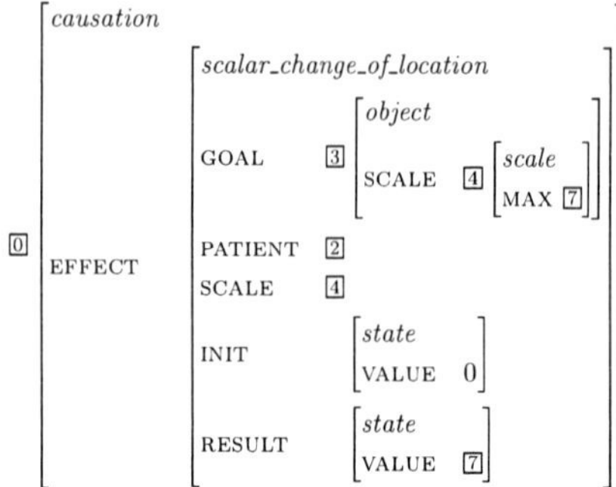

Figure 6: Frame for the ICC (English)

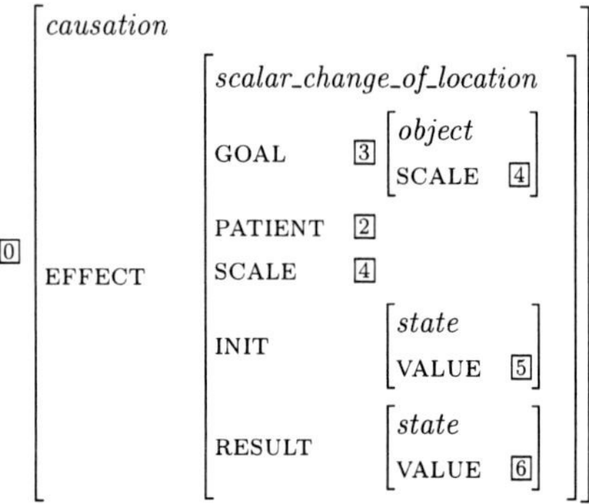

Figure 7: Frame for the ICC (Russian)

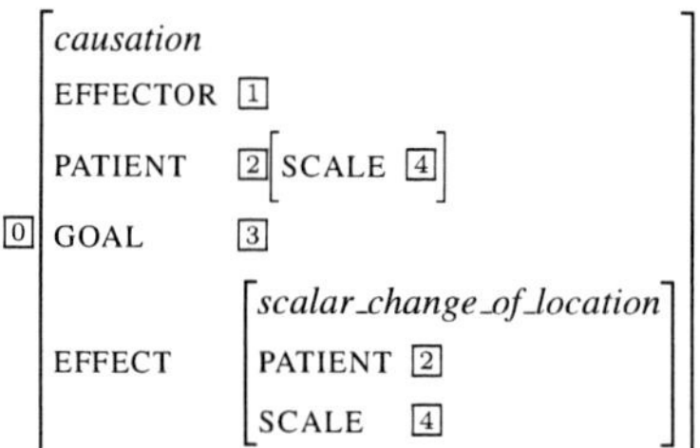

Figure 8: PPC frame (English, Russian)

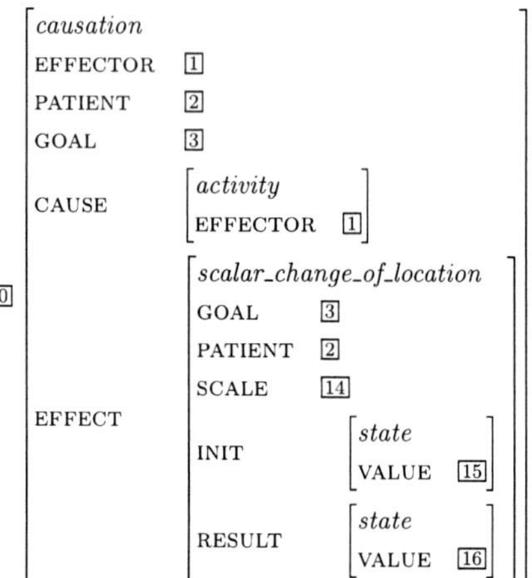

Figure 9: Frame for *load* (English, imperfective in Russian)

preposition *with* in English.[3]

Let us present our analysis by going through the decomposition of the verbal trees for (1) - (4).

Figures 6 and 7 show the frames for the unanchored trees for the ICC in English and Russian respectively. The frame for the PPC is common for both languages and represented in Fig. 8. In all three frames, the scalar change of location is embedded under the EFFECT attribute of the *causation* event that describes the meaning of the verbal construction. The ICC frame in Fig. 6 expresses that in the initial state there is nothing at the GOAL and in the result state the amount of PATIENT at the GOAL is equal to the maximum value specified in the SCALE inside the GOAL. This gives us the meaning that if the GOAL is a container and thus has a *capacity* scale, it's result state will be *full*. As already mentioned, in Russian this is not necessarily so. Therefore, in Fig. 7, the effect of the causation is less specified. The part which is

more specified in the English ICC construction, compared to the Russian one, comes with the perfectivizing prefixes, like *na-* and *za-*. The PPC frame (Fig. 8) expresses that the relevant scale for the change of location is provided by the patient.

4.3 Semantic Frame Composition

Let us first go through the full composition of (2). Fig. 9 gives the lexical semantics of *load*. When anchoring the ICC construction with *load*, yielding the tree in Fig. 10, the frames from Fig. 6 and Fig. 9 unify. The result is given in Fig. 11.

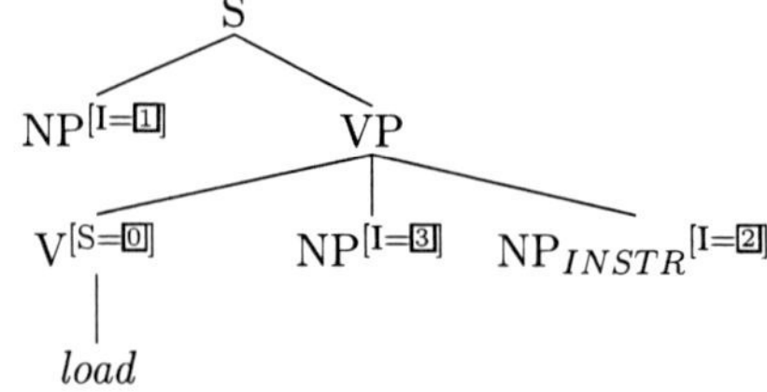

Figure 10: Elementary tree for *load*, ICC construction

---

[3]Note that, in order to adjoin VP modifiers, a more binary structure is actually needed. In this respect, our trees are slightly simplified for the sake of this paper.

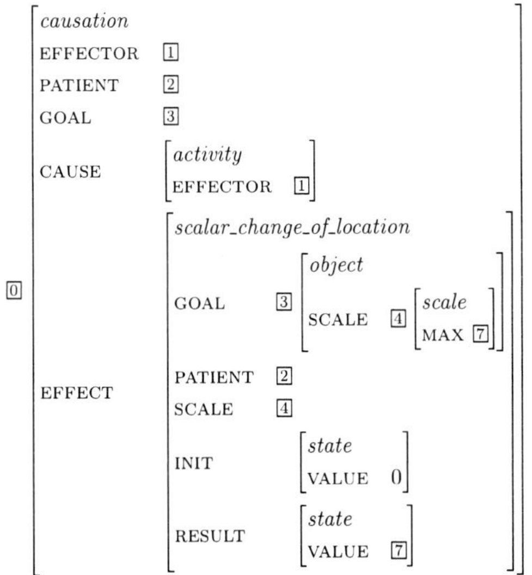

Figure 11: Frame for the *load* ICC tree (English)

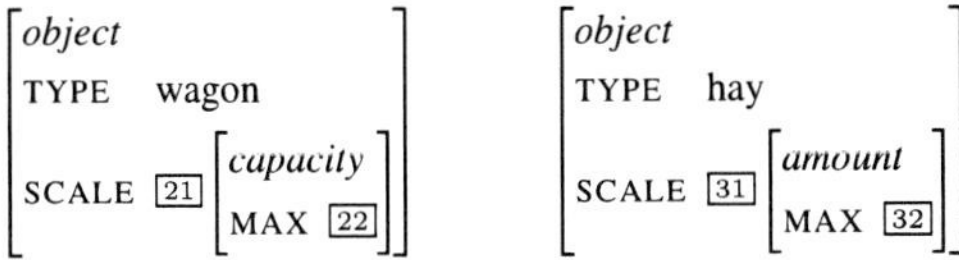

Figure 12: Frames for *wagon* and *hay*

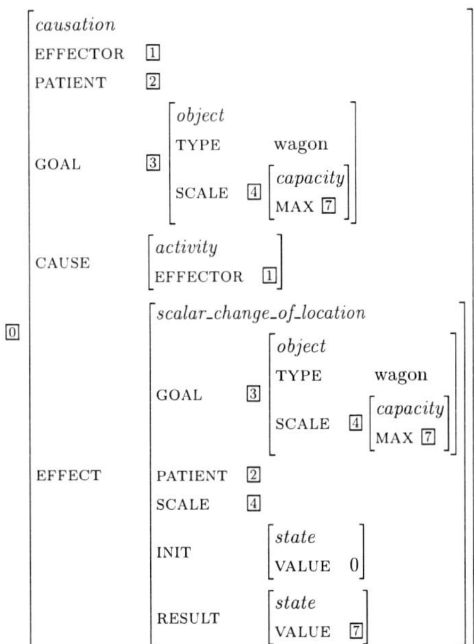

Figure 13: Frame for *load wagon* (ICC)

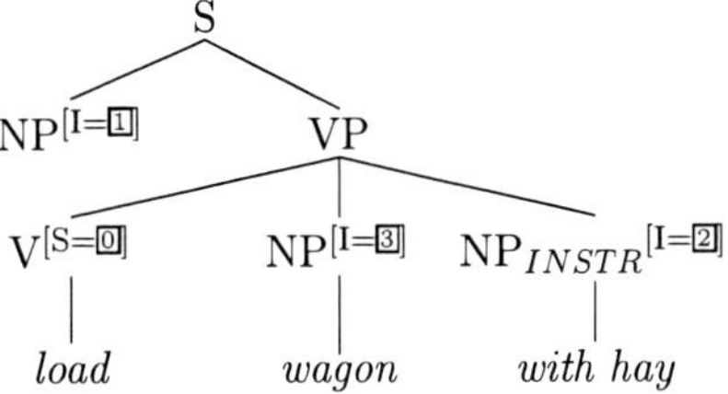

Figure 14: Tree for *load wagon with hay*

We assume that frames for nouns such as *wagon* or *hay* come with a SCALE attribute that can be for instance of type *capacity* as for *wagon* or *amount* as in the case of *hay*, see Fig. 12. When substituting the *wagon* into the direct object position, because of the linking I features, the value ③ of the GOAL feature in the frame in Fig. 11 is unified with the *wagon* frame. As a result, the maximal value on the *capacity* scale of the *wagon* provides the value of the result state, yielding the frame in 13. At the next step, *hay* is substituted into the instrumental object slot in the tree (see Fig. 14), causing a unification of its frame with the value ② of PATIENT. The resulting frame (Fig. 15) represents that in the result state the amount of hay in the wagon is equal to the maximal capacity of the wagon, in other words the wagon is full. As we have seen, the construction determines which scale is relevant for the result state; in an ICC construction it is the scale of the goal, i.e., the capacity of the wagon.

In contrast to this, in the PPC construction, the scale of the PATIENT is the relevant scale for the scalar change of location. In the case of *hay*, the change can be up to the total amount of hay. However, as expressed in the PPC frame, the RESULT value is not necessarily equal to the MAX value of the relevant scale. Consequently, no holistic effect arises in this case.

5 Morphological Decomposition

Let us now turn to the Russian examples (11) - (16). There are two questions we aim to answer:

- How does holistic meaning arise?
- Why does adding the prefix *za-* make some verbs eligible for both ICC and PPC?

The idea is that most verbs, for example *sypat'* 'to pour, but for non-liquids', have a restriction on the type of their relevant scale (see frame in Fig. 16), which does not allow them to combine with nouns that do not have an appropriate scale type, like *banka* 'can' whose frame is

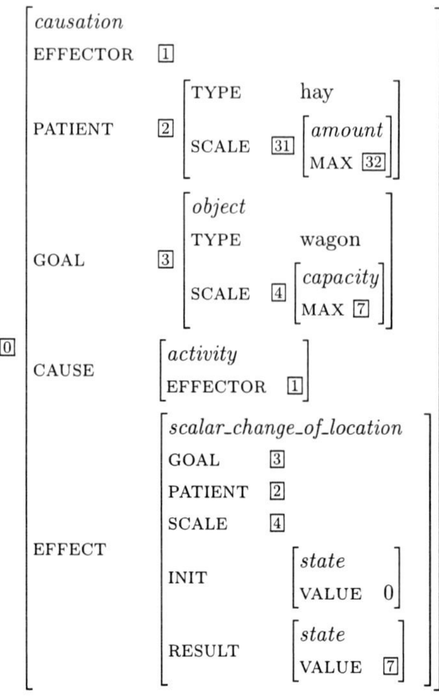

Figure 15: Resulting frame for the ICC and *load wagon with hay*

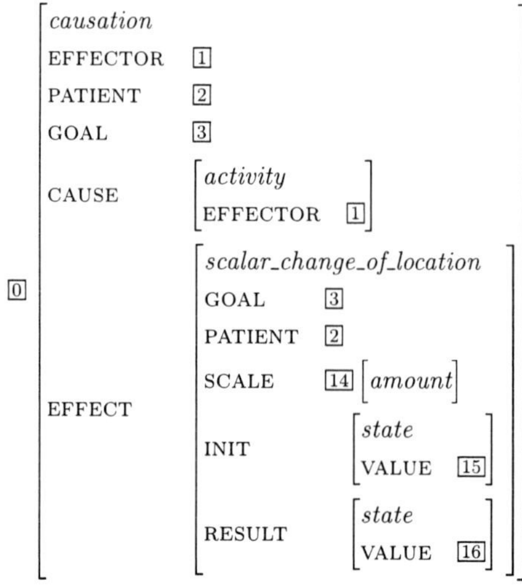

Figure 16: Frame for Russian verb *sypat'*

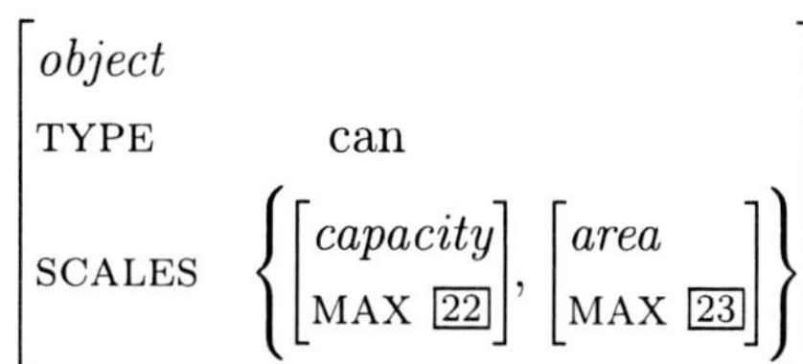

Figure 17: Frame for *banka* (can)

shown in Fig. 17. Note that, in contrast to the previous section, we now allow multivalued (i.e., set-valued) scale values for cases where several scales are possible. *Can* for instance has both a surface (*area*) that can be covered and a volume (*capacity*) that can be filled. When unifying with such a multivalued attribute, unification with one of the values must be successfull. When adding the noun in direct object position, the SCALE inside the *change_of_location* must unify with the SCALE of the noun. In the case of *sypat'* the unification fails since the type *amount* cannot unify with any of the two scale types of *can*.

What happens when a prefix is added? First, the perfective meaning is added (the part of the meaning that comes together with the ICC in English), see frames for both *na-* (Fig. 19) and *za-* (Fig. 18). Second, if the prefix *za-* is added, the scale restriction is removed (20). If the prefix *na-* is added, the restriction remains. As a preliminary analysis of this, let us introduce attributes that can overwrite something instead of unifying with it. This operation is allowed only on the morphological level and thus does not affect the compositionality of semantic derivation. The under-

lined SCALE attribute in the frame for *za-* prefix (Fig. 18) replaces the SCALE attribute in the verb frame and we obtain the resulting frame in 20 for the verb *zasypat'* 'to cover', 'to fill'.[4]

This analysis is in line with ideas from (Filip, 2000; Filip, 2003), where the meaning of Slavic prefixes is discussed. Both prefixes presented here derive a perfective verb from an imperfective one, but with different meanings: while *zasypat'* is a quantized verb, *nasypat'* (as well as *sypat'*) is a cummulative one and this leads to the restrictions on the direct object type (which is here expressed via the type of scales).

After the morphological step is computed, only standard unification is used. However, now the verb can participate in both the PPC and ICC constructions because it is now unifiable (after combination with the construction frames) with objects of container type (like *can*), as well as with objects of a content type (like *hay* or *sugar*).

---

[4]A more detailed investigation of the morphology-semantcs interface is planned for future research.

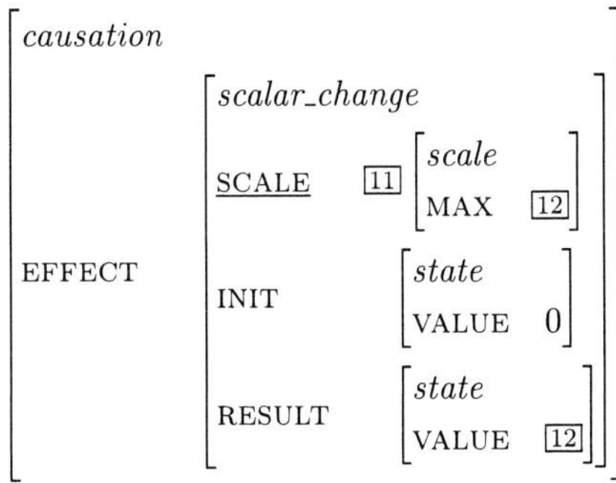

Figure 18: Frame for the prefix *za*

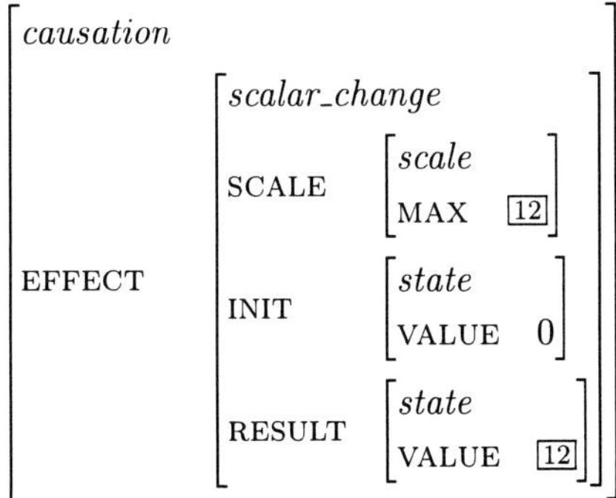

Figure 19: Frame for the prefix *na*

As mentioned above, at the moment we assume multiple values for the SCALE attribute of objects like *banka* 'can'. An alternative solution might be to store the object frame in the lexicon with characteristic attributes of this object, such as a CAPACITY attribute with a value of maximum capacity of the object, and then allow for such attributes to be transformed in the SCALE attribute. We leave this issue for future research.

Let us illustrate the multivalue approach that we currently assume by performing the substitution of the noun *banka* 'can', Fig. 17 into the tree for the verb *gruzit'* 'to load' in the ICC. There are two different scale types inside the object of *can* available for the unification while substituting *can* in a direct object position in the ICC, *capacity* and *area*. As there is no restriction on the type of the scale inside the verb, both unifications are possibe and lead to different interpretations of example (14): in case the capacity scale is selected, the result state of the can is *full* (Fig. 21) and in case the area scale is selected, the can is *covered* (Fig. 22).

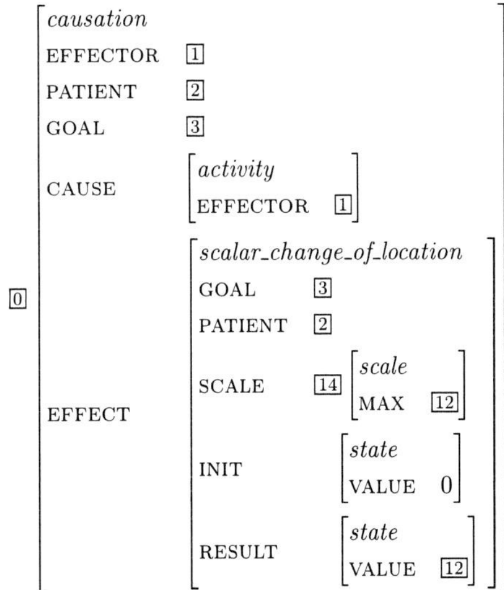

Figure 20: Frame for Russian verb *zasypat'*

6 Conclusion

In this paper we present an analysis of locative alternation phenomena in Russian and English using the combination of an LTAG and Frame Semantics. This analysis uses LTAG's mechanism of separation between unanchored elementary trees and lexical anchors to separate the contribution of the lexical meaning from the contribution of construction and follows the ideas expressed in (Kallmeyer and Osswald, 2012b). An advantage of combining LTAG with Frame Semantics is that LTAG's extended domain of locality allows direct linking of thematic roles of the arguments with corresponding syntactic slots. From the other side, Frame Semantics allows a reach meaning factorization, as is illustrated in the provided analysis of locative alternation.

Additionally, some ideas for morphological decomposition are presented, which is especially useful for languages with a rich morphology, such as Russian.

Acknowledgments

The work presented in this paper was financed by the Deutsche Forschungsgemeinschaft (DFG) within the CRC 991. For inspiring discussions and many useful comments we would like to thank Hana Filip, Timm Lichte and Rainer Osswald. Furthermore, we are grateful for the comments provided by three anonymous reviewers.

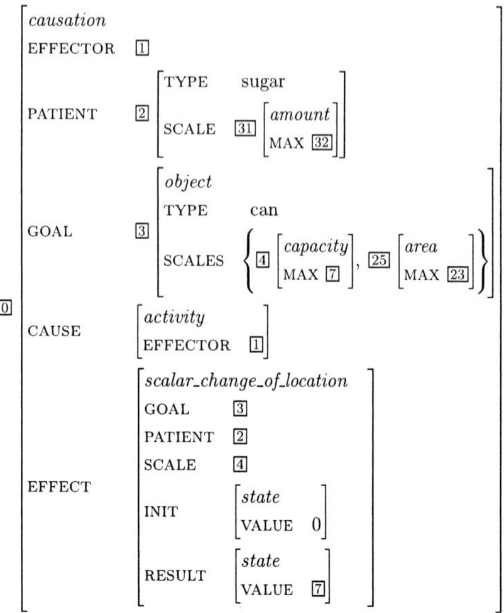

Figure 21: Frame for (14), 'fill' variant

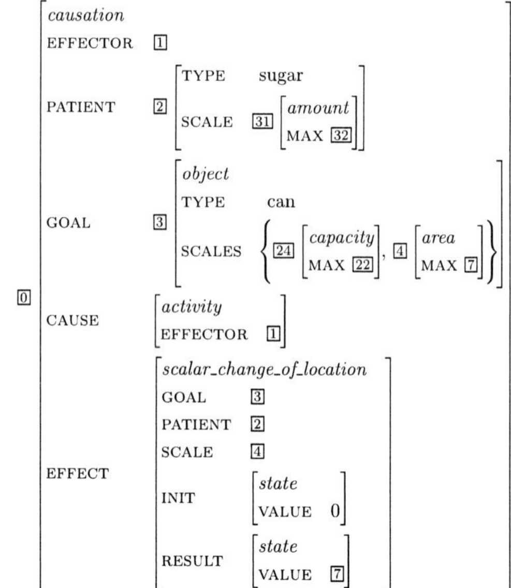

Figure 22: Frame for (14), 'cover' variant

References

Hana Filip. 2000. The quantization puzzle. In *Events as Grammatical Objects*, pages 3–60. CSLI Press, Stanford.

Hana Filip. 2003. Prefixes and the delimitation of events. *Journal of Slavic Linguistics*, 1(11):55–101.

Charles J. Fillmore. 1982. Frame semantics. In The Linguistic Society of Korea, editor, *Linguistics in the Morning Calm*, pages 111–137. Hanshin Publishing Co., Seoul.

Claire Gardent and Laura Kallmeyer. 2003. Semantic Construction in FTAG. In *Proceedings of EACL 2003*, pages 123–130, Budapest.

Adele E. Goldberg. 1995. *Constructions. A Construction Grammar Approach to Argument Structure*. Cognitive Theory of Language and Culture. The University of Chicago Press, Chicago and London.

Aravind K. Joshi and Yves Schabes. 1997. Tree-Adjoining Grammars. In G. Rozenberg and A. Salomaa, editors, *Handbook of Formal Languages*, pages 69–123. Springer, Berlin.

Taro Kageyama. 1997. Denominal verbs and relative salience in lexical conceptual structure. In T. Kageyama, editor, *Verb semantics and syntactic structure*, pages 45–96. Kurioso Publishers, Tokyo.

Laura Kallmeyer and Rainer Osswald. 2012a. An Analysis of Directed Motion Expressions with Lexicalized Tree Adjoining Grammars and Frame Semantics. In Luke Ong, editor, *Proceedings of WoLLIC*, Lecture Notes in Computer Science LNCS, September. To appear.

Laura Kallmeyer and Rainer Osswald. 2012b. A frame-based semantics of the dative alternation in lexicalized tree adjoining grammars. Submitted to Empirical Issues in Syntax and Semantics 9.

Laura Kallmeyer and Maribel Romero. 2008. Scope and situation binding in LTAG using semantic unification. *Research on Language and Computation*, 6(1):3–52.

Christopher Kennedy and Beth Levin. 2008. Measure of change: The adjectival core of degree achievements. In L. McNally and C. Kennedy, editors, *Adjectives and adverbs. syntax, semantics, and discourse*. Oxford University Press, Oxford.

Beth Levin and Malka Rappaport Hovav. 1998. Morphology and lexical semantics. In A. Spencer and A. M. Zwicky, editors, *Handbook of morphology*, pages 248–271. Blackwell Publishers, Oxford.

Rainer Osswald and Robert D. Van Valin, Jr. 2012. Framenet, frame structure, and the syntax-semantics interface. Manuskript Heinrich-Heine Universität.

Robert D. Van Valin and Randy J. LaPolla. 1997. *Syntax*. Cambridge University Press, Cambridge.

A Logical Characterization of Extended TAGs

Uwe Mönnich
Theoretische Computerlinguistik
Universität Tübingen
Wilhelmstr. 19
72074 Tübingen
`uwe.moennich@uni-tuebingen.de`

Abstract

Context-free tree grammars, originally introduced by Rounds ((Rounds, 1970)), are powerful grammar devices for the definition of tree languages. In the present paper, we consider a subclass of the class of context-free tree languages, namely the class of monadic simple context-free tree languages. For this class of context-free tree languages, a faithful rendering of extended TAGs, we show that it can be given a simple logical characterization in terms of monadic second-order transductions.

1 Introduction

The monadic simple context-free tree languages belong to the class of mildly context-sensitive languages. The intuitive notion of mild context-sensitivity has led to two competing candidates claiming to be an exact formal rendering of the intentions Joshi (1985) was trying to capture when introducing this concept. On the one hand multiple context-free grammars and their equivalents exhibiting a variety of wildly different specifications provide impressive evidence that this precise counterpart of the informal description of mild context-sensitivity constitutes a natural class. On the other hand the well-nested subclass of the multiple context-free grammars has recently been advertised as a formalization more in accordance with Joshi's original intentions ((Kanazawa, 2009; Kuhlmann, 2007)). Both candidates have counterparts in the realm of tree languages and it is in this context that they are easily recognized to provide a mathematically precise framework for the characterization of two leading linguistic models, minimalist syntax and tree adjoining grammars (cf. (Harkema, 2001), (Michaelis, 2001), (Kepser and Rogers, 2007), (Mönnich, 1997; Mönnich, 2007)).

The tree languages in question are the multiple regular tree languages ((Raoult, 1997)) and the simple context-free tree languages ((Engelfriet and Maneth, 2000)). Both language families are proper subfamilies of the tree languages generated by context-free hyperedge-replacement graph grammars and the latter family is identical with the output languages of logical tree-to-tree transductions applied to regular tree languages. The obvious question that poses itself is whether the two restricted rule formats or their corresponding tree transducers, finite-copying top-down tree transducers and simple macro/attributed tree transducers, respectively, can be given an equivalent logical characterization in terms of restrictions on the logical formulas defining the relations in the target structures of logical transductions. This is indeed the case. A central result in a paper by Bloem and Engelfriet (2000) states that the tree languages which are the output of finite-copying top-down tree transducers applied to regular tree languages are exactly the output tree languages of logical tree transducers which are direction preserving in the sense that edges in the output trees correspond to directed paths in the input trees. As a first step towards an analogous result for simple context-free tree languages the main theorem of the paper shows that their monadic subclass, which provides a formalization of the extended version of classical tree adjoining grammars ($TAGs$), has indeed an easy logical characterization that puts them on the same footing as their multiple regular counterparts and thereby closes the gap that

Proceedings of the 11th International Workshop on Tree Adjoining Grammars and Related Formalisms (TAG+11), pages 37–45,
Paris, September 2012.

has remained with respect to a model-theoretic description of $TAGs$.

The logical approach to the specification of language classes involves a lot of advantageous properties that have paved the way to its application to linguistic issues. Of particular importance in the present context is the restricted translational power of logical transductions. Monadic second-order definable tree translations are, by definition, of linear size increase. An output tree is at most k times as large as its input tree where k denotes the cardinality of the set of copy names. This bound on the copying power of transduction devices that are motivated by the model-theoretic idea of semantic interpretation is the main reason why the output languages of tree transductions definable in terms of monadic second-order logic satisfy in a particular perspicuous way the crucial criteria Joshi has suggested for the family of mildly context-sensitive languages.

One of our reviewers pointed out that there are recent attempts at relaxing the linearity condition of multiple context-free grammars and thus arriving at a larger class of languages for which it is claimed that they are still in accordance with the intuitions behind the notions of mild context-sensitivity. This extended class allows for a limited amount of copying (Cf.(Bourreau et al., To appear; Kallmeyer, 2010)). Whether such a formalization violates the criterion that poses a bound on cross-serial dependencies seems to be an open question. We favor a strong interpretation of this criterion and therefore are inclined to consider the realm of languages covered by logical translations as the the currently leading contender for an exact specification of Joshi's proposal.

There are two main sources that have influenced the ideas reported in this paper. Apart from the fundamental work on graph structure and monadic second-order logic due to Courcelle and Engelfriet (2012) we have to mention a previous attempt at giving a logical description of linear inside-out context-free tree languages (cf. (Kolb et al., 2000; Kolb et al., 2003)). This attempt relied on a particular technique of regularizing context-free tree grammars and does not lend itself to a treatment of arbitrary regular tree languages as input. The other principal source is provided by the characterization of tree transductions that are specifiable in monadic second-order logic in terms of attributed tree transducers with look-

ahead. This result was established by Bloem and Engelfriet (2000) and constitutes together with our own earlier proof of the equivalence between simple context-free tree grammars and simple attributed tree transducers (Mönnich, 2010) the basis for the main result of the present paper.

We have been at pains to expound the central notions of this paper in an informal way. Our emphasis has been on motivating examples and connections with recent work on syntax-directed semantics. We hope not to have traded formal rigour for transparency in the proof sketches below.

2 Preliminaries

This section defines familiar notions from the theory of syntax-directed semantics together with its model-theoretic counterpart, the theory of monadic second-order transductions.

For any set A, A^* is the set of all strings over A. ε is the empty string, $|w|$ is the length of a string w. N denotes the set $\{0, 1, 2, 3, \dots\}$ of nonnegative integers.

A *single-sorted* or *ranked alphabet* is a finite set Σ given with a mapping $rank : \Sigma \to N$ (the *rank* mapping). We usually write $\Sigma^{(n)}$ to denote the (unique) set of operators of rank $n \in N$; we also write $\sigma^{(n)}$ to indicate that $rank(\sigma) = n$. The elements of $\Sigma^{(0)}$ are also called *constants*. The set of trees T_Σ is defined recursively as follows. Each constant of Σ, i.e., each symbol of rank 0, is a tree. If σ is of rank k and $t_1, \dots, t_k$ are trees, then $\sigma(t_1, \dots, t_k)$ is a tree. A *tree language* $L \subseteq T_\Sigma$ over Σ is a subset of T_Σ. With each tree $t \in T_\Sigma$ we can associate a string $s \in \Sigma^{(0)*}$ by reading the leaves of t from left to right. This string is called the *yield* of t, denoted by $yd(t)$. More formally, $yd(t) = t$ if $t \in \Sigma^{(0)}$, and $yd(t) = yd(t_1) \cdots yd(t_k)$ whenever $t = \sigma(t_1, \dots, t_k)$ with $k \geq 1$. The yield of tree language L is defined straightforwardly as $yd(L) = \{yd(t) | t \in L\}$.

If A is a set (of symbols) disjoint from Σ, then $T_\Sigma(A)$ (alternatively $T(\Sigma, A)$) denotes the set of trees $T_{\Sigma \cup A}$ where all elements of A are taken as constants. Let $X = \{x_1, x_2, x_3, \dots\}$ be a fixed denumerable set of *input variables* and $Y = \{y_1, y_2, y_3, \dots\}$ be a fixed denumerable set of *parameters*. Let $X_0 = Y_0 = \emptyset$ and, for $k \geq 1$, $X_k = \{x_1, \dots, x_k\} \subset X$, and $Y_k = \{y_1, \dots, y_k\} \subset Y$. For $k \geq 0, m \geq 0, t \in T_\Sigma(X_k)$, and $t_1, \dots, t_k \in T_\Sigma(X_m)$, we denote by

$t[t_1, \ldots, t_k]$ the result of *substituting* t_i for x_i in t. Note that $t[t_1, \ldots, t_k]$ is in $T_\Sigma(X_m)$. Note also that for $k = 0$, $t[t_1, \ldots, t_k] = t$.

Definition 1. *A context-free tree (CFT) grammar is a tuple $G = (\mathcal{F}, \Omega, S, P)$ where $\mathcal{F}$ and Ω are ranked alphabets of non-terminals and terminals, respectively, $S \in \mathcal{F}^{(0)}$ is the start symbol and P is a finite set of productions of the form*

$$F(y_1, \ldots, y_m) \to \xi$$

where $F \in \mathcal{F}$ and ξ is a tree over $\mathcal{F}$, Ω and Y_m.

If for every $F \in \mathcal{F}^{(m)}$ each $y \in Y_m$ occurs exactly once on the right-hand side of the corresponding rule then the context-free tree grammar is called *simple in the parameters (sp)*. The family of tree languages which is generated by context-free tree grammars which are simple in their parameters is designated as CFT_{sp}. Of particular interest to us is the situation where all the non-terminals in a simple context-free tree grammar are at most of arity 1. We call this class of grammars *monadic simple* context-free grammars $CFT_{mon,sp}$.

Attributed tree transducers are a variant of attribute grammars in which all attribute values are trees. Besides *meaning names* which transmit information in a top-down manner, attributed tree transducers contain explicit *context names* which allow information to be passed up from a node to its mother. Consequently, arbitrary tree walks can be realized by attributed tree transducers.

Definition 2. *An attributed tree transducer (ATT) is a tuple*

$$A = (Syn, Inh, \Sigma, \Omega, \alpha_m, R),$$

where Syn and Inh are disjoint alphabets of synthesized and inherited attributes, respectively, Σ and Ω are ranked alphabets of input and output symbols, respectively, α_m is a synthesized attribute, and R is a finite set of rules of the following form: For every $\sigma \in \Sigma^{(m)}$, for every $(\gamma, \rho) \in ins_\sigma$ (the set of inside attributes of σ), there is exactly one rule in R_σ:

$$(\gamma, \rho) \to \xi$$

where $\xi \in T_{\Omega \cup out_\sigma}$ and out_σ is the set of outside attributes of σ. Rules where ξ is (γ', ρ') are called copy rules.

Definition 3. *For every $\sigma \in \Sigma^{(m)}$, the set of inside attributes is the set $ins_\sigma = \{(\alpha, \pi) | \alpha \in Syn\} \cup \{(\beta, \pi i) | \beta \in Inh, i \le m\}$ and the set of outside attributes is the set $out_\sigma = \{(\beta, \pi) | \beta \in Inh\} \cup \{(\alpha, \pi i) | \alpha \in Syn, i \le m\}$. π and ρ are path variables ranging over node occurrences in the input tree.*

$ATTs$ with rules R_σ at an input symbol σ in which each outside attribute occurs exactly once are called *simple* attributed tree transducers. We denote this class by $ATT_{ss,si}$.

The *dependencies* between attribute occurrences in an input tree s can be represented with the help of R_σ. An instance of an attribute occurrence (α', π') depends on another occurrence (α, π) if σ labels node u in s, R_σ contains the rule $(\alpha', \pi') \to \xi$ and (α, π) labels one of the leaves in ξ. The *dependency graph* $D(s)$ of an input tree $s \in T_\Sigma$ consists of the set of attribute occurrences together with the dependencies according to the rules in R. Reversing the direction of these dependencies leads to the notion of a *semantic graph* $S(s)$ of an input tree $s \in T_\Sigma$.

An attributed tree transducer is *noncircular* if the paths of attribute dependencies are noncircular. It is well known that noncircular $ATTs$ have unique *decorations dec*, functions which assign each attribute occurrence a tree over $\Omega \cup out_\sigma$ in accordance with the productions R_σ.

Definition 4. *The transduction realized by a noncircular attributed tree transducer A is the function*

$$\tau_A = \{(s, t) | s \in T_\sigma, t \in T_\Omega, t = dec_s(\alpha_m, \epsilon)\}$$

Declarative tree transductions are inspired by the model-theoretic technique of semantic interpretation (Rabin, 1965). The idea is to define a relational structure inside another structure in terms of monadic second-order formulas. Both the input and the output structures are finite trees regarded as finite models.

The language to be used for the specification of properties and relations satisfied by finite tree structures is a straightforward extension of first-order logic: monadic second-order logic (MSO). The language of this logic contains variables that range over subsets of the universe of discourse and quantifiers that bind these (monadic) predicate variables.

Given a ranked signature Σ the monadic second-order language over trees in T_Σ uses atomic formulas $lab_\sigma(x)$ $(\sigma \in \Sigma)$, $child_i(x,y)$, $x = y$ and $x \in X$ to convey the idea that node x has label σ, that node y is the i-th child of node x, that x and y are the same node and that node x is a member of the set of nodes X.

Besides this extension of the classical first-order logic the concept of a monadic second-order definable tree transducer ($MSOTT$) differs in two further aspects from the method of semantic interpretation as originally introduced by Rabin. First, an MSO formula ϕ serves to define the domain of the transducer. The second modification of the original method of semantic interpretation provides for a fixed number k of disjoint copies of the input tree. It is inside these disjoint copies that the output tree is to be defined.

Definition 5. *Given two ranked alphabets Σ and Ω and a finite set C of copy names, a monadic second-order definable* tree transducer *T from T_Σ to T_Ω is specified by the following formulas of the monadic second-order language over Σ:*

(i) a closed formula φ, the domain *formula*

(ii) formulas $\nu_c(x)$ with $c \in C$, the node *formulas*

(iii) formulas $\psi_{\delta,c}(x)$ with $c \in C$ and $\delta \in \Omega$, the labelling *formulas*

(iv) formulas $\chi_{i,c,d}(x,y)$ with $c,d \in C$ and $i \leq$ maximal arity of symbols in Ω, the edge *formulas*

In sharp contrast with the syntax-directed transformation devices a logic based tree transducer T does not translate its input trees in a recursive top-down manner. The translation τ_T realized by such a declarative transducer has to be defined in terms of the familiar ingredients of a relational structure.

Definition 6. *The tree translation τ_T realized by a monadic second-order definable tree transducer T from T_Σ to T_Ω is a partial function $\tau_T : T_\Sigma \to T_\Omega$ defined as follows. The domain of τ_T is $\{s \in T_\Sigma \mid s \models \varphi\}$. For every $s \in T_\Sigma$ in its domain $\tau_T(s)$ is the tree structure $t \in T_\Omega$ such that:*
$$D_t = \{(c,x) \in C \times D_s \mid s \models \nu_c(x)\}$$
is the tree domain of t
$$E_t = \{((c,x),i,(d,y)) \in D_t \times ar(\Omega) \times D_t \mid s \models \chi_{i,c,d}(x,y)\} \quad \text{is the edge relation of } t$$
where $ar(\Omega)$ denotes the rank of Ω
$$L_t = \{((c,x),\delta) \in D_t \times \Omega \mid s \models \psi_{c,\delta}(x)\}$$
is the labeling function of t

Logic based transducers are called *relabeling* if they just relabel the nodes of an input tree. Of particular interest regarding the logical analysis of monadic simple context-free tree grammars are logic based tree transducers that preserve or reverse the direction of the paths in the input tree in their definitions of edges of output trees. This family of tree transducers is designated by $MSOTT_{dir,rev}$. We depart slightly from this definition in allowing defining upwards paths between a leaf node and the daughter of a dominating branching node. In this situation we speak of a *slight modification* of $MSOTT_{dir,rev}$.

3 From $CFT_{mon,sp}$ to $1S, 1I - ATT_{ss,si}$

The proof of the logical characterization of monadic simple context-free tree languages is based on a procedural characterization of simple context-free tree languages as the output languages of simple attributed tree transducers with one synthesized attribute only (Cf. Mönnich, 2010). The simulation of attributed tree transducers by monadic second-order tree transducers along the lines of Bloem and Engelfriet (2000) then leads to the logical characterization of the (formal representation of) extended $TAGs$ in terms of extremely simple edge definitions on the input trees.

The translation below of a given $CFT_{mon,sp}$ G into an equivalent ATT_{sp} A is inspired by the proofs of Lemma 5.11 in (Fülöp and Vogler, 1998) and of Lemma 6.1 in (Engelfriet and Maneth, 1999).

Example 1. *Consider the $CFT_{mon,sp}$ $G = \langle\{S, S', \overline{S}, E, \overline{a}, \overline{b}, \overline{c}, \overline{d}\}, \{a,b,c,d,\varepsilon, S_t, S_t^0\}, S', P\rangle$ with P given as follows:*

$$
\begin{array}{ll}
S' \longrightarrow S_t(\overline{a}, S(\overline{S}(E)), \overline{d}) & \qquad \overline{a} \longrightarrow a \\
S(y) \longrightarrow S_t(\overline{a}, S(\overline{S}(y)), \overline{d}) & \qquad \overline{b} \longrightarrow b \\
S(y) \longrightarrow S_t^0(y) & \qquad \overline{c} \longrightarrow c \\
\overline{S}(y) \longrightarrow S_t(\overline{b}, y, \overline{c}) & \qquad \overline{d} \longrightarrow d \\
& \qquad E \longrightarrow \varepsilon
\end{array}
$$

This grammar generates the language $L = \{a^n b^n, c^n, d^n\}$. A derivation of the string $aabbccdd$ is shown in figure 1. We simplified the presentation in the sense that the last step involves the simultaneous application of several expansion rules.

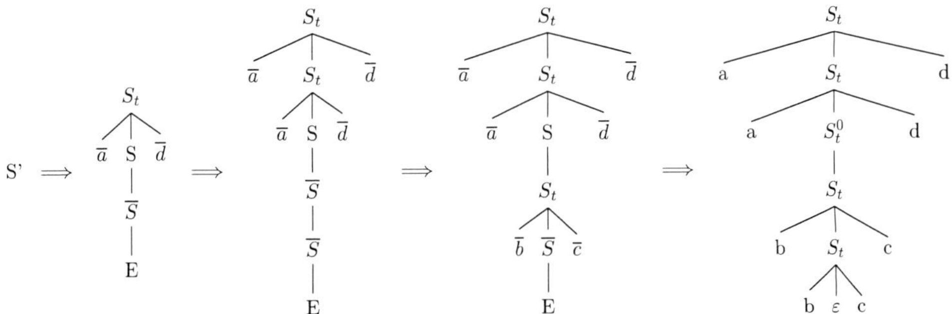

Figure 1: Derivation of yield *aabbccdd*

Inspecting the rules of the example grammar it turns out that they exhibit a particular normal form with a terminal symbol as head and a possibly empty string of non-terminals. This is not an accidental feature of our grammar, but a general characteristic of monadic simple context-free tree grammars. Context-free tree grammars in which the root of the right-hand side of each rule is labelled with a terminal symbol are in *Greibach* normal form. It is well known that there are context-free tree languages that do not admit grammars in Greibach normal form. In the case of tree languages generated by monadic simple context-free tree grammars, however, the classical proof for context-free word grammars goes through without any modification because of the isomorphism between strings and monadic trees. The preceding considerations lead to the following lemma:

Lemma 1. *For any monadic context-free tree grammar G, there is a monadic context-free tree grammar G' in Greibach normal form such that*

$$L(G') = L(G)$$

Given these preparations we arrive at the following translation procedure from monadic simple context-free tree grammars to simple attributed tree transducers.

Lemma 2. *For every $CFT_{mon,sp}$ G, there is an $1S, 1I - ATT_{ss,si}$ A_G that outputs the same language when applied to the derivation trees of G.*

Proof For a given $CFG_{mon,sp}$ $G = (\mathcal{F}, \Omega, S, P)$ an $1S, 1I - ATT_{ss,si} = (Syn, Inh, \Sigma, \Omega, \alpha_m, R)$ A_G that outputs the same language is defined from the rules of G in the following way.

- $Syn = \{0, 1\}$ with $\alpha = \alpha_m$ at the root node

- $Inh = \{y\}$

- Every symbol in the derivation trees is assigned one synthesized attribute.

- If $p : N \to \xi$ is an element of P then R'_p is specified for both the synthesized and inherited attributes by structural induction on the right-hand side ξ:

$$(q, \pi) \to \vartheta(\xi),$$

where $q = 0$ or $q = 1$ depending on the arity of N and ϑ substitutes a non-terminal M in ξ by $(q, \pi i)$ if the non-terminal M occurs in the i-th non-terminal position in ξ and y by (y, π)

$$(y_j, \pi_i) \to \vartheta'(\xi'),$$

where ξ' occurs in the argument position of some non-terminal L in ξ that itself occupies the i-th non-terminal position on the right-hand side of p and ϑ' is identical with ϑ except for erasing every y in ξ'.

⊣

Example 2. *Applying the construction just outlined to the context-free tree grammar of the last example we obtain the following attributed tree transducer $A = (Syn, Inh, \Sigma, \Omega, q_0, R')$:*

- $Syn = \{0, 1\}$

- $Inh = \{y\}$

- $\Sigma = \{p_0, \dots, p_9\}$

- $\Omega = \{a, b, c, d, \varepsilon, S_t, S_t^0\}$

- $q_0 = 0$

- $R' = \bigcup_{p_i} R'_{p_i}$

$$R'_{p_1} = \{(0, \pi) \to S_t((0, \pi 1), (1, \pi 2), (0, \pi 4)),$$
$$(y, \pi 2) \to (1, \pi 3)\}$$
$$R'_{p_2} = \{(1, \pi) \to S_t((0, \pi 1), (1, \pi 2), (0, \pi 4)),$$
$$(y, \pi 2) \to (1, \pi 3),$$
$$(y, \pi 3) \to (y, \pi)\}$$
$$R'_{p_3} = \{(1, \pi) \to S_t^0((y, \pi))\}$$
$$R'_{p_4} = \{|1, \pi) \to S_t((0, \pi 1), (y, \pi)(0, \pi 2))\}$$
$$R'_{p_5} = \{(0, \pi) \to a\}$$
$$R'_{p_6} = \{(0, \pi) \to b\}$$
$$R'_{p_7} = \{(0, \pi) \to c\}$$
$$R'_{p_8} = \{(0, \pi) \to d\}$$
$$R'_{p_9} = \{(1, \pi) \to \varepsilon\}$$

Given the constructed attributed tree transducer A that is equivalent to the previously considered monadic simple context-free tree grammar G we can now repeat the example derivation displayed in figure 1. We follow the conventional graphical representation for drawing attributed derivation trees together with the dependencies obtaining between synthesized and inherited attributes. Occurrences of synthesized and inherited attributes in conjunction with their tree values appear to the right and left, respectively, of the labelled nodes of the input tree. Dependencies among the attribute occurrences are indicated by arrows. Since dependency graphs indicate the connection between an attribute leaf and the tree which is to be substituted for it by building the output tree bottom-up we will depart from the conventional graphical representation in this respect and adopt instead the tradition of semantic graphs which construct the output tree top-down and therefore are direction preserving as far as relations between attribute values are concerned.

Under the stated conventions the graphical representation of the information transport in terms of the constructed attributed tree transducer A that corresponds to the example derivation of figure 1 looks as shown in figure 2. We have again simplified the presentation in the sense that the application of the "barred" rules is contracted into one single step.

4 Equivalence of $CFT_{mon,sp}$ with (a slight modification of) Non-Copying $MSOTT_{dir,rev}$

It was mentioned above that attributed tree transducers are attribute grammars with all their attribute values restricted to trees and their semantic functions to substitution of trees for dependent leaves. Second–order substitution for internal nodes of trees is achieved through the upward information transport that is made possible by the inherited attributes. An analysis of the paths in the semantic dependency graph of the attributed tree transducer that corresponds to a monadic simple context-free tree grammar in *Greibach* normal form reveals that these paths are either direction preserving as in the case of minimalist grammars or direction reversing.

Lemma 3. *For every $CFT_{mon,sp}$ G there is (a slight modification of) an equivalent non-copying reduced $MSOTT_{dir,rev}$ T.*

Proof (Sketch) The main idea of the proof is a careful case analysis of the translation procedure that produces an equivalent attributed tree transducer from a given monadic simple context-free tree grammar G. Inspection of this translation procedure in the proof of Lemma 2 reveals the following types of right-hand sides in the rules of a monadic simple context-free tree grammar. W.l.g we consider only terminals with at most arity one:

- $F \longrightarrow a$ The synthetic meaning attribute gets the value a at the node corresponding to the application of this rule.

- $F \longrightarrow a(N)$ The synthetic meaning attribute gets the value $a(\alpha, \pi)$ establishing a dependency on the synthetic value of the daughter.

- $F \longrightarrow a(N(M))$ In addition to the previous case a further dependency is established on the value of the sibling node corresponding to the application of a production with left-hand side M. This dependency is mediated by a copy rule at the inherited context attribute of the node corresponding to an application of a production with left-hand side N.

Iteration of the second case leads to further top-down semantic dependencies. If monadic instead

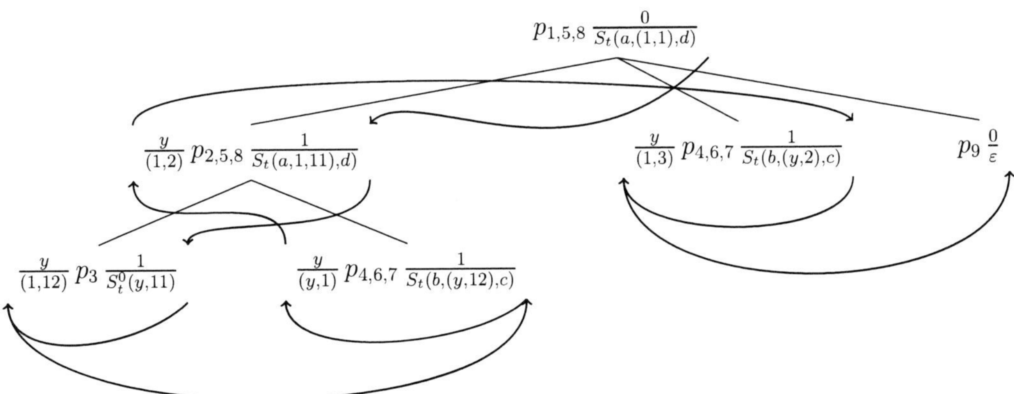

Figure 2: Attributed derivation tree with semantic dependency relations

of nullary non-terminals $F(y)$ are rewritten the parameter y mediates an one-step upwards information transport by means of inherited copy rules.

From this case analysis it follows immediately that all inherited rules are copy rules whereas all synthetic rules add material to the output tree. Furthermore, all upwards dependencies are mediated by an inherited rule establishing a dependency on the synthetic value of a sibling node.

Based on this intermediate simple ATT we can now define the equivalent MSO tree transducer T by specifying the edge formulas $\chi_{1,\gamma,\gamma'}(x,y)$ that represent the dependencies between the attributes and the node formulas $\psi_{d,\gamma}(x)$ that define the labels of the output tree. We assume again for simplicity that the terminals of the given grammar G are of arity at most one and that the copy rules introduce a new output symbol id. The set of copy nodes consists of the synthetic and the inherited attribute. The edge formulas mirror the information transport of rules of the form

$$(*) \qquad (\gamma, \rho) \to a(\gamma', \rho')$$

where (γ, ρ) is an inside, (γ', ρ') an outside attribute and a an output symbol or the new symbol id. Such an edge formula $\chi_{1,\gamma,\gamma'}(x,y)$ is the disjunction of all formulas $\exists z(lab_\sigma(z) \wedge edge_j(z,x) \vee edge_{j'}(z,y))$ for all input symbols σ with j, j' equal to 0 or 1 and $(\gamma, \pi j)$ depending on $(\gamma', \pi j')$ in R_σ. In the situation where $j, j' = 0$ $edge_0(x,y)$ is shorthand for $x = y$.

The node formula $\psi_{d,\gamma}(x)$ is the disjunction of all formulas $\exists z(lab_\sigma(z) \wedge edge_j(z,x))$ for all input symbols σ where the same stipulations hold

as for the edge formulas and R_σ contains the rule (*).

This easy transfer of the translation technique developed by Bloem and Engelfriet (2000) to the context of simple tree transducers with only one synthesised and one inherited attribute reveals immediately that the defined monadic second-order tree translation fulfills the condition of being *direction preserving/reversing* apart from the information flow to and fro between the the synthetic and inherited copies of the input trees.

Bloem and Engelfriet show how to prune all occurrences of these transitions. Since this makes the "inherited" copy of the input tree superfluous we can erase it completely and arrive thus at a *reduced* non-copying MSO-transduction in the sense that every node is the head or tail of an edge. The pruning step has introduced a slight modification of the upward paths by linking some leafs to the first daughter of a dominating branching node. $\dashv$

Applying the construction just outlined to the information transport illustrated by figure 2 we obtain the defined edges in the output of an MSO-transduction shown in figure 3.

Lemma 4. *For every (slight modification of a) non-copying reduced $MSOTT_{dir,rev}$ T there is an equivalent $CFT_{mon,sp}$ G_T.*

Proof (Sketch) We adapt again to the present situation the method of proof developed by Bloem and Engelfriet (2000). We assume with them that the root of the defined output tree of a given direction preserving/reversing MSO tree transducer T is identical to the root of the input tree. We as-

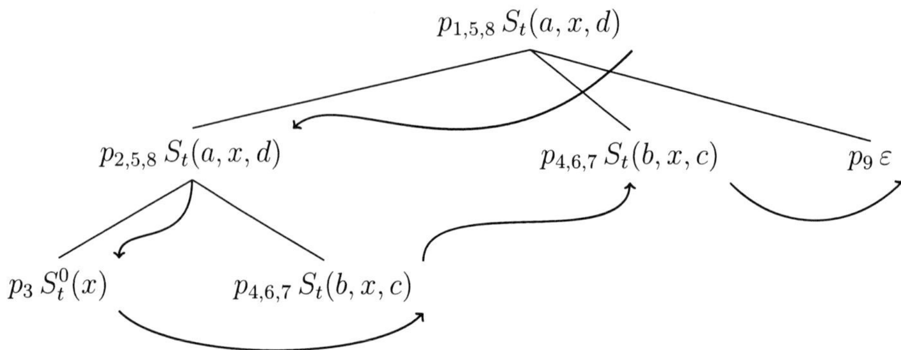

Figure 3: MSO-defined edges

sume furthermore that edges originate or end at every node of the input tree. For nodes occurring between endpoints of edges that correspond to direction preserving paths this assumption could be avoided by eliminating spurious rules like $N \longrightarrow M$ from the equivalent context-free tree grammar. Finally we observe that the upward edges of the output tree may still be established between nodes that are not immediate neighbours.

This non-local feature can be excluded by applying the inverse of the pruning action of the previous lemma. If there is a non-local upward edge from the leaf of the input tree to a sibling of the first daughter of a dominating branching node then we define a local path on an "inherited" copy of the input tree that connects the endpoints of the original non-local upward edge.

The specification of the equivalent ATT relies on information about the configuration of the (local) edges in its immediate neighbourhood. This information can be stored in the node labels by means of a relabeling $MSOTT$ T' that extends each label by a vector of truth values of the formulas for top-down and bottom-up edges and for edges between nodes and their twins in the other copy. To illustrate the simplest case for a unary output symbol a and a "synthesized" copy name γ: If the formula $\psi_{a,\gamma}(x)$ is true at a node with extended label σ' and the only true edge formula is $\chi_{1,\gamma,\gamma}(x,y)$ then $R_{\sigma'}$ contains just $(\gamma, \rho) \to a(\gamma, \rho 1)$.

From this intermediate attributed tree transducer the equivalent monadic simple context-free tree grammar G_T is then defined as follows where we use the notational conventions introduced in the preliminary section (cf. (Mönnich, 2010)):

- $\mathcal{F} = \Sigma$ where the arity of non-terminals is either zero or one depending on the occurrence of an inherited attribute assigned to them in the input tree.

- $\Omega = \Omega$

- $S = \{\sigma^{(0)}\}$ with $\sigma \in \Sigma$ labeling the root of an input tree.

- For every $\sigma \in \Sigma$ we construct a rule

$$\sigma(y_1, \ldots, y_n) \to t$$

where $t = COMP(\xi)$ and ξ is the right-hand side of the only synthesized attribute α in R_σ. The right-hand sides of rules in R_σ are designated by $rhs(\gamma\pi, \sigma)$ in the following:

(i) If $\xi = \alpha\pi i$ then

$$\sigma(y_1, \ldots, y_n) \to t$$

where $t = COMP(\xi)$ and ξ is the right-hand side of the only synthesized attribute α in R_σ. The right-hand sides of rules in R_σ are designated by $rhs(\gamma\pi, \sigma)$ in the following:

(i) If $\xi = \alpha\pi i$ then

$$COMP(\xi) = \rho(t)$$

where ρ labels the ith daughter of σ and

$$t = COMP(rhs(\beta\pi i, \sigma))$$

(ii) If $\xi = \beta\pi$ then

$$COMP(\xi) = y$$

(iii) If $\xi = f(\xi_1, \ldots, \xi_r)$ for $f \in \Omega^{(r)}$

$$\text{COMP}(\xi) = f(COMP(\xi_1), \ldots, COMP(\xi_r))$$

By a routine inspection it is easy to verify that the resulting grammar G_A is indeed simple and that it generates exactly the output language of T.

$\dashv$

By lemmas 4 and 4 we obtain our main result.

Theorem 1. *The monadic simple context-free tree languages are exactly the output languages (of a slight modification) of non-copying direction preserving/reversing MSO definable tree transductions.*

5 Envoi

The question of how to extend the logical characterization given in the present paper to the full class of simple context-free languages or to the family of well-nested tree languages, for that matter, is still open. Our conjecture is that a similar characterization holds for these languages. The main step towards such a result would consist in establishing a Greibach normal form for this larger class of languages.

References

Roderick Bloem and Joost Engelfriet. 2000. A Comparison of Tree Transductions Defined by Monadic Second-Order Logic and by Attribute Grammars. *J. Comp. System Sci.*, 61:1–50.

Pierre Bourreau, Sylvain Salvati, and Laura Kallmeyer. To appear. On io-copying and mildly context-sensitive formalisms. In *Proceedings of Formal Grammar 2012. Lecture Notes in Computer Science.*

Bruno Courcelle and Joost Engelfriet. 2012. *Graph Structure and Monadic Second-Order Logic. A Language-Theoretic Approach.* Cambridge University Press.

Joost Engelfriet and Sebastian Maneth. 1999. Macro Tree Transducers, Attribute Grammars, and MSO Definable Tree Translations. *Information and Computation*, 154:34–91.

Joost Engelfriet and Sebastian Maneth. 2000. Tree Languages Generated by Context-Free Graph Grammars. In Hartmut Ehrig et al., editor, *Graph Transformation*, number 1764 in LNCS, pages 15–29. Springer.

Zoltán Fülöp and Heiko Vogler. 1998. *Syntax-Directed Semantics - Formal Models Based on Tree Transducers.* Springer, New York and Berlin.

Hendrik Harkema. 2001. *Parsing Minimalist Languages.* Ph.D. thesis, University of California at Los Angeles.

Laura Kallmeyer. 2010. On mildly-context-sensitive non-linear rewriting. *Research on Language and Computation*, 8:341–363.

Makoto Kanazawa. 2009. The convergence of well-nested mildly context-sensitive grammar formalisms. In *14th Conference on Formal Grammar*. Slides available at http://research.nii.jp/˜kanazawa/.

Stephan Kepser and James Rogers. 2007. The equivalence of tree adjoining grammars and monadic linear context-free tree grammars. In M. Kracht, G. Penn, and E. Stabler, editors, *Mathematics of Language 10*.

Hans-Peter Kolb, Uwe Mönnich, and Frank Morawietz. 2000. Descriptions of cross-serial dependencies. *Grammars*, 3(2/3):189–216.

Hans-Peter Kolb, Jens Michaelis, Uwe Mönnich, and Frank Morawietz. 2003. An operational and denotational approach to non-context-freeness. *Theoretical Computer Science*, 293:261–289.

Marco Kuhlmann. 2007. *Dependency Structures and and Lexicalized Grammars.* Ph.D. thesis, Saarland University.

Jens Michaelis. 2001. *On Formal Properties of Minimalist Grammar*, volume 13 of *Linguistics in Potsdam*. Universität Potsdam.

Uwe Mönnich. 1997. Adjunction as substitution. In G-J. M. Kruijff, G. Morill, and R. Oehrle, editors, *Formal Grammar '97*, pages 169–178.

Uwe Mönnich. 2007. Minimalist syntax, multiple regular tree grammars and direction preserving tree transductions. In J. Rogers and S. Kepser, editors, *Proceedings Model Theoretic Syntax at 10*.

Uwe Mönnich. 2010. Well-nested tree languages and attributed tree transducers. In Srinivas Bangalore, Robert Frank, and Maribel Romero, editors, *TAG+10. Proceedings of the 10th International Workshop on Tree Adjoining Grammars and Related Formalims.*

Michael O. Rabin. 1965. A simple method for undecidability proofs and some applications. In Y. Bar-Hillel, editor, *Logic Methodology and Philosophy of Science II*, pages 58–68. North-Holland, Amsterdam.

Jean-Claude Raoult. 1997. Rational Tree Relations. *Bull. Belg. Math. Soc.*, 4:149–176.

William C. Rounds. 1970. Tree-oriented proofs of some theorems on context-free and indexed languages. In *2nd Annual ACM Symposium on Theory of Computing*, pages 109–116.

Synchronous Tree Unification Grammar

Timm Lichte
Collaborative Research Center 991
University of Düsseldorf
lichte@phil.hhu.de

Abstract

This paper presents a novel grammar formalism, Synchronous Tree Unification Grammar (STUG), that borrows ideas from two rather distinct exemplars of tree-based grammar formalisms, namely Synchronous Tree Adjoining Grammar and Tree Unification Grammar. At the same time STUG differs considerably from those in that it allows for a clean separation of syntax and valency. Exploiting this potential in the modelling of natural language grammar has a number of interesting consequences that we will sketch in the course of this paper.

1 Motivation

The underlying motivation for the development of Synchronous Tree Unification Grammar (STUG) is to model syntax and valency as separated, yet linked dimensions of natural language signs. This sharply contrasts with the lexical amalgamation of syntax and valency found within the TAG framework (and other main stream syntactic frameworks). Very generally speaking, we take *valency* to be a mapping from semantic roles to sets of morpho-syntactic properties and some marker for indicating necessity. Following common terminology, realizations of valency roles are also called *arguments*.

In TAG elementary trees, valency properties of the lexical anchor are commonly mapped bijectively onto non-terminal leaves due to well-formedness conditions (Abeillé, 1988; Frank, 1992; Abeillé and Rambow, 2000; Frank, 2002), while the realization of optional valency roles is reflected across the set of elementary trees with the same lexical anchor. However, the correspondence between elementary tree and valency frame is blurred by functional items such as complementizers, determiners and auxiliary verbs, which commonly anchor an elementary tree of their own.

This way of amalgamating elementary trees and valency information can be held responsible for a couple of difficulties that have shown up in various aspects of the TAG framework – amongst them the following:

Since elementary trees for predicative verbs enforce the surface realization of the verbal head and its obligatory arguments, TAG accounts have to cope with *elliptical structures* (i.e. with gapping) by means of more or less far reaching concessions: either tangled trees are generated from elementary trees using a non-trivial contraction operation (Sarkar and Joshi, 1996; Sarkar and Joshi, 1997), or one falls back on an infinitely ambiguous lexicon (Seddah, 2008; Seddah et al., 2010), or one includes empty words as a result of a deletion-like operation (Lichte and Kallmeyer, 2010) or as a result of lexical insertion using extra elementary trees (Sarkar, 1997; Seddah and Sagot, 2006).

Since alternative valency frames and alternative linearizations thereof multiply the set of (yet unanchored) tree templates (Prolo, 2002), the use of a metagrammar system in broad-coverage grammars is practically inevitable (XTAG Research Group, 2001; Duchier et al., 2004). Important syntactic generalisations are therefore not expressed directly in a TAG, but emerge indirectly across elementary trees. Furthermore the factorization by means of metagrammars makes the inclusion of empty words attractive, since they increase the reusability of tree fragments.

Finally, since elementary trees span over an ex-

Proceedings of the 11th International Workshop on Tree Adjoining Grammars and Related Formalisms (TAG+11), pages 46–54,
Paris, September 2012.

tended domain of locality and may relate a lexical anchor to more than one preceding constituent, it is far from obvious how incremental parsing can be performed. Proposals so far either add unlexicalized trees ("prediction trees") and a verification operation (Demberg and Keller, 2008; Demberg, 2010), or place the lexical anchor at the left edge of an elementary tree, the head of which can be left underspecified (Mazzei et al., 2007).

Each of these difficulties may seem resolvable in one of the mentioned ways. But in my view the sum of necessary adaptations and concessions makes it worth thinking about accounts that relate syntax and valency more indirectly. STUG represents the first result of this line of thought.

2 The STUG formalism

2.1 The elementary structures

STUG and Synchronous Tree-Adjoining Grammar (STAG) (Shieber and Schabes, 1990; Shieber, 1994; Nesson and Shieber, 2008) share the idea, that syntactic and semantic representations are joined in the lexicon by making up a set of pairs of trees or multi-component structures. Furthermore there is some way of directly linking nodes of the syntactic domain and the semantic domain within an elementary pair.

To provide an example, a STUG pair for the verb *laughs* is shown in Figure 1. We call the first element of the STUG pair the *syntactic tree*, and the second element the *valency tree*. While the syntactic tree corresponds to an elementary and derived tree known from TAG, the valency tree resembles a TAG derivation tree in that it is unordered and may have edge labels, which here indicate semantic roles. The valency tree for *laughs* in Figure 1 mentions two argument roles, namely A(GENT) and P(ATIENT), that are specified along the feature structures in the respective nodes. Note that features can be polarized in sense of (Guillaume and Perrier, 2009): features that must be specified carry an exclamation mark, while the #-symbol is attached to "neutralized" features which may not unify with another neutralized feature. Links, finally, are represented by circled numbers, i e. ①...ⓝ.

Speaking more formally, a STUG consists of tuples $\langle \sigma, \{\phi_1, \ldots, \phi_n\}, \frown \rangle$ with σ being a syntactic tree, with a set of valency trees $\{\phi_1, \ldots, \phi_n\}$ and a linking relation $\frown$, for which

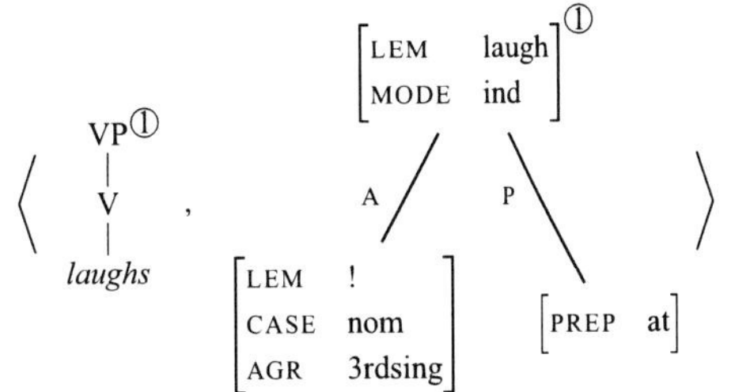

Figure 1: STUG pair for *laughs*.

the following holds:

- $\frown: P(V_\sigma) \to 2^{V_{\phi_1} \cup \ldots \cup V_{\phi_n}}$, where $P(V_\sigma)$ is the partition of the set of nodes from σ, and where $2^{V_{\phi_1} \cup \ldots \cup V_{\phi_n}}$ is the power set of the union of the sets of nodes from $\phi_1, \ldots, \phi_n$.

- For every valency tree $\phi_i \in \{\phi_1, \ldots, \phi_n\}$ with nodes V_i there exists at least one $\langle V_{syn}, V_{val} \rangle \in \frown$ with $V_i \cap V_{val} \neq \emptyset$.

In other words, (i) a link relates two sets of nodes, (ii) every syntactic node participates at most in one link and (iii) every valency tree must be linked with the syntactic tree. Note that we omit set braces around valency trees whenever a STUG pair includes only one valency tree, as is the case in Figure 1.

2.2 The combinatorial operations

While STAG uses substitution and adjunction in both domains, STUG combines syntactic trees by substitution and fusion, and valency trees by tree unification.

The *fusion operation* (Lichte, 2010) is a kind of tree unification where only single nodes unify, hereafter further limited to root nodes: When syntactic trees γ_i, γ_j with root nodes v_i, v_j are fused, the resulting syntactic tree γ' with root node v' only includes γ_i' and γ_j', where γ_i' is γ_i with v_i replaced by v', and where γ_j' is γ_j with v_j replaced by v'. Furthermore every node from γ_i' linearly precedes every node from γ_j'. A sample derivation of *John sometimes laughs* using fusion and substitution is shown in Figure 2, which also demonstrates, that fusion allows the generated syntactic structures to be flat.

The order of fusion is controlled via finite state automata (FSA) that are assigned to nodes based on their syntactic label. A sample FSA for label VP is depicted in Figure 3. It restricts the linear

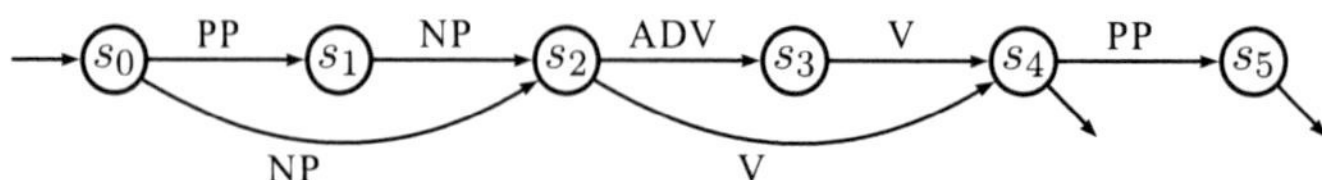

Figure 3: Sample finite state automaton for category VP.

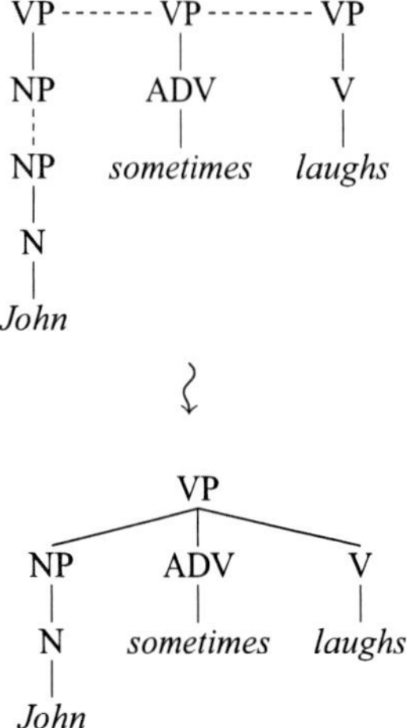

Figure 2: Derivation of *John sometimes laughs*. Dashed horizontal lines stand for fusion and dashed vertical lines stand for substitution.

order of daughter nodes in the following way: Let $l_V(v)$ be the label of v and let $fsa(l_V(v))$ be the FSA assigned to v. If $v_1 \ldots v_n$ is the sequence of daughter nodes of v in the final derived tree, the word $l_V(v_1) \ldots l_V(v_n)$ must be in $L(fsa(l_V(v)))$. To come back to our example, the derived tree in Figure 2 is licit, since the label sequence NP ADV V of the daughters of the VP node is in the language of the corresponding FSA shown in Figure 3.

In the process of fusion, links in the syntactic trees are collapsed in the following way: Let $\langle V_{syn_i}, V_{val_i} \rangle$ and $\langle V_{syn_j}, V_{val_j} \rangle$ be the links associated with nodes v_i, v_j that are replaced by v'. After fusion there is a new link $\langle V_{syn_i} \setminus v_i \cup V_{syn_j} \setminus \{v_j\} \cup \{v'\}, V_{val_i} \cup V_{val_j} \rangle$. Something similar applies during substitution.

The combination of valency trees falls back upon the more general notion of *(tree) unification*, as is known, e. g., from Tree Unification Grammar (TUG) (Popowich, 1989; Gerdes, 2004). Unifying trees γ_1 and γ_2 to obtain tree γ_3 implies that the unifying and the resulting nodes form one isomorphic subtree in γ_1, γ_2 and γ_3 respectively. In order to narrow down the space of results, only tree unifications with a maximal number of unified nodes are considered. In STUG, the linking structure poses further constraints on tree unification: (i) unifying valency trees must be co-linked; (ii) if two unifying nodes carry links, they must be co-linked. When two nodes unify, their features structures unify, just like the label of unifying edges.

Finally, it needs to be specified, what happens to the links when unifying nodes of valency trees. Roughly, the links of the resulting node form the set union of the links of the unifying nodes. More precisely, if nodes v_i, v_j are replaced by v, every link $\langle V_{syn}, V_{val} \rangle$ with $v_i \in V_{val}$ or $v_j \in V_{val}$ is replaced by $\langle V_{syn}, V_{val} \setminus \{v_i, v_j\} \cup \{v\} \rangle$.

Coming back to the STUG derivation of the sentence *John sometimes laughs*, Figure 4 displays the required elementary STUG pairs. Note that the valency structure of *sometimes* specifies a T(ENSE)-role and that the unlexicalized STUG pair solely serves to embed NPs in a VP. The STUG derivation can be processed in two steps: first the syntactic tree is generated according to Figure 2, and after that the collected valency trees get unified into one. This two step approach is pursued in Figure 5.

3 Expressive power

STUG is powerful enough to account for ill-nested dependencies such as in (1):

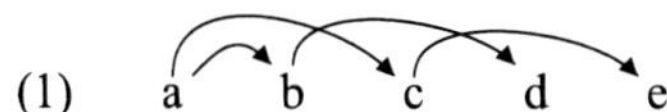

(1)   a   b   c   d   e

Assuming that the language contains only this string, the corresponding STUG in Figure 6 exploits the fact that all words differ and every word has a unique valency structure. Then in a flat structure, licensed by a simple FSA directly on the words, every node of the valency structure is linked to the S node, so that polarized features bring about the intended dependency relations and nothing more.

On the other side, STUG seems not capable of generating the counting language $\{a^n\, b^n | n > 0\}$ with crossed dependencies (and thus also

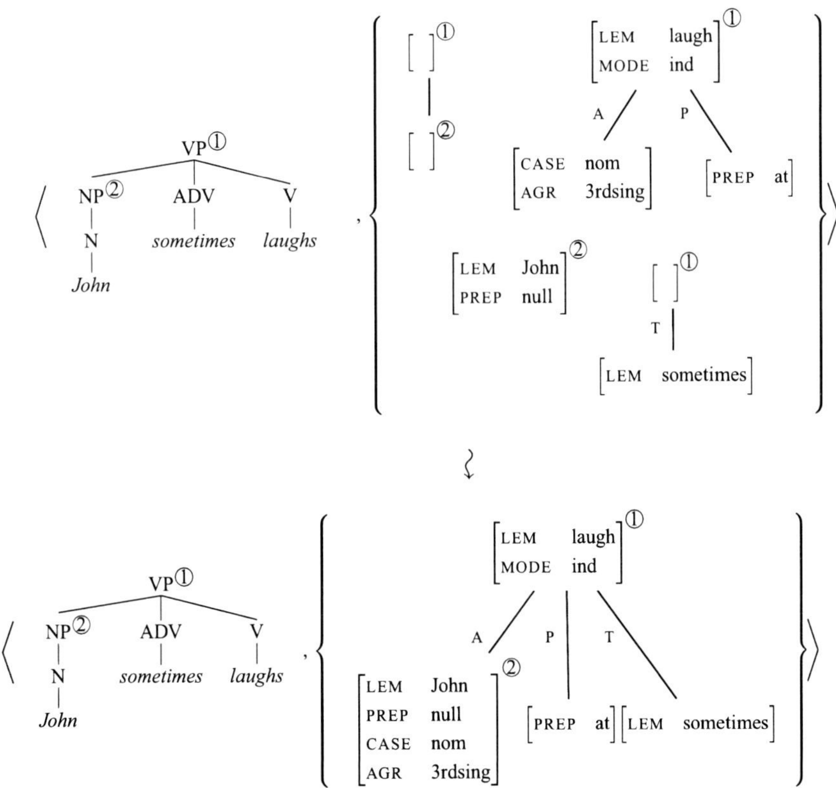

Figure 5: STUG derivation of *John sometimes laughs*.

not the copy language). Apparently linking is not selective enough to relate a^i only with b^i, while both can be in arbitrarily distant parts of the syntactic tree. Something similar also holds for the scrambling language $\mathrm{SCR}^{ind} = \{\sigma(NP_1, \ldots, NP_m)V_m \ldots V_1 | m \geq 1$ and σ is a permutation $\}$, where every $V_i + 1$ is supposed to govern V_i and which is beyond the expressive power of LCFRS (Becker et al., 1991). The counting language $\{a^n \, b^n | n > 0\}$ with nested dependencies is different is this respect, as can be seen from the STUG in Figure 7.

If we make use of neutralized polarity in features (indicated by #), which prevents unification of neutralized features and therefore helps to keep apart certain nodes in the valency tree, it is possible to generate the MIX-language, i.e. $\{w | w \in \{a, b, c\}^*, |a|_w = |b|_w = |c|_w\}$, as Figure 8 proves. Furthermore the grammar in Figure 8 can be easily adapted to derive the counting language $\{a^n \, b^n \, c^n \, d^n \, e^n | n > 0\}$ which also lies beyond the expressive power of TAG.

Hence, STUG seems to be both more and less powerful than TAG.

4 Formalism related questions

4.1 Valency structure = dependency structure?

The valency structure of a sentence and its dependency structure are not isomorphic. As Figure 9 shows, the contribution of functional elements such as the complementizer *that* and the passive auxiliary *is* can be diverse: *that* only contributes to the morpho-syntactic properties of the predicate node that is linked to the VP node in syntax; *is* furthermore specifies certain roles of the corresponding predicate. In both cases, however, functional elements do not get represented as nodes in the valency tree. This follows from the concept of valency as a mapping based solely on semantic roles. In contrast, the dependency structure would include also functional elements as single nodes, as it is a graph over words by definition.

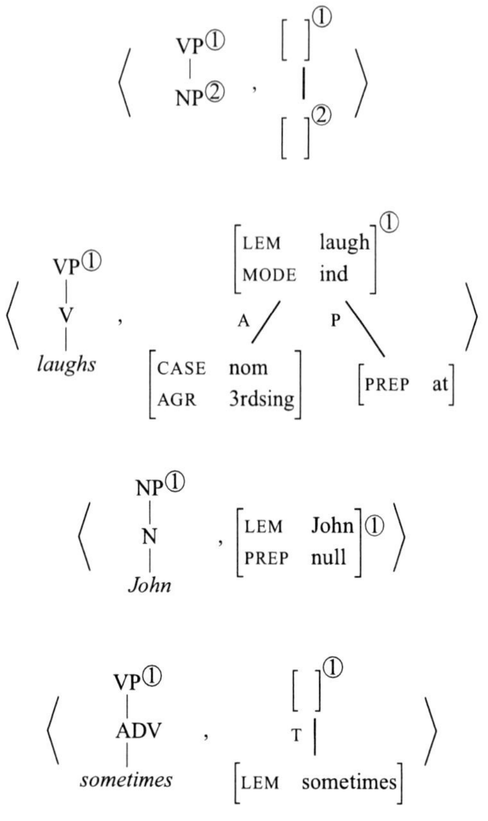

Figure 4: Elementary STUG pairs for *John sometimes laughs*.

One of the benefits in choosing valency structures might be that it circumvents the notoriously unclear (i.e. somewhat arbitrary) status of functional elements in dependency representations.

Note that derived valency structures do not only include semantic roles of arguments, but also semantic roles of adjuncts (see Figure 5). Consequently, they seem to have much in common with descriptions known from scenes-and-frames semantics (Fillmore, 1977a; Fillmore, 1977b).

4.2 Sister adjunction instead of fusion?

Both fusion and sister adjunction (Rambow et al., 1995; Chiang, 2003) support the generation of flat structures. However, they do not seem to be interchangeable in the context of STUG (see (Lichte, 2010) for a related discussion concerning TT-MCTAG). While fusion merges the root nodes of trees, sister adjunction rather draws a new edge between nodes. Choosing sister adjunction instead of fusion therefore considerably reduces the

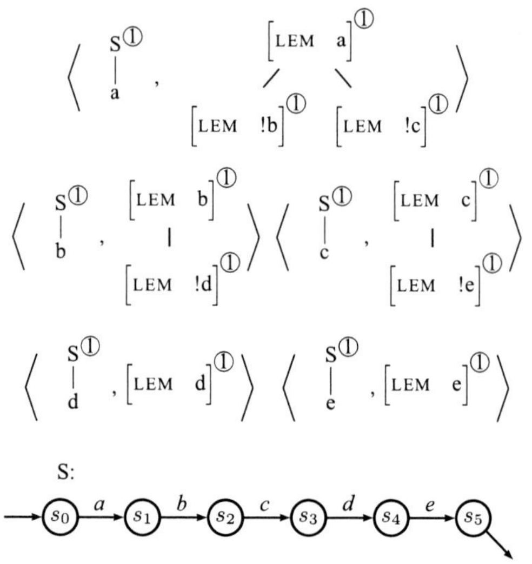

Figure 6: STUG for the ill-nested dependency structure in (1).

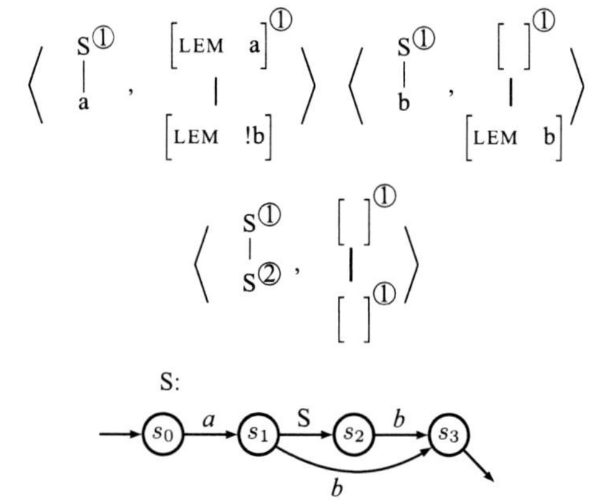

Figure 7: STUG for the string $a^n\ b^n$ with nested dependencies.

number of nodes, to which links can be attached in the lexicon. But since linking is a cornerstone of STUG, it is hard to see, how a STUG with sister adjunction for the mentioned cases would look like, let alone whether this would perform any better.

4.3 Feature structures instead of trees?

So far valency structures are represented as unordered trees whose edges carry role labels and stand for semantic relations, some of them functional in nature. It is thus debatable, whether one should choose a representation based on features structures instead, as they account for functional relations more straightforwardly. To give an ex-

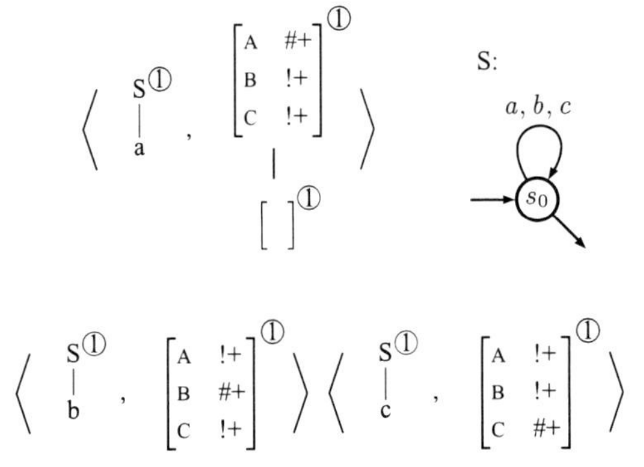

Figure 8: An STUG with neutralized features, marked up by exclamation marks, for deriving the MIX-language.

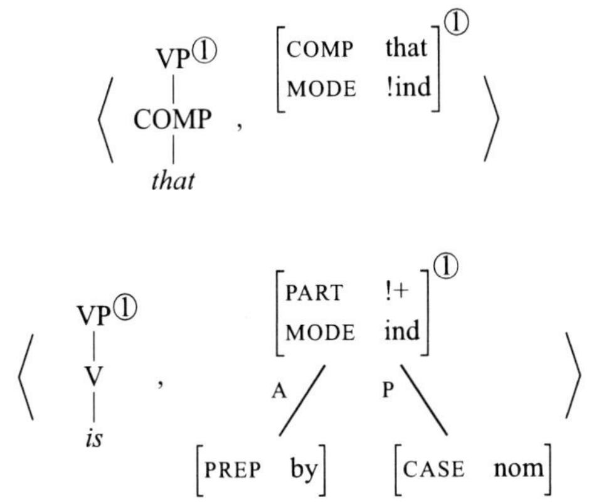

Figure 9: STUG pairs for complementizer *that* and passive auxiliary *is*. Exclamation marks indicate polarized features.

ample, the valency tree for *laughs* in Figure 1 could be replaced by the feature structure representation in Figure 10.

On the other side, a tree-based representation seems to pay off in cases where semantic roles are to be underspecified or where relations are non-functional, i.e. a single semantic role gets assigned to several constituents. The latter happens most prominently with temporal or locational roles.

5 Some consequences: ellipsis, grammar size and incrementality

Contrary to the amalgamation of syntax and valency in the TAG framework, STUG allows for a clear separation of syntax and valency, according to which syntax is only concerned with the

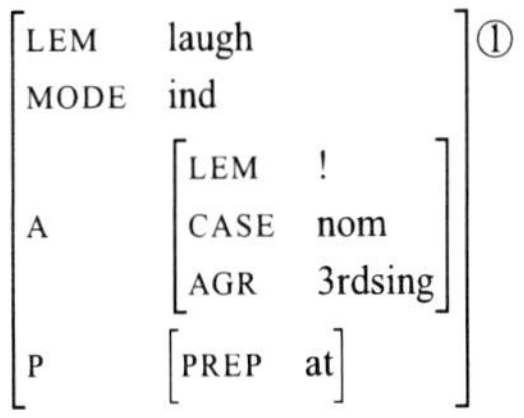

Figure 10: The valency tree of Figure 1 as feature structure.

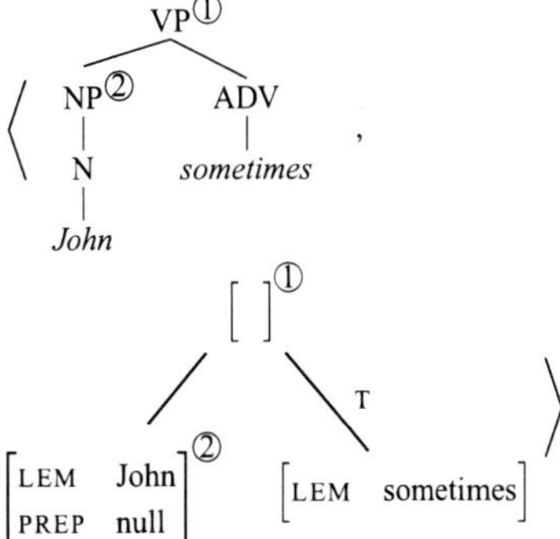

Figure 11: Derived STUG pair for *John sometimes*, which could be the fragmentary answer to the question *Who laughs?*, based on the elementary STUG pairs in Figure 4.

linearization of words (based on their syntactic category) and the determination of the local domain (based on the linking). Argument linking, however, completely rests on the unification of valency trees. This kind of separation has interesting consequences for the model of syntax. In the following we will discuss three of them involving ellipsis, grammar size and incrementality.

5.1 Ellipsis

Since syntactic trees can combine without there being any direct valency relation, STUG supports the base generation of ellipsis straightforwardly, as is shown in Figure 11 using the example of gapping. While the root node in the valency tree remains unspecified, the syntactic tree does not include any kind of empty placeholder for the missing verb. Furthermore neither extra rules nor extra lexical entries are involved in the process of derivation. Reconstruction, however, has to be guided by context, which can be thought of as set of more or less salient valency structures.

This analysis differs fundamentally from syntactic models that adhere to the amalgamation of syntax and valency. They start out from complete syntactic representations of valency frames, which they adapt in cases of incompleteness. In this respect TAG accounts behave similar to accounts from GB, CCG or HPSG. Either two complete syntactic representations are "contracted" (Sarkar and Joshi, 1996; Sarkar and Joshi, 1997), or one complete syntactic representation is augmented with empty words as a result of deletion (Lichte and Kallmeyer, 2010) or insertion (Seddah and Sagot, 2006), or the lexicon includes incomplete syntactic representations as defective variants (Sarkar, 1997). None of these strategies is pursued in STUG.

In favour of contraction accounts one could argue, that contraction and reconstruction of ellipsis go hand in hand. Hence no extra mechanism for reconstruction is required. However, contraction is only applicable in cases where ellipsis and its antecedent can be located in the same sentence. It is therefore hardly applicable to fragementary answers or fragmentary corrections (Ginzburg and Sag, 2001; Schlangen, 2003; Ginzburg and Cooper, 2004), not to speak of discourse-inital fragments (Stainton, 1998; Stainton, 2006). For these cases a separate reconstruction mechanism based on the surrounding discourse is needed anyways. (Lichte and Kallmeyer, 2010) propose to relate reconstruction to the derivation tree of the antecedent sentence.

Summing up it can be said that the sketched STUG account to ellipsis looks promising, as no extra syntactic mechanism is used and reconstruction relates to valency structures, which seem at least as suitable as derivation trees.

5.2 Grammar size

For generating and maintaining a large-coverage TAG, the use of a metagrammar system is almost inevitable due to the size of the grammar. Regarding, for example, XTAG (XTAG Research Group, 2001), (Prolo, 2002) counts 97 tree templates for intransitive, transitive and ditransitive subcategorization frames. Taking all subcategorization frames (including e. g. those for idioms) into account, XTAG contains even 1008 verbal tree templates. This is due to the fact, that alternative argument realizations tend to be derived by means of different tree templates. In other words, the set of tree templates is some subset of the "Cartesian product" (Prolo, 2002) of subcategorization frames, alternative linearizations and active/passive alternations.

On top of that, optional arguments further increase lexical ambiguity by joining different tree families. For example, the finite verb *laughs* anchors intransitive tree families with and without PP argument, thus at least ten tree templates: two of the base configuration, three for extraction including preposition stranding, and five for relative clauses.

STUG helps to eliminate these two sources for large grammars and lexical ambiguity. Alternative linearizations can be represented in one FSA, i. e. outside elementary structures, while optional and obligatory arguments can be differentiated locally within a valency tree. Therefore the number of elementary structures reduces substantially compared to TAG. This already becomes apparent with regard to the lexical STUG pair in Figure 1, which, in combination with the simplistic FSA in Figure 3, suffices to cover four out of the ten mentioned tree templates for the finite verb *laughs*.

But it is not only the reduction of elementary structures that makes STUG attractive. Another source for grammar complexity lies in the rich feature structures with which nodes of TAG elementary trees may be equipped. XTAG defines around 50 features and uses, for example, no less than nine features to get the sequencing of determiners in NPs right. But also the verbal projection is equipped with an impressive number of features. Some of them help to constrain linearization (e. g. INV and COMP), while others pass on case or agreement restrictions, such as ASSIGN-CASE and AGR, or just display morphological properties of a phrasal head, auch as MODE.

By contrast, the snippets of STUG presented above have already shown, that no features get percolated around in the syntax tree of a STUG pair. Instead their main purpose is to specify nodes in the valency tree directly. Accordingly, mediating features like ASSIGN-CASE seem to be obsolete, as even raising verbs can directly access the raised subject in the valency structure. This is exemplified in Figure 12. Finally, the work of features that constrain linearization is now done elsewhere, namely in FSAs, making them obsolete as well. Hence, STUG seems to allow for a more precise, more transparent use of features, and it also seems to require a smaller number of features compared to TAG/XTAG.

$$\left\langle \begin{array}{c} \mathrm{VP}^{①} \\ | \\ \mathrm{V} \\ | \\ \textit{seems} \end{array} \ , \ \begin{bmatrix} \mathrm{LEM} & \mathrm{seem} \\ \mathrm{MODE} & \mathrm{ind} \end{bmatrix}^{①} \atop \mathrm{TH} \right\rangle$$

Figure 12: Lexical STUG pair for the raising verb *seems*.

5.3 Incrementality

Following (Sturt and Lombardo, 2005) incremental processing does not only imply that a sentence is parsed left-to-right on a word-by-word basis, but also that a connected syntactic representation is available for every prefix of the sentence. (Sturt and Lombardo, 2005) call this property *full connectedness*. Parsing with TAG, however, does not meet full connectedness out of the box, since, e. g., elementary trees of an argument and a modifier cannot be connected when preceding their governor. To fill this gap, two TAG variants have been proposed so far, namely Dynamic TAG (Mazzei, 2005; Mazzei et al., 2007) and PLTAG (Demberg and Keller, 2008; Demberg, 2010). Note that this is not at all a problem specific to TAG, but also comparable grammar formalisms such as CCG and Dependency Grammar are affected (Demberg, 2010), which similarly pursue an amalgamation of syntax and valency.

Contrary to TAG, parsing with STUG can be conducted in a fully connected manner even for sentences like *John sometimes laughs*, as the derivation in Figure 2 can be read off from the left to the right. This is mainly due to three factors: (i) syntactic trees of governors are spinal (i. e., the extended domain of locality is not found in the syntactic trees, but in the valency trees) and (ii) arguments and modifiers can always be connected without mediation of the governor. Finally, (iii) the derivation of the syntactic tree and the valency tree can be done asynchronously. It remains to be seen, how STUG compares to advanced psycholinguistic models such as PLTAG. This seems particularly interesting, for STUG does not use traces and, moreover, has a stronger affinity for

free word order languages.

6 Conclusion

We presented a novel tree-based grammar formalism, Synchronous Tree Unification Grammar (STUG), which differs significantly from usual grammar formalisms such as TAG in that it allows for a separation of syntax and valency. After having described the functionality of STUG and having explored its expressive power, we briefly discussed some prospects concerning the modeling of ellipsis, the size and complexity of the grammar, and incremental, fully connected parsing. As encouraging as they may be, there is no doubt that many details are still unclear and need to be elaborated on in future work.

References

Anne Abeillé and Owen Rambow. 2000. Tree adjoining grammar: An overview. pages 1–68.

Anne Abeillé. 1988. A lexicalized tree adjoining grammar for French: The general framework. Technical Report MS-CIS-88-64, Department of Computer and Information Science , University of Pennsylvania.

Tilman Becker, Aravind K. Joshi, and Owen Rambow. 1991. Long-distance scrambling and tree adjoining grammars. In *Proceedings of EACL-91*.

David Chiang. 2003. Statistical parsing with an automatically extracted tree adjoining grammar. In Rens Bod, Remko Scha, and Khalil Sima'an, editors, *Data Oriented Parsing*, pages 299–316. CSLI Publications.

Vera Demberg and Frank Keller. 2008. A psycholinguistically motivated version of TAG. In *Proceedings of TAG+9*, pages 25–32, Tübingen.

Vera Demberg. 2010. *A Broad-Coverage Model of Prediction in Human Sentence Processing*. Ph.D. thesis, The University of Edinburgh.

Denys Duchier, Joseph Le Roux, and Yannick Parmentier. 2004. The Metagrammar Compiler: An NLP Application with a Multi-paradigm Architecture. In *Second International Mozart/Oz Conference (MOZ'2004)*.

Charles J. Fillmore. 1977a. The case for case reopened. In Peter Cole and Jerrold M. Sadock, editors, *Grammatical Relations*, volume 8 of *Syntax and Semantics*, pages 59–81. Academic Press, New York.

Charles J. Fillmore. 1977b. Scenes-and-frames semantics. In Antonio Zampolli, editor, *Linguistic Structures Processing*, volume 5, pages 55–81. North Holland, Amsterdam.

Robert Frank. 1992. *Syntactic Locality and Tree Adjoining Grammar: Grammatical, Acquisition and Processing Perspectives*. Ph.D. thesis, Department of Computer and Information Science, University of Pennsylvania.

Robert Frank. 2002. *Phrase Structure Composition and Syntactic Dependencies*. MIT Press, Cambridge,MA.

Kim Gerdes. 2004. Tree Unification Grammar. In Lawrence S. Moss and Richard T. Oehrle, editors, *Electronic Notes in Theoretical Computer Science*, volume 53. Elsevier. Proceedings of the joint meeting of the 6th Conference on Formal Grammar and the 7th Conference on Mathematics of Language.

Jonathan Ginzburg and Robin Cooper. 2004. Clarification, ellipsis, and the nature of contextual updates. *Linguistics and Philosophy*, 27(3):297–366.

Jonathan Ginzburg and Ivan A. Sag. 2001. *Interrogative Investigations: The Form, Meaning, and Use of English Interrogatives*. CSLI Publications, Stanford, CA.

Bruno Guillaume and Guy Perrier. 2009. Interaction Grammars. *Research on Language and Computation*, 7(2–4):171–208.

Timm Lichte and Laura Kallmeyer. 2010. Gapping through TAG derivation trees. In *Proceedings of TAG+10*, pages 93–100, New Haven, CT.

Timm Lichte. 2010. From partial VP fronting towards Spinal TT-MCTAG. In *Proceedings of TAG+10*, pages 85–92, New Haven, CT.

Alessandro Mazzei, Vincenzo Lombardo, and Patrick Sturt. 2007. Dynamic TAG and lexical dependencies. *Research on Language and Computation*, 5(3):309–332.

Alessandro Mazzei. 2005. *Formal and Empirical Issues of Applying Dynamics to Tree Adjoining Grammars*. Ph.D. thesis, University of Torino.

Rebecca Nesson and Stuart Shieber. 2008. Synchronous vector-TAG for natural language syntax and semantics. In *Proceedings of TAG+9*, Tübingen, Germany, 7–8 June.

Fred Popowich. 1989. Tree Unification Grammar. In *Proceedings of ACL-89*, pages 228–236, Vancouver, British Columbia, Canada, June.

Carlos A. Prolo. 2002. Generating the XTAG English grammar using metarules. In *Proceedings of COLING-02*, pages 814–820, Taipei. Taiwan.

Owen Rambow, K. Vijay-Shanker, and David Weir. 1995. D-tree grammars. In *Proceedings of ACL-95*, Cambridge, MA.

Anoop Sarkar and Aravind Joshi. 1996. Coordination in tree adjoining grammars: Formalization and implementation. In *Proceedings of COLING-96*, pages 610–615, Copenhagen, August 5-9.

Anoop Sarkar and Aravind Joshi. 1997. Handling coordination in a tree adjoining grammar. Longer version of paper in Proceedings of COLING 1996. Draft of August 19, 1997.

Anoop Sarkar. 1997. Seperating dependency from constituency in a tree rewriting system. In Tilman Becker and Hans-Ulrich Krieger, editors, *Proceedings of the Fifth Meeting on Mathematics of Language*, pages 153–160, Saarbrücken.

David Schlangen. 2003. *A Coherence-Based Approach to the Interpretation of Non-Sentential Utterances in Dialogue*. Ph.D. thesis, University of Edinburgh.

Djamé Seddah and Benoît Sagot. 2006. Modeling and analysis of elliptic coordination by dynamic exploitation of derivation forests in LTAG parsing. In *Proceedings of TAG+8*, pages 147–152, Syndey.

Djamé Seddah, Benoît Sagot, and Laurence Danlos. 2010. Control verb, argument cluster coordination and multi component TAG. In *Proceedings of TAG+10*, pages 101–109, New Haven, CT.

Djamé Seddah. 2008. The use of MCTAG to process elliptic coordination. In *Proceedings of TAG+9*, pages 81–88, Tübingen.

Stuart M. Shieber and Yves Schabes. 1990. Synchronous tree-adjoining grammars. In *Proceedings of COLING-90*, volume 3, pages 253–258, Helsinki, Finland.

Stuart M. Shieber. 1994. Restricting the weak-generative capacity of synchronous Tree-Adjoining Grammar. *Computational Intelligence*, 10(4):371–385.

Robert J. Stainton. 1998. Quantifier phrases, meaningfulness "in isolation", and ellipsis. *Linguistics and Philosophy*, 21:311–340.

Robert J. Stainton. 2006. *Words and Thoughts. Subsentences, Ellipsis, and the Philosophy of Language*. Oxford Univ. Press.

Patrick Sturt and Vicenzo Lombardo. 2005. Processing coordinated structures: Incrementality and connectedness. *Cognitive Science*, 29(2):291–305.

XTAG Research Group. 2001. A Lexicalized Tree Adjoining Grammar for English. Technical report, Institute for Research in Cognitive Science, University of Pennsylvania, Philadelphia, PA.

Synchronous Context-Free Tree Grammars

Mark-Jan Nederhof
School of Computer Science
University of St Andrews
KY16 9SX, UK

Heiko Vogler
Department of Computer Science
Technische Universität Dresden
D-01062 Dresden, Germany

Abstract

We consider pairs of context-free tree grammars combined through synchronous rewriting. The resulting formalism is at least as powerful as synchronous tree adjoining grammars and linear, nondeleting macro tree transducers, while the parsing complexity remains polynomial. Its power is subsumed by context-free hypergraph grammars. The new formalism has an alternative characterization in terms of bimorphisms. An advantage over synchronous variants of linear context-free rewriting systems is the ability to specify tree-to-tree transductions.

1 Introduction

Machine translation involves mappings between strings in two languages, formalized as *string transductions*. Early models of string transductions include syntax-directed translation schemata (Lewis II and Stearns, 1968; Aho and Ullman, 1969b; Aho and Ullman, 1969a). These are precursors of more recent models of translation, such as inversion transduction grammars (Wu, 1997), and models in the Hiero system (Chiang, 2007). The underlying assumption in such models is that source and target languages are context-free, which is often too restrictive for practical applications. Therefore, more powerful models have been investigated, such as synchronous tree adjoining grammars (STAGs) (Shieber and Schabes, 1990), which assume that the translation to be modelled is between two tree adjoining languages. Such grammars offer an *extended domain of locality*, beyond the power of context-free grammars.

All of the above models translate between string pairs via a hierarchical structure (i.e. a parse tree) imposed on the source string and another such structure imposed on the target string. These formalisms therefore involve a mapping between parse trees, in addition to a mapping between strings. STAGs also involve derivation trees next to parse trees.

Translations between trees, formalized as *tree transductions*, are the main focus of formalisms such as top-down tree transducers (Rounds, 1970; Thatcher, 1970) and bottom-up tree transducers (Thatcher, 1973). These have attracted much interest in the area of statistical machine translation (SMT) (Knight and Graehl, 2005). Recent developments include (Engelfriet et al., 2009; Maletti, 2011; Maletti, 2012).

The rationale for treating tree transductions as an isolated issue in machine translation is one of modularity: parsing a source sentence to produce a parse tree is challenging enough to be investigated as a separate task, next to the problem of transferring the source-language structure to the target-language structure.

The awareness that phrase structure may be discontinuous, and hence exceeds the power of context-free formalisms, has been growing steadily over the past few years, owing to treebanks for many different languages. See for example (Kallmeyer et al., 2009) for evidence that synchronous rewriting cannot be avoided. The 'gap degree' found in some treebanks in fact even exceeds the power of tree adjoining grammars (Gómez-Rodríguez et al., 2011). This suggests that more powerful formalisms such as linear context-free rewriting systems (LCFRSs) (Vijay-Shanker et al., 1987) may be needed.

While LCFRSs induce derivation trees, they lack a natural notion of derived trees. As a consequence, transduction between strings via synchronous LCFRSs do not, in any obvious

Proceedings of the 11th International Workshop on Tree Adjoining Grammars and Related Formalisms (TAG+11), pages 55–63,
Paris, September 2012.

way, involve source-language and target-language parse trees. This complicates modular design of machine translation systems, in which parsing/generation of the source/target languages is separated from transfer of structures across the two languages.

The purpose of the present paper is to remedy this by introducing a formalism that combines the flexibility of synchronous context-free and synchronous tree adjoining grammars, with some of the additional generative capacity offered by LCFRSs. The new formalism consists of pairs of simple context-free tree grammars (sCFTGs) (Rounds, 1970; Engelfriet and Schmidt, 1977; Engelfriet and Schmidt, 1978), which are coupled through synchronous rewriting. The relevance of sCFTG to natural language processing is suggested by recent findings involving lexicalization of tree adjoining grammars (Maletti and Engelfriet, 2012).

Among the properties that make the new formalism suitable for applications in machine translation are the following. First, it is based on tree transductions, but indirectly also describes string transductions. It can therefore be used to translate strings to strings, but also trees to trees, allowing separate modules to handle parsing/generation. Second, its generative capacity contains that of synchronous tree adjoining grammars, offering the potential to handle some difficult cases of non-projective linguistic structures. Third, parsing complexity is polynomial in the size of the input string or the input tree. Fourth, the formalism can be straightforwardly extended to assign probabilities to rules, whereby probability distributions can be defined, both on the set of pairs of trees, and on the set of pairs of strings.

2 Preliminaries

Let $\mathbb{N} = \{0, 1, 2, \ldots\}$ and $\mathbb{N}^+ = \mathbb{N}\backslash\{0\}$. For each $n \in \mathbb{N}$, we let $[n]$ stand for the set $\{1, \ldots, n\}$, with $[0] = \emptyset$.

A *ranked alphabet* is a finite set Σ of symbols, associated with a rank function assigning a number $\mathrm{rk}_\Sigma(\sigma) \in \mathbb{N}$ to each symbol $\sigma \in \Sigma$. We write rk for rk_Σ when the alphabet Σ is understood. We let $\Sigma^{(k)}$ denote $\{\sigma \in \Sigma \mid \mathrm{rk}_\Sigma(\sigma) = k\}$.

We fix an infinite list $x_1, x_2, \ldots$ of pairwise distinct *variables*. We write $X = \{x_1, x_2, x_3, \ldots\}$ and $X_k = \{x_1, \ldots, x_k\}$. We denote the set of all ordered, labelled *trees* over ranked alphabet Σ,

with variables in set $Y \subseteq X$, by $T_\Sigma(Y)$ We define T_Σ to be $T_\Sigma(\emptyset)$. If $\sigma \in \Sigma^{(0)}$, we may abbreviate $\sigma()$ to σ. Very often we will deal with sequences of variables such as $x_1, \ldots, x_k$, which we may then write in the abbreviated notation $x_{1,k}$. The same hold for sequences of trees; e.g. $t_{1,k} = t_1, \ldots, t_k$.

The *yield* of a tree t is the string of symbols in t that have rank 0, that is, the leaves, read from left to right. Positions in trees are identified by Gorn addresses, represented as strings of natural numbers as usual. The set of all positions in a tree t is denoted by $\mathrm{pos}(t)$. The *label* at position p of a tree $t \in T_\Sigma(Y)$ is denoted by $t(p)$ and the subtree of t at p is denoted by $t|_p$. The expression $t[s]_p$ denotes the tree obtained from t by replacing the subtree at position p by $s \in T_\Sigma(Y)$.

The set of positions in a tree t labelled by a symbol $a \in \Sigma \cup X$ is defined as $\mathrm{pos}_a(t) = \{p \mid t(p) = a\}$. For finite Y, the subset of $T_\Sigma(Y)$ consisting of those trees in which every variable in Y occurs precisely once is denoted by $C_\Sigma(Y)$.

If $t \in T_\Sigma(X_k)$ and $t_i \in T_\Sigma$ ($i \in [k]$), then the *first-order substitution* $t[t_{1,k}]$ denotes the tree t in which each occurrence of the variable x_i has been replaced by the corresponding tree t_i

If $t \in T_\Sigma(Y)$, $t(p) \in \Sigma^{(k)}$ and $s \in T_\Sigma(X_k)$, then the *second-order substitution* $t[\![s]\!]_p$ denotes the tree obtained from t in which the subtree at position p has been replaced by s, with the variables in s replaced by the corresponding immediate subtrees of $t|_p$, or formally $t[\![s]\!]_p = t[s[t|_{p1}, \ldots, t|_{pk}]]_p$.

3 CFTGs

A *context-free tree grammar (with states)* (CFTG) is a tuple $G = (Q, q_0, \Sigma, R)$, where:

- Q is a ranked alphabet (of *states*),

- $q_0 \in Q^{(0)}$ (*initial state*),

- Σ is a ranked alphabet (of *terminals*), such that $Q \cap \Sigma = \emptyset$, and

- R is a finite set (of *rules*), each of the form $q(x_{1,k}) \to \tau$, where $q \in Q^{(k)}$ and $\tau \in T_{Q \cup \Sigma}(X_k)$.

We write $\Rightarrow_G^{p,r}$ for the 'derives' relation, using rule $r = q(x_{1,k}) \to \tau$ at position p of a tree. Formally, we write $t \Rightarrow_G^{p,r} t'$ if $t \in T_{Q \cup \Sigma}$, $t(p) = q$

and $t' = t[\![\tau]\!]_p$. We write $t \Rightarrow_G t'$ if $t \Rightarrow_G^{p,r} t'$ for some p and r, and $\Rightarrow_G^*$ is the reflexive, transitive closure of $\Rightarrow_G$. The tree language induced by CFTG G is $[\![G]\!] = \{t \in T_\Sigma \mid q_0 \Rightarrow_G^* t\}$. The string language induced by G is $[G] = \{\mathrm{yield}(t) \mid t \in [\![G]\!]\}$.

In the sequel we will focus our attention on CFTGs where every rule is linear and nondeleting. Formally, a *simple* CFTG (sCFTG) is a CFTG where $\tau \in C_{Q \cup \Sigma}(X_k)$ for each rule $q(x_{1,k}) \to \tau$.

A CFTG G is a *regular tree grammar* (RTG) if $Q = Q^{(0)}$. We assume a normal form for RTG in which right-hand side trees contain precisely one terminal. The tree languages induced by RTGs are called *regular tree languages*.

Example 1 Fig. 1 shows a sCFTG allowing conjunctions, under the assumption that both parts share the same structure. The tree language contains:
$S(NP(John), VP(loves, and, eats))$, and
$S(NP(John), VP(VP(loves, haggis), and,$
$\qquad\qquad\qquad VP(eats, it)))$,
but not for example:
$S(NP(John), VP(VP(loves, haggis), and,$
$\qquad\qquad\qquad eats))$, nor
$S(NP(John), VP(loves, and, VP(eats, it)))$.

Note that if we modify the grammar to be recursive, for example by changing the first two occurrences of q_3 into q_2, then the string language is related to the copy language $\{ww \mid w \in \{a, b\}^*\}$. It is well-known that the copy language is induced by a tree adjoining grammar. However, the structure of the corresponding trees would be very different from the trees induced by our example sCFTG, and the latter arguably have a more direct linguistic interpretation. $\qquad\square$

4 Synchronous CFTGs

We now take a pair of simple CFTGs and synchronize their derivations. For this, we need to represent bijections between occurrences of states in two trees. This is realized by annotating states with *indices*. More precisely, we define $I(Q) = \{q^{\boxed{u}} \mid q \in Q, u \in \mathbb{N}^+\}$. For $t \in C_{I(Q) \cup \Sigma}(Y)$ and $u \in \mathbb{N}^+$, we let $\mathrm{pos}_u(t)$ denote the set of positions where u occurs as index of a state, or formally, $\mathrm{pos}_u(t) = \{p \mid \exists q[t(p) = q^{\boxed{u}}]\}$. For $n \in \mathbb{N}$, we define $I_{Q,\Sigma}^n(Y)$ to be the set of trees where each index from 1 to n occurs precisely once and no

$q_0 \to S(NP(John), q_1(loves, eats))$
$q_1(x_1, x_2) \to q_2(VP(x_1, haggis), VP(x_2, it))$
$q_1(x_1, x_2) \to q_2(x_1, x_2)$
$q_2(x_1, x_2) \to$
$\qquad q_3(VP(x_1, dearly), VP(x_2, often))$
$q_2(x_1, x_2) \to$
$\qquad q_3(VP(x_1, truly), VP(x_2, seldom))$
$q_2(x_1, x_2) \to q_3(x_1, x_2)$
$q_3(x_1, x_2) \to VP(x_1, and, x_2)$

Figure 1: Rules of an example sCFTG modelling two parts of a conjunction being developed in tandem, where $Q = \{q_0, q_1, q_2, q_3\}$, $\Sigma = \{S, NP, VP, John, loves, \ldots\}$.

other indices are present, or formally:

$$I_{Q,\Sigma}^n(Y) = \{t \in C_{I(Q) \cup \Sigma}(Y) \mid$$
$$\forall u[u \leq n \implies |\mathrm{pos}_u(t)| = 1,$$
$$u > n \implies |\mathrm{pos}_u(t)| = 0]\}$$

We let $I_{Q,\Sigma}^n$ denote $I_{Q,\Sigma}^n(\emptyset)$.

A pair $[t_1, t_2]$ of trees is called *synchronous* if each contains unique occurrences of all indices from 1 to n and no others, or formally, $t_1 \in I_{Q,\Sigma}^n(Y_1)$ and $t_2 \in I_{Q,\Sigma}^n(Y_2)$ for the same value of n. We call n the *synchronization breadth* of $[t_1, t_2]$.

A *synchronous (simple) CFTG* (SCFTG) is a tuple $G = (Q, q_0, \Sigma, R)$, where Q, q_0, and Σ are as for CFTGs, and R is a set of *synchronous rules*, each of which is of the form:

$$[q(x_{1,k}) \to \tau_1,\ q'(x_{1,m}) \to \tau_2] \qquad (1)$$

where $q \in Q^{(k)}$, $q' \in Q^{(m)}$, and $\tau_1 \in I_{Q,\Sigma}^n(X_k)$ and $\tau_2 \in I_{Q,\Sigma}^n(X_m)$ for some n. We note that $[\tau_1, \tau_2]$ is a synchronous tree pair. The *synchronization breadth* of a rule of the form (1) is the synchronization breadth of $[\tau_1, \tau_2]$.

In order to define the binary 'derives' relation $\Rightarrow_G^{u,r}$ between synchronous pairs of trees, we need the additional notion of *reindexing*. This is an injective function that replaces each existing index in the synchronous pair by another, making sure the new indices do not clash with those of a chosen rule r. More precisely, let t_1 and t_2 be two synchronous trees in $I_{Q,\Sigma}^{n'}$. Choose an index $u \in [n']$ and determine the unique positions p and p' such that $t_1(p) = q^{\boxed{u}}$ and $t_2(p') = q'^{\boxed{u}}$, for some q and q'. Further, choose a synchronous rule r of the form (1). Depending on u, we define the reindexing function f as follows:

- $f(v) = n' + v$ if $v < u$,

- $f(v) = n' + v - 1$ if $v > u$,

- the value of $f(u)$ can be arbitrarily chosen (it will be ignored in the rewriting step).

For $i = 1, 2$, let $f(t_i)$ be t_i in which every index v is replaced by $f(v)$. We can now formally define $[t_1, t_2] \Rightarrow_G^{u,r} [t'_1, t'_2]$ to hold if and only if $t'_1 = f(t_1)[\![\tau_1]\!]_p$ and $t'_2 = f(t_2)[\![\tau_2]\!]_{p'}$. It is easy to show that $t'_1, t'_2 \in I_{Q,\Sigma}^{n+n'-1}$. In other words, one derivation step turns a synchronous tree pair $[t_1, t_2]$ into another.

For SCFTG G, we write $[t_1, t_2] \Rightarrow_G [t'_1, t'_2]$ if $[t_1, t_2] \Rightarrow_G^{u,r} [t'_1, t'_2]$ for some u and r, and $\Rightarrow_G^*$ is the reflexive, transitive closure of $\Rightarrow_G$. The tree transduction induced by SCFTG G is $[\![G]\!] = \{[t_1, t_2] \in T_\Sigma \times T_\Sigma \mid [q_0, q_0] \Rightarrow_G^* [t_1, t_2]\}$. The string transduction induced by G is $[G] = \{[\mathrm{yield}(t_1), \mathrm{yield}(t_2)] \mid [t_1, t_2] \in [\![G]\!]\}$.

Example 2 Fig. 2 shows a SCFTG. On the input side it models inversion of subject and main verb following an adverbial phrase in German. $\quad\square$

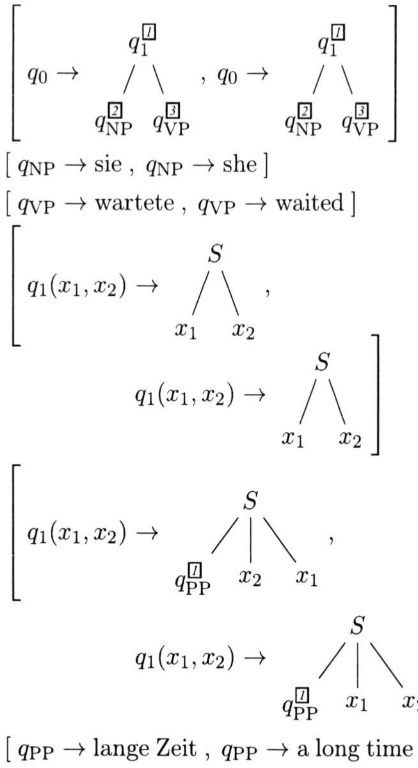

5 Bimorphism characterization

Next we investigate a characterization of SCFTG in terms of generalized bimorphisms (Arnold and Dauchet, 1976; Arnold and Dauchet, 1982). A *bitransformation* (BT) is a tuple $B = (g, L, h)$ where:

- $L \subseteq T_\Delta$ is a regular tree language (*center language*), and

- $g \subseteq T_\Delta \times T_\Sigma$ (*input transformation*) and $h \subseteq T_\Delta \times T_\Sigma$ (*output transformation*) are tree transformations.

The BT B computes the tree transformation $[\![B]\!] \subseteq T_\Sigma \times T_\Sigma$, which is defined by:

$$[\![B]\!] = g^{-1} \,; \mathrm{id}_L \,; h$$

where id_L is the binary identity relation on L and the semicolon denotes (left to right) composition of binary relations.

If the input and output tree transformation are tree homomorphisms, then the BT is a bimorphism in the sense of (Arnold and Dauchet, 1976;

Arnold and Dauchet, 1982) For our characterization of SCFTG in terms of bitransformations we need stronger input/output transformations however. For this we recall the concept of macro tree transducer (Engelfriet, 1980; Courcelle and Franchi-Zannettacci, 1982). It can be seen as the combination of the concepts of top-down tree transducer and context-free tree grammar, and serves as formal model for syntax-directed semantics (Engelfriet, 1982) in which context can be handled.

Formally, a *macro tree transducer* (MAC) is a tuple $N = (Q, q_0, \Delta, \Sigma, R)$ where Q is a ranked alphabet (of *states*) with $Q^{(0)} = \emptyset$, $q_0 \in Q^{(1)}$ (*initial state*), Δ and Σ are ranked alphabets (of *input symbols* and *output symbols*, resp.) with $Q \cap (\Delta \cup \Sigma) = \emptyset$, and R is a finite set of rules of the form:

$$q(\delta(y_{1,n}), x_{1,k}) \to \zeta \qquad (2)$$

where $n, k \geq 0$, $q \in Q^{(k+1)}$, $\delta \in \Delta^{(n)}$, $y_1, \ldots, y_n$ and $x_1, \ldots, x_k$ are input and output vari-

Figure 2: Rules of an SCFTG.

ables ranging over T_Δ and T_Σ, resp., and $\zeta \in$ RHS(n, k), where RHS(n, k) is the smallest subset RHS such that (i) $x_i \in$ RHS for every $i \in [k]$, (ii) $\sigma(\zeta_{1,m}) \in$ RHS for every $m \in \mathbb{N}$, $\sigma \in \Sigma^{(m)}$, and $\zeta_1, \ldots, \zeta_m \in$ RHS, and (iii) $q'(y_j, \zeta_{1,m}) \in$ RHS for every $j \in [n]$, $q' \in Q^{(m+1)}$, and $\zeta_1, \ldots, \zeta_m \in$ RHS.

A MAC M is *linear and nondeleting* if for each rule of the form (2), ζ contains exactly one occurrence of each y_j $(j \in [n])$ and one of each x_i $(i \in [k])$, and contains no other variables. It is *pure* if $|Q^{(m)}| \leq 1$ for every $m \in \mathbb{N}$. It is *monadic* if $Q = Q^{(1)} \cup Q^{(2)}$. It is *total and deterministic* if for each $q \in Q$ and $\delta \in \Delta$ there is exactly one rule with q and δ in its left-hand side. A MAC M is called an *enriched embedded tree transducer* (eEMB) if it is linear and nondeleting, pure, and total and deterministic; an eEMB M is called an *embedded tree transducer* (EMB) (Shieber, 2006) if it is monadic.

Based on the concept of term rewriting, we can define the binary derivation relation $\Rightarrow_N$ of N in the usual way. The tree transformation computed by N is the set $[\![N]\!] = \{[t_1, t_2] \in T_\Delta \times T_\Sigma \mid q_0(t_1) \Rightarrow_N^* t_2\}$.

Theorem 1. *Let $\mathcal{T} \subseteq T_\Delta \times T_\Delta$. Then the following are equivalent.*

1. *There is a SCFTG G such that $\mathcal{T} = [\![G]\!]$.*

2. *There are eEMBs M_1 and M_2 and a regular tree language L such that $\mathcal{T} = [\![([\![M_1]\!], L, [\![M_2]\!])]\!]$.*

Proof. $1 \Rightarrow 2$. Let $G = (Q, q_0, \Sigma, R)$ be a SCFTG. We construct the RTG $H = (Q \times Q, (q_0, q_0), R, R')$ where $\mathrm{rk}_R(r)$ is the synchronization breadth of r for each $r \in R$, and R' is constructed as follows. Let G contain a rule r of the form (1) with synchronization breadth n. Moreover, let $q_1^{\boxed{1}}, \ldots, q_n^{\boxed{n}}$ and $q_1'^{\boxed{1}}, \ldots, q_n'^{\boxed{n}}$ be all the occurrences of indexed states in τ_1 and τ_2, resp. Then R' contains the rule:

$$(q, q') \to r\big((q_1, q_1'), \ldots, (q_n, q_n')\big)$$

We construct the eEMB $M_1 = (Q_1, *_0, R, \Sigma, R_1)$ where $Q_1 = \{*_j \mid Q^{(j)} \neq \emptyset\}$ and $\mathrm{rk}_{Q_1}(*_j) = j + 1$. Let G contain a rule r of the form (1) as in the construction of H. Then R_1 contains the rule:

$$*_k(r(y_{1,n}), x_{1,k}) \to \tau_1'$$

where τ_1' is obtained from τ_1 by recursively replacing every subtree of the form $q_i^{\boxed{\ell}}(t_{1,\ell})$ by $*_\ell(y_i, t_{1,\ell}')$. In a similar way we can define the eEMB M_2 using τ_2 and m instead of τ_1 and k, resp. We can prove that $[\![G]\!] = [\![([\![M_1]\!], L(H), [\![M_2]\!])]\!]$.

Conversely, let $M_1 = (Q_1, q_{0,1}, \Delta, \Sigma, R_1)$ and $M_2 = (Q_2, q_{0,2}, \Delta, \Sigma, R_2)$ be two eEMBs and $H = (Q, q_0, \Delta, R)$ be a RTG in normal form. We construct the SCFTG $G = (Q', q_0', \Sigma, R')$ where $Q' = \{(q, i) \mid q \in Q, i \in \mathbb{N}^+, Q_1^{(i)} \cup Q_2^{(i)} \neq \emptyset\}$ and $\mathrm{rk}_{Q'}((q, i)) = i$. Now let:

$$q \to \delta(q_1, \ldots, q_n) \text{ be a rule in } R,$$
$$q'(\delta(y_{1,n}), x_{1,k}) \to \zeta_1 \text{ a rule in } R_1, \text{ and}$$
$$q''(\delta(y_{1,n}), x_{1,m}) \to \zeta_2 \text{ a rule in } R_2.$$

Then R' contains the rule:

$$[(q, k)(x_{1,k}) \to \zeta_1', (q, m)(x_{1,m}) \to \zeta_2']$$

where ζ_1' is obtained from ζ_1 by recursively replacing every subtree of the form $\bar{q}(y_j, t_{1,\ell})$ by $(q_j, \ell)^{\boxed{i}}(t_{1,\ell}')$. In a similar way we obtain ζ_2' from ζ_2. We can prove that $[\![G]\!] = [\![([\![M_1]\!], [\![H]\!], [\![M_2]\!])]\!]$. $\qquad\square$

6 Parsing

In SMT it has become commonplace to use a combination of relatively powerful syntactic models akin to context-free grammars, and weaker models of finite-state power. The theoretical foundation is the result by (Bar-Hillel et al., 1964), allowing the construction of a context-free grammar inducing the intersection of two languages, one induced by a given context-free grammar and another induced by a given finite automaton. The technique carries over to several other grammatical formalisms, and to tree languages next to string languages. In the realm of synchronous grammars, moreover, the technique generalizes to input products and output products.

The *input product* of a tree transformation $\mathcal{T} \subseteq T_\Sigma \times T_\Sigma$ and a tree language $L \subseteq T_\Sigma$, denoted by $L \lhd \mathcal{T}$, is defined as the tree transformation $\mathrm{id}_L; \mathcal{T}$. Similarly, we define the *output product* as $\mathcal{T} \rhd L = \mathcal{T}; \mathrm{id}_L$.

In this section, we consider application of the technique to SCFTGs and RTGs.

Theorem 2. *If G is a SCFTG and H is a RTG, then there are SCFTGs G' and G'' such that $[\![G']\!] = [\![H]\!] \lhd [\![G]\!]$ and $[\![G'']\!] = [\![G]\!] \rhd [\![H]\!]$.*

Proof. We prove closure under input product; the proof for output product is similar. By Theorem 1 there are eEMBs M_1 and M_2 and a regular tree language L such that $[\![G]\!] = [\![([\![M_1]\!], L, [\![M_2]\!])]\!] = [\![M_1]\!]^{-1}; \mathrm{id}_L; [\![M_2]\!]$. Therefore:

$$
\begin{aligned}
& [\![H]\!] \lhd [\![G]\!] \\
=\ & \mathrm{id}_{[\![H]\!]}; [\![M_1]\!]^{-1}; \mathrm{id}_L; [\![M_2]\!] \\
=\ & [\![M_1]\!]^{-1}; \mathrm{id}_{L \cap [\![M_1]\!]^{-1}([\![H]\!])}; [\![M_2]\!]
\end{aligned}
$$

Since the class of regular tree languages is closed under intersection and under the inverse of macro tree transformations (cf. Thm. 7.4 of (Engelfriet and Vogler, 1985)), $L' = L \cap [\![M_1]\!]^{-1}([\![H]\!])$ is a regular tree language. Hence $[\![H]\!] \lhd [\![G]\!] = [\![([\![M_1]\!], L', [\![M_2]\!])]\!]$ is induced by a SCFTG, once more by Theorem 1. $\square$

In the following, we give a direct construction of the SCFTG G' mentioned in Theorem 2 The style of the construction is close to that by (Büchse et al., 2011).

Let $G = (Q, q_0, \Sigma, R)$ be a SCFTG and $H = (Q_H, s_0, \Sigma, R_H)$ be a RTG. The constructed SCFTG G' is of the form $(Q', (q_0, s_0), \Sigma, R')$, where Q' is defined by $\bigcup_k Q^{(k)} \times Q_H^{k+1}$ and R' is defined below.

The intuition is that we explore all portions of trees that can be parsed simultaneously by H and by the CFTG that is composed of the input parts of the rules of G. For this purpose, we construct the RTG $H(r, s, \theta) = (Q_H, s, \Sigma \cup Q \cup X_k, R_\theta)$, for each rule $r \in R$ of the form (1), each $s \in Q_H$ and each function θ that maps:

- each indexed state $q^{\boxed{u}}$ in τ_1 to a sequence of $\mathrm{rk}(q) + 1$ states from Q_H, and

- each variable $x \in X_k$ to a state from Q_H.

The rules in R_θ include all rules from R_H and in addition:

- $s' \to q^{\boxed{u}}(s_1 \cdots s_{\mathrm{rk}(q)})$ for each indexed state $q^{\boxed{u}}$ in τ_1 such that $\theta(q^{\boxed{u}}) = s' s_1 \cdots s_{\mathrm{rk}(q)}$, and

- $s' \to x$ for each $x \in X_k$ such that $\theta(x) = s'$.

If τ_1 is in the tree language induced by $H(r, s, \theta)$, then we say that (s, θ) is *input-consistent* for r.
We can now define R' to contain one rule:

$$[q_1'(x_{1,k}) \to \tau_1', q_2(x_{1,m}) \to \tau_2]$$

for each rule r from R of the form:

$$[q_1(x_{1,k}) \to \tau_1, q_2(x_{1,m}) \to \tau_2] \qquad (3)$$

and each s and θ such that (s, θ) is input-consistent for r, where $q_1' = (q_1, s\theta(x_1) \ldots \theta(x_k))$ and τ_1' results from τ_1 by replacing each $q^{\boxed{u}}$ by $\theta(q^{\boxed{u}})^{\boxed{u}}$.

Let $q_1^{\boxed{u}}, \ldots, q_n^{\boxed{u}}$ be all indexed states in τ_1. Then there are up to $|Q_H|^C$ choices of (s, θ), where $C = 1 + k + \sum_{j \in [n]} 1 + \mathrm{rk}(q_j)$. Let $C_{\max}$ be the maximum value of C over different rules r. For checking whether a choice of (s, θ) is input-consistent for given r, we need to match at most $|R_H|$ rules at each position of $H(r, s, \theta)$ that is labelled with a terminal. Summing over all rules r, this means that R' can be constructed in time $\mathcal{O}(|G|_{in} \cdot |R_H| \cdot |Q_H|^{C_{\max}})$, where $|G|_{in}$ is defined as $\sum_{r \in R} |\mathrm{pos}(\tau_1(r))|$, where $\tau_1(r)$ denotes τ_1 assuming r is of the form (3). Deciding whether the input product is empty amounts to deciding whether all rules are useless. As for context-free grammars (Sippu and Soisalon-Soininen, 1988), this can be decided in linear time in the size of the grammar.

The input product can be used to realize recognition of strings, as follows. Given ranked alphabet Σ, one can construct a RTG H inducing T_Σ. Given a string $w = a_1 \cdots a_n$, with $a_i \in \Sigma^{(0)}$ for $i \in [n]$, one can construct the RTG H_w from H such that $[\![H_w]\!] = \{t \in [\![H]\!] \mid \mathrm{yield}(t) = w\}$, by the usual technique of intersection (Bar-Hillel et al., 1964). The number of rules of H_w is $\mathcal{O}(|\Sigma| \cdot n^{D+1})$, where D is $\max\{\mathrm{rk}(\sigma) \mid \sigma \in \Sigma\}$.

Deciding whether $(w, v) \in [G]$ for some v can now be done by deciding whether the input product of H_w and G is non-empty. By the above analysis, this can be done in polynomial time in n, assuming G and thereby Σ are fixed. As a side-effect of recognition, one obtains a SCFTG G' inducing the tree transduction $\{[t_1, t_2] \in [\![G]\!] \mid \mathrm{yield}(t_1) = w\}$. Appropriate output trees t_2 can subsequently be extracted from G'.

7 Relation to other formalisms

We now relate SCFTG to other formalisms that are relevant for machine translation. First, we return to macro tree transducers, which were discussed before in Section 5.

Theorem 3. *Linear, nondeleting macro tree transducers are strongly equivalent to SCFTGs in* *which rules have the form:*

$$[q \to \sigma(q_1^{\boxed{1}}, \ldots, q_k^{\boxed{k}}), \; q'(x_{1,m}) \to \tau] \quad (4)$$

Proof. Let $M = (Q, q_0, \Delta, \Sigma, R)$ be a linear, nondeleting MAC. We construct the SCFTG $G = (\bar{Q}, q_{\text{in}}, \Delta \cup \Sigma, R')$ where $\bar{Q} = Q \cup Q' \cup \{q_{\text{in}}\}$, $Q' = \{q' \mid q \in Q\}$, q_{in} is a new state, and $\text{rk}_{\bar{Q}}(q) = \text{rk}_Q(q) - 1$ and $\text{rk}_{\bar{Q}}(q') = 0$ for each $q \in Q$, and $\text{rk}_{\bar{Q}}(q_{\text{in}}) = 0$. Let $r \in R$ be of the form (2). For each $j \in [k]$, let p_j be the unique position such that $\zeta(p_j 1) = y_j$ and let $q_j = \zeta(p_j)$. Then R' contains the rule:

$$[q' \to \delta(q_1'^{\boxed{1}}, \ldots, q_k'^{\boxed{k}}), \; q(x_{1,n}) \to \zeta']$$

where ζ' is obtained from ζ by recursively replacing every subtree of the form $q_j(y_j, \zeta_{1,m})$ by $q_j^{\boxed{1}}(\zeta_{1,m}')$. In addition, R' contains the initial rule $[q_{\text{in}} \to q_0', q_{\text{in}} \to q_0]$. It can be proven that $[\![M]\!] = [\![G]\!]$.

Conversely, let $G = (Q, q_0, \Sigma, R)$ be a SCFTG in which each rule has the form (4). We construct the MAC $M = (Q', (q_0, q_0), \Sigma, \Sigma, R')$ where $Q' = Q \times Q$ and $\text{rk}_{Q'}((q, q')) = \text{rk}_Q(q') + 1$ for every $(q, q') \in Q'$, and if R contains a rule of the form (4), then R' contains the rule:

$$(q, q')(\sigma(y_{1,k}), x_{1,m}) \to \tau'$$

where τ' is obtained from τ by recursively replacing every subtree of the form $q''^{\boxed{1}}(\tau_{1,n})$ by $(q_j, q'')(y_j, \tau_{1,n}')$. It can be proven that $[\![G]\!] = [\![M]\!]$. $\square$

Synchronous tree-adjoining grammar (STAG) (Shieber and Schabes, 1990) captures mildly context-sensitive phenomena in natural languages. STAGs with states (Büchse et al., 2011; Büchse et al., 2012) are characterized by bitransformations in which the input and output transformations are EMBs (Shieber, 2006). Thus, in view of Theorem 1, every STAG with states can be simulated by a SCFTG.

Synchronous tree-substitution grammar (STSG) (Schabes, 1990) is STAG without adjoining. STSGs with states (Fülöp et al., 2010) are characterized by bitransformations in which the input and output transformations are linear, nondeleting tree homomorphisms (Shieber, 2004) (also cf. Thm. 4 of (Fülöp et al., 2010)).

Extended top-down tree transducers (XTOP) (Rounds, 1970; Arnold and Dauchet, 1976) and *extended bottom-up tree transducers* (XBOT) (Fülöp et al., 2011) are top-down tree transducers and bottom-up tree transducers, resp., in which the input patterns occurring in the left-hand sides of rules may have arbitrary depth. XTOPs have been used to specify e.g. English-Arabic translation (Maletti et al., 2009). The linear, nondeleting restrictions of XTOP and XBOT are denoted by ln-XTOP and ln-XBOT, respectively, and both classes are strongly equivalent (cf. Prop. 3.3 of (Fülöp et al., 2011)). Moreover, nl-XTOP (and hence, nl-XBOT) is strongly equivalent to STSG with states, because these classes have the same bimorphism characterization (Arnold and Dauchet, 1976) (also cf. Thm. 4.2 of (Fülöp et al., 2011)). Hence, the power of nl-XTOP and nl-XBOT is subsumed by SCFTG.

A *linear context-free rewriting system* (LCFRS) (Vijay-Shanker et al., 1987) is a string-generating device that can be thought of a context-free grammar in which each nonterminal has a fixed number of parameter positions, each of which contains a string. Moreover, each rule specifies how to synthesize the strings contained in the parameters on its right-hand side to make up the strings for the parameters on its left-hand side. In fact, LCFRSs are attribute grammars with synthesized attributes only (Knuth, 1968) interpreted over the set of strings with concatenation. LCFRGs are weakly equivalent to multiple context-free grammars (MCFGs) (Seki et al., 1991).

The string languages induced by linear CFTGs are the same as those induced by *well-nested* linear context-free rewriting systems (cf. footnote 3 of (Kanazawa, 2009)). A synchronous variant of well-nested LCFRSs can easily be defined in terms of generalized bimorphisms (see also (Bertsch and Nederhof, 2001)), but the connection to SCFTGs is yet to be clarified.

Context-free hypergraph grammars (CFHG) (Bauderon and Courcelle, 1987; Habel and Kreowski, 1987; Engelfriet and Heyker, 1991) are context-free grammars that generate hypergraphs. Each rule of a CFHG G specifies how a hyperedge, carrying a state and adjacent with n nodes, is replaced by a hypergraph with n port (or interface) nodes. The set of derivation trees of G is a regular tree language. The hypergraph language induced by G is the set of all hypergraphs that only contain hyperedges labelled by terminals.

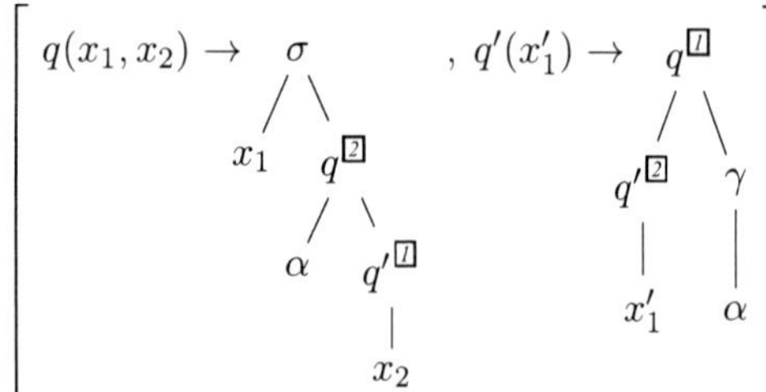

Figure 3: Rule of a SCFTG.

Every SCFTG G can be simulated by a CFHG H. Construction of H out of G is relatively straightforward, but available space does not allow a formal definition. Instead we give an example.

Example 3 Consider the SCFTG rule in Fig. 3, with states q and q' of rank 2 and 1, resp., and terminals σ, γ and α of rank 2, 1 and 0, resp.; the (only) variable in the output part is written x'_1 to distinguish it from x_1 in the input part. Fig. 4 shows the corresponding CFHG rule. A pair of synchronized states together form one hyperedge. Each pair of identically labelled nodes corresponds to a single node in the host graph to which this rule is applied, before and after the application. □

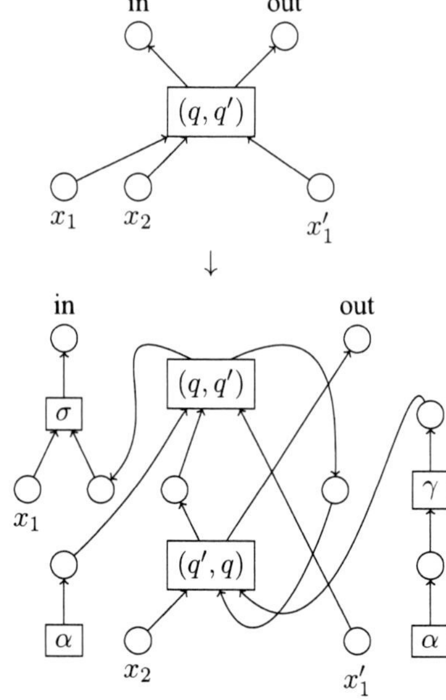

Figure 4: Rule of a CFHG.

References

A.V. Aho and J.D. Ullman. 1969a. Properties of syntax directed translations. *Journal of Computer and System Sciences*, 3:319–334.

A.V. Aho and J.D. Ullman. 1969b. Syntax directed translations and the pushdown assembler. *Journal of Computer and System Sciences*, 3:37–56.

A. Arnold and M. Dauchet. 1976. Bi-transduction de forêts. In S. Michaelson and R. Milner, editors, *Proc. 3rd International Colloquium on Automata, Languages and Programming*, pages 74–86. Edinburgh University Press.

A. Arnold and M. Dauchet. 1982. Morphismes et bimorphismes d'arbres. *Theoretical Computer Science*, 20:33–93.

Y. Bar-Hillel, M. Perles, and E. Shamir. 1964. On formal properties of simple phrase structure grammars. In Y. Bar-Hillel, editor, *Language and Information: Selected Essays on their Theory and Application*, chapter 9, pages 116–150. Addison-Wesley, Reading, Massachusetts.

M. Bauderon and B. Courcelle. 1987. Graph expressions and graph rewritings. *Mathematical Systems Theory*, 20:83–127.

E. Bertsch and M.-J. Nederhof. 2001. On the complexity of some extensions of RCG parsing. In *Proceedings of the Seventh International Workshop on Parsing Technologies*, pages 66–77, Beijing, China, October.

M. Büchse, M.-J. Nederhof, and H. Vogler. 2011. Tree parsing with synchronous tree-adjoining grammars. In *Proceedings of the 12th International Conference on Parsing Technologies*, pages 14–25, Dublin, Ireland, October.

M. Büchse, A. Maletti, and H. Vogler. 2012. Unidirectional derivation semantics for synchronous tree-adjoining grammars. In *Developments in Language Theory, 16th International Conference*, volume 7410 of *Lecture Notes in Computer Science*, Taipei, Taiwan. Springer-Verlag.

D. Chiang. 2007. Hierarchical phrase-based translation. *Computational Linguistics*, 33(2):201–228.

B. Courcelle and P. Franchi-Zannettacci. 1982. Attribute grammars and recursive program schemes. *Theoretical Computer Science*, 17:163–191.

J. Engelfriet and L. Heyker. 1991. The string generating power of context-free hypergraph grammars. *Journal of Computer and System Sciences*, 43:328–360.

J. Engelfriet and E.M. Schmidt. 1977. IO and OI. I. *Journal of Computer and System Sciences*, 15:328–353.

J. Engelfriet and E.M. Schmidt. 1978. IO and OI. II. *Journal of Computer and System Sciences*, 16:67–99.

J. Engelfriet and H. Vogler. 1985. Macro tree transducers. *Journal of Computer and System Sciences*, 31:71–146.

J. Engelfriet, E. Lilin, and A. Maletti. 2009. Composition and decomposition of extended multi bottom-up tree transducers. *Acta Informatica*, 46:561–590.

J. Engelfriet. 1980. Some open questions and recent results on tree transducers and tree languages. In R.V. Book, editor, *Formal language theory: perspectives and open problems*, pages 241–286. Academic Press, New York.

J. Engelfriet. 1982. Tree transducers and syntax-directed semantics. In *Proc. of 7th Colloquium on Trees in Algebra and Programming*, pages 82–107, Lille, France.

Z. Fülöp, A. Maletti, and H. Vogler. 2010. Preservation of recognizability for synchronous tree substitution grammars. In *Workshop on Applications of Tree Automata in Natural Language Processing*, pages 1–9, Uppsala, Sweden.

Z. Fülöp, A. Maletti, and H. Vogler. 2011. Weighted extended tree transducers. *Fundamenta Informaticae*, 111:163–202.

C. Gómez-Rodríguez, J. Carroll, and D. Weir. 2011. Dependency parsing schemata and mildly non-projective dependency parsing. *Computational Linguistics*, 37(3):541–586.

A. Habel and H.-J. Kreowski. 1987. Some structural aspects of hypergraph languages generated by hyperedge replacement. In *Proceedings of the 4th Annual Symposium on Theoretical Aspects of Computer Science*, volume 247 of *Lecture Notes in Computer Science*, pages 207–219. Springer-Verlag.

L. Kallmeyer, W. Maier, and G. Satta. 2009. Synchronous rewriting in treebanks. In *Proceedings of the 11th International Conference on Parsing Technologies*, pages 69–72, Paris, France, October.

M. Kanazawa. 2009. The pumping lemma for well-nested multiple context-free languages. In *Developments in Language Theory*, volume 5583 of *Lecture Notes in Computer Science*, pages 312–325, Stuttgart, Germany. Springer-Verlag.

K. Knight and J. Graehl. 2005. An overview of probabilistic tree transducers for natural language processing. In A.F. Gelbukh, editor, *Proceedings of the Sixth Conference on Intelligent Text Processing and Computational Linguistics*, volume 3406 of *Lecture Notes in Computer Science*, Mexico City, Mexico.

D.E. Knuth. 1968. Semantics of context-free languages. *Mathematical Systems Theory*, 2:127–145. Corrections in Math. Systems Theory 5 (1971), 95-96.

P.M. Lewis II and R.E. Stearns. 1968. Syntax-directed transduction. *Journal of the ACM*, 15(3):465–488, July.

A. Maletti and J. Engelfriet. 2012. Strong lexicalization of tree adjoining grammars. In *50th Annual Meeting of the ACL*, pages 506–515, Jeju Island, Korea, July.

A. Maletti, J. Graehl, M. Hopkins, and K. Knight. 2009. The power of extended top-down tree transducers. *SIAM Journal on Computing*, 39:410–430.

A. Maletti. 2011. How to train your multi bottom-up tree transducer. In *49th Annual Meeting of the ACL*, pages 825–834, Portland, Oregon, June.

A. Maletti. 2012. Every sensible extended top-down tree transducer is a multi bottom-up tree transducer. In *Conference of the North American Chapter of the ACL: Human Language Technologies*, pages 263–273, Montréal, Canada, June.

W.C. Rounds. 1970. Mappings and grammars on trees. *Mathematical Systems Theory*, 4:257–287.

Yves Schabes. 1990. *Mathematical and Computational Aspects of Lexicalized Grammars*. Ph.D. thesis, University of Pennsylvania.

H. Seki, T. Matsumura, M. Fujii, and T. Kasami. 1991. On multiple context-free grammars. *Theoretical Computer Science*, 88:191–229.

S.M. Shieber and Y. Schabes. 1990. Synchronous tree-adjoining grammars. In *Papers presented to the 13th International Conference on Computational Linguistics*, volume 3, pages 253–258.

S.M. Shieber. 2004. Synchronous grammars as tree transducers. In *Seventh International Workshop on Tree Adjoining Grammar and Related Formalisms*, pages 88–95, May.

S.M. Shieber. 2006. Unifying synchronous tree adjoining grammars and tree transducers via bimorphisms. In *Proceedings of the 11th Conference of the European Chapter of the ACL*, pages 377–384, Trento, Italy.

S. Sippu and E. Soisalon-Soininen. 1988. *Parsing Theory, Vol. I: Languages and Parsing*, volume 15 of *EATCS Monographs on Theoretical Computer Science*. Springer-Verlag.

J.W. Thatcher. 1970. Generalized^2 sequential machine maps. *Journal of Computer and System Sciences*, 4:339–367.

J.W. Thatcher. 1973. Tree automata: an informal survey. In A.V. Aho, editor, *Currents in the Theory of Computing*, pages 143–172. Prentice Hall, Englewood Cliffs.

K. Vijay-Shanker, D.J. Weir, and A.K. Joshi. 1987. Characterizing structural descriptions produced by various grammatical formalisms. In *25th Annual Meeting of the ACL*, pages 104–111, Stanford, California, USA, July.

D. Wu. 1997. Stochastic inversion transduction grammars and bilingual parsing of parallel corpora. *Computational Linguistics*, 23(3):377–404.

Incremental Neo-Davidsonian semantic construction for TAG

Asad Sayeed and Vera Demberg
Department of Computational Linguistics/MMCI Cluster of Excellence
Saarland University
66123 Saarbrücken, Saarland, Germany
`{asayeed,vera}@coli.uni-saarland.de`

Abstract

We propose a Neo-Davidsonian semantics approach as a framework for constructing a semantic interpretation simultaneously with a strictly incremental syntactic derivation using the PLTAG formalism, which supports full connectedness of all words under a single node at each point in time. This paper explains why Neo-Davidsonian semantics is particularly suitable for incremental semantic construction and outlines how the semantic construction process works. We focus also on quantifier scope, which turns out to be a particularly interesting question in the context of incremental TAG.

1 Introduction

Incremental processing formalisms have increasing importance due to the growing ubiquity of spoken dialogue systems that require understanding and generation in real-time using rich, robust semantics. Dialogue systems benefit from incremental processing in terms of shorter response time to the user's requests when the dialogue system can start interpreting and serving the request (e.g. by consulting databases, doing reference resolution, backchannelling or starting to generate an answer (Aist et al., 2007; Schuler et al., 2009; Skantze and Schlangen, 2009)) before the request is fully stated. Another use of formalisms that support strict incrementality is psycholinguistic modelling: As there is a substantial amount of evidence that human sentence processing is highly incremental, computational models of human sentence processing should be incremental to the same degree. Such models can then be used to calculate measures of human sentence processing difficulty, such as surprisal, which have been demonstrated to correspond to reading times (e.g., Levy, 2008; Mitchell et al., 2010).

Two strictly incremental versions of tree-adjoining grammar (TAG; Joshi et al., 1975) which have been proposed in recent years are DV-TAG (Mazzei et al., 2007) and PLTAG (Demberg-Winterfors, 2010). Incremental syntax is however only of limited interest without a corresponding mechanism for calculating the incremental semantic interpretation. And for that semantic model to be practically useful in psycholinguistic modelling or NLP applications such as speech recognition or dialogue systems, we believe that the semantic representation should ideally be simple, flat and usefully underspecified, in order to be used in the future in a context of compositional distributional semantics. We propose a framework in which semantic expressions are built synchronously with the syntactic tree. Simple rules are used to integrate an elementary tree's semantic expression with the semantic expression of the prefix tree at each stage. The semantic contribution of the new elementary tree is thereby added to the semantic output expression in a manner that reflects closely the order in which semantic material has arrived. The necessary semantic annotation of elementary trees can be obtained from subcategorization frame information (PropBank, FrameNet). We use a Neo-Davidsonian event-based semantics with minimal recursion.

Integrating incremental syntactic analysis with a framework of incremental semantic interpretation will allow one to model processing phenomena such as the decreased processing difficulty (1-b) (after Steedman, 2000) in comparison to

Proceedings of the 11th International Workshop on Tree Adjoining Grammars and Related Formalisms (TAG+11), pages 64–72,
Paris, September 2012.

(1-a) by downranking the main verb analysis of *sent* when the subject (like *flowers*) is unlikely to fill the sender role.

(1) a. The doctor sent for the patient arrived.
    b. The flowers sent for the patient arrived.

Incrementally generating the semantic interpretation requires the underspecification of the output semantics given the syntax, such as underspecifying the number of arguments of a verb or (to a greater extent than for non-incremental deviations, as we will discuss below) the scope of quantifiers.

This paper sets forth the initial proposal for this semantic formalism in terms of underlying desiderata, principles, and basic use cases. It provides one example derivation, and it outlines a way of dealing with the question of scope ambiguities, an issue which affects a number of aspects of the theoretical plausibility of a semantic formalism.

2 PLTAG Syntax

PLTAG (Demberg-Winterfors, 2010; Demberg and Keller, 2009, 2008) is a strictly incremental version of TAG. In order to achieve the strict incrementality (i.e., all words are always connected under a single root), the formalism uses *prediction trees*, which are usually not lexicalized. Each node of a prediction tree carries markers (see indices $_k$ and ^{k} in Figure 1(c)) which indicate that the predicted node has to be *verified* by a canonical (= non-predictive) TAG tree with matching structure at a later point in the derivation, in order to yield a valid derived tree.

This *verification* operation applies when an elementary tree arrives that structurally matches nodes in the prefix tree which are marked with the prediction markers. A structural match is thereby defined as the verification tree containing all nodes with identical index (i.e. all nodes that were contributed by a specific prediction tree). Additionally, the verification tree can have further nodes to the right of the spine (= the path from the root to the anchor). The prediction markers are removed, and the lexical item in the elementary tree is placed in the head of the prediction tree as in Figure 4, and any additional nodes of the verification tree which were not part of the prediction tree are inserted into the prefix tree. For more details

see Demberg-Winterfors (2010).

3 Semantic PLTAG

Consider the following ways of stating a command to a hypothetical restaurant reservation system:

(2) a. Send every restaurant a reservation request.
    b. Send a reservation request to every restaurant.

A system that derives syntax and semantics incrementally and simultaneously can partially disambiguate the ambiguity between the two elementary trees of "send" (see Figure 1(a)) by taking into account that restaurants are better recipients than reservation requests, while reservation requests are more typically sent. The following sections outline how we decorate the syntactic PLTAG trees with semantic annotations, how semantic expressions are composed, and how we deal with quantifier scope.

4 Neo-Davidsonian semantics

Neo-Davidsonian semantics (Parsons, 1990) is a form of first-order logic that uses existentially-bound event variables ($\exists e$) to connect verb predicates and their subcategorized arguments and separates predicate arguments into their own, separate event-modifying predicates connected through conjunctions. This permits a flexible means to underspecify function composition and argument structure (Hunter, 2009) by greatly limiting recursion (Example (3-a)) in semantic expressions.

(3) a. Happily(Eating(Candy))
    b. $\exists x_1 \exists e$ Candy(x_1)&Eaten(e, x_1)&
       Eating(e)&Happily(e)

The Neo-Davidsonian approach has been implemented in formalisms such as Robust Minimal Recursion Semantics (RMRS; Copestake, 2007). We use a variant exemplified in (3-b).

Neo-Davidsonian semantics has some advantages in the case of a strictly incremental parsing process: in incremental PLTAG parsing, the prediction trees do not always specify the full subcategorization frame of a predicate. For example, when processing the words *Peter often*, the NP tree for *Peter* and the auxiliary tree for *often* (see Fig. 1(b)) will be connected with a prediction

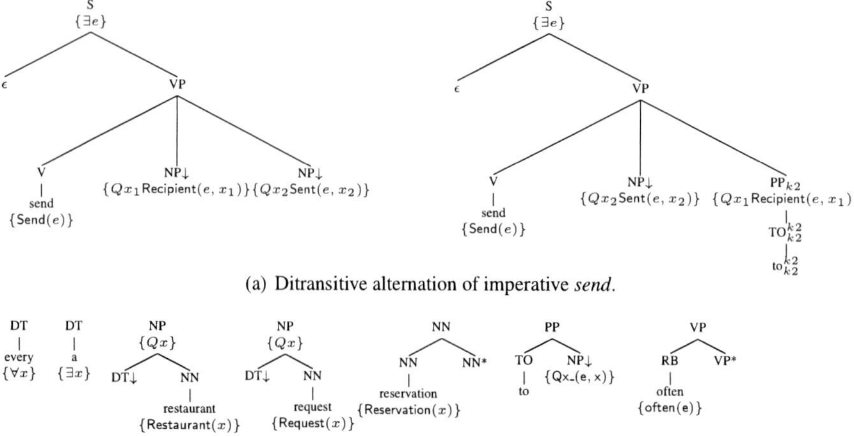

(a) Ditransitive alternation of imperative *send*.

(b) Canonical elementary trees for nominals, determiners, to-PP, adverbial.

(c) Prediction trees

Figure 1: Example Lexicon

tree, expressing that a verb phrase is expected and that the structure is going to root in S, see right hand tree in Fig. 1(c). It does however not specify the subcategorization frame of the verb that is going to be the head of the predicted verb phrase. Neo-Davidsonian semantics allows us to keep the same level of underspecification in the semantics, such that the verb-phrase prediction tree only introduces the event variable $\exists e$, which is then available to be unified with the unbound variable of *often*. Furthermore, the breaking up of n-ary predicates into an event predicate and a binary relation for each thematic role in Neo-Davidsonian semantics allows us to calculate the semantic contribution of a verb's argument before having seen all arguments.

The minimally-recursive nature of the formalism also permits the order of predicates in the formalism to reflect approximately the order in which their corresponding syntactic fragments were incorporated into the structure. In our PLTAG-based formalism, we tie each elementary tree to a neo-Davidsonian expression fragment which will be appended to the end of a semantic structure that grows along with the parse tree. This incorporates a notion of recency directly into our semantic expression construction, a characteristic relevant to semantic enhancements of PLTAG's syntactic prediction component.

This enables the produced expressions to be used directly in statistical prediction techniques where order may matter, including compositional distributional semantics (Mitchell and Lapata, 2010) or HMM-style sequence learning techniques. Its trade-off is that the semantic expressions are not always guaranteed to be immediately well-formed, particularly in the order of scopes. However, in the later sections we discuss ways to identify structure that needs to be rearranged, ways that can be applied at every incremental step.

4.1 Lexical construction and derivation

These are some relevant aspects of the lexicon's construction:

Verb trees are annotated at the root with an existentially-quantified event variable. The head node contains the verb's own predicate, and the nodes representing arguments have argument predicates with entity variables. The argument predicates correspond to thematic roles.

The semantic expressions associated with elementary trees consist of four types of variables, entity variables, written as x_n, first-order predicate variables, written as $\_$, quantifier variables, written as Q_n, and event variables, written as e_n. $\_$ variables are associated with the predictive component of PLTAG-based parsing and achieve their

Sentence: *Send* $\|$ *every restaurant a reservation request*

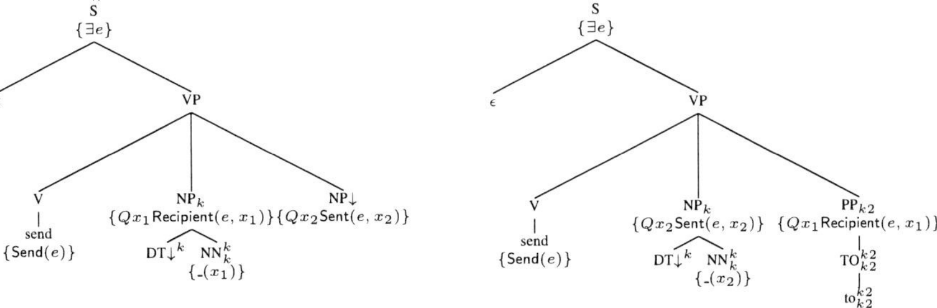

Semantics: $\exists e Q x_1 \mathsf{Recipient}(e, x_1) \&\_(x_1) \& Q x_2 \mathsf{Sent}(e, x_2) \& \mathsf{Send}(e)$

Semantics: $\exists e Q x_2 \mathsf{Sent}(e, x_2) \&\_(x_2) \& Q x_2 \mathsf{Recipient}(e, x_1) \& \mathsf{Send}(e)$

Figure 2: Ambiguous derivation when ditransitive *Send* is received.

values whenever a verification occurs that unifies a prediction tree with an elementary tree. Q_n variables are given concrete quantifier values whenever an elementary tree with a quantifier is substituted into a noun elementary tree that has the Q_n variable. e_n variables represent events and their connections to event participants through role predicates.

Determiners represent their own appropriate quantifier (e.g. $\forall x$). NP-rooted elementary trees for nouns have an unspecified Q quantifier at the root and a semantic predicate corresponding to the noun. Nominal adjuncts (such as the example *reservation* auxiliary tree) contain a corresponding predicate over an unbound entity variable.

4.2 Composition rules

We describe our procedure for incremental semantic parsing in terms of triggered procedures for the incorporation of the semantic expressions residing on nodes of the most recently attached elementary tree. We first describe some common characteristics of the composition procedure, and then we describe how some frequent types of elementary trees are semantically processed on arrival. One aspect of our approach is that most of the "work" in building the semantic expression is defined in terms of the derived tree, in contrast to other TAG semantics approaches that use the derivation tree. We found this the simplest way to align the verification step's role in giving values to prediction trees and the valuation of $\_$ variables in the semantic expressions. Expressions and variables in the derived tree are indexed to their corresponding forms in the semantic expression, so that they grow in parallel.

The semantic component proceeds through rules for unification and predicate emission. Semantic predicates are emitted as conjuncts from left to right, normally revising previous semantic structure based on unification events during PLTAG operations. Whenever an elementary tree is either substituted, adjoined, or predicted, the semantic expressions on that tree's nodes are emitted as conjuncts, once all unifications have been resolved.[1]

When an unbound variable joins the structure, it is unified with the nearest compatible variable the shortest distance above it in the structure. (Unbound variables generally appear in elementary trees representing adjunct structures like adjectives.) For the x_n entity variables, when they are unified, they will be assigned the same variable subscript. For Q quantifier variables, they will search for the nearest quantifier or quantifier variable, by the same standard of nearness. $\_$ variables are predictive and only bound during verification.

By default, all predicates are joined with conjunction operators, except in the case where a $\forall x_n$ is called for. Then a $\rightarrow$ conditional operator must be inserted when the universally-quantified NP is complete, with all adjuncts in the restrictor of the quantifier. We describe later a procedure to identify NP adjuncts directly from the semantic expression in order to insert the conditional operator as needed.

4.2.1 Example derivation

Figures 2-6 represent an example derivation based on the sentence *Send every restaurant a reservation request* using the lexicon in figure 1.

---

[1]We use the word "unification" in the sense of establishing strict structural identity and variable coindexation as in the Prolog programming language.

Sentence: *Send every ‖ restaurant a reservation request*

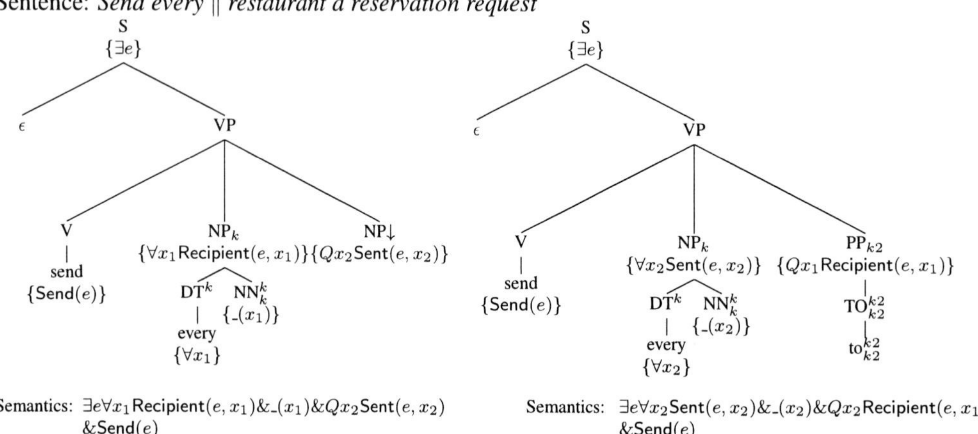

Semantics: $\exists e \forall x_1 \mathsf{Recipient}(e, x_1) \& \_(x_1) \& Q x_2 \mathsf{Sent}(e, x_2)$
$\& \mathsf{Send}(e)$

Semantics: $\exists e \forall x_2 \mathsf{Sent}(e, x_2) \& \_(x_2) \& Q x_2 \mathsf{Recipient}(e, x_1)$
$\& \mathsf{Send}(e)$

Figure 3: Derivation remains ambiguous after *every* is received.

Sentence: *Send every restaurant ‖ a reservation request*

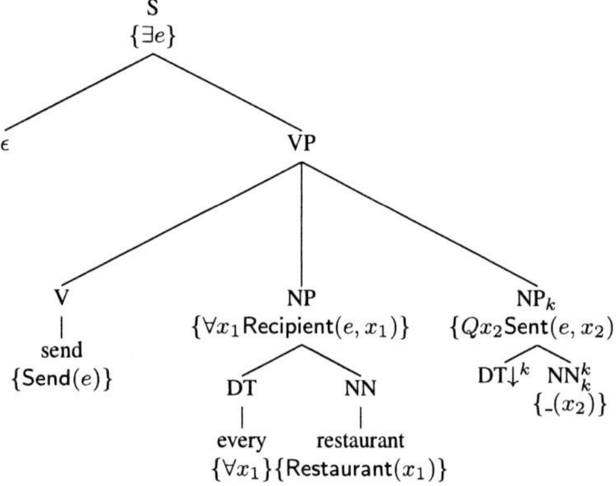

Semantics: $\exists e \forall x_1 \mathsf{Recipient}(e, x_1) \& \mathsf{Restaurant}(x_1)$
$\& Q x_2 \mathsf{Sent}(e, x_2) \& \mathsf{Send}(e) \& \_(x_2)$

Figure 4: The prediction NP tree is verified through unification with the tree for *restaurant*.

In figure 2, the two possible trees for *send* are introduced from the lexicon, and the semantic expressions associated with the nodes are emitted.

In figure 3, the derivation remains ambiguous after *every* is received. However, the quantifier $\forall$ unifies with the quantifier variable represented as Q in both the trees and in the resulting semantics.

Next, the prediction NP tree is verified through unification with the tree for *restaurant* (figure 4). The empty predicate $\_$ is also filled. Semantic selectional constraints abolish the second parallel derivation. The derivation is also now ready for the next NP prediction tree.

Prediction of a determiner and verification with *a* proceeds in analogy to the first NP. We then adjoin the noun *reservation* (figure 5). For brevity,

we omit the ambiguity created by the possible interpretation of *reservation* as an argument; we are illustrating the effect of adjunction. The variable in $\mathsf{Reservation}(x)$ unifies with the nearest quantified variable along the spine of the tree; nominal adjuncts generally do not bring entity variable bindings with them. The predicate is literally appended to the semantic expression as another conjunct.

Finally (figure 6), the prediction tree is verified by the arrival of *request*, which fills out the last $\_$ predicate variable. We demonstrate in this step an adjustment of the semantics to a form in which the event is quantified in the lowest position and the restrictor of $\forall$ is correctly placed before an inserted $\rightarrow$. We outline how to make this work in the next section.

4.3 Adjuncts and arguments

It is sometimes important to identify the parts of the output semantic expression that pertain to adjuncts, especially when interpreting the positions of variable scope bindings and satisfying the semantic conditions thereon. The order of strict incremental appearance of predicates and variables may be subject to further interpretive conditions that require limited reordering of sub-expressions, depending on the application. For example, Champollion (2011) notes that existentially-quantified events should be interpreted in the lowest possible position relative to the bindings of the event's arguments. This requires some ability to distinguish between argument and adjunct predicates. Similarly, in order to handle scope ambiguities soundly, the system

68

must also have the capacity to distinguish between the restrictor and the nuclear scope of a quantifier.

There are multiple ways to do this, including from the structure of the derived tree and the order in which the derivation proceeded, but we argue that most of the work can be done within the semantic expression itself. Most trivially, nominal adjuncts can be identified by the lack of an event argument to their predicates. Relative clause adjuncts will contain their own event variables, but will not refer to the exterior event directly. As an illustration:

(4) a. Some flower that some bride holds wilts.

    b. $\exists x_1 \mathsf{Flower}(x_1) \& [\exists x_2 \mathsf{Bride}(x_2)$
$\& \exists e_2 \mathsf{Hold}(e_2) \& \mathsf{Holder}(e_2, x_2)$
$\& \mathsf{Held}(e_2, x_1)] \& \exists e_1 \mathsf{Wilt}(e_1) \& \mathsf{Wilter}(e_1, x_1)$

Since e_1 is the root event, we know that the relative clause "that the bride holds" does not directly refer to it in its semantic expression and is an adjunct only of "the flower". We can even deduce from the expression that "the flower" is the host NP for the relative clause, because "the bride" is not directly connected to the root event as an argument. We can therefore correctly insert the $\rightarrow$ if the matrix subject had a universal quantifier.

(5) a. Every flower that some bride holds wilts.

    b. $\forall x_1 \mathsf{Flower}(x_1) \& [\exists x_2 \mathsf{Bride}(x_2)$
$\& \exists e_2 \mathsf{Hold}(e_2) \& \mathsf{Holder}(e_2, x_2) \& \mathsf{Held}(e_2, x_1)]$
$\rightarrow \exists e_1 \mathsf{Wilt}(e_1) \& \mathsf{Wilter}(e_1, x_1)$

A similar procedure can be applied to the distinction between argument clauses that appear after verbs like "say" and adjunct clauses heralded by "because." Argument clauses are heralded by an event variable that itself becomes an argument of a role predicate of the matrix argument, as here:

(6) a. Some professor says some student failed.

    b. $\exists x_1 \mathsf{Professor}(x_1) \& \exists e_1 \mathsf{Say}(e_1)$
$\& \mathsf{Speaker}(e_1, x_1) \& [\exists x_2 \mathsf{Student}(x_2)$
$\& \exists e_2 \mathsf{Spoken}(e_1, e_2) \& \mathsf{Fail}(e_2) \& \mathsf{Failer}(e_2, x_2)]$

In the case of an adjunct clause introduced with "because", there is no role predicate connecting the subordinate event to the matrix event, which is practically the definition of an adjunct.

4.4 Scope and Underspecification

Our example derivation in Figures 2 to 6 shows how a syntactic tree and semantic interpretation

Sentence: *Send every restaurant a reservation || request*

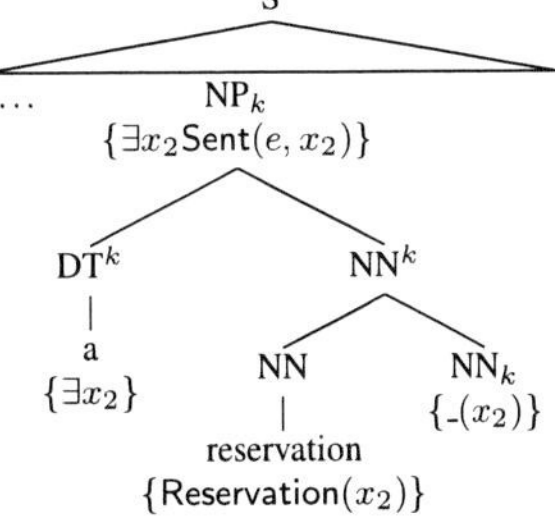

Semantics: $\exists e \forall x_1 \mathsf{Recipient}(e, x_1) \& \mathsf{Restaurant}(x_1)$
$\& \exists x_2 \mathsf{Sent}(e, x_2) \& \mathsf{Send}(e) \& \_(x_2) \& \mathsf{Reservation}(x_2)$

Figure 5: Prediction of a determiner and verification with *a* proceeds in analogy to the first NP. We then adjoin the noun *reservation*.

Sentence: *Send every restaurant a reservation request ||*

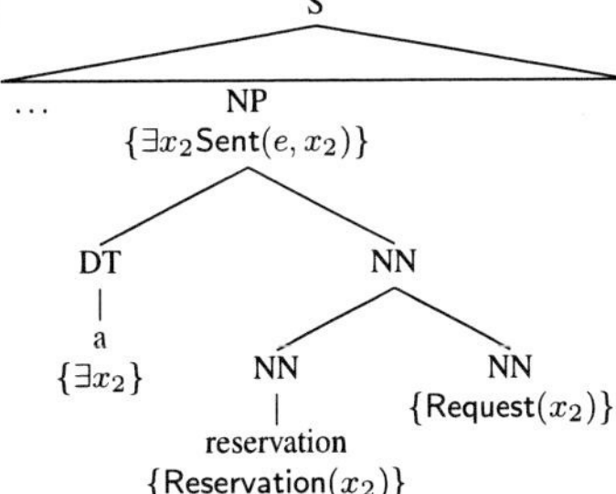

Semantics: $\forall x_1 \mathsf{Restaurant}(x_1) \rightarrow \exists x_2 \mathsf{Request}(x_2)$
$\& \mathsf{Reservation}(x_2) \& \exists e \mathsf{Recipient}(e, x_1)$
$\mathsf{Sent}(e, x_2) \& \mathsf{Send}(e)$

Figure 6: Finally, the prediction tree is verified by the arrival of *request*, which fills out the last _ predicate variable.

can be constructed for the sentences in (2-a). However, it only derives one possible reading for the sentence $\exists > \forall$, i.e. there exists a single reservation request, and that it is to be sent indiscriminately to all restaurants. This reading reflects the linear order that quantifiers occurred in. It misses the other interpretation $\forall > \exists$ (which was likely intended by the user). When sentences are derived incrementally, we cannot choose in the derivation to first substitute the second NP in order to get the other reading. Therefore, we need to systematically use *underspecification* to get both readings. Note that this problem also exists to a certain extent in standard LTAG (Joshi et al., 2007; Barker, 2010).

However, not all quantifier orderings are permissible given the syntax. Joshi et al. (2007) and Romero and Kallmeyer (2005) present an example of what can be seen as a challenge for current TAG-based and movementless approaches:

(7) Two politicians spied on some person from
every city.

They describe a situation where syntactic constraints prevent some readings out of all possible permutations of quantifiers. In order to forbid their hypothetical widest matrix scope reading of *every city*, we use dominance constraints (Koller et al., 2003) to implement restrictions based on the argument-adjunct distinction in preventing quantifier-raising.

Ruys and Winter (2010) describe two major approaches to developing a formal treatment of scope ambiguities. One of these approaches is the covert movement approach that comes from the Chomskyan generative tradition, sometimes known as Quantifier Raising (QR). In this approach, alternative scope readings are found by applying highly constrained operators over an intermediate representation. The other approach involves directly embedding the mechanism for the observed scope readings in the logical representation of the semantics, typically assisted by type-raising operators.

The QR approach stems from the observation that there appears to be a close relationship between *wh*-movement islands and the restrictions on scope readings, with *wh*-islands partially exhibited through restrictions on overt movement as well as covert movement. In other words, where an inverse scope reading is impossible, it is the case in languages that are not *wh in situ* that the overt *wh*-movement is also generally difficult or impossible.

This insight is difficult to capture in highly lexicalized, movement-less formalisms. Since *wh*-movement is overt, it is possible to lexicalize these types of structures and analyse them in a movement-less way, mostly from the surface structure. Quantifier scope ambiguity, however, "lives after the syntax" in some sense: further stipulations must be made in order to enable readings that do not come directly from the surface order. Multi-component TAG (MCTAG) formalisms achieve this by permitting TAG structures with ambiguous syntactic attachments for quantifiers; then it is possible to achieve scope ambiguity through the underspecification of the position of the quantifiers in the semantics (Joshi et al., 2007).

If, on the other hand, we need an explicit representation of the quantifier positions in syntax and semantics—for example, at every step in statistically-guided predictive parsing—then we need also to make the operations that convert semantic expressions from surface to inverse scope readings a little more explicit. Champollion (2011) presents a means of enabling quantifier raising in a Neo-Davidsonian semantic formalism without movement by optionally applying a type-shifting operator to quantified items. The change in type is propagated up the syntactic tree via lambda-calculus operations in order to provide an expression with the intended scope.

However, the potential bottom-up recalculation of the entire semantic expression is also not particularly friendly to a parsing technique that is striving to be meaningfully incremental and predictive. Instead, we propose to bring back, in a very limited fashion, a movement-based analysis of QR.

For the object noun phrase in example (7), both scopal readings are possible: there was a single person whose origin at some point has been every city ($\exists > \forall$), or for every city, there is a person from that city ($\forall < \exists$)—they are interchangeable. For the whole sentence, one of several available readings is that for every city, there is a person whom two politicians spied on ($\forall > \exists < 2$). However, a reading that is *not* available is $*\forall > 2 > \exists$—that every city has its own pair of politicians who are spying on some person in that city.[2]

---

[2]We can find a parallel for this distinction in *wh*-movement islands. Consider the following question, analogous to the $*\forall > 2 > \exists$:

(i) *From which cities did two politicians spy on some person? (with the interpretation that "from which cities" semantically applies to "some person").

Adjunct phrases are islands for *wh*-movement, leading to the ungrammaticality of the reading. However, it is possible to ask a highly emphatic multiple question:

(ii) Which people from which cities did two politicians spy on?

It is possible to bring the adjunct *wh* along with the argument *wh* in this case of overt movement. In fact, many languages (Boškovič, 2002) permit multiple *wh*-movement, constrained only by island restrictions such as adjunct islands. Multiple *wh*-movement by pied-piping is permitted in English when the lower question is a syntactic adjunct (Reich, 2002).

Furthermore, Romero and Kallmeyer (2005) present an

Focusing specifically on relations between quantifiers, we can define a representation and a set of constraints that limit the possible readings by looking at the relationships between variables in our semantic expression formalism. We construct a minimal spanning tree of variables connected to the event variable of the predicate in the main clause, which is then the root of the tree. Each edge in the variable tree, which is roughly analogous to a very stripped-down TAG derivation tree, represents a pair of arguments present in a binary predicate in the expression; parent-child relationships between event variables and entity variables are only permitted through role predicates to prevent the events of adjunct clauses from participating in scope relations. Each x_n variable would be annotated in the tree by its associated quantifier. For example, consider the following interpretation of example (7) in our formalism, after the lowering of the event scope and insertion of $\rightarrow$:

(8) $2x_1\mathsf{Politician}(x_1)\&\exists x_2\mathsf{Person}(x_2)\&\forall x_3$
$\mathsf{City}(x_3)\&\mathsf{From}(x_2, x_3) \rightarrow$
$\exists e\mathsf{Spyer}(e, x_1)\&\mathsf{SpiedUpon}(e, x_2)\&\mathsf{Spy}(e)$

The variable tree for this would be:

(9)

$$e$$
$$2x_1\widehat{\quad}\exists x_2$$
$$|$$
$$\forall x_3$$

We interpret surface scope order left to right and top down. Then we can express the interchangeability of $\exists$ and $\forall$ by declaring that variables in a

---

additional non-surface reading, $\exists > \forall, 2$, where $\forall$ is in the restrictor of $\exists$ (not surprising due to the adjunct status of "from every city"). While the requirement for pied-piping in English requires both *wh*-phrases to be fronted, this is a restriction that belongs to the syntax. Many analyses show that pied-piping restrictions do not necessarily hold at the level of logical form (von Stechow, 1996; Reich, 2002), even if island constraints do. Consequently, the additional valid reading is not ruled out by a QR analysis based in covert movement.

Given this parallelism, one could reasonably be tempted to advocate for the re-adoption of movement-based analyses in movementless grammatical formalisms, but at least in the case of TAG, actually doing so would break many of the properties of the formalism. Consequently, we only propose a form of movement-equivalent operation that focuses on representing ambiguities in semantic structure that are not easily accommodated in a monotonic, movementless incremental parsing system.

parent-child relationship can be interpreted interchangeably. Another important stipulation over variable trees is that only the immediate children of an event variable can change their relationship to the other descendants of the event variable, which would rule out $\forall$ immediately taking scope over 2 and $\exists$. This represents adjunct island restrictions on covert movement. The $\forall > \exists > 2$ reading can be licensed by actually allowing movement to occur in a manner somewhat analogous to the move operator in Minimalist accounts with no traces.

(10)
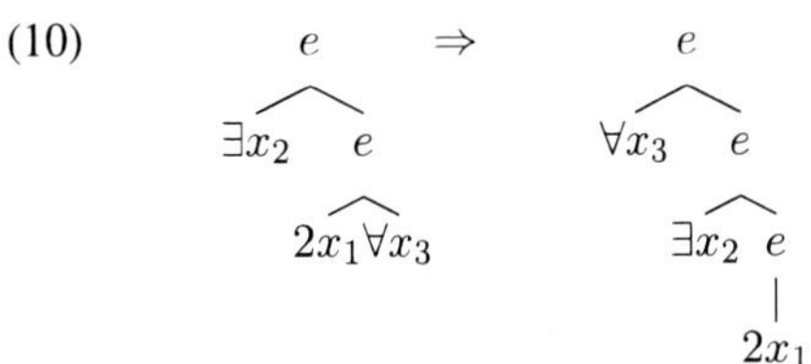

The last step is permissible because $\forall x_3$ is an immediate child of e in the previous step. Extending this analysis to, e.g., forbid QR from causing subjacency violations can be accomplished in approximately the following way: no entity variable can rise above its own nearest ancestor event variable except in the circumstance that the event variable is itself a child of another event variable (equivalent to successive-cyclic movement). These scope order changes can be reflected in the semantics, if necessary, by explicitly reordering the affected variable bindings in the expression. We leave a fuller exploration of the details of this proposal to future work.

5   Concluding remarks

We have proposed here a semantic extension to PLTAG, a syntactic formalism intended to enable robust, psychologically-plausible incremental parsing. This presented us the challenge of reconciling potentially conflicting goals, such as strict incrementality, semantic well-formedness, psycholinguistic plausiblity, and engineering applicability. Our solution consists of a variant of neo-Davidsonian semantics adjusted to support a close synchronisation between the composition of output semantic expressions and PLTAG operations such as the prediction/verification mechanism.

We illustrated the formalism with an example parse, and we described a way in which our approach can be adapted to handle ambiguous scope phenomena that constitute a challenge for robust semantic representation. Potential extensions of this work include semantic PLTAG lexicon extraction from treebanks and further formalisation of our variable tree representation of scope phenomena.

References

Aist, G., Allen, J., Campana, E., Gallo, C., Stoness, S., Swift, M., and Tanenhaus, M. (2007). Incremental dialogue system faster than and preferred to its nonincremental counterpart. pages 761–766.

Barker, C. (2010). Cosubstitution, derivational locality, and quantifier scope.

Boškovič, Ž. (2002). On multiple wh-fronting. *Linguistic inquiry*, 33:351–383.

Champollion, L. (2011). Quantification and negation in event semantics. *The Baltic international yearbook of cognition, logic, and communication*, 6(0).

Copestake, A. (2007). Semantic composition with (robust) minimal recursion semantics. In *Proc. of the Workshop on Deep Linguistic Processing*.

Demberg, V. and Keller, F. (2008). A psycholinguistically motivated version of TAG. In *Proc. of the 9th International Workshop on Tree Adjoining Grammars and Related Formalisms (TAG+9)*, Tübingen, Germany.

Demberg, V. and Keller, F. (2009). A computational model of prediction in human parsing: Unifying locality and surprisal effects.

Demberg-Winterfors, V. (2010). *A broad-coverage model of prediction in human sentence processing*. PhD thesis, School of Informatics, The University of Edinburgh.

Hunter, T. (2009). Deriving syntactic properties of arguments and adjuncts from neo-davidsonian semantics. In *Proc. of MOL 2009*, Los Angeles, CA, USA.

Joshi, A., Kallmeyer, L., and Romero, M. (2007). Flexible composition in ltag: quantifier scope and inverse linking. *Computing meaning*, pages 233–256.

Joshi, A., Levy, L., and Takahashi, M. (1975). Tree adjunct grammars. *Journal of the Computer and System Sciences*, 10.

Koller, A., Niehren, J., and Thater, S. (2003). Bridging the gap between underspecification formalisms: Hole semantics as dominance constraints. In *Proc. of EACL 2003*, pages 367–374.

Levy, R. (2008). Expectation-based syntactic comprehension. *Cognition*, 106(3):1126–1177.

Mazzei, A., Lombardo, V., and Sturt, P. (2007). Dynamic tag and lexical dependencies. *Research on Language and Computation, Foundations of Natural Language Grammar*, pages 309–332.

Mitchell, J. and Lapata, M. (2010). Composition in distributional models of semantics. *Cognitive Science*, 34(8):1388–1429.

Mitchell, J., Lapata, M., Demberg, V., and Keller, F. (2010). Syntactic and semantic factors in processing difficulty: An integrated measure. In *Proc. of the 48th Annual Meeting of the Association for Computational Linguistics*, pages 196–206, Uppsala, Sweden.

Parsons, T. (1990). *Events in the semantics of English*. MIT Press, Cambridge, MA, USA.

Reich, I. (2002). Pied piping and the syntax and semantics of wh-phrases. In Mauck, S. and Mittelstaedt, J., editors, *Georgetown University working papers in theoretical linguistics*, volume 2, pages 263–286.

Romero, M. and Kallmeyer, L. (2005). Scope and situation binding in ltag using semantic unification. In *Proc. of the 7th international workshop on computational semantics (IWCS)*.

Ruys, E. and Winter, Y. (2010). Scope ambiguities in formal syntax and semantics. In Gabbay, D. and Guenthner, F., editors, *Handbook of Philosophical Logic*, volume 16, pages 159–225.

Schuler, W., Wu, S., and Schwartz, L. (2009). A framework for fast incremental interpretation during speech decoding. *Computational Linguistics*, 35(3):313–343.

Skantze, G. and Schlangen, D. (2009). Incremental dialogue processing in a micro-domain. In *Proc. of the 12th Conference of the European Chapter of the Association for Computational Linguistics*, pages 745–753.

Steedman, M. (2000). *The syntactic process*. MIT Press.

von Stechow, A. (1996). Against LF pied-piping. *Natural Language Semantics*, 4(1):57–110.

Respresenting Focus in LTAG

Kata Balogh
Institut für Sprache und Information
Heinrich-Heine Universität Düsseldorf
Katalin.Balogh@hhu.de

Abstract

The paper proposes an LTAG semantic analysis to derive semantic representations for different focus constructions in a uniform way. The proposal is shown via examples of different narrow focus constructions, multiple foci and focus in questions.

1 Introduction

This paper proposes an analysis in Lexicalized Tree-Adjoining Grammar (LTAG) (Joshi and Schabes, 1997), that calculates the semantic representations of various focused sentences based on their syntactic structure and intonation pattern. The paper presents a proposal of extending the focus analysis of Balogh (2009) with the LTAG syntax-semantic interface from Kallmeyer & Romero (2008). Balogh (2009) provides a context-based approach of focusing, that gives a logical-semantic analysis of (narrow) focus constructions within the framework of Inquisitive Semantics (Groenendijk, 2009). One of the central claims of the analysis is that focusing leads to a special theme/rheme division of the utterance, that further relates it to the underlying context, and as such it regulates the coherent dialogue flow. This approach investigates the interpretation of focus from a semantic/pragmatic perspective, providing an analysis of phenomena as question-answer congruence and the exhaustive interpretation of answers. However, the analysis lacks an important part – the syntax-semantics interface –, that builds the semantic representations as theme-rheme structures of natural language sentences driven by their syntactic structure.

1.1 Aims

The main aim of the current paper is twofold. It wants to broaden the coverage of linguistics analyses in LTAG and as a primary aim it wants to fill this gap of Balogh (2009) by proposing an analysis of the syntax-semantics interface that provides the semantic representations of the different kinds of focus constructions. These representations can further be interpreted according to the desired semantic/pragmatic framework: Inquisitive Semantics (InqS) (Groenendijk, 2009). The choice for the logical-semantic system of InqS as opposed to, e.g., Alternative Semantics (Rooth, 1992)[1] has several motivations. One of the main aims in favor of InqS is, that its semantics and dialogue management system offers an elegant way to analyze various discourse-related phenomena involving focus such as: focusing in answers, question-answer relations, contrast in denial and specification by focusing. The analysis in this paper concentrates on narrow focus constructions, however a proposal of extending it to broad focus constructions and focus projection is also given.

2 Frameworks

The analysis proposed in this paper offers a compositional way to calculate the semantic representations for different (narrow) focus constructions in a uniform way. The analysis of the syntax-semantics interface as introduced here is provided within the framework of Lexicalized Tree-Adjoining Grammar, LTAG (Joshi and Schabes, 1997) with a semantic component as developed by Kallmeyer & Joshi (2003) and Kallmeyer & Romero (2008).

---

[1] As in the proposal from Babko-Malaya (2004), that integrates LTAG with Alternative Semantics.

Proceedings of the 11th International Workshop on Tree Adjoining Grammars and Related Formalisms (TAG+11), pages 73–81,
Paris, September 2012.

2.1 LTAG Semantics

For the semantic representation I adapt the LTAG semantics based on unification as introduced by Kallmeyer & Romero (2008). In this approach each elementary tree comes with a feature-structure and a (flat) semantic representation, each of them consisting of a set of labelled propositions and a set of scope constraints. These propositions and constraints contain meta-variables of individuals, propositions or situations, all of them given by boxed numbers. The feature structures are all linked to a semantic representation and by substitution and adjunction of the trees, feature structures get unified and the meta-variables get values. Also the semantic representation of the resulting tree is calculated by taking the union of the representations of the participating trees. For an illustration of LTAG semantics see Example 2.1, the derivation of the question *Who walks?* assigning the semantic representation as $?\exists x.walk(x)$.

Example 2.1 *Who walks?*

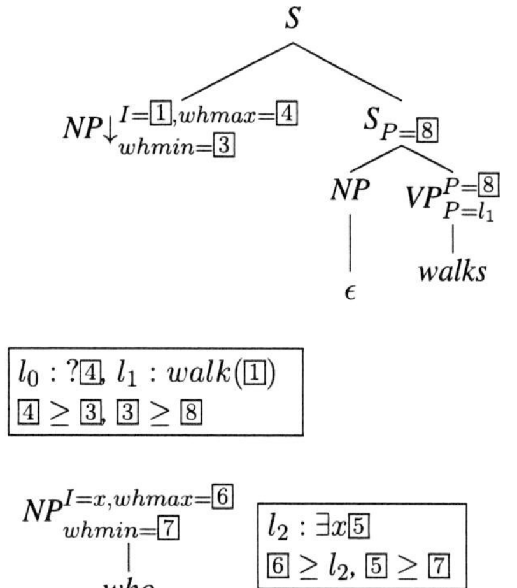

The S-tree of 'walks' comes with a semantic representation consisting of two propositions: l_0 contributes the question-operator applied to a proposition given here as the meta-variable $\boxed{4}$. The proposition l_1 says, that the predicate *walk* is applied to the individual variable $\boxed{1}$ that is contributed by the NP-tree substituted to the given position: given by $I = \boxed{1}$ on the feature structure of the substitution node. Here, two special features are introduced: WHMAX and WHMIN. These features are inspired by the idea of a wh-scope window from Romero & Kallmeyer & Babko-Malaya (2004) and by the MAXS and MINS fea-

tures from Kallmeyer & Romero (2008) that indicate the scope window of a given quantificational phrase. The features MAXS and MINS determine the maximum and minimum scope of quantificational NPs such as 'someone' or 'everyone', while WHMAX and WHMIN indicate the scope window for (wh-)questions and for focus. Separating these two different scope windows has the advantage to account for, e.g., quantifying into questions. Next to the propositions l_0 and l_1, the scope constrains $\boxed{4} \geq \boxed{3}$, $\boxed{3} \geq \boxed{8}$ are defined that determine the scope relations between the given propositions. The scope constrains are defined between the propositional meta-variables and the propositional labels.

The NP-tree of the wh-phrase gets substituted into the S-tree of 'walks' resulting in the equations $\boxed{1} = x, \boxed{4} = \boxed{6}, \boxed{3} = \boxed{7}$ and since nothing is adjoined at the VP node[2], we have $\boxed{8} = l_1$. After these equations the combination of the semantic representations results in:

$$\boxed{\begin{array}{l} l_0 : ?\boxed{4}, \; l_1 : walk(x), \; l_2 : \exists x\boxed{5} \\ \boxed{4} \geq \boxed{3}, \boxed{3} \geq l_1, \boxed{4} \geq l_2, \boxed{5} \geq \boxed{3} \end{array}}$$

Following these scope constraints, the possible plugging is: $\boxed{4} \mapsto l_2, \boxed{5} \mapsto l_1, \boxed{3} \mapsto l_1$, resulting in the semantic representation as $?\exists x.walks(x)$.

2.2 Inquisitive Semantics

In the semantic representation I follow the language of Inquisitive Semantics, serving the broader purpose to integrate the current analysis with a component of semantic-pragmatic interpretation and discourse modeling (e.g. modeling question-answer relations). The semantic representation $?\exists x.walks(x)$ is the translation of the wh-question *Who walks?* according to the logical system of InqS.

As already introduced before, in my analysis I adapt several ideas of the system of Inquisitive Semantics (Groenendijk, 2009). The main aim behind this framework is to create a logical system that models the flow of a coherent dialogue. The principal goal is to provide a model of information exchange as a cooperative process of raising and resolving issues. In the semantic interpretation of utterances, the main source of inquisitiveness is *disjunction*. The disjunction of two propositions

---

[2]To keep the examples easier, none of the following examples contain adjunction at the VP node, so in later examples I will skip the P features at the VP and S nodes.

is naturally interpreted as providing the information that one of the two propositions is true and also raising the issue *which one* of them is true. Hence the disjunction $p \vee q$ provides two *possibilites*: either p is true or q is true, while eliminating the option that both of them are false.

Consider now the meaning of a question. According to the classical theories[3], the meaning of a question is the set of its (true/complete) answers. Hence the meaning of the polar question *Is it raining?* ($?p$) is identified by the set of two propositions *it is raining* (p) and *it is not raining* ($\neg p$) and the questioner wants to know which one of the two holds. Since the questioner is interested whether p or $\neg p$ is the case, the question $?p$ can be defined as the disjunction of its two possibilities: $p \vee \neg p$, hence in general questions can be defined in terms of disjunction: $?\phi = \phi \vee \neg\phi$. The main conclusion that can be drawn here is that like questions, disjunctions have the characteristic of introducing possibilities, and they both get an alternative interpretation.

The system of InqS is developed in such a way that sentences can provide data (informativeness) and raise issues (inquisitiveness). In terms of these two notions three meaningful sentence types can be defined: (i) *assertions*: informative and not inquisitive, (ii) *questions*: inquisitive and not informative, and (iii) *hybrids*: informative and inquisitive. Such a hybrid type is the proposition $p \vee q$, that provides the information that $\neg p \wedge \neg q$ is not the case, while it raises the issue which one of p or q is true, thus it gives two possibilities. The question $?(p \vee q)$ is not informative, it does not exclude anything, it only raises the issue whether p or q or $\neg p \wedge \neg q$ is the case (three possibilities).[4] Similarly to $p \vee q$ the predicate logical expression $\exists x.\phi$ also provides the information that $\neg \exists x.\phi$ is not the case and additionally it raises the issue which individuals are ϕ. It leads to several possibilities depending on the number of individuals in the domain. Take, for example, the proposition $\exists x.P(x)$ and a small domain of three individuals $D = \{a, b, c\}$. The existential expression $\exists x.P(x)$ then excludes the option that none of a, b, c is P, and raises the issue which one is P. Relative to the given domain

D, this expression leads to the set of three possibilities: $P(a), P(b), P(c)$. Following this line, I assume the standard logical translation of a constituent question to be of the form $?\exists x.\phi$. A constituent question is interpreted as a set of possibilities, corresponding to its possible answers. I give a Hamblin-style interpretation of questions as sets of propositions, however with the crucial difference that in my analysis the set contains the proposition *nobody is P* as well. The wh-question *Who walks?* is translated as $?\exists x.walk(x)$ which is the same as the disjunction of the propositions (possibilities) $walk(d_1) \vee walk(d_2) \vee ... \vee walk(d_n) \vee \neg\exists x.came(x)$ relative to the given domain of individuals.

In the logical language of Inquisitive Semantics all utterances are claimed to be divided into a *theme* and a *rheme*, where the rheme corresponds to the information content of the given utterance and the theme to the issue that the utterance addresses. Balogh (2009) proposes an analysis of focused sentences claiming that focusing leads to a special theme-rheme division. Next to the parallelisms with the distinction of new and old information in the generative view, an important difference is that in this analysis the sentences itself are not split into two parts, but the way is defined how to signal the inherent issue (theme) of the utterance and the data it provides (rheme). The theme of an utterance is a question, and as such it is inquisitive, introducing two or more possibilities. In order to derive the special theme and rheme of a focused sentence Balogh (2009) defines the *Rule of Division* by focusing.

Definition 2.2 Rule of Division

Let α be an utterance in natural language, α' the translation of α in the language of InqS and $\natural$ the operation: $\varphi^\natural = \psi$ if $\varphi = ?\psi$, otherwise $\varphi^\natural = \varphi$.

Every utterance α is divided into a theme and rheme: $TH(\alpha); RH(\alpha)$ where

$$TH(\alpha) = ?\exists \vec{x}(\alpha'[a_F^{\rightarrow}{}'/\vec{x}])^\natural; \text{ and}$$
$$RH(\alpha) = \alpha'$$

This definition correctly derives the theme-rheme division of various narrow focus constructions, that further get interpreted in the system of InqS. This proposal provides a context-based analysis of focusing with special attention to question-answer congruence, exhaustivity, contrast in denials, and specification. However, the system of Balogh (2009) lacks the syntax-

---

[3]e.g. (Hamblin, 1973; Karttunen, 1977)

[4]Note, that $?\phi$ is not a separate category in the syntax of the logical language, but it is defined in terms of disjunction as given above.

semantics interface. As it can be seen in Definition 2.2, focus marking of constituents get directly translated in the logical language as ϕ_F not referring to the syntactic structure and the contribution of the focused constituent.

The analysis proposed in this paper wants to fill this gap defining the syntax-semantics interface, that provide the correct semantic representation (theme-rheme pair) on basis of the syntactic structure of the utterance.

3 Proposal

As a starting point, the current analysis suggests the semantic representations of utterances consisting of two components: one that represents the theme and one that represents the rheme. According to this, each S-tree comes with a semantic representation as the following:

$$\left\langle \begin{array}{|l|} \hline l_0 : ?\boxed{i}, l_1 : R^n(\boxed{t_1}, ..., \boxed{t_n}) \\ \{\boxed{i} \geq \boxed{j}, \boxed{j} \geq l_1, ...\} \\ \hline\hline l_1 : R^n(\boxed{t_1}, ..., \boxed{t_n}) \\ \{constraints\} \\ \hline \end{array} \right\rangle$$

In this two-component representation the above part is the representation of the theme, while the below one is the representation of the rheme. Defined in this way all S-trees come with a semantic representation, where the theme will lead to a question: the *issue behind*, and the rheme leads to a proposition: the *semantic content*.

3.1 Narrow focus constructions

The representation of focusing first of all has to provide different structures for the different (narrow) focus constructions. Consider first the basic cases of a sentence with a transitive verb: (i) none of the arguments is focused, (ii) the subject is focused or (iii) the object is focused. All these sentences lead to different theme-rheme divisions:

(1)   Pim likes Sam.
      $\leadsto$ TH: $?like(p, s)$ + RH: $like(p, s)$
      PIM_F likes Sam.
      $\leadsto$ TH: $?\exists x.like(x, s)$ + RH: $like(p, s)$
      Pim likes SAM_F.
      $\leadsto$ TH: $?\exists y.like(p, y)$ + RH: $like(p, s)$

Take first the sentence *Pim likes Sam* that is built of three elementary trees, the S-tree of the verb and two NP-trees of the two arguments.

Example 3.1 *Pim likes Sam*

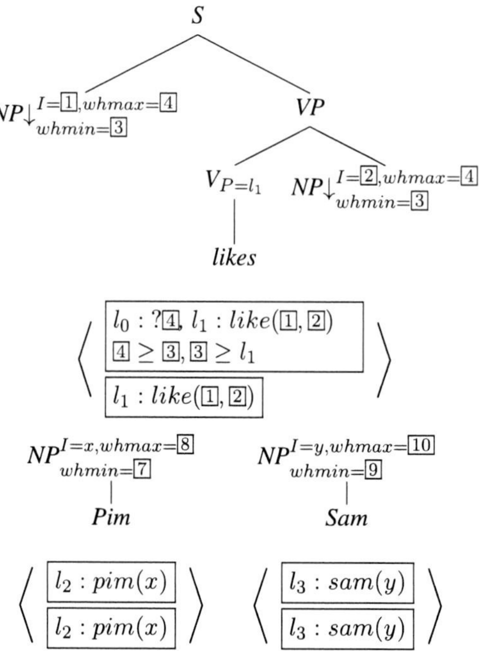

By substituting the NP-tree in the S-tree the features on the nodes get unified (thus $\boxed{1} = x, \boxed{2} = y$) and the corresponding semantic representations are combined, resulting in the semantic representation of the sentence as:

$$\left\langle \begin{array}{|l|} \hline l_0 : ?\boxed{4}, l_1 : like(x, y), l_2 : pim(x), \\ l_3 : sam(y), \boxed{4} \geq \boxed{3}, \boxed{3} \geq l_1 \\ \hline\hline l_1 : like(x, y), l_2 : pim(x), l_3 : sam(y) \\ \hline \end{array} \right\rangle$$

There is one way of plugging possible here: $\boxed{4} \mapsto l_1, \boxed{3} \mapsto l_1$, that derives the semantics representation of the given sentence as the following, where the theme corresponds to the polar question *Does Pim like Sam?* and the rheme corresponds to the proposition *Pim likes Sam*.

$$\left\langle \begin{array}{|l|} \hline ?like(x, y), pim(x), sam(y) \\ \hline\hline like(x, y), pim(x), sam(y) \\ \hline \end{array} \right\rangle$$

3.1.1 Subject / object in focus

Sentences consisting of a transitive verb have the possibilities of narrow focus: either the subject or the object (or both) can be focused. First, look at the sentences in (1) with single focus. The analysis derives the rheme as the proposition *Pim likes Sam* for both, while the different focus structures lead to two different themes corresponding to the inherent questions: *Who likes Sam?* and *Whom does Pim like?* respectively.

In the analysis of *PIM$_F$ likes Sam* with narrow focus on the subject, we take the S-tree of 'likes' as above and substitute two NP-trees: for the non-focused object the tree for 'Sam' as in Example 3.1, while for the focused subject we take the tree for 'Pim' with its special semantics:

$$\text{NP}^{I=x, whmax=\boxed{8}, foc=+}_{whmin=\boxed{7}}$$
$$|$$
$$\text{Pim}$$

$$\left\langle \begin{array}{c} \boxed{l_2 : \exists x \boxed{11}, \\ \boxed{8} \geq l_2, \boxed{11} \geq \boxed{7}} \\ \boxed{l_2 : pim(x)} \end{array} \right\rangle$$

The semantic representation of the focused NP contributes a special theme as an existential expression. The substitutions of the two NPs carried out and the respective meta-variables unified: $\boxed{1} = x, \boxed{2} = y, \boxed{8} = \boxed{4}, \boxed{7} = \boxed{3}$, that leads to the semantics:

$$\left\langle \begin{array}{c} \boxed{l_0 : ?\boxed{4}, l_1 : like(x,y), l_2 : \exists x\boxed{11}, \\ l_3 : sam(y), \boxed{4} \geq \boxed{3}, \boxed{3} \geq l_1, \\ \boxed{4} \geq l_2, \boxed{11} \geq \boxed{3}} \\ \boxed{l_1 : like(x,y), l_2 : pim(x), l_3 : sam(y)} \end{array} \right\rangle$$

Again, one way of plugging is possible here: $\boxed{4} \mapsto l_2, \boxed{11} \mapsto l_1, \boxed{3} \mapsto l_1$ providing the twofold semantic representation corresponding to the question *Who likes Sam?* as the theme and the proposition *Pim likes Sam* as the rheme of the utterance.

$$\left\langle \begin{array}{c} \boxed{?\exists x.like(x,y), sam(y)} \\ \boxed{like(x,y), pim(x), sam(y)} \end{array} \right\rangle$$

The analysis of *Pim likes SAM$_F$* is similar, we take the sam S-tree for the non-focused subject we substitute the tree for 'Pim' as before and for the focused object we substitute the tree for 'Sam' as:

$$\text{NP}^{I=y, whmax=\boxed{10}, foc=+}_{whmin=\boxed{9}}$$
$$|$$
$$\text{Sam}$$

$$\left\langle \begin{array}{c} \boxed{l_3 : \exists y\boxed{12} \\ \boxed{10} \geq l_3, \boxed{12} \geq \boxed{9}} \\ \boxed{l_3 : sam(y)} \end{array} \right\rangle$$

The two substitutions here lead to the semantic representations before and after plugging:

$$\left\langle \begin{array}{c} \boxed{l_0 : ?\boxed{4}, l_1 : like(x,y), l_2 : pim(x), \\ l_3 : \exists y\boxed{12}, \boxed{4} \geq \boxed{3}, \boxed{3} \geq l_1, \\ \boxed{4} \geq l_3, \boxed{12} \geq \boxed{3}} \\ \boxed{l_1 : like(x,y), l_2 : pim(x), l_3 : sam(y)} \end{array} \right\rangle$$

$$\left\langle \begin{array}{c} \boxed{?\exists y.like(x,y), pim(x)} \\ \boxed{like(x,y), pim(x), sam(y)} \end{array} \right\rangle$$

Similarly to the previous example, this representation corresponds to the question *Whom does Pim like?* as the theme and to the proposition *Pim likes Sam* as the rheme.

3.2 Multiple focus

After showing the basic cases, let us now turn to more complex examples such as multiple focus. In sentences formed of a transitive verb, not only single focusing is possible, but also both arguments can be focused in the same time: *PIM$_F$ likes SAM$_F$*. The rheme or information content of this sentence is again the proposition *Pim likes Sam*, while the theme or underlying issue is the multiple wh-question *Who likes whom?* The analysis derives the correct theme-rheme division straightforwardly, by substituting the NP-trees of the focused arguments (see in the previous section) into the S-tree of 'likes' (see Example 3.1). The substitutions of the focused subject and object lead to the semantic representation:

$$\left\langle \begin{array}{c} \boxed{l_0 : ?\boxed{4}, l_1 : like(x,y), l_2 : \exists x\boxed{11}, \\ l_3 : \exists y\boxed{12}, \boxed{4} \geq \boxed{3}, \boxed{3} \geq l_1, \boxed{4} \geq l_2, \\ \boxed{11} \geq \boxed{3}, \boxed{4} \geq l_3, \boxed{12} \geq \boxed{3}} \\ \boxed{l_1 : like(x,y), l_2 : pim(x), l_3 : sam(y)} \end{array} \right\rangle$$

Here, two different pluggings are possible: (i) $\boxed{4} \mapsto l_2, \boxed{11} \mapsto l_3, \boxed{12} \mapsto l_1, \boxed{3} \mapsto l_1$ and (ii) $\boxed{4} \mapsto l_3, \boxed{12} \mapsto l_2, \boxed{11} \mapsto l_1, \boxed{3} \mapsto l_1$, yielding two semantic representations, where the representations of the theme are slightly different: at plugging (i) $?\exists x \exists y.like(x,y)$ and at (ii) $?\exists y \exists x.like(x,y)$. Since we have existential expressions, these two representations are equivalent, both corresponding to the question *Who likes whom?*

3.3 Focus in questions

The analysis proposed above gives also a straightforward derivation of a special construction, when an argument is focused within a wh-question as, e.g. *'Who likes SAM$_F$?'* Such examples appear in, e.g., answering strategies , where the goal is to resolve a question, which can be reached via answering all of its (easier) sub-questions. As Roberts (1996) shows, the question 'Who likes whom?' can be resolved by the strategy of replacing the original question with its sub-questions, where the sub-question is only felicitous if it is appropriately focused. For an illustration, consider the answering strategy of the multiple wh-question 'Who likes whom?':

(2)   Who likes whom?
        Who likes SAM$_F$?
          Does Sam like Sam?
          Does Tom like Sam?
        . . .

In the derivation of 'Who likes SAM$_F$?' we take the S-tree of 'likes' (example 3.2) and substitute the elementary trees of the wh-phrase 'who' and the focused object 'Sam' (example 3.3):

Example 3.2

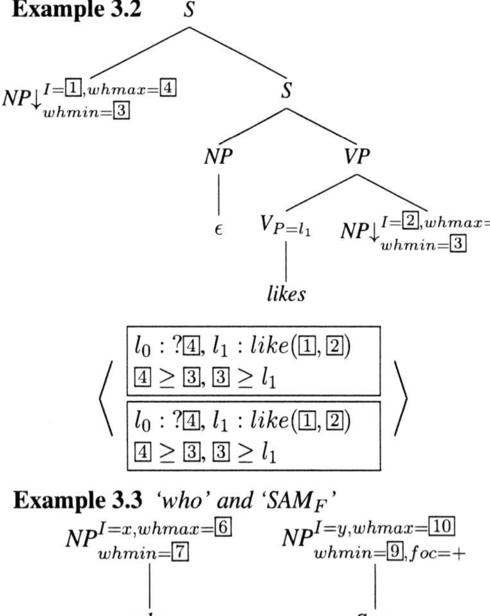

Example 3.3 *'who' and 'SAM$_F$'*

By substitution of the two NP-trees we get the equations $\boxed{1} = x, \boxed{2} = y, \boxed{4} = \boxed{6} = \boxed{10}, \boxed{3} = \boxed{7} = \boxed{9}$ on the theme side and $\boxed{1} = x, \boxed{2} = y, \boxed{4} =$

$\boxed{6}, \boxed{3} = \boxed{7}$ on the rheme side. This gives us the still underspecified semantic representation:

$$\left\langle \begin{array}{l} \boxed{l_0 : ?\boxed{4},\, l_1 : like(x,y),\, l_2 : \exists x\boxed{5},\, l_3 : \exists y\boxed{12}} \\ \boxed{4} \geq \boxed{3},\, \boxed{3} \geq l_0,\, \boxed{4} \geq l_2,\, \boxed{5} \geq \boxed{3}, \\ \boxed{4} \geq l_3,\, \boxed{12} \geq \boxed{3} \\[4pt] l_0 : ?\boxed{4},\, l_1 : like(x,y),\, l_2 : \exists x\boxed{5},\, l_3 : sam(y) \\ \boxed{4} \geq \boxed{3},\, \boxed{3} \geq l_0,\, \boxed{4} \geq l_2,\, \boxed{5} \geq \boxed{3} \end{array} \right\rangle$$

Similarly to the example with multiple foci, at the theme side of this example two pluggings are possible, that derive the representations $?\exists x \exists y. like(x,y)$ and $?\exists y \exists x. like(x,y)$ that are equivalent. On the rheme side only one plugging is possible, that derives the representation $?\exists x. like(x,y), pim(y)$. Hence, the analysis correctly derives the theme and the rheme of 'Who likes PIM$_F$?' as the multiple wh-question 'Who likes whom?' and the single wh-question 'Who likes Pim?' respectively.

4   Conclusion and further issues

The approach introduced here is a proposal towards an analysis of focus constructions using LTAG with a unification based semantics. The analysis derives the theme/rheme divisions of different (narrow) focus constructions including multiple foci and focusing in questions.

(3)   Pim likes Sam.
       $\leadsto$ TH: $?like(x,y), pim(x), sam(y)$
       $\leadsto$ RH: $like(x,y), pim(x), sam(y)$

       PIM$_F$ likes Sam.
       $\leadsto$ TH: $?\exists x. like(x,y), sam(y)$
       $\leadsto$ RH: $like(x,y), pim(x), sam(y)$

       Pim likes SAM$_F$.
       $\leadsto$ TH: $?\exists y. like(x,y), pim(x)$
       $\leadsto$ RH: $like(x,y), pim(x), sam(y)$

       PIM$_F$ likes SAM$_F$.
       $\leadsto$ TH: $?\exists x \exists y. like(x,y)$
       $\leadsto$ RH: $like(x,y), pim(x), sam(y)$

The advantage of this analysis is that all four sentences bear the same propositional content (rheme), while the different focus structures lead to different inherent issues (theme) indicating that these sentences are felicitous in different contexts. Consequently, they relate to four different wh-questions, which offers a straightforward way to deal with the basic cases of question-answer congruence. This analysis follows the core ideas of the context-based approach of Balogh (2009), that concentrates merely on the interpretation of different focus structures. The above analysis provides an extension to the syntax-semantics interface of Kallmeyer & Romero (2008). It determines the semantic representations as assumed in Balogh (2009) on basis of the syntactic structures of the sentences in a straightforward, intuitive and compositional way.

Since this paper is a report of a work in progress, several loose ends can be pointed out. First of all an analysis of the relation of accent placement and focus has to be given to deal with, among others, the phenomenon of Focus Projection (Selkirk, 1996). The second important issue to investigate is the relation of focusing and quantifier scope as one of the main reasons of choosing LTAG as the framework of the syntax-semantics interface. The semantic component of LTAG as introduced by Kallmeyer & Romero (2008) offers an analysis of scope ambiguities. In their analysis scope windows are introduced for quantificational NPs by the features MAXS and MINS signalling the maximal and minimal scope sides. Focus and questions also bear scope properties, different from the scope properties of quantificational NPs. To offer a uniform analysis of the similarities and differences of these scope sides, this paper introduces the features WHMAX and WH-MIN as the scope window for focus and questions (inspired by Romero & Kallmeyer & Babako-Malaya (2004)). The distinction of the two different scope windows gives the possibility to deal with the relation of focusing and quantifiers as well as quantifying into questions.

4.1 Focus marking and accenting

In section 2, the proposal of the analysis of narrow focus constructions was introduced, deriving a two-fold semantics of utterances representing the theme (underlying issue) and the rheme (propositional content). Focused constituents contribute a special semantics to the theme of the sentence meaning, yielding the corresponding wh-question. Each elementary tree of a focused constituent came with a different semantic representation as their non-focused counterpart. Focus marking can be signaled within the feature structure of the given elementary tree, introducing the feature FOC with possible values + and - for focused and non-focused occurences.

In the previous examples all NP arguments are proper names with an elementary tree of a noun phrase without further inner structure and the focus feature can appear at the maximal projection. However, for an elegant account for focusing we need to be able to give an analysis of the placement of the pitch accent and the focus marking. Hence, we have to account for Focus Projection as well as focus marking within a complex NP. Following Selkirk's (1996) Focus Projection principle, the same accenting can receive different focus marking, hence different focus interpretation. As her focus marking principles suggest, pitch accent on the noun can lead to a narrow focus interpretation or to a broadad (VP) focus interpretation:

(4) a. John rented [a BICYCLE]$_F$.

  b. John [rented a BICYCLE]$_F$.

An important issue for the current approach is, how to analyze the relation between the placement of the pitch accent and the marking of the focused constituent. For this we need to introduce two features FOC and PITCH that stand for focus marking and accenting respectively. The placement of the pitch accent is given by the feature $pitch = +$ coming from the lexicon together with the lexical anchor. The value of the pitch accent is then passed to the FOC feature that appears on some nodes of the elementary tree of the noun phrase.

$$\text{NP}_{foc=\boxed{1}}$$
$$|$$
$$\text{N}\Diamond^{foc=\boxed{1}}_{foc=\boxed{1},pitch=\boxed{1}}$$

As for the focus projection, the + value of the FOC feature can be optionally passed up from the rightmost NP argument to the higher VP node marking the possible focus projection (FPP). This is not possible from the subject position (or from the not right-most argument), the focused NP in that position gets narrow focus intrepretation.

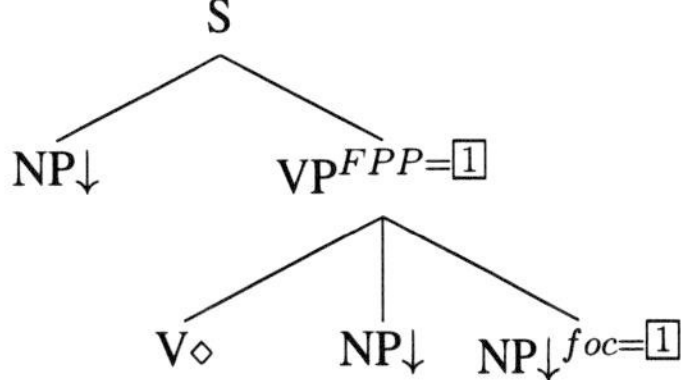

However, the picture is more complex, since by focusing we have to deal with (at least two) different issues: (i) the information structure of the sentence: which part of the content is the

Focus / Topic / Background as defined in formal pragmatic terms; (ii) the coherent discourse: what is "given / retrievable" and "non-given / no-retrievable" information.

Towards an account of these issues, first of all, we take *focus* as a pragmatic notion, defined as the part of the answer that corresponds to the wh-part of a question. Following this definition, the FOC feature is passed to the maximal projection of the noun phrase, marking the whole NP as the focus of the sentence. This raises the issue how we can deal with complex NPs like 'a green bicycle' where either the noun or the adjective gets the accent. In case the noun is accented 'a green BICYCLE$_F$', it passes the focus marking to its maximal projection, and the whole noun phrase will be in focus. In case, that the adjective is accented 'a GREEN$_F$ bicycle' we can still mark the whole NP as focus, however we have to deal with the notion of *giveness* as well. Consider the following examples:

(5) **context1**: John attended a conference where the participants rented vehicles to move around.
What did John rent?

   a. John rented [a BICYCLE]$_F$.

   b. John rented [a green BICYCLE]$_F$.

(6) **context2**: John attended a conference where all participants rented different kinds of bicycles to move around.
What did John rent?

   a. #John rented [a BICYCLE]$_F$.

   b. #John rented [a green BICYCLE]$_F$.

   c. John rented [a GREEN bicycle]$_F$.

   d. John rented [a TANDEM]$_F$.

In context 2, the wh-question is approporiate although the information that the rented vehicles are all bicycles is given. The answer in (6c) is felicitous with the focus marking of the whole NP as the corresponding to the wh-phrase of the question. Focus marking of the whole NP is thus possible even if some part of the NP is already given. Consequently, we need to distinguish the notions of *focus* and *given information*. This example supports the notion of *focus* in pragmatic terms and the proposed analysis of focus marking.

4.2 Focus and quantifier scope

The paper introduces the special scope window for focus and questions by the new features WH-MAX and WHMIN. These features follow the idea of MAXS and MINS from Kallmeyer & Romero (2008), however, in the previous examples we only discussed cases having only the focus window. In case we have both a quantificational NP and a focused constituent in the sentence, the distinction of the two scope windows get relevant and important. Consider, for example, the sentence *SOMEONE$_F$ walks.* as an answer of the wh-question *Who walks?* In this example a quantificational NP is in focus, and its theme (issue) refers to the focus/question-window by the features WHMAX/WHMIN, while its rheme (content) makes use of the scope window by MAXS/MINS.

Example 4.1

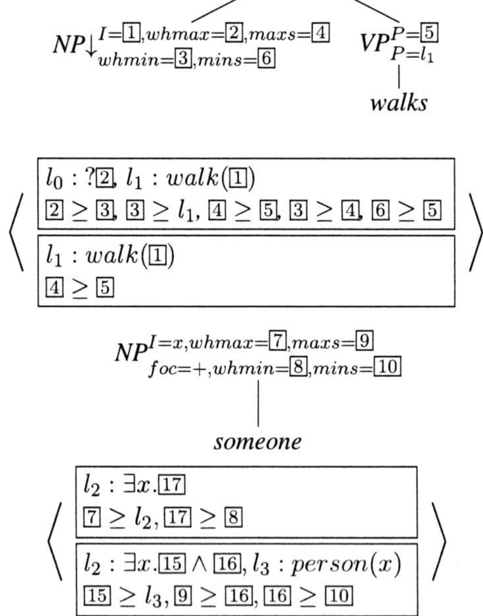

By substitution of the NP-tree of 'someone' (with focus) into the S-tree of 'walk', we derive the semantic representation of the sentence *SOMEONE$_F$ walks* as the following.

That correctly derives – after plugging – the theme of the sentence as the wh-question *Who walks?* while the rheme as the proposition *someone walks*.

$$\left\langle \begin{array}{|l|} \hline ?\exists x.walk(x) \\ \hline \exists x.person(x) \wedge walk(x) \\ \hline \end{array} \right\rangle$$

Acknowledgments

I would like to thank the anonymous reviewers for their comments on the abstract of this paper and would like to express my special thanks to Laura Kallmeyer for all her comments and help, especially on the LTAG formalism.

References

Olga Babko-Malaya. 2004. Ltag semantics of focus. In Chung-hye Han and Anoop Sarkar, editors, *Proceedings of TAG+7: Seventh International Workshop on Tree Adjoining Grammar and Related Formalisms*, Vancouver, BC, Canada.

Kata Balogh. 2009. *Theme with Variations. A Context-based Analysis of Focus.* Ph.D. thesis, ILLC, University of Amsterdam, Amsterdam.

Jeroen Groenendijk. 2009. Inquisitive semantics: Two possibilities for disjunction. In Peter Bosch, David Gabelaia, and Jérôme Lang, editors, *Logic, Language and Computation. 7th International Tbilisi Symposium on Logic, Language and Computation. Revised Selected Papers.*, Berlin-Heidelberg. Springer-Verlag.

C. L. Hamblin. 1973. Questions in montague english. *Foundations of Language*, 10.

Aravind K. Joshi and Yves Schabes. 1997. Tree-Adjoning Grammars. In G. Rozenberg and A. Salomaa, editors, *Handbook of Formal Languages*, pages 69–123. Springer, Berlin.

Laura Kallmeyer and Aravind K. Joshi. 2003. Factoring predicate argument and scope semantics: Underspecified semantics with ltag. *Research on Language and Computation*, 1(1-2).

Laura Kallmeyer and Maribel Romero. 2008. Scope and situation binding in LTAG using semantic unification. *Research on Language and Computation*, 6(1):3–52.

Lauri Karttunen. 1977. Syntax and semantics of questions. *Linguistics and Philosophy*, 1.

Craige Roberts. 1996. Information structure: Towards an integrated formal theory of pragmatics. In Jae-Hak Yoon and Andreas Kathol, editors, *OSUWPL: Papers in Semantics*, volume 49. Ohio State University, Columbus.

Maribel Romero, Laura Kallmeyer, and Olga Babko-Malaya. 2004. LTAG Semantics for Questions. In Chung-hye Han and Anoop Sarkar, editors, *Proceedings of TAG+7: Seventh International Workshop on Tree Adjoining Grammar and Related Formalisms*, Vancouver, BC, Canada.

Mats Rooth. 1992. A theory of focus interpretation. *Natural Language Semantics*, 1.

Elisabeth Selkirk. 1996. Sentence prosody: Intonation, stress, and phrasing. In John A. Glodsmith, editor, *The Handbook of Phonological Theory*. Blackwell Publishing, Cambridge, MA / Oxford, UK.

Describing São Tomense Using a Tree-Adjoining Meta-Grammar

Emmanuel Schang[1], Denys Duchier[2], Brunelle Magnana Ekoukou[1],

Yannick Parmentier[2], Simon Petitjean[2]

(1) LLL, Université d'Orléans - 10, rue de Tours 45067 Orléans Cedex 2 – France

(2) LIFO, Université d'Orléans - 6, rue Léonard de Vinci 45067 Orléans Cedex 2 – France

`firstname.lastname@univ-orleans.fr`

Abstract

In this paper, we show how the interactions between the tense, aspect and mood preverbal markers in São Tomense can be formally and concisely described at an abstract level, using the concept of projection. More precisely, we show how to encode the different valid orders of preverbal markers in an abstract description of a Tree-Adjoining Grammar of São Tomense. This description is written using the XMG meta-grammar language (Crabbé and Duchier, 2004).

1 Introduction

São Tomense[1] is a Portuguese-based Creole language spoken on São Tomé Island (RDSTP). Like many (if not all) Creole Languages, it has preverbal markers expressing Tense and Aspect (TMA markers in the classical literature on Creole languages, see (Holm, 1989)), as shown in (1):

(1)   a.   tataluga xiga.
             turtle   come
             'The turtle came.'
    b.   tataluga ka   xiga.
             turtle   IMPF *come*
             'The turtle is coming.'
    c.   tataluga tava   ka   xiga
             turtle   Anterior IMPF *come*
             'The turtle was coming.'

Several approaches have been proposed to formally describe the combinations of TMA markers in São Tomense, including tree-based descriptions such as Tree-Adjoining Grammar (TAG) (Schang,

---

[1]The abbreviations are: ST (São Tomense) ; IMPF (imperfective) ; Asp (Aspect).

2000). Schang's TAG uses adjunction (*i.e.*, auxiliary trees) to encode the ordering of the TMA markers. As we shall see in Section 5, this is not satisfactory for several reasons. In this paper, we propose to shift the description of TMA markers to a meta-level, using the XMG language (Crabbé and Duchier, 2004). The paper is structured as follows. In section 2, we describe São Tomense TMA system. In Section 3, we introduce the XMG language. Section 4 focuses on the syntactic properties of the TMA markers. In Section 5, we then show how to control the TMA markers' combinations in an XMG meta-grammar. This meta-grammar is then compiled in order to produce a TAG where verbal elementary trees only contain correctly ordered TMA markers (realised as lexical nodes).

2 TMA system

Before describing the TMA markers and their combination, let us first look at the bare verbs.

2.1 Bare Verbs

As in many languages (and as in most of the Creoles), bare verbs are used to express the past perfective (or preterite) with dynamic processes (as in (1-a)) and express the present tense with stative verbs, as in (2).

(2)   n   konse mana bo.
          1sg know sister your
          'I know your sister.' (*'I knew your sister')

Stative verbs are often considered to collide with the TMA markers (Ferraz, 1979), but several uses of both have been noticed in ST spoken corpora

Proceedings of the 11th International Workshop on Tree Adjoining Grammars and Related Formalisms (TAG+11), pages 82–89,
Paris, September 2012.

(Schang, 2000), triggering an inchoative meaning (3).

(3)　e　ka　sa yo　godu.
　　　3sg IMPF *be very fat*
　　　'He is going to be very fat."

(Schang, 2000, p. 193) shows that bare verbs in São Tomense are literally "bare" and that no information on Tense or Aspect is attached to them, and that no functional projection (containing a zero morphem) is needed to account for the various uses of bare verbs. By contrast, the preverbal markers bear such temporal and aspectual features.

2.2 Aspect

ka is the most-used aspectual marker in São Tomense[2]. (Hagemeijer, 2007) and (Ferraz, 1979) provide several examples of its uses in various contexts, triggering habitual reading (4-a) , future tense (4-b) and conditionality (4-c):

(4)　a.　Zon ka　kanta ni gleza.
　　　　　John Asp sing　in church
　　　　　'John uses to sing at church.'
　　b.　Zoze ka　xiga amanha.
　　　　　José Asp come tomorrow
　　　　　'José will come tomorrow.'
　　c.　xi bo **ka** bi　amanha,　bo ka
　　　　　if 2sg Asp come tomorrow 2sg Asp
　　　　　be mu.
　　　　　see me
　　　　　'If you come tomorrow, you'll see me.'

(Schang, 2000, p. 193) shows that all the various interpretations of *ka* boil down to an imperfective reading, which is the core meaning of this marker.

2.3 Tense

Two Tense markers occupy the same position: *tava* (anterior) and *sa* (present). Both markers derive from the Portuguese verb *estar* 'to be', in its 3sg imperfect indicative tense form and 3sg present tense form respectively. They inherit from the temporal value of the etymon.

While *tava* can freely combine with the verb, *sa* goes together with *ka*, often pronounced *xka*,[3] see (5).

(5)　a.　e　tava　bi.
　　　　　3sg Tense come
　　　　　'He had come.'
　　b.　e　sa　ka　bi.
　　　　　3sg Tense Asp come
　　　　　'He is coming.'
　　c.　e　tava ka　bi.
　　　　　3sg Tense Asp come
　　　　　'He was coming.'
　　d.　*e sa bi.

(5-b) illustrates the *sa ka* or *xka* (its short form) combination which triggers the progressive reading. Any other combination is blocked,[4] see (6).

(6)　a.　*e ka tava bi.
　　b.　*e sa tava bi.
　　c.　*e ka sa bi.

To summarize, São Tomense combines a few preverbal markers in order to derive a rich range of semantic interpretations.

3　eXtensible Meta-Grammar

As mentioned above, in this paper, we show how to move the description of TMA markers in a São Tomense TAG from the syntactic level (*i.e.*, the TAG elementary trees) to a meta-level, using the *eXtensible Meta-Grammar* (XMG) framework. This move makes it possible for the linguist to concisely describe the valid TMA orders.[5]

XMG is a declarative language for specifying tree-based grammars at a meta-level (Crabbé and Duchier, 2004). Basically, XMG allows to abstract over tree structures (*i.e.*, to capture generalizations) by defining (i) elementary tree fragments and (ii) conjunctive / disjunctive combinations of these fragments. Such an abstraction over a (tree) grammar is generally called a *meta-grammar*. It is compiled in order to automatically produce the underlying grammar.[6]

---

[4](Hagemeijer, 2007) reports some other combinations (*sa xka, ka ka, tava sa xka*) which are firmly rejected by our informants and absent from the fieldwork recordings we have. It suggests that some variation exists. But as we focus on standard ST we don't take it into account. Note however that these combinations can be seen as relaxed constraints on the system, and do not invalidate our analyses.

[5]This move presupposes that TMA markers should rather be treated as co-anchors of verbal elementary trees than anchors of auxiliary trees. This is motivated in Section 4.

[6]The compiler for the XMG language is also called XMG, and is freely available at `https://launchpad. net/xmg`.

---

[2]Leaving aside its allomorph *ga*.

[3]It can also be pronouced 'e ska bi'.

The elementary tree fragments of the XMG language correspond to tree descriptions and are encapsulated within *classes*. Such a class provides the linguist with a mean to refer to a given tree description, *e.g.*, in order to reuse it in distinct contextes. These tree descriptions can contain (node or feature) variables, dominance and precedence constraints on nodes, and labelling constraints (association of a node with some feature structure). Note that the combinations of these tree descriptions are also encapsulated within classes, and that the default scope of a variable is the class. XMG is also equipped with an inheritance mechanism, which allows to import the content of a class and access directly its variables.

The compilation of an XMG specification amounts to (i) accumulating tree descriptions and then (ii) solving accumulated tree descriptions. As a result, a fully redundant grammar is generated (*i.e.*, TAG trees grouped into tree families).

The XMG language reveals expressive enough to describe a large amount of syntactic structures in a compact way, as shown by the various tree grammars designed with XMG for French (Crabbé, 2005; Perrier, 2007; Gardent, 2008), English (Alahverdzhieva, 2008) and German (Kallmeyer et al., 2008).

A particularly interesting feature of the XMG language is that it comes with a set of built-in *linguistic principles* that the linguist can activate in order to ensure the validity of the output structures (Crabbé et al., To appear). These principles not only guaranty the well-formedness of the grammar with respect to linguistic invariants, but also help the linguist to highly factorise her/his meta-grammar. Indeed, principles allow the linguist to avoid defining numerous alternative descriptions for exceptions, but to rather catch them during the compilation of the meta-grammar.

In the meta-grammar for ST described in Section 5, we use the unifications over feature structures labelling nodes, which are triggered during tree description solving, to rule out invalid TMA orders. In a future work, we plan to rather describe valid TMA orders via a dedicated linguistic principle.

4 Projecting Aspect and Tense

Prior to describing our meta-grammar of ST, let us describe interesting properties of TMA markers, which will motivate our formal description of ST.

(Schang, 2000) and (Hagemeijer, 2007) propose a description of the properties of the TMA markers that we complete below. Contrary to the full verb *sa* and *tava* ('be'), which can be used as copula, as in (7), *sa* and *tava* as TMA do not have the properties of the verbs they originate from, a fact we will show below.

(7)   a.   kafe sa kentxi.
           coffee be hot
           'The coffee is hot.'
     b.   kafe   tava   kentxi.
           coffee be.Anterior hot
           'The coffee was hot.'

The question we address here is the nature of *ka*, *sa* and *tava*. We present a series of tests which shows that TMA markers behave differently from verbs (auxiliaries included), adverbs and adjectives (note that hereafter we use the reduced form *xka* instead of the full form *sa ka*).

- Coordination

  Contrary to lexical items, TMA markers cannot be coordinated (neither overtly nor covertly):

  (8)   *Zon sa   i/o   tava ka kume.
          John Tense and/or Tense Asp eat
          'John is and/or was eating.'

  Note that the TMA markers don't show the properties of French and English auxiliaries with regard to coordination.

- Reiteration

  TMA markers cannot be reiterated on the same verb (9), contrary to adverbs for instance (see (Schang, 2012) for a study of lexical reiteration in ST).

  (9)   *Zon sa   sa   ka kume / *Zon
          John Tense Tense Asp eat   / John
          ka ka kume
          Asp Asp eat

- Negation

  Sentential negation in ST is double-headed. The first particle comes to the immediate left of the TMA markers and the second one comes in sentence-final position (see (Hagemeijer, 2007) and (Schang, 2000) for a description).

(10)   Zon **na** xka (*na) kume loso
        John Neg1 TMA (Neg1) eat   rice
        fa.
        Neg2
        'John doesn't eat the rice.'

However, *fa* is used without *na* in partial negation (contrastive negation):

(11)   a.   ami fa!
              me Neg2
              'Not me!'
        b.   karu fa!
              car Neg2
              'Not the car!'
        c.   kume fa!
              eat   Neg2
              'Not eating!'
        d.   glavi   fa!
              beautiful Neg2
              'Not beautiful!'
        e.   leve-leve fa!
              slowly   Neg2
              'Not slowly'
        f.   isa fa!
              this Neg2
              'Not this one!'

(12)   *{ka/xka/tava/tava ka} fa!
        [Tense and Asp markers negated]

The TMA markers cannot be negated (12) while pronouns, nouns, verbs, adjective, adverbs and strong demonstratives can, as in (11-a-f).
While English auxiliaries for instance can be negated, TMA markers cannot (13):

(13)   a.   Zon tava   ka kume?
              John Tense Asp eat
              'Was he eating?'
        b.   *Inon, e   na   tava   ka
              no   3sg Neg1 Tense Asp
              fa.
              Neg2
              'No, he wasn't.'

- Participle-like constructions

  Some verbs of Portuguese origin have been incorporated in ST lexicon with their past participle form (ex. Port.: chegadu > ST: xigadu). While they can be complement of a full verb (*fika* 'to stay', or sa 'to be' (the full verb used as copula), they cannot appear with TMA markers, as shown in (14) (adapted from (Hagemeijer, 2007, p.132)) :

(14)   a.   *kinte   ka/xka balidu.
              garden TMA   swept
        b.   kinte   sa/fika balidu.
              garden is/stays swept
              'The garden has been/remains swept'

- Question-answer pairs

  TMA markers cannot form a minimal answer:

(15)   a.   Zon ka/xka bali   kinte?
              John TMA   sweep garden
              'Does John sweep/is sweeping the garden?'
        b.   efan, e   ka/xka *(bali).
              yes   he TMA   sweep
              'Yes, he does.'

- VP-fronting:

(16)   a.   bo ka/xka bali   kinte.
              you TMA   sweep garden
              'you (sweep/are sweeping) the garden.'
        b.   bali   kinte so   bo
              sweep garden FOCUS you
              ka/xka *(bali)
              TMA   sweep
              'SWEEP THE GARDEN is what he does/is doing.'

- Pseudo-cleft

(17)   a.   kume/dansa/kanta sa kwa
              eat/dance/sing   is thing
              ku   e   ka/xka fe.
              that he TMA   do
              'Eating/dancing/singing   is what he does/is doing.'

b. *ka kume/dansa/kanta sa
   Asp eat/danse/sing   is
   kwa ku e ka fe.
   thing that 3sg Asp do

In the fronted position where only the lexical verb (without its functional projections) is allowed, the TMA are excluded. No ellipsis is allowed for the inflected verb. To describe it in classic words, it shows that the material copied to the focus position originates below INFL.

We conclude from these tests that the TMA markers are clearly functional elements, as inflectional affixes in English and French are.

The reason why TMA markers are not represented as prefixes in the relevant litterature comes from adverb placement. The adverb *kwaji* can be inserted between Tense and Aspect, as in:

(18)   Tataluga sa   kwaji ka koda.
       turtle   Tense almost Asp wake-up
       'The turtle is about to wake up.'

(19)   Tataluga (??kwaji) xka (*kwaji) koda.

(19) shows that when *kwaji* is inserted, *sa* and *ka* cannot freely agglutinate as *xka/ska*. Note incidentally that the agglutinated form *xka* is thus built post-syntactically in phonology.

5 Describing Tense and Aspect in São Tomense using a Meta-Grammar

(Schang, 2000) proposes an analysis in the TAG framework which treats the TMA markers as adjuncts to V and uses Tense and Aspect features on the foot node of the adjunct tree to reject invalid combinations. However, a description based on the concept of Extended Projections (Grimshaw, 1991) (see also (Frank, 2004) for a similar approach) better reflects the fact that TMA markers are not adjuncts such as adjectives or adverbs are. Consequently, we treat here TMA markers as extended projections of V, which can remain bare or be stretched with Tense and Aspect projections.

Thus, Tense and Aspect markers are not stored in the Lexicon (they don't anchor any tree) but are co-anchors of the elementary tree associated with verbs.

Let us consider (21), which illustrates the structure of (20).

(20)   e tava ka kume.
       3sg Tense Asp eat
       'He was eating.'

(21)

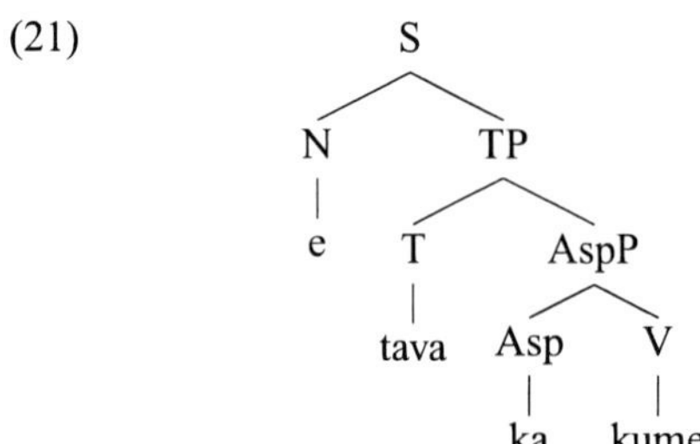

In (21), S is a projection of V, the maximal functional stretching of the verb.

These facts can easily be recast in XMG's framework. To this aim, the structure (20) is broken down into four pieces (*i.e.* classes) each containing minimal information. These Classes are listed below.

- *CanSubject*: to express what is usually called the External Argument of the verb. It is described in (22-a) .

- *Intransitive* verb: the minimal projection of V. It is described in (22-e) .

- *Aspect*: as a projection of the aspectual marker. It is described in (22-b) .

- *Tensed*: as a projection of Tense. Note that *Tensed* refers to a disjunction of two tree fragments, which differ according to the *past* feature labelling the Tense marker. This distinction allows us to treat the case where a non-past Tense marker must precede an Aspect marker. The corresponding two tree fragments are described in (22-c) and (22-d).

(22)   a.

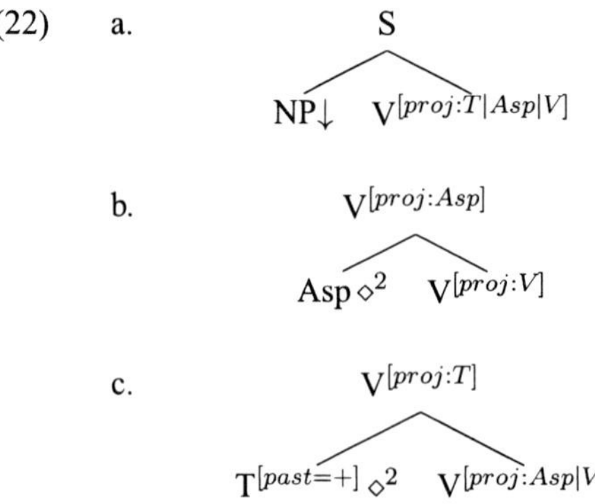

d.

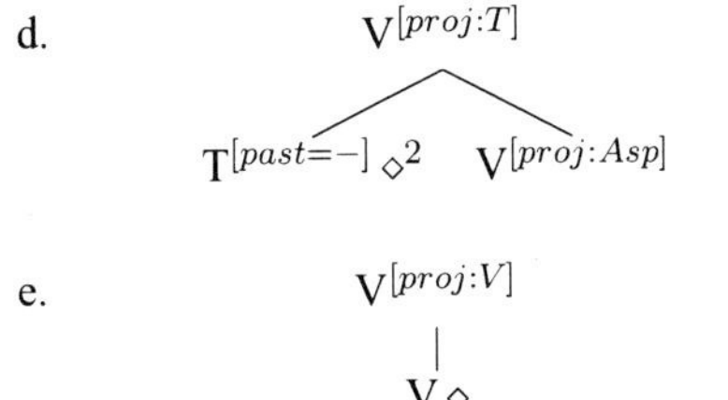

e. $V^{[proj:V]}$
|
$V\diamond$

Thus, (21) is built up from the following conjunction of Classes:

$$CanSubject \wedge Intransitive \wedge Aspect \wedge Tensed$$

The feature *proj(ection)* is used here to rule out invalid combinations in the output elementary tree.[7] As mentioned in Section 3, during the compilation of the meta-grammar, the accumulated tree descriptions are solved in order to produce minimal tree models (which correspond to the elementary TAG trees of the grammar being described). In the present case of TMA markers, the tree description solver will compute verbal elementary trees by identifying nodes belonging to the tree fragments introduced in (22). For such a node identification to succeed, the nodes need to be labelled with feature structures, which unify. While giving a linguistically motivated account of the properties of TMA markers, the *proj* feature will help the meta-grammar compiler to only produce valid elementary trees (recall that Tense must dominate/precede Aspect and V).

From the conjunction of classes given above, the result of the meta-grammar compilation are elementary trees for intransitive verbs, including the tree associated with *kume* 'to eat' depicted in (23).

(23)

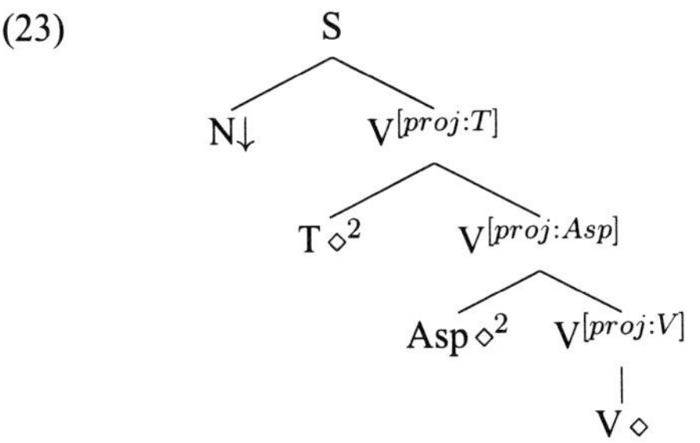

To fill the Tense and Aspect slots, this verb appears in the Lexicon as associated with two co-anchor equations (*cf*, $\diamond$-nodes refer to anchors and $\diamond^2$-nodes to co-anchors in (23)):[8]

- T$\rightarrow tava\ [past = +]$

- Asp $\rightarrow ka$

A felicitous side-effect of incorporating the TMA markers in the elementary tree of the verb appears when looking at the derivation tree of the sentence "e tava ka kume" (24) where functional information such as Tense and Aspect do not appear as adjuncts but are hold by the verb (tree $\alpha 1$, tree $\alpha 2$ being the elementary tree of the pronoun *e* '3sg').

(24) $\alpha 1$-kume$[tense{:}past, aspect{:}Impf]$
|
$\alpha 2$-e

It is interesting to notice that, in this context, TMA markers can be treated similarly to Tense and Aspect affixes in some agglutinative languages (see (Duchier et al., 2012) for an analysis of Ikota – Bantu B25 – with XMG), diverging only in the way they combine.

Of course, treating TMA markers as co-anchors raises the question of the production of the numerous elementary trees and the computational efficiency of parsing with these.

Regarding the production of elementary trees, the use of the XMG framework makes it possible to concisely describe elementary trees (including TMA markers), the XMG compiler being in charge of producing the redundant elementary trees.[9]

Regarding the computational efficiency of parsing with TAG grammars having TMA markers embedded in verbal elementary trees, it may not be a problem for the following reasons. While this treatment of TMA markers causes the grammar to have a much higher number of elementary trees (TMA markers are no longer factored out, as it is the case when using auxiliary trees), it is worth considering two points.

First, Creoles are known to have little morphology (McWhorter, 2001) and ST does not allow many transformations (no voice and no argumental affixation). The extra cost of enlarging the

---

⁷In the values associated with feature proj, "|" refers to disjunction.

⁸Here, we adopt a grammar-lexicon interface comparable

to that of the XTAG project (XTAG Research Group, 2001), where the grammar is made of unanchored trees, anchoring being realized at parsing.

⁹The question on how to produce the large lexicon used to anchor the grammar (that is, containing the co-anchor equations) remains to be answered, nonetheless one option would be to use techniques for automatic lexicon acquisition such as that of (Sagot, 2005).

grammar size is thus low (and make ST grammar size still reasonable).

Second, when replacing auxiliary trees with co-anchoring equations, the parsing complexity is somehow moved from the actual parsing step (where adjunction is processed) to the lexical selection and anchoring step (which is done prior to actual parsing, see *e.g.* (Gardent et al., 2011)). In other words, the complexity here raises when selecting the right lexical entries, and anchoring the many trees associated with these entries. But, once the elementary trees are anchored, it will be possible to select a pertinent subgrammar (that is, to remove useless trees with respect to the sentence to parse) using techniques such as polarity-based filtering (Gardent et al., 2011).

6 Conclusion

In this paper, we have shown how to implement the concept of projection at an abstract level (the meta-grammar) in order to describe a crucial domain of the syntax of São Tomense, namely the TMA markers. We claim that the TMA markers have to be integrated in the TAG elementary trees of verbs instead of anchoring auxiliary trees, as it was done before (Schang, 2000). This comes from the fact these markers can be considered as functional elements.

In this context, we chose to use a meta-grammatical framework, namely the XMG system, in order to facilitate the description of verbal elementary trees equipped with nodes for TMA markers. By *facilitate*, we do not only mean that the meta-grammar compiler will take care of the tedious task of producing the numerous elementary trees concerned with TMA markers, but also (and mainly) that an abstract level may be the right place to implement a linguistic theory such as that of projection used here.

Acknowledgments

We are grateful to the three anonymous reviewers for their helpful comments.

References

Katya Alahverdzhieva. 2008. XTAG using XMG. Master Thesis, Nancy Université.

Benoît Crabbé and Denys Duchier. 2004. Metagrammar redux. In *Constraint Solving and Language Processing, First International Workshop (CSLP 2004)*, volume 3438 of *Lecture Notes in Computer Science*, pages 32–47, Roskilde, Denmark. Springer.

Benoît Crabbé, Denys Duchier, Claire Gardent, Joseph Le Roux, and Yannick Parmentier. To appear. XMG: eXtensible Meta-Grammar. *Computational Linguistics*.

Benoît Crabbé. 2005. *Représentation informatique de grammaires fortement lexicalisées : Application à la grammaire d'arbres adjoints*. Ph.D. thesis, Université Nancy 2.

D. Duchier, B.M. Ekoukou, Y. Parmentier, S. Petitjean, E. Schang, et al. 2012. Describing Morphologically-rich Languages using Metagrammars: a Look at Verbs in Ikota. In *Workshop on 'Language technology for normalisation of less-resourced languages', 8th SALTMIL Workshop on Minority Languages and the 4th workshop on African Language Technology*, pages 55–60.

Luiz Ivens Ferraz. 1979. *The Creole of Sao Tome*. Witwatersrand University Press, Johannesburg.

Robert Frank. 2004. *Phrase structure composition and syntactic dependencies*, volume 38. Mit Press.

Claire Gardent, Yannick Parmentier, Guy Perrier, and Sylvain Schmitz. 2011. Lexical Disambiguation in LTAG using Left Context. In *5th Language & Technology Conference - LTC'11*, pages 395–399, Poznań, Poland.

Claire Gardent. 2008. Integrating a Unification-Based Semantics in a Large Scale Lexicalised Tree Adjoining Grammar for French. In *Proceedings of the 22nd International Conference on Computational Linguistics (Coling 2008)*, pages 249–256, Manchester, UK.

Jane Grimshaw. 1991. Extended projection. Master thesis, Brandeis University.

Tjerk Hagemeijer. 2007. *Clause structure in Santome*. Ph.D. thesis, University of Lisbon.

J.A. Holm. 1989. *Pidgins and Creoles*, volume 1&2. Cambridge Univ Pr.

Laura Kallmeyer, Timm Lichte, Wolfgang Maier, Yannick Parmentier, and Johannes Dellert. 2008. Developing a TT-MCTAG for German with an RCG-based Parser. In *The sixth international conference on Language Resources and Evaluation (LREC 08)*, pages 782–789, Marrakech, Morocco.

J.H. McWhorter. 2001. The worlds simplest grammars are creole grammars. *Linguistic typology*, 5(2-3):125–166.

Guy Perrier. 2007. A French Interaction Grammar. In *proceedings of the 6th Conference on Recent Advances in Natural Language Processing (RANLP 2007)*, pages 463–467, Borovets, Bulgaria.

Benoît Sagot. 2005. Automatic acquisition of a Slovak Lexicon from a Raw Corpus. In *Proceedings of the 8th International Conference on Text, Speech and Dialogue (TSD'05)*, volume 3658 of *Lecture*

Notes in Artificial Intelligence, pages 156–163, Karlovy Vary, Czech Republic. Springer-Verlag.

Emmanuel Schang. 2000. *L'émergence des créoles portugais du golfe de Guinée*. Ph.D. thesis, Université Nancy 2.

Emmanuel Schang. 2012. Reduplication in São Tomense. *The Morphosyntax of Reiteration in Creole and Non-Creole Languages*, pages 235–250.

XTAG Research Group. 2001. A lexicalized tree adjoining grammar for english. Technical Report IRCS-01-03, IRCS, University of Pennsylvania.

An Attempt Towards Learning Semantics:
Distributional Learning of IO Context-Free Tree Grammars

Ryo Yoshinaka

Kyoto University, Japan

`ry@i.kyoto-u.ac.jp`

Abstract

Solid techniques based on distributional learning have been developed targeting rich subclasses of CFGs and their extensions including linear context-free tree grammars. Along this line we propose a learning algorithm for some subclasses of IO context-free tree grammars.

1 Introduction

Several efficient algorithms have been proposed to learn different subclasses of context-free grammars (CFGs) based on *distributional learning* (e.g. (Clark and Eyraud, 2007; Yoshinaka, 2011b)). Distributional learning models and exploits the distribution of strings in contexts. Those techniques have soon been generalized to *mildly context-sensitive formalisms*: multiple CFGs (Yoshinaka, 2011a) and simple (non-deleting linear) context-free tree grammars (CFTGs) (Kasprzik and Yoshinaka, 2011). Those formalisms can be naturally encoded by abstract categorial grammars (ACGs) (de Groote and Pogodalla, 2004), which are based on the simply typed linear lambda calculus. By the flexible nature of lambda terms, ACGs can generate various types of data like strings, trees, meaning representations and their combinations. The distributional learning of ACGs is discussed in (Yoshinaka and Kanazawa, 2011).

It is quite recently shown that interesting subclasses of *parallel* MCFGs are also learnable by a distributional learning technique (Clark and Yoshinaka, 2012). PMCFGs are a non-linear extension of MCFGs, whose production rules may copy arguments. They are not considered to be an MCS formalism, but can model some (controversial) non-semilinear syntactic phenomena reported in linguistics.

Non-linear operations are more commonly required in generating semantic representations than in syntax. Consequently it is a natural direction of research to enhance the distributional learning techniques for ACGs to non-linear extensions of ACGs so that we can learn pairs of words and their meanings as lambda terms in the style of Montague semantics. However, treating general lambda terms involves technical difficulties. Instead, this paper discusses an easier case – the distributional learning of IO-CFTGs (Rounds, 1970; Engelfriet and Schmidt, 1977), which are also a non-linear formalism. Although trees are not satisfactory enough compared with lambda-terms, trees can be used as primitive models of meaning expressions. An example of an IO-CFTG that generates meaning representations of English sentences is found in Figure 1. For the sake of simplicity, this paper does not target the learning of word-meaning pairs, but it is possible to apply the technique presented in this paper to a natural formalism that generates pairs of a string and a tree through the same context-free derivation tree. We will concentrate on the distributional learning of IO-CFTGs.

Every grammar formalism for which distributional learning techniques have been proposed so far generate their languages through context-free derivation trees, whose nodes are labeled by production rules. The formalism and grammar rules determine how a context-free derivation tree t is mapped to a derived object $\phi(t) = T$. A context-free derivation tree t can be decomposed into a subtree s and a tree-context c with $t = c[s]$. The

Proceedings of the 11th International Workshop on Tree Adjoining Grammars and Related Formalisms (TAG+11), pages 90–98,
Paris, September 2012.

	CFG rules	;	IO-CFTG rules	
π_1	$\langle \quad I \to NP\ VP$;		$I \to VP(NP)$	$\rangle$
π_2	$\langle \quad VP \to V\ NP$;		$VP(x_1) \to V(x_1, NP)$	$\rangle$
π_3	$\langle \quad VP \to V$ himself ;		$VP(x_1) \to V(x_1, x_1)$	$\rangle$
π_4	$\langle \quad V \to$ loves ;		$V(x_1, x_2) \to \textbf{Love}(x_1, x_2)$	$\rangle$
π_5	$\langle \quad V \to$ hates ;		$V(x_1, x_2) \to \textbf{Hate}(x_1, x_2)$	$\rangle$
π_6	$\langle \quad V \to$ kills ;		$V(x_1, x_2) \to \textbf{Kill}(x_1, x_2)$	$\rangle$
π_7	$\langle \quad V \to V$ and V ;		$V(x_1, x_2) \to \wedge(V(x_1, x_2), V(x_1, x_2))$	$\rangle$
π_8	$\langle \quad NP \to$ Adam ;		$NP \to \textbf{Adam}$	$\rangle$
π_9	$\langle \quad NP \to$ Eve ;		$NP \to \textbf{Eve}$	$\rangle$
π_{10}	$\langle \quad NP \to$ Steve ;		$NP \to \textbf{Steve}$	$\rangle$

Figure 1: An IO-CFTG generating meanings expressions together with a CFG for sentences, where I is the initial symbol.

subtree determines a constituent $S = \phi(s)$ and the tree-context determines a contextual structure $C = \phi(c)$ in which the constituent is plugged to form the derived object $T = C \odot S$, where we represent the plugging operation by $\odot$. For example, in the CFG case, C is a string pair $\langle l, r \rangle$ and S is a string u and $\langle l, r \rangle \odot u = lur$, which may correspond to a derivation $I \overset{*}{\Rightarrow} lAr \overset{*}{\Rightarrow} lur$ where I is the initial symbol and A is a nonterminal symbol. A learner does not know how a positive example T is derived by the target grammar. A learner based on distributional learning simply tries all the possible decompositions of a positive example into arbitral two parts C' and S' such that $T = C' \odot S'$ where some grammar may derive T thorough a derivation tree $t' = c'[s']$ with $\phi(c') = C'$ and $\phi(s') = S'$. Based on observation on the relation between potential constituents S' and contextual structures C' collected from given examples, she constructs her hypothesis grammar.

The literature has proposed several distributional properties that give learnable subclasses of a concerned formalism. Those properties can be classified into two: One, which we call *primal*, assumes that the language generated by each nonterminal is characterized by a finite number of constituents, whereas they are characterized by contextual structures in the other type, which we call *dual*. Those approaches show a tidy symmetry in the learning of CFGs (Yoshinaka, 2011b).

An important property of a formalism that makes distributional learning approach tractable is the *linearity*. A constituent S corresponding to a subtree s of a derivation tree will not be duplicated through the derivation process — S "occurs" in $C \odot S$ just once. This property makes the decomposition of a positive example tractable. The PMCFGs are not a linear formalism in this sense. Some components of a constituent S of a PMCFG may be duplicated during the derivation process and appear more than once in $C \odot S$. However, still the linearity property holds on the other side. That is, no components from the contextual structure C will be duplicated in $C \odot S$ through the interaction with S. Based on the linearity on the constituent side, Clark and Yoshinaka (2012) have shown that PMCFGs are learnable by a straightforward modification of an existing dual approach of distributional learning, while they discussed difficulties in learning PMCFGs by a primal approach due to the non-linearity of the contextual structure side.

The formalism this paper targets is IO-CFTGs, where copying operations are embedded into both constituent and contextual sides, which contrasts the case of PMCFGs. Therefore, the difficulty pointed out by Clark and Yoshinaka confronts both primal and dual approaches. This paper discusses how we can overcome the difficulty at the expense of restriction on our learning target. Clark and Yoshinaka's result on the learning of PMCFGs is a strict generalization of the learnability results on (M)CFGs, but our learner for IO-CFTGs does not learn some languages which are learnable by Kasprzik and Yoshinaka's algorithm for simple CFTGs. In fact, some finite languages are not learnable by our technique despite the strong learning scheme. Our result is presented as a first step towards learning word-meaning pairs by distributional learning techniques.

2 Preliminaries

We denote the set of nonnegative integers by $\mathbb{N}$. For a *ranked* alphabet Σ, we denote by Σ_m the set of letters of rank $m \in \mathbb{N}$. The set $\mathbb{T}_\Sigma$ of *trees* on Σ is the smallest set s.t. $f(t_1, \ldots, t_m) \in \mathbb{T}_\Sigma$ whenever $f \in \Sigma_m$ and $t_1, \ldots, t_m \in \mathbb{T}_\Sigma$ where $m \geq 0$. For $t \in \mathbb{T}_\Sigma$ and $\Delta \subseteq \Sigma$, we denote the number of occurrences of symbols from Δ in t by $|t|_\Delta$. We drop the subscript Δ if $\Sigma = \Delta$. For a finite set D of trees, we define $\|D\| = \sum_{t \in D} |t|$. Let X be a countably infinite set of rank 0 *variables* $x_1, x_2, \ldots$. An m-*stub* s is a tree in $\mathbb{T}_{\Sigma \cup \{x_1, \ldots, x_m\}}$ in which every variable x_i ($1 \leq i \leq m$) occurs at least once. Thus 0-stub is a variable-free tree. An m-stub is said to be p-*copying* if every variable occurs at most p times. A 1-copying stub is also called a *linear* stub. The set of p-copying m-stubs is denoted by $\mathbb{S}_\Sigma^{m,p}$. We will use $*$ to denote unlimitedness: e.g. $\mathbb{S}_\Sigma^{m,*} = \bigcup_{p \in \mathbb{N}} \mathbb{S}_\Sigma^{m,p}$. A *leaf substitution* σ is a mapping from $\{x_1, \ldots, x_m\}$ to $\mathbb{T}_\Sigma$ for some m, whose domain is extended to stubs in the standard way: $s\sigma$ is the tree obtained from $s \in \mathbb{S}_\Sigma^{m,p}$ by substituting $\sigma(x)$ for every occurrence of $x \in X$ in t. Let Y be another ranked alphabet of variables, whose elements are denoted by y with or without subscripts: $y, y_1, y_2, \ldots$ etc. This paper flexibly assumes their ranks depending on the context.

An *infix substitution* θ is a partial map from Y to $\mathbb{S}_\Sigma^{*,*}$ such that $y \in Y_m$ implies $y\theta \in \mathbb{S}_\Sigma^{m,*}$ (if defined), which is extended so that $f(t_1, \ldots, t_m)\theta = f(t_1\theta, \ldots, t_m\theta)$ if $f \notin \mathrm{dom}(\theta)$ and $f(t_1, \ldots, t_m)\theta = \theta(f)\sigma$ where $\sigma(x_i) = t_i\theta$ for each i if $f \in \mathrm{dom}(\theta)$. By assuming that the order of the variables of the domain of θ is understood, a substitution $\{ y_i \mapsto s_i \mid 1 \leq i \leq n \}$ is often specified as $[s_1, \ldots, s_n]$. Moreover when $s_i = B_i(x_1, \ldots, x_{m_i})$ for some $B_i \in \Sigma_{m_i}$, we write it by $[B_1, \ldots, B_n]$. An m-*environment* e is a tree in $\mathbb{T}_{\Sigma \cup \{y\}}$ in which all subtrees rooted by y of rank m are identical: i.e., $e = e'[x_1 \mapsto y(t_1, \ldots, t_m)]$ for some trees $t_i \in \mathbb{T}_\Sigma$ and a stub $e' \in \mathbb{S}_\Sigma^{1,*}$, where the rank of y is m. If y occurs at most p times in e, we call it p-copying. The set of p-copying m-environments is denoted by $\mathbb{E}_\Sigma^{m,p}$. For an m-environment $e \in \mathbb{E}_\Sigma^{m,*}$ and an m-stub $s \in \mathbb{S}_\Sigma^{m,*}$, $e \odot s$ denotes the tree $e[s]$. The operation $\odot$ is naturally extended to sets so that $E \odot S = \{ e \odot s \mid e \in E \text{ and } s \in S \}$ for $E \subseteq \mathbb{E}_\Sigma^{m,*}$ and $S \subseteq \mathbb{S}_\Sigma^{m,*}$. When the alphabet Σ is

understood, we write $\mathbb{S}^{m,p}$ for $\mathbb{S}_\Sigma^{m,p}$ and so on.

For a tree set $D \subseteq \mathbb{T}_\Sigma$, we define

$$\mathrm{Sub}^{m,p}(D) = \{ s \in \mathbb{S}_\Sigma^{m,p} \mid \exists e \in \mathbb{E}_\Sigma^{m,*}, e \odot s \in D \},$$
$$\mathrm{Env}^{m,p}(D) = \{ e \in \mathbb{E}_\Sigma^{m,p} \mid \exists s \in \mathbb{S}_\Sigma^{m,*}, e \odot s \in D \}.$$

We note that $\mathrm{Sub}^{0,*}(D)$ is the set of *subtrees* of elements of D in the usual sense.

Lemma 1.

$$\mathrm{Sub}^{m,p}(D) = \{ s \in \mathbb{S}_\Sigma^{m,p} \mid \exists e \in \mathbb{E}_\Sigma^{m,1}, e \odot s \in D \},$$
$$\mathrm{Env}^{m,p}(D) = \{ e \in \mathbb{E}_\Sigma^{m,p} \mid \exists s \in \mathbb{S}_\Sigma^{m,1}, e \odot s \in D \}.$$

Proof. We prove the first claim. The second one can be shown in a similar manner. Suppose that $e \odot s \in D$ with $s \in \mathbb{S}^{m,p}$ and $e \in \mathbb{E}^{m,n}$ for some $n > 1$, where y occurs just n times in e, i.e.,

$$e = f[\overbrace{y(\vec{t}), \ldots, y(\vec{t})}^{n\text{-times}}] \in \mathbb{E}^{m,n} \text{ for some } f \in \mathbb{S}^{1,n},$$

where $\vec{t}$ denotes a sequence of trees of length m. For $e' = f[y(\vec{t}), s[\vec{t}], \ldots, s[\vec{t}]] \in \mathbb{E}^{m,1}$, which is obtained from e by substituting s for all but one occurrence of y, we have $e' \odot s \in D$ and thus $s \in \mathrm{Sub}^{m,p}(D)$. $\qquad\square$

Lemma 2. *For fixed m and p, one can enumerate all elements of $\mathrm{Sub}^{m,p}(D)$ and $\mathrm{Env}^{m,p}(D)$ in polynomial time.*

Proof. We prove the first claim only. Suppose that $t = e \odot s \in D$ for some $e = e'[y(t_1, \ldots, t_m)] \in \mathbb{E}_\Sigma^{m,1}$ and $s \in \mathbb{S}^{m,p}$. Let $n_i \leq p$ be the number of occurrences of x_i in s. Then s can be written as $s'[x_1^{n_1}, \ldots, x_m^{n_m}]$ with a linear stub s' where $x_i^{n_i}$ denotes the sequence of x_i of length n_i. We have $t = e[s'[t_1^{n_1}, \ldots, t_m^{n_m}]]$. Hence such a pair $\langle e, s \rangle$ can be uniquely specified by the positions where s' and t_i occur in t, which are at most $1 + n_1 + \cdots + n_m \leq 1 + mp$ positions in total. Therefore, there are at most $\|t\|^{1+mp}$ elements in $\mathrm{Sub}^{m,p}(\{t\})$ by Lemma 1 and one can enumerate all in polynomial time. $\qquad\square$

An IO-CFTG[1] is a tuple $G = \langle \Sigma, N, P, I \rangle$ where N and Σ are disjoint ranked alphabets of *nonterminals* and *terminals*, respectively, P is the set of rules and $I \subseteq N_0$ is the set of initial symbols. Each rule in P has the form $A(x_1, \ldots, x_m) \to s$ with $A \in N_m$ and $s \in \mathbb{S}_{\Sigma \cup N}^{m,*}$ for some m, which will be abbreviated as $A \to s$. We stipulate that hereafter when we denote a rule

---

[1] We consider only non-deleting CFTGs.

as $A \to s'[A_1, \ldots, A_n]$ with $A_i \in N$ for each i, it means that $|s'[A_1, \ldots, A_n]|_N = n$. For example a rule $A \to B(B(c))$ may be denoted as $A \to s_1[B, B]$ with $s_1 = y_1(y_2(c))$ but is never denoted as $A \to s_2[B]$ with $s_2 = y_1(y_1(c))$ or $s_2 = B(y_1(c))$.

We define the derivation of an IO-CFTG in a non-standard way. Derivation trees of G are defined as follows.

- for every rule $\pi = (A \to s)$ with $s \in \mathbb{S}_\Sigma^{*,*}$, π is an A-derivation tree and its *yield* is $\phi(\pi) = s$;

- for a rule $\pi = (A \to s[B_1, \ldots, B_n])$ and B_i-derivation trees τ_i for $i = 1, \ldots, n$, the tree $\pi(\tau_1, \ldots, \tau_n)$ is an A-derivation tree and its yield is $\phi(\pi(\tau_1, \ldots, \tau_n)) = s[\phi(\tau_1), \ldots, \phi(\tau_n)]$;

- nothing else is an A-derivation tree.

An A-derivation tree is simply called a *derivation tree* if $A \in I$. The *language* $\mathcal{L}(G, A) \subseteq \mathbb{S}^{m,*}$ generated by $A \in N_m$ is defined to be

$$\mathcal{L}(G, A) = \{\, \phi(\tau) \mid \tau \text{ is an } A\text{-derivation tree} \,\}.$$

The *language* of G is defined to be $\bigcup_{A \in I} \mathcal{L}(G, A)$. A *derivation tree-context* is a tree χ with exactly one occurrence of a rank 0 variable z such that $\chi[z \mapsto \tau]$ is a derivation tree for some A-derivation tree τ for some $A \in N$. The mapping ϕ is naturally applied to a derivation tree-context by $\phi(z) = y$ so that $\phi(\chi) \odot \phi(\tau) = \phi(\chi[\tau])$, where $\phi(\chi) \in \mathbb{E}^{m,*}$ with m the rank of both A and y.

Example 3. Figure 1 includes a CFG on the left column and an IO-CFTG on the right with common rule labels. $\pi_1(\pi_8, \pi_2(\pi_4, \pi_9))$ is a derivation tree, which yields a string Adam loves Eve by the CFG and a tree **Love(Adam, Eve)** by the IO-CFTG.

Another derivation tree $\pi_1(\pi_8, \pi_3(\pi_7(\pi_4, \pi_5)))$ yields Adam loves and hates himself and $\wedge(\textbf{Love(Adam, Adam)}, \textbf{Hate(Adam, Adam)})$.

Corollary 4. *Let τ be a derivation tree that has an A-derivation tree τ' as a subtree. There is $e \in \mathbb{E}^{m,1}$ such that $\phi(\tau) = e[\phi(\tau')]$ where m is the rank of A.*

Proof. By Lemma 1. $\qquad\square$

Lemma 5. *Suppose that G_* generates L_*, and $t \in L_*$ is derived using a rule $A_0 \to s[A_1, \ldots, A_n]$ with $A_0 \in N_m$. Then there are $s_i \in \mathbb{S}_\Sigma^{m_i,1}$ such that $s[s_1, \ldots, s_n] \in \mathrm{Sub}^{m,p}(t)$.*

Proof. The idea of the proof is common to the one for Lemma 1 except that copies of arguments by other arguments require a little care. We prove the lemma only for a special case for understandability, which will easily be generalized. Suppose that we have a rule π of the form

$$A_0 \to s[A_1, A_2]$$

where $s[y_1, y_2] = y_1(a(y_2(b, x_1)), c)$. Let τ_1 and τ_2 be A_1- and A_2-derivation trees such that $\phi(\tau_1) = u_1 = u_1'[x_1, x_1, x_2] \in \mathcal{L}(G_*, A_1)$ and $\phi(\tau_2) = u_2 = u_2'[x_1, x_2, x_2] \in \mathcal{L}(G_*, A_2)$, where u_1 contains just two occurrences of x_1 and one occurrence of x_2 and so on. We then have

$$\begin{aligned}
\phi(\pi(\tau_1, \tau_2)) &= s[u_1, u_2] \\
&= u_1'[a(u_2'[b, x_1, x_1]), a(u_2'[b, x_1, x_1]), c] \\
&\qquad\qquad \in \mathcal{L}(G, A_0).
\end{aligned}$$

Now let us consider a derivation tree τ that has $\pi(\tau_1, \tau_2)$ as a subtree. Let $t = \phi(\tau)$ and $u = \phi(\pi(\tau_1, \tau_2))$. By Lemma 4, $t = e[u]$ for some $e = t'[y(t'')] \in \mathbb{E}^{m,1}$. We then have

$$\begin{aligned}
t &= e[u_1'[a(u_2'[b, t'', t'']), a(u_2'[b, t'', t'']), c]] \\
&= e[s[s_1, s_2]]
\end{aligned}$$

for

$$s_1 = u_1'[x_1, a(u_2'[b, t'', t'']), x_2] \in \mathbb{S}^{2,1},$$
$$s_2 = u_2'[x_1, x_2, t''] \in \mathbb{S}^{2,1}. \qquad\square$$

By $\mathbb{G}(p, q, r)$ we denote the class of IO-CFTGs G such that $N = \bigcup_{m=1}^r N_m$ and for every rule $A \to s$, we have $s \in \mathbb{S}^{*,p}$ and $|s|_N \leq q$. We will consider only grammars in $\mathbb{G}(p, q, r)$ with fixed and small numbers p, q, r.

Proposition 6. *The uniform membership problem for $\mathbb{G}(p, q, r)$ for fixed p, q, r can be solved in polynomial time.*

Proof. This proposition is a corollary to known results. Particularly Kanazawa's technique that reduces membership problems to datalog queries will give an elegant parsing algorithm (Kanazawa, 2007; Beeri and Ramakrishnan, 1991). Yet to make this paper self-contained, we give a brief sketch of a CKY-style algorithm for the problem. Let $\langle G, t \rangle$ with $G \in \mathbb{G}(p, q, r)$ and $t \in \mathbb{T}_\Sigma$ be an instance of the problem. For each nonterminal symbol A of rank m, we compute a set $Q_A \subseteq (\mathrm{Sub}^{0,*}(\{t\}))^{1+m}$ of $(1 + m)$-tuples of subtrees of t so that $\langle t_0, t_1, \ldots, t_m \rangle \in Q_A$ iff $s[t_1, \ldots, t_m] = t_0$ for some $s \in \mathcal{L}(G, A)$. We initialize those sets Q_A to be empty and then monotonically and recursively expand the sets by referring to the rules of G. We have $t \in \mathcal{L}(G)$ if $t \in Q_A$ for some initial symbol $A \in I$. When all sets converge without satisfying this condition, we conclude $t \notin \mathcal{L}(G)$. Note that the bounds q and r play a crucial role for the polynomial-time computability. $\qquad\square$

3 Learning IO-CFTGs

Our learning scheme is *identification in the limit from positive data and membership queries* following Clark (2010). The learner is given an infinite sequence consisting of all and only trees from a learning target L_* and each time the learner gets a tree, it outputs an IO-CFTG as its conjecture. The learner has access to a membership oracle, which answers whether an arbitrary tree belongs to L_*. The sequence of the conjectures must eventually converge to an IO-CFTG representing L_*.

Hereafter we fix a target language L_*. Distributional learning observes the distribution of stubs in environments with respect to L_*. Let us define dual polar maps as follows. For $S \subseteq \mathbb{S}^{m,*}$ and $E \subseteq \mathbb{E}^{m,*}$,

$$S^\triangleright = \{\, e \in \mathbb{E}^{m,*} \mid e \odot S \subseteq L_* \,\},$$
$$E^\triangleleft = \{\, s \in \mathbb{S}^{m,*} \mid E \odot s \subseteq L_* \,\}.$$

We write $S^{\triangleright\triangleleft}$ for $(S^\triangleright)^\triangleleft$ and so on. One can easily see that $S^{\triangleright\triangleleft\triangleright} = S^\triangleright$ and $E^{\triangleleft\triangleright\triangleleft} = E^\triangleleft$. A learner extracts stubs and environments from given positive examples and ask the oracle which combination of those give grammatical trees in L_*. When a positive example t is derived by a derivation tree τ that has a A-derivation subtree τ' for some A, in general there is no bound p such that $\mathcal{L}(G, A) \subseteq \mathbb{S}^{m,p}$ where m is the rank of A. That is, there exist exponentially many potential constituents $s' \in \mathrm{Sub}^{m,*}(\{t\})$ and extracting all such stubs is not tractable. The same holds for the environment side. In stead we consider only p-copying stubs and environments. We define restricted polar maps as follows:

$$S^{(E)} = S^\triangleright \cap E \text{ and } E^{(S)} = E^\triangleleft \cap S.$$

Among the two types of approaches in the distributional learning, we first discuss the so-called primal one.

3.1 Primal property

The following definition is an easy translation of the k-FKP for CFGs (Yoshinaka, 2011b) to IO-CFTGs.

Definition 7. We say that an IO-CFTG G has *the (k, p)-kernel property* $((k, p)$-KP$)$ if every nonterminal A of rank m admits a set $S_A \subseteq \mathbb{S}^{m,p}$ s.t. $|S_A| \le k$ and $S_A^{\triangleright\triangleleft} = \mathcal{L}(G, A)^{\triangleright\triangleleft}$. We call such a set S_A a *characterizing (stub) set* of A.

In the CFG case, Clark et al. (2009) showed that CFGs with the 1-FKP generate all regular languages and other simple CFLs including the Dyck language. However the $(1, p)$-KP is still too strong to describe non-linear languages.

Example 8. Let an IO-CFTG consist of the following rules, where $\Sigma_0 = \{a\}$, $\Sigma_1 = \{b\}$, $\Sigma_2 = \{c\}$, $N_0 = \{I, A\}$, $N_1 = \{C\}$:

$$I \to C(A), \; C \to C(c(x_1, x_1)), \; C \to x_1,$$
$$A \to b(A), \; A \to a,$$

Let $b^0(a) = a$ and $b^{i+1}(a) = b(b^i(a))$. The defined language consists of trees of the form $s[y \mapsto b^k(a)]$ where s is a balanced binary tree whose internal nodes and leaves are labeled by c and y, respectively. The nonterminal A does not have a singleton characterizing set. Any element $b^k(a)$ of $\mathcal{L}(G, A)$ admits its unique environment $e = c(y, b^k(a))$, in the sense that $\{e\}^\triangleleft \cap \mathcal{L}(G, A) = b^k(a)$. Thus the $(1, p)$-KP does not hold. On the other hand, one can easily see that $\{a, b(a)\}$, $\{x_1, c(x_1, x_1)\}$ and $\{a, c(a, a)\}$ characterize A, C and I, respectively (2-KP).

The primal approaches use environments to check the correctness of constructed rules. In the linear case, we can extract all required environments, which are linear, from given examples in polynomial time, but in our general setting, we have to collect non-linear environments as well, which is computationally intractable. We further require the following condition.

Definition 9. We say that a language L_* has *the (p, r, k)-fiducial environment property* ((p, r, k)-FEP) if for any $S \subseteq \mathbb{S}^{m,p}$ with $m \leq r$ and $|S| \leq k$, we have $(S^{(\mathbb{E}^{m,p})})^{\triangleleft} = S^{\triangleright\triangleleft}$.

The (p, r, k)-FEP means that to validate whether a stub s may occur in every environment that accepts S, it is enough to confirm that it is the case for every p-copying environment. Actually the (p, r, k)-FEP is rather strong for $k > 1$. The finite language $\{a(d), b(d), c(d), a^{p+1}(d), b^{p+1}(d)\}$ does not have the $(p, 1, 2)$-FEP ($c(x_1) \in S^{(\mathbb{E}^{1,p})\triangleleft} \setminus S^{\triangleright\triangleleft}$ for $S = \{a(x_1), b(x_1)\}$). On the other hand, one can show that the $(p, r, 1)$-FEP is satisfied by every language. Our first learning target is the following class:

$$\mathbb{P}(p, q, r, k) = \{\, G \in \mathbb{G}(p, q, r) \text{ with the}$$
$$(p, k)\text{-KP and } (p, r, k)\text{-FEP} \,\}$$

The above discussion on the property shows that the defined language class does not cover the class of simple CFTGs with k-FKP. Checking the property FEP is cumbersome even for the very simple IO-CFTG in Figure 1. Yet the author found no evidence suggesting that the grammar does not belong to $\mathbb{P}(2, 2, 2, 2)$.

3.2 Primal learner

Our learner (Algorithm 1) computes its conjecture $\mathcal{G}(T, F)$ from $T = \bigcup_{0 \leq m \leq r} T_m$ with $T_m \subseteq \mathrm{Sub}^{m,p}(D)$ and $F = \bigcup_{0 \leq m \leq r} F_m$ with $F_m = \mathrm{Env}^{m,p}(D)$ for a finite tree set $D \subseteq L_*$. The nonterminal set is $N^T = \bigcup_{0 \leq m \leq r} N_m^T$ where $N_m^T = \{ [\![S]\!] \mid S \subseteq T_m \wedge |S| \leq k \}$. $[\![S]\!] \in I$ if $S \subseteq L_*$. We have a rule of the form

$$[\![S_0]\!] \to s[[\![S_1]\!], \ldots, [\![S_n]\!]]$$

iff for some $m_0, \ldots, m_n \leq r$, $[\![S_i]\!] \in N_{m_i}^T$ for $i = 0, \ldots, n$, $s \in \mathbb{S}_{\Sigma \cup \{y_1, \ldots, y_n\}}^{m_0, p}$ in which each of $y_1, \ldots, y_n$ occurs just once in s with $n \leq q$,

1. there are $s_i \in \mathbb{S}_{\Sigma}^{m_i, 1}$ for $i = 1, \ldots, n$ such that $s[s_1, \ldots, s_n] \in T_{m_0}$,

2. $S_0^{(F_m)} \odot s[S_1, \ldots, S_n] \subseteq L_*$.

Lemma 10. *One can construct $\mathcal{G}(T, F)$ in polynomial time in $\|D\|$ with the aid of a membership oracle.*

<hr>

Algorithm 1 $\mathcal{A}(p, q, r, k)$

Data: trees $t_1, t_2, \cdots \in L_*$
Result: IO-CFTGs $G_1, G_2, \ldots$
let $D := T := F := \varnothing$; $\hat{G} := \mathcal{G}(T, F)$;
for $n = 1, 2, \ldots$ **do**
    let $D := D \cup \{t_n\}$; $F := \bigcup_{0 \leq m \leq r} \mathrm{Env}^m(D)$;
    if $D \not\subseteq \mathcal{L}(\hat{G})$ **then**
        let $T := \bigcup_{0 \leq m \leq r} \mathrm{Sub}^{m,p}(D)$;
    end if
    output $\hat{G} = \mathcal{G}(T, F)$ as G_n;
end for

<hr>

Proof. By Lemma 2, one can compute T and F in polynomial time in $\|D\|$.

We discuss the first condition of the rule construction. For each $t \in T_m$, there are at most $|t|^{1+m_1}$ pairs of $s_1 \in \mathbb{S}^{m_1, 1}$ and t_1 with just one occurrence of y_1 such that $t = t_1[y_1 \mapsto s_1]$, since such a pair corresponds to at most $1 + m_1$ positions on a path from the root to a leaf of t. Recursively one can determine $s_2, s_3, \ldots, s_n \in \mathbb{S}^{m_1, 1}$ such that $t_i = t_{i+1}[y_{i+1} \mapsto s_{i+1}]$ and $y_1, \ldots, y_i$ occur in t_{i+1}. t_n will be what we would like. There can be at most $|t|^{n+m_1+\cdots+m_n}$ possible choices and the enumeration can be done in polynomial time.

It is easy to see that checking the second condition can be done in polynomial time with the aid of a membership oracle. $\qquad\square$

A rule of the form $[\![S_0]\!] \to s[[\![S_1]\!], \ldots, [\![S_n]\!]]$ is said to be *incorrect* if $S_0^{\triangleright} \odot s[S_1, \ldots, S_n] \not\subseteq L_*$. We say that $F \subseteq \mathbb{E}^{*,*}$ is *fiducial* on T (with respect to L_*) if $\mathcal{G}(T, F)$ has no incorrect rules. Clearly, if F is fiducial on T then so is every superset of F.

Lemma 11. *Every T admits a fiducial set $F \subseteq \mathbb{E}^{*,p}$ such that*

- *the cardinality $|F|$ is polynomially bounded by the description size of T,*

- *for each $e \in F_m$ there is $s \in \mathbb{S}^{m,p}$ such that $e \odot s \in L_*$.*

Proof. Suppose a rule $[\![S_0]\!] \to s[[\![S_1]\!], \ldots, [\![S_n]\!]]$ is incorrect, which by the (p, r, k)-FEP means $S_0^{(\mathbb{E}^{m,p})} \odot s[S_1, \ldots, S_n] \not\subseteq L_*$. There is $e \in \mathbb{E}^{m,p}$ such that $e \odot S_0 \subseteq L_*$ and $e \odot s[S_1, \ldots, S_n] \not\subseteq L_*$. If e is in F, such a rule is excluded from $\mathcal{G}(T, F)$. In this case, we have $e \odot s \in L_*$ for any $s \in S_0 \subseteq \mathbb{S}^{m,p}$. $\qquad\square$

Lemma 12. *Let $\hat{G} = \mathcal{G}(T, F)$ with F fiducial on T. For any $[\![S_0]\!] \in N_m^T$ and $e \in \mathbb{E}^{m,*}$,*

$$e \odot S_0 \subseteq L_* \implies e \odot \mathcal{L}(\hat{G}, [\![S_0]\!]) \subseteq L_* .$$

Proof. Suppose that $e \odot S_0 \subseteq L_*$. We prove by induction on the derivation of $s_0 \in \mathcal{L}(\hat{G}, [\![S_0]\!])$ that $e \odot s_0 \in L_*$. Let $s_0 \in \mathcal{L}(\hat{G}, [\![S_0]\!])$ be derived by a rule $[\![S_0]\!] \to s[[\![S_1]\!], \ldots, [\![S_n]\!]]$ with $s_i \in \mathcal{L}(\hat{G}, [\![S_i]\!])$ and $s_0 = s[s_1, \ldots, s_n]$. Since the rule is correct by the assumption, we have

$$e \odot s[S_1, \ldots, S_n] \subseteq L_* ,$$

which implies

$$(e \odot s[y_1, S_2, \ldots, S_n]) \odot S_1 \subseteq L_*$$
$$\implies (e \odot s[y_1, S_2, \ldots, S_n]) \odot s_1$$
$$= e \odot s[s_1, S_2 \ldots, S_n] \subseteq L_*$$

by the induction hypothesis on $[\![S_1]\!]$. By repeatedly applying the same argument, we finally obtain

$$e \odot s[s_1, \ldots, s_n] = e \odot s_0 \in L_* . \qquad \square$$

Lemma 13. *If F is fiducial on T, then $\mathcal{L}(\mathcal{G}(T, F)) \subseteq L_*$.*

Proof. Apply Lemma 12 to an initial symbol $[\![S]\!] \in I$ with $e = y$. $\qquad \square$

Suppose that $G_* \in \mathbb{P}(p, q, r, k)$ generates L_*, We say that $T \subseteq \mathrm{Sub}^{*,*}(L_*)$ is *adequate* if (i) T_m includes a characterizing stub set S_A for every nonterminal $A \in N_m$ of G_* and (ii) for every rule $A \to s[A_1, \ldots, A_n]$ of G_*, there are $s_i \in \mathbb{S}_\Sigma^{m_i, 1}$ such that $s[s_1, \ldots, s_n] \in T_m$. Clearly if T is adequate, every superset of T is adequate.

Lemma 14. *There is a finite set $D \subseteq L_*$ such that $\bigcup_{0 \le m \le r} \mathrm{Sub}^{m,p}(D)$ is adequate and $|D|$ is polynomially bounded by the description size of G_*.*

Proof. By Lemmas 4 and 5. $\qquad \square$

Lemma 15. *If T is adequate, $\mathcal{L}(G_*) \subseteq \mathcal{L}(\mathcal{G}(T, F))$ for any F.*

Proof. We show that for every rule $A_0 \to s[A_1, \ldots, A_n]$ of G_*, $\hat{G}$ has a rule $[\![S_0]\!] \to s[[\![S_1]\!], \ldots, [\![S_n]\!]]$ where S_i are characterizing sets of A_i for $i = 0, \ldots, n$. Suppose that $e \odot S_0 \subseteq L_*$ for $e \in F_m$. Since S_0 is a characterizing set for A_0, we have $e \odot \mathcal{L}(G_*, A_0) \subseteq L_*$.

The fact $S_i \subseteq \mathcal{L}(G_*, A_i)$ for $i = 1, \ldots, n$ implies $s[S_1, \ldots, S_n] \subseteq \mathcal{L}(G_*, A_0)$ and thus $e \odot s[S_1, \ldots, S_n] \subseteq L_*$. Hence $\mathcal{G}(T, F)$ has the rule $[\![S_0]\!] \to s[[\![S_1]\!], \ldots, [\![S_n]\!]]$. $\qquad \square$

Corollary 16. *If T is adequate and F is fiducial on T, then $\mathcal{L}(\mathcal{G}(T, F)) = L_*$.*

Proof. By Lemmas 12 and 15. $\qquad \square$

Proposition 17. *Algorithm 1 for fixed p, q, r, k identifies $\mathbb{P}(p, q, r, k)$ in the limit from positive data and membership queries.*

Proof. We first show that the conjecture never converges to a wrong grammar. If the current conjecture $\hat{G} = \mathcal{G}(T, F)$ is such that $\mathcal{L}(G_*) \not\subseteq \mathcal{L}(\hat{G})$, at some point some $t \in \mathcal{L}(G_*) \setminus \mathcal{L}(\hat{G})$ will be given, which expands the conjecture. If $\mathcal{L}(\hat{G}) \not\subseteq \mathcal{L}(G_*)$, Lemma 13 implies that F is not fiducial on T and $\hat{G}$ has an incorrect rule $[\![S_0]\!] \to s[[\![S_1]\!], \ldots, [\![S_n]\!]]$. Lemma 11 implies that there is $e \in \mathrm{Env}^{m,p}(L_*)$ such that $e \odot S_0 \subseteq L_*$ and $e \odot s[S_1, \ldots, S_n] \not\subseteq L_*$, which rejects the rule. The conjecture cannot be changed infinitely many times. At some point T will be adequate by Lemma 14, which fixes the nonterminal set of $\hat{G}$. Once T is fixed, expansion of F causes deletion of rules, which can happen at most finitely many times. Therefore, the conjecture converges to a grammar representing the target. $\qquad \square$

All in all, Algorithm 1 learns $\mathbb{P}(p, q, r, k)$ efficiently for small p, q, r, k.

3.3 Dual property

The dual properties of the (k, p)-KP and (p, r, k)-FEP are given as follows.

Definition 18. We say that an IO-CFTG G has *the (k, p)-environment property* $((k, p)$-EP$)$ if every nonterminal A of rank m admits a set $E_A \subseteq \mathbb{E}^{m,p}$ s.t. $|E_A| \le k$ and $E_A^{\oplus} = \mathcal{L}(G, A)^{\triangleright}$. We call such a set E_A a *characterizing (environment) set* of A.

A language L_* has *the (p, r, k)-fiducial stub property* $((p, r, k)$-FSP$)$ if for any $E \subseteq \mathbb{E}^{m,p}$ with $m \le r$ and $|E| \le k$, we have $(E^{(\mathbb{S}^{m,p})})^{\triangleright} = E^{\oplus}$.

The grammar of Example 8 satisfies the 1-EP, whereas 1-KP does not hold. The environment sets $\{b(y)\}$, $\{y(c(a, a))\}$ and $\{y\}$ characterize A, C and I, respectively. Hence, one might think the dual approach is somewhat better. However, while every tree language satisfies the $(p, r, 1)$-FEP, it is not the case for $(p, r, 1)$-FSP. For the language $\{a(c(d,d)), b(c(d,e)), b(c(e,d))\}$, one sees that $b(y(e)) \in \{a(y(d))\}^{\mathbb{S}^{1,1}\triangleright} \setminus \{a(y(d))\}^{\oslash}$.

We target the following class of tree languages by a dual approach.

$$\mathbb{D}(p,q,r,k) = \{\, G \in \mathbb{G}(p,q,r) \text{ with the}$$
$$(p,k)\text{-EP and } (p,r,k)\text{-FSP}\,\}\,.$$

3.4 Dual learner

Algorithm 2 is our learner for $\mathbb{D}(p,q,r,k)$, which is quite symmetric to Algorithm 1. It computes its conjecture $\mathcal{G}(H,F,T)$ from $H \subseteq D$, $F = \bigcup_{0 \leq m \leq r} F_m$, and $T = \bigcup_{0 \leq m \leq r} T_m$ with $F_m \subseteq \mathrm{Env}^{m,p}(D)$ and $T_m = \mathrm{Sub}^{m,p}(D)$ for a finite tree set $D \subseteq L_*$. The nonterminal set is $N^F = \bigcup_{0 \leq m \leq r} N_m^F$ where $N_m^F = \{\, [\![E]\!] \mid E \subseteq F_m \wedge |E| \leq k \,\}$ and the initial symbol set is the singleton $I = \{[\![\{y\}]\!]\}$. We have a rule of the form

$$[\![E_0]\!] \to s[\![E_1]\!], \ldots, [\![E_n]\!]]$$

iff for some $m_0, \ldots, m_n \leq r$, $[\![E_i]\!] \in N_{m_i}^F$ for $i = 0, \ldots, n$, $s \in \mathbb{S}_{\Sigma \cup \{y_1, \ldots, y_n\}}^{m_0, p}$ in which each of $y_1, \ldots, y_n$ occurs just once with $n \leq q$,

1. there are $s_i \in \mathbb{S}_\Sigma^{m_i, 1}$ for $i = 1, \ldots, n$ such that $s[s_1, \ldots, s_n] \in \mathrm{Sub}^{m_0, p}(H)$,

2. $E_0 \odot s[E_1^{(T_{m_1})}, \ldots, E_n^{(T_{m_n})}] \subseteq L_*$.

Algorithm 2 $\mathcal{B}(p,q,r,k)$

Data: trees $t_1, t_2, \cdots \in L_*$
Result: IO-CFTGs $G_1, G_2, \ldots$
let $D := H := F := T := \varnothing$; $\hat{G} := \mathcal{G}(H,F,T)$;
for $n = 1, 2, \ldots$ **do**
    let $D := D \cup \{t_n\}$; $T := \bigcup_{0 \leq m \leq r} \mathrm{Sub}^m(D)$;
    if $D \nsubseteq \mathcal{L}(\hat{G})$ **then**
        let $H := D$ and $F := \bigcup_{0 \leq m \leq r} \mathrm{Env}^{m,p}(D)$;
    end if
    output $\hat{G} = \mathcal{G}(H,F,T)$ as G_n;
end for

The following lemmas, corollary and proposition are exactly in parallel with those in the primal approach, namely, Lemmas 10 to 15, Corollary 16 and Proposition 17.

Lemma 19. *One can construct $\mathcal{G}(H,F,T)$ in polynomial time in $\|D\|$ with the aid of a membership oracle.*

A rule of the form $[\![E_0]\!] \to s[\![E_1]\!], \ldots, [\![E_n]\!]]$ is said to be *incorrect* if $E_0 \odot s[E_1^\triangleleft, \ldots, E_n^\triangleleft] \nsubseteq L_*$. We say that $T \subseteq \mathbb{S}^{*,*}$ is *fiducial* on $\langle H, F \rangle$ (with respect to L_*) if $\mathcal{G}(H,F,T)$ has no incorrect rules. Clearly, if T is fiducial on $\langle H, F \rangle$ then so is every superset of T.

Lemma 20. *Every $\langle H, F \rangle$ admits a fiducial set $T \subseteq \mathbb{E}^{*,p}$ such that*

- *the cardinality $|T|$ is polynomially bounded by the description size of $\langle H, F \rangle$,*

- *for each $s \in T_m$ there is $e \in \mathbb{E}^{m,p}$ such that $e \odot s \in L_*$.*

Lemma 21. *Suppose that T is fiducial on $\langle H, F \rangle$. For every $[\![E]\!] \in F_m^T$ we have*

$$E \odot \mathcal{L}(\mathcal{G}(H,F,T), [\![E]\!]) \subseteq L_* \,.$$

Lemma 22. *If T fiducial on $\langle H, F \rangle$, then $\mathcal{L}(\mathcal{G}(H,F,T)) \subseteq L_*$.*

Suppose that $G_* \in \mathbb{D}(p,q,r,k)$ generates L_*, We say that a pair of $F \subseteq \mathrm{Env}^{*,*}(L_*)$ and $H \subseteq L_*$ is *adequate* if F_m includes a characterizing environment set E_A for every nonterminal $A \in N_m$ of G_* and for every rule $A \to s[A_1, \ldots, A_n]$ of G_*, there are $e \in \mathbb{E}^{n,1}$ and $s \in \mathbb{S}_{\Sigma \cup \{y_1, \ldots, y_n\}}^{m_0, p}$ such that $e \odot s \in H$ and each of $y_1, \ldots, y_n$ occurs just once in s with $n \leq q$. Clearly if $\langle H, F \rangle$ is adequate, every pair $\langle H', F' \rangle$ with $H' \supseteq H$ and $F' \supseteq F$ is adequate.

Lemma 23. *There is a finite set $D \subseteq L_*$ such that $\langle D, \bigcup_{0 \leq m \leq r} \mathrm{Env}^{m,p}(D) \rangle$ is adequate and $|D|$ is polynomially bounded by the description size of G_*.*

Lemma 24. *If $\langle H, F \rangle$ is adequate, $\mathcal{L}(G_*) \subseteq \mathcal{L}(\mathcal{G}(H,F,T))$ for any T.*

Corollary 25. *If $\langle H, F \rangle$ is adequate and T is fiducial on $\langle H, F \rangle$, then $\mathcal{L}(\mathcal{G}(H,F,T)) = L_*$.*

Proposition 26. *Algorithm 2 for fixed p, q, r, k identifies $\mathbb{D}(p,q,r,k)$ in the limit from positive data and membership queries.*

All in all, Algorithm 2 learns $\mathbb{D}(p,q,r,k)$ efficiently.

4 Discussion

Motivated for investigating the learning of meanings with words, we in this paper have discussed how distributional learning techniques can be applicable to IO-CFTGs. Copying operations seem very important for generating natural meaning representations in spite of technical difficulties in learning non-linear structures. The approaches presented in this paper are rather naive applications of existing techniques with additional conditions, the fiducial environment property and fiducial stub property, which are convenient assumptions for making our learners run in polynomial-time. It is not clear whether the introduced conditions are too much restrictive for meaning representations. The author hopes this paper to become a basis for other distributional properties more reasonable for expressivity and learnability.

Generalizing the learning of IO-CFTGs to *almost linear* ACGs must be very important future work. A simply typed lambda term is said to be almost linear if it has no vacuous λ-abstraction and only variables assigned atomic types may occur more than once. It is shown that almost linear lambda terms inherit nice properties of linear lambda terms (Kanazawa, 2007; Kanazawa, 2011). Targeting almost linear ACGs seems quite promising.

Clark (Clark, 2011) has proposed an algorithm that learns an interesting subclass of synchronous CFGs from positive data only, where languages in the class satisfy functionality. Though the relation between words and meanings in natural languages are not a function, the relation is very sparse. Therefore combination of Clark's and our approaches is an interesting direction of further research for a basic model of natural language acquisition taking syntax-semantics interface into account.

References

Catriel Beeri and Raghu Ramakrishnan. 1991. On the power of magic. *Journal of Logic Programming*, 10(3&4):255–299.

Alexander Clark and Rémi Eyraud. 2007. Polynomial identification in the limit of substitutable context-free languages. *Journal of Machine Learning Research*, 8:1725–1745.

Alexander Clark and Ryo Yoshinaka. 2012. Beyond semilinearity: Distributional learning of parallel multiple context-free grammars. In Jeffrey Heinz, Colin de la Higuera, and Tim Oates, editors, *Proceedings of the Eleventh International Conference on Grammatical Inference*, volume 21 of *JMLR Workshop and Conference Proceedings*, pages 84–96.

Alexander Clark, Rémi Eyraud, and Amaury Habrard. 2009. A note on contextual binary feature grammars. In *EACL 2009 workshop on Computational Linguistic Aspects of Grammatical Inference*, pages 33–40.

Alexander Clark. 2010. Learning context free grammars with the syntactic concept lattice. In José M. Sempere and Pedro García, editors, *ICGI*, volume 6339 of *Lecture Notes in Computer Science*, pages 38–51. Springer.

Alexander Clark. 2011. Inference of inversion transduction grammars. In Lise Getoor and Tobias Scheffer, editors, *ICML*, pages 201–208. Omnipress.

Philippe de Groote and Sylvain Pogodalla. 2004. On the expressive power of abstract categorial grammars: Representing context-free formalisms. *Journal of Logic, Language and Information*, 13(4):421–438.

Joost Engelfriet and Erik Meineche Schmidt. 1977. IO and OI. I. *J. Comput. Syst. Sci.*, 15(3):328–353.

Makoto Kanazawa. 2007. Parsing and generation as datalog queries. In John A. Carroll, Antal van den Bosch, and Annie Zaenen, editors, *ACL*. The Association for Computational Linguistics.

Makoto Kanazawa. 2011. Parsing and generation as datalog query evaluation.

Anna Kasprzik and Ryo Yoshinaka. 2011. Distributional learning of simple context-free tree grammars. In Jyrki Kivinen, Csaba Szepesvári, Esko Ukkonen, and Thomas Zeugmann, editors, *Algorithmic Learning Theory*, volume 6925 of *Lecture Notes in Computer Science*, pages 398–412. Springer.

William C. Rounds. 1970. Mappings and grammars on trees. *Mathematical Systems Theory*, 4(3):257–287.

Ryo Yoshinaka and Makoto Kanazawa. 2011. Distributional learning of abstract categorial grammars. In Sylvain Pogodalla and Jean-Philippe Prost, editors, *LACL*, volume 6736 of *Lecture Notes in Computer Science*, pages 251–266. Springer.

Ryo Yoshinaka. 2011a. Efficient learning of multiple context-free languages with multidimensional substitutability from positive data. *Theoretical Computer Science*, 412(19):1821–1831.

Ryo Yoshinaka. 2011b. Towards dual approaches for learning context-free grammars based on syntactic concept lattices. In Giancarlo Mauri and Alberto Leporati, editors, *Developments in Language Theory*, volume 6795 of *Lecture Notes in Computer Science*, pages 429–440. Springer.

Delayed Tree Locality and the Status of Derivation Structures

Joan Chen-Main
Institute for Research in Cognitive Science
University of Pennsylvania
Philadelphia, PA 19104, USA
chenmain@seas.upenn.edu

Abstract

While the derived trees yielded by TAG derivations are uncontroversially taken to correspond to phrase structure, the status of TAG derivation structures as more than a record of TAG operations is less certain. An attractive possibility is to interpret the derivation structure as some representation of semantic meaning, such as a dependency analysis. However, the literature has identified cases where doing so is problematic (Rambow et al., 1995, Candito and Kahane, 1998, Frank and van Genabith, 2001, Gardent and Kallmeyer, 2003, Kallmeyer and Romero 2008), including what has been referred to as the Missing Link Problem: predicates which should have a dependency link are unconnected in the derivation structure. This paper shows that delayed tree-local MC-TAG (Chiang and Scheffler, 2008) provides a solution for certain types of missing links. Further, we observe that the regular form 2-level TAG solutions to the Missing Link Problem given in (Dras et al., 2004) can be reinterpreted using delayed tree-local MC-TAG: the object level derivations of the 2-level TAG derivations can be converted into legal 1-delayed tree-local MCTAG derivations. Thus, delayed tree-locality maintains the possibility that TAG derivation structures can be more meaning-laden than solely a record of the combination of trees.

1 Introduction

In the mainstream generative approaches to grammatical structure, there is typically no distinction between a derivation of a sentence and its phrase structure. For example, in Chomsky's (1995) Minimalist Program (formalized by Stabler (1997) and its precusors, the history of a valid derivation is taken to be the phrase structure of a grammatical construction: composition determines constituency. In contrast, a derivation in a tree-rewriting formalism, such as TAG, allows for an additional level of representation. As a mathematical object, each TAG derivation yields a string, a derived tree, and a derivation structure. When TAG is used for linguistic analysis, the string and derived tree uncontroversially correspond to the grammatical sentence and its phrase structure, respectively, but the status of the derivation structure as more than a record of TAG operations is less certain.

An attractive possibility is to interpret the derivation structure as some representation of semantic meaning, such as a dependency analysis (e.g. Rambow and Joshi, 1997), and, indeed, there is body of work that explores the degree to which it is possible to equate the TAG derivation tree with a dependency analysis. This line of inquiry has identified cases where doing so is problematic (Rambow et al., 1995, Candito and Kahane, 1998, Frank and van Genabith, 2001, Gardent and Kallmeyer, 2003, Kallmeyer and Romero 2008), including what has been referred to as the Missing Link Problem. This particular mismatch stems from the way extraction is handled in TAG-style analyses when part of a lower clause ends up in the higher clause. In such cases, clausal complementation is carried out using adjoining. The resulting "stretching apart" of substructure in the tree for the lower clause eliminates the need for traces, and is a hallmark of TAG accounts of phenomena such as raising and successive-cyclic *wh*-movement in English.

Proceedings of the 11th International Workshop on Tree Adjoining Grammars and Related Formalisms (TAG+11), pages 99–107,
Paris, September 2012.

The problem arises when more than one instance of this kind of adjoining occurs in the same tree.

The proposed solutions to the Missing Link Problem can be divided into two kinds of approaches. The Missing Link Problem naturally led to the question of how to address the computation of TAG semantics in general, and the first kind of response can be roughly characterized as modification of the object on which semantics is computed, for example, by "enriching" the derivation structure with additional links (Kallmeyer, 2002), computing meaning based on the derived phrase structure tree instead of the derivation tree (Gardent and Kallmeyer, 2003, Frank and van Genabith, 2001), and encoding meaning in both the derivation and derived tree (Kallmeyer and Romero, 2008). The development of TAG semantics is a significant and related contribution, but for the purposes of this paper, it is important to note that the status of the derivation tree is not the primary concern of this area of research.

A second type of solution to the Missing Link Problem can roughly be characterized as modifications to the grammar such that the derivation structures better align with the desired dependency analyses. These include proposals that are more powerful that TAGs, such as set-local MCTAGs (Weir, 1988) and D-tree Substitution Grammar (Rambow et al., 1995), as well as some that are weakly TAG-equivalent., such as regular form 2-level TAG (Dras et al., 2004). These proposals do not include a full semantics for TAG, but they preserve the intuition that the derivation structure is a meaning-carrying level of representation. The derivation structure need not be the object over which semantics is computed to be useful. Note, for example, that the Prague Dependency Treebank (PDT 2.0) is annotated with multiple layers, with the analytical layer encoding what are deemed "dependency relations" and the tectogrammatical layer encoding what is taken to be the "underlying deep structure" of the sentence (Hajič et al, 2006). It is also worth noting that when the derivations of TAGs and TAG variants are converted into the form of dependency structures (in the style of Kulhmann, 2007, Bodirsky et al., 2005), their formal properties as a class inform us with respect to coverage of dependency treebanks (Chen-Main and Joshi, 2012).

The observations reported here fall under the second kind of response. The big picture goal is to understand the role of the derivation structure. With the intuition that the derivation structure's role reaches beyond a record of operations as a backdrop, this paper begins to pursue the kind of answers afforded us by the recently introduced delayed tree-local MC-TAG formalism (Chiang and Scheffler, 2008). Delayed tree-local MCTAG is weakly-equivalent to standard TAG,[1] but it permits linguistic dependencies to be retained that are not necessarily retained in alternative TAG variants. This has already proven useful in linguistic analyses of anaphor binding (Chiang and Scheffler, 2008), non-local right node raising (Han et al., 2010), binding variables (Storoshenko and Han, 2010), and clitic climbing (Chen-Main et al. 2012). Here, we explore how the formalism deals with constructions whose standard TAG (or MCTAG) derivations result in missing links. We also observes that the solutions to the Missing Link Problem given in (Dras et al., 2004) can be reinterpreted as 1-delayed tree-local MCTAG derivations. We see that the increased flexibility of delayed tree-locality is advantageous not only for syntactic analyses, but also for maintaining the possibility that TAG derivation structures can be more meaning-laden than solely a record of the combination of trees.

This paper is structured as follows. Section 2 reviews two situations in which The Missing Link Problem arises. Section 3 first reviews delayed tree-local MCTAG before turning to a solution to one of the types of the Missing Link Problem. Section 4 addresses the second type of the Missing Link Problem. Following a brief review the regular form 2-level TAG solution to given in (Dras et al., 2004), we see how the solution can be recast as a delayed tree-local MCTAG derivation. Section 5 includes further discussion, raising some open questions, and concludes the paper.

2 The Missing Link Problem Revisited

Consider the construction in (1) (from Dras et al., 2004), in which raising and cyclic *wh*-movement co-occur.

---

[1] Delayed tree-local MCTAG is related to tree-local MCTAG with flexible composition (Joshi et al., 2003). Chiang and Scheffler (2008) show their weak equivalence by showing how any derivations in MCTAG with flexible composition can be converted into a 2-delayed tree-local MCTAG derivation. However, delayed tree-local MCTAG is not a formalization of MCTAG with flexible composition.

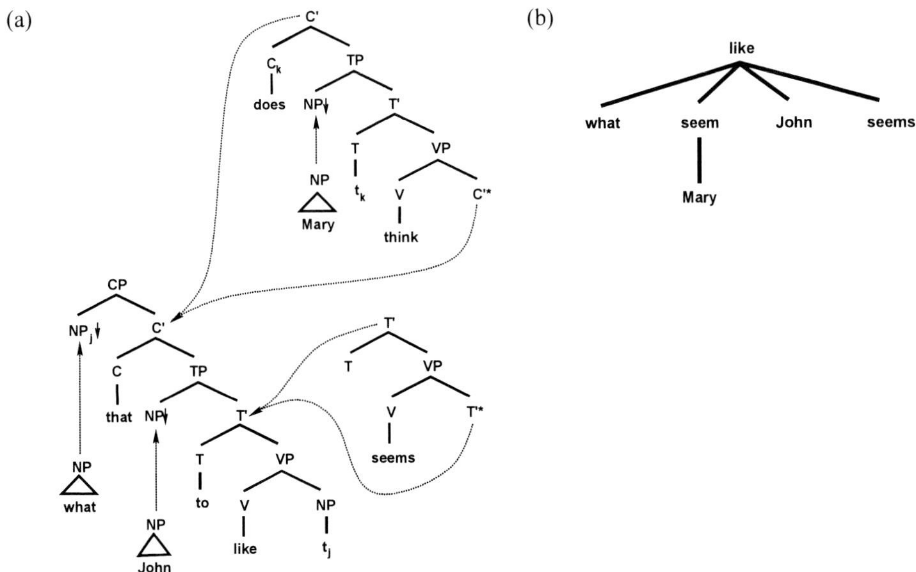

Figure 1. a) TAG derivation for *What does Mary think that John seems to like?*
b) Derivation structure for (a)

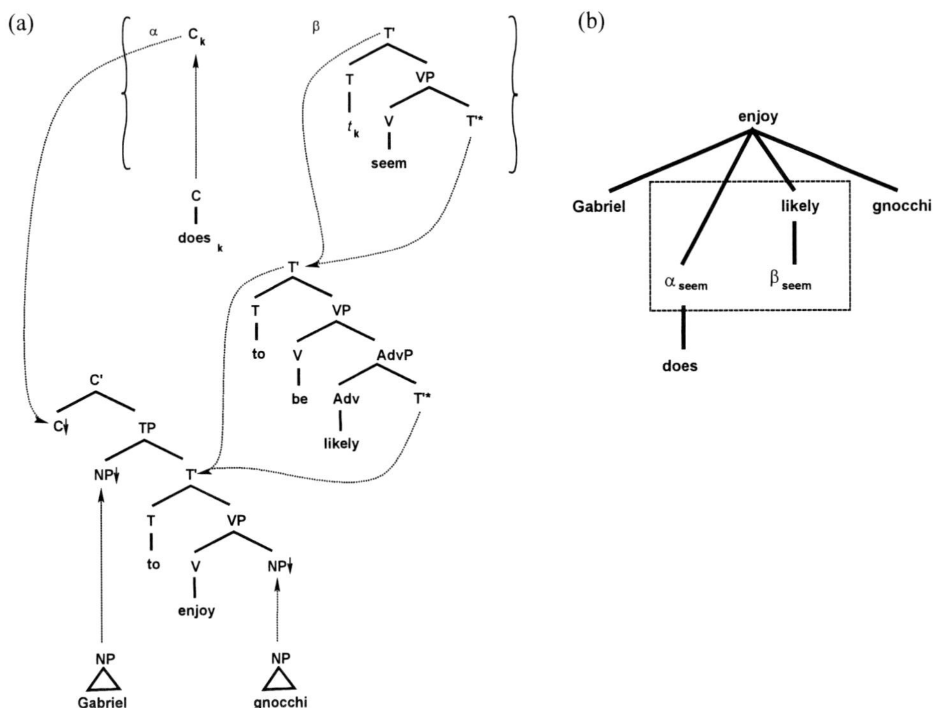

Figure 2. a) Derivation for *Does Gabriel seem to be likely to enjoy gnocchi?*: Legal in 1-delayed tree-local MCTAG, illegal in tree-local and set-local MCTAG
(b) Derivation structure for (a) with delay marked with a dashed box

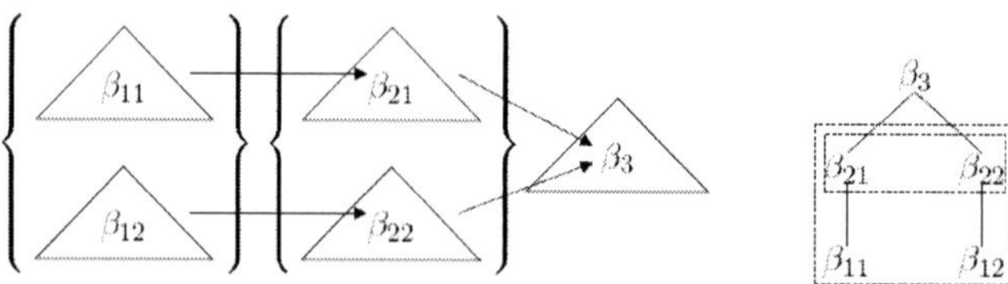

Figure 3: A 2-delayed tree-local MCTAG derivation. Delays are marked with dashed boxes.
(Figure taken from Chiang and Scheffler (2008).)

(1) What does Mary think that John seems to like?

The derivation for (1), shown in Figure 1a, combines the standard TAG treatment of both these phenomena: Both the *seems*-tree for the raising construction and the *thinks*-tree for the bridge construction adjoin into the *like*-tree. The resulting two-fold problem can be seen in the corresponding derivation structure shown in Figure 1b: 1) the bridge verb *think* and the most embedded verb *like,* which have no semantic dependency, are connected with an edge while 2) the bridge verb *think* and the raising verb *seems,* which should have a semantic dependency, are unconnected.

This case is an example of the more general problem that can arise when several trees are adjoined into distinct nodes of the same tree. Thus, we also see the Missing Link Problem arise when other long distance dependencies co-occur with raising, e.g. Rambow et al.'s (1995) example, given in (2), in which topicalization out of an embedded clause interacts with raising.

(2) Small spicy hotdogs, he claims Mary seems to adore.

Dras et al. (2004) discuss a similar case involving subject-auxiliary inversion in conjunction with raising. A yes-no question like (3) is typically handled used multi-component TAG, with the structure for *does* and structure of *seem* as members of the same elementary tree set. The difficulty arises when another level of embedding is added, as in (4).

(3) Does Gabriel seem to enjoy gnocchi?
(4) Does Gabriel seem to be likely to enjoy gnocchi?

A dependency ought to link *seem* to *to be likely,* with another link between *to be likely* and *enjoy.*

To derive (4) with the desired dependencies, the tree set containing *does* and *seem* must combine with *to be likely* before combing into the *enjoy*-tree. This derivation is shown in Figure 2. However, this derivation is neither tree-local nor set-local. (The *to be likely* tree cannot adjoin into the *seem* tree without adjoining into a foot node, and would also not yield the desired dependencies.) An alternative would be to permit multiple adjoining (Schabes and Shieber, 1994), but with predicative trees. A derivation structure for such a derivation, however, would link both *seem* and *to be likely* directly to *enjoy,* without the desired link between *seem* and *to be likely.*

3 Delayed Tree-Local MCTAG and Desired Links

3.1 *k*-Delayed Tree-Local MCTAG

The delayed tree-local variant of MCTAG specifies a way to relax the restriction that all components of a multi-component set must combine into the same tree during the same derivational step. Each use of a multicomponent set introduces a *delay* into the derivation. A delay is the union of the paths in the derivation structure from each component of an MC-set S to the lowest node that dominates all members of S. A k-delayed tree-local MCTAG permits each node in the derivation structure to be a member of at most k delays. Figure 3 replicates the example of a 2-delayed tree-local derivation given in Chiang and Scheffler (2008). The dashed boxes mark the delays. Thus, a valid k-delayed tree local MCTAG derivation permits members of the same MC set to compose into different trees, so long as all members of the MC set eventually compose into the same tree without requiring any node to belong to more than k delays.

3.2 A Solution for Raising and Subj-Aux Inversion

In contrast to the traditional tree-local and set-local variants of MCTAG, 1 delayed tree-local MCTAG does permit the derivation given in Figure 2 for our problematic raising and subj-aux inversion example. The derivation structure is given in Figure 2b, with the delay indicated by a dashed box. The two components of the *seem* tree set eventually both combine into the *enjoy* tree. However, the β component first adjoins into the *to be likely* tree and the combined phrase structure adjoins into the *enjoy* tree, while the α component (into which *does* substitutes) combines directly into the *enjoy* tree. This yields a link *seem* between *to be likely* and a link between *to be likely* and *enjoy*.[2]

This example illustrates how delayed tree-locality provides a straightforward solution in cases where two predicative trees are ultimately contiguous in the derived tree, but tree-locality and set-locality do not permit a derivation. The added flexibility of delayed tree-locality allows for a derivation in which the two predicative trees are combined, yielding the desired link in the derivation structure.

4 Borrowing from Regular Form Two-level TAG

We turn now to how to deal with the more typical cases of the Missing Link Problem, where several trees are adjoined into distinct nodes of the same tree. To allow the predicative trees to combine in the desired order, we will need to modify the shapes of the tree. The strategy is to conform the derivational shape of this case to the derivational shape of the case above where the two predicative trees are ultimately contiguous in the derived tree. We appeal to the solution given in Dras et al. (2004) and show how it can be recast as a 1-delayed tree-local MCTAG derivation.

4.1 Regular Form Two-level TAG Solution for Raising and Wh-movement

Dras et al. (2004) propose a regular form 2-level TAG, with a meta-level grammar that generates possible derivation structures and an object level grammar that yields derived phrase structures. Consider the object level derivation given in Figure 5 for example (1). At the object level, the derivation looks similar to a standard TAG derivation in that the combinatory operations combine pieces of phrase structure. The derivation structure for the object level (shown in Figure 5b), however, is the end product of a derivation at the meta-level. At the meta-level, the trees are pieces of object-level derivations. Figure 4a shows how the meta-level grammar generates the object-level derivation structure in Figure 5b. Figure 4b shows the history of this meta-level derivation. It is the derivation structure at this level which Dras et al. (2004) take to encode dependencies. Their goal is to match the meta-level derivation structure with a reasonable dependency analysis.

A key aspect to their analysis is that the tree anchored by a verb can be split into two parts. Consider the $\mathcal{A}[like]$ meta-level tree in Figure 4a. The $\alpha_S[like]$ node and $\beta_{S/VP}[like]$ node correspond to separate pieces of structure at the object level. As can be seem in Figure 5a, the $\alpha_S[like]$ tree contains the verb itself while the $\beta_{S/VP}[like]$ tree contains the position for the subject. It is in the meta-grammar that the two parts are elementary tree local. As the authors themselves note, this is strikingly similar to a multi-component TAG approach, but their proposed derivation would not be tree-local in the original sense.

Note also that Dras et al. (2004) modifies the shapes of the trees by using a feature unification TAG where all non-terminals have the label X, but have top and bottom features that must be identical at the end of the derivation. A non-terminal node's part-of-speech or phrasal category is no longer its label, but rather, one of its features. However, in the figures that follow, the part-of-speech or phrasal category feature is graphically represented as a node label. It is crucial to adopt the modified shape of the trees to allow the predicative trees to combine as desired. The material that previously intervened between the *think* tree and the *seem* tree, forcing the two trees to be adjoined into different nodes in the *like* tree in Figure 1, is moved in two ways: 1) "that" is moved into a different tree, the *seems* tree, and 2) the position for the subject of *like* is extracted from the *like* tree as a separate piece of structure. Now, *think* may adjoin into *seems*, which later adjoins into *like*. The subject position

---

[2] When using multi-component sets, the question arises as to how to interpret multiple links from the same set. I assume that the link between the component containing the lexical anchor of the set and its target is the primary link for the set. Something more may need to be said about links to the other components, but my chief concern here is to ensure that the previously missing links are now present.

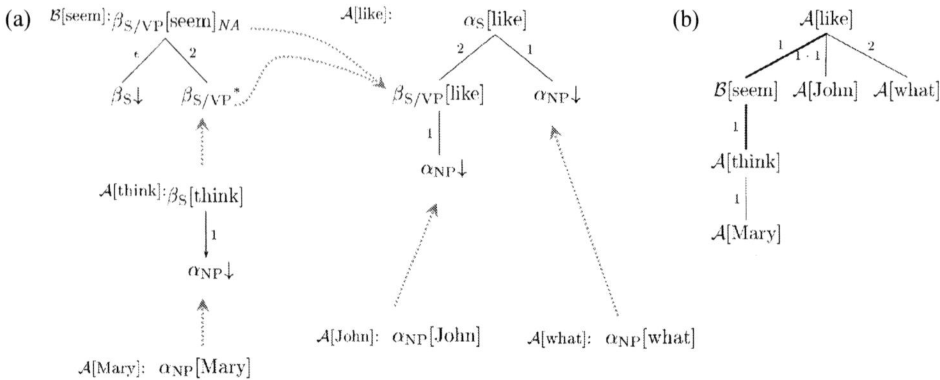

Figure 4: a) 2LTAG meta-level derivation for *What does Mary think that John seems to like?*
b) derivation structure for (a)
(Adapted from Dras et al. (2004))

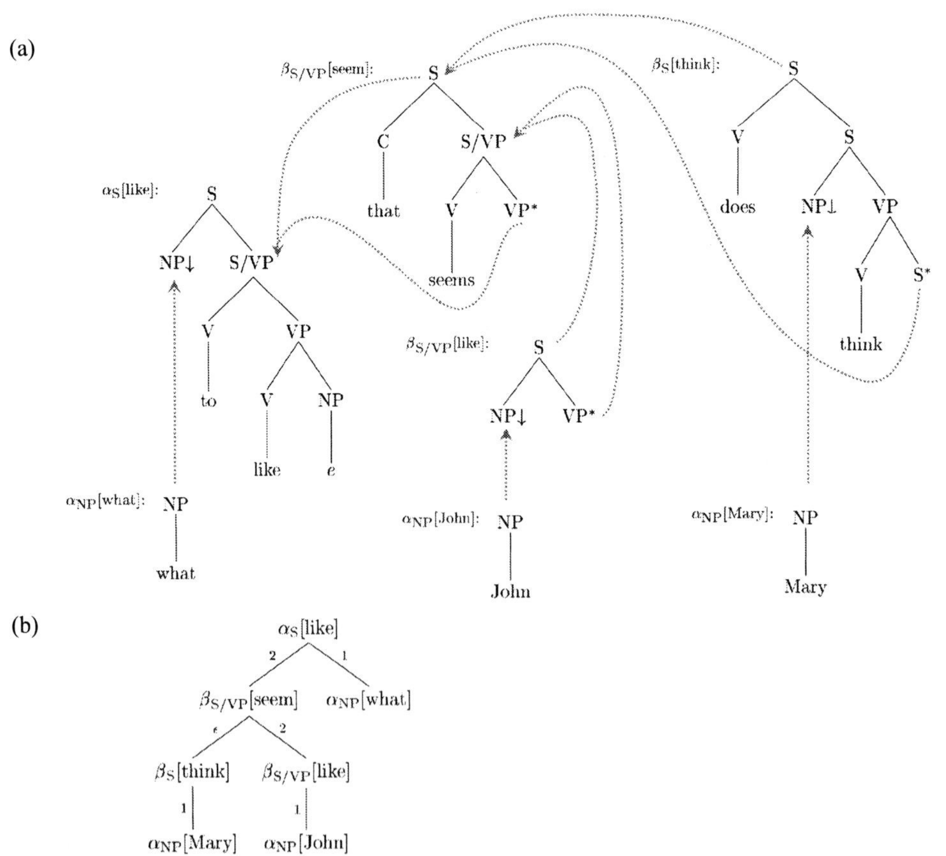

Figure 5: a) 2LTAG object-level derivation for *What does Mary think that John seems to like?*
b) derivation structure for (a)
(Adapted from Dras et al. (2004))

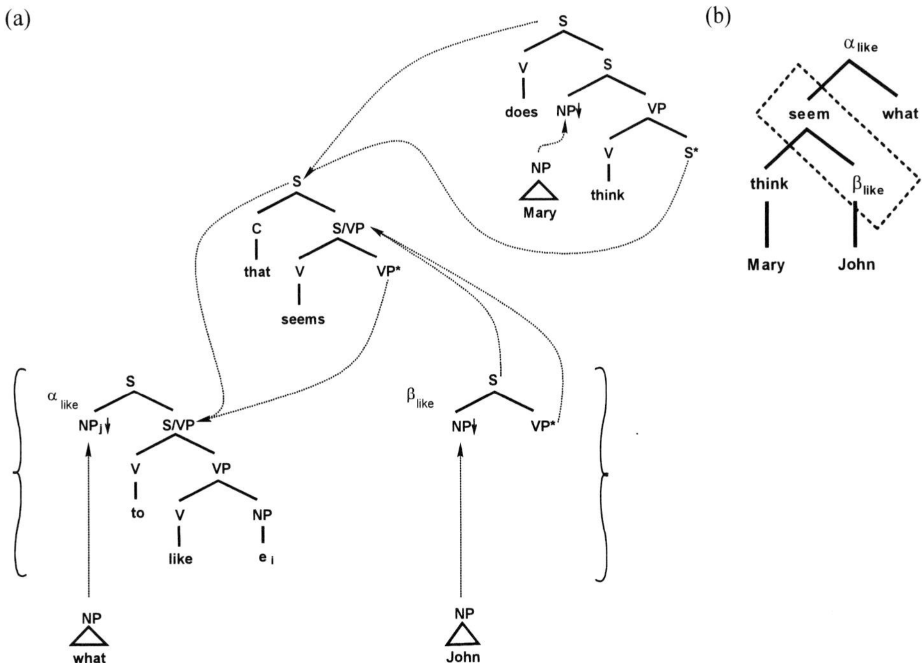

Figure 6. (a) 1-delayed tree-local MC-TAG Derivation for *What does Mary think that John seems to like?* (b) Derivation structure for (a) with delay marked with a dashed box

of *like* adjoins into *seems*, achieving the correct word order.

4.2 Translating into Delayed Tree-local MCTAG

It is straightforward to convert Dras et al.'s object level derivation into an MC-TAG derivation that abides by 1-delayed tree-locality. Instead of treating the tree for *like* and the tree for its subject as part of the same object at the meta-level, the delayed tree-local approach treats the elementary object for *like* as a 2-component set. Figure 6 is almost identical to Figure 5. The only differences are the braces denoting the 2-component set and the dashed box indicating the delay. [3] Note that delayed tree-locality as formalized in (Chiang and Scheffler, 2008) does permit a component to be combine into another component from the same MC-set. This means that the derivational steps that were prohibited under tree-locality and set-locality, i.e. the β component of the *like* set adjoins into the *seems* tree, which in turn adjoins into the α component

of the *like* set, are now legal. As in the regular form 2-level TAG solution, the desired link between *think* and *seems* is no longer missing and the undesired link between *think* and *like* is no longer present

We have already presented a solution for constructions involving both raising and subject-Aux inversion, but we note that the alternative regular form 2-level TAG solution given in Dras et al. (2004) can also be converted into a 1-delayed tree-local derivation.

5 Conclusion and Discussion

The observation that delayed tree-locality can provide a solution for at least two types of missing links bears on questions specific to the formalism as well as more general issues. With respect to *k*-delayed tree-local MCTAG, we can frame this work as complementing work exploiting the formalism for linguistic analysis. Whereas the analyses in Chiang and Scheffler (2008), Han et al., (2010), Storoshenko and Han (2010), and Chen-Main et al. (2012) can tell us something about the coverage of *k*-delayed tree-local MCTAG (for a specific *k*) at the phrase

---

[3] See footnote 2 for comments on interpreting links from the same MC-set.

structure level, this paper demonstrates the kind of "coverage" that the formalism provides at the derivation structure level.

We also see how one of the derivational sequences that is, thus far, unique to delayed tree-local MCTAGs can be utilized. As shown in Figure 6, one component of an MC set ultimately combines into another component belonging to the same set. This allows what other TAG variants previously treated as contiguous pieces of structure to be treated instead as a multicomponent set.

Additionally, the observation that the regular form 2-level TAG derivations given by Dras et al. (2004) can be straightforwardly viewed as legal 1-delayed tree-local MCTAG derivations adds a linguistic dimension to Chiang and Scheffler's (2008) assertion that it is possible to give a formulation of TAG with flexible composition as a special case of regular-form 2-level TAG. As suggested by a reviewer, a sensible future avenue would be to see if other analyses that use multiple levels (or dimensions) can be restated in delayed tree-local MCTAG, particularly for phenomena that have been challenging for standard TAG (e.g. Rogers' (2004) analysis of scrambling).

Turning to broader issues, this paper revisits the question of what linguistic information, if any, is encoded in a derivation structure. It also raises the related question of what exactly a dependency analysis is and what linguistic information it carries. Chen-Main and Joshi (2012) show how TAG derivation structures (interpreted in the form of dependency structures) can be the basis for measuring complexity and a means for assessing coverage of large scale corpora, but they steer away from claims about the meaning that might be encoded. As noted in the introduction, work on TAG semantics appears to have reached a consensus that the derivation structure is not the appropriate representation for computing semantics. The introduction of delayed tree-local MCTAG, however, renews the viability of interpreting the derivation tree as a dependency analysis. The degree to which this is possible can lead to two additional research avenues. One is that we retain the current non-derivation structure based approach to TAG semantics and wrestle with distinguishing between a dependency analysis and semantic analysis. The other is to reevaluate the coverage that is possible when TAG semantics uses a delayed tree-local MCTAG derivation structure as the object on which

semantics is computed. Either avenue should lead to a greater understanding of the role of the derivation structure.

Acknowledgments

The author would like to thank Aravind K. Joshi and the TAG+ reviewers for their comments, despite not yet having found the time to properly address them.

References

Manuel Bodirsky, Marco Kuhlmann, and Mathias Möhl. 2005. Well-nested drawings as models of syntactic structure. In *10th Conference of Formal Grammar and 9th Meeting on Mathematics of Language*, Edinburgh, UK.

Marie-Hélène Candito and Sylvain Kahane. 1998. Can the TAG derivation tree represent a semantic graph? An answer in the light of Meaning-Text Theory. In *Proceedings of TAG+4,* Philadelphia, USA.

Joan Chen-Main, Tonia Bleam, and Aravind K. Joshi. 2012. Delayed Tree-Locality, Set-locality, and Clitic Climbing. In *Proceedings of TAG+11*, Paris, France.

Joan Chen-Main and Aravind.K. Joshi. 2012. A Dependency Perspective on the Adequacy of Tree Local Multi-component Tree Adjoining Grammar. *Journal of Logic and Computation.* doi:10.1093/logcom/exs012

David Chiang and Tatjana Scheffler. 2008. Flexible Composition and Delayed Tree-Locality. In *Proceedings of TAG+9*, Tübingen, Germany.

Noam Chomsky. 1995. *The Minimalist Program.* MIT Press, Boston, Massachusetts.

Mark Dras, David Chiang and William Schuler. 2004. On Relations of Constituency and Dependency Grammars. *Research on Language and Computation* 2(2), 281-305. Hermes Science Publishers, Paris, France.

Anette Frank and Josef van Genabith. 2001 GlueTag: Linear Logic based Semantics for LTAG - and what it teaches us about LFG and LTAG. In M. Butt and T. Holloway King, editors, *Proceedings of the LFG01 Conference,* Hong Kong. p 104-126.

Claire Gardent and Laura Kallmeyer. 2003. Semantic Construction in FTAG. In *Proceedings of EACL 2003,* Budapest, Hungary. 123-130.

Jan Hajič, Jarmila Panevová, Eva Hajičová, Jarmila Panevová, Petr Sgall, Petr Pajas, Jan ?těpánek, Jiří Havelka, and Marie Mikulová. 2006. *Prague Dependency Treebank 2.0* LDC2006T01, Linguistic Data Consortium, Philadelphia

Chung-Hye Han, David Potter, and Dennis Ryan Storoshenko. 2010. Non-local Right Node Raising: an Analysis Using Delayed Tree-Local MC-TAG. In *Proceedings of TAG+10*, New Haven, USA.

Aravind K. Joshi, Laura Kallmeyer, and Maribel Romero. 2003. Flexible composition in LTAG: quantifier scope and inverse linking. In H. Bunt and R. Muskens (eds.), *Computing Meaning 3*. Kluwer.

Laura Kallmeyer. 2002. Using an Enriched TAG Derivation Structure as Basis for Semantics In *Proceedings of TAG+6*, Universitá di Venezia.

Laura Kallmeyer and Maribel Romero. 2008. Scope and Situation Binding in LTAG using Semantic Unification. *Research on Language and Computation* 6(1), 3-52. Kluwer Academic Publishers, the Netherlands.

Marco Kuhlmann. 2007. Dependency Structures and Lexicalized Grammars. PhD thesis, Saarland University, Saarbrücken, Germany.

Owen Rambow and Aravind K. Joshi. 1997 A formal look at dependency grammars and phrase structure grammars, with special consideration of word-order phenomena. In L. Wanner, ed. *Recent Trends in Meaning-Text Theory*, 167-190. John Benjamins, Amsterdam and Philadelphia.

Owen Rambow, K, Vijay-Shanker, and David Weir. 1995. D-Tree grammars. In *Proceeding of the 33rd Annual Meeting of the Association for Computational Linguistics (ACL-95)*, Cambridge, USA. 151-158.

James Rogers. 2004. On scrambling, another perspective. In *Proceedings of TAG+7*, Vancouver, Canada.

Yves Schabes and Stuart Shieber. 1994. An alternative conception of tree-adjoining derivation. *Computational Linguistics*, 20(1), 91-121.

Edward P. Stabler. 1997. Derivational minimalism. In *Proceedings of Logical Aspects of Computational Linguistics*, 68-95.

Dennis Ryan Storoshenko and Chung-Hye Han. 2010. Binding Variables in English: An Analysis using Delayed Tree Locality. In *Proceedings of TAG+10*, New Haven, USA.

David Weir. 1988. *Characterizing mildly context-sensitive grammar formalisms*. PhD dissertation, University of Pennsylvania, Philadelphia, USA.

A Formal Model for Plausible Dependencies
in Lexicalized Tree Adjoining Grammar

Laura Kallmeyer
Heinrich-Heine-Universität Düsseldorf
Universitätsstr. 1
40225 Düsseldorf, Germany
`kallmeyer@phil.uni-duesseldorf.de`

Marco Kuhlmann
Uppsala University
Box 635
751 26 Uppsala, Sweden
`marco.kuhlmann@lingfil.uu.se`

Abstract

Several authors have pointed out that the correspondence between LTAG derivation trees and dependency structures is not as direct as it may seem at first glance, and various proposals have been made to overcome this divergence. In this paper we propose to view the correspondence between derivation trees and dependency structures as a tree transformation during which the direction of some of the original edges is reversed. We show that, under this transformation, LTAG is able to induce both ill-nested dependency trees and dependency trees with gap-degree greater than 1, which is not possible under the direct reading of derivation trees as dependency trees.

1 Introduction

In lexicalized tree adjoining grammar (LTAG), the operations of substitution and adjunction establish an asymmetric relation between two lexical items: The elementary tree for one item is substituted or adjoined into the elementary tree for another one. In many cases, this relation can be interpreted as a relation of syntactic dependency (complementation or adjunction), and it is natural then to try to interpret LTAG derivations as dependency trees. However, as several authors have pointed out, the correspondence between derivation trees and dependency structures is not as direct as it may seem at first glance (Rambow et al., 1995; Candito and Kahane, 1998; Frank and van Genabith, 2001). Examples of mismatches are in particular those where predicates adjoin into their arguments, an analysis that is chosen whenever an argument allows for long extractions. In these cases, the edge

in the derivation tree and the syntactic dependency have opposite directions.

Different strategies have been adopted to obtain linguistically plausible dependency structures using LTAG. Some proposals adopt variants of the formalism with different derivation operations (Rambow et al., 2001; Chen-Main and Joshi, 2012); others retrieve the missing dependencies from the derivation tree and the derived tree (Kallmeyer, 2002; Gardent and Kallmeyer, 2003). In this paper we follow the second line of work in that we take a two-step approach: To get a dependency tree, we first construct a derivation tree, and then obtain the dependencies in a postprocessing step. However, in contrast to previous work we retain the property that dependencies should form a tree structure: We do not regard the missing dependencies as additions to the derivation tree, but view the correspondence between derivation trees and dependency structures as a tree-to-tree mapping. The crucial feature of this mapping is that it can reverse some of the edges in the derivation tree. In particular it can 'correct' the directions of predicate–argument adjunctions.

The paper is structured as follows. We start by reviewing the divergence between derivation trees and dependency trees in Section 2. In Section 3 we present the basic ideas behind our transformation. A formalization of this transformation is given in Section 4. In Section 5 we examine the structural properties of the dependency trees that can be induced using our transformation. We propose in particular analyses for some examples of ill-nested dependencies and of dependencies of gap degree > 1. Under the direct interpretation, LTAG induces the class of well-nested dependency trees with gap-degree at most 1 (Bodirsky et

Proceedings of the 11th International Workshop on Tree Adjoining Grammars and Related Formalisms (TAG+11), pages 108–116,
Paris, September 2012.

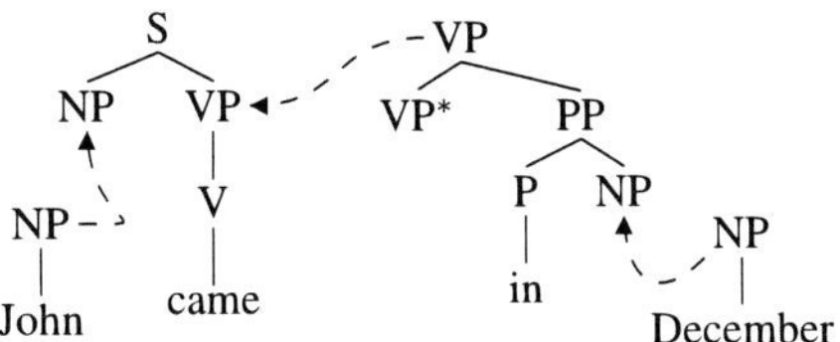

derived tree:

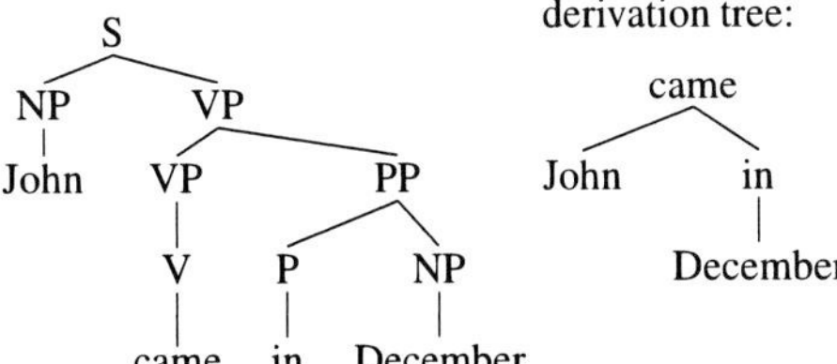

derivation tree:

Figure 1: A sample derivation

al., 2005). With our transformation, both ill-nested dependency trees and dependency trees with gap-degree > 1 can be induced. Section 6 discusses related work and Section 7 concludes.

2   Derivations and Dependencies

A lexicalized tree adjoining grammar (LTAG, Joshi and Schabes (1997)) consists of a finite set of *elementary trees*, each of which has at least one leaf with a lexical item. Starting from the elementary trees, larger trees are derived by the operations of *substitution* (which replaces a leaf with a new tree) and *adjunction* (which replaces an internal node with a new tree). In case of an adjunction, the tree being adjoined has exactly one leaf that is marked as the *foot node*. Such a tree is called an *auxiliary* tree. To license its adjunction to a node n, the root and foot node must have the same label as n. When adjoining an auxiliary tree at a node n, in the resulting tree, the subtree with root n from the old tree is attached to the foot node of the auxiliary tree. Non-auxiliary elementary trees are called *initial* trees. A complete derivation starts with an initial tree and produces a derived tree in which all leaves have terminal labels. The history of a derivation is captured in its *derivation tree*. The nodes of this tree correspond to the elementary trees that have been used in the derivation; the edges correspond to the operations performed. Fig. 1 shows a sample derivation.

As can be seen from Fig. 1, in many cases the LTAG derivation tree corresponds to a dependency structure. However, the correspondence

between derivation trees and dependency structures is not always a direct one. Examples of mismatches are in particular those where a) an adjunction of a predicate into one of its arguments occurs and b) furthermore, a higher predicate adjoins into the same argument (Rambow et al., 1995). Consider the following example:

(1)   John Bill claims Mary seems to love.

A derivation of this sentence, together with the corresponding derivation tree and a dependency tree, is shown in Fig. 2. Here, we have a long-distance topicalization of one of the arguments of *love*. In order to account for this in a satisfying way, in particular without violating any of the linguistic assumptions underlying the form of LTAG elementary trees, one has to realize the substitution node for *John* in the elementary tree for *to_love* while making sure that *claim* can end up in between. Therefore, standardly, *claim* adjoins to an S node in the *to_love* tree. Concerning raising verbs such as *seems*, the standard analysis is to adjoin them to the VP node of the sentence to which they contribute finiteness and tense. In this example, *seems* adjoins to the VP node of *to_love*.

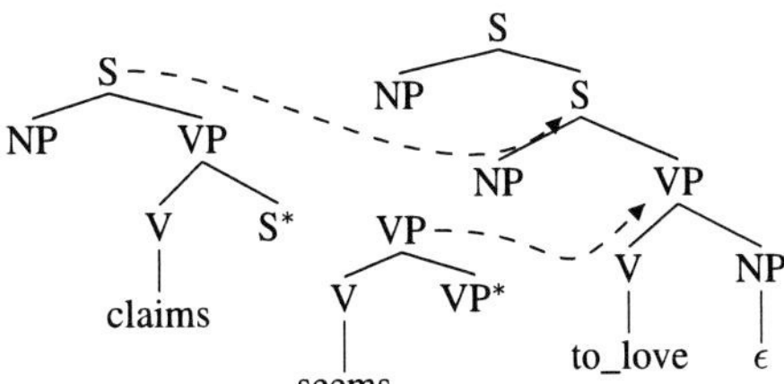

derivation tree: dependency tree:

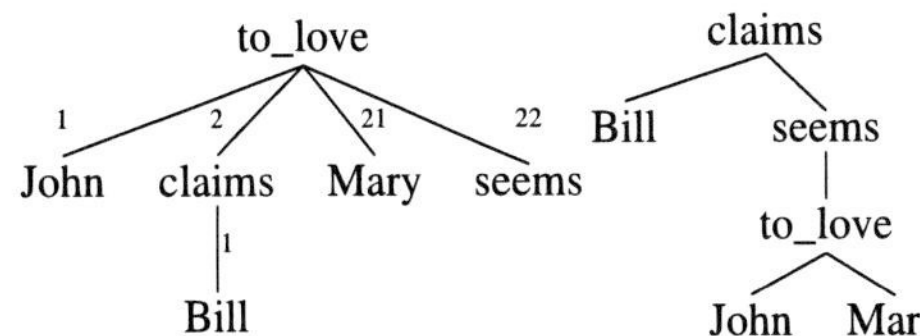

Figure 2: Derivation for (1), together with the corresponding derivation tree and a dependency tree

3   From Derivation to Dependency Trees

Let us inspect the derivation and dependency trees in Fig. 2 more closely in order to understand what the difference is. Concerning substitution nodes, the two trees show the same predicate–argument

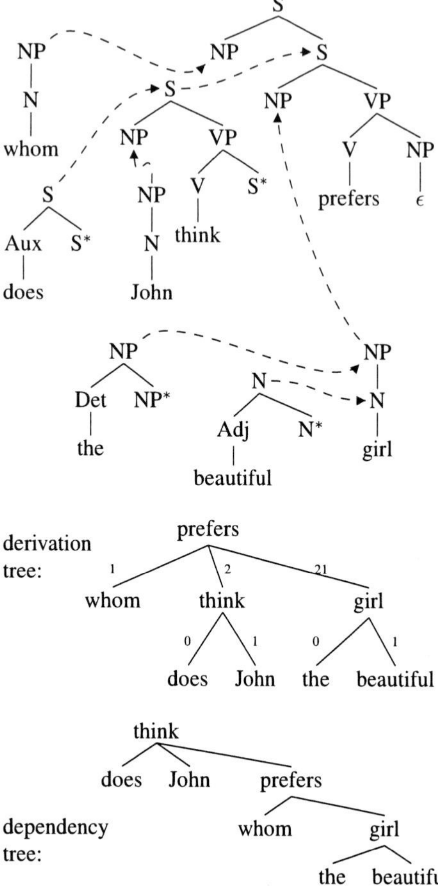

Figure 3: Derivation for (2)

dependencies: *John* and *Mary* are daughters of *to_love*, and *Bill* is a daughter of *claims*. The edge between *seems* and *to_love* has the opposite direction in the derivation tree. This is due to *seems* adjoining into the complement clause that it embeds, which is separated into two discontinuous parts. So, as a first attempt to characterize the relation between LTAG derivation trees and dependency trees, we can say that we should reverse any derivation tree edges originating from complement-taking adjunctions.[1] More precisely, we should replace every complement-adjoining edge $\gamma \to \gamma'$ with the reverse edge, and redirect the previous incoming edge of γ (if it existed) into γ'.

This transformation works in many cases. As an example consider the following:

(2) Whom does John think the beautiful girl prefers?

The derivation of (2) is given in Fig. 3. There are different types of adjunctions: The adjunction of *think* into *prefers* is a complement-taking adjunction, whose edge gets reversed. All the other adjunctions (of *does*, *the*, and *beautiful*) are not complement-taking, and therefore their edges remain unchanged. As a result, we obtain the desired dependency tree after the tree transformation.

Now let us go back to Fig. 2. Here we have the additional complication that there are *two* complement-taking adjunctions that target the *to_love* tree, and that we get different dependency trees depending on which of the edges we reverse first. A look at the desired tree tells us that *claim* should dominate *seems*. Our hypothesis is that this is related to the fact that *claim* adjoins higher on the head projection line in the *to_love* tree than *seems*.[2] The address of the verbal head (i.e., the anchor) is 221, so the verbal projection line is $\varepsilon, 2, 22, 221$. The edge reversals proceed from higher complement-taking adjunctions to lower ones, i.e., in Fig. 4, first the adjunction of *claim* is reversed and then the adjunction of *seems*. More generally, for our transformation to be deterministic, we need to assume a total order on complement-taking adjunctions on the head projection line. Figure 4 shows the two steps of the transformation of the derivation tree for (1) that yields the desired dependency tree.

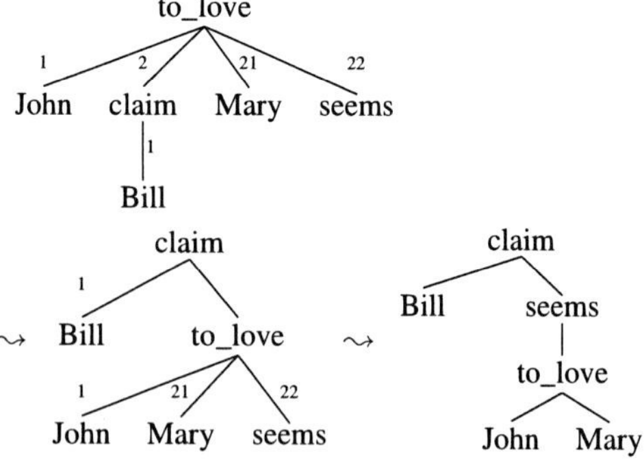

Figure 4: Transformation of the derivation tree for (1)

---

[1] The observation that complement-taking adjunction edges need to be reversed in order to retrieve the correct dependency goes back to Rambow and Joshi (1994).

[2] Kallmeyer and Romero (2008) use specific features on the head projection line of verbs (the *verbal spine* in their terminology) in order to retrieve the missing dependency links.

4 Formal Version of the Transformation

In this section we give a formal account of the transformation sketched above.

4.1 Derivation Trees as Terms

We represent derivation trees as *terms*, formal expressions over a signature of operation symbols (Vijay-Shanker et al., 1987). For example, we represent the derivation in Fig. 2 by the term t_0:

$$t_0 = \text{to\_love}(\text{John}, \text{claims}(\text{Bill}), \text{Mary}, \text{seems})$$

Here 'to_love' is an operation symbol with rank 4; this corresponds to the fact that during the derivation, four trees are substituted/adjoined into the elementary tree for *to_love*. We will use the term t_0 as a running example in this section.

Note that in order to capture all information contained in a derivation tree, each operation symbol needs to encapsulate not only an elementary tree γ but also the specific addresses at which trees were substituted/adjoined into γ. Since adjunctions may be optional, there will in general be several (albeit a bounded number) of operation symbols per elementary tree, and in particular several different versions of the symbol 'to_love'. To simplify our notation, we ignore this aspect of the term representation in this paper.

4.2 Yield Functions

Each derivation tree t encodes the derivation of a derived tree γ. This can be formalized by interpreting the operation symbols in t as operations on derived trees: The symbol to_love for example can be interpreted as a function that takes four derived trees as arguments and returns the tree obtained by substituting/adjoining these trees at the specified nodes of the elementary tree for *to_love*. To compute the derived tree corresponding to t_0, for example, one applies the operation corresponding to to_love to the derived trees corresponding to the subderivations John, claims(Bill), Mary and seems, respectively.

Let the *yield* of a derived tree γ be defined as follows. If γ is a derived initial tree, then its yield is the one-component tuple $\langle w \rangle$, where w is the string consisting of the symbols at the frontier of γ. If γ is a derived auxiliary tree, then its yield is the pair $\langle w_1, w_2 \rangle$, where w_1 and w_2 are the strings corresponding to the parts of the frontier of γ to the left and to the right of the foot node,

respectively. The yield of the derived tree corresponding to a derivation tree t can be obtained by associating with each operation symbol in t a *yield function* (Weir, 1988). To illustrate the idea, suppose that the yields of the four subterms of t_0 are given as $\langle John \rangle$, $\langle Bill\ claims, \varepsilon \rangle$, $\langle Mary \rangle$, and $\langle seems, \varepsilon \rangle$, respectively. Then the full yield (1) is obtained by assigning the following yield function to 'to_love':

$$\text{to\_love}(\langle x_{11} \rangle, \langle x_{21}, x_{22} \rangle, \langle x_{31} \rangle, \langle x_{41}, x_{42} \rangle) =$$
$$\langle x_{11}\ x_{21}\ x_{31}\ x_{41}\ \textit{to\_love}\ x_{42}\ x_{22} \rangle$$

In the context of our transformation, yields may consist of more than two strings, so yield functions will be operations on arbitrary (finite) tuples of strings. We only require that they are non-copying and non-deleting, as in LCFRSs (Weir, 1988). This means that each yield function f can be defined by an equation of the form

$$f(\vec{x}_1, \ldots, \vec{x}_m) = \langle \alpha_1, \ldots, \alpha_k \rangle$$

where the $\vec{x}_i$ are vectors of variables and $\alpha_1 \cdots \alpha_k$ is a string over these variables and symbols from the yield alphabet in which each variable occurs exactly once. We adopt the convention that the variables in the vector $\vec{x}_i$ should be named $x_{i1}, \ldots, x_{ik_i}$. In this case, the defining equation of a yield function is uniquely determined by the tuple on its right-hand side. We call this tuple the *template* of f, and use it as a unique name for f. This means that we can talk about e.g. the standard binary concatenation function as 'the yield function $\langle x_{11}\ x_{21} \rangle$'.

The yield function associated with an operation symbol in a derivation tree can be extracted in a systematic way; see Boullier (1999) for a procedure that performs this extraction in the formalism of range concatenation grammars.

4.3 Direct Interpretation

The direct interpretation of a derivation tree as a dependency tree can be formalized by interpreting symbols as operations on dependency trees (Kuhlmann, 2013). Continuing our running example, suppose that for each subtree of t_0 we are not only given a string or a pair of strings as before, but also a corresponding dependency tree. Then the symbol to_love has a straightforward reading as constructing a new dependency tree for the full sentence (1): Preserve all the old dependencies, and add new edges from *to_love* to the roots of the dependency trees associated with the subterms.

4.4 Transformation

We illustrate the formal transformation by means of our running example. In order to convey the intuitive idea, we first present the transformation as an iterative procedure, in much the same way as in Section 3. Then, in a second step, we show how the transformation can be carried out in a single top–down traversal of the initial derivation tree.

Starting from the tree t_0, we will reverse some edges and change some operation symbols to obtain the modified tree

$$t_1 = \text{claims}'(\text{seems}'(\text{to\_love}'(\text{John}, \text{Mary})), \text{Bill})$$

When interpreting this transformed tree as outlined in Section 4.3, we will obtain the plausible dependency tree shown in Fig. 2.

In a first step, we want to reverse the direction of the edge from *to_love* to *claims*, so the transformed derivation tree should have the form

$$t_0' = \text{claims}'(\text{to\_love}''(\text{John}, \text{Mary}, \text{seems}), \text{Bill})$$

However, the yield of t_0 and t_0' should be the same. To achieve this, we change the yield functions of to_love and claims from

$$\text{to\_love} \rightsquigarrow \langle x_{11}\, x_{21}\, x_{31}\, x_{41}\, \textit{to\_love}\, x_{42}\, x_{22}\rangle$$
$$\text{claims} \rightsquigarrow \langle x_{11}\, \textit{claims}, \varepsilon\rangle$$

in the source derivation tree t_0 to

$$\text{claims}' \rightsquigarrow \langle x_{11}\, x_{21}\, \textit{claims}\, x_{12}\, x_{13}\rangle$$
$$\text{to\_love}'' \rightsquigarrow \langle x_{11}, x_{21}\, x_{31}\, \textit{to\_love}\, x_{32}, \varepsilon\rangle$$

in the target derivation tree t_0'.

The idea is illustrated in Fig. 5, which shows the schematic structure of the yield of a derived tree that results from the adjunction of an auxiliary tree β_2 (grey part) into an auxiliary tree β_1 (white parts). In the term representation, the yield functions associated with β_1 and β_2 take the forms

$$f_1 = \langle v_1\, x_1\, v_2, v_3\, x_2\, v_4\rangle \quad \text{and} \quad f_2 = \langle w_1, w_2\rangle,$$

respectively, where the variables x_1, x_2 in f_1 are placeholders for the two components of the tuple returned by f_2. When we now reverse the edge between β_1 and β_2, but want the resulting term to have the same yield as before, then we need to change the yield functions into

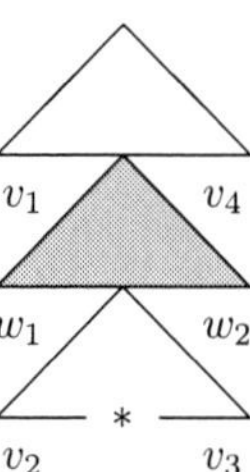

Figure 5: Schematic structure of the yields involved in an adjunction

$$f_2' = \langle x_1\, w_1\, x_2, x_3\, w_2\, x_4\rangle \quad f_1' = \langle v_1, v_2, v_3, v_4\rangle.$$

In the second step, we want to reverse the direction of the edge from *to_love* to *seems* and obtain

$$t_1 = \text{claims}(\text{seems}(\text{to\_love}(\text{John}, \text{Mary})), \text{Bill})$$

as above. Again, the yield of t_0' and t_1 should be the same. We therefore change the yield functions of to_love and seems from

$$\text{to\_love}'' \rightsquigarrow \langle x_{11}, x_{21}\, x_{31}\, \textit{to\_love}\, x_{32}, \varepsilon\rangle$$
$$\text{seems} \rightsquigarrow \langle \textit{seems}, \varepsilon\rangle$$

in the source derivation tree t_1 to

$$\text{seems}' \rightsquigarrow \langle x_{11}, x_{12}\, \textit{seems}\, x_{13}\, x_{14}, x_{15}\rangle$$
$$\text{to\_love}' \rightsquigarrow \langle x_{11}, x_{21}, \textit{to\_love}, \varepsilon, \varepsilon\rangle$$

in the target derivation tree t_1. Note that the yield of *to_love''* no longer has the schematic structure of Fig. 5, but consists of *three* discontinuous segments (even though the third segment is empty). More generally, each step of our transformation may increase the *fan-out* of the yield functions that are involved.

4.5 Macro Tree Transducers

To implement our transformation in a single pass over the initial derivation tree, we use a *macro tree transducer* (Engelfriet and Vogler, 1985). Macro tree transducers extend standard top–down tree transducers by the ability to pass the output of the translation of a subtree to the translation of another subtree as an argument. We illustrate how we take advantage of this ability by means of the derivation tree t_0. To obtain the tree t_1, we apply the following rule to t_0:

$$\langle q_0, \text{to\_love}(x_1, x_2, x_3, x_4)\rangle \rightarrow$$
$$\langle q_2, x_2\rangle(\langle q_4, x_4\rangle(\text{to\_love}'(\langle q_1, x_1\rangle, \langle q_3, x_3\rangle)))$$

The informal reading of this rule is: 'To translate an input tree of the form to_love(t_1, t_2, t_3, t_4): translate the subtrees t_1 and t_3 (corresponding to *John* and *Mary*); attach the outputs of these translations as arguments of the modified symbol to_love$'$; attach the resulting tree to the output of the translation of t_4 (*seems*); and attach the tree resulting from that to the output of the translation of t_2 (*claims*). The q_i are states that can be used to communicate a limited amount of contextual information to the translations of the subtrees. In our case, they are used to transport information about how to modify the yield functions. Each rule of the macro tree transducer encapsulates the full set of modifications to the yield functions that are necessary to simulate the reversals of the complement-taking adjunctions.

In the macro tree transducer for our running example, the rules for the translations of *seems* and *claims* have access to a special variable y that will be instantiated with the output of the translation of the subtrees for *to_love* and *seems*, respectively:

$$\langle q_4, \text{seems} \rangle(y) \rightarrow \text{seems}'(y)$$
$$\langle q_2, \text{claims}(x_1) \rangle(y) \rightarrow \text{claims}'(y, \langle q_{21}, x_1 \rangle)$$

These rules produce the following output trees:

$$seems \rightsquigarrow \text{seems}'(\text{to\_love}'(\text{john}, \text{mary}))$$
$$claims \rightsquigarrow \text{claims}'(\text{seems}'(\cdots), \text{bill})$$

Concerning the complexity of parsing, our transformation is linear in the size of the derivation tree. Consequently, parsing (i.e., obtaining derived, derivation, and dependency tree for a given input) is still polynomial both in the size of the input string and in the size of the grammar, as in the case of standard TAG. This is a difference compared to tree-local MCTAG where, due to the fact that adjunctions at different nodes of an elementary tree are no longer completely independent from each other, the universal recognition problem is NP-complete (Søgaard et al., 2007).

5 Structural Properties

In this section, we reconsider some examples involving ill-nested dependency structures and dependency structures with gap-degree > 1 that have been argued to be problematic for TAG. If we assume that LTAG derivation trees are dependency trees, TAG is limited to well-nested dependency trees of gap-degree ≤ 1 (Bodirsky et al.,

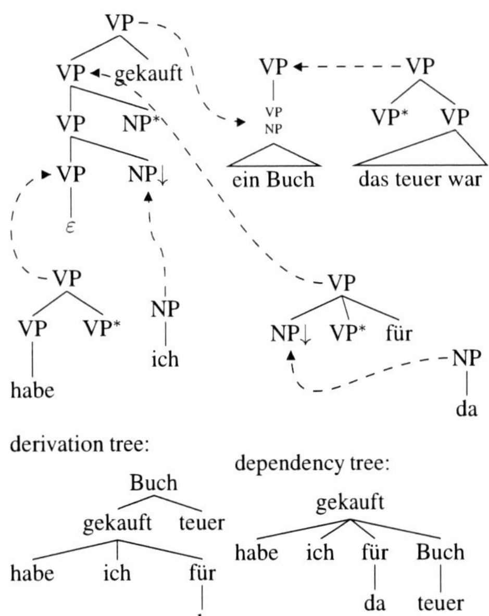

Figure 6: LTAG derivation for (3)

2005). We will see that if the transformation described above is applied to a TAG derivation tree, then this limit is no longer given.

5.1 Ill-Nestedness

Consider the following ill-nested dependency structures in German, both taken from Chen-Main and Joshi (2012). (3) combines a *dafür*-split with an NP containing an extraposed relative clause. (4) combines a split quantifier with an NP having an extraposed relative clause.

(3) Da habe ich ein Buch für gekauft das
    that have I   a   book for bought which
    teuer   war
    expensive was
    'for that I bought a book which was expensive'

(4) Bücher hat der Student drei   gekauft
    books has the student three bought
    der am meisten Geld hatte
    who the most money had
    'the student with the most money bought three books'

Assuming that adjunctions to complements have to be reversed in order to obtain the correct dependencies, we can analyze (3) with the TAG derivation from Fig. 6. The adjunction of *gekauft* to *Buch* then has to be reversed. As a result, we

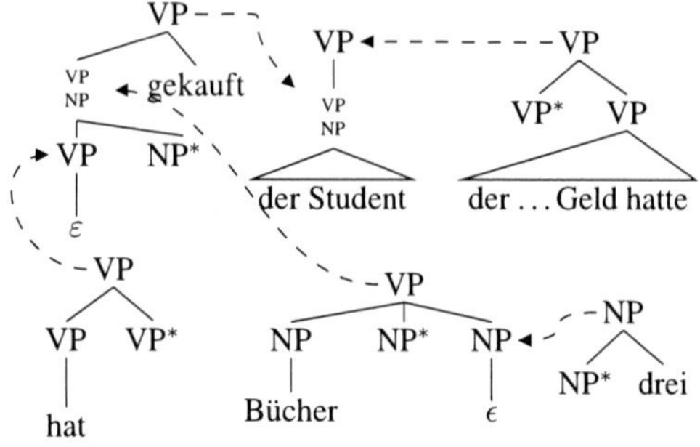

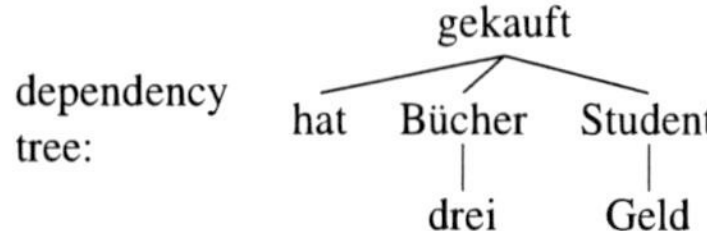

Figure 7: Derivation for (4)

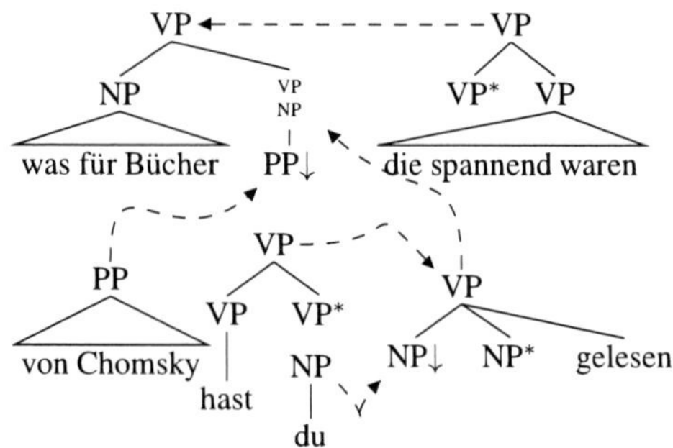

Figure 8: LTAG derivation for (5)

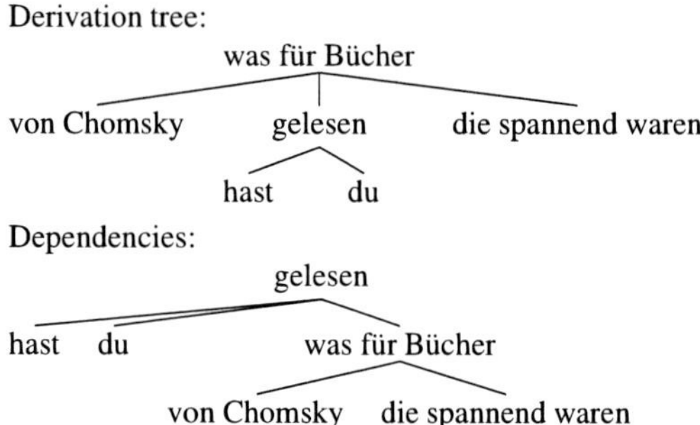

Figure 9: Derivation tree and dependencies for (5)

obtain the dependency tree in the lower part of Fig. 6. Note that we assume a feature structure based TAG where the CAT (= category) feature can be different in the top and bottom structures of a node, requiring an adjunction. In Fig. 6 the *Buch* tree requires the adjunction of a VP tree that takes an NP-complement.[3]

The second example for ill-nested dependencies, (4), is slightly more complicated since both split constituents are arguments of the same verb. In order to deal with this, we need to adjoin one of the arguments. This is a major change to standard TAG analyses since there is no argument slot in the sense of substitution or foot node for this argument. The selection of this argument has to be done via the features, namely via the CAT feature of the node where the argument adjoins. The derivation is shown in Fig. 7. Here, the only complement taking adjunction is the adjunction of *gekauft* into *der Student*; the corresponding edge is reversed by our transformation. This yields the correct dependency tree.

5.2 Gap-Degree > 1

Now let us move to examples of gap-degree greater than 1, such as (5). The analysis of this sentence involves an NP that is split into three non-adjacent parts, *was für Bücher von Chomsky die spannend sind*. This is again an example from Chen-Main and Joshi (2012).

(5) Was für   Bücher hast du von Chomsky
    what type of books have you by Chomsky
    gelesen die   spannend sind
    read   which exciting are
    'what type of books by Chomsky have you read
    that are exciting'

This example could be analyzed as in Fig. 8. Again, we assume that an adjunction into a complement (here *gelesen* adjoins into its object *Bücher*) is an adjunction that needs to be reversed. As a result, we obtain the derivation and dependency structures in Fig. 9.[4]

5.3 Generalization

From these examples we have already seen that, under the new interpretation of derivation trees as dependency structures, TAG can generate ill-nested dependencies and dependencies of gap degree > 1. A question is whether the gap-degree is limited at all. And here the answer is no. Or rather, there is a grammar-dependent limit on the maximal number of gaps a derivation can generate.

---

[3]With this feature-based modeling of adjunction constraints, the requirement that root and foot node have the same labels in auxiliary trees is no longer assumed.

[4]Note that this example involves a complement-taking adjunction that does not take place above the lexical anchor. We leave the investigation of possible nodes for complement-taking adjunctions for future research.

As we have seen, gaps arise from complement-taking adjunctions where each of these adjunctions can introduce two new gaps (to the left and right of the spine of the auxiliary tree). Furthermore, the number of such adjunctions is limited by the maximal number of internal nodes per elementary tree. In addition to this, the tree itself can be a non-complement taking auxiliary tree that contains a gap below its foot node. Consequently, the following holds under our transformation:

Claim. Let G be an LTAG, and let k be the maximal number of internal nodes in a tree of G. Then the gap-degree of the dependency trees induced by G is upper-bounded by $2(k-2)+1$.

This is actually surprising, given that previous assumptions were that LTAG is too limited to generate the dependency structures needed for natural languages (Kuhlmann, 2010). As shown in this paper, instead of moving to a TAG variant different from standard LTAG, one can also use standard LTAG and assume the transformation described in this paper as the operation that induces the underlying dependency structure. In this sense, this paper opens a different perspective on LTAG, showing that the claim about the limitations of LTAG concerning dependency trees is not valid if the induction of dependencies is taken to be an operation on the derivation tree that is different from just the identity.

6   Related Work

The mismatch between TAG derivation trees and dependency structures has been known for a long time, and several solutions have been proposed. These fall, roughly, into two classes. On the one hand, several authors have proposed to use a variant of TAG that yields different derivation trees than standard TAG. On the other hand, some approaches keep standard TAG while exploring ways to obtain the missing links from the derivation tree. Our approach falls into the second class.

Concerning the first class, one of the earliest proposals was D-Tree Substitution Grammar (Rambow et al., 2001). The idea is to use tree descriptions instead of trees. These tree descriptions contain dominance links whenever different parts of an elementary tree can be split. Arguments are added by substitution but an 'extracted' part of an argument, linked to the lower part by a dominance link, can be separated from this lower part

and end up much higher. This gives more flexibility concerning the modeling of discontinuities and non-projective dependencies.

Another LTAG variant that has been discussed a lot recently in the context of the 'missing link problem' is tree-local MCTAG with flexible composition (Joshi et al., 2007; Chen-Main and Joshi, 2012), formalized by the notion of delayed tree-locality (Chiang and Scheffler, 2008). The idea is roughly to perform the reversal of complement-taking adjunctions not on the derivation tree, but already during derivation. More precisely, instead of considering such an operation as a standard adjunction, it is considered as a wrapping operation directed from the adjunction site to the auxiliary tree. Consider for instance the derivation in Fig. 3. If we take the adjunction of the *think* tree into the *prefer* tree to be a wrapping of *prefer*, split at its internal S node, around the *think* tree. If this is reflected in the derivation tree by an edge from *prefer* to *think*, then one obtains the lower tree in Fig. 3 as a derivation tree. Chen-Main and Joshi (2012) provide analyses for the examples from Section 6 using tree-local MCTAG with flexible composition. In contrast to their approach, in our proposal flexible composition is replaced by a transformation on the derivation trees. As a result, for the construction of the derivation tree, we keep standard TAG and we can still use its parsing techniques. The choice to remain with standard TAG however requires some relaxation of the predicate argument cooccurrence principle since, as we have seen in with the analysis of (4), we sometimes have to adjoin arguments and express their selection via features of an internal node.

Concerning the use of TAG with some additional means to retrieve the desired dependencies from the derivation tree, this has been pursued by Kallmeyer (2002), where the derivation tree is explicitly enriched with additional links, and by Gardent and Kallmeyer (2003) and Kallmeyer and Romero (2008), where these links are indirectly constructed via feature percolation. However, these approaches do not provide an explicit transformation from derivation trees to dependency structures.

7   Conclusion

In this paper we have addressed the relation between LTAG derivation trees and linguistically plausible dependency trees. We have formalized the correspondence between the two as an edge-reversing tree transformation, and shown that, under this transformation, LTAG can induce dependency trees that cannot be induced under the direct interpretation.

We used our approach to analyze some of the problematic examples from the literature. It turned out that, given our transformation, these examples can be treated using only TAG, i.e., without multiple components. This is a nice result since it means that parsing (yielding derived, derivation and dependency tree) is polynomial both in input and grammar size. The latter is not the case for tree-local MCTAG.

In future work we hope to address the question whether there are linguistic phenomena that are not covered by our approach, and to carry out a more systematic and comprehensive comparison of the various proposals that have been put forward to address the 'missing link problem'.

References

Manuel Bodirsky, Marco Kuhlmann, and Mathias Möhl. 2005. Well-nested drawings as models of syntactic structure. In *Proceedings of the 10th Conference on Formal Grammar (FG) and Ninth Meeting on Mathematics of Language (MOL)*, pages 195–203, Edinburgh, UK.

Pierre Boullier. 1999. On TAG parsing. In *Traitement Automatique des Langues Naturelles (TALN)*, pages 75–84, Cargèse, France.

Marie-Hélène Candito and Sylvain Kahane. 1998. Can the TAG derivation tree represent a semantic graph? an answer in the light of Meaning-Text Theory. In *Fourth International Workshop on Tree Adjoining Grammars and Related Frameworks, IRCS Report 98–12*, pages 25–28, University of Pennsylvania, Philadelphia.

Joan Chen-Main and Aravind Joshi. 2012. A dependency perspective on the adequacy of tree local multi-component tree adjoining grammar. *Journal of Logic and Computation Advance Access*, June.

David Chiang and Tatjana Scheffler. 2008. Flexible composition and delayed tree-locality. In *TAG+9 Proceedings of the Ninth International Workshop on Tree-Adjoining Grammar and Related Formalisms (TAG+9)*, pages 17–24, Tübingen, June.

Joost Engelfriet and Heiko Vogler. 1985. Macro tree transducers. *Journal of Computer and System Sciences*, 31(1):71–146.

Anette Frank and Josef van Genabith. 2001. GlueTag. Linear logic based semantics for LTAG – and what it teaches us about LFG and LTAG. In Miriam Butt and Tracy Holloway King, editors, *Proceedings of the LFG01 Conference*, Hong Kong.

Claire Gardent and Laura Kallmeyer. 2003. Semantic Construction in FTAG. In *Proceedings of EACL 2003*, pages 123–130, Budapest.

Aravind K. Joshi and Yves Schabes. 1997. Tree-Adjoining Grammars. In Grzegorz Rozenberg and Arto Salomaa, editors, *Handbook of Formal Languages*, volume 3, pages 69–123. Springer.

Aravind K. Joshi, Laura Kallmeyer, and Maribel Romero. 2007. Flexible Composition in LTAG: Quantifier Scope and Inverse Linking. In Reinhard Muskens and Harry Bunt, editors, *Computing Meaning Volume 3*, volume 83 of *Studies in Linguistics and Philosophy*, pages 233–256. Springer.

Laura Kallmeyer and Maribel Romero. 2008. Scope and situation binding in LTAG using semantic unification. *Research on Language and Computation*, 6(1):3–52.

Laura Kallmeyer. 2002. Using an Enriched TAG Derivation Structure as Basis for Semantics. In *Proceedings of the Sixth International Workshop on Tree Adjoining Grammars and Related Frameworks (TAG+6)*, pages 127–136, Venice, May.

Marco Kuhlmann. 2010. *Dependency Structures and Lexicalized Grammars*, volume 6270 of *LNCS*. Springer.

Marco Kuhlmann. 2013. Mildly non-projective dependency grammar. *Computational Linguistics*, 39(2). Just Accepted publication August 22, 2012.

Owen Rambow and Aravind K. Joshi. 1994. A processing model for free word order languages. In Charles J. Clifton, Lyn Frazier, and Keith Rayner, editors, *Perspectives on sentence processing*. L. Erlbaum Associates.

Owen Rambow, K. Vijay-Shanker, and David Weir. 1995. D-Tree Grammars. In *Proceedings of ACL*.

Owen Rambow, K. Vijay-Shanker, and David Weir. 2001. D-Tree Substitution Grammars. *Computational Linguistics*, 27(1):87–121.

Anders Søgaard, Timm Lichte, and Wolfgang Maier. 2007. The complexity of linguistically motivated extensions of tree-adjoining grammar. In *Recent Advances in Natural Language Processing 2007*, Borovets, Bulgaria.

K. Vijay-Shanker, David J. Weir, and Aravind K. Joshi. 1987. Characterizing structural descriptions produced by various grammatical formalisms. In *Proceedings of the 25th Annual Meeting of the Association for Computational Linguistics (ACL)*, pages 104–111, Stanford, CA, USA.

David J. Weir. 1988. *Characterizing Mildly Context-Sensitive Grammar Formalisms*. Ph.D. thesis, University of Pennsylvania, Philadelphia, USA.

Using FB-LTAG Derivation Trees to Generate Transformation-Based Grammar Exercises

Claire Gardent
CNRS/LORIA
Nancy, France
Claire.Gardent@loria.fr

Laura Perez-Beltrachini
Université de Lorraine/LORIA
Nancy, France
Laura.Perez@loria.fr

Abstract

Using a Feature-Based Lexicalised Tree Adjoining Grammar (FB-LTAG), we present an approach for generating pairs of sentences that are related by a syntactic transformation and we apply this approach to create language learning exercises. We argue that the derivation trees of an FB-LTAG provide a good level of representation for capturing syntactic transformations. We relate our approach to previous work on sentence reformulation, question generation and grammar exercise generation. We evaluate precision and linguistic coverage. And we demonstrate the genericity of the proposal by applying it to a range of transformations including the Passive/Active transformation, the pronominalisation of an NP, the assertion / yes-no question relation and the assertion / wh-question transformation.

1 Introduction

Textbooks for language learning generally include grammar exercises. For instance, *Tex's French Grammar* [1] includes at the end of each lecture, a set of grammar exercises which target a specific pedagogical goal such as the one shown in Figure 1 for learning to form questions. The aim of those exercises is to facilitate the acquisition of a specific grammar point by presenting the learner with *exercises made up of short sentences involving a simple syntax and a restricted vocabulary.*

As argued in (Perez-Beltrachini et al., 2012), most existing work on the generation of grammar exercises has concentrated on the automatic creation of exercises whose source sentences are "real life sentences" extracted from an existing corpus. In contrast, we aim at generating textbook style exercises i.e., exercices whose syntax and lexicon are controlled to match the linguistic content already acquired by the learner.

Moreover, in computer aided language learning (CALL), much of the work towards generating exercices has focused on so-called objective test items i.e., test items such as multiple choice questions, fill in the blank and cloze exercise items, whose answer is strongly constrained and can therefore be predicted and checked with high accuracy. Thus, (Chen et al., 2006) describes a system called FAST which supports the semi-automatic generation of Multiple-Choice and Error Detection exercises while (Aldabe et al., 2006) presents the ArikiTurri automatic question generator for constructing Fill-in-the-Blank, Word Formation, Multiple Choice and Error Detection exercises.

Few studies, however, have been conducted on the generation of transformation based exercices such as illustrated in Figure 1.

In this paper, we present an approach for generating transformation exercices such as (1), where the query (Q) is a sentence and the solution (S) is related to the query by a syntactic transformation.

(1) Instruction: *Modify Q so that the underlined verb is in passive.*
Q: John hopes that Mary <u>likes</u> Peter.

---

[1] *Tex's French Grammar* http://www.laits.utexas.edu/tex/ is an online pedagogical reference grammar which is arranged like many other traditional reference grammars with the parts of speech (nouns, verbs, etc.) used to categorize specific grammar items (gender of nouns, irregular verbs). Individual grammar items are explained in English, exemplified in a dialogue, and finally tested in self-correcting, fill-in-the-blank exercises.

Proceedings of the 11th International Workshop on Tree Adjoining Grammars and Related Formalisms (TAG+11), pages 117–125,
Paris, September 2012.

```
Interrogative pronouns. Transform each sentence into the corresponding question.
Example: Rita parle DE LA POLITIQUE. You write: De quoi est-ce que Rita parle?
1. Bette parle DE TAMMY.
2. Corey a besoin D'UNE BIERE.
3. Fiona téléphone A RITA.
4. Joe-Bob sort AVEC TEX.
5. LE PROF dérange Joe-Bob.
6. LES DEVOIRS dérangent Joe-Bob.
7. Paw-Paw fait UNE SIESTE (nap).
8. Tammy cherche TEX.
9. TAMMY cherche Tex.
```

Figure 1: Grammar exercises from the *Tex's French Grammar* textbook

S: John hopes that Peter is liked by Mary.

To control the syntax and the lexicon of the exercices produced, we take a grammar based approach and make use of generation techniques. More specifically, we generate sentences using a Feature-Based Lexicalised Tree Adjoining Grammar (FB-LTAG) for French (SemTAG). We show that the rich linguistic information associated with sentences by the generation process naturally supports the identification of sentence pairs related by a syntactic transformation. In particular, we argue that the derivation trees of the FB-LTAG grammar provide a level of representation that captures both the formal and the content constraints governing transformations. The content words and the grammatical functions labelling the tree nodes permit checking that the two sentences stand in the appropriate semantic relation (i.e., fully identical content or identical content modulo some local change). Further, the syntactic properties labelling these nodes (names of FB-LTAG elementary tree names but also some additional information provided by our generator) permits ensuring that they stand in the appropriate syntactic relation.

The structure of the paper is the following. We start (Section 2) by discussing related work focusing on studies that target the production of syntactic reformulations. We then go on to present our approach and show that it permits generating different types of transformations (Section 3). In Section (4), we discuss results concerning linguistic coverage, precision and recall. Section (5) concludes with pointers for further research.

2 Related work

In linguistics, transformations (Harris, 1957; Chomsky, 1957) model recurrent linguistic relations between sentence pairs. For instance, a transformation can be used to define the relation between the active and the passive voice version of the same sentence. Formally, transformations were stated as tree-transducers on phrase structure trees and they defined either structure changing or structure building (generalised transformation) operations.

In computational linguistics, transformations and more generally, structure changing and structure building rules have been used in such tasks as text simplification (Siddharthan, 2010), text summarising (Cohn and Lapata, 2009) and question generation (Piwek and Boyer, 2012). In these approaches however, the transformation relation is not necessarily defined on phrase structure trees. For instance, for the question generation task, (Yao et al., 2012) has argued that Assertion/WH-Question transformations are best defined on semantic representations. Conversely, for text simplification, (Siddharthan, 2010) has convincingly shown that dependency trees are better suited as a representation on which to define text simplification rules than both phrase structure trees and semantic representations.

(Siddharthan, 2011) presents a user evaluation comparing different re-generation approaches for sentence simplification. He notes in particular that annotators preferred those transformations that are closer in syntax to the original sentence. To achieve this, rules for word ordering are either added to the transform rules or coded as constraints within the input to a generator. In contrast, in our approach, syntactic similarity can be deduced by tree comparison using the rich linguistic information associated by the generator with the FB-LTAG derivation trees.

(Chandrasekar and Srinivas, 1997) describes an algorithm by which generalised rules for simplification are automatically induced from annotated training material. Similar to our work, their approach makes use of TAG derivation trees as a

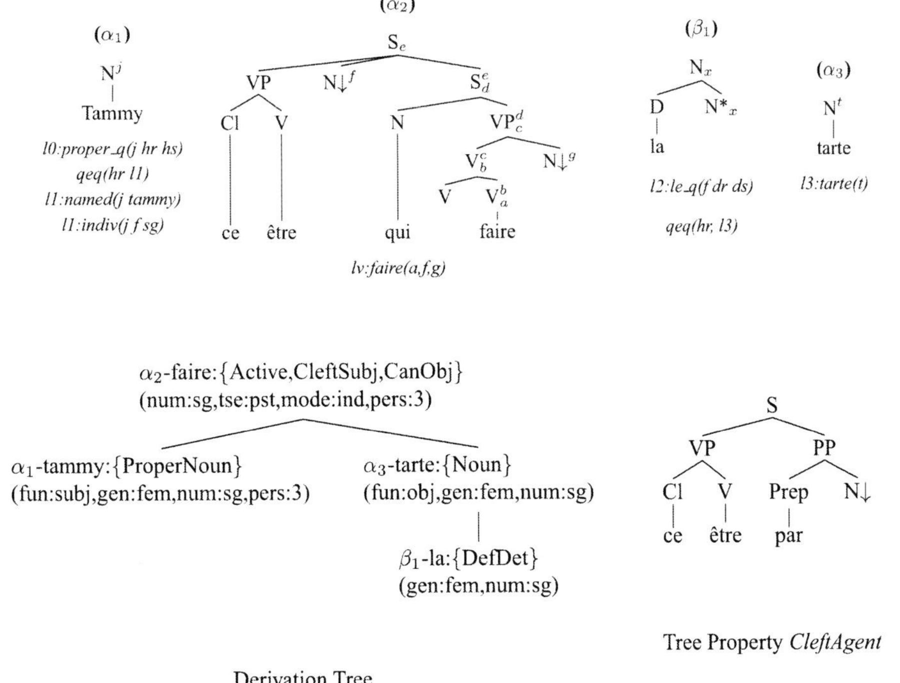

Figure 2: Grammar, Derivation Tree and Example Tree Property (Bottom right) for the sentence *C'est Tammy qui fait la tarte* (It is Tammy who bakes the pie)

base representation. Using a corpus of complex sentences parsed and aligned with the corresponding simplified sentences, the tree comparison algorithm they propose permit inducing simplification rules between dependency trees derived from TAG derivation trees. Although similar to our approach, (Chandrasekar and Srinivas, 1997)'s proposal differs from ours in several ways. First, while we focus on transformations, they work on simplifications relating e.g., a sentence containing a relative clause to two base clauses. Second, the trees on which they define their transformations are reconstructed in a rather ad hoc manner from the TAG derivation trees and from information extracted from the TAG derived trees. In contrast, we make use of the derivation trees produced by the *GraDe* algorithm. Third, while their work is limited to sentences containing relative clauses, we consider a wider range of transformations. Fourth, their approach targets the automatic acquisition of simplification rules while we manually define those.

3 Generating Transformation-related sentences

To generate pairs of sentences that are related by a transformation, we proceed in two main steps.

First, we construct a generation bank by generating sentences from underspecified semantic representations using the *GraDe* algorithm (Gardent and Kruszewski, 2012). This generation bank stores sentences that have been generated using *GraDe* together with the detailed linguistic information associated by this algorithm with each sentence in particular, its derivation tree.

Second, filters are used to retrieve from the generation bank sentence pairs that provide the query and the solution to a given transformation type exercise. These filters are defined on derivation trees and make use of the rich linguistic information associated by our generator with those derivation trees.

In what follows, we start by describing the grammar used and the information contained in the derivation trees produced by *GraDe* . We then go on to motivate the use of derivation trees as a structure on which to base the identification of

119

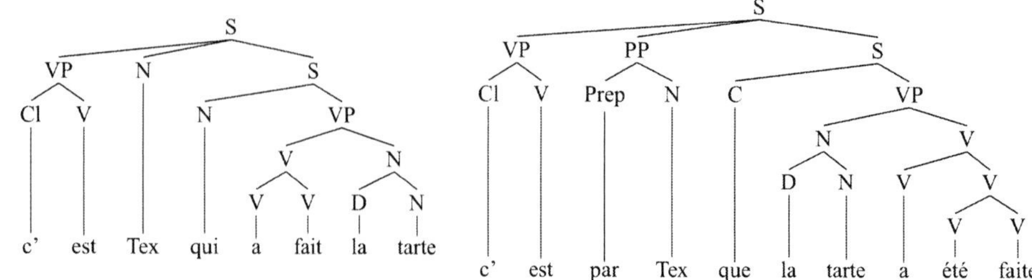

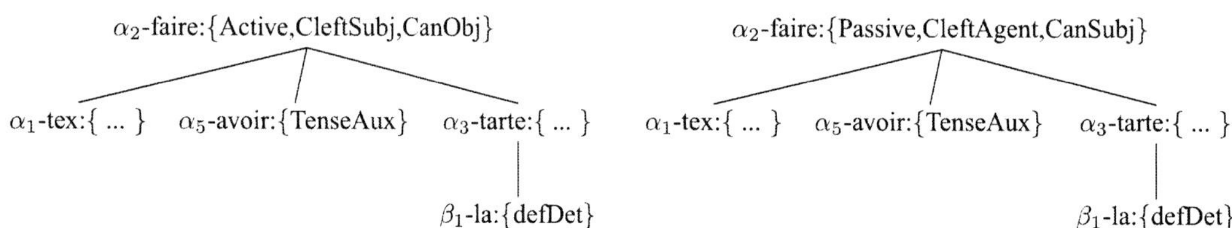

Figure 3: Derived (top) and Derivation (bottom) Trees for the active voiced sentence *C'est Tex qui a fait la tarte* (It is Tex who baked the pie) and its passive variant

transformationally related sentences. Finally, we present the derivation tree filters used to identify pairs of transformationally related sentences.

3.1 Grammar

The grammar used by the surface realiser is called *SemTAG*. It is a Feature-Based Lexicalised Tree Adjoining Grammar (FB-LTAG, (Vijay-Shanker and Joshi, 1988)) for French augmented with a unification-based compositional semantics as described in (Gardent and Kallmeyer, 2003).

Figure 2 shows an example FB-LTAG grammar and the derivation tree associated with the sentence *C'est Tammy qui fait la tarte* (It is Tammy who bakes the pie).

The basic elements of FB-LTAG are called *elementary trees*. Each elementary tree is labelled with feature structures and is associated with at least one lexical item called the *anchor* of that tree. Elementary trees are of two types: auxiliary (to model recursion) and initial (to capture predicate/argument dependencies). They are combined using two operations, *substitution* and *adjunction*. The result of combining elementary trees together is both a derived tree (representing phrase structure) and a derivation tree (describing the process by which a derived tree was produced). More

specifically, an FB-LTAG derivation tree indicates which FB-LTAG elementary trees were used to construct the parse tree and how they were combined: each node in a derivation tree is labelled with the name of an elementary trees used in the derivation and each edge indicates which operation (substitution or adjunction) was applied to combine the two trees related by the edge.

As shown in Figure 2, the derivation trees produced by *GraDe* contain additional information[2]. Nodes are labelled not only with the name of an elementary tree but also with the lemma anchoring that tree, the feature structure associated with the anchor of that tree and the *tree properties* of that tree.

We use feature structure information to identify the grammatical function of an argument and to verify that two transformationally related sentences are syntactically and morpho-syntactically identical up to the transformed part.

Tree properties are abstractions over tree descriptions. These properties are produced by the grammar compiler computing the grammar out of a more abstract grammar specification. They name the tree descriptions that were used to build

---

[2]In Figure 2, edge labels are omitted for simplicity.

the FB-LTAG elementary trees. Thus, for instance, the tree property *CleftAgent* names the tree description appearing at the bottom right of Figure 2; and the elementary tree α_2 in Figure 2 is associated with the tree properties *Active, CleftSubj,CanObj* indicating that this tree was built by combining together the tree descriptions named *Active, CleftSubj* and *CanObj*.

3.2 Why Derivation Trees?

As discussed in Section 2, previous work on syntactic transformations has experimented with different levels of representation on which to define transformations namely, dependency trees, phrase structure tree and semantic representations. While providing detailed information about the syntax and the informational content of a sentence, FB-LTAG derivation trees provide both a more abstract description of this information than derived trees and a richer representation than semantic formulae.

Figure 3 illustrates the difference between derived and derivation trees by showing those trees for the sentences *C'est Tex qui a fait la tarte (It is Tex who baked the pie)* and *C'est par Tex que la tarte a été faite (It is by Tex that the pie was baked)*. While the derived trees of these two sentences differ in their overall structure (different structure, different number of nodes), their derivation trees are identical up to the tree properties of the verb. Moreover, the tree properties of the active ($\{Active,CleftSubj,CanObj\}$) and of the passive ($\{passive,cleftAgent,canSubj\}$) verb capture the changes in argument and verb realisation typical of a passive transformation. In other words, derivation trees provide a level of description that is simpler (less nodes) and that better supports the identification of tranformationally related sentences (more similar configurations and explicit description of changes in argument and verb realisation).

Derivation trees are also better suited than semantic formulae to capture transformations as, in some cases[3], the semantic representations of two transformationally related sentences

---

[3]Whether two syntactically distinct sentences share the same semantics depends on the grammar. In the grammar we use, the semantic representations aims to capture the truth conditions of a sentence not their pragmatic or informational content. As a result, Passive/Active variations do share the same semantics.

may be identical. For instance, in our grammar, Active/Passive, canonical/inverted subject and cleft/non cleft argument variations are assigned the same semantics. As shown above, for those cases, the tree properties labelling the derivation trees provide a direct handle for identifying sentences related by these transformations.

3.3 Derivation Tree Filters

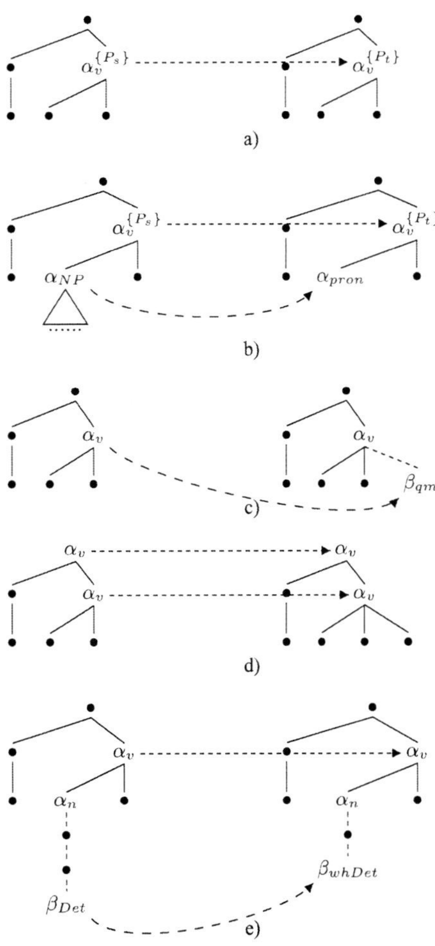

Figure 4: Tree filter types (tree schemas on the left depict source sentence derivation trees and those to their right their transform)

To identify transformationally related sentences, we define tree filters on derivation trees. These filters make use of all the information present in the FB-LTAG derivation trees produced by *GraDe* namely, the tree names, the lemmas, the feature structures and the tree properties la-

121

belling the nodes of these trees.

Figure 4 shows the general filtering patterns we used to handle four types of transformations used in language learning: Active/Passive, NP/pronoun (pronominalisation), NP/Wh-NP (WH-questions) and Assertion/Yes-No questions.

Filters (a) and (d) are used for the Active/Passive and for the canonical/inverted subject variations. Filter (a) relates two trees which are identical up to either one node differing in its tree properties. It applies for instance to the derivation trees shown in Figure 3. Filter (d) is used for cases such as *John wants Mary to like him / John wants to be liked by Mary* where the two derivation trees differ both in the tree properties assigned to *want* (*CanSubj, CanObj, SentObj ↔ CanObj, SentObj*) and in the tree properties assigned to *like* (*InfSubj, CanObj ↔ InfSubj, CanAgent*); and where an additional node is present due to the presence of the pronoun *him* in the active sentence and its absence in the passive variant.

Filter (b) is used for the NP/Pronoun transformation and relates two trees which in addition to having one node with different tree properties also differ in that an NP node and its subtree maps to a pronoun node.

Filter (c) relates two trees which are identical up to the addition of an auxiliary tree of type β_{qm}. As we shall see below, this is used to account for the relation between an assertion and a question including a question phrase (i.e., *n'est ce pas / Isn't it, est ce que*, inverted *t'il* or question mark).

Finally, Filter (e) is used for the assertion/wh-question transformation and matches pairs of trees such that an NP containing n modifiers in one tree becomes a WH-NP with any number of these n modifiers in the other tree.

We now discuss in more detail the derivation tree filters specified for each type of transformations.

3.4 Meaning Preserving Transformations

In SemTAG, semantic representations aim to capture the truth conditions of a sentence not their pragmatic or informational content. As a result, some sentences with different syntax share the same semantics. For instance, all sentences in (2b) share the semantics in (2a).

(2) a. L0:proper_q(C HR HS) L1:named(C tammy)
L1:indiv(C f sg) qeq(HR L1) L3:love(EL TX C) L3:event(EL pst indet ind) L4:proper_q(TX

HRX HSX) L5:named(TX tex) L5:indiv(TX m sg) qeq(HRX L5)

b. *Tex loves Tammy, It is Tex who loves Tammy, It is Tammy whom Tex loves, Tammy is loved by Tex, It is Tammy who is loved by Tex, It is by Tex that Tammy is loved, etc.*

The syntactic and pragmatic differences between these semantically identical sentences is captured by their derivation trees and in particular, by the tree properties labelling the nodes of these derivation trees. More generally, Active/Passive sentence pairs, canonical/cleft (e.g., *Tex loves Tammy / It is Tex who loves Tammy* and Canonical/Inverted Subject variations (e.g. *C'est Tex que Tammy adore / C'est Tex qu'adore Tammy* may lead to derivation trees of identical structure but distinct tree properties. In such cases, the transformationally related sentence pairs can therefore be captured using the first type of derivation filter i.e., filters which related derivation trees with identical structure but distinct tree properties. Here, we focus on the Active/Passive variation.

The differences between an active voice sentence and its passive counterpart include lexical, morphological and syntactic differences. Thus for instance, (3a) differs from (3b) in that the verb agrees with the proper name *Tammy* rather than the pronoun *il*; the clitic is in the oblique case (*lui*) rather that the nominative (*il*); the subject NP *Il* has become a PP headed by the preposition *par*; the passive auxiliary *être* and the preposition *par* have been added to support the passive voice construction.

(3) a. Il regarde Tammy (*He watches Tammy*)
b. Tammy est regardée par lui
  (*Tammy is watched by him*)

In (Siddharthan, 2010), these variations are handled by complex node deletion, lexical substitution, insertion, and node ordering rules. By contrast, to identify `Active / Passive` variations, we search for pairs of derivation trees that are related by an Active/Passive derivation tree filter namely, a filter that relates two trees which are identical up to a set of tree properties labelling a single node pair. We specify as many Active/Passive tree property patters as there are possible variations in argument realisations. For instance, for a transitive verb, some of the defined tree property patterns are as follows:

Active/Passive Tree Property Patterns

$\{Active, CanSubj, CanObj\}$
$\leftrightarrow \{Passive, CanSubj, CanAgent\}$
$\{Active, CliticSubj, CanObj\}$
$\leftrightarrow \{Passive, CanSubj, CanAgent\}$
$\{Active, WhSubj, CanObj\}$
$\leftrightarrow \{Passive, InvertedSubj, WhAgent\}$
$\{Active, RelSubj, CanObj\}$
$\leftrightarrow \{Passive, CanSubj, RelAgent\}$
$\{Active, CleftSubj, CanObj\}$
$\leftrightarrow \{Passive, CanSubj, CleftAgent\}$

In sum, in our approach, the possible differences in morphological agreement between active and passive sentences are accounted for by the grammar; differences in argument realisation (Object/Subject, Subject/Agent) are handled by the tree filters; and lexical differences due to additional function words fall out of the FB-LTAG coanchoring mechanism.

As should be clear from the derivation tree below, our approach supports transformations at any level of embedding. For instance, it permits identifying the pair *Tammy sait que Tex a fait la tarte / Tammy sait que la tarte a été faite par Tex (Tammy knows that Tex has baked the pie / Tammy knows that the pie has been baked by Tex)*.

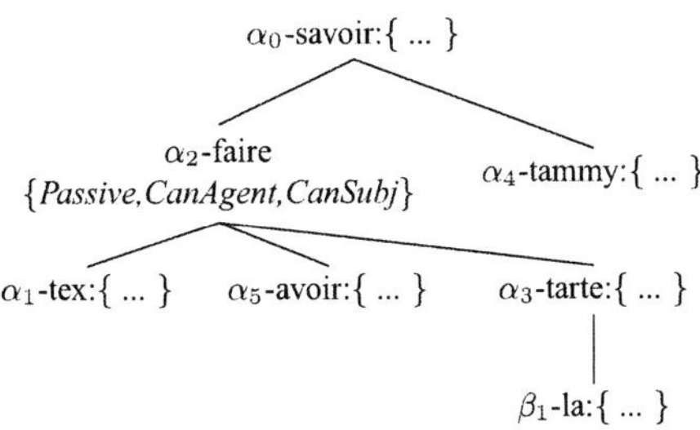

It also supports a fine grained control of the Active/passive variants allowing both for cases with multiple variants (4a) and for transitive configurations with no passive counterpart (4b,d).

(4) a. C'est la tatou qu'il adore
   C'est par lui que la tatou est adorée
   C'est lui par qui la tatou est adorée
   It is the tatoo that he loves / It is the tatoo that is loved by him

   b. Tex veut faire une tarte
   ** Une tarte veut être faite par Tex
   *Tex wants to bake a pie / ** A pie wants to be baked by Tex*

   c. Tex semble faire une tarte
   Une tarte semble être faite par Tex
   Tex seems to bake a pie / A pie seems to be baked by Tex

   d. Tex mesure 1.80m
   ** 1.80m est mesuré par Tex
   *Tex measures 1.80m ** 1.80m is measured by Tex*

(4a) is accounted for by specifying a tree filter including the tree property mapping *CleftSubject* $\leftrightarrow$ *CleftAgent* where *CleftAgent* subsumes the two types of clefts illustrated in (4a).

The lack of passive in (4b) and (4d) is accounted for by the grammar: since (4b) does not licence a passive, the starred sentence will not be generated. Similarly, because the verb *mesurer / to be X tall* is not passivable, the starred sentence in (4d) will not be produced.

3.5   Meaning Altering Transformations

When the content of two sentences differs, in particular, when a content word is deleted or added, the derivation trees of these sentences may have a different structure. In those cases, we use filters that relate derivation trees with distinct tree structures namely, filters (b), (c), (d) and (e) in Figure 4.

NP/Pronoun   To handle the NP/Pronoun, we use the filter sketched in Figure (4b) which relates derivation trees that are identical up to an NP subtree replaced by a node labelled with a pronoun. In this way the difference between the derivation tree of *le tatou* (two nodes) and *qui* (one node) does not prevent the identification of sentence pairs such as (5a).

(5) a. Le tatou chante
   Il chante   (*Personal pronoun*)
   The tatoo sings/He sings

   b. Quel tatou chante ?
   Qui chante ?   (*WH-Personal Pronoun*)
   Which tatoo sings?/Who sings?

NP/Wh-NP   For wh-questions, the main difficulty is to account for variations such as (6) below where a complex NP with several modifiers can map to a Wh-NP with different numbers of modifiers. To capture these various cases, we use two tree filters. The first filter is similar to filter

(b) in Figure 4 and matches NP/WH-Pronoun sentences (e.g., 6a-b where the NP *Le grand tatou avec un chapeau qui dort sous le palmier* maps to a WH-Pronoun *qui*). The second tree filter is sketched in Figure (4e). It matches NP/Wh-NP sentences (e.g., 6a-c/f) where an NP matches to a WH-NP headed by a WH-Determiner, the head noun and any number of modifiers.

(6) a. Le grand tatou avec un chapeau qui dort sous le palmier ronfle.
   Qui ronfle ? Quel tatou ronfle ? Quel grand tatou ronfle? Quel tatou avec un chapeau ronfle ? Quel tatou qui dort sous un palmier ronfle ? etc.
   The big tatoo with a hat who sleeps under the palmtree snores/ Who snores? Which tatoo snores? Which tatoo with a hat snores? Which tatoo who sleeps snores? etc.

Yes-No Question. In French, yes/no questions can be formed in several ways:

(7) a. Le tatou chante
   Le tatou chante t'il? (*Inverted t'il*)
   Est ce que le tatou chante ? (*est ce que*)
   Le tatou chante? (*Intonation*)
   Le tatou chante n'est ce pas? (*n'est ce pas (isn't it)*)
   The tatoo sings / Does the tatoo sing? The tatoo sings? The tatoo sings doesn't it?

   b. Vous chantez
   Chantez vous? (*Inverted Subject*)
   You sing/Do you sing?

For cases such as (7b), we require the derivation trees to be identical up to the tree property mapping *CliticSubject* ↔ *InvertedCliticSubject*. For cases such as (7a) on the other hand, we use the filter sketched in Figure (4c) that is, a filter which requires that the derivation trees be identical up to a single additional node licenced by a question phase (i.e., *t'il, est ce que, n'est ce pas* or a question mark).

4   Evaluation

We carried out an experiment designed to assess the genericity, the correctness, the coverage and the recall of the approach. In what follows, we describe the grammar and lexicon used in that experiment; the sentence set used for testing; and the results obtained.

Grammar and Lexicons. The *SemTAG* grammar used contains around 1300 elementary trees and covers auxiliaries, copula, raising and small clause constructions, relative clauses, infinitives, gerunds, passives, adjuncts, wh-clefts, PRO constructions, imperatives and 15 distinct subcategorisation frames. The syntactic and morphosyntactic lexicons used for generating were tailored to cover basic vocabulary as defined by the lexicon used in *Tex's French Grammar*. The syntactic lexicon contains 690 lemmas and the morphological lexicon 5294 forms.

Generated Sentences. To populate the generation bank, we input *GraDe* with 52 semantic formulae corresponding to various syntactic and semantic configurations and their interactions[4]: including all types of realisations for verb arguments (cleft, pronominalisation, relative, question arguments); Intransitive, Transitive and ditransitive verbs; Control, raising and embedding verbs; Nouns, common nouns, personal strong and weak pronouns; standard and Wh- determiners.

From these 52 semantic formulae, *GraDe* produced 5748 sentences which we stored in a database together with their full semantics and their derivation tree.

Results. Table 1 summarises the results of our experiment. It indicates the number of source sentences manually selected so as to test different syntactic configurations for each type of transformation considered (S), the number of transformations found for these source sentences (T), the number of tree filters used for each type of transformation (TF) and the precision obtained (ratio of correct transformations).

The low number of tree filters relative to the number of syntactic configurations explored indicates a good level of genericity: with few filters, a transformation can be captured in many distinct syntactic contexts. For instance, for the Active/passive transformation, 8 filters suffice to capture 43 distinct syntactic configurations.

As expected in an approach where the filters are defined manually, precision is high indicating that the filters are accurate. The generated pairs marked as incorrect by the annotator are all cases where the transformed sentence was ungrammatical; in other words, the filters were accurate.

---

[4]We restrict the tense of the verb of the main clause to present and indicative mode

	S	T	TF	Precision
Active/passive	43	38	8	88.5
Pronominalisation	36	33	7	73
Wh-Questions	25	20	7	88
YN-Questions	24	20	5	90.5

Table 1: Source Sentences (S), Transformations of Source Sentences (T), Number of Filters (F) and Precision (Ratio of correct transformations)

Finally, the relatively low number of transformations found relative to the number of source sentences (e.g., 38 transforms for 43 source sentences in the Active/passive case) is mainly due to transformed sentences that are missing from the generation bank either because the corresponding input semantics is missing or because of gaps in the grammar or the lexicon. However, for few cases missing filters were identified as well.

5 Conclusion

We presented an approach which is, to the best of our knowledge, the first approach for generating grammar exercices covering a wide range of structure changing transformations. And we argued that FB-LTAG derivation trees naturally support the identification of sentences that are related by a syntactic transformation.

In current work, we are pursuing two main directions. First, we are investigating how to account for more complex transformations such as *Tom ate because of his hunger* and *His hunger caused Tom to eat*. In particular, we plan to explore in how far the approach developed on dependency trees by (Siddharthan, 2010) can be ported to Sem-TAG derivation trees. Second, drawing on (Chandrasekar and Srinivas, 1997)'s work, we are investigating how to develop an algorithm that can induce derivation tree filters from FB-LTAG derivation trees.

Acknowledgments

The research presented in this paper was partially supported by the European Fund for Regional Development within the framework of the INTER-REG IV A Allegro Project. We would also like to thank German Kruszewski and Elise Fetet for their help in developing and annotating the test data.

References

I. Aldabe, M. Lopez de Lacalle, M. Maritxalar, E. Martinez, and L. Uria. 2006. Arikiturri: an automatic question generator based on corpora and nlp techniques. In *Proceedings of the 8th international conference on Intelligent Tutoring Systems*, ITS'06, pages 584–594, Berlin, Heidelberg. Springer-Verlag.

R. Chandrasekar and B. Srinivas. 1997. Automatic induction of rules for text simplification. *Knowledge-Based Systems*, pages 183–190.

C. Chen, H. Liou, and J. Chang. 2006. Fast: an automatic generation system for grammar tests. In *Proceedings of the COLING/ACL on Interactive presentation sessions*, pages 1–4, Stroudsburg, PA, USA.

N. Chomsky. 1957. *Syntactic Structures*. Mouton.

T. Cohn and M. Lapata. 2009. Sentence compression as tree transduction. *Journal of Artificial Intelligence Research*, 34:637–674.

C. Gardent and L. Kallmeyer. 2003. Semantic construction in FTAG. In *10th EACL*, Budapest, Hungary.

C. Gardent and G. Kruszewski. 2012. Generation for grammar engineering. In *INLG 2012, The seventh International Natural Language Generation Conference*, Starved Rock, Illinois, USA.

Z.S. Harris. 1957. Co-occurrence and transformation in linguistic structure. *Language*, 33(3):283–340.

L. Perez-Beltrachini, C. Gardent, and G. Kruszewski. 2012. Generating Grammar Exercises. In *NAACL-HLT 7th Workshop on Innovative Use of NLP for Building Educational Applications*, Montreal, Canada.

P. Piwek and K. E. Boyer. 2012. Varieties of question generation: introduction to this special issue. *Dialogue and Discourse, Special Issue on Question Generation*.

A. Siddharthan. 2010. Complex lexico-syntactic reformulation of sentences using typed dependency representations. In *Proceedings of the 6th International Natural Language Generation Conference*, INLG '10, pages 125–133, Stroudsburg, PA, USA.

A. Siddharthan. 2011. Text simplification using typed dependencies: a comparison of the robustness of different generation strategies. In *Proceedings of the 13th European Workshop on Natural Language Generation*, ENLG '11, pages 2–11, Stroudsburg, PA, USA.

K. Vijay-Shanker and AK Joshi. 1988. Feature Structures Based Tree Adjoining Grammars. *Proceedings of the 12th conference on Computational linguistics*.

X. Yao, G. Bouma, and Y. Zhang. 2012. Semantics-based question generation and implementation. *Dialogue and Discourse, Special Issue on Question Generation*.

PLCFRS Parsing Revisited: Restricting the Fan-Out to Two

Wolfgang Maier, **Miriam Kaeshammer** and **Laura Kallmeyer**
Institut für Sprache und Information
University of Düsseldorf
Universitätsstr. 1, 40225 Düsseldorf, Germany
{maierwo,kaeshammer,kallmeyer}@phil.hhu.de

Abstract

Linear Context-Free Rewriting System (LCFRS) is an extension of Context-Free Grammar (CFG) in which a non-terminal can dominate more than a single continuous span of terminals. Probabilistic LCFRS have recently successfully been used for the direct data-driven parsing of discontinuous structures. In this paper we present a parser for binary PLCFRS of fan-out two, together with a novel monotonous estimate for A* parsing, with which we conduct experiments on modified versions of the German NeGra treebank and the Discontinuous Penn Treebank in which all trees have block degree two. The experiments show that compared to previous work, our approach provides an enormous speed-up while delivering an output of comparable richness.

1 Introduction

In many constituency treebanks, the syntactic annotation takes the form of Context-Free Grammar (CFG) derivation trees, i.e., of trees with no crossing branches. Discontinuous structures (Huck and Ojeda, 1987) cannot be modeled with CFG and are therefore handled by an additional mechanism in such an annotation. In the Penn Treebank (PTB) (Marcus et al., 1993), for instance, a combination of trace nodes and co-indexation labels is used in order to establish implicit edges. In other treebanks, e.g., the German NeGra (Skut et al., 1997) and TIGER (Brants et al., 2002) treebanks, crossing branches are allowed.[1] This way, all parts of a discontinuous constituent can

---

[1]The annotation differences between TIGER and NeGra are minor and can be neglected for the purpose of this work.

be grouped under a single node. There is no fundamental difference between both representations: PTB-style annotation can be converted into a NeGra/TIGER-style annotation. This has been done in the Discontinuous Penn Treebank (DPTB) (Evang and Kallmeyer, 2011).

For data-driven parsing with Probabilistic CFG (PCFG), the annotation information concerning discontinuities must be discarded, because it exceeds the expressivity of CFG. For NeGra, there exist two methods, namely (i) attaching non-head daughters of discontinuous constituents to higher positions in the tree, such that the crossing branches disappear (the NeGra distribution contains a version of the treebank in which this transformation is readily carried out), or (ii) introducing an additional non-terminal node for each continuous part of a discontinuous constituent (Boyd, 2007). As an example, figure 1 shows the annotation of (1) before and after both transformations.

(1)   Der CD wird bald ein Buch folgen
      The CD will soon a   book follow
      "Soon, the CD will be followed by a book."

For PCFG parsing with the PTB, trace nodes and co-indexation are simply discarded. With either of these transformations, discontinuities are lost and cannot be restored from the parser output. However, the fact that about 25%, resp. 20% of all sentences in NeGra, resp. the PTB contain discontinuities (Maier and Lichte, 2011; Evang and Kallmeyer, 2011) shows that this is an undesirable situation and that these structures warrant a proper treatment.

Linear Context-Free Rewriting System (LCFRS), an extension of CFG, has been established as an appropriate candidate for modeling

Proceedings of the 11th International Workshop on Tree Adjoining Grammars and Related Formalisms (TAG+11), pages 126–134,
Paris, September 2012.

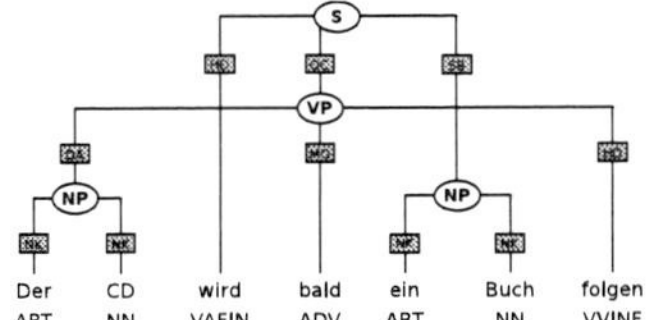

Crossing branches, original NeGra tree

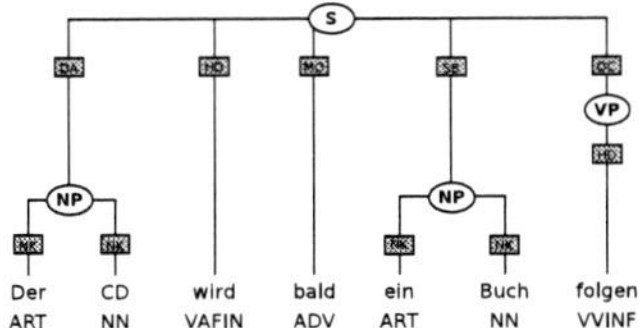

Resolved crossing branches, NeGra distribution

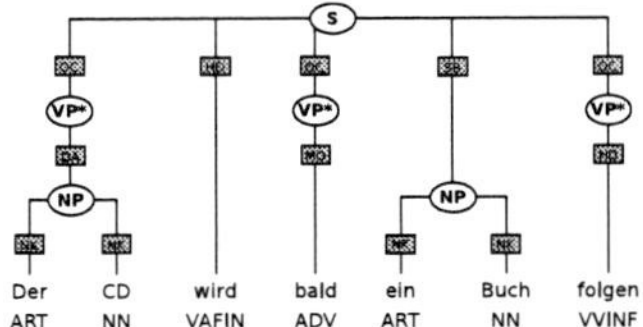

Resolved crossing branches, Boyd (2007)

Figure 1: Crossing branches removal for NeGra. Note that the argument structure is changed as a result of the removal of the crossing branches.

discontinuities (Maier and Lichte, 2011). In LCFRS, a single non-terminal can span $k \geq 1$ continuous blocks of a string. A CFG is simply a special case of an LCFRS in which $k = 1$. k is called the *fan-out* of the non-terminal, and a corresponding constituent is said to have *block degree k*. It has been shown that probabilistic data-driven parsing on the basis of Probabilistic LCFRS (PLCFRS) is feasible and gives good results while preserving discontinuity information (Kallmeyer and Maier, 2010; Maier, 2010; van Cranenburgh et al., 2011; Evang and Kallmeyer, 2011; van Cranenburgh, 2012; Maier, 2012).

The major problem of PLCFRS parsing is its high computational complexity. A binarized PCFG can be parsed in $\mathcal{O}(n^3)$, parsing a binarized LCFRS takes $\mathcal{O}(n^{3k})$ (Seki et al., 1991), where k is the fan-out of the grammar (the maximal fan-out of any of its non-terminals). The parsers from the literature allow for an unbounded k. This leads to parsing times beyond practically acceptable values for sentences longer than 25 to 30 words.

In this paper, our goal is to show that by re-

stricting the block degree, resp. the fan-out to two, (i) one can express almost all the information contained in the discontinuous treebank annotation of NeGra and the DPTB, and (ii) one can obtain a parser which is faster by an order of magnitude.

We proceed as follows. In section 2, we present definitions of PLCFRS, as well as of trees and the notion of block degree. In section 3, we describe how to bring the trees of both the DPTB and NeGra to block degree two. Unlike the transformations used for PCFG parsing, our transformations preserve the discontinuity information in almost all cases. Section 4 introduces PLCFRS as a formalism for data-driven parsing. In section 5, we present a data-driven parser for binary PLCFRS of fan-out two which uses an efficient case-by-case strategy, together with a new outside estimate for A* parsing. Section 6 contains experiments on the transformed NeGra as well as on the Discontinuous Penn Treebank. We use both the new parser and `rparse`, the parser used in our previous work (Kallmeyer and Maier, 2010). Our experiments show that given equal conditions, we achieve an enormous speed-up while obtaining an output of a comparable richness. Finally, section 7 concludes the article.

2 Definitions

We notate LCFRS with the syntax of Simple Range Concatenation Grammars (SRCG) (Boullier, 1998), a formalism equivalent to LCFRS.

An LCFRS (Vijay-Shanker et al., 1987) is a tuple $G = (N, T, V, P, S)$ where a) N is a finite set of non-terminals with a function dim: $N \rightarrow \mathbb{N}$ determining the *fan-out* of each $A \in N$; b) T and V are disjoint finite sets of terminals and variables; c) $S \in N$ is the start symbol with $dim(S) = 1$; d) P is a finite set of rewriting rules

$$A(\alpha_1, \ldots, \alpha_{dim(A)}) \rightarrow A_1(X_1^{(1)}, \ldots, X_{dim(A_1)}^{(1)})$$
$$\cdots A_m(X_1^{(m)}, \ldots, X_{dim(A_m)}^{(m)})$$

where $A, A_1, \ldots, A_m \in N$, $X_j^{(i)} \in V$ for $1 \leq i \leq m, 1 \leq j \leq dim(A_i)$ and $\alpha_i \in (T \cup V)^*$ for $1 \leq i \leq dim(A)$, for a *rank $m \geq 0$*. For all $r \in P$, every variable X occurring in r occurs exactly once in the left-hand side (LHS) and exactly once in the right-hand side (RHS). The *rank* of G is the maximal rank of any of its rules, its *fan-out* is the maximal fan-out of any of its non-terminals. If G has rank u and fan-out v, then G is an (u, v)-LCFRS.

$$A(ab, cd) \rightarrow \varepsilon \qquad (\langle ab, cd \rangle \text{ in yield of } A)$$
$$A(aXb, cYd) \rightarrow A(X, Y) \qquad (\text{if } \langle X, Y \rangle \text{ in yield of } A,$$
$$\text{then also } \langle aXb, cYd \rangle \text{ in yield of } A)$$
$$S(XY) \rightarrow A(X, Y) \qquad (\text{if } \langle X, Y \rangle \text{ in yield of } A,$$
$$\text{then } \langle XY \rangle \text{ in yield of } S)$$
$$L = \{a^n b^n c^n d^n \mid n > 0\}$$

Figure 2: Sample LCFRS

A rewriting rule describes how to compute the yield of the LHS non-terminal from the yields of the RHS non-terminals. The yield of S is the language of the grammar. See figure 2 for a sample LCFRS.

A *probabilistic LCFRS* (PLCFRS) is a tuple $\langle N, T, V, P, S, p \rangle$ such that $\langle N, T, V, P, S \rangle$ is a LCFRS and $p : P \rightarrow [0..1]$ a function such that for all $A \in N$: $\Sigma_{A(\vec{x}) \rightarrow \vec{\Phi} \in P} p(A(\vec{x}) \rightarrow \vec{\Phi}) = 1$.

A *tree* over a sentence $w = w_1 \cdots w_n$, $n \geq 1$, is a labeled ordered directed graph $\mathcal{D} = (V, E, r)$ with V a set of nodes, $E : V \times V$ a set of edges and $r \in V$ a single dedicated root node, where every $v \in V \setminus \{r\}$ has exactly one incoming edge and r has no incoming edges. All $v_l \in V$ with no outgoing edges are called *leaves* or *terminals*, and V_l is the set of all leaves or terminals. The *labeling* of $\mathcal{D}$ is given by a function $\Lambda : V \rightarrow N \cup \{1, \ldots, n\}$, where N a set of non-terminal labels, for all $v_i \in V_l$, $1 \leq i \leq n$, $\Lambda(v_i) = i$, and for all $v \in V \setminus V_l$, $\Lambda(v) \in N$. The function π gives the *yield* of the node; more precisely, for all $v \in V$, $\pi(v) = \{i \in \Lambda(u) \mid u \in V \text{ is a leaf and there is a } \langle v, u \rangle \in E^*\}$. The *ordering* of $\mathcal{D}$ is given by the relation $\prec$ which is such that for all v_1, v_2, $v_1 \prec v_2$ iff $min(\pi(v_1)) \leq min(\pi(v_2))$.

The yield *blocks* of v are given by a partition of $\pi(v)$ into maximal continuous sequences of integers. The *block degree* of v is the number of blocks of v, its *gap degree* is its block degree minus one. A gap of v is a tuple (i, k) such that $i \in \pi(v)$, $k + 1 \in \pi(v)$ and $j \notin \pi(v)$ for $i + 1 \leq j \leq k$.

3 Treebanks with Block-Degree Two

3.1 Removing Spurious Gaps

In the DPTB as used by Evang and Kallmeyer (2011),[2] the maximal block degree is three. Mo-

tivated by the suspicion (Evang, p.c.) that the cases of block degree three are spurious, i.e., caused only by punctuation, we move all punctuation terminals to the least common ancestor of their resp. left and right non-punctuation terminal neighbors. This is essentially the algorithm of Levy (2005), pp. 163. It leaves us with only 11 sentences containing nodes with more than one (non-spurious) gap. For our experiments, we remove those sentences; an investigation of their properties is left for future work.

In the NeGra annotation, punctuation and a very small number of other elements such as parts of ungrammatical sentences are not included in the annotation, i.e., the corresponding nodes are attached at the root node. They cause a very high, linguistically meaningless block degree of 40. In order to avoid gaps which contain nothing but those elements, we attach them lower.[3] Since aside from (punctuation) terminals, non-terminals may be concerned, we extend Levy's strategy as follows. Let n be a node originally attached to the root node, furthermore let $n_{l_1}, \ldots, n_{l_k}, n_{r_1}, \ldots, n_{r_m}, k, m \geq 0$, be all left, resp. right siblings of n for which it holds that both $\mathcal{S}_l = \{min(\pi(n))\} \cup (\bigcup_{i=1}^{k} \pi(n_{l_i}))$ and $\mathcal{S}_r = \{max(\pi(n))\} \cup (\bigcup_{j=1}^{m} \pi(n_{r_j}))$ are continuous sequences of integers. We select as an attachment target the least common ancestor node of the terminals t_l, t_r with $\pi(t_l) = \{(min(\mathcal{S}_l) - 1)\}$ and $\pi(t_r) = \{(max(\mathcal{S}_r) + 1)\}$. If t_r or t_l do not exist, we do not move n. This algorithm improves over the strategy from Maier (2012), pp. 189, in the sense that the latter does not remove all spurious gaps. We call the new strategy T_1.

3.2 Block Degree Two for NeGra

For NeGra, we introduce a novel series of linguistically motivated transformations which ensures that all resulting trees have block degree two. The block degrees of the treebank after each transformation are listed in table 1.

Verbs There is no consensus about the analysis of German verb phrases (VPs) and auxiliaries in particular, cf. Bouma and van Noord (1998) for a discussion. In the interest of a small block degree of the trees in NeGra, we change the VP anno-

---

[2]Thanks to Kilian Evang for providing us with his original data.

[3]This is a necessary preprocessing step for PCFG parsing as well since those elements are equally unattached in the version of NeGra with resolved crossing branches.

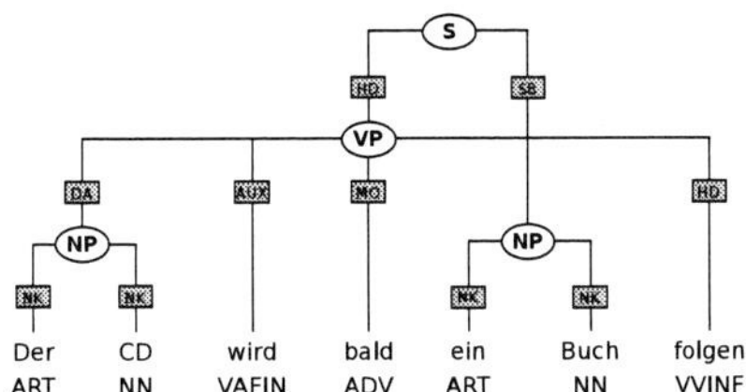

Figure 3: Verb transformation on original tree from fig. 1

Blocks	Orig.	T_1	T_2	T_3	T_4
1	7,704	14,927	10,898	10,944	10,944
2	5,275	4,988	9,333	9,361	9,658
3	3,585	679	370	297	-
4	1,917	8	1	-	-
5	998	-	-	-	-
≥ 6	1123	-	-	-	-

Table 1: Number of sentences in NeGra with a certain block degree before and after transformations

tation principles and group auxiliary verbs under the same VP as the corresponding full verb. We furthermore insert a VP for all finite verbs and their dependents except the subject (identified by the labels in the treebank), since in the original NeGra annotation, only non-finite verbs project to a VP. See figure 3 for an example.

The positions of the newly introduced VPs influences the attachment points for the punctuation attachment. As the second transformation T_2 we therefore first perform the verb transformation we just described, followed by T_1.

Parentheticals Parenthetical sentences such as (2) are annotated as embedding the enclosing sentence and therefore lead to an additional gap in the latter.

(2) ..., so argumentierten die Richter, ...
      ..., as argued   the judges, ...
      "..., the judges argued, ..."

We structurally identify them (not lexically) and attach them as low as necessary such that they do not create a gap. This is motivated by the annotation of TüBa-D/Z (Telljohann et al., 2012), another German treebank, where parenthetical sentences are left unattached. T_3 consists of T_2, followed by the parenthetical transformation.

Remainder Eventually, T_4 consists of T_3 followed by a transformation inspired by the standard crossing branches resolution for NeGra. We re-attach material to higher positions iff it causes a block degree higher than two. Thereby, we first consider sentential modifiers, then modifiers in general and only finally constituents of any sort. T_4 only treats a tiny fraction of all sentences; however, it does change structures for which a block degree higher than two can be linguistically justified, such as di-transitive adjectives and verbs in particular word order configurations. A more

careful investigation of T_4 is left for future work.

4 PLCFRS for Data-Driven Parsing

LCFRSs can be extracted directly from treebanks with a direct annotation of discontinuities (Maier and Søgaard, 2008). The difference between treebank PLCFRS and PCFG extraction is, intuitively, that in PLCFRS variables are used to describe the blocks which are dominated by a nonterminal. In other words, an argument boundary in a production corresponds to a block boundary of the corresponding non-terminal in the tree, and the fan-out of an extracted rule is equal to the block degree of the treebank non-terminal corresponding to the rule's LHS non-terminal. Consider again the original tree from figure 1. From the discontinuous VP *Der CD ... bald ... folgen* we extract the rule $VP(X_1, X_2, X_3) \rightarrow NP(X_1) ADV(X_2) VVINF(X_3)$. The LHS nonterminal has fan-out three due to the fact that the VP has block degree three.

When applied to a treebank of block degree two, the extraction algorithm yields grammars of fan-out two. In order to obtain a $(2, 2)$-PLCFRS, i.e., for rank reduction, we use the *optimal binarization* algorithm of Kallmeyer (2010), p. 150, which yields a minimal fan-out, resp. number of variables per binarized rule. As in PCFG parsing, we use markovization (Kallmeyer and Maier, 2010). We use standard Maximum Likelihood estimation. See section 6 for further experimental details.

5 A CYK Parser for $(2, 2)$-PLCFRS

5.1 The Parser

Just as Kallmeyer and Maier (2010), we use a probabilistic CYK parser (Seki et al., 1991). The general CYK deduction system is shown in figure 4. Its items have the form $[A, \vec{\rho}]$, with $A \in N$ and

Scan: $$\frac{}{0 : [A, \langle\langle i, i+1\rangle\rangle]} \quad A \text{ POS tag of } w_{i+1}$$

Unary: $$\frac{in : [B, \vec{\rho}]}{in + |\log(p)| : [A, \vec{\rho}]} \quad p : A(\vec{\rho}) \to B(\vec{\rho}) \in P$$

Binary: $$\frac{in_B : [B, \vec{\rho_B}], in_C : [C, \vec{\rho_C}]}{in_B + in_C + |\log(p)| : [A, \vec{\rho_A}]}$$

where $p : A(\vec{\rho_A}) \to B(\vec{\rho_B})C(\vec{\rho_C})$ is an instantiated rule.

Goal: $[S, \langle\langle 0, n\rangle\rangle]$

Figure 4: Weighted CYK deduction system for LCFRS

ID	Type	G30T	E30
1	A(X) → B(X)	49	235
2	A(X,Y) → B(X,Y)	1	4
3	A(XY) → B(X) C(Y)	14,430	11,777
4	A(X,Y) → B(X) C(Y)	1,644	312
5	A(XYZ) → B(X,Z) C(Y)	621	205
6	A(X,YZ) → B(X,Y) C(Z)	100	45
7	A(X,YZ) → B(X,Z) C(Y)	142	94
8	A(XY,Z) → B(X,Z) C(Y)	172	10
9	A(XY,Z) → B(X) C(Y,Z)	582	108
10	A(XY,ZU) → B(X,Z) C(Y,U)	7	0
11	A(XY,ZU) → B(X,U) C(Y,Z)	0	0
12	A(X,YZU) → B(X,Z) C(Y,U)	12	3
13	A(XYZ,U) → B(X,Z) C(Y,U)	12	2
14	A(XYZU) → B(X,Z) C(Y,U)	13	6

Figure 5: LCFRS rule types and numbers of occurrence in binarized grammars (cf. section 6)

$\vec{\rho}$ a vector of ranges characterizing all components of the span of A. We specify a simpler, specialized deduction system which takes advantage of the fact that due to our maximum fan-out of two, we can rely on only encountering rules of certain forms. The second column of figure 5 schematically displays all 14 different rule types the parser must handle.

In the specialized deduction system, *unary items* now take the form $[A, i, j]$ and *binary items* take the form $[A, i, j, k, l]$, where $A \in N$ and i, j, resp. k, l are spans dominated by A with $0 \leq i < j < k < l \leq n$. The goal item is $[S, 0, n]$. We replace the old Unary and Binary deduction rules in figure 4 with 14 new rules, one per production type. Figure 6 shows the new scan rule and the complete rules for type 1, type 6 and type 10, which should make the basic idea clear. Note that there is no need to refer to instantiations anymore. Our case-by-case strategy is similar to the one employed by Kato et al. (2006).

As in our previous work, we specify the set

Scan: $$\frac{}{0 : [A, i, i+1]} \quad A \text{ POS tag of } w_{i+1}$$

Complete1: $$\frac{in : [B, i, j]}{in + |\log(p)| : [A, i, j]}$$

where $p : A(X) \to B(X) \in P$.

Complete6: $$\frac{in_B : [B, i, j, k, l], in_C : [C, l, u]}{in_B + in_C + |\log(p)| : [A, i, j, k, u]}$$

where $p : A(X, YZ) \to B(X, Y)C(Z) \in P$.

Complete10: $$\frac{in_B : [B, i, x, k, y], in_C : [C, x, j, y, l]}{in_B + in_C + |\log(p)| : [A, i, j, k, l]}$$

where $p : A(XY, ZU) \to B(X, Z)C(Y, U) \in P$

Figure 6: Weighted CYK deduction rules for 2-LCFRS

of parse items using the algorithm of weighted deductive parsing (WDP) (Nederhof, 2003). In WDP, one maintains a priority queue of items, sorted by the resp. Viterbi inside scores. The topmost item is always processed first. WDP guarantees optimality, i.e., that the best parse is found.

5.2 A Novel Outside Estimate

One can speed up parsing by adding to the Viterbi inside score of an item an estimate of its Viterbi outside score, in other words, an estimate of the cost of completion of the item to a complete parse. This has proven to be successful for both PCFG (Klein and Manning, 2003) and PLCFRS (Kallmeyer and Maier, 2010). As outside estimate, one uses the outside probability of a summary of the item, i.e., of an equivalence class of parse items. The difficulty for PLCFRS is to choose the summary such that optimality is maintained through the two estimate properties *admissibility* and *monotonicity* (Klein and Manning, 2003).

Here, we present the novel *LN estimate*, which is based on a summary that records only the sum of the span lengths and the length of the entire sentence. It is the first practically computable estimate which allows for maintaining optimality.

The estimate is computed offline up to a certain maximal sentence length len_{max}. We specify the estimate computation with the deduction system in figure 7.[4] The items have the form $[X, len, slen]$ with $X \in N$, $dim(X) \leq len \leq slen$. The value $in(X, l)$ for a non-terminal X and a length l, $0 \leq l \leq len_{max}$ is an estimate of

---

[4] A simpler deduction system for the estimate computation for $(2, 2)$-LCFRS would be possible as well, along the lines of the simplification of the CYK parser.

$$\text{Axiom}: \quad \frac{}{0:[S,len,len]} \quad 1 \leq len \leq len_{max}$$

$$\text{Unary}: \quad \frac{w:[X,l_X,slen]}{w+|\log(p)|:[A,l_X,slen]}$$
$$\text{where } p: X(\vec{\alpha}) \rightarrow A(\vec{\alpha}) \in P$$

$$\text{Binary-right}: \quad \frac{w:[X,l_X,slen]}{w+in(A,l_X-l_B)+|\log(p)|:[B,l_B,slen]}$$

$$\text{Binary-left}: \quad \frac{w:[X,l_X,slen]}{w+in(B,l_X-l_A)+|\log(p)|:[A,l_A,slen]}$$
$$\text{where, for both rules,}$$
$$p: X(\vec{\alpha}) \rightarrow A(\vec{\alpha_A})B(\vec{\alpha_B}) \in P.$$

Figure 7: LN estimate (span and sentence length)

$$\text{POS tags}: \quad \frac{}{0:[A,1]} \quad A \text{ a POS tag}$$

$$\text{Unary}: \quad \frac{in:[B,l]}{in+|\log(p)|:[A,l]} \quad p:A(\vec{\alpha})\rightarrow B(\vec{\alpha})\in P$$

$$\text{Binary}: \quad \frac{in_B:[B,l_B],in_C:[C,l_C]}{in_B+in_C+|\log(p)|:[A,l_B+l_C]}$$
$$\text{where either } p: A(\vec{\alpha_A}) \rightarrow B(\vec{\alpha_B})C(\vec{\alpha_C}) \in P \text{ or}$$
$$p: A(\vec{\alpha_A}) \rightarrow C(\vec{\alpha_C})B(\vec{\alpha_B}) \in P.$$

Figure 8: Inside estimate with total span length

the inside score of an X category with a span of length l. Its computation is specified in figure 8.

The outside estimate for a sentence length n and for some predicate C with a span $\vec{\rho} = \langle\langle l_1, r_1\rangle, \ldots, \langle l_{dim(C)}, r_{dim(C)}\rangle\rangle$ where $len = \Sigma_{i=1}^{dim(C)}(r_i - l_i)$ is then the minimal weight of $[C, len, n]$.

We will show in the following that the LN estimate maintains optimal search by being both admissible and monotonic. Since the weight of the outside estimate for an item is always lower or equal to the actual outside probability, given the input, the weight of an item in the agenda is always lower or equal to the log of the actual product of inside and outside probability of the constituent represented by the item. Therefore, the LN estimate is admissible. In order to prove that the estimate is also monotonic, we look at the CYK deduction rules when being augmented with the estimate. Only *Unary* and *Binary* are relevant since *Scan* does not have antecedent items. The two rules are now as follows:

$$\text{Unary}: \quad \frac{in_B+out_B:[B,\vec{\rho}]}{in_B+|\log(p)|+out_A:[A,\vec{\rho}]}$$
$$\text{where } p: A(\vec{\alpha}) \rightarrow B(\vec{\alpha}) \in P.$$

$$\text{Binary}: \quad \frac{in_B+out_B:[B,\vec{\rho_B}],in_C+out_C:[C,\vec{\rho_C}]}{in_B+in_C+|\log(p)|+out_A:[A,\vec{\rho_A}]}$$
$$\text{where } p: A(\vec{\rho_A}) \rightarrow B(\vec{\rho_B})C(\vec{\rho_C}) \text{ is an instan-}$$
tiated rule. (Here, out_A, out_B and out_C are the respective outside estimates of $[A, \vec{\rho_A}]$, $[B, \vec{\rho_B}]$ and $[C, \vec{\rho_C}]$.)

We have to show that for every rule, if this rule has an antecedent item with weight w and a consequent item with weight w', then $w \leq w'$.

We start with *Unary*. To show: $in_B + out_B \leq in_B + |\log(p)| + out_A$. Because of the *Unary* rule for computing the outside estimate and because of the unary production, we obtain that, given the outside estimate out_A of $[A, \vec{\rho}]$, the outside estimate out_B of the item $[B, \vec{\rho}]$ is at most $out_A + |\log(p)|$, i.e., $out_B \leq |\log(p)| + out_A$. $\square$

Now we consider the rule *Binary*. We treat only the relation between the weight of the C antecedent item and the consequent. The treatment of the antecedent B is symmetric. To show: $in_C + out_C \leq in_B + in_C + |\log(p)| + out_A$. Assume that l_B is the length of the components of the B item and n is the sentence length. Then, because of the *Binary-right* rule in the computation of the outside estimate and because of our instantiated rule $p: A(\vec{\rho_A}) \rightarrow B(\vec{\rho_B})C(\vec{\rho_C})$, we have that the outside estimate out_C of the C-item is at most $out_A + in(B, l_B) + |\log(p)|$. Furthermore, $in(B, l_B) \leq in_B$. Consequently $out_C \leq in_B + |\log(p)| + out_A$. $\square$

6 Experiments

We have implemented the parser within the API of *rparse* in order to provide equal conditions. The new parser will be made available under GNU GPL.[5] For all experiments, we have used the newest Oracle Java 7, running on Debian Linux on a series of Intel Xeon X5690 nodes at 3.46GHz.

6.1 Data and Experimental Setup

We perform experiments with both the English DPTB and the German NeGra. The names of the data sets will have the prefixes E (for the DPTB)

---

[5]See `http://www.phil.hhu.de/rparse` for more information.

and G (for NeGra). We create two versions of Ne-Gra in which we limit the sentence lengths to 30 and 40 words respectively and investigate the treebank after T_4 (data set name suffix T) (only for 30 words) and after T_1 (data set name suffix O) (for 30 and 40 words). The names of the data sets are consequently: G30O (for the 30-word data set after T_1) and G30T, resp. G40T (for the 30- and 40-word data sets after T_4). As for the DPTB, we create one data set E30 with a sentence length limit of 30. In E30, we reattach punctuation tokens as described in section 3.1. For training, resp. testing we use the first 90%, resp. the last 10% of each data set. The parser is provided with gold POS tags.

We extract PLCFRSs from our data sets as described before and binarize them using the optimal binarization algorithm from Kallmeyer (2010). For E30 we cannot resort to deterministic left-to-right binarization as done by Evang and Kallmeyer, since it results in a binarized grammar of fan-out three. Note that in general, given an unbinarized LCFRS production with a fan-out of two, finding a binarization which does not increase the fan-out cannot be guaranteed if its RHS has a length > 3 (Gómez-Rodríguez et al., 2010; Rambow and Satta, 1999). However, with the optimal algorithm, we have not observed an increased fan-out in practice, neither for NeGra, nor for the DPTB. Figure 5 shows the occurrence counts of the 14 different production types in the binarized grammars of G30T and E30. For the choice of the remaining parsing parameters, we exploit the results of Maier (2012): We do not use unary rules during binarization and markovize the binarized grammars with $v = 1, h = 2$.

6.2 Parsing Speed

We first investigate the speed of the new parser on both NeGra and the DPTB.

NeGra The upper graph in figure 9 shows the average parsing times of both parsers on G40T. The speed-up provided by the case-by-case strategy of the new parser is enormous. The average parsing time for a sentence of length 40 (a common upper length limit in PCFG parsing literature, see, e.g., Klein and Manning (2003)) drops from several hours with `rparse` to slightly under 3 minutes with the new parser. Note that the parsing complexity is not changed. The speed gain

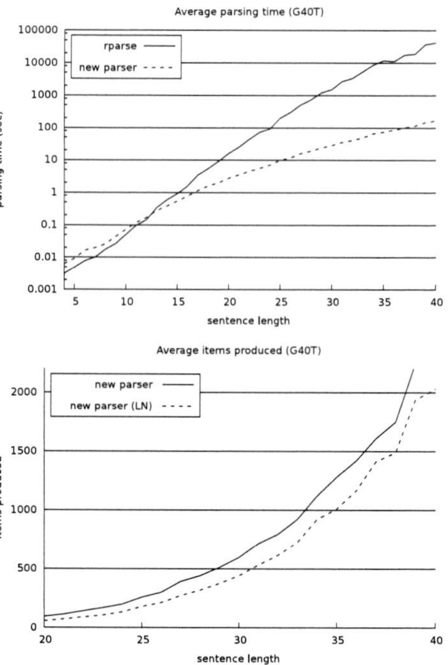

Figure 9: Average parsing times and items for G40T

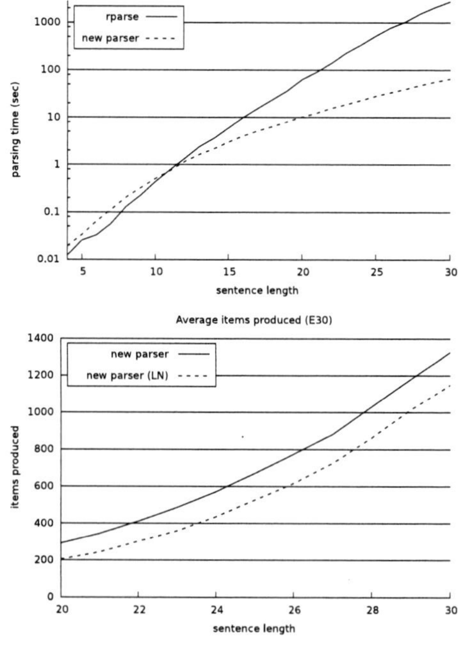

Figure 10: Average parsing times and items for E30

	Precision	Recall	F_1
G30O	74.6	74.5	74.5
G30T	71.8	71.7	71.8
G30O-S	73.6	73.8	73.7
G30T-V	73.5	73.6	73.5

Table 2: Parsing results for NeGra

can be attributed to the fact that it is much cheaper to perform the simple integer comparisons of the specialized *Complete* rules (fig. 6) than to provide a comparison operation for range vectors of an arbitrary length (Maier, 2012, p. 176). This becomes more clear when regarding the pseudo-code formulation of the similar case-by-case strategy of Kato et al. (2006).

As for the LN estimate, we can observe that it effectively reduces the number of items which are produced (cf. the lower graph in fig. 9). However, it has less effect than the estimates presented in previous work (Kallmeyer and Maier, 2010). This indicates that the context summary consisting of the sum of the span lengths and the total sentence length provides too few information. For $(2, 2)$-LCFRS, unlike for full LCFRS, the full SX estimate from Kallmeyer and Maier should be computable and should deliver better results. We postpone this to future work.

DPTB The upper graph in figure 10 shows the average parsing times for both parsers on E30. We can see that the speed gain with the new parser is similar to the one we obtain on NeGra. The behavior of the LN estimate is also similar to its behavior in the NeGra experiments (cf. the lower graph in fig. 10).

6.3 Output Quality

For the qualitative evaluation of the parser output, we use the extended `evalb` measure for PLCFRS (Maier, 2010). We report labeled precision, recall and F_1.

NeGra In order to investigate how the transformed treebank behaves compared to the unmodified treebank, we run `rparse` on G30O and the new parser on G30T. Intuitively, one might expect that the less flat annotation of the transformed treebank leads to better results (Rehbein and van Genabith, 2007), however, as can be seen in table 2, the results on G30T are worse. We can identify

two major reasons for this: The status of subjects and different types of verb phrases.

Subjects can be identified structurally in the transformed treebank, because they are attached below S while other arguments are part of the newly introduced VPs. In the original treebank, when disregarding grammatical functions (such as we do), subject NPs are indistinguishable from other NPs. In other words, with the transformed treebank, the parser must cope with the additional tasks of identifying subjects. We therefore produce a minimally modified version of G30O, G30O-S, in which subjects can be identified by node labels. In the original annotation, the edge label SB designates subjects. We rename all NPs with an SB edge to NP-SB. Subjects which consists only of a single word are attached directly to the sentence in the original annotation, we project them to a new single NP-SB node instead. The results get about 0.8 points worse (cf. tab. 2), reflecting the difficulty of the task.

Verb phrases also have a different status in the transformed treebank. While per definition in the original annotation, the VP label only designates non-finite VPs, in the transformed treebank, we have both finite and non-finite VPs. We therefore produce a modified version of G30T, G30T-V, in which we change the label of a VP to VPFIN if it has a finite lexical head. Similar linguistically motivated splits have successfully been used before (Maier, 2010). It turns out that the results for G30T-V and G30O-S lie very close together (again cf. tab. 2).

DPTB For the sake of completeness we report the results for the DPTB as well. On E30, we obtain LP 76.15, LR 70.94, and therefore a LF_1 of 73.45. Our parameter settings have not been tried before on the DPTB (Evang, 2011; Evang and Kallmeyer, 2011), therefore there are no previous result to compare to.

7 Conclusion

The goal of this paper on data-driven PLCFRS parsing was to show that by restricting the block degree of trees used for grammar extraction, resp. the fan-out of the resulting grammars to two, (i) one can express almost all the information contained in the discontinuous treebank annotation of NeGra and the DPTB, and (ii) one obtains a parser which is much faster than a parser for general

LCFRS on the same data. The first contribution of this paper is a series of treebank transformations for NeGra and the DPTB which produces trees of a block degree of at most two. Unlike transformations for PCFG parsing, our transformations almost completely preserve the annotation information on discontinuities. The second contribution is an efficient data-driven parser for $(2, 2)$-PLCFRS, to be extracted from the converted treebanks. The evaluation of experiments with this parser on both NeGra and the Penn Treebank shows that an enormous speed-up has been achieved in comparison to earlier PLCFRS parsers, all while obtaining an output of comparable richness.

References

Pierre Boullier. 1998. Proposal for a Natural Language Processing syntactic backbone. Technical Report 3342, INRIA.

Gosse Bouma and Gertjan van Noord. 1998. Word Order Constraints on Verb Clusters in German and Dutch. In Erhard Hinrichs, Tsuneko Nakazawa, and Andreas Kathol, editors, *Complex predicates in Nonderivational Syntax*. Academic Press.

Adriane Boyd. 2007. Discontinuity revisited: An improved conversion to context-free representations. In *Proceedings of The Linguistic Annotation Workshop*.

Sabine Brants, Stefanie Dipper, Silvia Hansen, Wolfgang Lezius, and George Smith. 2002. The TIGER Treebank. In *Proceedings of TLT*.

Kilian Evang and Laura Kallmeyer. 2011. PLCFRS parsing of English discontinuous constituents. In *Proceedings of IWPT*.

Kilian Evang. 2011. Parsing discontinuous constituents in English. Master's thesis, University of Tübingen.

Carlos Gómez-Rodríguez, Marco Kuhlmann, and Giorgio Satta. 2010. Efficient parsing of well-nested Linear Context-Free Rewriting Systems. In *Proceedings of HLT-NAACL*.

Geoffrey Huck and Almerindo Ojeda, editors. 1987. *Discontinuous constituency*. Academic Press.

Laura Kallmeyer and Wolfgang Maier. 2010. Data-driven parsing with Probabilistic Linear Context-Free Rewriting Systems. In *Proceedings of COLING*.

Laura Kallmeyer. 2010. *Parsing beyond Context-Free Grammar*. Springer.

Yuki Kato, Hiroyuki Seki, and Tadao Kasami. 2006. Stochastic multiple Context-Free Grammar for RNA pseudoknot modeling. In *Proceedings of TAG+8*.

Dan Klein and Christopher D. Manning. 2003. A* parsing: Fast exact viterbi parse selection. In *Proceedings of NAACL*.

Roger Levy. 2005. *Probabilistic Models of Word Order and Syntactic Discontinuity*. Ph.D. thesis, Stanford University.

Wolfgang Maier and Timm Lichte. 2011. Characterizing discontinuity in constituent treebanks. In *FG 2009, Revised Selected Papers*, volume 5591 of *LNAI*. Springer.

Wolfgang Maier and Anders Søgaard. 2008. Treebanks and mild context-sensitivity. In Philippe de Groote, editor, *Proceedings of Formal Grammar*. CSLI.

Wolfgang Maier. 2010. Direct parsing of discontinuous constituents in German. In *Proceedings of SPMRL*.

Wolfgang Maier. 2012. *Parsing Discontinuous Structures*. Ph.D. thesis, University of Tübingen.

Mitchell P. Marcus, Beatrice Santorini, and Mary Ann Marcinkiewicz. 1993. Building a large annotated corpus of English: The Penn Treebank. *Computational Linguistics*, 19(2):313–330.

Mark-Jan Nederhof. 2003. Weighted deductive parsing and Knuth's algorithm. *Computational Linguistics*, 29(1):1–9.

Owen Rambow and Giorgio Satta. 1999. Independent parallelism in finite copying parallel rewriting systems. *Theoretical Computer Science*, 223(1-2):87–120.

Ines Rehbein and Josef van Genabith. 2007. Evaluating evaluation measures. In *Proceedings of NODALIDA-2007*.

Hiroyuki Seki, Takashi Matsumura, Mamoru Fujii, and Tadao Kasami. 1991. On Multiple Context-Free Grammars. *Theoretical Computer Science*, 88(2):191–229.

Wojciech Skut, Brigitte Krenn, Thorsten Brants, and Hans Uszkoreit. 1997. An annotation scheme for free word order languages. In *Proceedings of ANLP*, pages 88–95.

Heike Telljohann, Erhard W. Hinrichs, Sandra Kübler, Heike Zinsmeister, and Kathrin Beck. 2012. Stylebook for the Tübingen Treebank of Written German (TüBa-D/Z). Technical report, University of Tübingen.

Andreas van Cranenburgh, Remko Scha, and Federico Sangati. 2011. Discontinuous data-oriented parsing: A mildly context-sensitive all-fragments grammar. In *Proceedings of SPMRL*.

Andreas van Cranenburgh. 2012. Efficient parsing with linear context-free rewriting systems. In *Proceedings of EACL*.

K. Vijay-Shanker, David Weir, and Aravind K. Joshi. 1987. Characterising structural descriptions used by various formalisms. In *Proceedings of ACL*.

Decomposing TAG Algorithms Using Simple Algebraizations

Alexander Koller
Dept. of Linguistics
University of Potsdam, Germany
koller@ling.uni-potsdam.de

Marco Kuhlmann
Dept. of Linguistics and Philology
Uppsala University, Sweden
marco.kuhlmann@lingfil.uu.se

Abstract

We review a number of different 'algebraic' perspectives on TAG and STAG in the framework of interpreted regular tree grammars (IRTGs). We then use this framework to derive a new parsing algorithm for TAGs, based on two algebras that describe strings and derived trees. Our algorithm is extremely modular, and can easily be adapted to the synchronous case.

1 Introduction

Much of the early and recent literature on tree-adjoining grammars (TAG) is concerned with working out the formal relationships between TAG and other grammar formalisms. A common approach in this line of research has been to conceive the way in which TAG generates a string or a derived tree from a grammar as a two-step process: first a derivation tree is generated, then this derivation tree is mapped into a term over some algebra and evaluated there. Under this view, one can take different perspectives on how the labour of generating a string or derived tree should be divided between the mapping process and the algebra. In a way that we will make precise, linear context-free rewriting systems (LCFRSs, Weir (1988)) push much of the work into the algebra; Shieber (2006)'s analysis of synchronous TAG as bimorphisms puts the burden mostly on the mapping procedure; and a line of research using context-free tree languages (CFTLs), of which Maletti (2010) is a recent representative, strikes a balance between the other two approaches.

This research has done much to clarify the formal connections between TAG and other formalisms in terms of *generative capacity*. It has not been particularly productive with respect to finding new *algorithms* for parsing, training, and (in the synchronous case) decoding. This is regrettable because standard parsing algorithms for TAG (Vijay-Shanker and Joshi, 1985; Shieber et al., 1995) are complicated, require relatively involved correctness proofs, and are hard to teach. A similar criticism applies to parsing algorithms for LCFRSs (Burden and Ljunglöf, 2005). So far, no new parsing algorithms have arisen from Shieber's work on bimorphisms, or from the CFTL-based view. Indeed, Maletti (2010) leaves the development of such algorithms as an open problem.

This paper makes two contributions. First, we show how a number of the formal perspectives on TAG mentioned above can be recast in a uniform way as *interpreted regular tree grammars* (IRTGs, Koller and Kuhlmann (2011)). IRTGs capture the fundamental idea of generating strings, derived trees, or other objects from a regular tree language, and allow us to make the intuitive differences in how different perspectives divide the labour over the various modules formally precise.

Second, we introduce two new algebras. One captures TAG string languages; the other describes TAG derived tree languages. We show that both of these algebras are *regularly decomposable*, which means that the very modular algorithms that are available for parsing, training, and decoding of IRTGs can be applied to TAG. As an immediate consequence we obtain algorithms for these problems (for both TAG and STAG) that consist of small modules, each of which is simpler to understand, prove correct, and teach than a monolithic parser. As long as the grammar is binary, this comes at no cost in asymptotic parsing complexity.

Proceedings of the 11th International Workshop on Tree Adjoining Grammars and Related Formalisms (TAG+11), pages 135–143,
Paris, September 2012.

The paper is structured as follows. In Section 2, we introduce some formal foundations and review IRTGs. In Section 3, we recast three existing perspectives on TAG as IRTGs. In Sections 4 and 5, we present algebras for derived trees and strings in TAG; we apply them to parsing in Section 6. Section 7 concludes and discusses future work.

2 Interpreted Regular Tree Grammars

We start by introducing some basic concepts.

2.1 Foundations

A *signature* is a finite set Σ of function symbols f, each of which has been assigned a non-negative integer called its *rank*. We write $f|_n$ to indicate that f has rank n. For the following, let Σ be a signature.

A *tree* over Σ takes the form $t = f(t_1, \ldots, t_n)$, where $f|_n \in \Sigma$ and $t_1, \ldots, t_n$ are trees over Σ. We write T_Σ for the set of all trees over Σ. The *nodes* of a tree can be identified by paths $\pi \in \mathbb{N}^*$ from the root: The root has the address ε, and the ith child of the node with the address π has the address πi. We write $t(\pi)$ for the symbol at path π in the tree t, and $t \downarrow \pi$ for the subtree of t at π.

A *context* over Σ is a tree $C \in T_{\Sigma \cup \{\bullet\}}$ which contains a single leaf labeled with the *hole* $\bullet$. $C[t]$ is the tree in T_Σ which is obtained by replacing the hole in C by some tree $t \in T_\Sigma$. We write C_Σ for the set of all contexts over Σ.

A Σ-*algebra* $\mathcal{A}$ consists of a non-empty set A called the *domain* and, for each function symbol $f|_n \in \Sigma$, a total function $f^{\mathcal{A}} : A^n \to A$, the *operation* associated with f. Symbols of arity 0 are also called *constants*. The trees in T_Σ are called the *terms* of this algebra. We can *evaluate* a term $t \in T_\Sigma$ to an object $[\![t]\!]_{\mathcal{A}} \in A$ by executing the operations:

$$[\![f(t_1, \ldots, t_n)]\!]_{\mathcal{A}} = f^{\mathcal{A}}([\![t_1]\!]_{\mathcal{A}}, \ldots, [\![t_n]\!]_{\mathcal{A}}).$$

One algebra that we will use throughout the paper is the *string algebra* A^* over some alphabet A. Its elements are the strings over A; it has one binary operation "·", which concatenates its two arguments, and one constant for each symbol in A which evaluates to itself. Another important algebra is the *term algebra* T_Σ over some ranked signature Σ. The domain of the term algebra is T_Σ, and for each symbol $f|_n \in \Sigma$, we have $f^{T_\Sigma}(t_1, \ldots, t_n) = f(t_1, \ldots, t_n)$, i.e. every term evaluates to itself.

If some function $f^{\mathcal{A}}$ is partial, then $\mathcal{A}$ is a *partial* algebra; in this case there may be terms that do not have a value.

A *(tree) homomorphism* is a total function $h: T_\Sigma \to T_\Delta$ that expands symbols of Σ into trees over Δ while following the structure of the input tree. Formally, h is specified by pairs $(f, h(f))$, where $f \in \Sigma$ is a symbol with some rank n, and $h(f) \in T_{\Delta \cup \{x_1, \ldots, x_n\}}$ is a term with variables. The value of a term $t = f(t_1, \ldots, t_n) \in T_\Sigma$ under h is

$$h(f(t_1, \ldots, t_n)) = h(f)[h(t_1)/x_1, \ldots, h(t_n)/x_n].$$

2.2 Regular Tree Languages

Sets of trees can be specified by *regular tree grammars (RTGs)* (Gécseg and Steinby, 1997; Comon et al., 2008). Formally, an RTG is a construct $\mathcal{G} = (N, \Sigma, P, S)$ where N and Σ are signatures of nonterminal and terminal symbols, $S \in N$ is a start symbol, and P is a finite set of production rules of the form $A \to t$, where $A \in N$ and $t \in T_{N \cup \Sigma}$. Every nonterminal has rank 0. The language generated by $\mathcal{G}$ is the set $L(\mathcal{G}) \subseteq T_\Sigma$ of all trees with only terminal symbols that can be obtained by repeatedly applying the production rules, starting from S.

The class of languages that can be generated by regular tree grammars are called *regular tree languages (RTLs)*. They share many of the closure properties that are familiar from regular string languages. In particular, if L_1 and L_2 are regular and h is a homomorphism, then $L_1 \cap L_2$ and $h^{-1}(L)$ are also regular. If h is linear, then $h(L_1)$ is regular as well.

2.3 Interpreted RTGs

Koller and Kuhlmann (2011) extend RTGs to *interpreted regular tree grammars (IRTGs)*, which specify relations between arbitrary algebras. In this paper, we will focus on relations between strings and (derived) trees, but IRTGs can be used also to describe languages of and relations between other kinds of algebras.

Formally, an IRTG $\mathbb{G}$ is a tuple $(\mathcal{G}, I_1, \ldots, I_k)$ consisting of an RTG $\mathcal{G}$ and $k \geq 1$ *interpretations* $I_1, \ldots, I_k$. Each interpretation I_i is a pair $(h_i, \mathcal{A}_i)$ of an algebra $\mathcal{A}_i$ and a tree homomorphism h_i that maps the trees generated by $\mathcal{G}$ to terms over $\mathcal{A}_i$ (see Fig. 1). The *language* $L(\mathbb{G})$ is then defined as

$$L(\mathbb{G}) = \{([\![h_1(t)]\!]_{\mathcal{A}_1}, \ldots, [\![h_k(t)]\!]_{\mathcal{A}_k}) \mid t \in L(\mathcal{G})\}.$$

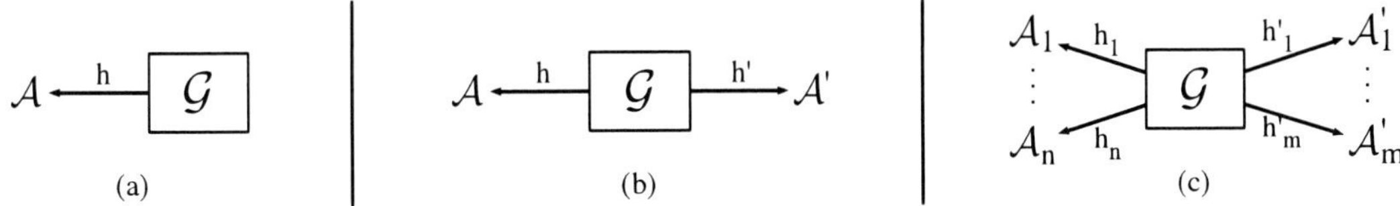

(a)   (b)   (c)

Figure 1: Schematic view of some IRTGs. (a) Monolingual grammar, $k = 1$, $L(\mathbb{G}) \subseteq \mathcal{A}$; (b) synchronous grammar, $k = 2$, $L(\mathbb{G}) \subseteq \mathcal{A} \times \mathcal{A}'$; (c) generalized synchronous grammar with n "input" and m "output" interpretations, $k = m + n$, $L(\mathbb{G}) \subseteq \mathcal{A}_1 \times \ldots \times \mathcal{A}_n \times \mathcal{A}'_1 \times \ldots \mathcal{A}'_m$.

The trees in $L(\mathcal{G})$ correspond to derivation trees in TAG; the elements of $L(\mathbb{G})$ are the objects described by the grammar. For instance, all context-free string languages can be described using $k = 1$ and the string algebra mentioned above (see Fig. 1a). String relations defined by synchronous CFGs or STSGs are exactly those described by IRTGs with $k = 2$ and two such algebras (Fig. 1b).

When parsing IRTGs, we are given input objects on a number of interpretations, and look for those derivation trees $t \in L(\mathcal{G})$ that are consistent with these input objects. Consider the case where we have an input object $a \in \mathcal{A}_1$ for a single interpretation; we are looking for the trees $t \in L(\mathcal{G})$ such that $[\![h_1(t)]\!]_{\mathcal{A}_1} = a$. Many important algebras (including the string and term algebras) are *regularly decomposable*: for each $a \in \mathcal{A}_1$, there is an RTG $D(a)$ – the *decomposition grammar* of a – such that $L(D(a))$ is the set of all terms over $\mathcal{A}_1$ that evaluate to a. Then the set of parses is $L(\mathcal{G}) \cap h_1^{-1}(L(D(a)))$. Using the closure properties of RTLs, this can be computed with a variety of generic algorithms, including bottom-up and top-down algorithms for intersection.

Under the IRTG perspective, the distinction between "monolingual" and synchronous grammars boils down to the choice of $k = 1$ (Fig. 1a) vs. $k > 1$ (Fig. 1b,c). The parsing algorithm generalizes easily to the synchronous case, and supports both the synchronous parsing of multiple input interpretations and the decoding into multiple output interpretations. See Koller and Kuhlmann (2011) for details.

3 Perspectives on TAG

There is an extensive literature on relating TAG to other grammar formalisms. In this section, we provide a uniform view on some of the most important such analyses by recasting them as IRTGs.

Derivation Trees. The fundamental insight that enables us to convert TAGs into IRTGs is that the set of derivation trees of a TAG G forms a regular tree language (Vijay-Shanker et al., 1987). In the formulation of Schmitz and Le Roux (2008), we can obtain an RTG $\mathcal{G}$ describing the derivation trees by using a nonterminal set $\{N_S, N_A \mid N \text{ nonterminal of } G\}$; the start symbol is S_S. $\mathcal{G}$ is defined over a signature whose symbols are the names of the elementary trees in G. The production rules encode the way in which these elementary trees can be combined using substitution (by expanding a nonterminal of the form N_S) and adjunction (by expanding a nonterminal of the form N_A). In this way, the derivation trees of the example grammar from Fig. 2a are described by an RTG $\mathcal{G}_0 = (N_0, \Sigma_0, P_0, S_0)$ with productions

$$S_S \rightarrow \alpha_1(NP_S, S_A, VP_A)$$
$$NP_S \rightarrow \alpha_2(NP_A)$$
$$VP_A \rightarrow \beta_1(VP_A)$$
$$S_A, VP_A, NP_A \rightarrow \text{nop}$$

Notice that every node at which an adjunction may take place is represented by a nonterminal symbol, which must be expanded by a production rule. If no adjunction takes place, we expand it with a rule of the form $N \rightarrow \text{nop}$, which is available for every nonterminal N (see Fig. 2b).

LCFRS. The view of TAG as a linear context-free rewriting system (LCFRS; Weir (1988)) can be seen as an IRTG as follows. Consider a Σ_0-algebra $\mathcal{A}_L$ whose values are the derived trees of the TAG grammar G. $\mathcal{A}_L$ interprets each symbol in the derivation tree as a complex tree-building operation which spells out the derived trees. For instance, $\alpha_1^{\mathcal{A}_L}$ is a function (on three arguments, because α_1 has rank 3) which takes an initial tree t_1 and two auxiliary trees t_2 and t_3 as arguments, and returns the tree which results

137

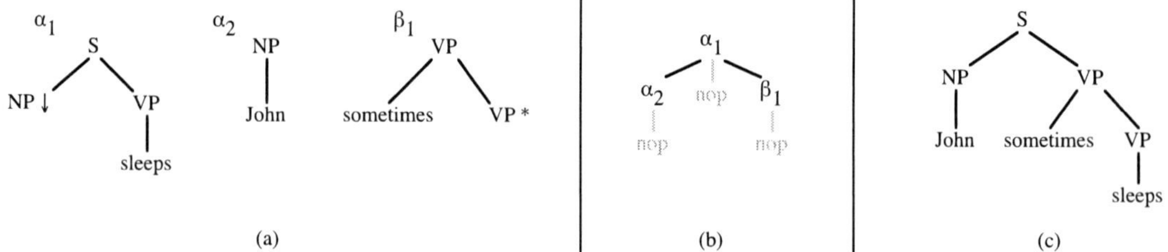

Figure 2: A TAG grammar (a), together with a derivation tree (b) and a derived tree (c). The "nop" nodes in the derivation tree indicate that no adjunction took place where one was possible, and are only needed for technical reasons.

from substituting and adjoining t_1, t_2, and t_3 into α_1 at appropriate places. Using such functions, one can directly interpret the tree $\alpha_1(\alpha_2(\text{nop}), \text{nop}, \beta_1(\text{nop}))$ as the derived tree in Fig. 2c. Therefore, for the IRTG $\mathbb{G}_L = (\mathscr{G}_0, (\text{id}, \mathscr{A}_L))$, where id is the identity homomorphism on T_{Σ_0}, $L(\mathbb{G}_L)$ is exactly the set of derived trees of G. One could instead obtain an IRTG for describing the string language of G by using an interpretation into a Σ_0-algebra of strings and string tuples in which the elementary trees evaluate to appropriate generalized concatenation operations.

STAG as Bimorphisms. Shieber (2004) proposes a different perspective on the generative process of synchronous tree substitution grammar (STSG). He builds upon earlier work on bimorphisms and represents an STSG as an IRTG $(\mathscr{G}_0, (h_1, T_{\Delta_1}), (h_2, T_{\Delta_2}))$, where T_{Δ_1} and T_{Δ_2} are appropriate term algebras. In this construction, the homomorphisms must carry some of the load: In an STSG whose left-hand side contains the trees α_1 and α_2 from Fig. 2a, we would have $h_1(\alpha_1) = S(x_1, VP(\text{sleeps}))$. Shieber (2006) later extended this approach to STAG by replacing the tree homomorphisms with embedded push-down transducers, a more powerful tree rewriting device.

Context-Free Tree Languages. Finally, Mönnich (1998) noticed that the language of derived trees of a TAG grammar is always a (monadic) context-free tree language (CFTL). It has been known since the seminal paper of Engelfriet and Schmidt (1977) that every CFTL can be generated by evaluating the trees of a regular tree language in a specific tree algebra that Engelfriet and Schmidt call the "tree substitution algebra"; we will call it the *YIELD algebra* T_Σ^Y here to avoid confusion, after the name of the evaluation function. Using this insight, we can capture Mön-

nich's perspective by describing the derived trees of a TAG grammar with an IRTG $(\mathscr{G}_0, (h, T_\Sigma^Y))$, where h is a homomorphism that spells out the elementary trees. Essentially, TAG derived trees are generated by using a TSG of "building instructions" (spelled out by the homomorphisms in a way that is similar to Shieber's), and evaluating the derived trees of the TSG in the YIELD algebra. This idea was made explicit for TAG by Morawietz and Mönnich (2001) and applied to STAG by Maletti (2010).

Discussion. These three different perspectives on TAG as IRTGs are summarized in Fig. 3. The choice of perspective has a significant impact on the algorithms that are natural for it, and the challenges one faces in developing them. The LCFRS view pushes the work of constructing a derived tree almost entirely into the algebra, which is relatively complicated and not binary. This makes it tricky to define a uniform algorithm for computing $D(w)$ for an input string w. When an LCFRS is used to encode an STAG grammar, it is also inconvenient to define a parsing or decoding algorithm that only gets a left string as its input. Shieber's perspective pushes almost all of the work into the translation from derivation trees to derived trees. Parsing involves computing the pre-image of $D(w)$ under embedded push-down transducers, which is harder than for ordinary homomorphisms. The YIELD approach strikes a balance between these two extremes, in that the workload is more evenly balanced between the (ordinary) homomorphism and the algebra. To our knowledge, no parsing or decoding algorithms for strings based on this perspective have been worked out; Maletti (2010) leaves this as an open problem. In the remainder of this paper we will fill this gap.

	homomorphisms	algebras	parsing	synchronous
LCFRSs	identity	complex	+	(+)
bimorphisms	embedded pushdown	term	-	+
CFTLs	tree homomorphisms	YIELD	-	+
this paper	tree homomorphisms	YIELD (simplified)	+	+

Figure 3: Perspectives on TAG.

4   An Algebra for Derived Trees

We will first introduce an algebra for derived trees and show how it can be used to cast TAG as an IRTG. We will then introduce a suitable TAG string algebra in Section 5.

4.1   The Tree Algebra T_Δ^D

The intuition of the derived tree algebra is that adjunction can be modeled using two substitutions of trees into a context. Take an auxiliary tree as a context C with a hole in place of the foot node, and say we want to adjoin it at some node π in the tree t. This can be done by splitting t into a context application $C'[t']$, where C' is the context in t with root ε and hole π. The result of the adjunction is then simply $C'[C[t]]$. In the derivation tree algebra, we use a special symbol @, which inserts its second argument into the hole of its first argument. Thus, in this algebra the term $@(C', @(C, t))$ evaluates to the result of the adjunction. The @ operation is a special case of the composition symbols $c_{n,k}$ used in the YIELD algebra of Engelfriet and Schmidt (1977). A similar intuition underlies the idea of "lifting" in Morawietz and Mönnich (2001), and the work of Maletti (2010).

Let Δ be a ranked signature of node labels. We define the algebra T_Δ^D of all TAG derived trees over Δ as a partial algebra whose domain contains all trees over Δ and all contexts over Δ; that is, the domain is $T_\Delta \cup C_\Delta$. Every $f|_k \in \Delta$ is a k-place operation in T_Δ^D. It takes k arguments $t_1, \ldots, t_k \in T_\Delta \cup C_\Delta$. It is defined if either $t_1, \ldots, t_k$ are all trees, or at most one of them is a context. In either case, it returns the result $f(t_1, \ldots, t_k)$. In addition, T_Δ^D has a constant $*$ that evaluates to the empty context $\bullet$. Finally, the binary operation @ substitutes an element of T_Δ^D into a context. It is defined for arguments C, t where t is a context and t is either a context or a tree. It returns $C[t]$; this is a tree if t is a tree, and a context otherwise.

4.2   An IRTG for TAG Derived Tree Languages

For any given TAG grammar G that uses some alphabet Δ of node labels in its derived trees, we can now construct an IRTG $\mathbb{G} = (\mathcal{G}, (h_t, T_\Delta^D))$ such that $L(\mathbb{G})$ consists of exactly the derived trees that are generated by G. We choose $\mathcal{G}$ to be a Σ-RTG that describes exactly the derivation trees of G, and we need to construct the homomorphism h_t that maps derivation trees into "building instructions" for derived trees, i.e. terms of T_Δ^D.

Each node in the derivation tree is labeled with the name α of an elementary tree (or nop); the subtrees below it describe trees that are combined with this elementary tree using substitution and adjunction. The purpose of $h_t(\alpha)$ is to spell out the way in which α does this combining. Substitution is modeled by simply leaving a variable in $h_t(\alpha)$ in the appropriate place; it will be filled with the initial tree when h_t is evaluated. Adjunction is modeled through the @ operator, as indicated above. Formally, let

$$A \to \alpha(B_S^1, \ldots, B_S^k, B_A^{k+1}, \ldots, B_A^n)$$

be the (unique) rule in $\mathcal{G}$ that contains the symbol α. Let i be a function that maps each substitution node π in α to the position of the nonterminal occurrence that corresponds to π in the right-hand side of this rule, i.e. to a number between 1 and k. Likewise, let i map each node at which an adjunction may take place to the position of the adjunction nonterminal, i.e. a number between $k + 1$ and n. We define a function h_α for each α that maps nodes π of α to terms over T_Δ^D, and let $h_t(\alpha) = h_\alpha(\varepsilon)$. Then $h_\alpha(\pi) = x_{i(\pi)}$ if π is a substitution node; $h_\alpha(\pi) = a$ if π is a lexical leaf with label a; $h_\alpha(\pi) = *$ if π is a foot node, and

$$h_\alpha(\pi) = @(x_{i(\pi)}, f(h_\alpha(\pi 1), \ldots, h_\alpha(\pi n))$$

if π is a non-leaf with label f. In this way, we can construct $h_t(\alpha)$ for each elementary tree α.

We illustrate this construction by converting the grammar of Fig. 2a into an IRTG $\mathbb{G} = (\mathcal{G}_0, (h_t, T_\Delta^D))$, where $\Delta = \{S_2, NP_1, VP_2, VP_1, \mathsf{John}_0, \mathsf{sometimes}_0, \mathsf{sleeps}_0\}$. The subscripts are needed to distinguish occurrences of the label same "VP" in Fig. 2c with different ranks. The homomorphism h_t looks as follows:

$$h_t(\alpha_1) = @(x_2, S_2(x_1, @(x_3, VP_1(\mathsf{sleeps}))))$$
$$h_t(\alpha_2) = @(x_1, NP_1(\mathsf{john}))$$
$$h_t(\beta_1) = @(x_1, VP_2(\mathsf{sometimes}, *))$$
$$h_t(\mathsf{nop}) = *$$

Notice how the ability of α_1 to allow adjunction at the S_2 and VP_2 nodes translates into uses of $@$, which perform the adjunctions by inserting the contexts (= auxiliary trees) that are passed in x_2 and x_3, respectively, in the right places. The NP substitution happens by simply inserting the tree (= initial tree) that is passed in x_1. The term $h_t(\beta_1)$ illustrates how the contexts that model the auxiliary trees are built by combining $*$ (which stands for the empty context containing just one hole) into larger structures. The term $h_t(\mathsf{nop})$ simply evaluates to the empty context; adjoining it anywhere leaves a tree unchanged.

When applied to the derivation tree in Fig. 2b, the homomorphism h_t returns the term $@(*, S_2(@(*, NP_1(\mathsf{john})), @(@(*, VP_2(\mathsf{sometimes}, *)), VP_1(\mathsf{sleeps}))))$. This term evaluates to the derived tree in Fig. 2c.

5 A String Algebra for TAG

Now consider how the basic ideas from Section 4 can be applied to obtain an algebra for TAG string languages. The domain of any such algebra must contain both strings (for the yields of initial trees) and pairs of strings (for the yields of auxiliary trees: one string to the left of the foot node and one string to the right). We have several options in defining the operations on such an algebra. One option is to use the same signature as for the derived tree algebra from Section 4. Unfortunately, this has the effect that the algebra contains operations of rank greater than two, which increases the parsing complexity.

5.1 The TAG String Algebra A^T

We choose to instead build a binary string algebra. The string algebra A^T for TAG over the finite alphabet A is a partial algebra whose domain contains all strings and all pairs of strings over A; that is, the domain is $A^* \cup (A^* \times A^*)$. We write w for a string and $\overline{w} = (w_1, w_2)$ for a string pair.

Every element a of A is a constant of A^T with $a^{A^T} = a$. There is also a constant $*$ with $*^{A^T} = (\varepsilon, \varepsilon)$. A^T has a binary partial concatenation operation conc, which is defined if at least one of its two arguments is a string. When defined, it concatenates strings and string pairs as follows:

$$\mathsf{conc}^{A^T}(w_1, w_2) = w_1 w_2$$
$$\mathsf{conc}^{A^T}(w_1, \overline{w_2}) = (w_1 w_{21}, w_{22})$$
$$\mathsf{conc}^{A^T}(\overline{w_1}, w_2) = (w_{11}, w_{12} w_2)$$

Finally, there is a binary partial wrapping operation wrap, which is defined if its first argument is a string pair. This operation wraps its first argument around the second, as follows:

$$\mathsf{wrap}^{A^T}(\overline{w_1}, w_2) = w_{11} w_2 w_{12}$$
$$\mathsf{wrap}^{A^T}(\overline{w_1}, \overline{w_2}) = (w_{11} w_{21}, w_{22} w_{12})$$

Notice that these operations closely mirror the operations for well-nested LCFRSs with fan-out 2 that were used in Gómez-Rodríguez et al. (2010).

5.2 An IRTG for TAG String Languages

We can use A^T to construct, for any given TAG grammar G over some alphabet A of terminal symbols, an IRTG $\mathbb{G} = (\mathcal{G}, (h_s, A^T))$ such that $L(\mathbb{G})$ consists of exactly the strings that are generated by G. We again describe the derivation trees using a Σ-RTG $\mathcal{G}$. Say that A^T is a Δ-algebra. It remains to construct a homomorphism h_s from T_Σ to T_Δ.

This is most easily done by defining a second homomorphism h_{st} that maps from T_Δ^D to A^T. h_{st} effectively reads off the yield of a tree or context, and is defined by mapping each operation symbol of T_Δ^D to a term over A^T. In particular, it breaks tree-constructing symbols $f \in \Delta$ in T_Δ^D up into sequences of binary concatenation operations. Thus $h_s = h_{st} \circ h_t$ becomes a homomorphism from Σ into terms of A^T.

$$
\begin{aligned}
h_{st}(f) &= \mathsf{conc}(x_1, \ldots, \mathsf{conc}(x_{k-1}, x_k)) && \text{if } k \geq 2 \\
h_{st}(f) &= x_1 && \text{if } f|_1 \\
h_{st}(f) &= f && \text{if } f|_0 \\
h_{st}(@) &= \mathsf{wrap}(x_1, x_2) \\
h_{st}(*) &= *
\end{aligned}
$$

To describe the string language Fig. 2a, we can use the IRTG $(\mathcal{G}_0, (h_s, A^T))$, for the alphabet $A = \{\text{john}, \text{sometimes}, \text{sleeps}\}$. The homomorphism h_s comes out as follows:

$$h_s(\alpha_1) = \text{wrap}(x_2, \text{conc}(x_1, \text{wrap}(x_3, \text{sleeps})))$$
$$h_s(\alpha_2) = \text{wrap}(x_1, \text{john})$$
$$h_s(\beta_1) = \text{wrap}(x_1, \text{conc}(\text{sometimes}, *))$$
$$h_s(\text{nop}) = *$$

Each $h_s(\alpha)$ encodes the operation of the elementary tree α as a generalized concatenation function on strings and string pairs. Applying h_s to the derivation tree in Fig. 2b produces the term $\text{wrap}(*, \text{conc}(\text{wrap}(*, \text{john}), \text{wrap}(\text{wrap}(*, \text{conc}(\text{sometimes}, *)), \text{sleeps})))$. This term evaluates in A^T to "John sometimes sleeps."

5.3 Synchronous Grammars

In summary, for any TAG grammar G, we can obtain an IRTG $(\mathcal{G}, (h_s, A^T))$ for the strings described by G, and an IRTG $(\mathcal{G}, (h_t, T_\Delta^D))$ for the derived trees. Both IRTGs use the same central RTG $\mathcal{G}$. This means that we can combine both views on TAG in a single IRTG with two interpretations, $\mathbb{G} = (\mathcal{G}, (h_s, A^T), (h_t, T_\Delta^D))$.

We can take this idea one step further in order to model synchronous TAG grammars. An STAG grammar can be seen as an RTG generating the derivation trees, plus two separate devices that build the left and right derived tree from a given derivation tree (Shieber, 2004; Shieber, 2006). Each "half" of the STAG grammar is simply an ordinary TAG grammar; they are synchronized with each other by requiring that in each STAG derivation, the individual TAG components must use the same derivation tree. As we have seen, an individual TAG grammar can be represented as an IRTG with two interpretations. We can therefore represent an STAG grammar as an IRTG with four interpretations, $\mathbb{G} = (\mathcal{G}, (h_s^1, A_1^T), (h_t^1, T_{\Delta_1}^D), (h_s^2, A_2^T), (h_t^2, T_{\Delta_2}^D))$. The language of $\mathbb{G}$ consists of four-tuples containing two derived trees and their two associated string yields – one each for the left and right-hand side of the STAG grammar. Notice that unlike in the LCFRS view on STAG, the four individual components are kept separate at all points, and decoding any combination of inputs into any combination of outputs is straightforward.

6 Decomposing the Parsing Algorithm

With these two algebras in place, all that remains to be done to define parsing and decoding algorithms for TAG and STAG is to show that A^T and T_Δ^D are regularly decomposable; then the generic algorithms for IRTG can do the rest.

6.1 Decomposition in the String Algebra

A term t that evaluates to some string or string pair w in the string algebra A^T describes how w can be built recursively from smaller parts using concatenation and wrapping. Just as in a CKY parser, these parts are either spans $[i, k]$ identifying the substring $w_i \ldots w_{k-1}$, or span pairs $[i, j, k, l]$ identifying the pair $(w_i \ldots w_{j-1}, w_k \ldots w_{l-1})$ of substrings.

We can obtain a decomposition grammar $D(w)$ for w by using these spans and span pairs as nonterminals. The production rules of $D(w)$ spell out how larger parts can be built from smaller ones using concatenation and wrapping operations, as follows:

$$[i, k] \rightarrow \text{conc}([i, j], [j, k])$$
$$[i, j, k, l] \rightarrow \text{conc}([i, j'], [j', j, k, l])$$
$$[i, j, k, l] \rightarrow \text{conc}([i, j, k, k'], [k', l])$$
$$[i, l] \rightarrow \text{wrap}([i, j, k, l], [j, k])$$
$$[i, j, k, l] \rightarrow \text{wrap}([i, i', l', l], [i', j, k, l'])$$
$$[i, i + 1] \rightarrow w_i$$
$$[i, i, j, j] \rightarrow *$$

The start symbol of $D(w)$ is the span that corresponds to the entire string or string pair w. If w is a string of length n, it is $[1, n + 1]$; for a string pair $\overline{w} = (w_1 \ldots w_{m-1}, w_m \ldots w_n) \in A^T$, the start symbol is $[1, m, m, n + 1]$. Notice that the size of $D(w)$ is $O(n^6)$ because of the second wrapping rule, and the grammar can also be computed in time $O(n^6)$.

6.2 Decomposition in the Derived Tree Algebra

The parts from which a term over the derived tree algebra T_Δ^D builds some derived tree or context $\tau \in T_\Delta^D$ are the subtrees or the contexts within τ. Each subtree can be identified by its root node π in τ; each context can be identified by its root π and its hole π'.

Thus we can obtain a decomposition grammar $D(\tau)$ using a nonterminal A_π to indicate the subtree starting at π and a nonterminal $B_{\pi/\pi'}$ to indicate the context from π to π'. As above, the rules spell out the ways in which larger subtrees and contexts can be constructed from smaller parts:

$$A_\pi \to f(A_{\pi 1}, \ldots, A_{\pi n}) \qquad t(\pi) = f|_n$$
$$A_\pi \to @(B_{\pi/\pi'}, A_{\pi'}) \qquad \pi' \text{ node in } t \downarrow \pi$$
$$B_{\pi/\pi'} \to f(A_{\pi 1}, \ldots, B_{\pi i/\pi'}, \ldots, A_{\pi n}) \quad \pi i \le \pi', t(\pi) = f|_n$$
$$B_{\pi/\pi'} \to @(B_{\pi/\pi''}, B_{\pi''/\pi'}) \qquad \pi < \pi'' \le \pi'$$
$$B_{\pi/\pi} \to *$$

Again, the start symbol is simply the representations of τ itself. If τ is a tree, it is A_ε; for a context with hole π, the start symbol is $B_{\varepsilon/\pi}$. If τ has n nodes, the grammar $D(\tau)$ has $O(n^3)$ rules because of the second rule for $@$.

6.3 Decomposing the TAG Parsing Algorithm

To illustrate the use of these decomposition grammars in the context of the parsing algorithm of Section 2, we parse the string $w = $ "John sometimes sleeps" using the IRTG $\mathbb{G} = (\mathscr{G}_0, (h_s, A^T))$ for the string perspective on the example grammar from Fig. 2 (cf. Section 5).

Step 1: Decomposition Grammar. First, the parser computes the decomposition grammar $D(w)$. As explained above, this grammar has the start symbol $[1, 4]$ and rules given in Fig. 4 (among others). The complete grammar generates a set of 72 terms over A^T, each of which evaluates to w. The term that is important here is wrap($*$, conc(wrap($*$, john), wrap(wrap($*$, conc(sometimes, $*$)), sleeps))). Crucially, the TAG grammar is completely irrelevant at this point: $L(D(w))$ consists of *all* terms over A^T which evaluate to w, regardless of whether they correspond to grammatical derivation trees or not.

Step 2: Inverse Homomorphism. Next, we compute an RTG $\mathscr{G}'$ for $h_s^{-1}(L(D(w)))$. This grammar describes all trees over Σ that are mapped by h_s into terms that evaluate to w. Its nonterminal symbols are still spans and span pairs, but the terminal symbols are now names of elementary trees. The grammar has the start symbol $[1, 4]$ and the following rules:

$$[1, 4] \to \alpha_1([1, 2], [1, 1, 4, 4], [2, 3, 4, 4])$$
$$[1, 2] \to \alpha_2([1, 1, 2, 2])$$
$$[2, 3, 4, 4] \to \beta_1([2, 2, 4, 4])$$
$$[1, 1, 4, 4] \to \text{nop}$$
$$[1, 1, 2, 2] \to \text{nop}$$
$$[2, 2, 4, 4] \to \text{nop}$$

$$[1, 2] \to \text{john}$$
$$[2, 3] \to \text{sometimes}$$
$$[3, 4] \to \text{sleeps}$$
$$[1, 1, 2, 2] \to *$$
$$[1, 2] \to \text{wrap}([1, 1, 2, 2], [1, 2])$$
$$[3, 3, 4, 4] \to *$$
$$[2, 3, 4, 4] \to \text{conc}([2, 3], [3, 3, 4, 4])$$
$$[2, 2, 4, 4] \to *$$
$$[2, 3, 4, 4] \to \text{wrap}([2, 2, 4, 4], [2, 3, 4, 4])$$
$$[2, 4] \to \text{wrap}([2, 3, 4, 4], [3, 4])$$
$$[1, 4] \to \text{conc}([1, 2], [2, 4])$$
$$[1, 4] \to \text{wrap}([1, 1, 4, 4], [1, 4])$$
$$[1, 1, 4, 4] \to *$$

Figure 4: The decomposition grammar.

An algorithm that computes $\mathscr{G}'$ is given by Koller and Kuhlmann (2011). The basic idea is to simulate the backwards application to the rules of $D(w)$ on the right-hand sides of the rules of the homomorphism h_s. As an example, consider the rule

$$h_s(\alpha_1) = \text{wrap}(x_2, \text{conc}(x_1, \text{wrap}(x_3, \text{sleeps})))$$

If we instantiate the variables x_2, x_1, x_3 with the spans $[1, 2]$, $[1, 1, 4, 4]$ and $[2, 3, 4, 4]$, respectively, then the backwards application of $D(w)$ yields $[1, 4]$. This warrants the first production of $\mathscr{G}'$.

Step 3: Intersection. $\mathscr{G}'$ is an RTG that represents all derivation trees that are consistent with the input string; these are not necessarily grammatical according to $\mathbb{G}$. On the other hand, $\mathscr{G}_0$ generates exactly the grammatical derivation trees, including ones that do not describe the input string. To obtain an RTG for the derivation trees that are grammatical *and* match the input, we intersect $\mathscr{G}_0$ and $\mathscr{G}'$. This yields a grammar $\mathscr{G}''$ whose nonterminals are pairs of nonterminals from $\mathscr{G}_0$ and $\mathscr{G}'$ and the following rules:

$$S_{[1,4]} \to \alpha_1(NP_{[1,2]}, S_{[1,1,4,4]}, VP_{[2,3,4,4]})$$
$$NP_{[1,2]} \to \alpha_2(NP_{[1,1,2,2]})$$
$$VP_{[2,3,4,4]} \to \beta_1(VP_{[2,2,4,4]})$$
$$S_{[1,1,4,4]} \to \text{nop}$$
$$NP_{[1,1,2,2]} \to \text{nop}$$
$$VP_{[2,2,4,4]} \to \text{nop}$$

As expected, $L(\mathscr{G}'')$ contains a single tree, namely the derivation tree in Fig. 2b.

Discussion. $\mathscr{G}''$ is essentially a standard TAG parse chart for w. We have obtained it in three steps. Step 1 was an algebra-specific decomposition step; this was the only step in the parsing algorithm that was particular to TAG. Steps 2 and 3 then performed generic operations on RTGs, and are exactly the same whether we would parse with respect to TAG, context-free grammars, or a grammar formalism that describes objects in some other algebra. Thus this is a TAG parsing algorithm which decomposes into three parts, each of which is easier to understand, teach, and prove correct than a monolithic algorithm.

The runtime of the overall algorithm is $O(n^6)$ as long as both the algebra and the underlying RTG are binary. The string algebra was binary by design; furthermore, the RTG of every IRTG that encodes a TAG can be brought into a binary normal form (Gómez-Rodríguez et al., 2010). If we are parsing input on several interpretations simultaneously, e.g. in STAG parsing, binarization is not always possible (Huang et al., 2009), and the parsing algorithm takes exponential runtime. See also Koller and Kuhlmann (2011) for a discussion of binarization.

7 Conclusion

We have shown how a variety of formal perspectives on TAG can be uniformly understood in terms of IRTGs. By introducing two new, regularly decomposable algebras for strings and derived trees, we have shown how to obtain a modular parsing algorithm for TAG and STAG. This algorithm can be adapted to support synchronous parsing and decoding. For IRTGs with weighted RTGs, which are capable of capturing PTAG (Resnik, 1992) and synchronous PTAG, we can also perform Viterbi parsing and EM training on the parse chart.

The general advantage of the parsing algorithm presented here is that it decomposes into simple components. Recombining these yields an algorithm that is essentially identical to the standard CKY parser for TAG (Shieber et al., 1995). We can obtain other parsing algorithms by varying the way in which intersection and inverse homomorphisms are computed.

Acknowledgments. We thank Matthias Büchse, John Hale, Andreas Maletti, Heiko Vogler, and our reviewers for helpful comments, and Thutrang Nguyen for an initial implementation.

References

H. Burden and P. Ljunglöf. 2005. Parsing linear context-free rewriting systems. In *Proc. of the 9th IWPT*.

H. Comon, M. Dauchet, R. Gilleron, F. Jacquemard, D. Lugiez, C. Löding, S. Tison, and M. Tommasi. 2008. Tree automata techniques and applications. Available on http://tata.gforge.inria.fr/.

J. Engelfriet and E. Schmidt. 1977. IO and OI. I. *Journal of Computer and System Sciences*, 15(3):328–353.

F. Gécseg and M. Steinby. 1997. Tree languages. In G. Rozenberg and A. Salomaa, editors, *Handbook of Formal Languages*, volume 3, pages 1–68. Springer.

C. Gómez-Rodríguez, M. Kuhlmann, and G. Satta. 2010. Efficient parsing of well-nested linear context-free rewriting systems. In *Proc. of HLT/NAACL*.

L. Huang, H. Zhang, D. Gildea, and K. Knight. 2009. Binarization of synchronous context-free grammars. *Computational Linguistics*, 35(4):559–595.

A. Koller and M. Kuhlmann. 2011. A generalized view on parsing and translation. In *Proc. of the 12th IWPT*.

A. Maletti. 2010. A tree transducer model for synchronous tree-adjoining grammars. In *Proc. of the 48th ACL*.

U. Mönnich. 1998. Adjunction as substitution. an algebraic formulation of regular, context-free, and tree-adjoining languages. In *Proc. of FG*.

F. Morawietz and U. Mönnich. 2001. A model-theoretic description of tree adjoining grammars. *Electronic Notes in Theoretical Computer Science*, 53.

P. Resnik. 1992. Probabilistic tree-adjoining grammar as a framework for statistical natural language processing. In *Proc. of COLING*.

S. Schmitz and J. Le Roux. 2008. Feature unification in TAG derivation trees. In *Proc. of the 9th TAG+ Workshop*.

S. Shieber, Y. Schabes, and F. Pereira. 1995. Principles and implementation of deductive parsing. *Journal of Logic Programming*, 24(1–2):3–36.

S. Shieber. 2004. Synchronous grammars as tree transducers. In *Proc. of the 7th TAG+ Workshop*.

S. Shieber. 2006. Unifying synchronous tree-adjoining grammars and tree transducers via bimorphisms. In *Proc. of the 11th EACL*.

K. Vijay-Shanker and A. Joshi. 1985. Some computational properties of Tree Adjoining Grammars. In *Proc. of the 23rd ACL*.

K. Vijay-Shanker, D. Weir, and A. Joshi. 1987. Characterizing structural descriptions produced by various grammatical formalisms. In *Proc. of the 25th ACL*.

D. Weir. 1988. *Characterizing Mildly Context-Sensitive Grammar Formalisms*. Ph.D. thesis, University of Pennsylvania, Philadelphia, USA.

Practical Parsing of Parallel Multiple Context-Free Grammars

Peter Ljunglöf

Department of Computer Science and Engineering
University of Gothenburg and Chalmers University of Technology
Gothenburg, Sweden
`peter.ljunglof@gu.se`

Abstract

We discuss four previously published parsing algorithms for parallell multiple context-free grammar (PMCFG), and argue that they are similar to each other, and implement an Earley-style top-down algorithm. Starting from one of these algorithms, we derive three modifications – one bottom-up and two variants using a left corner filter. An evaluation shows that substantial improvements can be made by using the algorithm that performs best on a given grammar. The algorithms are implemented in Python and released under an open-source licence.

We start by introducing the necessary concepts. Then we discuss four previously published PMCFG algorithms, and argue that they are similar. We take Angelov (2009) as a starting point for introducing three new parsing strategies. Finally we discuss various optimizations of the parsing strategies and give a small evaluation.

1 Background

1.1 PMCFG

Let Σ and N be sets of terminal and nonterminal symobls, respectively. A *parallel multiple context-free grammar* (PMCFG) (Seki et al., 1991) consists of a set of context-free production rules $A \to f(\vec{B})$, where $A \in N$ and $\vec{B} = B_1, \ldots, B_n \in N$ are nonterminals. f is a *linearization* function:

$$f \ : \ (\Sigma^*)^{\delta(B_1)} \times \cdots \times (\Sigma^*)^{\delta(B_n)} \to (\Sigma^*)^{\delta(A)}$$

where $\delta(X)$ is the *fan-out*, or *dimension*, of the non-terminal X. The linearization function f is

$$
\begin{array}{ll}
S \to f(A) & f(\langle x, y \rangle) = \langle x\,y \rangle \\
A \to g(A) & g(\langle x, y \rangle) = \langle a\,x\,b,\ c\,y\,d \rangle \\
A \to h() & h() = \langle a\,b,\ c\,d \rangle
\end{array}
$$

Figure 1: A grammar that recognizes the langauge $\{a^n b^n c^n d^n \mid n > 0\}$.

$$
\begin{array}{lll}
S \to f(A) & f.1 = \langle 1.1 \rangle \langle 1.2 \rangle & \\
A \to g(A) & g.1 = a\,\langle 1.1 \rangle\,b & g.2 = c\,\langle 1.2 \rangle\,d \\
A \to h() & h.1 = a\,b & h.2 = c\,d
\end{array}
$$

Figure 2: The same grammar in variable-free form.

normally written like this:

$$f\left(\langle x_{1,1}\ldots x_{1,\delta(B_1)}\rangle, \ldots, \langle x_{n,1}\ldots x_{n,\delta(B_n)}\rangle\right) = \langle \alpha_1, \ldots, \alpha_{\delta(A)}\rangle$$

where each α_i is sequence of terminal symbols and bound variables. However, in this paper we write the linearizations in variable-free form, where each bound variable $x_{d,r}$ is written as a pair of the form $\langle d.r \rangle$. We use $f.s$ to denote the sth constituent of the linearization, i.e. α_s.

Figure 1 contains an example grammar recognizing the language $a^n b^n c^n d^n$, and its variable-free form is shown in figure 2. The fanouts of this grammar are $\delta(S) = 1$ and $\delta(A) = 2$.

1.2 MCFG and LCFRS

A linearization function is *linear* if no argument constituent $\langle d.r \rangle$ occurs more than once in the right-hand side. It is *non-erasing* if all possible argument constituents occurs in the right-hand side.

A *multiple context-free grammar* (MCFG) is a PMCFG where all linearization functions are linear. A *linear context-free rewriting system* (LCFRS) (Vijay-Shanker et al., 1987) is a linear and non-erasing PMCFG. Erasingness does not

Proceedings of the 11th International Workshop on Tree Adjoining Grammars and Related Formalisms (TAG+11), pages 144–152,
Paris, September 2012.

add to the expressive power, and therefore LCFRS and MCFG are weakly equivalent. However, reduplication does give extra expressive power, so PMCFG is a proper extension of MCFG/LCFRS (Seki et al., 1991).

1.3 Emptiness and left corners

We define the *context-free approximation* of a PMCFG rule $A \to f(\vec{B})$ to be $\delta(A)$ context-free rules $A.r \to \beta_r$, where β_r is the linearization $f.r$ with every occurrence of $\langle d.s \rangle$ replaced by $B_d.s$. The nonterminals of the context-free approximation are of the form $A.r$.

We define $(\Rightarrow)$ as the standard reflexive and transitive rewriting relation on the context-free approximation. We say that a constituent $A.r$ is *empty* if $A.r \Rightarrow \epsilon$. We define the *left corner* relation as: $A.r \triangleright x$ iff $A.r \Rightarrow x\,\beta$ for some β, where x is either a terminal w or a constituent $B.s$.

1.4 Non-empty grammars

Our algorithms can handle all kinds of PMCFG grammars, but the two bottom-up variants work much better if the grammar has no empty linearizations, i.e., if $A.r \not\Rightarrow \epsilon$ for all constituents $A.r$. This is discussed further in section 4.3.

All grammars with empty linearizations can be transformed to nonempty grammars (Seki et al., 1991). We use an adaptation of an algorithm for context-free grammars. The transformation does not lose any important information, and it is straightforward to translate parse trees back into the original grammar efficiently.

2 Existing parsing algorithms

Most existing parsing algorithms require that the grammar is a LCFRS or a subclass thereof (Burden and Ljunglöf, 2005; de la Clergerie, 2002; Gómez-Rodríguez et al., 2008; Kallmeyer, 2010; Kallmeyer and Maier, 2009; Kanazawa, 2008), often in some kind of normal form such as a *binarized* or an *ordered* LCFRS. There are some algorithms that can handle general PMCFG grammars (Angelov, 2009; Boullier, 2004; Ljunglöf, 2004), including the algorithms presented in this paper. This is important when parsing Grammatical Framework (GF) grammars (Ranta, 2011), since the algorithm for converting a GF grammar results in an erasing PMCFG (Ljunglöf, 2004).

In this section we give an informal introduction to the algorithm by Angelov (2009), and dis-

$$
\boxed{
\begin{array}{llll}
S \to A_1\,A_2 & S \to A_1'\,A_2' & S \to A_1''\,A_2'' & \dots \\
A_1 \to a\,b & A_1' \to a\,A_1\,b & A_1'' \to a\,A_1'\,b & \dots \\
A_2 \to c\,d & A_2' \to c\,A_2\,d & A_2'' \to c\,A_2'\,d & \dots
\end{array}
}
$$

Figure 3: Infinite context-free equivalent of the example PMCFG in figure 1.

cuss its similarities with three other algorithms (Kallmeyer and Maier, 2009; Kanazawa, 2008; Ljunglöf, 2004). We argue that all four algorithms implement the same basic Earley-style top-down parsing algorithm.

2.1 Angelov's top-down algorithm

Angelov (2009) views a PMCFG as a CFG with a possibly infinite number of nonterminals and rules. Note that the term "infinite CFG" is an oxymoron, since such a grammar can recognize non-context-free languages. E.g., the infinite CFG shown in figure 3 is equivalent to the grammar in figure 1, which recognizes a non-context-free language.

Since this CFG is infinite, it cannot be calculated from the PMCFG beforehand. But given a certain input string, there are only a finite number of nonterminals and rules that are used in the final parse trees. Angelov's idea is to dynamically create nonterminals and rules during parsing: Whenever the parser has recognized a new constituent r of a nonterminal A, between input positions $i{-}j$, it creates a new nonterminal $A' = A(i, j, r)$, and new grammar rules for A'.

2.2 Similarity with other approaches

Angelov's dynamic CFG is not conceptually different from the parsing algorithms described by other authors. The new nonterminals are all of the form $A' = A(i_1, j_1, r_1) \dots (i_n, j_n, r_n)$, which is equivalent to the PMCFG nonterminal A, coupled with a sequence of the constituents that have been found during parsing. This is similar to how other algorithms store their found constituents:

- Angelov (2009) uses an ordered sequence where the constituents are stored in the order they are found.

- Ljunglöf (2004, section 4.6) separates the nonterminal A from the "range record" Γ, which is a set containing the found constituents.

Angelov	**Ljunglöf**	**K&M**	**Kanazawa**
$A(i_1, j_1, r_1)$	$\{r_1 : i_1\text{-}j_1\}$	$\langle i_1\text{-}j_1, ?, \ldots, ?\rangle$	$A_1(i_1, j_1)$
$A(i_1, j_1, r_1) \ldots (i_n, j_n, r_n)$	$\{r_1 : i_1\text{-}j_1, \ldots, r_n : i_n\text{-}j_n\}$	$\langle i_1\text{-}j_1, \ldots, i_n\text{-}j_n\rangle$	$A_n(i_1, j_1, \ldots, i_n, j_n)$

Table 1: How different algorithms denote similar derived facts.

- Kallmeyer and Maier (2009) also separates the nonterminal A from the "range vector" Φ, which is a ordered tuple of ranges. In a range vector, the constituents that are not yet found are uninstantiated.

- Kanazawa (2008) derives successively increasing Datalog facts of arity (2 × the number of found constituents).

In table 1 we can see how the different authors denote similar derived facts. The first row corresponds to when the first constituent r_1 of a nonterminal A has been found spanning the positions $i_1 - j_1$. The second row corresponds to when the parser has found all n constituents of A.

All the discussed algorithms use the same general top-down parsing strategy: First they predict the toplevel nonterminal, followed by its children, and further down until they reach the lexical rules. Then they try to match the lexical rules with the next input token, and so on. This strategy is a PMCFG version of Earley's context-free parsing algorithm (Earley, 1970).

2.3 Bottom-up parsing

However, there are alternative context-free parsing strategies which have not been adopted for PMCFG parsing (Sikkel and Nijholt, 1997; Moore, 2004). Ljunglöf (2004, section 4.6.1) makes an attempt at bottom-up prediction, but it is not very efficient. The problem with a pure bottom-up approach is that the algorithm will recognize all constituents independently, and then it is very costly to combine the constituents further up in the parse tree.

The solution we adopt in the next section is to always use a top-down parsing strategy to recognize additional constituents. This means that the different prediction strategies in sections 3.4–3.6 only apply when recognizing the first constituent of a grammar rule.

3 Three new algorithms

We describe our parsing algorithms as deductive parsing systems (Shieber et al., 1995; Sikkel, 1998), where we infer a set of parse items called a *chart*. Furthermore, we assume that the input is given as n input tokens $w_1 w_2 \ldots w_n$.

3.1 Parse items

We use four different kinds of parse items, and we divide the chart into four indexed sets, $\mathbf{A}_{j,k}$, $\mathbf{F}_{j,k}$, $\mathbf{P}_k$ and $\mathbf{R}_k$, where $j \leq k$ are input positions. The fundamental item is the *active item*:

$$[r : \alpha \bullet \beta \mid A \to f(\vec{B})] \in \mathbf{A}_{j,k}$$

which says that the parser is trying to find the constituent $A.r$ using the linearization $f.r = \alpha\beta$. It has already found α between the positions j and k, but is still looking for β.

The other parse items are strictly not necessary, but they simplify our presentation of the algorithms. The following *predict item* says that the parser is looking for a constituent $A.r$ starting in position k:

$$[?A.r] \in \mathbf{P}_k$$

When the parser finds the constituent $A.r$ between j and k, it creates a new nonterminal $A' = A(j, k, r)$, and infers both a *dynamic grammar rule* and a *passive item*:

$$[A' \to f(\vec{B})] \in \mathbf{R}_k \qquad [A.r : A'] \in \mathbf{F}_{j,k}$$

The dynamic rule is used whenever a parent searches for a new constituent of a partly recognized A child. The passive item says that $A.r$ has been found between j and k, and is used when the parser combines the recognized constituent with an active item looking for $A.r$.

We have reformulated Angelov's algorithm slightly so that it fits better with our alternative parsing strategies. Angelov does not use predict items, but we have added them since they simplify the filtered bottom-up parsing strategy (Moore, 2004). Another difference is that we separate the original (static) grammar rules $A \to f(\vec{B})$ from the dynamic rules $[A' \to f(\vec{B})]$.

$$
\begin{array}{cc}
\textit{predict-item} & \dfrac{[\,r : \alpha \bullet \langle d.s \rangle\ \beta \mid A \to f(\vec{B})\,] \in \mathbf{A}_{j,k}}{[\,?B_d.s\,] \in \mathbf{P}_k}
\end{array}
$$

$$
\begin{array}{cc}
\textit{predict-next} & \dfrac{[\,A \to f(\vec{B})\,] \in \mathbf{R}_j \quad [\,?A.r\,] \in \mathbf{P}_k}{[\,r :\ \bullet\,\beta \mid A \to f(\vec{B})\,] \in \mathbf{A}_{k,k}} \quad f.r = \beta,\, j \le k
\end{array}
$$

$$
\begin{array}{cc}
\textit{scan} & \dfrac{[\,r : \alpha \bullet w_k\ \beta \mid A \to f(\vec{B})\,] \in \mathbf{A}_{j,k-1}}{[\,r : \alpha\ w_k \bullet \beta \mid A \to f(\vec{B})\,] \in \mathbf{A}_{j,k}}
\end{array}
$$

$$
\begin{array}{cc}
\textit{complete} & \dfrac{[\,r : \alpha \bullet\ \mid A \to f(\vec{B})\,] \in \mathbf{A}_{j,k}}{[\,A' \to f(\vec{B})\,] \in \mathbf{R}_k \quad [\,A.r : A'\,] \in \mathbf{F}_{j,k}} \quad A' = A(j,k,r)
\end{array}
$$

$$
\begin{array}{cc}
\textit{combine} & \dfrac{[\,r : \alpha \bullet \langle d.s \rangle\ \beta \mid A \to f(\vec{B})\,] \in \mathbf{A}_{i,j} \quad [\,B_d.s : B_d'\,] \in \mathbf{F}_{j,k}}{[\,r : \alpha\ \langle d.s \rangle \bullet \beta \mid A \to f(\vec{B}[d := B_d'])\,] \in \mathbf{A}_{i,k}}
\end{array}
$$

Figure 4: General inference rules

3.2 General inference rules

Most of the inference rules will be reused by the alternative algorithms, so we split the inference rules into general rules (which are used by all algorithms), and algorithm-specific rules. The general inference rules are shown in figure 4. Since we want to be able to use different prediction strategies for the first constituent, and still predict additional constituents top-down, we have split Angelov's top-down prediction into two separate inference rules. The rule that predicts additional constituents is included here as *predict-next*.

The inference rules *predict-item*, *scan* and *complete* are mutually exclusive, since their antecedent is an active item which either looks for a nonterminal, a terminal, or nothing at all. The rule *predict-item* infers a predict item for $B_d.s$ from an active item looking for $\langle d.s \rangle$. The *scan* rule moves the dot forward if the active item is looking for the next input token w_k. The *complete* rule applies when the dot is at the end of the linearization, and it derives a dynamic rule and a passive item, together with a fresh dynamic nonterminal $A' = A(j,k,r)$.

The fundamental inference rule is *combine*, which takes one active item looking for a nonterminal $B_d.s$ starting in position j, and one passive item that has found $B_d.s$ between j and k. The *combine* rule moves the dot of the active item forward, but it also updates the nonterminal child B_d to $B_d' = B_d(j,k,s)$.

Now, if the active item that is inferred by *combine*, in a later parsing stage wants to find another constituent of B_d' (say $B_d'.u$ starting in position $p \ge k$), the item $[\,?B_d'.u\,] \in \mathbf{P}_p$ is infered by *predict-item*. This in turn triggers *predict-next* to look for a dynamic rule $[\,B_d' \to g(\ldots)\,]$. But since that rule was inferred at the same time as the passive item $[\,B_d.s : B_d'\,] \in \mathbf{F}_{j,k}$, *predict-next* will start recognizing the constituent $B_d'.u$.

3.3 Top-down prediction

The only infenrence rules that are specific to a parsing strategy are the prediction rules. Angelov's (2009) unfiltered top-down strategy consists of the two rules shown in figure 5. Whenever there is a predict item looking for $A.r$ (where A is a grammar nonterminal, not a dynamic one), *predict-topdown* finds all A rules in the grammar and adds them as active items.

The parsing process is initiated by *init-topdown*, which predicts the starting nonterminal S at the beginning of the string.

3.4 Bottom-up prediction

In bottom-up parsing we predict a nonterminal constituent only when its first symbol has been found (Ljunglöf and Wirén, 2010, section 4.4.4). There are three possibilities, depending on whether the first symbol is a terminal, a nonterminal, or if the constitutent is empty. They constitute the inference rules *predict-bottomup*, *scan-bottomup* and *scan-empty*, respectively.

$$\text{init-topdown} \qquad \frac{}{[\,?S.r\,] \in \mathbf{P}_0} \ \ \text{start}(S)$$

$$\text{predict-topdown} \qquad \frac{[\,?A.r\,] \in \mathbf{P}_k}{[\,r:\ \bullet\,\beta \mid A \to f(\vec{B})\,] \in \mathbf{A}_{k,k}} \ \ A \to f(\vec{B}),\, f.r = \beta$$

Figure 5: Top-down prediction

$$\text{predict-bottomup} \qquad \frac{[\,B_d.s : B'_d\,] \in \mathbf{F}_{j,k}}{[\,r: \langle d.s\rangle\,\bullet\,\beta \mid A \to f(\vec{B}[d := B'_d])\,] \in \mathbf{A}_{j,k}} \ \ A \to f(\vec{B}),\, f.r = \langle d.s\rangle\,\beta$$

$$\text{scan-bottomup} \qquad \frac{}{[\,r: w_k\,\bullet\,\beta \mid A \to f(\vec{B})\,] \in \mathbf{A}_{k-1,k}} \ \ A \to f(\vec{B}),\, f.r = w_k\,\beta$$

$$\text{scan-empty} \qquad \frac{}{[\,r:\ \bullet\ \mid A \to f(\vec{B})\,] \in \mathbf{A}_{k,k}} \ \ A \to f(\vec{B}),\, f.r = \epsilon$$

Figure 6: Bottom-up prediction

The rule *predict-bottomup* is triggered when we have found a passive item covering the first constituent $\langle d.r\rangle$ of $f.r$. Since $B_d.r$ is found, we can directly move the dot past $\langle d.r\rangle$, but then we have to update the nonterminal B_d to the dynamic nonterminal B'_d, in the same way as *combine* does.

One problem with this algorithm is that *scan-empty* adds an item for every empty constituent $A.r$ and every position k in the input. Depending on the grammar, this can lead to a very large chart. There are several ways to solve this: One is to let *scan-bottomup* and *predict-bottomup* skip over initial empty constituents, similar to the context-free GHR algorithm (Graham et al., 1980). Another possibility is to only infer an empty constituent $A.r$ if it can be followed by the input token starting in position k. Our solution is to use the left corner relation as a filter, see section 3.6.

3.5 Filtered top-down prediction

The problem with the top-down algorithm is that it predicts lots of useless items that cannot possibly be inferred from the input tokens. So, we augment *predict-topdown* with a filter, shown in figure 7. Using this filter the parser can only predict a new $A.r$ item in position k if the next input token w_{k+1} is a left corner ($A.r \rhd w_{k+1}$), or if the constituent is empty ($A.r \Rightarrow \epsilon$).

This filter is not as strict as it can be, since it doesn't test empty constituents against the input.

One way of making it stricter would be to only predict empty constituents that can be followed by the next input token w_{k+1}.

3.6 Filtered bottom-up prediction

A problem with bottom-up prediction is that it infers lots of items that cannot be used in a final parse tree. We adapt a context-free left corner strategy (Moore, 2004) to our bottom-up algorithm. The modified inference rules are shown in figure 8.

Each inference rule now requires a predict item $[\,?D.u\,]$, such that $D.u \rhd A.r$. In other words, the parser will only predict a constituent $A.r$ if it is the left corner of another constituent $D.u$ that the parser is already looking for. To initialize this left corner filter, we borrow the *init-topdown* rule from the top-down strategy.

3.7 Other possible filters

Kallmeyer and Maier (2009) discuss two additional filters. The *length filter* prohibits parse items that are too long to fit in the sentence. The *terminal filter* checks that all terminals in a linearization occurs among the input tokens, and in the same order.

We have not incorporated their filters in our parser implementations, but we see no reason why this could not be done.

$$\text{init-topdown} \quad \frac{}{[\,?S.r\,] \in \mathbf{P}_0} \ \ \text{start}(S)$$

$$\text{predict-topdown} \quad \frac{[\,?A.r\,] \in \mathbf{P}_k}{[\,r :\ \bullet\, \beta \mid A \to f(\vec{B})\,] \in \mathbf{A}_{k,k}} \quad \begin{cases} A \to f(\vec{B}),\, f.r = \beta \\ A.r \Rightarrow \epsilon \ \ \lor \ \ A.r \triangleright w_{k+1} \end{cases}$$

Figure 7: Top-down prediction with bottom-up filtering

$$\text{init-topdown} \quad \frac{}{[\,?S.r\,] \in \mathbf{P}_0} \ \ \text{start}(S)$$

$$\text{predict-bottomup} \quad \frac{[\,?D.u\,] \in \mathbf{P}_j \quad [\,B_d.s : B'_d\,] \in \mathbf{F}_{j,k}}{[\,r : \langle d.s \rangle \bullet \beta \mid A \to f(\vec{B}[d := B'_d])\,] \in \mathbf{A}_{j,k}} \quad \begin{cases} A \to f(\vec{B}),\, f.r = \langle d.s \rangle\, \beta \\ D.u \triangleright A.r \end{cases}$$

$$\text{scan-bottomup} \quad \frac{[\,?D.u\,] \in \mathbf{P}_{k-1}}{[\,r : w_k \bullet \beta \mid A \to f(\vec{B})\,] \in \mathbf{A}_{k-1,k}} \quad \begin{cases} A \to f(\vec{B}),\, f.r = w_k\, \beta \\ D.u \triangleright A.r \end{cases}$$

$$\text{scan-empty} \quad \frac{[\,?D.u\,] \in \mathbf{P}_k}{[\,r :\ \bullet \mid A \to f(\vec{B})\,] \in \mathbf{A}_{k,k}} \quad \begin{cases} A \to f(\vec{B}),\, f.r = \epsilon \\ D.u \triangleright A.r \end{cases}$$

Figure 8: Bottom-up prediction with left corner filtering

4 Incrementality and optimizations

Let us define *stage* k to be all sets $\mathbf{A}_{i,k}$, $\mathbf{F}_{i,k}$, $\mathbf{P}_k$ and $\mathbf{R}_k$ that end in position k. Then we can say that a parser is *incremental* if all sets in stage k are computed before it starts computing the sets in stage $k+1$. All our inference rules are straightforward to implement incrementally, since no antecedent belongs to a later stage than the state belonging to the consequent item.

If we assume that the implementation is incremental, we can make some optimizations, some more obvious than others. One immediate consequence is that *predict-next* never needs to check if $j \leq k$ since it is trivially satisfied. But there are more things that can be optimized.

4.1 Dynamic rules

As the rule is stated in figure 4, if *predict-next* is triggered by the predict item, it will have to search through all sets $\mathbf{R}_0, \ldots, \mathbf{R}_k$ to find a matching dynamic rule. However, if parsing is performed incrementally, we do not have to separate the rules into different sets, but we can instead add all dynamic rules to one big set $\mathbf{R}$.

4.2 Optimizing previous stages

The passive sets $\mathbf{F}_{j,k}$ are only used in stage k. This means that when the parser starts building the $k+1$ sets, it can discard all sets $\mathbf{F}_{j,k}$ from stage k. The same holds for the predict items $\mathbf{P}_k$, except in the filtered bottom-up algorithm.

Furthermore, since all dynamic nonterminals $A' = A(j, k, r)$ are created in stage k, they become static in later stages. This means that when stage k is completed, we can replace all stage k nonterminals with atomic values, such as fresh integers. It is more efficient to compare atomic values than to compare sequences of the form $A(i_1, j_1, r_1) \ldots (i_n, j_n, r_n)$.

Angelov (2009) implements both these optimizations, and also the previous one merging the dynamic rule sets into one big set $\mathbf{R}$.

4.3 Filtered bottom-up and empty rules

If the grammar contains empty constituents, the filtered bottom-up strategy in figure 8 could be very slow. This is because every time a new predict item $[\,?D.u\,] \in \mathbf{P}_k$ is inferred, *predict-bottomup* tries to find some passive item $[\,B_d.s : B'_d\,] \in \mathbf{F}_{k,k}$ that is a left corner of $D.u$. Most of the time this fails, or the active item that is

	English Resource	English FraCaS	Swedish FraCaS
Nr. terminals (w)	1,549	1,549	208
Nr. nonterminals (A)	189	194	274
Nr. constituents ($A.r$)	4,663	4,728	3,178
Nr. grammar rules ($A \to f(\vec{B})$)	43,910	2,992	1,967
Nr. linearizations ($f.r = \alpha$)	256,855	74,709	35,365
Nr. left corner pairs ($D.u \triangleright A.r$)	323,471	256,865	915,650

Table 2: The grammars used for testing

	English Resource	English FraCaS	Swedish FraCaS
Nr. terminals (w)	1,549	1,549	208
Nr. nonterminals (A)	211	231	468
Nr. constituents ($A.r$)	20,669	22,422	8,017
Nr. grammar rules ($A \to f(\vec{B})$)	45,919	135,121	103,334
Nr. linearizations ($f.r = \alpha$)	567,818	1,318,915	3,701,923
Nr. left corner pairs ($D.u \triangleright A.r$)	400,657	424,709	2,288,044

Table 3: The test grammars with empty constituents removed

the consequence will already be in the chart. In the end, lot of useless work will be performed by *predict-bottomup*.

This problem completely disappears if the grammar does not have any empty constituents. In that case all passive items will span at least one input token, i.e., $j < k$, and the predict items will always be from an earlier parsing state.

4.4 Building the sets in stages

Especially the bottom-up strategies benefit from a grammar without empty constituents. In that case, the bottom-up strategies have no use *scan-empty*, and the side condition in *predict-topdown* can be simplified. Furthermore, *combine* can only be triggered by the passive item, since the active item will be from an earlier parsing state.

If the grammar is non-empty, the inference rules also say something about in which order the sets can be built. As an example, if the grammar is non-empty, the set $\mathbf{A}_{k,k}$ can only be created by predict-next from $\mathbf{P}_k$ which on the other hand is built by predict-item from $\mathbf{A}_{jk}$ ($j \leq k$). This means that $\mathbf{A}_{k,k}$ and $\mathbf{P}_k$ depend on each other.

By analyzing all inference rules, we come to the following build order, where $j < k$:

$$\mathbf{A}_{j,j}, \mathbf{P}_j \Rightarrow \mathbf{A}_{j,k}, \mathbf{F}_{j,k} \Rightarrow \mathbf{R}_k \Rightarrow \mathbf{A}_{k,k}, \mathbf{P}_k$$

This ordering suggests the following pseudo-code for parsing n tokens using a non-empty grammar:

1. Build the sets $\mathbf{P}_0$ and $\mathbf{A}_{0,0}$
   [*init-topdown, pred.-topdown, pred.-item*]

2. For each k between 1 and n:

   (a) Build $\mathbf{A}_{j,k}$ and $\mathbf{F}_{j,k}$ (for all $j < k$)
       [*complete, combine, scan, scan-bottomup, pred.-bottomup*]
       As a side-effect, this will also add new rules to $\mathbf{R}$

   (b) Build $\mathbf{P}_k$ and $\mathbf{A}_{k,k}$
       [*pred.-topdown, pred.-item, pred.-next*]

5 Evaluation

We performed a small evaluation of our four parsing strategies. We tested two English grammars and one Swedish grammar written in GF (Ranta, 2011) on 100 randomly selected sentences from the FraCaS textual inference problem set (Cooper et al., 1996). One of the English grammars is the GF English Resource grammar (Ranta, 2009) with the FraCaS lexicon added. The other two grammars and the Swedish translations of the sentences are taken from the FraCaS GF Treebank (Ljunglöf and Siverbo, 2011).

	English Resource			English FraCaS			Swedish FraCaS		
	chart	time	/item	chart	time	/item	chart	time	/item
Top-down	721,000	9,2 s	13 μs	96,000	1,7 s	18 μs	96,000	1,7 s	18 μs
Bottom-up	144,000	2,5 s	17 μs	51,000	1,1 s	21 μs	167,000	3,8 s	23 μs
Filtered top-down	239,000	3,2 s	13 μs	38,000	0,8 s	21 μs	27,000	0,5 s	20 μs
Filtered bottom-up	27,000	0,5 s	17 μs	8,000	0,2 s	20 μs	17,000	0,6 s	34 μs

Table 4: Average chart size per sentence, parse time per sentence and parse time per chart item.

5.1 Non-empty bottom-up grammars

As explained in section 4.3, the bottom-up strategies perform especially poorly if the grammars contain empty constituents. So we also created non-empty versions of the grammars. Table 2 contains some statistics about the grammars and table 3 about their non-empty versions. The tables show that the size of the grammar can explode quite dramatically when removing empty constituents, but it depends on the grammar. E.g., the number of rules in the FraCaS grammars increase by 50 times, while the Resource grammar is almost unaffected.

Despite the dramatic increase of the grammar size, the non-empty grammars always outperform the empty grammars when doing bottom-up parsing. On the other hand, the top-down strategies perform much worse on the empty grammars. Therefore we tested the bottom-up strategies on the empty grammars, and the top-down strategies on the original grammars.

5.2 Test results

We tested each of the four parsing strategies on each of the three grammars and their test sentences. The results are given in table 4, which contains the average size of the chart after parsing each test sentence, together with the average parsing time and the average parsing time per chart item. The tests were run on a 2GHz Intel Core2Duo processor with 4GB RAM.

It is clear from the table that the filtered algorithms outperform the unfiltered ones, and that the filtered bottom-up algorithm is the fastet most of the time. However, we have only tested on three quite similar grammars, so the results could very well be different when testing on other grammars.

Note the increase in parsing time per item for the filtered bottom-up algorithm on the Swedish grammar. This is most certainly caused by the extreme size of the non-empty Swedish grammar,

forcing the Python interpreter to perform garbage collection much more often than usual.

6 Final remarks

We compared four previously published PM-CFG/LCFRS parsing algorithms, and argued that they all implement the same top-down Earley style algorithm without bottom-up filtering. From Angelov's (2009) algorithm we derived three new PMCFG parsing algorithms, one pure bottom-up variant and two variants using a left corner filter. An initial evaluation suggested that these new algorithms can increase PMCFG parsing performance dramatically, at least for some grammars.

6.1 The correct-prefix property

An algorithm satisfies the correct-prefix property (CPP) if it aborts and reports a failure as soon as it reads a prefix that is not a prefix of any correct string in the grammar (Nederhof, 1999).

Angelov's (2009) original top-down algorithm already satisfies CPP, and since the filtered top-down algorithm does not add any additional parse items it also satisfies CPP.

The filtered bottom-up algorithm would also be prefix-correct if the left corner relation was perfect. But we extract the left corners from a context-free approximation, which means that the relation is over-generating. Therefore some non-CPP parse items can be pass through the left corner filter, which means that neither of the bottom-up algorithms satisfy CPP.

6.2 Implementation

We have implemented all four algorithms as a library in the programming language Python. The library is released under an open-source licence and can be downloaded or forked from the following URL:

http://github.com/heatherleaf/MCFParser.py

Acknowledgments

I would like to thank Krasimir Angelov and three anonymous reviewers for insightful and valuable comments and suggestions.

References

Krasimir Angelov. 2009. Incremental parsing with parallel multiple context-free grammars. In *EACL'09, 12th Conference of the European Chapter of the Association for Computational Linguistics*, pages 69–76, Athens, Greece.

Pierre Boullier. 2004. Range concatenation grammars. In Harry Bunt, John Carroll, and Giorgio Satta, editors, *New developments in parsing technology*, pages 269–289. Kluwer Academic Publishers.

Håkan Burden and Peter Ljunglöf. 2005. Parsing linear context-free rewriting systems. In *IWPT'05, 9th International Workshop on Parsing Technologies*, Vancouver, Canada.

Robin Cooper, Dick Crouch, Jan van Eijck, Chris Fox, Josef van Genabith, Jaspars Jan, Hans Kamp, David Milward, Manfred Pinkal, Massimo Poesio, Steve Pulman, Ted Briscoe, Holger Maier, and Karsten Konrad. 1996. Using the framework. Deliverable D16, FraCaS Project.

Éric Villemonte de la Clergerie. 2002. Parsing mildly context-sensitive languages with thread automata. In *COLING'02, 19th International Conference on Computational Linguistics*.

Jay Earley. 1970. An efficient context-free parsing algorithm. *Communications of the ACM*, 13(2):94–102.

Carlos Gómez-Rodríguez, John Carroll, and David Weir. 2008. A deductive approach to dependency parsing. In *ACL'08: HLT, 46th Annual Meeting of the Association for Computational Linguistics: Human Language Technologies*, Columbus, Ohio.

Susan Graham, Michael Harrison, and Walter Ruzzo. 1980. An improved context-free recognizer. *ACM Trans. Program. Lang. Syst.*, 2(3):415–462.

Laura Kallmeyer and Wolfgang Maier. 2009. An incremental Earley parser for simple range concatenation grammar. In *IWPT'09, 11th International Workshop on Parsing Technologies*, Paris, France.

Laura Kallmeyer. 2010. *Parsing Beyong Context-Free Grammars*. Springer.

Makoto Kanazawa. 2008. A prefix-correct Earley recognizer for multiple context-free grammars. In *TAG+9, 9th International Workshop on Tree Adjoining Grammar and Related Formalisms*, Tübingen, Germany.

Peter Ljunglöf and Magdalena Siverbo. 2011. A bilingual treebank for the FraCaS test suite. CLT project report, University of Gothenburg.

Peter Ljunglöf and Mats Wirén. 2010. Syntactic parsing. In Nitin Indurkhya and Fred J. Damerau, editors, *Handbook of Natural Language Processing, 2nd edition*, chapter 4. CRC Press, Taylor and Francis. ISBN 978-1420085921.

Peter Ljunglöf. 2004. *Expressivity and Complexity of the Grammatical Framework*. Ph.D. thesis, University of Gothenburg and Chalmers University of Technology, Gothenburg, Sweden.

Robert C. Moore. 2004. Improved left-corner chart parsing for large context-free grammars. In Harry Bunt, John Carroll, and Giorgio Satta, editors, *New Developments in Parsing Technology*, pages 185–201. Kluwer Academic Publishers.

Mark-Jan Nederhof. 1999. The computational complexity of the correct-prefix property for TAGs. *Computational Linguistics*, 25(3):345–360.

Aarne Ranta. 2009. The GF resource grammar library. *Linguistic Issues in Language Technology*, 2.

Aarne Ranta. 2011. *Grammatical Framework: Programming with Multilingual Grammars*. CSLI Publications, Stanford.

Hiroyuki Seki, Takashi Matsumara, Mamoru Fujii, and Tadao Kasami. 1991. On multiple context-free grammars. *Theoretical Computer Science*, 88:191–229.

Stuart M. Shieber, Yves Schabes, and Fernando C. N. Pereira. 1995. Principles and implementation of deductive parsing. *Journal of Logic Programming*, 24(1–2):3–36.

Klaas Sikkel and Anton Nijholt. 1997. Parsing of context-free languages. In G. Rozenberg and A. Salomaa, editors, *The Handbook of Formal Languages*, volume II, pages 61–100. Springer-Verlag.

Klaas Sikkel. 1998. Parsing schemata and correctness of parsing algorithms. *Theoretical Computer Science*, 199:87–103.

K. Vijay-Shanker, David Weir, and Aravind K. Joshi. 1987. Characterizing structural descriptions produced by various grammatical formalisms. In *ACL'87, 25th Annual Meeting of the Association for Computational Linguistics*, Stanford, California.

Idioms and extended transducers

Gregory M. Kobele
University of Chicago
kobele@uchicago.edu

Abstract

There is a tension between the idea that idioms can be both listed in the lexicon, and the idea that they are themselves composed of the lexical items which seem to inhabit them in the standard way. In other words, in order to maintain the insight that idioms actually contain the words they look like they contain, we need to derive them syntactically from these words. However, the entity that should be assigned a special meaning is then a derivation, which is not the kind of object that can occur in a lexicon (which is, by definition, the atoms of which derivations are built), and thus not the kind of thing that we are able to assign meanings directly to. Here I will show how to resolve this tension in an elegant way, one which bears striking similarities to those proposed by psychologists and psycholinguists working on idioms.

1 Introduction

One standard conception of the lexicon is that it is a set of form-meaning pairs, usually just the bare minimum needed to derive in a systematic way all the other form-meaning pairings constitutive of the language (Di Sciullo and Williams, 1987). Under this conception of the lexicon, an idiom, as its meaning is by definition not predictable given its form, must be a lexical item. Given that idioms are able to occur in syntactic environments where their parts are separated by arbitrarily large amounts of material, as in 1, it then follows, under this conception of the lexicon, that lexical items must (be able to) have complex internal structure, of the sort that is amenable to syntactic manipulation.

(1) *The cat* seems to have been *let out of the bag*.

This treatment of idioms is unsatisfying in the following way. It is natural to think that the word '*cat*' occurs in the idiom '*let the cat out of the bag*', and not just a synchronically unrelated string of phonemes /c/, /a/, /t/. However, as idioms are simply entered *en masse* into the lexicon,

and are therefore not derived objects, they cannot be said to contain the words they look like they contain. In other words, the word '*cat*' occurs in '*let the cat out of the bag*' under this conception of the lexicon to the very same degree it occurs in '*catastrophe*' (i.e. not at all).

In order for the word '*cat*' to actually occur in the idiomatic expression '*let the cat out of the bag*', the idiomatic expression must have a derivation that uses the word '*cat*'.[1] But then it would seem that we must assign a non-predictable meaning to a non-lexical item.

There are thus two (mutually incompatible) roles that a lexicon plays. It is on one hand the set of syntactic building blocks, and on the other the repository of form-meaning pairings. In this paper I will show how the transductive ('two-step') approach to grammar (Morawietz, 2003) disentangles these two notions. The transductive approach to grammar defines the expressions generated in two steps: first, in terms of a set of derivation trees, and second, in terms of operations turning these derivation trees into the objects (sounds, and meanings) that they are the derivations of. We propose that the mapping between derivation tree and derived object be not a simple transduction, but rather an *extended* one in the sense of Graehl et al. (2008). These transducers implement exactly the kind of 'bounded subderivation' translation suggested by Shieber (1994). This ennables us to dissolve the tension between listing idioms on the one hand, and allowing them to be derived, on the other – they are derivationally complex, but interpretatively atomic.

Compare this approach with the general picture painted by Chomsky (1995):

> A language, in turn, determines an infinite set of linguistic expressions (SDs),

---

[1]This is true by definition: an expression *A* contains all and only those expressions that its immediate constituents contain, along with its immediate constituents. (Note that this implicitly involves identifying an expression with its derivation; we don't say of ambiguous expressions that they contain all the expressions that occur in any of their derivations, but rather that under one reading, the expression contains one set of expressions, and under another, another.)

Proceedings of the 11th International Workshop on Tree Adjoining Grammars and Related Formalisms (TAG+11), pages 153–161,
Paris, September 2012.

each a pair $\langle \pi, \lambda \rangle$ drawn from the interface levels (PF,LF), respectively.

According to the two-step approach, each language determines an infinite set of linguistic expressions d, which are then mapped to interface interpretable elements π and λ by operations Π and Λ, respectively. Λ will be viewed as the repository of atomic syntax-meaning pairings, and Π as the repository of atomic syntax-form pairings, while these may make reference to syntactic atoms, they are defined over entire derivation trees, and thus can make reference to larger chunks than single nodes.

The remainder of this paper is structured as follows. In section 2 we present some formal preliminaries. Our proposal is presented in more detail in §3. Section 5 explores linguistic aspects of idioms from this perspective. Section 6 is the conclusion.

2 Background

Lambda terms provide a simple and uniform presentation of structured objects (trees, strings) and of mappings between them. Given a denumerably infinite set X of variables, and a set C of constants, the set of lambda terms over C is defined by the following grammar:

$$M ::= X \mid C \mid (MM) \mid \lambda X.M$$

The usual notions of β, η, and α reduction apply (Barendregt, 1984), and we do not distinguish between terms which are β, η, or α equivalent.

We are interested in lambda terms which can be (simply) typed. Given a finite set A (of atomic types), we define the set $\mathcal{T}(A)$ of types as the closure of A under pairing. When writing elements of $\mathcal{T}(A)$, we treat pairing as associating to the right; $(a, (b, c))$ will be written simply as abc. We write $t^0 := t$ and $t^{n+1} := tt^n$. The order of an atomic type is 1, and of a function type ab is the greater of $\mathsf{ord}(a) + 1$ and $\mathsf{ord}(b)$. A linear Higher Order Signature (HOS) is a triple $\Sigma = \langle C, A, \tau \rangle$ where C and A are finite sets (of constants and atomic types, respectively), and $\tau : C \to \mathcal{T}(A)$ is a function assigning types over A to each $c \in C$. We adopt the notational convention that a HOS Σ_i consists of C_i, A_i, and τ_i. A HOS is of order n just in case the highest order type assigned to any constant is n.

$$\frac{}{x : \alpha \vdash_\Sigma x : \alpha} \qquad \frac{\Gamma \vdash_\Sigma M : \alpha\beta \quad \Delta \vdash_\Sigma N : \alpha}{\Gamma, \Delta \vdash_\Sigma (MN) : \beta}$$

$$\frac{\Gamma, x : \alpha \vdash_\Sigma M : \beta}{\Gamma \vdash_\Sigma \lambda x.M : \alpha\beta} \qquad \frac{}{\vdash_\Sigma c : \tau(c)}$$

Figure 1: Deriving typing judgments

A typing context Γ is a finite map from variables to types. We write $x : \alpha$ to indicate the typing context defined only on x, mapping x to α. Given typing contexts Γ, Δ, their union Γ, Δ is defined iff they have disjoint domains (i.e. no variable is assigned a type in both Γ and Δ). A typing judgment $\Gamma \vdash_\Sigma M : \alpha$ indicates that M has type α in context Γ, with respect to HOS Σ. A typing judgment is derivable just in case it is licensed by the inference system in figure 1.[2] The language $\Lambda_\alpha(\Sigma)$ at type α of HOS Σ is defined to be the set of lambda terms which have the type α in the empty context $(\Lambda_\alpha(\Sigma) := \{M : \vdash_\Sigma M : \alpha\})$. We write $\Lambda(\Sigma)$ to denote the set of all well-typed lambda terms over Σ.

A tree is a first order term (i.e. a term of atomic type) over a second order HOS (which we will call a *tree signature*). Here a constant corresponds to a node of a tree, and its arguments (which are themselves trees) to its daughters. A tree context is a second order term over a second order HOS. A set of trees is regular iff it is the language $\Lambda_\alpha(\Sigma)$ at some atomic type α of some tree signature Σ. The atomic types in this case correspond to states of a tree automaton, and a constant c of type $a_1 a_2 \cdots a_n a$ corresponds to a production $c(a_1, \ldots, a_n) \to a$. A string is a second order term over a second order HOS all of whose constants have type $\alpha\beta$ for some atomic types α, β (which we will call a *string signature*). As an example, $\lambda x.x$ represents the empty string, and $\lambda x.a(b(x))$ the string "ab". As before, the types correspond to states of an NFA, and the function type $\alpha\beta$ assigned to a constant c to a transition from α to β reading c (without ϵ transitions). A set of strings is regular iff it is the language $\Lambda_{\alpha\beta}(\Sigma)$ of some string signature Σ, for α, β atomic types

---

[2]Because the rules for variables and constants require particular typing contexts, lambda bindings are necessarily non-vacuous. Furthermore, because contexts are finite maps, and context union is only defined over disjoint contexts, lambda bindings are necessarily linear.

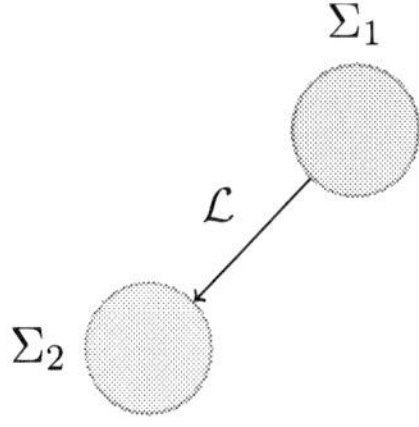

Figure 2: ACGs, graphically

(here α is the start state of the NFA, and β the (unique) final state).

A linear homomorphism $\mathcal{L}$ from HOS Σ_1 to HOS Σ_2 is a pair of maps $F : A_1 \to \mathcal{T}(A_2)$ and $G : C_1 \to \Lambda(\Sigma_2)$ such that for any $c \in C_1, \vdash_{\Sigma_2} G(c) : \hat{F}(\tau_1(c))$, where $\hat{F}$ is F extended pointwise over $\mathcal{T}(A_1)$; this simply demands that the lambda term a constant is mapped to has a type which is appropriately related to the type of the original constant. The order of a linear homomorphism $\mathcal{L}$ is the maximum order of the image under it of an atomic type.[3]

Our proposal is formalized using abstract categorial grammars (ACGs). An ACG (de Groote, 2001) $G = \langle \Sigma_1, \Sigma_2, \mathcal{L}, \alpha \rangle$ consists of a pair of higher order signatures Σ_1 (called its *abstract* vocabulary) and Σ_2 (its *concrete* vocabulary), a linear homomorphism $\mathcal{L}$ (called a *lexicon*) between them, and a designated type α in A_1. The *abstract language* of an ACG G is the set $\Lambda_\alpha(\Sigma_1)$, and its *concrete language* is the set $\mathcal{L}(\Lambda_\alpha(\Sigma_1)) := \{\mathcal{L}(M) : M \in \Lambda_\alpha(\Sigma_1)\}$. It will be convenient to depict ACGs graphically, as in figure 2.

We write $\mathcal{G}(m, n)$ for the set of ACGs G with m the order of its abstract vocabulary, and n the order of its lexicon. Thinking of the abstract vocabulary as the 'derivation structures', ACGs with a second order abstract vocabulary (i.e. those in $\mathcal{G}(2) := \bigcup_{n \in \mathbb{N}} \mathcal{G}(2, n)$) represent grammar formalisms with regular derivation tree languages (de Groote and Pogodalla, 2004). The set of concrete tree languages defined by $\mathcal{G}(2)$ is exactly the set of tree languages generated by hyperedge replacement grammars (Kanazawa, 2010), and the concrete string languages defined by $\mathcal{G}(2)$ is exactly the set of multiple context free languages (Salvati, 2007).

$${}^3\mathtt{ord}(\mathcal{L}) := \mathtt{max}(\{\mathtt{ord}(\mathcal{L}(a)) : a \in A_1\})$$

3 Proposal

We focus on grammars with regular derivation tree languages; in particular tree adjoining grammars (Joshi, 1987) and minimalist grammars (Stabler, 1997).

The derived structures generated by a grammar in both of these grammar formalisms can be given in terms of a transducer of a particular sort acting on a regular set of derivation trees – in the case of tree adjoining grammars the transducer is a simple macro tree transducer (Shieber, 2006), and in the case of minimalist grammars it is a linear deterministic multi-bottom up tree transducer (Kobele et al., 2007; Mönnich, 2007).

Importantly, natural semantic analyses for both grammar formalisms can be given in terms of a similar tree transduction over the derivation (Nesson, 2009; Kobele, 2006), allowing a 'synchronous' representation whereby lexical items ℓ are represented as triples of the form $\langle h_1(\ell), \mathtt{cat}(\ell), h_2(\ell)\rangle$, where h_1, h_2 are the derived structure and semantic structure transductions respectively, and $\mathtt{cat}(\ell)$ is the relevant categorical information (the state the regular tree automaton recognizing the well-formed derivation trees is in upon scanning ℓ).[4] The 'standard' approach to idioms in (synchronous) TAG is to enter them directly into the lexicon (Shieber and Schabes, 1990) – this amounts to introducing a new atomic lexical item ℓ_{idiom}, with (possibly complex) images under h_1 and h_2. While idiomatic expressions have not been handled in published work on MGs, this is also the obvious approach here too. While judicious choice of the derived structures associated with ℓ_{idiom} may allow for the ability of idiomatic material to be affected by syntactic operations, it does not capture the intuition that idioms actually contain the words it seems they do. To do this, we move to extended transductions (we discuss for simplicity homomorphisms: transductions without state). The kernel of an extended homomorphism is a finite relation between tree contexts: $H \subset T_\Sigma(X) \times T_\Delta(X)$. This kernel is thus the repository of non-predictable interpretations of derivation tree contexts. Intuitively, H will map kick(the(bucket)) directly to $\mathtt{die}$, as well as, indirectly via its

---

[4]The second component, $\mathtt{cat}(\ell)$, is only implicit in the standard presentations of synchronous TAGs, e.g. (Shieber and Schabes, 1990) (but is partially indicated by the links).

components, to $\text{kick}(\iota x.\text{bucket}(x))$. Note that, in the case we are primarily interested in here in which only the semantic map is 'non-compositional', we have two objects which can be weighted – the set of lexical items, and the kernel of the semantic homomorphism. This is in line with the psycholinguistic findings (more on which in §5.2) (Titone and Connine, 1999) that (1) idioms seem to behave as though they are syntactically complex (weights over the lexicon) and (2) idioms themselves have different frequencies which subjects are sensitive to (weights over the extended transducers). In the remainder of this paper, we use abstract categorial grammars to work out this approach to idioms.

4 An ACG perspective

Viewing extended transducers from the perspective of abstract categorial grammars (ACGs) (de Groote, 2001) gives us a uniform way of visualizing this approach to idioms, one which explains the attraction of treating idioms as complex lexical items. Simply put, applying an extended transducer to a term t is the same as applying a non-extended transducer to the inverse homomorphic image of t under the map $h_{ex} : \Sigma \cup \Delta \to T_\Sigma(X)$, which maps elements of Σ to themselves, and elements of Δ to contexts over Σ. (Δ represents the idioms as atomic objects.) (Second order) ACGs provide a uniform notation for the macro and the multi bottom-up transducers mentioned above – both are defined in terms of a common set A of 'abstract λ-terms' which are mapped via homomorphism $\mathcal{L}$ to a set of 'concrete λ-terms' C. The differences between macro and multi bottom-up transductions are cashed out in terms of the homomorphisms and the nature of the concrete terms (de Groote and Pogodalla, 2004). Synchronous grammars are given in terms of two ACGs sharing the same abstract language A, but with different homomorphisms $\mathcal{L}_\Pi$ and $\mathcal{L}_\Lambda$ to different concrete languages C_1 (derived syntax) and C_2 (semantics) respectively as illustrated in figure 3 (cf. (Pogodalla, 2007)).

An ACG representation of an extended transduction τ from the terms of HOS A to those of HOS C is obtained as follows. First, we create a HOS X, whose constants represent the left hand sides of the extended transducer rules, and a homomorphism $\mathcal{L}_X$ expanding constants in X to the terms over A which they represent. Then

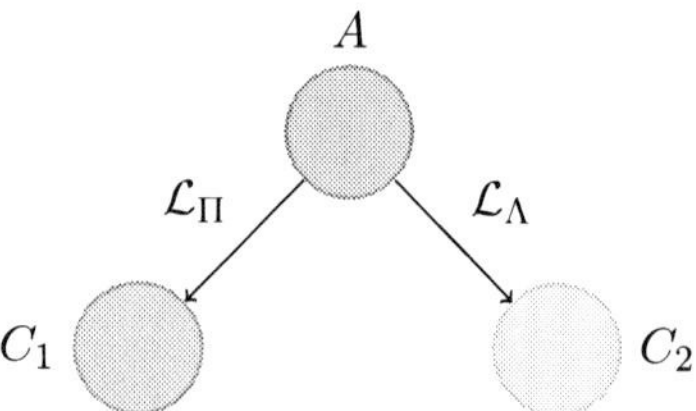

Figure 3: An ACG Perspective on Synchronous Grammars

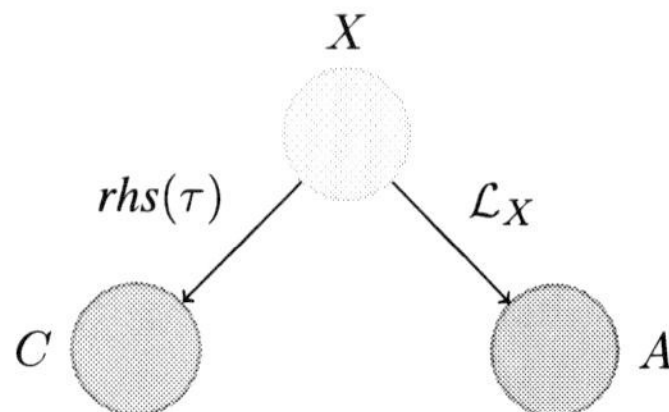

Figure 4: Representing an extended transducer τ

the right hand sides of the extended transducer rules are implemented via a homomorphism from X to C. In the degenerate case where τ is a non-extended transduction, A and X are the same and the map $\mathcal{L}_X$ is the identity function. This is shown in figure 4. As a concrete example, consider an extended (linear) bottom-up transducer t from T_Σ to T_Δ. The HOS A has a single atomic type o, and constants $\sigma \in \Sigma$ of type $o^{\text{rank}(\sigma)}$, similarly for C and Δ. The atomic types of the HOS X are the states of the transducer. For each rule $\rho = q(D[x_1, \ldots, x_n]) \to E[q_1(x_1), \ldots, q_n(x_n)]$, we have in X a constant c_ρ of type $q_1 \cdots q_n q$, whose image under $\mathcal{L}_X : X \to A$ is $\lambda x_1, \ldots, x_n.E(x_1) \cdots (x_n)$, and whose image under $\mathcal{L} : X \to C$ is $\lambda x_1, \ldots, x_n.D(x_1) \cdots (x_n)$.

From the synchronous perspective, it is natural to begin with the non-extended case, as shown in figure 3. Adding 'extension' on the semantic side, so as to describe idioms, we must introduce a new abstract language X, which is simply the original abstract language of derivation terms A with an extra atomic constant for each idiom. Then the semantic homomorphism $\mathcal{L}_\Lambda$ is defined from X to C_2, and the derived syntactic homomorphism is the composition of the mapping $\mathcal{L}_X$ from X to A, which maps elements of A to themselves, and

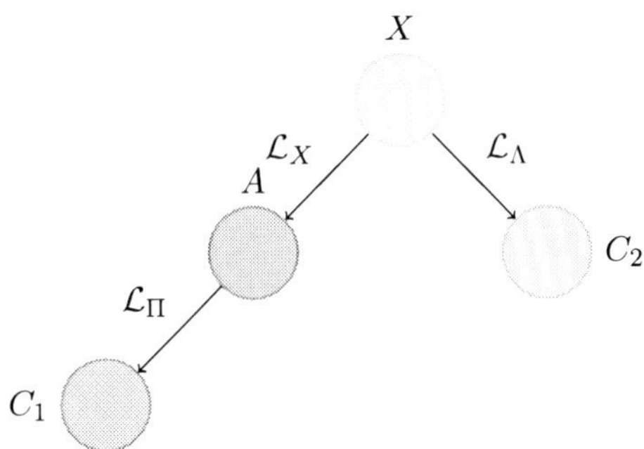

Figure 5: Semantically Extended Synchronous Grammars

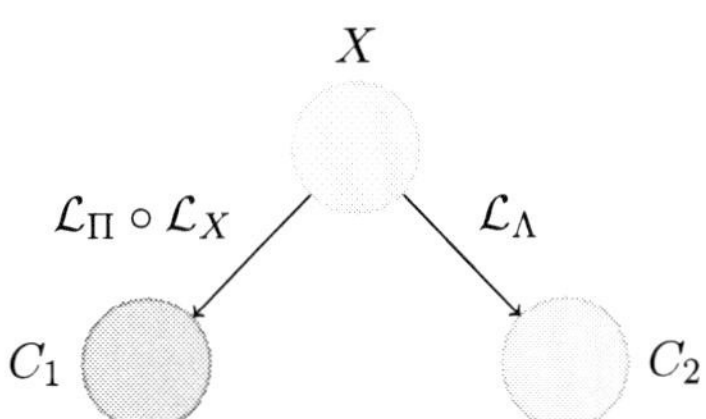

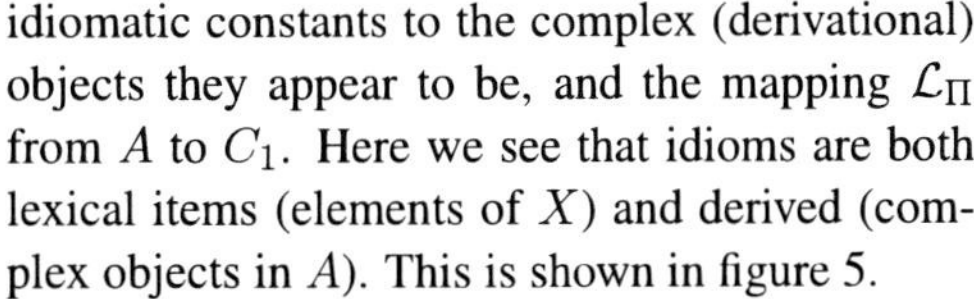

Figure 6: An ACG Perspective on Idioms as Lexical Items

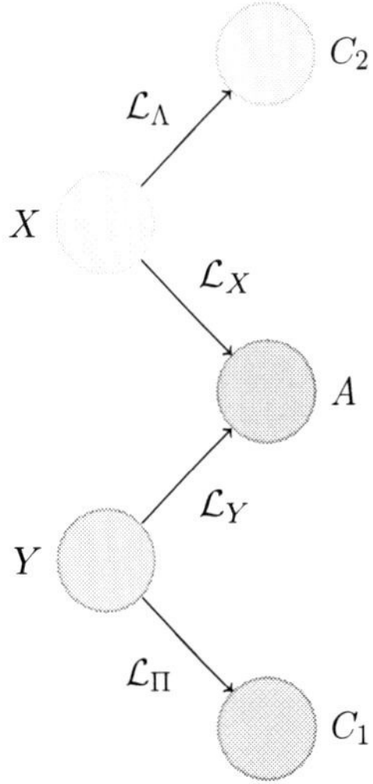

Figure 7: A w-shaped ACG

idiomatic constants to the complex (derivational) objects they appear to be, and the mapping $\mathcal{L}_\Pi$ from A to C_1. Here we see that idioms are both lexical items (elements of X) and derived (complex objects in A). This is shown in figure 5.

Indeed, the standard approach to idioms, whereby they are simply lexical items, is obtained from ours by eliminating the HOS A by composing the maps $\mathcal{L}_X$ and $\mathcal{L}_\Pi$, as shown in figure 6. Distinguishing between A and X, as we propose here, does however have two (potential) benefits, as discussed in sections 4.1, where we propose a similar approach to morphological suppletion, and 5.2, where we suggest that our approach has some psychological plausibility.

4.1 Interface Uniformity

In decompositional (i.e. non-lexicalist) approaches to syntax, the notion of word-hood is divorced from the notion of syntactic terminal – words are conceived of as syntactically complex objects. In this sort of approach, an additional interface is needed to mediate between syntax and morphology, so as to permit suppletive forms

(go + Past $\rightsquigarrow$ went). A natural idea is to take both the mapping from syntax to semantics and the one from syntax to morphology to be of the same kind; an extended transduction.

In our ACG setting, this amounts to introducing a new abstract language Y, and a new lexicon $\mathcal{L}_Y$ mapping terms in Y to terms in A. The lexicon Π from A to C_1, the concrete language of strings, is replaced by one from Y to C_1. This gives rise to a new 'w-shaped' way of combining ACGs, shown in figure 7. In the figure, we see that the derivation tree language is no longer directly mapped to any derived structure language (and has become therefore a concrete language). Instead, it serves only to coordinate the abstract languages X and Y, making sure that the strings and meanings they produce are 'of the same derivation'. Note also that we are no longer able to eliminate the HOS A (and recover the standard approach to idioms outlined in figure 6) as the relation between X and C_1 (or between Y and C_2) is no longer functional.

Parsing in a w-shaped ACG is a matter of computing the inverse image of $\mathcal{L}_\Pi$, then its image under $\mathcal{L}_Y$, then its inverse image under $\mathcal{L}_X$, and then finally its image under $\mathcal{L}_\Lambda$; in other words, the composition $\mathcal{L}_\Lambda \circ \mathcal{L}_X^{-1} \circ \mathcal{L}_Y \circ \mathcal{L}_\Pi^{-1}$. Whereas application of a lambda homomorphism to a recognizable set of terms does not usually preserve recognizability, here the mappings $\mathcal{L}_X$ and $\mathcal{L}_Y$

are both first order (as they map atomic types to atomic types) and lexicalized (abstract constants are mapped to non-combinators), and thus do indeed preserve recognizability. Hence a regular set of strings (over the concrete HOS C_1) is mapped to a regular set of trees over the abstract HOS X.

The fact that the maps $\mathcal{L}_X$ and $\mathcal{L}_Y$ are first order distinguishes our proposal formally from the related one proposed by Dras (1999) in the context of textual paraphrase, which, from our perspective, introduces a sequence of ever more abstract languages, which are related to each other by maps of the same complexity as the maps $\mathcal{L}_\Pi$ and $\mathcal{L}_\Lambda$. (There it is described as deriving tree languages which are then interpreted as derivation tree languages and so on.)

5 Linguistics

5.1 Constraints on Idiomatic Structure

Linguists have formulated various constraints on possible idioms, in particular that dependents of a head can belong to an idiom only if the head belongs as well (Koopman and Sportiche, 1991; O'Grady, 1998). This constraint is naturally implemented in the present context by adopting a TAG-like perspective on derivations, whereby the operations of the grammar are left implicit, and the lexical items are treated as constants of higher rank. Then any first order subterm of a derivation tree satisfies this constraint. This move additionally rules out completely unlexicalized idioms and constructions.[5] This perspective on derivation trees can be easily adapted into the minimalist grammar framework, where the rank of each lexical item is the number of positive selector features[6] it has.[7] Although the set of well-formed minimalist derivation trees is not the algebra freely generated over this signature, it is a regular subset thereof.

[5]For example, $\lambda x, y.\mathbf{merge}(\mathbf{move}(y), z)$ is a first order term over a HOS for (standard presentations of) minimalist derivations. It could be the image of some idiom under the map $\mathcal{L}_S$.

[6]Recall that minimalist grammar categories are finite lists of syntactic features, which are either positive or negative versions of either licensing (for the **move** operation) or selection (for **merge**) feature types.

[7]It is also not necessary in the TAG framework, where one could treat elementary trees as nullary function symbols, and **adjoin** and **substitute** as binary ones.

5.1.1 Syntactic Permeability

Empirical 'puzzles' about idioms, such as their variable permeability to syntactic operations (Nunberg et al., 1994), must be dealt with by fine-tuning the syntactic analysis; canonical analyses of voice phenomena in MGs (as in (Kobele, 2006)) treat the voice head as taking a verb phrase as an argument – an idiom which is not passivizable must include the voice head, whereas one which is must not.

As an example, consider the idiom *"kick the bucket"* ('die'), which cannot be passivized.[8] Adopting the naïve formalization of standard transformational analyses from Kobele (2006), we could represent the idiomatic interpretation of this phrase by means of a unary abstract constant $c_{kick\ the\ bucket}$, which is interpreted semantically as **die**, and derivationally as $\lambda x.\mathtt{act}(\mathtt{kick}(\mathtt{the}(\mathtt{bucket})))(x)$.[9] On the other hand, idioms like *"let the cat out of the bag"* ('reveal a secret') can be passivized (and then subject to raising, and other transformations). While there is no analysis of prepositions in Kobele (2006), we can treat *let* as a raising to object verb, and adapt a small clause analysis of the following form:[10]

$$[_V let\ [_{sc}[_D the\ cat]\ out\ [_P of\ the\ bag]]]$$

We represent this in terms of a nullary abstract constant $c_{let\ cat\ out\ of\ bag}$, which is semantically interpreted as $\lambda x.\mathsf{some}(\mathsf{secret})(\lambda y.\mathsf{reveal}(y)(x))$, and which is derivationally interpreted as $\mathtt{let}(\mathtt{out}(\mathtt{P}(\mathtt{of}(\mathtt{the}(\mathtt{bag})))))(\mathtt{the}(\mathtt{cat}))$

Finally, an idiom like "throw the book at" ('punish severely') illustrates the need for constants corresponding not to subtrees, but to derivation tree contexts. Adopting again an overly simplistic approach to prepositions, we represent this passivizible idiom using the unary abstract constant $c_{throw\ book\ at}$, which is semantically interpreted as $\lambda x.\mathsf{severely}(\mathsf{punish}(x))$,

[8]This means that sentences like *"The bucket was kicked"* can have only a literal interpretation.

[9]Lexical entries:
$\langle act, =V\ +k\ =d\ v\rangle$ $\langle kick, =d\ V\rangle$
$\langle the, =n\ d\ -k\ -q\rangle$ $\langle bucket, n\rangle$

[10]Lexical entries:
$\langle let, =sc\ V\rangle$ $\langle out, =p\ =d\ sc\rangle$
$\langle of, =d\ +k\ +q\ P\rangle$ $\langle P, =P\ p\rangle$
$\langle bag, n\rangle$ $\langle cat, n\rangle$

and is interpreted as the derivational term $\lambda x.\mathtt{Adj}(\mathtt{throw}(\mathtt{the}(\mathtt{book})))(\mathtt{P}(\mathtt{at}(x)))$.[11]

5.1.2 Transformationalism

In general, treating idioms via extended transducers (as done here) puts great pressure on the type system of the grammar formalism (if it is desired to have a single abstract constant representing the idiom in all of its glory). As one of the arguments for transformational analysis continues to be the variety of syntactic contexts which permits idiomatic interpretation, it is perhaps no surprise that the minimalist analyses sketched here go some ways in achieving the ideal of assigning a single type to the idiomatic abstract constant. However, the particular constraints on idiom shape in place here rule out certain otherwise reasonable transformational analyses, such as the implementation of the raising analysis of relative clauses in Kobele (2006).

5.2 Psycholinguistics

Adopting a 'levels' perspective on the relation between grammar and parser (Marr, 1982), a 'search' perspective on parsing still needs a way to order nodes in the agenda. A natural strategy here is to use weights assigned to lexical entries. Perhaps the main substantive difference between our proposal and 'standard' treatments of idioms is the availability of *two* 'lexica' – the HOSs A (for derivations) and X (for idioms) – for differential weighting (see figure 5). The standard treatment, according to which idioms are lexical items (as in figure 6), does not have access to the HOS A. We will need to make a linking theory precise, but, generally speaking, this setup will predict that idioms behave in certain respects as though they were indeed composed of the syntactic atoms it appears they contain. We claim that the literature on priming is consistent with this prediction (Cutting and Bock, 1997; Titone and Connine, 1999; Peterson et al., 2001; Sprenger et al., 2006; Konopka and Bock, 2009). Priming is the phenomenon whereby a prior exposure to some linguistic object token facilitates the comprehension of another token of that type, and increases the likelihood of producing a token of that type.

In order to account for the fact that words can prime idioms which contain them, and vice versa, Sprenger et al. (2006) (following Cutting and Bock (1997)) propose that the mental lexicon is structured as a graph; the lexicon contains idioms, along with links to their constituent parts. Priming works by increasing the weights attached not only to a single node, but to all of its immediate neighbors. (And thus *kick* will prime the node kick as well as its neighbors kick the bucket, kick the can, …) One defect of this account is that it does not explain *why* certain nodes are linked to others. Still, it bears an obvious resemblance to the ACG account presented here – its nodes are the elements of HOS X (which is the HOS A with extra constants for idioms), and the links are given by the lexicon $\mathcal{L}_X$.

First, a (sketch of a) naïve linking theory. We assume that priming effects are to be captured by updating weights on lexical items, and that the weights of all and only the lexical items in a successful parse are increased.[12] Under this view, priming effects come about due to an increased weight of the primed lexical item as a result of having used it previously in a successful parse. For our preliminary purposes here, we will say that a derivation d' primes derivation d (of sentence s) given grammar G just in case $\mathtt{Weight}_{G_{d'}}(d) > \mathtt{Weight}_G(d)$, where G_x is the result of updating the weights of lexical items in parse x (i.e. the weight of d is higher in the reweighted grammar than in the original grammar).

Now, taking the unique derivation d' of the sentence "John kicked Mary" as our primer, and the idiomatic derivation d of the sentence "Susan will kick the bucket" as our primee, we have that the weight of d in the 'idiomatic' HOS X is the same as in $X_{d'}$, but that the weight in the 'derivational' HOS A is less than in $A_{d'}$ (as the weight of the constant c_{kick} was increased after parsing d'). Taking the overall weight of a term t in G to be a monotonic function f of its weight in X and its weight in A, we have that d is primed.

---

[11] Lexical entries:
$\langle\text{throw}, =\text{d V}\rangle$ $\langle\text{Adj}, =\text{V} =\text{p V}\rangle$
$\langle\text{at}, =\text{d} +\text{k} +\text{q P}\rangle$ $\langle\text{P}, =\text{P p}\rangle$
$\langle\text{book}, \text{n}\rangle$ $\langle\text{cat}, \text{n}\rangle$

[12] This is an 'off-line' implementation of priming effects, which neglects the role played by alternative parses of the sentence; Slevc and Ferreira (to appear) demonstrate that priming may occur from *failed parses*.

6 Conclusion

The noncompositional aspect of idiomatic expressions is most naturally dealt with in terms of extended transducers. The ACG perspective allows for a generalization to a wide variety of transducer types, and language families. In addition to being a principled formal account of idioms, the present story allows for a natural connection to the psycholinguistic data.

What we have not explained is the intuition that, in some idioms (such as *let the cat out of the bag*), certain parts of the idioms (e.g. *the cat*) seem to be associated with certain parts of the idiomatic meaning (e.g. *the secret*). That this intuition may in fact be deserving of an explanation is suggested by Horn (2003) (building on work by Nunberg et al. (1994)), who argues that this sort of 'semantic transparency' is a good predictor of whether the internal structure of an idiom can be subject to syntactic manipulation.

References

Hendrik Barendregt. 1984. *The Lambda Calculus: Its syntax and semantics*, volume 103 of *Studies in Logic and the Foundations of Mathematics*. Elsevier, Amsterdam.

Noam Chomsky. 1995. *The Minimalist Program.* MIT Press, Cambridge, Massachusetts.

J. Cooper Cutting and Kathryn Bock. 1997. That's the way the cookie bounces: Syntactic and semantic components of experimentally elicited idiom blends. *Memory and Cognition*, 25(1):57–71.

Philippe de Groote and Sylvain Pogodalla. 2004. On the expressive power of Abstract Categorial Grammars: Representing Context-Free formalisms. *Journal of Logic, Language and Information*, 13(4):421–438.

Philippe de Groote. 2001. Towards abstract categorial grammars. In *Association for Computational Linguistics, 39th Annual Meeting and 10th Conference of the European Chapter, Proceedings of the Conference*, pages 148–155.

Anna Maria Di Sciullo and Edwin Williams. 1987. *On the definition of word*, volume 14 of *Linguistic Inquiry Monographs*. MIT Press.

Mark Dras. 1999. *Tree Adjoining Grammar and the Reluctant Paraphrasing of Text*. Ph.D. thesis, Macquarie University.

Jonathan Graehl, Kevin Knight, and Jonathan May. 2008. Training tree transducers. *Computational Linguistics*, 34(3):391–427.

George M. Horn. 2003. Idioms, metaphors and syntactic mobility. *Journal of Linguistics*, 39:245–273.

Aravind K. Joshi. 1987. An introduction to tree adjoining grammars. In A. Manaster-Ramer, editor, *Mathematics of Language*. John Benjamins, Amsterdam.

Makoto Kanazawa. 2010. Second-order abstract categorial grammars as hyperedge replacement grammars. *Journal of Logic, Language and Information*, 19:137–161.

Gregory M. Kobele, Christian Retoré, and Sylvain Salvati. 2007. An automata theoretic approach to minimalism. In James Rogers and Stephan Kepser, editors, *Proceedings of the Workshop Model-Theoretic Syntax at 10; ESSLLI '07*, Dublin.

Gregory M. Kobele. 2006. *Generating Copies: An investigation into structural identity in language and grammar*. Ph.D. thesis, University of California, Los Angeles.

Agnieszka E. Konopka and Kathryn Bock. 2009. Lexical of syntactic control of sentence formulation? Structural generalizations from idiom production. *Cognitive Psychology*, 58:68–101.

Hilda Koopman and Dominique Sportiche. 1991. The position of subjects. *Lingua*, 85:211–258.

David Marr. 1982. *Vision*. W. H. Freeman and Company, New York.

Uwe Mönnich. 2007. Minimalist syntax, multiple regular tree grammars and direction preserving tree transductions. In James Rogers and Stephan Kepser, editors, *Proceedings of the Workshop Model-Theoretic Syntax at 10; ESSLLI '07*, Dublin.

Frank Morawietz. 2003. *Two-Step Approaches to Natural Language Formalisms*, volume 64 of *Studies in Generative Grammar*. Mouton de Gruyter.

Rebecca Nesson. 2009. *Synchronous and Multicomponenet Tree-Adjoining Grammars: Complexity, Algorithms and Linguistic Applications*. Ph.D. thesis, Harvard University.

Geoffrey Nunberg, Ivan A. Sag, and Thomas Wasow. 1994. Idioms. *Language*, 70(3):491–538.

William O'Grady. 1998. The syntax of idioms. *Natural Language and Linguistic Theory*, 16:279–312.

Robert R. Peterson, Curt Burgess, Gary S. Dell, and Kathleen M. Eberhard. 2001. Dissociation between syntactic and semantic processing during idiom comprehension. *Journal of Experimental Psychology: Learning, Memory, and Cognition*, 27(5):1223–1237.

Sylvain Pogodalla. 2007. Generalizing a proof-theoretic account of scope ambiguity. In J. Geertzen, E. Thijsse, H. Bunt, and A. Schiffrin, editors, *Proceedings of the 7th International Workshop on Computational Semantics (IWCS)*, pages 154–165.

Sylvain Salvati. 2007. Encoding second order string acgs with deterministic tree walking transducers. In Shuly Wintner, editor, *Proceedings of FG 2006: the*

11th conference on Formal Grammar, pages 143–156. CSLI Publications.

Stuart M. Shieber and Yves Schabes. 1990. Synchronous tree-adjoining grammars. In *Proceedings of the 13th International Conference on Computational Linguistics (COLING)*, volume 3, pages 253–258, Helsinki,Finland.

Stuart M. Shieber. 1994. Restricting the weakgenerative capacity of synchronous tree-adjoining grammars. *Computational Intelligence*, 10(4):371–385.

Stuart M. Shieber. 2006. Unifying synchronous treeadjoining grammars and tree transducers via bimorphisms. In *Proceedings of the 11th Conference of the European Chapter of the Association for Computational Linguistics (EACL-2006)*, pages 377–384, Trento.

L. Robert Slevc and Victor S. Ferreira. to appear. To err is human; to structurally prime from errors is also human. *Journal of Experimental Psychology: Learning, Memory, and Cognition.* doi:10.1037/a0029525.

Simone A. Sprenger, Willem J. M. Levelt, and Gerard Kempen. 2006. Lexical access during the production of idiomatic phrases. *Journal of Memory and Language*, 54:161–184.

Edward P. Stabler. 1997. Derivational minimalism. In Christian Retoré, editor, *Logical Aspects of Computational Linguistics*, volume 1328 of *Lecture Notes in Computer Science*, pages 68–95. SpringerVerlag, Berlin.

Debra A. Titone and Cynthia M. Connine. 1999. On the compositional and noncompositional nature of idiomatic expressions. *Journal of Pragmatics*, 31:1655–1674.

Creating a Tree Adjoining Grammar
from a Multilayer Treebank

Rajesh Bhatt
Univ. of Massachusetts
Amherst, MA 01003, USA
bhatt@linguist.umass.edu

Owen Rambow
CCLS, Columbia University
New York, NY 10115, USA
rambow@ccls.columbia.edu

Fei Xia
Univ. of Washington
Seattle, WA 98195, USA
fxia@uw.edu

Abstract

We propose a method for the extraction of a Tree Adjoining Grammar (TAG) from a dependency treebank which has some representative examples annotated with phrase structures. We show that the resulting TAG along with corresponding dependency structure can be used to convert a dependency treebank to a TAG-based phrase structure treebank.

1 Introduction

In this paper, we address the problem of extracting a Tree Adjoining Grammar (TAG) from a treebank which has been annotated manually for dependency structure (DS), and which has a small set of representative example sentences manually annotated for both DS and phrase structure (PS). There has been much work on TAG extraction from PS treebanks (e.g., (Xia, 1999; Chen, 1999)). In those studies, heuristics are used to "cut up" the PS trees of entire sentences into elementary trees, which are then collected into a grammar.

This paper extends the previous work and makes the following novel contributions:

- We present a method for extracting a TAG from a DS treebank augmented with a set of representative examples of (DS, PS) pairs.

- We show that the resulting TAG paired with DS subtrees can be interpreted as conversion rules for converting the DS treebank to a PS treebank.

The structure of the paper is as follows. In Section 2, we review the relevant properties of the Hindi Treebank, which serves as the source of our examples in this paper. We then discuss the crucial notion of "consistency" in Section 3, and present

our basic algorithm in Section 4. We then discuss two issues which require extensions to our agorithm: empty categories (Section 5) and long-distance word order variations (Section 6). These extensions are sketched, but we do not present them in full detail due to lack of space. Finally, we discuss remaining issues in Section 7 and then conclude.

2 The Hindi Treebank

In this paper, we use the Hindi Treebank (HTB) (Palmer et al., 2009) as an example, but the principles we present are language-independent. Compared to other existing treebanks, the HTB is unusual in that it contains three layers: dependency structure (DS), PropBank-style annotation (PB) (Kingsbury et al., 2002) for predicate-argument structure, and an independently motivated phrase-structure (PS) annotation which is automatically derived from the DS plus the PB. The treebank is created in three steps. The first step is the manual annotation of DS. The second step is PropBanking, which focuses on adding the lexical predicate-argument structure on top of DS. The third step is the automatic creation of PS, which is done by a DS-to-PS conversion process that takes DS and PB as input and generates PS as output.

Figure 1 (top row) shows the three layers for Ex (1), a sentence with the unaccusative verb *break*. Because the three layers are independently motivated, they have a certain freedom in choosing how they represent syntactic phenomena. In this example, the DS layer decides to treat unaccusative verbs the same way as unergative (such as *sleep*), and marks their subjects as a *k1*. In contrast, the PB makes the distinction, marking the subject of an unaccusative verb as an *ARG1*, not *ARG0* (as is the case for the subjects of unergative verbs); PS also makes the distinction, by in-

Proceedings of the 11th International Workshop on Tree Adjoining Grammars and Related Formalisms (TAG+11), pages 162–170,
Paris, September 2012.

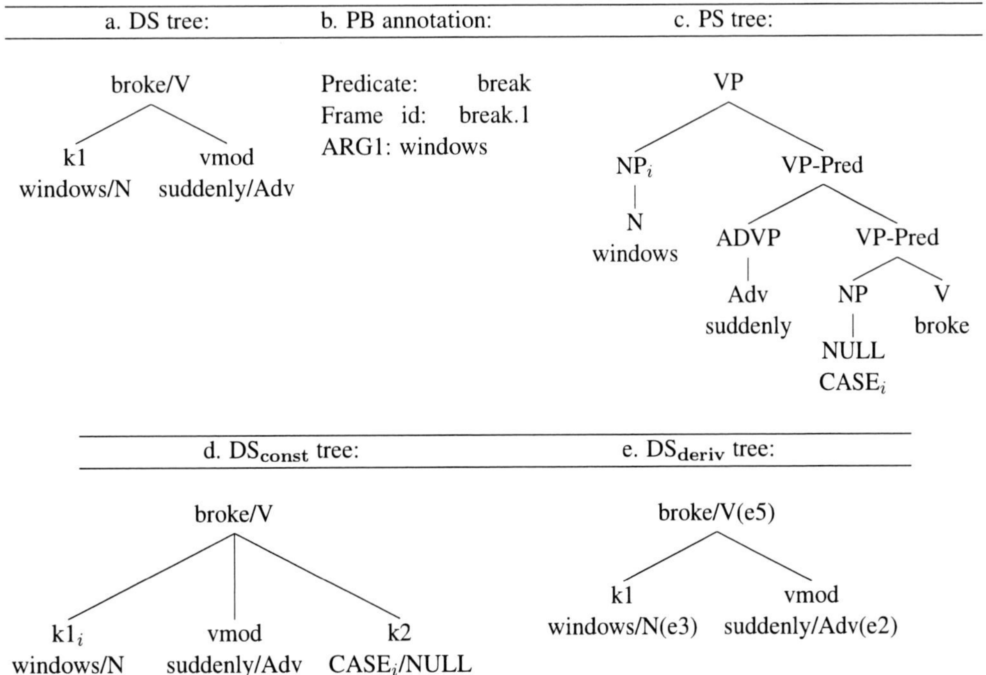

Figure 1: The three annotation levels of the HTB: Dependency Structure, PropBank, and Phase Structure (top row); the consistent DS (DS_{const}) and the derivation tree (DS_{deriv}) obtained from these structures (bottom row); e_i in the DS_{deriv} tree refers to elementary trees in Figures 5-6.

dicating *movement* from the object position to the subject position using a coindexed trace.

(1) khiṛkiyā: acaanak   ṭuuṭī:
     windows.F suddenly broke.FPl

     'The windows broke suddenly.'

3 Consistency between DS and PS

In our previous study (Xia et al., 2009; Bhatt et al., 2011), we proposed a DS-to-PS conversion algorithm, which extracts conversion rules from a small number of (DS, PS) pairs, and then applies the rules to a new DS to generate a PS for the DS.

The algorithm introduces two concepts: *consistency* and *compatibility*. A DS and a PS tree are *consistent* if and only if there exists an assignment of head words for the internal nodes in the PS such that after merging all the (head child, parent) nodes in the PS, the new PS is identical to the DS. In Figure 1, the DS in (a) and the PS in (c) are not consistent because the empty category *CASE* appears only in (c). In contrast, the dependency structure in (d), where *CASE* is added to the original DS as a *k2* dependent of the verb, is consistent with the PS in (c). A DS and a PS analysis

for a linguistic phenomenon are *compatible* if the (DS,PS) tree pairs for the sentences with that phenomenon are consistent.

Bhatt and Xia (2012) demonstrate that automatic, high-quality DS-to-PS conversion is facilitated when the analyses chosen by the DS and PS guidelines for most linguistic phenomena are compatible; for the phenomena with incompatible analyses, manually written rules transform DS to an intermediate representation called DS_{const} (*const* stands for *consistency*). The process of creating DS_{const} from a DS is explained in that paper.

We are currently using the algorithm to automatically generate the PS trees in the HTB, given the manual annotation of the DS and PB layers. The process is illustrated in Figure 2.[1] The process assumes that there is a small set of sentences with all three layers of annotation, which are used in the training stage of the conversion to extract

---

[1] PB is part of the input for the conversion process because it provides certain information (e.g., unaccusative vs. unergative distinction) that is not present in the DS. For the sake of simplicity, we still call the process "DS-to-PS conversion", though "DS+PB-to-PS conversion" would be more complete.

conversion rules. The rules are then applied to the DS and PB for the new sentences in the test stage to generate PS. For instance, if the DS and PB in Figure 1a. and 1b. are the input to the training stage, the system will create DS_{const} in Figure 1d. From the (DS_{const}, PS) pair (Figure 1d. and 1c.), the system will automatically extract the conversion rules in Figure 3. If these rules are applied to the same DS_{const} tree in the test stage, the PS created by the system will be identical to the one in Figure 1c. The details of the algorithm can be found in (Xia et al., 2009; Bhatt and Xia, 2012).

(a) Training stage

(b) Test stage

Figure 2: The flow chart for DS-to-PS conversion

4 Basic TAG Extraction Algorithm

Given a dependency treebank *DTB* and a set of (DS, PS) pairs, the goals of this study are (1) to design the algorithm that extracts a TAG from the DTB, and (2) transforms the DTB into a treebank for the extracted TAG–that is, for each sentence in the DTB, we want to create a derivation tree and a derived tree for the sentence based on the extracted TAG with the requirement that the derived tree is consistent with the DS_{const} for the sentence.

One possible approach works as follows: (1) run the DS-to-PS conversion algorithm described in Section 3 on the DTB to generate a PS treebank; (2) extract a TAG from the PS treebank by adapting an existing grammar extraction algorithm (e.g., (Xia, 1999; Chen, 1999)); (3) run a TAG parser to generate a set of parse trees for each sentence in the DTB; (4) for each sentence in the DTB, to maintain the dependency relation in its DS, a filter is needed to throw away all the parse trees generated in (3) that are not consistent with the DS_{const} for that sentence.

This approach has several limitations. First, it requires adapting a grammar extraction algorithm

in Step (2) and writing a filter in Step (4). Second, it is highly inefficient; for instance, many parse trees generated in Step (3) will later be thrown away in Step (4). Third, the connection between dependency relation in the DTB and elementary trees in the extracted TAG is not represented as the latter is extracted from the PS produced in Step (1), not from the DS directly.

We propose a new approach (see Figure 4), which not only extracts a TAG from a dependency treebank directly, but also provides a new way for converting DS to PS. Compared to the DS-to-PS conversion algorithm (see Figure 2), the second modules in the training and test stages are different and the definition of conversion rules is extended. In the original definition, the lefthand side of a conversion rule is a dependency link, and the righthand side is similar to a context-free rule. In the new definition, the lefthand side is a subtree of a DS that includes a head and either all its arguments or one adjunct with the adjunct's arguments, and the righthand side is an elementary tree. We call the new rule *etree-based rule* (*etree* for elementary tree).

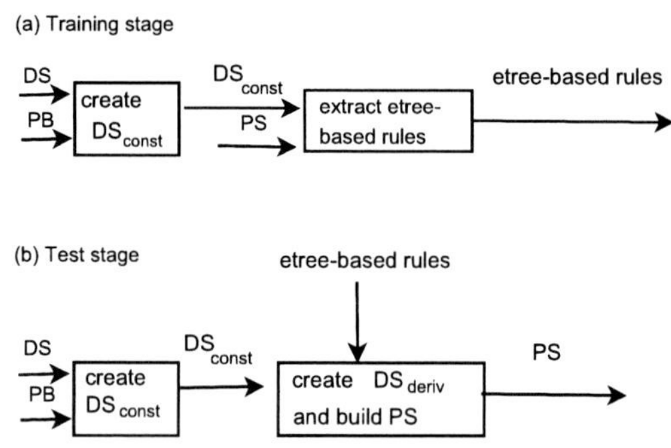

Figure 4: The flow chart for converting the HTB into a TAG-based treebank

4.1 Extracting *etree-based* conversion rules and TAGs

The training stage, as in Figure 4(a), has two modules. The first module is the same as the first module in the DS-to-PS conversion algorithm and is described in (Bhatt and Xia, 2012). The second module takes (DS_{const},PS) pairs as input and outputs etree-based rules, and Table 1 shows its pseudocode.

Xia et al. (1999) described an algorithm that extracts TAGs from a PS treebank. Given a phrase structure T, the algorithm extracts a TAG in four

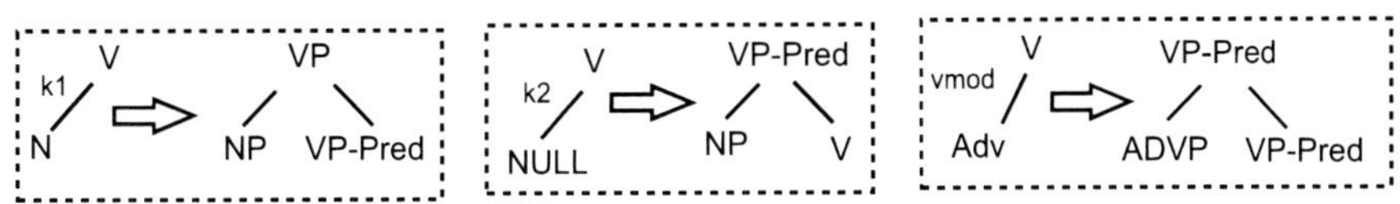

Figure 3: Conversion rules extracted from the (DS$_{\text{const}}$,PS) pair in Figure 1, which is produced by the DS-to-PS conversion process in Figure 2.

Input: *TreePairs* is a set of (DS$_{\text{const}}$, PS) pairs
        ArgTable is a set of (head-POS-tag, dep-types)

Output: *ConvRules* is a set of *etree-based* conversion rules

Algorithm: ExtConvRules(TreePairs, ArgTable)
(1) *ConvRules* = ϕ;
(2) for each (DS$_{\text{const}}$, PS) pair in *TreePairs*
(3)   // Step 1: Make argument/adjunct distinction in the DS$_{\text{const}}$
(4)   for each internal node h in DS$_{\text{const}}$
(5)   mark each child d of h as argument or adjunct based on *ArgTable*

(6)   // Step 2: Choose head child and make argument/adjunct distinction in the PS
(7)   for each dependency link (d, h) in DS$_{\text{const}}$, do the following in the PS
(8)   find the lowest ancestor of d and h in PS and call it Y
(9)   let X_d be Y's child that dominates d and X_h be Y's child that dominates h
(10)   mark X_h as the head child of Y
(11)   mark X_d as an argument or adjunct child of Y based on the label of d in line (5)

(12)   // Step 3: deflat the PS and extract *etrees* from it
(13)   *deflat* the PS so that arguments and adjuncts are not siblings
(14)   extract *etrees* from the deflatted PS

(15)   // Step 4: create conversion rules
(16)   for each node h in DS$_{\text{const}}$
(17)   for each adjunct child d of h
(18)   create a rule where the lefthand side is a subtree of DS$_{\text{const}}$ with dependency
(19)   link (d, h) and links between d and all its argument children (if any),
(20)   and the righthand side is the corresponding auxiliary tree anchored by d
(21)   if (h is the root of DS$_{\text{const}}$) or (h is not marked as an adjunct child of its parent)
(22)   create a rule where the lefthand side is h with all its argument children in the
(23)   DS$_{\text{const}}$, and the righthand side is the corresponding initial tree anchored by h
(24)   add the rules to *ConvRules*

(25) return *ConvRules*

Table 1: Algorithm for extracting *etree-based* conversion rules

Input: *ConvRules* which is extracted from the training stage
        ArgTable is the same as the one used in the training stage
        A new DS_{const}

Output: A set of PSs for the input DS_{const}

Algorithm: BuildPS(ConvRules, ArgTable, DS_{const})
(1) $DS_{deriv} = DS_{const}$
(2) DS_{deriv} has an extra field EtreeSet[n] that stores the possible etrees for node n

(3) // Step 1: make argument/adjunct distinction in DS_{const}
(4) for each internal node h in DS_{deriv}
(5)   mark each child d of h as argument or adjunct based on *ArgTable*

(6) // Step 2: Find *etrees* for the nodes in DS_{const}
(7) for each node h in DS_{const}
(8)   for each adjunct child d of h
(9)   find rules in *ConvRules* whose lefthand side is a subtree of DS_{const} that
(10)   includes the dependency link (d, h) and links between d and its arguments
(11)   EtreeSet[d] = the etrees in these matched rules
(12)   if (h is the root of DS_{const}) or (h is not marked as an adjunct child of its parent)
(13)   find rules in *ConvRules* whose lefthand side is a subtree of DS_{const} that
(14)   includes h and all its argument children (if any)
(15)   EtreeSet[h] = the etrees in these matched rules

(16) // Step 3: Build PSs from DS_{deriv}
(17) PSset = ϕ
(18) for each combination of etrees in DS_{deriv}
(19) (In a *combination*, one etree is picked from EtreeSet[n] for each node n in DS_{deriv})
(20)   generate PSs from the combination
(21)   add these PSs to PSset

(22) return PSset

Table 2: Algorithm for building PSs for a given DS_{const}

steps: (i) for each internal node n in T, select one of its children as head child according to a head percolation table; (ii) for other children of n, determine whether each child is an argument or an adjunct of n using an argument table; (iii) *deflat* the PS so that arguments and adjuncts are not siblings; (iv) extract etrees from deflatted PS by decomposing the PS into pieces and gluing some pieces together to form etrees.

The algorithm in Table 1 can be seen as an extension of the algorithm in (Xia, 1999). First, because its input includes DS_{const}, the dependency relation is already given between words so Step (i) is no longer needed; second, argument/adjunct distinction is made on DS_{const} first (see Step 1) and then carried over to PS (see Step 2). Step 1 uses an argument table which specifies what kind of dependents are considered as arguments of a head. For instance, if dependents with *k1*, *k2*, or *k4* role labels are considered arguments of a verb, the argument table will include an entry *(v, k1/k2/k4)*. Step 2 makes the argument/adjunct distinction in the PS based on the decision made in the DS. Step 3 is identical to Steps (iii)-(iv) and it extracts etrees from the deflatted PS. Step 4 links subtrees in the DS_{const} to extracted etrees to form etree-based rules. Each subtree in an etree-based rule includes a head and either all its arguments (this determines how many substitution nodes the etree has) or one adjunct of the head and the adjunct's arguments (if any). The righthand side of the etree-based rules form a TAG.

Given the (DS_{const}, PS) pair in Figure 1d and 1c, the extracted rules are shown in Figure 5. Compared to the rules in Figure 3, etree-based rules have extended locality.

4.2 Generating PS from DS

The test stage (see Figure 4(b)) also has two modules: the first one is the same as the one in the training stage. Table 2 shows the algorithm for the second module. The algorithm has three steps. The first step makes argument/adjunct distinction in the input DS_{const}.

The second step finds the etrees that each word in the DS_{const} could anchor. This is done by forming a subtree of DS_{const} that a word belongs to (similar to Step 4 in Table 1) and then selecting conversion rules that match that subtree. The etrees in those selected conversion rules are stored with the node in DS_{const}, resulting in

a new tree called DS_{deriv}. The subscript *deriv* in DS_{deriv} stands for *derivation tree* because DS_{deriv} is just like the derivation tree in the TAG except that it does not include the positions of substitution/adjoining operations and which etree the word anchors in the current sentence is not determined.

The third step produces a set of PSs from the DS_{deriv}. The set could have more than one PS due to various types of ambiguity. In principle, one could imagine that there is already a one-to-many mapping between the DS_{const} the PS. We do not handle ambiguities that have such a source as we consider these to be a treebank design flaw. Either side should be enriched or modified during the design process to eliminate intrinsically ambiguous mappings. However, ambiguity can arise despite careful design of the levels of representation. For example, in Hindi adverbs can occur before or after the subject. From the DS and PS trees for a sentence such as (1), the rule with adjunction at the VP-Pred-level will be extracted (the second rule in Figure 5), while the DS and PS trees for *acaanak khiṟkiyā: ṭuuṭī:* ("suddenly the windows broke") yields a rule with adjunction at the VP-level. Thus, we have an ambiguous rule. Most of the time this does not matter since word order resolves the adjunction level, but if the subject is empty we obtain two possible derivations using two different etrees. Another, related type of ambiguity arises when there are multiple instances of a node label in one tree, allowing for multiple derivation using the *same* etrees. Consider a simple case of a verb that has a left adjunct as well as a right adjunct: **L V R**. Let us assume that, according to the conversion rules, both **L** and **R** can adjoin at the VP level. This will lead to two PSs, one with **L** attached higher than **R**, and the other with **R** attached higher than **L**.

5 Empty Categories

In the basic algorithm outlined in Section 4, DS_{deriv} is isomorphic to DS_{const} by design. The problem with that design is that DS_{const} may include nodes labeled with empty categories (ECs) (see Figure 1d.), meaning that some etrees in the resulting TAG would be "lexicalized" by an EC and that could cause difficulty when using the TAG for parsing.

To solve this problem, we make two minor revisions to the basic algorithm: in the rule extraction

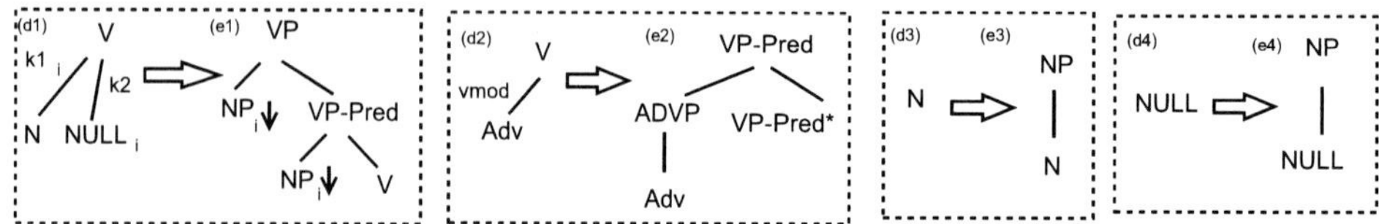

Figure 5: Etree-based rules extracted by the algorithm in Table 1 from the (DS$_{const}$,PS) pair in Ex (1)

module (see Table 1), if in the DS$_{const}$ a head has a dependent which is an EC, then the EC (along with its phrase structure projection, if any) is included in the etree for the head word (see the etree in Figure 6). Similarly, in the creating DS$_{deriv}$ module (see Table 2), the EC leaf node will be removed from DS$_{deriv}$ as it is already included in the etree for its parent node.

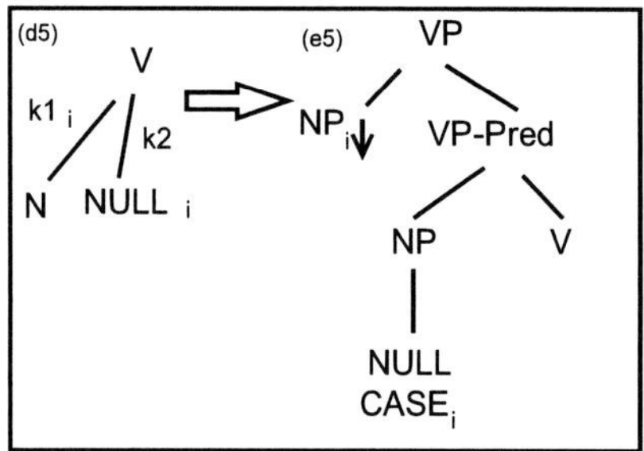

Figure 6: The new etree-based rule extracted from the (DS$_{const}$, PS) pair in Figure 1. It will replace the first and last rules in Figure 5

In the case of our unaccusative example, the extracted TAG will include the rule in Figure 6, which replace the first and last rules in Figure 5. The new DS$_{deriv}$ is in Figure 1e., where e_2 and e_3 are two etrees in Figure 5, and e_5 is the etree in Figure 6.[2]

6 Issues in Word Order

It has been known for a long time that in a lexicalized TAG, the derivation tree is a lexical dependency tree (since the nodes are bijectively identified with the words of the sentence), and that this dependency structure is not necessarily the linguistically plausible structure (Rambow and Joshi, 1997; Candito and Kahane, 1998; Rambow et al., 2001). Consider the following example (2):

[2]It is not a coincident that in this example DS$_{deriv}$ and DS are isomorphic, as the DS-to-DS$_{const}$ module involves adding ECs and DS$_{const}$-to-DS$_{deriv}$ involves removing ECs. But in theory, DS$_{deriv}$ and DS are not necessarily always isomorphic as the DS-to-DS$_{const}$ module is not limited to adding ECs.

(2) kitaabẽ mẼ-ne khariid-nii caah-ii
     books.F I-Erg buy-Inf.F want-Pfv.F
     'Books, I had wanted to buy.'

Here, the standard analysis is that the matrix clause anchored on *want* is adjoined into the embedded clause anchored on *buy*, which results in a derivation structure in which the *buy* node dominates the *want* node, contrary to the dependency representation. Furthermore, it has been known that if we want the etrees and the derivation structure to have a linguistic interpretation, then certain word orders in free word order languages cannot be derived using a TAG (Rambow, 1994; Chen-Main and Joshi, 2008). Consider the following example.

(3) mẼ-ne yeh kitaab sab-se khariid-ne-ko
     I-Erg this book all-Instr buy-Inf-Acc
     kah-aa
     say-Pfv
     'I told everyone to buy this book.'

In (3), *this book* is an argument of the embedded verb *buy*, and is placed between the matrix verb's two arguments. While this can be derived by a TAG, it would require an etree headed by *buy* to have a VP foot node, which has no plausible linguistic interpretation (since *buy* does not have a clausal argument).

Both problems have a common solution: non-local multicomponent TAGs with dominance links (nlMC-TAG-DL), for example in the definition given in (Rambow et al., 2001) as D-Tree Substitution Grammars (DSG). In a DSG, there is only the substitution operation, but all links in trees are interpreted as non-immediate dominance links; in fact, the trees can be seen as tree descriptions rather than as trees; this allows components of trees to move up and be inserted into other trees. For large-scale grammar development in DSG, see (Carroll et al., 1999).

There are good reasons to want to try and restrict the generative power of a formal system used for the description of syntax: on the one hand, we may want to restrict the formal power in order to obtain parsing algorithms of certain restricted complexities (Kallmeyer, 2005), and on the other hand, we may want to make assumptions about the underlying formalism in order to make predictions about what word orders are grammatical (or plausible) (Chen-Main and Joshi, 2008). However, in this paper we do not address the tradeoff between non-local and restricted MC-TAG systems, and we do not present empirical arguments from Hindi in order to address the issue of what formal complexity is required for the syntactic description of Hindi. We leave those issues to future work. Instead, we assume a simple framework in which we can explore the issue of grammar extraction.

The algorithm for extraction of a TAG can be extended straightforwardly to an algorithm for extracting a DSG: whenever in DS_{const} we have a node labeled with an empty category which is co-indexed with a node which is higher in the tree (in a c-command relationship), then we put the two etrees resulting from those two nodes into one set, and add a dominance relation. The step for creating DS_{deriv} should also be revised accordingly to indicate that the two etrees belong to one set.

7   Conclusion

We have given a basic algorithm for the extraction of a TAG from a dependency treebank which has some representative examples annotated with phrase structures. This TAG can be used for any purpose TAGs can be used, such as parsing or generation, but we can also use etree-based conversion rules to convert the entire DS treebank to a TAG-based treebank. We have also sketched how this basic algorithm can be extended to handle empty categories and word order variation.

There are several important remaining issues. The first issue is ambiguity. Ideally, we want to have exactly one PS and one TAG derivation tree for each DS_{const} in the test stage because we can then transform the original dependency treebank into a treebank for the extracted TAG. However, as discussed in Section 4.2, the second module in the test stage may produce multiple PSs for a given DS_{const}. One possible way to reduce spurious ambiguity is to look at the PS trees in the training data where ambiguity of attachment can arise. If there are regularities in these situations (for example, lowest attachment possible, and a certain

order for attaching left and right adjuncts), then that information could be passed to the test stage to reduce ambiguity.

The second issue is unseen rules. The etree-based rules are extracted from the (DS_{const}, PS) pairs in the training stage. If the number of such representative examples is small, it is unlikely that the rules extracted from the pairs are complete enough to cover the DS_{const} subtrees in the test stage. Some kind of backoff strategy is needed to handle such cases. We will study both issues in the future.

Acknowledgment This work is supported by NSF grants CNS-0751089, CNS-0751171, and CNS-0751213. We would like to thank the anonymous reviewers for helpful comments and our colleagues on the Hindi-Urdu Treebank Project for their support.

References

Rajesh Bhatt and Fei Xia. 2012. Challenges in converting between treebanks: a case study from the hutb. In *Proceedings of META-RESEARCH Workshop on Advanced Treebanking, in conjunction with LREC-2012*, Istanbul, Turkey.

Rajesh Bhatt, Owen Rambow, and Fei Xia. 2011. Linguistic phenomena, analyses, and representations: Understanding conversion between treebanks. In *Proceedings of the 5th International Joint Conference on Natural Language Processing (IJCNLP)*, pages 1234–1242, Chiang Mai, Thailand.

Marie-Hélène Candito and Sylvain Kahane. 1998. Can the TAG derivation tree represent a semantic graph? An answer in the light of Meaning-Text Theory. In *Proceedings of the Fourth International Workshop on Tree Adjoining Grammars and Related Frameworks (TAG+4)*, IRCS Report 98–12, pages 21–24. Institute for Research in Cognitive Science, University of Pennsylvania.

John Carroll, Nicolas Nicolov, Olga Shaumyan, Martine Smets, and David Weir. 1999. Parsing with an extended domain of locality. In *Ninth Conference of the European Chapter of the Association for Computational Linguistics (EACL'99)*, pages 217–224.

Joan Chen-Main and Aaravind K. Joshi. 2008. Flexible composition, multiple adjoining and word order variation. In *Proceedings of the 9th International Workshop on Tree Adjoining Grammars and Related Formalisms (TAG+ 9), Tübingen, Germany*.

John Chen. 1999. An Investigation into Efficient Statistical Parsing Using Lexicalized Grammatical Information. Thesis proposal, University of Delaware.

Laura Kallmeyer. 2005. Tree-local multicomponent tree-adjoining grammars with shared nodes. *Comput. Linguist.*, 31(2):187–226, June.

Paul Kingsbury, Martha Palmer, and Mitch Marcus. 2002. Adding semantic annotation to the Penn Tree-Bank. In *Proceedings of the Human Language Technology Conference (HLT-2002)*, San Diego, CA.

Martha Palmer, Rajesh Bhatt, Bhuvana Narasimhan, Owen Rambow, Dipti Misra Sharma, and Fei Xia. 2009. Hindi Syntax: Annotating Dependency, Lexical Predicate-Argument Structure, and Phrase Structure. In *Proceedings of ICON-2009: 7th International Conference on Natural Language Processing*, Hyderabad.

Owen Rambow and Aravind Joshi. 1997. A formal look at dependency grammars and phrase-structure grammars, with special consideration of word-order phenomena. In Leo Wanner, editor, *Recent Trends in Meaning-Text Theory*, pages 167–190. John Benjamins, Amsterdam and Philadelphia.

Owen Rambow, K. Vijay-Shanker, and David Weir. 2001. D-Tree Substitution Grammars. *Computational Linguistics*, 27(1).

Owen Rambow. 1994. *Formal and Computational Aspects of Natural Language Syntax*. Ph.D. thesis, Department of Computer and Information Science, University of Pennsylvania, Philadelphia. Available as Technical Report 94-08 from the Institute for Research in Cognitive Science (IRCS) and also at ftp://ftp.cis.upenn.edu/pub/rambow/thesis.ps.Z .

Fei Xia, Owen Rambow, Rajesh Bhatt, Martha Palmer, and Dipti Misra Sharma. 2009. Towards a multi-representational treebank. In *The 7th International Workshop on Treebanks and Linguistic Theories (TLT-7)*, Groningen, Netherlands.

Fei Xia. 1999. Extracting Tree Adjoining Grammars from Bracketed Corpora. In *Proc. of 5th Natural Language Processing Pacific Rim Symposium (NLPRS-1999)*, Beijing, China.

Search Space Properties for Learning a Class of Constraint-based Grammars

Smaranda Muresan

School of Communication and Information

Rutgers University

4 Huntington St, New Brunswick, NJ, 08901

smuresan@rutgers.edu

Abstract

We discuss a class of constraint-based grammars, Lexicalized Well-Founded Grammars (LWFGs) and present the theoretical underpinnings for learning these grammars from a representative set of positive examples. Given several assumptions, we define the search space as a complete grammar lattice. In order to prove a learnability theorem, we give a general algorithm through which the top and bottom elements of the complete grammar lattice can be built.

1 Introduction

There has been significant interest in grammar induction on the part of both formal languages and natural language processing communities. In this paper, we discuss the learnability of a recently introduced constraint-based grammar formalism for deep linguistic processing, Lexicalized Well-Founded Grammars (LWFGs) (Muresan, 2006; Muresan and Rambow, 2007; Muresan, 2011). Most formalisms used for deep linguistic processing, such as Tree Adjoining Grammars (Joshi and Schabes, 1997) and Head-driven Phrase Structure Grammar (HPSG) (Pollard and Sag, 1994) are not known to be accompanied by a formal guarantee of polynomial learnability. While stochastic grammar learning for statistical parsing for some of these grammars has been achieved using large annotated treebanks (e.g., (Hockenmaier and Steedman, 2002; Clark and Curran, 2007; Shen, 2006)), LWFG is suited to learning in *resource-poor settings*. LWFG's learning is a relational learning framework which characterizes the importance of substructures in the model not simply by frequency, as in most previous work, but rather linguistically, by defining a notion of *representative examples* that drives the acquisition process.

LWFGs can be seen as a type of Definite Clause Grammars (Pereira and Warren, 1980) where: 1) the Context-Free Grammar backbone is extended by introducing a *partial ordering relation* among *delexicalized* nonterminals (well-founded), 2) nonterminals are augmented with strings and their syntactic-semantic representations; and 3) grammar rules have two types of constraints: one for semantic composition and one for ontology-based semantic interpretation (Muresan, 2006). In LWFG every string w is associated with a syntactic-semantic representation called semantic molecule $\binom{h}{b}$. We call the tuple $(w, \binom{h}{b})$ a *syntagma*:

$$\left(\text{big table}, \begin{array}{c} h\begin{bmatrix} \text{cat} & \text{np} \\ \text{head} & X \\ \text{nr} & sg \end{bmatrix} \\ b\langle X_1.\text{isa} = \text{big}, X.Y = X_1, X.\text{isa=table} \rangle \end{array}\right)$$

The language generated by a LWFG consists of syntagmas, and not strings.

There are several properties and assumptions that are essential for LWFG learnability: 1) partial ordering relation on the delexicalized nonterminal set (well-founded property); 2) each string has its linguistic category known (e.g., np for the phrase *big table*); 3) LWFGs are unambiguous; 4) LWFGs are non-terminally separable (Clark, 2006). Regarding unambiguity, we need to emphasize that unambiguity is relative to a set of syntagmas (pairs of strings and their syntactic-semantic representations) and not to a set of natural language strings. For example, the sentence *I saw the man with a telescope* is ambiguous at the string level (PP-attachment ambiguity), but it is unambiguous if we consider the syntagmas associated with it.

Proceedings of the 11th International Workshop on Tree Adjoining Grammars and Related Formalisms (TAG+11), pages 171–179,
Paris, September 2012.

In this paper, for clarity of presentation, we make abstraction of the semantic representation and grammar constraints, and discuss the theoretical underpinnings of Well-Founded Grammars (WFGs), which have all the properties of LWFGs that assures polynomial learnability. By defining the operational and denotational semantics of WFGs, we are able to formally define the representative set of WFGs. Giving several assumptions, we define the search space for WFG learning as a complete grammar lattice by defining the least upper bound and the greatest lower bound operators. The grammar lattice preserves the parsing of the representative set. We give a theorem showing that this lattice is a complete grammar lattice. In order to give a learnability theorem, we give a general algorithm through which the top and the bottom elements of the complete grammar lattice can be built. The theoretical results obtained in this paper hold for the LWFG formalism. This theoretical result proves that the practical algorithms introduced by Muresan (2011) converge to the same target grammar.

2 Well-Founded Grammars

Well-Founded Grammars are a subclass of Context-Free Grammars where there is a partial ordering relation on the set of non-terminals.

Definition 1. *A Well-Founded Grammar (WFG) is a 5-tuple, $G = \langle \Sigma, N_G, \succeq, P, S \rangle$ where:*

1. *Σ is a finite set of terminal symbols.*
2. *N_G is a finite set of nonterminal symbols, where $N_G \cap \Sigma = \emptyset$.*
3. *$\succeq$ is a partial ordering relation on the set of nonterminals N_G*
4. *P is the set of grammar rules, $P = P_\Sigma \cup P_G$, $P_\Sigma \cap P_G = \emptyset$, where:*

   a) *P_Σ is the set of grammar rules whose right-hand side are terminals, $A \rightarrow w$, where $A \in N_G$ and $w \in \Sigma$ (empty string cannot be derived). We denote $pre(N_G) \subseteq N_G$ the set of pre-terminals, $pre(N_G) = \{A | A \in N_G, w \in \Sigma, A \rightarrow w \in P_\Sigma\}$.*

   b) *P_G is the set of grammar rules $A \rightarrow B_1 \ldots B_n$, where $A \in (N_G - pre(N_G))$, $B_i \in N_G$. For brevity, we denote a rule by $A \rightarrow \beta$, where $A \in (N_G - pre(N_G)), \beta \in N_G^+$. For every grammar rule $A \rightarrow \beta \in P_G$ there is a direct relation between the left-hand side nonterminal A and all the nonterminals on the right-hand side $B_i \in \beta$ (i.e.,*

$\Sigma = \{0, 1, 2, 3, 4, 5, 6, 7, 8, 9, +, -, *, \div, (,)\}$
$N_G = \{D, Sum, Prod, Lbr, Rbr, N, F, T, E\}$
$pre(N_G) = \{D, Sum, Prod, Lbr, Rbr\}$

P_Σ	P_G
$D \rightarrow 0|1|2|3|4|5|6|7|8|9$	$N \rightarrow D$
$Sum \rightarrow +|-$	$N \rightarrow N\,D$
$Prod \rightarrow *|\div$	$F \rightarrow N$
$Lbr \rightarrow ($	$F \rightarrow Lbr\;E\;Rbr$
$Rbr \rightarrow)$	$T \rightarrow F$
	$T \rightarrow T\;Prod\;F$
	$E \rightarrow T$
	$E \rightarrow E\;Sum\;T$

Figure 1: A WFG for Mathematical Expressions

$A \succeq B_i$, or $B_i \succeq A$). If for all $B_i \in \beta$ we have that $A \succeq B_i$ and $A \neq B_i$, the grammar rule $A \rightarrow \beta$ is an ordered non-recursive rule. Each nonterminal symbol $A \in (N_G - pre(N_G))$ is a left-hand side in at least one ordered non-recursive rule. In addition, the empty string cannot be derived from any nonterminal symbol and cycles are not allowed.

5. *$S \in N_G$ is the start nonterminal symbol, and $\forall A \in N_G, S \succeq A$ (we use the same notation for the reflexive, transitive closure of $\succeq$).*

Besides the partial ordering relations $\succeq$, in WFGs the set of production rules P is split in P_Σ and P_G. For learning, P_Σ is given, while the grammar rules in P_G are learned.

In Figure 1 we give a WFG for Mathematical Expressions that will be used as a simple illustrative example to present the formalism and the foundation of the search space for WFG learning.

Every CFG $G = \langle \Sigma, N_G, P_\Sigma \cup P_G, S \rangle$ can be efficiently tested to see whether it is a Well-Founded Grammar.

The derivation in WFGs is called *ground derivation* and it can be seen as the bottom up counterpart of the usual derivation. Given a WFG, G, the *ground derivation* relation, $\overset{*G}{\Rightarrow}$, is defined as: $\dfrac{A \rightarrow w}{A \overset{*G}{\Rightarrow} w}$ $(A \rightarrow w \in P_\Sigma)$, and $\dfrac{B_i \overset{*G}{\Rightarrow} w_i,\, i=1,\ldots,n \quad A \rightarrow B_1 \ldots B_n}{A \overset{*G}{\Rightarrow} w \quad w = w_1 \ldots w_n}$ $(w \in \Sigma^+)$.

The language of a grammar G is the set of all strings generated from the start symbol S, i.e., $L(G) = \{w | w \in \Sigma^+, S \overset{*G}{\Rightarrow} w\}$. The *set of all strings* generated by a grammar G is $L_w(G) = \{w | w \in \Sigma^+, \exists A \in N_G, A \overset{*G}{\Rightarrow} w\}$. Extending the notation, the set of strings generated by *a nonterminal* A of a grammar G is $L_w(A) = \{w | w \in \Sigma^+, A \in N_G, A \overset{*G}{\Rightarrow} w\}$, and the set of strings generated by *a rule* $A \to \beta$ of a grammar G is $L_w(A \to \beta) = \{w | w \in \Sigma^+, (A \to \beta) \overset{*G}{\Rightarrow} w\}$, where $(A \to \beta) \overset{*G}{\Rightarrow} w$ denotes the ground derivation $A \overset{*G}{\Rightarrow} w$ obtained using the rule $A \to \beta$ in the last derivation step. For a WFG G, we call a set of substrings $E_w \subseteq L_w(G)$ a sublanguage of G.

Operational Semantics of WFGs. It has been shown that the operational semantics of a CFG corresponds to the language of the grammar (Wintner, 1999). Analogously, the operational semantics of a WFG, G, is the set of all strings generated by the grammar, $L_w(G)$.

Denotational Semantics of WFGs. As discussed in literature (Pereira and Shieber, 1984; Wintner, 1999), the denotational semantics of a grammar is defined through a fixpoint of a transformational operator associated with the grammar. Let $I \subseteq L_w(G)$ be a subset of all strings generated by a grammar G. We define the *immediate derivation operator* $T_G \colon 2^{L_w(G)} \to 2^{L_w(G)}$, s.t.: $T_G(I) = \{w \in L_w(G) | \text{ if } (A \to B_1 \ldots B_n) \in P_G \wedge B_i \overset{*G}{\Rightarrow} w_i \ \wedge \ w_i \in I \text{ then } A \overset{*G}{\Rightarrow} w\}$. If we denote $T_G \uparrow 0 = \emptyset$ and $T_G \uparrow (i+1) = T_G(T_G \uparrow i)$, then we have that for $i = 1, T_G \uparrow 1 = T_G(\emptyset) = \{w \in L_w(G) | A \in pre(N_G), A \overset{*G}{\Rightarrow} w\}$. This corresponds to the strings derived from preterminals, i.e., $w \in \Sigma$. T_G is analogous with the immediate consequence operator of definite logic programs (i.e., no negation) (van Emden and Kowalski, 1976; Denecker et al., 2001). T_G is monotonous and hence the least fixpoint always exists (Tarski, 1955). This least fixpoint is unique, as for definite logic programs (van Emden and Kowalski, 1976). We have $lfp(T_G) = T_G \uparrow \omega$, where ω is the minimum limit ordinal. Thus, the denotational semantics of a grammar G can be seen as the least fixpoint of the immediate derivation operator. An assumption for learning WFGs is that the rules corresponding to grammar preterminals, $A \to w \in P_\Sigma$, are given, i.e., $T_G(\emptyset)$ is given.

As in the case of definite logic programs, the denotational semantics is equivalent with the operational one, i.e., $L_w(G) = lfp(T_G)$. Based on T_G we can define the *ground derivation length (gdl)* for strings and the *minimum ground derivation length (mgdl)* for grammar rules, which are key concepts in defining the representative set E_R of a WFG.

$$gdl(w) = \min_{w \in T_G \uparrow i} (i)$$

$$mgdl(A \to \beta) = \min_{w \in L_w(A \to \beta)} (gdl(w))$$

2.1 Properties and Principles for WFG Learning

In this section we present the main properties of WFGs, discussing their importance for learning.

1) Partial ordering relation $\succeq$ (well-founded). In WFGs, the partial ordering relation $\succeq$ on the nonterminal set N_G allows the total ordering of grammar nonterminals and grammar rules, which allows the bottom-up learning of WFGs. WFG rules can be ordered or non-ordered, and they can be recursive or non-recursive. In addition, from the definition of WFGs, every non-terminal is a left-hand side in at least one ordered non-recursive rule, cycles are not allowed and the empty string cannot be derived, properties that guarantee the termination condition for learning.

2) Category Principle. Wintner (Wintner, 1999) calls observables for a grammar G all the derivable strings paired with the non-terminal that derives them: $Ob(G) = \{\langle w, A \rangle | w \in \Sigma, A \in N_G, A \overset{*G}{\Rightarrow} w\}$, i.e., $w \in L_w(A)$. We call w a *constituent* and A its *category*. For example, we can say that *1+1* is a constituent having the category *expression (E)*, *1*1* is a constituent having the category *term (T)*, and *1* is a constituent having the categories *digit(D), number (N), factor (F), term (T), expression (E)*. The Category Principle for WFGs states that *the observables are known a-priori*. When learning WFGs, the input to the learner are observables $\langle w, A \rangle$. The category is used by the learner as the name of the left-hand side (lhs) nonterminal of the learned grammar rule. The Category Principle is met for natural language, where observables (i.e., constituents and their linguistic categories) ca be identified: e.g., $\langle formal\ proposal, NP \rangle$, $\langle very\ loud, ADJP \rangle$.

3) Representative Set of a WFG (E_R). Given an unambiguous[1] Well-Founded Grammar G, a set of observables E_R is called a **representative set** of G iff for each rule $(A \to \beta) \in P_G$ there is a unique observable $\langle w, A \rangle \in E_R$ s.t.

---

[1] A WFG G is unambiguous if every string in $L(G)$ has only one derivation.

ID	E_R	$E_{gen} - E_R$
1	$\langle 1, N \rangle$	
2	$\langle 11, N \rangle$	$\langle 111, N \rangle$
3	$\langle 1, F \rangle$	$\langle 11, F \rangle$
4	$\langle (1), F \rangle$	$\langle (11), F \rangle$ $\langle ((1)), F \rangle$ $\langle (1 * 1), F \rangle$ $\langle (1 + 1), F \rangle$
5	$\langle 1, T \rangle$	$\langle 11, T \rangle$ $\langle (1), T \rangle$
6	$\langle 1 * 1, T \rangle$	$\langle 1 * 11, T \rangle$ $\langle 11 * 1, T \rangle$ $\langle 1 * (1), T \rangle$ $\langle (1) * 1, T \rangle$ $\langle 1 * 1 * 1, T \rangle$
7	$\langle 1, E \rangle$	$\langle 11, E \rangle$ $\langle (1), E \rangle$ $\langle 1 * 1, E \rangle$
8	$\langle 1 + 1, E \rangle$	$\langle 11 + 1, E \rangle$ $\langle 1 + 11, E \rangle$ $\langle (1) + 1, E \rangle$ $\langle 1 + (1), E \rangle$ $\langle 1 * 1 + 1, E \rangle$, $\langle 1 + 1 * 1, E \rangle$ $\langle 1 + 1 + 1, E \rangle$

Figure 2: Examples for Learning the WFG in Figure 1

$gdl(w) = mgdl(A \rightarrow \beta)$, where $w \in L_w(G)$. The nonterminal A is the category of the string w. E_R contains the most simple strings ground derived by the grammar G paired with their categories. From this definition it is straightforward to show that $|E_R| = |P_G|$. The partial ordering relation on the nonterminal set induces a total order on the representative set E_R as well as on the set of grammar rules P_G.

For the WFG induction, the representative set E_R will be used by the learner to generate hypotheses (i.e., grammar rules). The category will give the name of the left-hand side nonterminals (lhs) of the learned grammar rules. An example of a representative set E_R for the mathematical expressions grammar from Figure 1 is given in Figure 2. For generalization the learner will use a generalization set of observables $E_{gen} = \{\langle w, A \rangle | A \in N_G \wedge A \overset{*G}{\Rightarrow} w\}$, where $E_R \subseteq E_{gen}$. An example of a generalization set E_{gen} for learning the WFG from Figure 1 is given in Figure 2.

4) Semantics of a WFG reduced to a generalization set E_{gen}. Given a WFG G and a generalization set E_{gen} (not necessarily of G) the set $\mathbb{S}(G) = \{\langle w, A \rangle | \langle w, A \rangle \in E_{gen} \wedge A \overset{*G}{\Rightarrow} w\}$ is called the semantics of G reduced to the generalization set E_{gen}. In other words, $\mathbb{S}(G)$ will contain all the pairs $\langle w, A \rangle$ in the generalization set whose strings w can be ground-derived by the grammar G, $w \in L_w(G)$. Given a grammar rule $r_A \in P_G$, we call $\mathbb{S}(r_A) = \{\langle w, A \rangle | \text{lhs}(r_A) = A \wedge \langle w, A \rangle \in E_{gen} \wedge r_A \overset{*G}{\Rightarrow} w\}$ the semantics of r_A reduced to E_{gen}. The cardinality of $\mathbb{S}$ is used during learning as performance criterion.

5) E_R-parsing-preserving. We present the *rule specialization step* and the *rule generalization step* of unambiguous WFGs, such that they are E_R-*parsing-preserving* and are the inverse of each other. The property of E_R-parsing-preserving means that both the initial and the spe-

cialized/generalized rules ground-derive the same string w of the observable $\langle w, A \rangle \in E_R$. The **rule specialization step**:

$$\frac{A \rightarrow \alpha B \gamma \qquad B \rightarrow \beta}{A \rightarrow \alpha \beta \gamma}$$

is E_R-**parsing-preserving**, if there exists $\langle w, A \rangle \in E_R$ and $r_g \overset{*G}{\Rightarrow} w$ and $r_s \overset{*G'}{\Rightarrow} w$, where $r_g = A \rightarrow \alpha B \gamma$, $r_B = B \rightarrow \beta$, $r_s = A \rightarrow \alpha \beta \gamma$ and $r_g \in P_G$, $r_B \in P_G \cap P_{G'}$, $r_s \in P_{G'}$. We write $r_g \overset{r_B}{\vdash} r_s$.[2] The rule generalization step, which is also E_R-parsing-preserving, is defined as the inverse of the rule specialization step and denoted by $r_s \overset{r_B}{\dashv} r_g$.

Since $\langle w, A \rangle$ is an element of the representative set, w is derived in the minimum number of derivation steps, and thus the rule r_B is always an ordered, non-recursive rule. Examples of E_R-parsing-preserving rule specialization steps are given in Figure 3, where all rules derive the same representative example *1+1*. In the derivation step $E \rightarrow N \; Sum \; D \overset{N \rightarrow D}{\vdash} E \rightarrow D \; Sum \; D$ the ordered, non recursive rule $r_B = N \rightarrow D$ is used. If the recursive rule $N \rightarrow N \; D$ were used, we would obtain a specialized rule $E \rightarrow N \; D \; Sum \; D$ which does not preserve the parsing of the representative example *1+1*.

From both the specialization and the generalization step we have that $L_w(r_g) \supseteq L_w(r_s)$.

The goal of the rule specialization step is to obtain a new target grammar G' from G by specializing a rule of G ($G \overset{r}{\vdash} G'$). Extending the notation to allow for the transitive closure of rule specialization, we have that $G \overset{*}{\vdash} G'$, and we say that the grammar G' is **specialized** from the grammar G, using a finite number of rule specialization steps that are E_R-*parsing-preserving*. Similarly, the goal of the rule generalization step is to

---

[2]Grammar G is non-terminally separable (Clark, 2006).

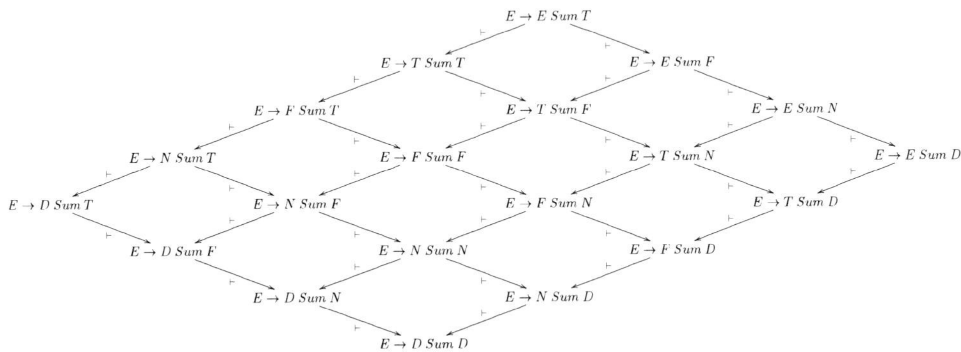

Figure 3: E_R-parsing preserving rule specialization steps for the grammar in Figure 1.

obtain a new target grammar G from G' by generalizing a rule of G'. Extending the notation to allow for transitive closure of rule generalization, we have that $G' \overset{*}{\dashv} G$, and we say that the grammar G is **generalized** from the grammar G' using a finite number of rule generalization steps that are E_R-*parsing-preserving*. That is, E_R is a representative set for both G and G'. The E_R-parsing-preserving property allows us to define a class of grammars that form a complete grammar lattice used as search space for WFGs induction, as detailed in the next section.

6) Conformal Property. A WFG G is called *normalized* w.r.t. a generalization set E_{gen}, if none of the grammar rules r_s of G can be further generalized to a rule r_g by the rule generalization step such that $\mathbb{S}(r_s) \subset \mathbb{S}(r_g)$. A WFG G is **conformal w.r.t. a generalization set** E_{gen} iff $\forall \langle w, A \rangle \in E_{gen}$ we have that $w \in L_w(G)$, and G is unambiguous and normalized w.r.t. E_{gen} and the rule specialization step guarantees that $\mathbb{S}(r_g) \supset \mathbb{S}(r_s)$ for all grammars specialized from G. This property allows learning only from positive examples.

7) Chains. We define a *chain* as a set of ordered unary branching rules: $\{B_k \to B_{k-1}, \ldots, B_2 \to B_1, B_1 \to \beta\}$ such that all these rules ground-derive the same string $w \in \Sigma^+$ (i.e., $B_k \succ B_{k-1} \cdots \succ B_1$ and $B_0 = \beta$, such that $B_i \overset{*G}{\Rightarrow} w$ for $0 \leq i \leq k$, where $B_i \in N_G$ for $1 \leq i \leq k$). For our grammar $\{E \to T, T \to F, F \to N, N \to D\}$ is a chain, all these rules ground-deriving the string *1*. Chains are used to generalize grammar rules during WFG learning (Fig. 3).

All the above mentioned properties are used to define the search space of WFG learning as a complete grammar lattice.

2.2 Grammar Lattice as Search Space

In this section we formally define a grammar lattice $\mathfrak{L} = \langle \mathcal{L}, \sqsupseteq \rangle$ that will be the search space for WFG learning. We first define the set of lattice elements $\mathcal{L}$.

Let $\top$ be a WFG conformal to a generalization set E_{gen} that includes the representative set E_R of the grammar $\top$ ($E_{gen} \supseteq E_R$). Let $\mathcal{L} = \{G | \top \overset{*}{\vdash} G\}$ be the set of grammars specialized from $\top$. We call $\top$ the *top element* of $\mathcal{L}$, and $\bot$ the *bottom element* of $\mathcal{L}$, if $\forall G \in \mathcal{L}, \top \overset{*}{\vdash} G \wedge G \overset{*}{\vdash} \bot$. The bottom element, $\bot$, is the grammar specialized from $\top$, such that the right-hand side of all grammar rules contains only preterminals. We have $\mathbb{S}(\top) = E_{gen}$ and $\mathbb{S}(\bot) \supseteq E_R$.

There is a partial ordering among the elements of $\mathcal{L}$ (the subsumption $\sqsupseteq$), which we define below.

Definition 2. *If* $G, G' \in \mathcal{L}$, *we say that* G *subsumes* G', $G \sqsupseteq G'$, *iff* $G \overset{*}{\vdash} G'$ *(i.e.,* G' *is specialized from* G, *and* G *is generalized from* G'*)*

We have that for $G, G' \in \mathcal{L}$, if $G \sqsupseteq G'$ then $\mathbb{S}(G) \supseteq \mathbb{S}(G')$. That means that the subsumption relation is semantic based.

In sum, the set $\mathcal{L}$ contains the grammars specialized from $\top$, while the binary subsumption relation $\sqsupseteq$ establishes a partial ordering in $\mathcal{L}$. The top element of the lattice $\top$ is a normalized WFG, the bottom element $\bot$ is a grammar specialized from $\top$, whose rules' right-hand sides consist of preterminals, and all the other lattice elements are WFGs that preserve the parsing of the representative set. In Figure 3, the rule $(E \to E\ Sum\ T) \in P_\top$, the rule $(E \to D\ Sum\ D) \in P_\bot$ and all rules ground-derive the representative string *1+1*.

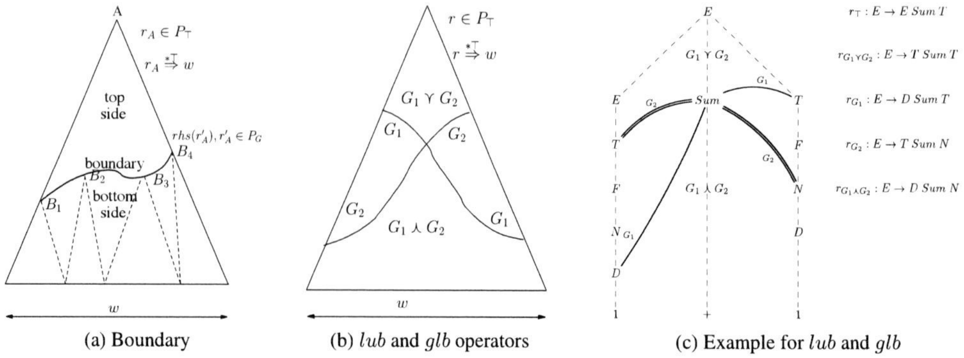

(a) Boundary   (b) lub and glb operators   (c) Example for lub and glb

Figure 4

In order for $\mathfrak{L} = \langle \mathcal{L}, \sqsupseteq \rangle$ to form a lattice, we must define two operators: the *least upper bound* (*lub*), $\curlyvee$ and the *greatest lower bound* (*glb*), $\curlywedge$, such that for any two elements $G_1, G_2 \in \mathcal{L}$, the elements $G_1 \curlyvee G_2 \in \mathcal{L}$ and $G_1 \curlywedge G_2 \in \mathcal{L}$ exist (Tarski, 1955).

We first introduce the concept of boundary. Let $r_A \in P_\top$ be a rule in grammar $\top$, and r'_A its specialized rule in grammar G ($\top \sqsupseteq G$) (see Figure 4a). Let $pt(r_A \overset{*\top}{\Rightarrow} w)$ be the parse tree corresponding to the ground-derivation $r_A \overset{*\top}{\Rightarrow} w$. We call **boundary** of a grammar $G \in \mathcal{L}$ relative to $pt(r_A \overset{*\top}{\Rightarrow} w)$,[3] the right-hand side of the corresponding rule $r'_A \in P_G, r'_A \overset{*G}{\Rightarrow} w$, i.e. $bd(G) = \{B | r'_A \in P_G \wedge B \in rhs(r'_A)\}$[4] (see Figure 4a). For the example in Figure 4c, the rule in grammar $\top$ is $E \rightarrow E\ Sum\ T$, the rule in grammar G_1 is $E \rightarrow D\ Sum\ T$. Thus, $bd(G_1) = \{D, Sum, T\}$ We define the **bottom-side** $bs(G)$ of a grammar G relative to the parse tree $pt(r_A \overset{*\top}{\Rightarrow} w)$, as the forest composed of all the subtrees in $pt(r_A \overset{*\top}{\Rightarrow} w)$ whose roots are on $bd(G)$ (e.g., subtrees with roots at B_1, B_2, B_3, B_4 in Figure 4a). For the example in Figure 4c, $bs(G_1)$ will be the forest of subtrees of the parse tree $pt(r_\top \overset{*\top}{\Rightarrow} 1+1)$ with the roots D, Sum and T on the boundary $bd(G_1)$ of grammar G_1. We define the **top-side** $ts(G)$ of a grammar G relative to the parse tree $pt(r_A \overset{*\top}{\Rightarrow} w)$, as the subtree in $pt(r_A \overset{*\top}{\Rightarrow} w)$ rooted at A and whose leaf nodes are on $bd(G)$ (e.g., B_1, B_2, B_3 and B_4 in Figure 4a). For the example in Figure 4c, $ts(G_1)$ will be the subtree of the parse tree $pt(r_\top \overset{*\top}{\Rightarrow} 1+1)$ rooted at E and the leaf nodes D, Sum and T on the boundary $bd(G_1)$ of the grammar G_1. We have that $ts(G) \cap bs(G) = bd(G)$, $ts(G) \cup bs(G) = pt(r_A \overset{*\top}{\Rightarrow} w)$.

For any two elements $G_1, G_2 \in \mathcal{L}$, the *lub* element of G_1, G_2 is the minimum element that has the boundary above the boundaries of G_1 and G_2. The *glb* element of G_1, G_2 is the maximum element that has the boundary below the boundaries of G_1 and G_2. Thus, *lub* and *glb* are defined such that for all grammar rules we have:

$$ts(G_1 \curlyvee G_2) = ts(G_1) \cap ts(G_2)$$
$$bs(G_1 \curlywedge G_2) = bs(G_1) \cap bs(G_2) \tag{1}$$

as can be seen in Figure 4b, 4c.[5] In order to have a complete lattice, the property must hold $\forall \mathcal{G} \subseteq \mathcal{L}$:

$$ts(\curlyvee_{G \in \mathcal{G}}G) = \bigcap_{G \in \mathcal{G}} ts(G)$$
$$bs(\curlywedge_{G \in \mathcal{G}}G) = \bigcap_{G \in \mathcal{G}} bs(G) \tag{2}$$

Lemma 1. $\mathfrak{L} = \langle \mathcal{L}, \sqsupseteq \rangle$ *together with the lub and glb operators guarantees that for any two grammars* $G_1, G_2 \in \mathcal{L}$ *the following property holds:* $G_1 \curlyvee G_2 \sqsupseteq G_1, G_2 \sqsupseteq G_1 \curlywedge G_2$

Theorem 1. $\mathfrak{L} = \langle \mathcal{L}, \sqsupseteq \rangle$ *together with the lub and glb operators forms a complete lattice.*

Proof. Besides the property given in Lemma 1, *lub* and *glb* operators are computed w.r.t. (2), such that we have $ts(\curlyvee_{G \in \mathcal{L}}G) = \bigcap_{G \in \mathcal{L}} ts(G) =$

---

[3] All grammars $G \in \mathcal{L}$ are E_R-parsing-preserving and all boundaries of G are in the parse trees of the ground derivations of $\top$ grammar rules.

[4] The notation of $bd(G), ts(G), bs(G)$ ignores the rule relative to which these concepts are defined, and in the remainder of this paper we implicitly understand that the relations hold for all grammar rules.

[5] The intersection of two trees is the maximum common subtree of those two trees, and similarly for forests of trees.

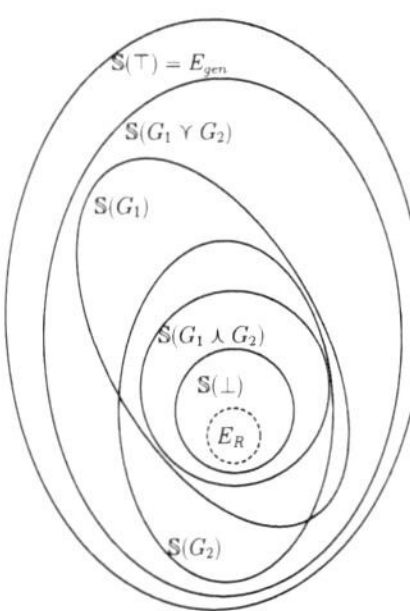

Figure 5: WFG semantics reduced to E_{gen}

$ts(\top)$, $bs(\lambda_{G \in \mathcal{L}} G) = \bigcap_{G \in \mathcal{L}} bs(G) = bs(\bot)$, which gives the uniqueness of $\top$ and $\bot$ elements. □

Similar to the subsumption relation $\sqsupseteq$, the *lub* $\curlyvee$ and *glb* $\curlywedge$ operators are semantic-based. In the complete lattice $\mathfrak{L} = \langle \mathcal{L}, \sqsupseteq \rangle$, $\forall G_1, G_2 \in \mathcal{L}$ we have:

$$\mathbb{S}(G_1 \curlyvee G_2) \supseteq \mathbb{S}(G_1) \cup \mathbb{S}(G_2). \tag{3}$$
$$\mathbb{S}(G_1 \curlywedge G_2) \subseteq \mathbb{S}(G_1) \cap \mathbb{S}(G_2)$$

Thus, the complete grammar lattice is semantic-based (Figure 5). It is straightforward to prove that $\mathfrak{L} = \langle \mathcal{L}, \sqsupseteq \rangle$ has all the known properties (i.e., idempotency, commutativity, associativity, absorption, $\top$ and $\bot$ laws, distributivity).

2.3 Learnability Theorem

In oder to give a learnability theorem we need to show that $\bot$ and $\top$ elements of the lattice can be built. Through Algorithm 1 we show that giving the set of examples E_R and E_{gen}, the $\bot$ grammar can be built and the $\top$ grammar can be learned by generalizing the $\bot$ grammar. The grammar generalization is determinate if the rule generalization step is determinate. Before describing Algorithm 1 we introduce the concepts of *determinate generalizable* and give a lemma that states that given a grammar $\top$ conformal with E_{gen}, for any grammars G specialized from $\top$, all the grammar rules are determinate generalizable if all the chains of the $\top$ grammar are known.

Definition 3. *A grammar rule $r'_A \in P_G$ is determinate generalizable if for $\beta \in rhs(r'_A)$ there exists a unique rule $r_B = (B \to \beta)$ such that $r'_A \overset{r_B}{\dashv} r_A$ with $\mathbb{S}(r'_A) \subset \mathbb{S}(r_A)$. We use the notation $r'_A \overset{1\subset}{\dashv} r_A$ for the determinate generalization step with semantic increase.*

The only rule generalization steps allowed in the grammar induction process are those which guarantee the relation $\mathbb{S}(r_s) \subset \mathbb{S}(r_g)$ that ensures that all the generalized grammars belong to the grammar lattice. This property allows the grammar induction based only on positive examples. We use the notation $r'_A \overset{r_B \subset}{\dashv} r_A$ for the generalization step with semantic increase.

This step can be nondeterminate due to chain rules. Let $ch_\top$ be a chain of rules in a WFG $\top$ conformal w.r.t a generalization set E_{gen}, $ch_\top = \{B_k \to B_{k-1}, \ldots, B_2 \to B_1, B_1 \to \beta\}$. All the chain rules, but the last, are unary branching rules. The last rule is the minimal chain rule. For our example, $ch_\top = \{E \to T, T \to F, F \to N, N \to D\}$. For the $\bot$ grammar of a lattice that has $\top$ as its top element, the aforementioned chain becomes $ch_\bot = \{B_k \to \beta_\bot, \ldots, B_2 \to \beta_\bot, B_1 \to \beta_\bot\}$, where $\beta_\bot$ contains only preterminals and the rule order is unknown. By the E_R-parsing-preserving property of the rule specialization step, the same string is ground-derived from the $ch_\bot$ rules. Thus, the $\bot$ grammar is ambiguous. For our example, $ch_\bot = \{E \to D, T \to D, F \to D, N \to D\}$.

We denote by $ch = \{r_k, \ldots, r_2, r_1\}$, one or more chains in any lattice grammar, where the rule order is unknown. The minimal chain rules r_m can always be determined if $r_m \in ch$ s.t. $\forall r \in ch - \{r_m\} \wedge r_m \overset{r}{\dashv} r_{mg}$ we have that $\mathbb{S}(r_m) = \mathbb{S}(r_{mg})$ (see also `MinRule` algorithm). By the consequence of the conformal property, the generalization step $r_m \overset{r}{\dashv} r_{mg}$ is not allowed, since it does not produce any increase in rule semantics. That is, a minimal chain rule cannot be generalized by any other chain rule with an increase in its semantics. Given $ch_\bot$ and the aforementioned property of the minimal chain rules we can recover $ch_\top$ by `Chains_Recovery` algorithm.

Lemma 2. *Given a WFG $\top$ conformal w.r.t a generalization set E_{gen}, for any grammar G derived from $\top$ all rules are determinate generalizable if all chains of the grammar $\top$ (i.e., all $ch_\top$) are known (i.e., recovered by `Chains_Recovery` algorithm).*

Proof. The only case of rule generalization step nondeterminism with semantic increase is introduced by the derivation of the unary branching rules of ordered $ch_\top$, which yields the unordered

ID	$P_\perp$	$P_\top$
1	$N \to D$	$N \to D$
2	$N \to D\,D$	$N \to N\,D$
3	$F \to D$	$F \to N$
4	$F \to Lbr\,D\,Rbr$	$F \to Lbr\,E\,Rbr$
5	$T \to D$	$T \to F$
6	$T \to D\,Prod\,D$	$T \to T\,Prod\,F$
7	$E \to D$	$E \to T$
8	$E \to D\,Sum\,D$	$E \to E\,Sum\,T$

Figure 6: Examples of $P_\perp$ and learned $P_\top$

$ch_\perp$, where $B_i \to \beta_\perp \stackrel{B_j \to \beta_\perp \subset}{\dashv} B_i \to B_j$ holds for all $B_j \prec B_i$. Thus, keeping (or recovering) the ordered $ch_\top$ in any grammar G derived from $\top$, all the other grammar rules are determinate generalizable. $\qquad\square$

We now introduce Algorithm 1, which given the representative set E_R and the generalization set E_{gen}, builds the $\perp$ and $\top$ grammars. First, an assumption in our learning model is that the rules corresponding to the grammar preterminals (P_Σ) are given. Thus, for a given representative set E_R, we can build the grammar $\perp$ in the following way: for each observable $\langle w, A \rangle \in E_R$ the category A gives the name of the left-hand side nonterminal of the grammar rule, while the right-hand side is constructed using a bottom-up active chart parser (Kay, 1973) (line 1 in Algorithm 1). For our mathematical expressions example, given E_R in Figure 2 and P_Σ in Figure 1, the rules of the bottom grammar $P_\perp$ are given in Figure 6.

Algorithm 1 Top (E_R, E_{gen})

1: $P_\perp \leftarrow Bottom(E_R)$
2: $P_\top \leftarrow$ Chains_Recovery $(P_\perp, E_R, E_{gen})$
  {$P_\top$ is determinate generalizable }
3: **while** $\exists r \in P_\top$ s.t. $r \stackrel{1\subset}{\dashv} r_g$ **do**
4: $\quad r \leftarrow r_g$;
5: **end while**
6: **return** $P_\top$

In order to build the $\top$ element (lines 2-5 in Algorithm 1), we first need to apply the Chain_recovery algorithm to the lattice $\perp$ grammar (line 2 in Algorithm 1). Chains_Recovery first detects all $ch = ch_\perp$ which contain rules with identical right-hand side (line 5-6). Then, all $ch_\perp$ rules are transformed in $ch_\top$ by generalizing them through the minimal chain rule (lines 10-17). The generalization step $r \stackrel{r_m\subset}{\dashv} r_g$ guar-

---

Algorithm 2 Chains_Recovery

1: **Input:** $P_\perp, E_R, E_{gen}$
2: **Output:** $P_\perp$ which contains all $ch_\top$
3: **while** $E_R \neq \emptyset$ **do**
4: $\quad \langle w, c \rangle \leftarrow first(E_R)$
5: $\quad ch \leftarrow \{r \in P_\perp | r \stackrel{*\perp}{\Rightarrow} w\}$ $\qquad\quad \{ch = ch_\perp\}$
6: $\quad lch \leftarrow \{lhs(r) | r \in ch\}$
7: $\quad$ **for each** $c \in lch$ **do**
8: $\qquad E_R \leftarrow E_R - \{\langle w, c \rangle\}$
9: $\quad$ **end for**
10: $\quad$ **while** $|ch| > 1$ **do**
11: $\qquad r_m \leftarrow$ MinRule(ch)
12: $\qquad ch \leftarrow ch - \{r_m\}$
13: $\qquad lch \leftarrow lch - \{lhs(r_m)\}$
14: $\qquad$ **for each** $r \in P_\perp \wedge lhs(r) \in lch$ s.t. $r \stackrel{r_m\subset}{\dashv} r_g$ **do**
15: $\qquad\quad r \leftarrow r_g$
16: $\qquad$ **end for**
17: $\quad$ **end while**
18: **end while**
19: **return:** $P_\perp$

Algorithm 3 MinRule

1: **Input:** the chain ch
2: **for each** $r_m \in ch$ **do**
3: $\quad find \leftarrow true$
4: $\quad$ **for each** $r \in ch - \{r_m\}$ **do**
5: $\qquad$ **if** $r_m \stackrel{r}{\dashv} r_{mg} \wedge \mathbb{S}(r_m) \subset \mathbb{S}(r_{mg})$ **then**
6: $\qquad\quad find \leftarrow false$
7: $\qquad$ **end if**
8: $\quad$ **end for**
9: $\quad$ **if** $find == true$ **then**
10: $\qquad$ **return** r_m
11: $\quad$ **end if**
12: **end for**

---

antees the semantic increase $\mathbb{S}(r_g) \supset \mathbb{S}(r)$ for all the rules r which are generalized through r_m, thus being the inverse of the rule specialization step in the grammar lattice. The rules r are either chain rules or rules having the same left-hand side as the chain rules. The returned set $P_\perp$ contains all unary branching rules ($ch_\top$) of the $\top$ grammar. The efficiency of Chain_Recovery algorithm is $O(|E_R| * |\beta| * |E_{gen}|)$. Therefore, in Algorithm 1 the set $P_\top$ initially contains determinate generalizable rules and the while loop (lines 3-5, Alg 1) can determinately generalize all the grammar rules. In Figure 6, the grammar $P_\top$ is learned by Algorithm 1, based only on the examples in Figure 2 and P_Σ in Figure 1.

Theorem 2 (Learnability Theorem). *If E_R is*

the representative set of a WFG G conformal w.r.t a generalization set $E_{gen} \supseteq E_R$, then Top(E_R, E_{gen}) algorithm computes the lattice $\top$ element such that $\mathbb{S}(\top) = E_{gen}$.

Proof. Since G is normalized, none of its rule can be generalized with increase in semantics. Starting with the $\bot$ element, after `Chains_Recovery` all rules that can be generalized with semantic increase through the rule generalization step, are determinate generalizable. This means that the grammar generalization sequence $\bot, G_1, \ldots, G_n, \top$, ensures the semantic increase of $\mathbb{S}(G_i)$ so that the generalization process ends at the semantic limit $\mathbb{S}(\top) = E_{gen}$. $\square$

For WFGs which have rules that can be either left or right recursive, the top element is unique only if we impose a direction of generalization in the rule's right-hand side (e.g., left to right). Another way to guarantee uniqueness of the top element is to add constraints at the grammar rules. In our example, if we augment de grammar nonterminals with expression values (semantic interpretation) and we add constraints at the grammar rules we have $E(v) \rightarrow E(v_1) \; Sum(op) \; T(v_2): \{v \leftarrow v_1 \; op \; v_2\}$. With the generalization example $\langle 5 - 3 - 1, E(1) \rangle \in E_{gen}$ we can generalize the rule $E \rightarrow T \; Sum \; T$ only to $E \rightarrow E \; Sum \; T$ and not to $E \rightarrow T \; Sum \; E$ because $1 = (5 - 3) - 1$ and $1 \neq 5 - (3 - 1)$. For our Lexicalized Well-Founded Grammars this problem is solved by associating strings with their syntactic-semantic representations and by having semantic compositional constraints at the grammar rule level.

3   Conclusions

In this paper, we discussed the learnability of Lexicalized Well-Founded Grammars. We introduced the class of well-founded grammars and presented the theoretical underpinnings for learning these grammars from a representative set of positive examples. We proved that under several assumptions the search space for learning these grammars is a complete grammar lattice. We presented a general algorithm which builds the top and the bottom elements of the complete grammar lattice and gave a learnability theorem. The theoretical results obtained in this paper hold for the LWFG formalism, which is suitable for deep linguistic processing.

References

Stephen Clark and James R. Curran. 2007. Wide-coverage efficient statistical parsing with ccg and log-linear models. *Computational Linguistics*, 33(4).

Alexander Clark. 2006. PAC-learning unambiguous NTS languages. In *Proceedings of the 8th International Colloquium on Grammatical Inference (ICGI 2006)*, pages 59–71.

Marc Denecker, Maurice Bruynooghe, and Victor W. Marek. 2001. Logic programming revisited: Logic programs as inductive definitions. *ACM Transactions on Computational Logic*, 2(4):623–654.

Julia Hockenmaier and Mark Steedman. 2002. Generative models for statistical parsing with combinatory categorial grammar. In *Proceedings of the ACL '02*, pages 335–342.

Aravind Joshi and Yves Schabes. 1997. Tree-Adjoining Grammars. In G. Rozenberg and A. Salomaa, editors, *Handbook of Formal Languages*, volume 3, chapter 2, pages 69–124. Springer, Berlin,New York.

Martin Kay. 1973. The MIND system. In Randall Rustin, editor, *Natural Language Processing*, pages 155–188. Algorithmics Press, New York.

Smaranda Muresan and Owen Rambow. 2007. Grammar approximation by representative sublanguage: A new model for language learning. In *Proceedings of ACL'07*.

Smaranda Muresan. 2006. *Learning Constraint-based Grammars from Representative Examples: Theory and Applications*. Ph.D. thesis, Columbia University.

Smaranda Muresan. 2011. Learning for deep language understanding. In *Proceedings of IJCAI-11*.

Fernando C. Pereira and Stuart M. Shieber. 1984. The semantics of grammar formalisms seen as computer languages. In *Proceeding of the ACL 1984*.

Fernando C. Pereira and David H.D Warren. 1980. Definite Clause Grammars for language analysis. *Artificial Intelligence*, 13:231–278.

Carl Pollard and Ivan Sag. 1994. *Head-Driven Phrase Structure Grammar*. University of Chicago Press, Chicago, Illinois.

Libin Shen. 2006. *Statistical LTAG Parsing*. Ph.D. thesis, University of Pennsylvania, Philadelphia, PA, USA. AAI3225543.

Alfred Tarski. 1955. Lattice-theoretic fixpoint theorem and its applications. *Pacific Journal of Mathematics*, 5(2):285–309.

Maarten H. van Emden and Robert A. Kowalski. 1976. The semantics of predicate logic as a programming language. *Journal of the ACM*, 23(4):733–742.

Shuly Wintner. 1999. Compositional semantics for linguistic formalisms. In *Proceedings of the ACL'99*.

State-Split for Hypergraphs with an Application to Tree-Adjoining Grammars

Johannes Osterholzer and **Torsten Stüber**
Department of Computer Science
Technische Universität Dresden
D-01062 Dresden
{johannes.osterholzer,torsten.stueber}@tu-dresden.de

Abstract

In this work, we present a generalization of
the state-split method to probabilistic hypergraphs. We show how to represent the derivational stucture of probabilistic tree-adjoining
grammars by hypergraphs and detail how
the generalized state-split procedure can be
applied to such representations, yielding a
state-split procedure for tree-adjoining grammars.

1 Introduction

The *state-split* method (Petrov et al., 2006) allows
the successive refinement of a probabilistic context-
free grammar (PCFG) for the purpose of natural
language processing (NLP). It employs automatic
subcategorization of nonterminal symbols: in an
iteration of a *split-merge cycle,* every nonterminal of the PCFG is split into two, along with the
corresponding grammar rules, whose probabilities
are distributed uniformly to the split rules. The resulting PCFG's rule probabilities are then trained
on an underlying treebank using the *Expectation-
Maximization* algorithm (Dempster et al., 1977)
for maximum-likelihood estimation on incomplete
data. Finally, split nonterminal symbols which do
not contribute to a significant increase in likelihood
are merged back together. This counteracts an exponential blowup in the number of nonterminals
and prevents, to some degree, the phenomenon of
overfitting.

The in-house developed statistical machine translation toolkit *Vanda* (Büchse et al., 2012) offers
state-splitting for the refinement of its language
models. Vanda's internal representation of the
various weighted tree grammar, automaton and
transducer formalisms utilized for translation is
by means of probabilistic *hypergraphs,* i.e., graphs

consisting of *vertices* and *hyperedges,* where each
of the latter connects a (possibly empty) sequence
of *tail vertices* to a *head vertex* and is assigned a
probability. Hence, our implementation of state-
split operates on such hypergraphs as underlying
data structures. The connection between parsing
and hypergraphs is well-known in the field of NLP
(Klein and Manning, 2004), where a hypergraph
represents the derivation forest of a certain word. In
our system, however, we use such a probabilistic hypergraph to represent the *whole* derivational structure of a grammar, with a one-to-one correspondence between hyperpaths and grammar derivations. We apply well-known product constructions
from the theory of weighted automata, going back
to Bar-Hillel et al. (1961) and generalized to the
case of weighted tree automata by Maletti and Satta
(2009), to restrict them to the derivations of a given
word.

The mildly context-sensitive generative capacity
of *tree-adjoining grammars (TAG)* is well-suited to
the purpose of NLP (Joshi and Schabes, 1991). tree-
adjoining grammars allow two basic operations
to rewrite and derive trees: *substitution,* where a
tree's leaf node is replaced with another tree, and
adjoining, which can be seen as the second-order
substitution of a context (called an auxiliary tree)
into another tree.

Probabilistic tree-adjoining grammars (PTAG)
(Schabes, 1992; Resnik, 1992) assign to every derived tree an associated probability. They can also
be incorporated into Vanda by an appropriate representation with hypergraphs. Such PTAGs can
be extracted from treebank corpora, as detailed by
Chen et al. (2006). The idea to refine these grammars furthermore by executing the already implemented state-split procedure on their hypergraph
representations arises naturally. The main contribution of the work at hand is a formalization of this

Proceedings of the 11th International Workshop on Tree Adjoining Grammars and Related Formalisms (TAG+11), pages 180–188,
Paris, September 2012.

idea. However, one should note that our proposed method does not just apply to PTAG, but should carry over to many grammar formalisms that can be represented by hypergraphs. In our formalization, we have to deal with a complication, introduced by the nature of adjunction in TAG. For this purpose, we introduce *split relations*.

An alternative to our approach to state-splitting PTAG is the one taken by Shindo et al. (2012), where a method for symbol refinement of probabilistic tree substitution grammars is presented. Since tree substitution grammars are just tree-adjoining grammars without adjoining sites (and indeed, adjoining can be simulated by the combination of a tree substitution grammar which encodes adjoining explicitly, and a yield function which performs these encoded operations, cf. (Maletti, 2010)), it is possible that their technique can be adapted to the more general setting. This would have the additional advantage that smoothing by backoff to simpler context-free grammar rules is incorporated in their system, increasing performance in the case of sparse data, while we do not cover smoothing in the work at hand.

Note that, although most of the preliminaries may be safely skimmed, we want to point out that our definitions of first- and second-order substitution are slightly non-standard (but they enable a concise formalization of TAG).

2 Preliminaries

In the following, we will denote the set of non-negative integers by $\mathbb{N}$. The set $\{1, \ldots, k\}$ shall be abbreviated by $[k]$. The set of the non-negative real numbers will be denoted by $\mathbb{R}_{\geq 0}$, and the closed interval between two reals a and b by $[a, b]$.

The set of finite words over a set A is written as A^*, $\varepsilon \in A^*$ is the empty word and $A^+ = A^* \setminus \{\varepsilon\}$. The reflexive-transitive closure of a binary relation R shall be denoted by R^*.

2.1 Unranked Trees

We call a finite set Σ of *symbols* an *alphabet*. Given a finite set A and alphabet Σ, let Σ_A denote the alphabet of all σ_a with $\sigma \in \Sigma$, $a \in A$. Note that the new symbol σ_a is merely a syntactic construct and should be identified neither with σ nor a.

Presuming an alphabet Σ and set A, the set $U_\Sigma(A)$ of *unranked trees over Σ indexed by A* is the smallest set U such that $A \subseteq U$ and for every $n \in \mathbb{N}$, $t_1, \ldots, t_n \in U$, and $\sigma \in \Sigma$, also

$\sigma(t_1, \ldots, t_n) \in U$. For a tree $\sigma()$ we will just write σ and $U_\Sigma(\emptyset)$ will be denoted by U_Σ. The set of *positions* $\text{pos}(t)$ of a tree $t \in U_\Sigma(A)$ is defined by $\text{pos}(\sigma(t_1, \ldots, t_n)) = \{\varepsilon\} \cup \{iw \mid i \in [n], w \in \text{pos}(t_i)\}$ and $t(w)$ denotes the *label* of t at position w.

Throughout the rest of the paper, let $X = \{x_1, x_2, \ldots\}$ denote an infinite set of variables and, for $n \in \mathbb{N}$, let $X_n = \{x_1, \ldots, x_n\}$. Similarly, let $Y = \{y_1, y_2, \ldots\}$, let $Y_n = \{y_1, \ldots, y_n\}$ for $n \in \mathbb{N}$, and $Z = \{z\}$. Given $k \in \mathbb{N}$, we call a tree $t \in U_\Sigma(A \cup \Delta_X)$ (resp. $t \in U_{\Sigma \cup \Delta_Y}(A)$) *proper in X_k (resp. Y_k)* if for every $i > k$, there is no appearance of δ_{x_i} (resp. of δ_{y_i}) in t, and for every $i \in [k]$, there is exactly one position in t labeled with δ_{x_i} (resp. δ_{y_j}), for some $\delta \in \Delta$. This unique $\delta \in \Delta$ will be denoted by $\text{lb}_t(x_i)$ (resp. $\text{lb}_t(y_j)$).

For an alphabet Σ and $k \in \mathbb{N}$, we denote first-order substitution of the trees $s_1, \ldots, s_k \in U_\Sigma$ into $t \in U_\Sigma(\Sigma_{X_k})$ by $t[x_1/s_1, \ldots, x_k/s_k] \in U_\Sigma$, abbreviated by $t[\boldsymbol{x}/\boldsymbol{s}]$. The tree $t[\boldsymbol{x}/\boldsymbol{s}]$ is the result of replacing every node in t which is labeled by σ_{x_i}, for $i \in [k]$ and some $\sigma \in \Sigma$, by the tree s_i. Similarly, for $s \in U_\Sigma(A)$ and $t \in U_\Sigma(Z)$, let $t[z/s]$ denote the tree obtained from t by replacing every node that is labelled with z by s.

For every alphabet Σ and $k \in \mathbb{N}$, second-order substitution of the trees $s_1, \ldots, s_k \in U_\Sigma(Z)$ into the tree $t \in U_{\Sigma \cup \Sigma_{Y_k}}$ will be denoted by $t[\![y_1/s_1, \ldots, y_k/s_k]\!] \in U_\Sigma$, or shorter, by $t[\![\boldsymbol{y}/\boldsymbol{s}]\!]$. For every symbol $\sigma \in \Sigma$ and variable $y_i \in Y_k$, we define $\sigma_{y_i}(t_1, \ldots, t_n)[\![\boldsymbol{y}/\boldsymbol{s}]\!] = s_i[z/\sigma(t_1[\![\boldsymbol{y}/\boldsymbol{s}]\!], \ldots, t_n[\![\boldsymbol{y}/\boldsymbol{s}]\!])]$, and we define $\sigma(t_1, \ldots, t_n)[\![\boldsymbol{y}/\boldsymbol{s}]\!] = \sigma(t_1[\![\boldsymbol{y}/\boldsymbol{s}]\!], \ldots, t_n[\![\boldsymbol{y}/\boldsymbol{s}]\!])$ for $\sigma \in \Sigma$.

2.2 Hypergraphs

A *hypergraph* is a tuple (V, E, μ, g) where the set V contains the graph's *vertices* and E the *hyperedges* (or just *edges*). Edge connectivity is denoted by the function $\mu \colon E \to V^+$ and $g \in V$ is the graph's *goal vertex*. For a hyperedge e with $\mu(e) = a_0 a_1 \cdots a_n$, we define its *head* as $\text{hd}(e) = a_0$, its *tail* as $\text{tl}(e) = a_1 \cdots a_n$ and its *arity* as $\text{ar}(e) = n$. The set of *a-hyperpaths* H_G^a of a hypergraph $G = (V, E, \mu, g)$, $a \in V$, is the largest set of trees $H \subseteq U_E$ such that for every $d \in H$, $w \in \text{pos}(d)$, we have $\text{hd}(d(\varepsilon)) = a$, $|\{v \in \text{pos}(d) \mid v = wi, i \in \mathbb{N}\}| = |\text{tl}(e)|$, and $\text{tl}(d(w)) = \text{hd}(d(w1)) \cdots \text{hd}(d(wn))$, where

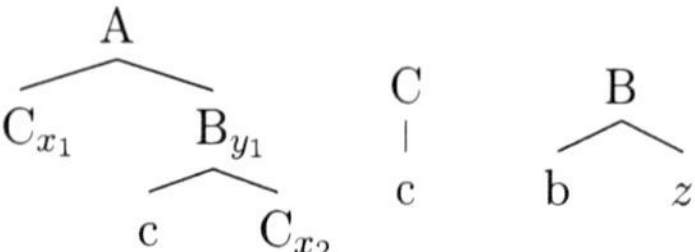

Figure 1: PTAG $\mathcal{G}$ with trees α_1, α_2 and β

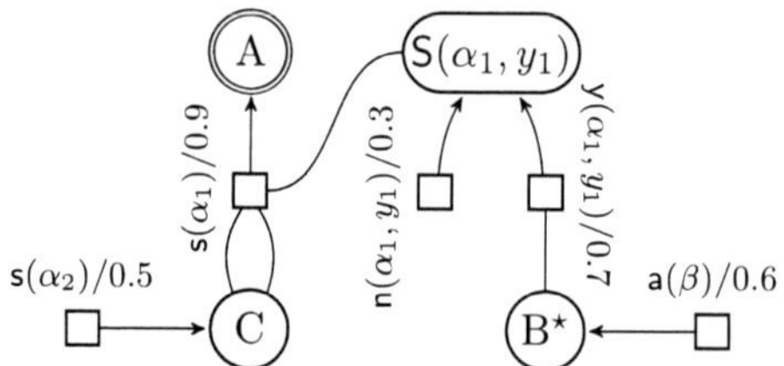

Figure 2: Hypergraph representation of $\mathcal{G}$

$n = |\mathrm{tl}(e)|$. The *hyperpaths* of G are its g-hyperpaths: $H_G = H_G^g$.

A tuple (V, E, μ, g, p) is called a *probabilistic hypergraph (phg)* if (V, E, μ, g) is a hypergraph and $p\colon E \to [0,1]$ assigns a *probability* to every hyperedge. We will denote the class of all probabilistic hypergraphs by $\mathcal{H}$ and assume definitions for unweighted hypergraphs to carry over to the probabilistic case. The *probability* of a derivation $d \in H_G$ is defined to be

$$P(d \mid G) = \prod_{w \in \mathrm{pos}(d)} p(d(w)).$$

In the following, we will fix the phg G (resp. G', G'') to be of the form (V, E, μ, g, p) (resp. (V', E', μ', g', p'), etc.).

2.3 Tree-Adjoining Grammars

In our definition of tree-adjoining grammars, the variable x_i (resp. y_j) in a symbol σ_{x_i} (resp. σ_{y_j}) will be used to tag σ with the information that it labels the ith substitution (resp. jth adjoining) site of the respective tree. The variable z in an auxiliary tree denotes the tree's foot node. This formalization allows us, among others, to give a straightforward definition of derived trees.

A *tree-adjoining grammar (TAG)* is a tuple $\mathcal{G} = (\Sigma, S, \mathcal{S}, \mathcal{A})$ where Σ is an alphabet, $S \in \Sigma$ is called the *start symbol*, $\mathcal{S} \subseteq U_\Gamma(\Delta)$ the set of *initial trees*, and $\mathcal{A} \subseteq U_\Gamma(\Delta \cup Z)$ the set of *auxiliary trees*, with $\Gamma = \Sigma \cup \Sigma_Y$ and $\Delta = \Sigma_X$. We demand for every $t \in \mathcal{S} \cup \mathcal{A}$ that $t(\varepsilon) \in \Sigma$, and that there are $n, m \in \mathbb{N}$ such that t is proper in X_n and in Y_m. In the following, we will denote these unique n and m by $\mathrm{rk}_1(t)$, resp. $\mathrm{rk}_2(t)$. Moreover, we require that for every $t \in \mathcal{A}$, z appears exactly once in t.

A *probabilistic tree-adjoining grammar (PTAG)* is then a tuple $\mathcal{G} = (\Sigma, S, \mathcal{S}, \mathcal{A}, P, Q)$ such that $(\Sigma, S, \mathcal{S}, \mathcal{A})$ is a TAG, $P\colon \mathcal{S} \cup \mathcal{A} \to [0,1]$ maps trees to their probabilities and $Q = (Q_t\colon Y_{\mathrm{rk}_2(t)} \to [0,1])_{t \in \mathcal{S} \cup \mathcal{A}}$ assigns to adjoining sites the probability of their activation. We will denote the class of all PTAG by $\mathcal{T}$.

In the following, the PTAG $\mathcal{G}$ (resp. $\mathcal{G}'$) will be assumed to be of the form $(\Sigma, S, \mathcal{S}, \mathcal{A}, P, Q)$ (resp. $(\Sigma', S', \mathcal{S}', \mathcal{A}', P', Q')$).

Let us examine an example PTAG $\mathcal{G}$, with $\Sigma = \{A, B, C, c, b\}$, $S = A$, initial trees $\mathcal{S} = \{\alpha_1, \alpha_2\}$, and an auxiliary tree $\mathcal{A} = \{\beta\}$. Refer to Fig. 1, which depicts the tree α_1 with two substitution sites labeled, resp., with symbols A and C, as well as one adjoining site, labeled with B. To the right are the initial tree α_2 and the auxiliary tree β, both with no substitution or adjoining sites. The foot node of β is indicated by z.

We denote the conditional probability that an elementary tree t with root symbol A is used to rewrite substitution or adjoining sites that are labeled with A by $P(t)$. For $\mathcal{G}$, e.g., let $P(\alpha_1) = 0.9$, $P(\alpha_2) = 0.5$, and $P(\beta) = 0.6$. The probability that the adjoining site in α_1, tagged with y_1, is activated during a derivation, is denoted by $Q_{\alpha_1}(y_1)$. In the case of this running example, let $Q_{\alpha_1}(y_1) = 0.7$.

3 Hypergraph Representations

For every PTAG $\mathcal{G}$, we can construct a hypergraph $G = \mathrm{hg}(\mathcal{G})$, whose hyperpaths stand in a one-to-one correspondence to the grammar's derivations. Hence, we will call G a *hypergraph representation* of $\mathcal{G}$.

In our following definition, such a hypergraph $\mathrm{hg}(\mathcal{G})$ can contain three different types of vertices. The vertices of the first type model the derivation of initial trees. These vertices are just copies of the symbols of $\mathcal{G}$: for every symbol $A \in \Sigma$, a vertex A is introduced. Refer to Fig. 2, which depicts the hypergraph $\mathrm{hg}(\mathcal{G})$ that represents the derivational structure of the PTAG $\mathcal{G}$ from our running example. Its A- and C-hyperpaths model derivation of initial trees with respective root symbols. Other, irrelevant, vertices of this form are omitted from the figure.

The second vertex type helps in the derivation of auxiliary trees. For each $A \in \Sigma$, the hypergraph contains a corresponding vertex $A^\star$. In Fig. 2, the only relevant vertex of this form is $B^\star$, whose hyperpaths represent derivations of auxiliary trees with root symbol B.

Lastly, for every adjoining site that appears in an elementary tree t and is tagged with y_i, we include a vertex $\mathsf{S}(t, y_i)$. This vertex is used to explicitly model the decision to activate or not to activate the corresponding adjoining site. In the figure, there is only one such vertex, $\mathsf{S}(\alpha_1, y_1)$.

The hyperedges of $\mathrm{hg}(\mathcal{G})$ can also be classified by their intended meaning: a hyperedge of the form $\mathsf{s}(\alpha)$ signifies the substitution of the initial tree α during a derivation. Its head vertex is its root symbol. Its tail vertices are, in order, the labels of α's substitution sites (indicating that the derivation must continue with derivations of trees with the respective symbols at their root) and the vertices $\mathsf{S}(\alpha, y_i)$ modelling its adjoining sites (these indicate the necessary decision on activating the sites). In Fig. 2, we see, among others, $\mathsf{s}(\alpha_1)$, whose head vertex A corresponds to α_1's root symbol, while its two tail vertices C stand for its respective substitution sites, and $\mathsf{S}(\alpha_1, y_1)$ for its adjoining site.

Hyperedges of the form $\mathsf{a}(\beta)$, with β an elementary auxiliary tree, possess essentially the same structure as the former, but signify derivation of auxiliary trees. In the figure, the only edge of this form is $\mathsf{a}(\beta)$. Its head vertex is $B^\star$ because β's root symbol is B, and it has no tail vertices, since there are no sites in β.

Finally, the hyperedge $\mathsf{y}(t, y_i)$ (resp. $\mathsf{n}(t, y_i)$) encodes the information that an adjoining site in t was activated (deactivated). Both have $\mathsf{S}(t, y_i)$ as head, and while $\mathsf{n}(t, y_i)$ has no tail, the tail of $\mathsf{y}(t, y_i)$ signifies that the derivation should continue with the adjoining of an auxiliary tree. In Fig. 2, e.g., $\mathsf{y}(\alpha_1, y_1)$ models the activation of the site that corresponds to its head vertex $\mathsf{S}(\alpha_1, y_1)$, and has the tail vertex $B^\star$, because that site is labeled with B.

The probabilities of these hyperedges are taken over from P and Q in the obvious way. Formally, we define $\mathrm{hg}(\mathcal{G}) = G$ with

$$V = \{A, A^\star \mid A \in \Sigma\}$$
$$\cup \{\mathsf{S}(t, y_i) \mid t \in \mathcal{S} \cup \mathcal{A}, i \in [\mathrm{rk}_2(t)]\},$$

$$E = \{\mathsf{s}(t) \mid t \in \mathcal{S}\} \cup \{\mathsf{a}(t) \mid t \in \mathcal{A}\}$$
$$\cup \{\mathsf{y}(t, y_i), \mathsf{n}(t, y_i) \mid t \in \mathcal{S} \cup A, i \in [\mathrm{rk}_2(t)]\},$$

goal vertex $g = S$, and

$$\mu(\mathsf{s}(t)) = A\, B_1 \cdots B_n\, \mathsf{S}(t, y_1) \cdots \mathsf{S}(t, y_m),$$
$$\mu(\mathsf{a}(t)) = A^\star\, B_1 \cdots B_n\, \mathsf{S}(t, y_1) \cdots \mathsf{S}(t, y_m),$$
$$\mu(\mathsf{y}(t, y_j)) = \mathsf{S}(t, y_j)\, C_j^\star,$$
$$\mu(\mathsf{n}(t, y_j)) = \mathsf{S}(t, y_j),$$

where $n = \mathrm{rk}_1(t)$, $m = \mathrm{rk}_2(t)$, $A = t(\varepsilon)$, $B_i = \mathrm{lb}_t(x_i)$ for $i \in [n]$, and $C_j = \mathrm{lb}_t(y_j)$ for $j \in [m]$, while

$$p(\mathsf{s}(t)) = P(t), \quad p(\mathsf{y}(t, y_j)) = Q_t(y_j),$$
$$p(\mathsf{a}(t)) = P(t), \quad p(\mathsf{n}(t, y_j)) = 1 - Q_t(y_j).$$

Note that for our simple running example from Fig. 1, there are only two possible derivations of trees with root symbol A: in the first one, we substitute two instances of α_2 into α_1, and, after activation of the adjoining site in α_1, adjoin β into this site. The corresponding A-hyperpath in Fig. 2 is $d_1 = \mathsf{s}(\alpha_1)\big(\mathsf{s}(\alpha_2), \mathsf{s}(\alpha_2), \mathsf{y}(\alpha_1, y_1)\big(\mathsf{a}(\beta)\big)\big)$. Alternatively, we can ignore the adjoining site, and arrive at the corresponding derivation $d_2 = \mathsf{s}(\alpha_1)\big(\mathsf{s}(\alpha_2), \mathsf{s}(\alpha_2), \mathsf{n}(\alpha_1, y_1)\big)$.

Given such a hyperpath that represents a PTAG derivation, we can compute the derivation's derived tree in a bottom-up manner with the function $\mathrm{yd} \colon H_{\mathrm{hg}(\mathcal{G})} \to U_\Sigma(X \cup Z)$ defined by

$$\mathrm{yd}(\mathsf{s}(t)(d_1, \ldots, d_n, d_1', \ldots, d_m'))$$
$$= t[\boldsymbol{x}/\mathrm{yd}(\boldsymbol{d})][\![\boldsymbol{y}/\mathrm{yd}(\boldsymbol{d}')]\!]$$
$$\mathrm{yd}(\mathsf{a}(t)(d_1, \ldots, d_n, d_1', \ldots, d_m'))$$
$$= t[\boldsymbol{x}/\mathrm{yd}(\boldsymbol{d})][\![\boldsymbol{y}/\mathrm{yd}(\boldsymbol{d}')]\!]$$
$$\mathrm{yd}(\mathsf{y}(t, y_j)(d)) = \mathrm{yd}(d)$$
$$\mathrm{yd}(\mathsf{n}(t, y_j)) = z,$$

where again $n = \mathrm{rk}_1(t)$, $m = \mathrm{rk}_2(t)$, and $\mathrm{yd}(\boldsymbol{d})$ denotes the element-wise application of yd to all $d_1, \ldots, d_n$, analogously for $\mathrm{yd}(\boldsymbol{d}')$.

For example, for d_1 from above, we can compute its derived tree as

$$\mathrm{yd}(d_1) = \alpha_1[x_1/\alpha_2, x_2/\alpha_2][\![y_1/\beta]\!]$$
$$= \mathrm{A}\big(\mathrm{C}(c), \mathrm{B}_{y_1}(c, \mathrm{C}(c))\big)[\![y_1/\beta]\!]$$
$$= \mathrm{A}\big(\mathrm{C}(c), \beta[z/\mathrm{B}(c, \mathrm{C}(c))]\big)$$
$$= \mathrm{A}\big(\mathrm{C}(c), \mathrm{B}(b, \mathrm{B}(c, \mathrm{C}(c)))\big).$$

4   State-Split Hypergraphs

In this section, we will detail how to generalize the state-split method presented by Petrov et al. to hypergraphs that represent PTAGs.

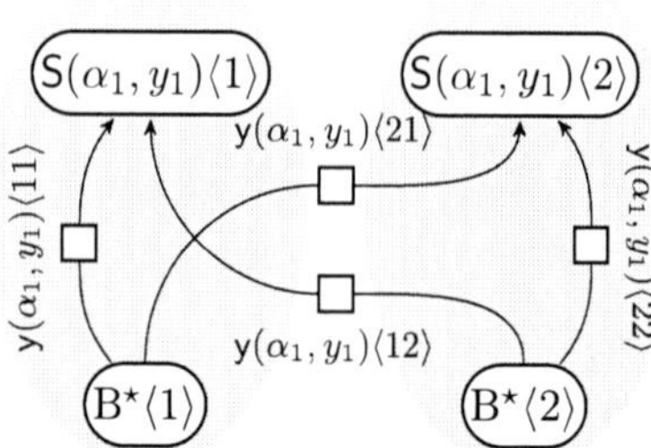

Figure 3: Crossing hyperedges

As explained in the introduction, the state-split algorithm proceeds in three distinct phases: first of all, it splits every vertex into two, and then it trains the probabilities of the resulting hyperedges on a given treebank corpus, using the EM algorithm. In a third step, vertices which do not increase likelihood are merged back together. However, due to the nature of adjunction in tree-adjoining grammar, the splits and merges cannot be quite as liberal as in the case of context-free grammars.

The reason for this will be shown immediately, but first and foremost, let us define how to represent split vertices. Given a hypergraph G, for any $a \in V$, and $b \in \{0, 1, 2\}$, define

$$a\langle b \rangle = \begin{cases} (a, b) & \text{if } b \in \{1, 2\} \\ a & \text{if } b = 0. \end{cases}$$

For a vertex a, the so-defined $a\langle 1 \rangle$ and $a\langle 2 \rangle$ will denote the two vertices which result from splitting a, while $a\langle 0 \rangle$ is just a notation for the merged-back-together vertex a. We will also have to annotate split hyperedges in this way: for a hyperedge $e \in E$ with $\mathrm{ar}(e) = n$, as well as a tuple $\boldsymbol{b} \in \{0, 1, 2\}^{n+1}$, we introduce the syntax $e\langle \boldsymbol{b} \rangle$, which stands for $(e, \boldsymbol{b})$.

Given this notation, we can examine the mentioned complication of the state-split procedure, which arises when splitting hyperedges of the form $\mathsf{y}(t, y_j)$. Let us assume that the vertices $\mathsf{S}(\alpha_1, y_1)$, $\mathsf{B}^\star$, as well as the hyperedge $\mathsf{y}(\alpha_1, y_1)$ from Fig. 2 are to undergo subcategorization.

If we split the vertices and hyperedges indiscriminately, we arrive at the situation displayed in Fig. 3: each of the vertices has been split into two copies, and four new y-hyperedges were introduced. What is the meaning of these hyperedges? In a hyperpath representing a PTAG derivation, the appearance of the hyperedge $\mathsf{y}(\alpha_1, y_1)\langle 11 \rangle$ signifies that the adjoining site in α_1, labeled with the split symbol

$\mathsf{B}\langle 1 \rangle$, is activated, and next, an auxiliary tree with equal root symbol must be adjoined into it.

However, there is a problem with the hyperedge $\mathsf{y}(\alpha_1, y_1)\langle 21 \rangle$ which crosses the shaded ellipses in the figure (and, analogously, with $\mathsf{y}(\alpha_1, y_1)\langle 12 \rangle$). This hyperedge can be interpreted as activation of the mentioned adjoining site, labeled with $\mathsf{B}\langle 1 \rangle$, and preparation of adjoining an auxiliary tree with root symbol $\mathsf{B}\langle 2 \rangle$. This stands in conflict to the concept of adjoining, where the label of the node to be replaced must be identical to the symbol at the root of the auxiliary tree.

There are several distinct possibilities to handle this complication. First of all, one could just do away with the above condition regarding adjoining. Actually, such a relaxation of the formalism was already proposed by Rogers (2003), resulting in *non-strict* tree-adjoining grammars.

As a second option, the formalism of TAG could be extended by introducing states (cf. (Büchse et al., 2011) for synchronous TAG). In this modification, the derivational structure of the grammar is no longer dependent on the labels of adjoining and substitution sites, this information is instead encoded into the states, which only appear as intermediate symbols in a derivation. Performing the splits and merges on such states, instead of symbols, could also remedy the problem.

However, for this work, we chose to stick to a conceptually simpler solution, thus staying close to the established notion of tree-adjoining grammar: we just disallow the creation of such crossing hyperedges during the split-merge cycle; or, to put it differently, we only introduce a hyperedge $\mathsf{y}(t, y)\langle i\,j \rangle$ into the split hypergraph if $i = j$. Hence, in Fig. 3, only the two hyperedges $\mathsf{y}(\alpha_1, y_1)\langle 11 \rangle$ and $\mathsf{y}(\alpha_1, y_1)\langle 22 \rangle$, which are both "within" the two shaded ellipses, would be generated.

To formalize this idea, we augment the state-split method with what we call *split relations*. Given a hypergraph G which is to undergo a split-merge cycle, a split relation on G is a symmetric relation $R \subseteq V \times V$ on the graph's vertices. If a hyperedge e from G connects, among others, two vertices a_1 and a_2 such that $a_1 R a_2$, then the idea is to split e only into such hyperedges which connect either only $a_1\langle 1 \rangle$ and $a_2\langle 1 \rangle$, or only $a_1\langle 2 \rangle$ and $a_2\langle 2 \rangle$, but not, e.g., $a_1\langle 1 \rangle$ and $a_2\langle 2 \rangle$.

This invariant must also be heeded when we merge back together parts of the hypergraph: for example, if $a_1 R a_2$, we cannot merge back together

$a_1\langle 1\rangle$ and $a_1\langle 2\rangle$ but leave $a_2\langle 1\rangle$ and $a_2\langle 2\rangle$ split at the same time. Hence, what we must consider is merging all elements which are (in-)directly related by R simultaneously together. More succinctly, the objects considered to be merged must be the equivalence classes of the reflexive-transitive closure R^* of R, which we also call *split classes*.

4.1 Splitting

When we split the vertices of a hypergraph, we must take care that the created hyperedges respect the supplied split relation R, as explained above.

This is achieved by the following function split_R, which splits every node and introduces new hyperedges respecting R. Given a hypergraph G and split relation $R \subseteq V \times V$, we let $\mathrm{split}_R(G) = G'$ with

$$V' = \{a\langle b\rangle \mid a \in V, b \in \{1,2\}\},$$
$$E' = \{e\langle b_0, \ldots, b_k\rangle \mid e \in E, \mu(e) = a_0 \cdots a_k,$$
$$b_0, \ldots, b_k \in \{1,2\},$$
$$a_i R a_j \text{ implies } b_i = b_j\},$$
$$\mu'(e\langle b_0, \ldots, b_k\rangle) = a_0\langle b_0\rangle \cdots a_k\langle b_k\rangle,$$
$$\text{where } \mu(e) = a_0 \cdots a_k,$$
$$g' = g\langle 1\rangle, \text{ and}$$
$$p'(e\langle b_0, \ldots, b_k\rangle) = \frac{p(e)}{2^c}$$
$$\text{where } c = |\{e\langle \boldsymbol{b'}\rangle \in E' \mid \boldsymbol{b'} = b_0 \cdots b_k\}|.$$

Note that the probabilities of hyperedges are distributed uniformly to their split copies in G'. In an implementation, these should be slightly randomized to give starting values for the EM algorithm, as mentioned by Petrov et al. (2006).

The split hypergraph's number of hyperedges is exponential in their arity. We can try to mitigate the problem of this exponential blowup by binarizing the trees of the TAG which was initially extracted from a corpus, following the description of Lang (1994).

4.2 Merging

As explained above, we have to merge all elements of a split class back together simultaneously. This will be denoted with the following function. Let $G' = \mathrm{split}_R(G)$ be a hypergraph resulting from a split, $R \subseteq V \times V$ a split relation, and $C \in V/R^*$ one of its split classes. The hypergraph which results from merging C back together is denoted by $G'' = \mathrm{merge}_R^C(G')$ with

$$V'' = V' \setminus \{a\langle b\rangle \mid a \in C, b \in \{1,2\}\} \cup C,$$

$$E'' = \{e\langle b_0', \ldots, b_k'\rangle \mid e\langle b_0, \ldots, b_k\rangle \in E',$$
$$\mu(e) = a_0 \cdots a_k,$$
$$a_i \in C \text{ implies } b_i' = 0,$$
$$a_i \notin C \text{ implies } b_i' = b_i\},$$

where we write $o(e\langle b_0', \ldots, b_k'\rangle) = e\langle b_0, \ldots, b_k\rangle$ for the relation of $e\langle b_0', \ldots, b_k'\rangle$ to $e\langle b_0, \ldots, b_k\rangle$,

$$\mu''(e\langle b_0, \ldots, b_k\rangle) = a_0\langle b_0\rangle \cdots a_k\langle b_k\rangle,$$
$$\text{where } \mu(e) = a_0 \cdots a_k,$$

$$g'' = \begin{cases} g & \text{if } g \in C \\ g' & \text{otherwise, and} \end{cases}$$

$$p''(e'') = \begin{cases} \displaystyle\sum_{e' \in o^{-1}(e'')} p'(e')/2 & \text{if } \mathrm{hd}(e) \in C \\ \displaystyle\sum_{e \in o^{-1}(e'')} p'(e) & \text{otherwise} \end{cases}$$

Note that the probabilities of hyperedges which are merged back together are summed up. In the case that a hyperedge's head vertex is merged, we have to normalize the resulting probability.

4.3 Treebank Corpora and Likelihood

During the split-merge procedure, we want to train the split hypergraph representations on a supplied treebank. Following the presentation of Prescher (2005), we will abstract away from the concrete data structures which might be used to represent a collection of trees, and just define a treebank corpus as a function $K : U_\Sigma \to \mathbb{R}_{\geq 0}$, assigning to every tree over an alphabet Σ a certain *frequency*, such that the set of trees with non-zero frequency is finite.

Let us assume that $G_0 = \mathrm{hg}(\mathcal{G})$ is the hypergraph representation of a PTAG $\mathcal{G}$ and G_n is the result of n split-merge cycles on G_0. Then we can define the likelihood of a corpus $K : U_\Sigma \to \mathbb{R}_{\geq 0}$ on G_n as

$$L(K \mid G_n) = \prod_{\substack{t \in U_\Sigma}} \Bigg(\sum_{\substack{d \in H_{G_n} \\ \mathrm{yd}(u_n(d))=t}} P(d \mid G_n)\Bigg)^{K(t)}$$

$$= \prod_{\substack{t \in U_\Sigma}} \Bigg(\sum_{\substack{d' \in H_{G_0} \\ \mathrm{yd}(d')=t}} \Big(\sum_{\substack{d \in H_{G_n} \\ u_n(d)=d'}} P(d \mid G_n)\Big)\Bigg)^{K(t)}. \quad (1)$$

Hereby, the function u_n removes n levels of annotation from an annotated derivation, for every $n \in \mathbb{N}$. It is defined as the homomorphic extension of the function $\tilde{u}_n$ on hyperedges to unranked trees, where $\tilde{u}$ is defined for every hyperedge e by $\tilde{u}_0(e) = e$, and for $n > 1$, $\tilde{u}_n(e\langle \boldsymbol{b}\rangle) = \tilde{u}_{n-1}(e)$.

Algorithm 1 The state-split algorithm	**Algorithm 2** A split-merge cycle
Require: phg G, $n \in \mathbb{N}$, corpus $K : U_\Sigma \to \mathbb{R}_{\geq 0}$	**Require:** phg G, $R \subseteq V \times V$, corpus $K : U_\Sigma \to \mathbb{R}_{\geq 0}$
1: **function** STATESPLIT(G, n, K)	1: **function** SPLITMERGE(G, R, K)
2: $G_0 \leftarrow G$	2: $G' \leftarrow \mathrm{split}_R(G)$
3: **compute** split relation R_0	3: $G' \leftarrow \mathrm{EMTRAIN}(G', K)$
4: **for all** $i \in [n]$ **do**	4: **for all** $C \in V/R^*$ **do**
5: $G_i \leftarrow$ SPLITMERGE(G_{i-1}, R_{i-1}, K)	5: $G'' \leftarrow \mathrm{merge}_R^C(G')$
6: **update** split relation R_{i-1} to R_{i-1}	6: **if** $L(G'' \mid K)/L(G' \mid K) \geq \lambda$ **then**
7: **end for**	7: $G' \leftarrow G''$
8: **return** G_n	8: **end if**
9: **end function**	9: **end for**
	10: **return** G'
	11: **end function**

Note that in (1), for every $t \in U_\Sigma$ with non-zero frequency, there are only finitely many derivations $d' \in H_{G_0}$, which can be determined by employing a TAG parser at the beginning of the state-split process. For each of these d' we can compute the value of the innermost sum in a bottom-up manner, similarly to the computation of inside probabilities as described by Petrov et al. (2006).

In the following, given a hypergraph G_n, $n > 0$, we will identify $\mathrm{yd}(d)$ with $\mathrm{yd}(u_n(d))$, for every $d \in H_{G_n}$.

4.4 Overview of the Algorithm

Now we can denote the state-split algorithm for hypergraphs in pseudocode, cf. Alg. 1. After computing the initial split relation, the algorithm's outer loop (ll. 4–7) executes n split-merge cycles on G using the treebank corpus K for training. Additionally, in each step it updates the split relation to the newly generated hypergraph.

Note that the concrete computation of split classes depends strongly on the grammar formalism represented by the hypergraph, hence we leave it abstract in the general formulation of the algorithm. In our case, where we use tree-adjoining grammars as underlying formalism, we can instantiate it as follows: R_0 is defined as the finest symmetric relation R such that, for every vertex of the form $\mathsf{S}(t, y_i)$ in G_0, we have $(\mathsf{S}(t, y_i), \mathrm{lb}_t(y_i)^\star) \in R$. Similarly, given a split relation R_{i-1}, the updated split relation R_i is the finest symmetric relation R such that, for every $b \in \{0, 1, 2\}$ and pair $a_1\langle b \rangle$, $a_2\langle b \rangle$, if $a_1\langle b \rangle$ and $a_2\langle b \rangle$ are vertices in G_i such that $a_1 R_{i-1} a_2$, then $a_1\langle b \rangle R a_2\langle b \rangle$.

The split-merge cycle (cf. Alg. 2) can be considered as the core of the state-split algorithm. Supplied with a phg G, split relation R on G, and treebank corpus K, SPLITMERGE first of all splits the nodes of G, as defined in section 4.1. Then it

uses the EM algorithm for maximum likelihood estimation on incomplete data to train the newly-split phg on the treebank K. Finally, in ll. 4–9, each split class is tentatively merged back together, and if the concomitant loss in likelihood does not fall below a certain factor $\lambda \in [0, 1]$, this merge is taken over permanently. As noted by Petrov et al., this combats the exponential blow-up of the hypergraph, as well as the phenomenon of overfitting.

For the sake of completeness, let us give a rough sketch of the EM algorithm for training state-split hypergraphs on treebank corpora, following the exposition of Prescher (2005). Given a phg G and a treebank corpus K, the EM algorithm alternatingly repeats two computations, called the *Expectation step (E-step)* and the *Maximization step (M-step)*, until the increase in likelihood of the newly-computed hypergraph on the corpus K falls beneath a certain threshold $\delta \in \mathbb{R}$.

Note that the EM algorithm is not guaranteed to find the actual global maximum of the likelihood, however, as already shown by Dempster et al. (1977), the likelihoods of the respective grammars are monotonically non-decreasing, and so at least a local maximum can be approximated.

In the algorithm's E-step, a complete-data corpus $C : H_G \to \mathbb{R}_{\geq 0}$ on the hyperpaths of G is generated by distributing the frequencies of every derived tree $t \in U_\Sigma$ in the corpus K to the hyperpaths representing derivations of t, weighted by their conditional probability given t. The M-step then uses this complete-data corpus to compute hyperedge probabilities by relative frequency estimation. Thereby, $\mathrm{ct}_e(d)$ denotes the number of appearances of the hyperedge e in the derivation d,

Algorithm 3 EM for (state-split) hypergraphs

Require: phg G, corpus $K\colon U_\Sigma \to \mathbb{R}_{\geq 0}$

1: **function** EMTRAIN(G, K)
2:     **repeat**
3:         $G' \leftarrow G$
4:         **E-Step:** define $C\colon H_G \to \mathbb{R}$ by:
5:         $C(d) = K(\mathrm{yd}(d)) \cdot P\big(d \mid \mathrm{yd}(d), G\big)$
6:         **M-step:** set new probabilities:
7:         **for all** $e \in E$ **do**
8:           $p(e) \leftarrow \dfrac{\sum_{d \in H_G} C(d)\cdot\mathrm{ct}_e(d)}{\sum_{d \in H_G} C(d)\cdot\mathrm{ct}_{\mathrm{hd}(e)}(d)}$
9:         **end for**
10:    **until** $L(G|K) - L(G'|K) < \delta$
11:    **return** G
12: **end function**

and $\mathrm{ct}_{\mathrm{hd}(e)}(d)$ the number of appearing hyperedges with the same head vertex as e.

One might remark that this concise, but formulaic presentation of EM is not immediately suitable for implementation, but, using the derivation employed by Gupta and Chen (2011), it is straightforward to bring it into the form of the well-known *Inside-Outside algorithm*, which has been adapted to PTAG by Schabes (1992).

5 State-Split preserves Hypergraph Representations

After all these definitions, we might ask ourselves the following question: given a hypergraph representation G of some PTAG $\mathcal{G}$, does the hypergraph which results from an application of the split-merge cycle to G still represent a PTAG? This question indeed arises quite naturally, after all it is an important requirement for the correctness of the state-split procedure for PTAGs with hypergraphs.

If we denote the result of a split-merge cycle on a phg G by $\mathrm{sm}(G)$, and the class of all hypergraph representations of probabilistic tree-adjoining grammars by $\mathcal{H}_\mathcal{T}$, then this question can essentially be answered by proving the inclusion

$$\mathrm{sm}(\mathcal{H}_\mathcal{T}) \subseteq \mathcal{H}_\mathcal{T}. \tag{2}$$

But the validity of this inclusion does certainly depend on the formal definition of $\mathcal{H}_\mathcal{T}$. Indeed, for the definition which comes to mind first, in which we just fix $\mathcal{H}_\mathcal{T}$ to be the set $\{\mathrm{hg}(\mathcal{G}) \mid \mathcal{G} \in \mathcal{T}\}$, i.e. the image of the class of all PTAGs under hg, the inclusion is *not* valid! This is due to the annotation of vertices and hyperedges in a split-merge cycle: hypergraphs that contain, for example, a vertex

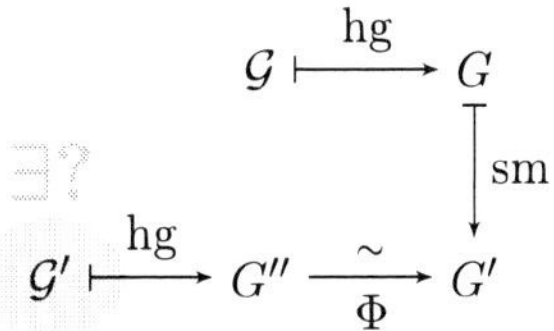

Figure 4: Proof idea

$A\langle 2\rangle$, which was generated by splitting a vertex A, are arguably not in the image of hg!

However, one can show that the *structure* of a split-and-merged hypergraph still corresponds to the image of a PTAG $\mathcal{G}$ under hg. We will capture this structural identity by means of hypergraph isomorphisms.

A *hypergraph isomorphism* $\Phi\colon G \xrightarrow{\sim} G'$ is a tuple (Φ_1, Φ_2), where $\Phi_1\colon V \to V'$ and $\Phi_2\colon E \to E'$ are bijections such that $\Phi_1(g) = g'$ and $\mu'(\Phi_2(e)) = \Phi_1(a_0) \cdots \Phi_1(a_n)$ if $\mu(e) = a_0 \cdots a_n$. We write $G \cong G'$ if there is an isomorphism $\Phi\colon G \xrightarrow{\sim} G'$.

We define the set of all possible hypergraph representations of PTAG as

$$\mathcal{H}_\mathcal{T} = \{G \in \mathcal{H} \mid \exists \mathcal{G} \in \mathcal{T}.\, \mathrm{hg}(\mathcal{G}) \cong G\}.$$

Obviously, for every PTAG $\mathcal{G}$, $\mathrm{hg}(\mathcal{G}) \in \mathcal{H}_\mathcal{T}$, i.e., it is indeed a hypergraph representation according to this definition. As visualized in Fig. 4, the core of the proof of (2) is then as follows: Given $\mathcal{G} \in \mathcal{T}$, $G \in \mathcal{H}$, and $G' = \mathrm{sm}(G)$, we have to construct a PTAG $\mathcal{G}'$ and hypergraph isomorphism $\Phi\colon \mathrm{hg}(\mathcal{G}') \xrightarrow{\sim} G'$.

We construct $\mathcal{G}'$ so that the trees of $\mathcal{G}'$ are relabelings of those in $\mathcal{G}$, generated by incorporating the annotations to the hyperedges in G to substitution and adjoining sites:

$$\mathcal{S}' = \{t\langle \boldsymbol{b}\rangle \mid \mathsf{s}(t)\langle \boldsymbol{b}\rangle \in E'\},$$
$$\mathcal{A}' = \{t\langle \boldsymbol{b}\rangle \mid \mathsf{a}(t)\langle \boldsymbol{b}\rangle \in E'\},$$

where $t\langle a\, b_1 \cdots b_{\mathrm{rk}_1(t)}\, c_1 \cdots c_{\mathrm{rk}_2(t)}\rangle$ is the result of replacing the root symbol A of t by $A\langle a\rangle$, every substitution site A_{x_i} in t by $A\langle b_i\rangle_{x_i}$, and every adjoining site A_{y_j} by $A\langle c_j\rangle_{y_j}$, for $i \in [\mathrm{rk}_1(t)]$ and $j \in [\mathrm{rk}_2(t)]$. The probabilities $P(t)$ of elementary trees t, as well as the activation probabilities $Q_t(y_i)$ are just read off from $p(\mathsf{s}(t))$, $p(\mathsf{a}(t))$, resp. $p(\mathsf{y}(t, y_i))$.

The hypergraph isomorphism Φ then just reverses this relabeling. Given nodes or hyperedges from $\mathrm{hg}(\mathcal{G}')$ with annotations in them, it removes them from the contained symbols resp. elementary trees and moves them "to the back", i.e.,

$$\Phi_1(A\langle b\rangle) = A\langle b\rangle, \quad \Phi_1\big((A\langle b\rangle)^{\star}\big) = A^{\star}\langle b\rangle,$$

$$\Phi_1\big(\mathsf{S}(t\langle\boldsymbol{b}\rangle, y_i)\big) = \mathsf{S}(t, y_i)\langle b^{(i)}\rangle$$

and

$$\Phi_2\big(\mathsf{s}(t\langle\boldsymbol{b}\rangle)\big) = \mathsf{s}(t)\langle\boldsymbol{b}\rangle,$$

$$\Phi_2\big(\mathsf{s}(t\langle\boldsymbol{b}\rangle)\big) = \mathsf{s}(t)\langle\boldsymbol{b}\rangle,$$

$$\Phi_2\big(\mathsf{y}(t\langle\boldsymbol{b}\rangle, y_i)\big) = \mathsf{y}(t, y_i)\langle b^{(i)}\boldsymbol{b}^{(i)}\rangle,$$

$$\Phi_2\big(\mathsf{n}(t\langle\boldsymbol{b}\rangle, y_i)\big) = \mathsf{n}(t, y_i)\langle b^{(i)}\rangle,$$

where, in all three cases, $b^{(i)} = \boldsymbol{b}(\mathrm{rk}_1(t) + i)$.

Now, Φ can indeed be proven to be a hypergraph isomorphism between $\mathcal{G}'$ and $\mathrm{sm}(G)$, but for reasons of space, we will omit these details from this work. Note that the construction of $\mathcal{G}'$ and Φ can alternatively be interpreted as the definition of a *read-off* procedure, which allows our system *Vanda* to convert back its internal state-split hypergraph representation into a probabilistic tree-adjoining grammar, e.g. to display the resulting grammars for means of debugging. Thus, it also has a hands-on relevance for implementation.

Acknowledgements We thank the anonymous reviewers for their valuable comments, and our colleagues Toni Dietze and Matthias Büchse for fruitful discussions.

References

Yehoshua Bar-Hillel, Micha A Perles, and Eli Shamir. 1961. On formal properties of simple phrase structure grammars. *Zeitschrift für Phonetik, Sprachwissenschaft und Kommunikationsforschung*, 14:143–172.

Matthias Büchse, Mark-Jan Nederhof, and Heiko Vogler. 2011. Tree Parsing with Synchronous Tree-Adjoining Grammars. In *Proceedings of the 12th International Conference on Parsing Technologies*, pages 14–25, Dublin, Ireland, October. Association for Computational Linguistics.

Matthias Büchse, Toni Dietze, Johannes Osterholzer, Anja Fischer, and Linda Leuschner. 2012. Vanda – A Statistical Machine Translation Toolkit. In *Proceedings of the 6th International Workshop Weighted Automata: Theory and Applications*, pages 36–37.

John Chen, Srinivas Bangalore, and K Vijay-Shanker. 2006. Automated Extraction of Tree-Adjoining Grammars from Treebanks. *Natural Language Engineering*, 12(3):251.

Arthur P Dempster, Nan McKenzie Laird, and Donald B Rubin. 1977. Maximum Likelihood from Incomplete Data via the EM Algorithm. *Journal of the Royal Statistical Society*, B(39):1–38.

Maya R Gupta and Yihua Chen. 2011. Theory and Use of the EM Algorithm. *Foundations and Trends in Signal Processing*, 4(3):223–296.

Aravind K Joshi and Yves Schabes. 1991. Tree-Adjoining Grammars and Lexicalized Grammars. In Maurice Nivat and Andreas Podelski, editors, *Definability and Recognizability of Sets of Trees*, pages 409–431. Elsevier.

Dan Klein and Christopher D Manning. 2004. Parsing and Hypergraphs. In Harry Bunt, John Carroll, and Giorgio Satta, editors, *New Developments in Parsing Technology*, volume 23 of *Text, Speech and Language Technology*, pages 351–372. Springer Netherlands.

Bernard Lang. 1994. Recognition can be Harder than Parsing. *Computational Intelligence*, 10(4):486–494.

Andreas Maletti and Giorgio Satta. 2009. Parsing Algorithms based on Tree Automata. In Harry Bunt, editor, *Proceedings of the 11th International Conference on Parsing Technologies*, pages 1–12. Association for Computational Linguistics.

Andreas Maletti. 2010. A Tree Transducer Model for Synchronous Tree-Adjoining Grammars. In *Proceedings of the 48th Annual Meeting of the Association for Computational Linguistics*, pages 1067–1076. Association for Computational Linguistics.

Slav Petrov, Leon Barrett, Romain Thibaux, and Dan Klein. 2006. Learning Accurate, Compact, and Interpretable Tree Annotation. In *Proceedings of the 21st International Conference on Computational Linguistics and 44th Annual Meeting of the Association for Computational Linguistics*, pages 433–440, Sydney, Australia. Association for Computational Linguistics.

Detlef Prescher. 2005. A Tutorial on the Expectation-Maximization Algorithm Including Maximum-Likelihood Estimation and EM Training of Probabilistic Context-Free Grammars. Technical report, 15th European Summer School in Logic, Language, and Information.

Philip Resnik. 1992. Probabilistic Tree-Adjoining Grammar As A Framework For Statistical Natural Language Processing. In *Proceedings of the 14th Conference on Computational Linguistics*, pages 418–424.

James Rogers. 2003. wMSO theories as grammar formalisms. *Theoretical Computer Science*, 293(2):291–320, February.

Yves Schabes. 1992. Stochastic Tree-Adjoining Grammars. In *Proceedings of the Workshop on Speech and Natural Language*, HLT '91, pages 140–145, Stroudsburg, PA, USA. Association for Computational Linguistics.

Hiroyuki Shindo, Yusuke Miyao, Akinori Fujino, and Masaaki Nagata. 2012. Bayesian Symbol-Refined Tree Substitution Grammars for Syntactic Parsing. In *Proceedings of the 50th Annual Meeting of the Association for Computational Linguistics*, pages 440–448.

Is Syntactic Binding Rational?

Thomas Graf
Department of Linguistics
University of California, Los Angeles
3125 Campbell Hall
Los Angeles, CA 90095-1543, USA
tgraf@ucla.edu

Natasha Abner
Department of Linguistics
University of California, Los Angeles
3125 Campbell Hall
Los Angeles, CA 90095-1543, USA
nabner@ucla.edu

Abstract

Recent results show that both TAG and Minimalist grammars can be enriched with rational constraints without increasing their strong generative capacity, where a constraint is rational iff it can be computed by a bottom-up tree automaton. This raises the question which aspects of syntax can be adequately formalized using only such constraints. One of hardest phenomena commonly studied by syntacticians is binding theory. In this paper, we give a high-level implementation of (the syntactic parts of) binding theory in terms of rational constraints, and we argue that this implementation is sufficiently powerful for natural language. This conclusion is backed up by data drawn from English, German, and American Sign Language.

1 Introduction

Finite-state methods and tools are ubiquitous in computational linguistics due to their ease of use, attractive closure properties, and efficient runtime behavior. At the level of trees, they are represented by *rational constraints*. A constraint is called rational iff it defines a regular tree language iff it can be computed by a bottom-up tree automaton iff it is definable in monadic second-order logic with predicates for immediate dominance and linear precedence (Gécseg and Steinby, 1997).

Recently it was demonstrated that rational constraints can be added to TAG as well as Minimalist grammars (MGs; Stabler, 2011) without increasing their strong generative capacity (Rogers, 2003; Mönnich, 2006; Graf, 2011; Kobele, 2011). At least in the case of MGs it is also known that rational constraints are the most powerful class of constraints for which this result holds. Therefore any aspect of syntax that cannot be expressed in terms of rational constraints requires a proper extension of the framework. Quick surveys in Graf (2011) and Kobele (2011) suggest that rational constraints are powerful enough for a rich variety of modifications and embellishment put forward in the syntactic literature. One problematic area, however, is binding theory, which is sometimes claimed to be NP-complete (Ristad, 1993) and thus firmly outside the realm of finite-state computability. In this paper we give a high-level implementation of (syntactic) binding theory in terms of rational constraints; we also argue that this implementation is sufficiently powerful for natural language and discuss potential counterexamples from several languages, foremost English and American Sign Language (ASL).

Organization. The paper is laid out as follows. In Sec. 2 we discuss the limitations of rational theories of binding and what they nonetheless need to be capable of accounting for. The major stumbling block turns out to be the disjoint reference requirement on pronouns. We give a finite-state implementation in Sec. 3 that successfully captures this condition as long as there is an upper bound on the number of antecedents needed for all the pronouns in a specific domain. Sec. 4 demonstrates that this assumption is empirically feasible.

2 Object Domain

Binding theory is a very active research area, with proposals ranging from the purely syntactic to the purely discourse-driven and covering almost every shade in between. Thus it isn't particularly surprising that there is no consensus as to what

Proceedings of the 11th International Workshop on Tree Adjoining Grammars and Related Formalisms (TAG+11), pages 189–197,
Paris, September 2012.

exactly a theory of binding needs to account for. In this section we delineate the scope of a rational theory of binding and highlight the main empirical issue such an approach faces. We will see that there are parts of binding theory that provably cannot be recast as rational constraints, but also that those aren't the aspects formal grammar formalisms like TAG or MGs should be concerned with.

A distinction is often made in the linguistic literature between syntactic binding and discourse binding (Reinhart, 1983; Kiparsky, 2002; Reuland, 2011). Syntactic binding regulates the distribution of pronominals on a structural level and thus is sensitive to c-command and locality effects.[1] Discourse binding, on the other hand, is agnostic about structure and cares mostly about the compatibility of certain readings with an established common ground and various pragmatic considerations. For example, *John* cannot syntactically bind *him* in *John likes him* due to a locality constraint, but discourse binding might be possible nonetheless if the sentence is a facetious reply to the statement that nobody likes John. The conditions on discourse binding are rather ephemeral (see Heim, 1998 for further examples) and must be evaluated with respect to highly detailed models of the context of utterance. Thus it should come as no surprise that we consider discourse binding beyond the reach of rational constraints and focus only on syntactic binding.

The decision to ignore any kind of non-syntactic binding is also motivated by the formal results of Ristad (1993). Ristad gives a proof that canonical binding theory is NP-complete, which entails that it cannot be captured by finite-state devices. But his proof relies on configurations where arguably no syntactic binding is involved, such as weak crossover, ellipsis and Principle C effects, all of which are assumed to be (at least partially) regulated by semantics nowadays.

Syntactic binding is still a fuzzy concept, though: does it regulate the availability of specific readings *modulo* discourse considerations, or merely determine the syntactic distribution of pronominals? The former implies the latter, but not the other way round — verifying that a particular reading is available is not the same thing as ensuring that a given sentence is grammatical

---

[1]We use *pronominal* as a catch-all term to refer to anaphors and reflexives as well as pronouns.

under some interpretation. Seeing how both TAG and MGs are primarily formal models of syntax, we opt for the latter interpretation. A rational theory of binding determines for any given sentence whether it has some grammatical reading, while the computation of available readings is relegated to a dedicated semantic apparatus (Bonato, 2005; Kobele, 2006).

This decision is further corroborated by an observation by Rogers (1998). Rogers implements Principles A and B of the canonical binding theory (Chomsky, 1981) in terms of rational constraints and proves that any rational binding theory must be index-free. In the absence of indices one can only guarantee that a suitable antecedent exists for any given pronominal, but not which specific constituent in the tree serves this role (unless there is exactly one).

Index-Free A rational binding theory does not evaluate specific indexations. It only ensures that some grammatical assignment of indices exists.

This condition is at odds with common practice among linguists, where sentences are analyzed with respect to specific readings.

At least for English, though, the distinction is irrelevant if one is interested only in regulating the distribution of pronominals rather than their interpretation. First of all, Index-Free is inconsequential for anaphora such as *himself*, whose distribution is regulated by Principle A. Principle A requires for every anaphor to be syntactically bound within its binding domain, but crucially, two anaphors contained in the same binding domain may share an antecedent. Therefore we do not need to know whether two anaphors have the same referent, and indices — whose sole purpose is to denote referents — are redundant.

This leaves us with the case of pronouns. According to the standard binding theory, a pronoun must not be coreferent with any material in the same binding domain. Hence a sentence like *John told Mary that he likes him* is ungrammatical if both pronouns are supposed to be bound by *John*. However, pronouns can always get an interpretation from discourse; the pronouns in the example sentence might refer to male individuals distinct from John. Pronouns do not need a syntactic antecedent at all, and hence they have the same distribution as normal DPs. This means that Principle B can be ignored and Index-Free is once again irrelevant.

One might be tempted to conclude, then, that Rogers's rational binding theory is empirically adequate despite the mandatory absence of indices and consider the issue solved. But the arguments above do not hold in full generality. English has a rather impoverished inventory of pronominals, and the bifurcation into anaphors and pronouns is too simple from a cross-linguistic perspective. Kiparsky (2002; 2012) proposes to stratify pronominals depending on the maximum size of their binding domain and whether there are configurations in which they must be disjoint in reference from other DPs. Pronominals with such a disjointness requirement are *obviative* or, equivalently, *show obviation*. Kiparsky's system gives rise to ten distinct types, eight of which are attested empirically (see Tab. 1).

Our previous argument that Index-Free is unproblematic for anaphors because they need not be disjoint in reference carries over to all pronominals that lack obviation effects. Likewise, indices aren't required for any pronominals that do not need a syntactic antecedent, for the reasons we just discussed. This still leaves us with two attested subclasses, though: I) long-distance reflexives such as Swedish *sig* that need an antecedent which belongs to the same finite clause but is not a coargument, and II) pronouns like Marathi *aapaṇ* that cannot receive a referent from context or discourse. In neither case can the problem of determining the correct distribution be separated from obviation, so that Rogers's implementation is insufficient in its current form.

What is needed, then, is a strategy for dealing with obviation effects that can be implemented with rational constraints. In combination with suitable modifications of the definition of binding domain in Rogers (1998), this would be enough to cover all instances of syntactic binding identified by Kiparsky (the first three columns in Tab. 1).

Note that this is relevant even if one is only interested in English. While unrestricted *him* can appear in the same positions as standard DPs (i.e. R-expressions), the distributions of discourse bound *him* and syntactically bound *him* are incomparable (more on that in Sec. 4). At the same time, unrestricted *him* is mostly restricted to deictic uses, which are comparatively rare. Since *him* is actually bound in most instances and the type

of binding gives rise to different distributions, an efficient mechanism for syntactic binding is essential under more realistic conditions where not every pronoun can be assumed to introduce a new referent.

In sum, the basic duty of binding theory from the perspective of formal grammars is to regulate the distribution of various pronominal forms (where, depending on the ultimate goals, one might want to distinguish between homophonous pronouns that belong to distinct classes). More ambitious goals, such as computing specific meanings or incorporating conditions imposed by discourse, are beyond the reach of rational constraints and best left to additional machinery. This does not mean that the task at hand is trivial, though. Since rational constraints cannot keep track of indexations, it is unclear how the requirements of obviative pronouns are to be handled. The next section offers a simple solution to this issue.

3 Computing Obviation

As just discussed, the only challenge to a rational binding theory is posed by pronominals that both need a syntactic antecedent and show obviation effects. Other pronominals either do not involve syntactic binding or are easily reigned in by extending the size of the binding domain in Rogers's (1998) definition of Principle A. For the problematic subclass of pronominals — be it Swedish *sig*, Marathi *aapaṇ*, or syntactically bound pronouns in English — there are two constraints to be taken care of: I) every pronoun has an antecedent, and II) no two pronouns that must be disjoint in reference have the same antecedent.

Suppose that we have some well-defined notion of *obviation domain* such that every pronominal belongs to at least one obviation domain and only pronominals belonging to the same one can (but need not) be required to be disjoint in reference. In addition, there is some procedure A such that for each pronominal p in tree t, $A(p, t)$ is the set of viable antecedents of p in t. In the case of canonical binding theory, the two would be supplied by the definition of binding domains on the one hand and c-command on the other. Then I) and II) can be verified as follows.

Given a tree t and sequence $P :=$ $\langle p_1, \ldots, p_{i-1} \diamond p_i, \ldots, p_n \rangle$ of pronominals in t, $n \geq 0$, the *debt* of P is

		Size of Binding Domain			
	Subject Domain	Finite Clause	Sentence	Discourse	Unrestricted
No Obviation	English *himself*	Russian *sebja*	Icelandic *sig*	Turkish *kendisi*	—
Obviation	—	Swedish *sig*	Marathi *aapaṇ*	Greek *o idhios*	English *him*

Table 1: Cross-linguistic classification of pronominals according to Kiparsky (2002; 2012)

- 0 if $i - 1 = n$,

- $0 + debt(\langle p_1, \ldots, p_i \diamond p_{i+1}, \ldots, p_n \rangle)$ if there is some p_j, $j < i$, such that p_j and p_i need not be disjoint in reference in t,

- $1 + debt(\langle p_1, \ldots, p_i \diamond p_{i+1}, \ldots, p_n \rangle)$ otherwise.

Assume t contains obviation domains $O_1, \ldots, O_n$, $n \geq 1$, and let $pro(O_i)$ be the set of pronominals contained by O_i, $1 \leq i \leq n$. Furthermore, let ϕ be some arbitrary procedure for totally ordering any given set $P \subseteq pro(O_i)$, $debt(P) := debt(\langle \diamond \rangle \cdot \phi(P))$, and $A(P, t) := |\bigcup_{p \in P} A(p, t)|$. Then conditions I) and II) above are satisfied in t iff for every $1 \leq i \leq n$ and $P \subseteq pro(O_i)$, $A(P, t) \geq debt(P)$.

Proof. Suppose $A(P, t) \geq debt(P)$ for every $P \subseteq pro(O_i)$. Then in particular $A(\{p\}, t) \geq debt(\{p\})$ for every $p \in pro(O_i)$, implying I). As for II), let Ω be the smallest set containing all obviative $p \in pro(O_i)$. By assumption $A(P, t) \geq debt(P)$ for all $P \subseteq \Omega$, too, which entails that for any arbitrary choice of $p_1, \ldots p_n \in \Omega$, $n \geq 2$, there are at least n available antecedents. It follows immediately that no two $p_i, p_j \in \Omega$ need to share an antecedent.

In the other direction, we prove the contrapositive: violation of I) or II) implies that $A(P, t) < debt(P)$ for some $P \subseteq pro(O_i)$. If I) does not hold, then there is some p such that $A(\{p\}, t) = 0 < 1 = debt(\{p\})$. Now let Ω be defined as before. It is easy to see that if II) is necessarily violated, then for some $P \subseteq \Omega$, $A(P, t) < debt(P)$. $\qquad\square$

Intuitively, our condition states that for every collection of mutually obviative pronominals, there are enough antecedents such that no two pronominals need to share a referent. It is crucial that we consider every subset of a given obviation domain, for otherwise a pronominal with many available antecedents could pay off debt induced by other pronominals. For example, if $A(p_1, t) = 2$ and $A(p_2, t) = 0$, then $A(\{p_1, p_2\}, t) = 2 = debt(\{p_1, p_2\})$ yet p_2 has no viable antecedents at all and thus cannot be bound.

Let us quickly work through an example. Consider the clause *that he wants him to entertain him*. According to standard linguistic assumptions, it consists of two overlapping obviation domains, $O_1 :=$ *that he wants him* and $O_2 :=$ *him to entertain him*. Each obviation domain has a debt of 2, and each pronoun needs at least one possible antecedent. Any masculine singular DP that c-commands the entire clause is a viable antecedent for the pronouns. Hence we correctly predict (1b) but not (1a) to be grammatical if all pronouns are meant to be syntactically bound.

(1)   a.   * John said that he wants him to entertain him.

       b.   John told Bill that he wants him to entertain him.

Note that almost all morphological requirements on the antecedent (gender, animacy, etc.) can be encoded as part of the procedure A if one considers them relevant to syntax. The major exception is number, which also needs to be taken into account in the definition of the debt function. At first sight this seems rather trivial: instead of a single debt value, the function now returns a pair encoding the minimum required number of singular and plural antecedents. However, a plural pronominal can be bound by two singular DPs, so every time one is encountered there is a choice of either increasing the singular antecedent threshold by 2 or the plural antecedent threshold by 1. Rather than a pair of values, then, we actually need to keep track of a set of such constantly updated pairs, and the cardinality of said set doubles with every new plural pronominal. Singular and plural antecedents must be counted separately, too, and for every obviation domain O and $P \subseteq O$ there must be some pair $d := \langle sg, pl \rangle \in debt(P)$ such that sg and pl do not exceed the number of singular and plural antecedents, respectively.

Things might be even more involved, because at least some sentences seem to marginally allow for a singular pronoun to partially overlap in reference with a plural pronominal, even in cases where the former should be obviative.

(2) John$_i$ and Peter$_j$ agreed that they$_{i+j}$ like him$_i$.

Unfortunately the binding properties of plural pronominals (let alone dual) still aren't particularly well understood, so we have to leave it to future research for now.

Even when the complications introduced by plural are taken into account, though, the procedure proposed here can be computed by rational constraints iff the following holds.

Rational Base Obviation domains, mandatory disjointness in reference, and possible antecedents can be determined by rational constraints.

Limited Obviation There is some finite upper bound k on the range of *debt*.

The relevance of Rational Base is obvious in both directions. The necessity of Limited Obviation follows immediately from the fact that rational constraints are computable by bottom-up tree automata, which by virtue of being finite-state can only count up to some fixed threshold k. In the right-to-left direction, it suffices to observe that both the debt function and the cardinality comparison $A(P,t) \geq debt(P)$ can easily be stated in monadic second-order logic — definability in which is equivalent to being rational — if Limited Obviation holds together with Rational Base.

To our knowledge, Rational Base is satisfied for all theories of binding commonly entertained in the literature (cf. Rogers's implementation). Whether Limited Obviation is tenable is an empirical question. Is there an upper bound on the number of required antecedents per obviation domain?

4 Empirical Evaluation

In this section we investigate a range of data drawn primarily from English in an attempt to elicit a counterexample to Limited Obviation. Since Limited Obviation can be falsified only by instances of syntactic binding, we assume that pronouns are indeed syntactically bound unless there is evidence to the contrary. We also make heavy use of quantified DPs, which aren't as amenable to discourse binding as their non-quantified counterparts. In particular, DPs quantified by *no* are viable antecedents for syntactic binding, but not for discourse binding, as it evidenced by the paradigm in (3).

(3) a. Every player was given a card. He was delighted.

b. * No player was given a card. He was upset.

c. Every/No player was upset that he wasn't given a card.

Discourse binding is the only option in (3a) and (3b) (besides introducing an entirely new referent), whereas (3c) also allows for syntactic binding. A *no*-quantified DP is a licit antecedent in the latter example, but not the former.

Besides the restriction to syntactic binding, it is also clear from our definitions that Limited Obviation is trivially satisfied for every obviation domain that may only contain a bounded number of pronouns. So if there exists a counterexample to Limited Obviation in natural language, it must involve an obviation domain without such a bound. The literature on binding contains not a single mention of a language where obviation domains are larger than a single CP (keep in mind that we only consider pronominals here; there are of course instances of obviation domains extending beyond several CPs, but those involve R-expressions such as proper names). There are three ways of accommodating an unbounded number of pronouns inside a single CP: adjunction, TP/VP/DP-recursion, and coordination. Let's consider one after another.

4.1 Adjuncts

In English, pronouns inside adjuncts usually do not show obviation effects. Native speakers of English agree that the sentence below has a reading in which the pronoun is bound by the quantified DP.

(4) Every/No/Some woman put the box down in front of her.

Even speakers that prefer a reflexive instead of the pronoun still consider this sentence grammatical under the intended reading.

In cases where obviation occurs, pronouns contained by distinct adjuncts do not obviate each other, so debt is increased by at most one point, irrespective of the number of adjuncts.

(5) a. * Every/No/Some priest sacrificed a goat for him/in honor of him.

   b. Every/No/Some Egyptian goddess asked of some priest that he sacrifice a goat for her in honor of her.

In (5a), the pronoun must introduce a new referent or be at least discourse-bound. Otherwise it would be locally bound by the *priest*-DP, and this reading is not available. In the perfectly acceptable (5b), on the other hand, the same adjuncts are clause mates and each one contains a pronoun that is bound by the quantified subject of the next higher clause. Note that in the minimally different (6) below, the pronouns inside the adjunct must still be disjoint in reference from the embedded subject. Consequently, they can be bound by *priest* iff *he* is bound by *god* (this reading, albeit odd, is indeed available).

(6) Every/No/Some Egyptian god asked of some priest that he sacrifice a goat for him in honor of him.

Taken together the data corroborates our initial claim: pronouns inside adjuncts usually aren't obviative, but when they are the obviation effect does not extend to adjuncts contained in the same clause. This guarantees that debt is increased by only one point no matter how many adjuncts are present.

A similar pattern emerges in German, where some speakers treat pronouns inside PP-adjuncts as obviative yet pronouns contained by distinct PPs do not obviate each other.

(7) a. * Jeder/Kein/Irgendein Student hat
      every/no/some   student has
      für ihn/neben   ihm
      for him.ACC/next to him.DAT
      einen Spickzettel versteckt.
      a   book   hidden
      'Every/no/some student hid a cheat sheet for himself/next to himself.'

   b. Jeder/Kein/Irgendein Student hat
      every/no/some   student has
      seine Schwester gebeten, dass sie
      his   sister   asked   that she

      für ihn neben ihm einen
      for him next to him a
      Spickzettel versteckt.
      cheat   sheet   hides
      'Every/no/some student asked his sister to hide a cheat sheet next to him for him.'

4.2 TP-Recursion

Nested TPs do not endanger the empirical adequacy of Limited Obviation. This is witnessed by the paradigm in (8).

(8) a. * Every/No/Some patient said [$_{CP}$ that [$_{TP}$ he wants [$_{TP}$ him to be sedated]]].

   b. * Every/No/Some patient said that he wants him to sedate him.

   c. Every/No/Some patient told some doctor that he wants him to sedate him.

   d. Every/No/Some patient told some doctor that he incorrectly believes him to want him to sedate him.

The ungrammaticality (8a) shows that the ECM subject must be disjoint from the subject of the embedded clause, so obviation domains span at least an entire TP and may partially overlap. At the same time it is clear that the embedded subject pronoun can be bound by the matrix subject, indicating that obviation domains do not extend beyond CPs. Comparing (8b) to (8c), we see that the overlap in nested TPs is limited to Spec,TP, since two antecedents are enough for three pronouns, which implies that the embedded subject and the object of the ECM clause can have the same referent. This conclusion is further corroborated by (8d), in which two antecedents are sufficient to satisfy the binding requirements of four pronouns. It follows, then, that the debt of n nested TPs, $n \geq 1$, is determined by the maximum of the debts of the individual TPs. As long as the debt of individual TPs is finitely bounded, so is the debt of nested TPs.

4.3 VP-Recursion

It is commonly assumed that English does not allow for VPs to be nested without an intervening TP. To the degree that one is willing to entertain

VP-recursion as a possible analysis for some constructions in English, it seems to behave exactly like TP-recursion.

(9) a. *Every/No/Some patient said that he made him operate on him.

     b. Every/No/Some doctor told some patient that he made him watch him operate on him.

4.4 DP-Recursion

The absence of obviation effects with pronouns inside DPs in English is a well-established fact.

(10) Every/No/Some politician liked the (photographer's) picture of him.

(11) Every/No/Some politician enjoyed the (consultant's) presentation to him.

It is a contentious issue whether the observed behavior is due to DPs establishing new obviation domains or pronouns losing their obviative properties in these configurations. For our purposes, though, the underlying cause of this pattern is irrelevant as long as it carries over to nested DPs, which is indeed the case.

(12) Every/No/Some post-modern artist must paint at least one [picture of [him and a picture of him]].

(13) Every/No/Some facetious client wanted to see a [presentation of [a presentation to him] to him].

The first sentence has a grammatical reading in which every post-modern artist a must paint a picture that depicts both a and some other picture of a. In order for this reading to be licensed the two pronouns inside the DP need to be coreferent, wherefore they do not obviate each other. One could wonder whether this might be due to the presence of a conjunction, but this objection does not apply to (13), which has an analogous reading. Some speakers dislike both sentences, but their judgment is independent of a specific interpretation and thus has no bearing on determining obviation requirements. We conclude that nested DPs do not give rise to unbounded debt.

4.5 Coordination

Coordination exhibits a very peculiar pattern that to our knowledge has gone unnoticed in the empirical literature so far: coordination of syntactically bound pronouns is grammatical iff the coordinated pronouns are distinct.

(14) a. Every/No/Some football player told every/no/some cheerleader that the coach wants to see him and her in the office.

     b. *Every/No/some football player told every/no/some masseur that the coach wants to see him and him in the office.

It is unclear what exactly the relevant notion of distinctness is. Several languages have distinct pronouns with identical morphological feature specifications that differ with respect to degrees of discourse salience, e.g. Latin *is*, *iste*, *ille*, and *dieser* and *jener* in German. Marcel den Dikken (p.c.) points out that a similar contrast exists in Dutch and that the Dutch analogue of (14b) seems well-formed if one coordinated pronoun is replaced by one of these alternate pronouns.

We are unsure whether the same holds true of German, but fascinating as this question might be, it is ultimately orthogonal to the issue at hand, *viz.* whether coordination can lead to unbounded debt. Latin, German, and Dutch still have only a finite inventory of distinct pronoun types, so unless arbitrarily many identical tokens of one of these types can be coordinated, we are still guaranteed a finite bound on debt even if the pronouns would all obviate each other.

4.6 American Sign Language

Curiously, the analogue of (14b) is well-formed in ASL, so identical pronouns may indeed be coordinated.

(15) [all wrestler]$_i$ inform [someone swimmer]$_j$ that *pro$_i$* and *pro$_j$* will ride-in-vehicle limo go-to dance
      'Every wrestler told some swimmer that the two of them would ride in a limo to the dance.'

It is important to keep in mind, however, that ASL's binding mechanism differs in essential respects from that of English. Foremost, it has distinctively deictic flavor to it. Referential expressions are assigned distinct *loci* in front of the speaker, and a pronoun is realized by pointing at a previously established locus. So in (15), the signer would first map *every wrestler* and *some swimmer* to specific loci, which we indicate by the subscripts i and j, respectively. In order to refer back to them in the coordination, the signer simply points at the intended loci. That is to say, pro_i and pro_j in the sentence above represent only the act of retrieving referents from their loci via pointing, no discrete morphological forms beyond that are involved. Pronouns are pointers.

Considering the deictic nature of all pronouns in ASL, one might suspect that (15) involves discourse binding rather than syntactic binding. After all, (14b) is perfectly grammatical in English if the pronouns are used deictically by simultaneously pointing at two specific individuals. Moreover, binding in ASL lacks several properties of syntactic binding. Foremost, the denotational domain of a pronoun must be non-empty, meaning that a DP quantified by *no* is not a suitable antecedent.

(16)   a.   [each politics person]$_i$ tell-story pro_i want win

       b.   * [no politics person]$_i$ tell-story pro_i want win

            'Every/No politician$_i$ said he$_i$ wants to win.'

As we saw at the beginning of this chapter, discourse binding across sentences in English is subject to a similar restriction, making it rather unlikely that these instances of binding in ASL are truly syntactic. Further evidence along these lines is presented by Schlenker (2011; 2012). Recent work of Rudnev and Kimmelman (2011) on Russian Sign Language also suggests that it is the norm for binding conditions in signed languages to differ from those of spoken languages, rather than the exception.

When these observations are added to our own, it seems that neither English nor ASL furnish a decisive counterexample to Limited Obviation. Consequently, a rational theory of binding seems empirically feasible.

5   Conclusion

We have shown that if one is content with a theory that can only verify the existence of some grammatical reading for a given phrase structure tree — rather than evaluating specific readings — the major challenge to a rational theory of binding is posed by pronouns that need a syntactic antecedent yet must not be coreferent with any other material within the bounds of some locality domain. This problem can be tackled by a system that builds on obviation domains, antecedents, and the notion of debt, which represents the number of antecedents that must be present in order to satisfy all binding requirements. As long as the debt of obviation domains is finitely bounded, the proposed system is finite-state computable. No convincing counterexample to this assumption could be found in English or ASL. While it is difficult to estimate from the existing binding literature whether this result will carry over to other languages due to the scarcity of pertinent data, we are confident that potential counterexamples will also turn out not to be truly syntactic in nature.

Acknowledgments

For their helpful comments and criticism, we are greatly indebted to Marcel den Dikken, Ed Keenan, Craig Sailor, Dominique Sportiche, Ed Stabler, the three anonymous reviewers, and the audiences at WCCFL30, CLS48, and FEAST 2012.

References

Roberto Bonato. 2005. Towards a computational treatment of binding theory. In *Logical Aspects of Computational Linguistics, 5th International Conference, LACL 2005, Bordeaux, France, April 28-30, 2005*.

Noam Chomsky. 1981. *Lectures on Government and Binding: The Pisa Lectures*. Foris, Dordrecht.

Thomas Graf. 2011. Closure properties of minimalist derivation tree languages. In Sylvain Pogodalla and Jean-Philippe Prost, editors, *LACL 2011*, volume 6736 of *Lecture Notes in Artificial Intelligence*, pages 96–111.

Ferenc Gécseg and Magnus Steinby. 1997. Tree languages. In Gregorz Rozenberg and Arto Salomaa, editors, *Handbook of Formal Languages*, volume 3, pages 1–68. Springer, New York.

Irene Heim. 1998. Anaphora and semantic interpretation: A reinterpretation of Reinhart's approach. In Uli Sauerland and O. Percus, editors, *The Interpretive Tract*, volume 25 of *MIT Working Papers in Linguistics*, pages 205–246. MIT Press, Cambridge, Mass.

Paul Kiparsky. 2002. Disjoint reference and the typology of pronouns. In Ingrid Kaufmann and Barbara Stiebels, editors, *More than Words*, volume 53 of *Studia Grammatica*, pages 179–226. Akademie Verlag, Berlin.

Paul Kiparsky. 2012. Greek anaphora in cross-linguistic perspective. *Journal of Greek Linguistics*, 12:84–117.

Gregory M. Kobele. 2006. *Generating Copies: An Investigation into Structural Identity in Language and Grammar*. Ph.D. thesis, UCLA.

Gregory M. Kobele. 2011. Minimalist tree languages are closed under intersection with recognizable tree languages. In Sylvain Pogodalla and Jean-Philippe Prost, editors, *LACL 2011*, volume 6736 of *Lecture Notes in Artificial Intelligence*, pages 129–144.

Uwe Mönnich. 2006. Grammar morphisms. Ms. University of Tübingen.

Tanya Reinhart. 1983. *Anaphora and Semantic Interpretation*. Croon-Helm, Chicago University Press.

Eric Reuland. 2011. *Anaphora and Language Design*. MIT Press, Cambridge, Mass.

Eric Sven Ristad. 1993. *The Language Complexity Game*. MIT Press, Cambridge, Mass.

James Rogers. 1998. *A Descriptive Approach to Language-Theoretic Complexity*. CSLI, Stanford.

James Rogers. 2003. Syntactic structures as multi-dimensional trees. *Research on Language and Computation*, 1(1):265–305.

Pavel Rudnev and Vadim Kimmelman. 2011. Breaking the coreference rule: Reflexivity in Russian Sign Language. Submitted to Semantics & Pragmatics.

Philippe Schlenker. 2011. Donkey anaphora: The view from sign language (ASL and LSF). To appear in *Linguistics & Philosophy*.

Philippe Schlenker. 2012. Complement set anaphora and structural iconicity in ASL. To appear in *Snippets*.

Edward P. Stabler. 2011. Computational perspectives on minimalism. In Cedric Boeckx, editor, *Oxford Handbook of Linguistic Minimalism*, pages 617–643. Oxford University Press, Oxford.

Incremental Derivations in CCG

Vera Demberg
Cluster of Excellence Multimodal Computing and Interaction
Saarland University, Saarbrücken, Germany
vera@coli.uni-saarland.de

Abstract

This paper presents a research note on the degree to which strictly incremental derivations (that is derivations which are fully connected at each point in time) are possible in Combinatory Categorial Grammar (CCG). There has been a recent surge of interest in incremental parsing both from the psycholinguistic community in a bid to build psycholinguistically plausible models of language comprehension, and from the NLP community for building systems that process language greedily in order to achieve shorter response times in spoken dialogue systems, for speech recognition and machine translation. CCG allows for a variety of different derivations, including derivations that are almost fully incremental. This paper explores the syntactic constructions for which full incrementality is not possible in standard CCG, a point that recent work on incremental CCG parsing has glossed over.

1 Introduction

In recent years, there has been an increasing interest in (strictly) incremental and connected processing, both from a cognitive modelling perspective (Mazzei et al., 2007; Demberg and Keller, 2008; Schuler et al., 2008; Reitter et al., 2006) and from a perspective of NLP applications like spoken dialogue system (e.g., Purver and Kempson, 2004; Schlangen and Skantze, 2009; Atterer and Schlangen, 2009), machine translation (Hassan et al., 2008; Hefny et al., 2011) and speech recognition (Roark, 2001) that set out to process linguistic input in real time and therefore require the greedy generation of hypotheses about the input without delaying decisions about how words are connected.

CCG (Steedman, 1996, 2000) as a grammar formalism seems particularly well-suited for incremental connected processing due to its flexible constituency structure and direct syntax-semantic interface, which allows to simultaneously construct an incremental syntactic and semantic derivation. Indeed, Steedman (2000, p. 226) claims that "combinatory grammars are particularly well suited to the incremental, essentially word-by-word assembly of semantic interpretations".

However, existing work on using CCG incrementally (Reitter et al., 2006; Hefny et al., 2011) either did not use fully connected incremental derivations, or introduced additional operations which are not part of the standard CCG rule set. From the existing literature, it remains largely unclear in what kinds of cases a fully connected incremental analysis is impossible (with the exception of coordination, see Sturt and Lombardo, 2005). Milward (1995) notes in a footnote that "CCG doesn't provide a type for all initial fragments of sentences. For example, it gives a type to *John thinks Mary* but not to *John thinks each*". While Demberg and Keller (2008) briefly mentions that object relative clauses (like *The woman that the man saw laughed.*) are problematic to process strictly incrementally with CCG, they do not provide a detailed explanation. The goal of this paper is to provide an overview of the different cases and explain in detail when and why fully connected word-by-word derivations are not possible with standard CCG.

This paper will first discuss the concept of full connectedness (Sec. 2) and provide an overview of CCG (Sec. 3), and then discuss in which cases CCG fails to derive a sentence prefix incrementally (Sec. 4). A discussion and comparison to other grammar formalisms is provided in Sec. 5.

Proceedings of the 11th International Workshop on Tree Adjoining Grammars and Related Formalisms (TAG+11), pages 198–206,
Paris, September 2012.

2   Incrementality and Connectedness

There are different interpretations of what "incremental processing" on the syntax level means. The most general interpretation is that it involves left-to-right processing on a word by word basis. But then the question arises, how "complete" that left-to-right processing should be. In the less strict interpretation of incremental processing, words can be partially connected and these partial structures stored on a stack until further evidence for how to connect them is encountered. The strongest form of incrementality, which we will refer to as *strict incrementality* or *full connectedness* entails that all words which have been perceived so far are connected under a single syntactic node, which means that the relations between all words that have so far been processed have been specified.

In this section, we will review arguments for full connectedness first from a psycholinguistic perspective and then from a practical perspective of eager processing for real-time dialogue systems.

2.1   Psycholinguistic Evidence for Connectedness

What does it mean from a CCG perspective to derive a sentence strictly incrementally? Because CCG implements the *strict competence hypothesis* (Steedman, 2000), any string of words that is connected under a single node must be semantically interpretable. So in order to show that full connectedness is necessary at a specific point in the sentence, we would need to show that humans have built the syntactic and semantic interpretation up to exactly that point.

Evidence that human sentence processing is incremental and at least to some degree connected comes from visual world studies. One example is a study by Kamide et al. (2003), where participants listened to sentences like the ones shown in Example (1) while looking at a visual scene that included four objects, three of which were mentioned in the sentence (e.g. a cabbage, a hare and a fox with respect to the "eat" relation), and a distractor object. They found that people would gaze at the cabbage upon hearing a sentence like (1-a) just before actually hearing the second noun phrase, and would respectively gaze at the fox in sentences like (1-b). This means that people were

anticipating the correct relationship between the hare and the eating event. One can therefore conclude that role assignment has been achieved at the point when the verb (*frisst* in example sentences (1)) is processed. If we assume that the syntactic relations have to be established before role assignment can be performed, the evidence from these experiments suggests full connectedness at the verb.

(1) a.   Der Hase frisst gleich den Kohl.
        The Hare-nom will eat soon the cabbage-acc.
    b.   Den Hasen frisst gleich der Fuchs.
        The Hare-acc will eat soon the fox-nom.

Evidence from experiments on Japanese furthermore indicates that humans build compositional structures by connecting NPs in a grammatically constrained fashion in advance of encountering the verb, which is the head of the sentence and establishes the connection between the NPs (Aoshima et al., 2007).

Evidence for full connectedness furthermore comes from findings such as the one presented by Sturt and Lombardo (2005), see Example (2).

(2) a.   The pilot embarrassed John and put himself in an awkward situation.
    b.   The pilot embarrassed Mary and put herself in an awkward situation.
    c.   The pilot embarrassed John and put him in an awkward situation.
    d.   The pilot embarrassed Mary and put her in an awkward situation.

The experimental items are constructed in order to test for a gender default mismatch effect in condition (2-b), where the pronoun herself refers back to *the pilot*. If people have connected all parts of the syntactic structure completely at this point, the c-command relation between the *pilot* and the pronoun should be established. In the experiment, the gender mismatch effect occurs directly when the reflexive pronoun is encountered (and not just at the end of the sentence), suggesting that the syntactic c-command relation link must have been created at the point of processing *herself*. Conditions (2-c) and (2-d) were included to rule out a structurally-blind strategy for connecting the pronoun, in which the pronoun would be connected to the first noun in the sequence.

Further evidence comes also from an English

eye-tracking experiment by Sturt and Yoshida (2008). In (3-c) the negative element c-commands and thus licenses the use of the word *ever* later on in the sentence. This is not the case for sentences like (3-a), where processing difficulty can thus be expected at the point where the mismatch is detected. Reading times are indeed found to be longer for the word *ever* in condition (3-a). This indicates that the structural relations necessary for computing the scope of negation in sentences like (3) were available early during the processing of the relative clause, in particular before its verbal head had been processed. Thus, the modifiers *ever* or *never* must have been immediately incorporated into the structure.

(3) a. Tony doesn't believe it, but Vanity Fair is a film which I ever really want to see.

b. Tony doesn't believe it, but Vanity Fair is a film which I never really want to see.

c. Tony doesn't believe that Vanity Fair is a film which I ever really want to see.

d. Tony doesn't believe that Vanity Fair is a film which I never really want to see.

While the above phenomena provide evidence for a strong degree of connectedness, there are also findings from other studies that suggest that sentence processing is not fully incremental, or at least that the valid prefix property, meaning that only analyses that are compatible with the interpretation so far are followed, is not always observed by humans. *Local coherence effects* (see e.g. Tabor et al., 2004) are often interpreted as evidence that humans adopt a locally coherent interpretation of a parse, or experience interference effects by locally coherent structures which are however not compatible with the incremental interpretation of the sentence. Local coherence effects have been successfully modelled using a bottom-up CCG parser (Morgan et al., 2010) which does however not implement full connectedness. Some people have also suggested (e.g., Gibson, 2006) that the difficulty in local coherences arises because of a conflict between the incremental analysis and the bottom-up part-of-speech tag, an explanation which is still compatible with fully incremental processing.

While there is a considerable amount of supporting evidence for connectedness in human sentence processing, these studies can only make claims about connectedness at a specific point in a particular construction, but cannot answer the question whether human processing is fully connected at every point in every sentence.

2.2 Connectedness for fast Interpretation in Dialogue Systems

Dialogue systems which interact with the user in real time have been shown to exhibit more natural behaviour when they process the language input incrementally (Schlangen and Skantze, 2009; Skantze and Schlangen, 2009; Skantze and Hjalmarsson, 2010). They can then start constructing hypotheses of what is being said, and react to the language input (e.g. by searching a database, formulating a response, a backchannel or a clarification question) much more quickly than if they wait for the whole utterance to be completed. If the partial derivation of a sentence is fully connected at each point in time, a semantic interpretation will be available more quickly, and the system can thus react more quickly than in a non-connected system. Similarly, speech recognition and machine translation systems can profit from interpretations (and their probabilities) that are available early on.

In order for such real-time applications to really profit from the fast interpretation, it is however necessary to make sure that the quality and reliability of the analysis is high – feeding into the other processing layers interpretations which later turn out to be incorrect causes frequent revisions and corrections in all processing layers, which can be very costly. Because connecting all words generally means to spell out the different ways in which the words might be connected while still lacking some of the evidence, a significant amount of uncertainty concerning which interpretation is correct can be expected. In praxis, one therefore has to consider the trade-off between the degree of incrementality or connectedness and accuracy (see for example Baumann et al., 2009; Kato et al., 2004).

3 CCG

Combinatory Categorial Grammar (CCG, Steedman, 1996, 2000) consists of a lexicalized grammar and a small set of rules that allow the lexical entries to be combined into parse trees. Each word in the lexicon is assigned one or more categories that define its behaviour in the sentence. Categories for a word can either be atomic e.g., *NP*,

Forward Application:	X/Y	Y	$\Rightarrow_>$	X
Backward Application:	Y	X\Y	$\Rightarrow_<$	X
Forward Composition:	X/Y	Y/Z	$\Rightarrow_{>B}$	X/Z
Backward Composition:	Y\Z	X\Y	$\Rightarrow_{<B}$	X\Z
Forward Generalized Composition:	X/Y	(Y/Z)/\$_1	$\Rightarrow_{>B^n}$	(X/Z)/\$_1
Backward Crossed Composition:	Y\Z	X\Y	$\Rightarrow_{<B_x}$	X/Z
Forward Type-raising:	X		$\Rightarrow_T$	T/(T\X)
Coordination:	X conj	X	$\Rightarrow_\phi$	X

Figure 1: Standard CCG Rules for English.

S, PP, or complex like the category $(S\backslash NP)/NP$. Complex categories X/Y and $X\backslash Y$ designate a functor-argument relationship between X and Y, where the directionality of the relation is indicated by the forward slash / and the backward slash \. For example, category X/Y takes category Y as an argument to its right and yields category X, while category $X\backslash Y$ takes category Y as an argument to its left to result in category X. These two rules are referred to as forward and backward functional application (marked as > and < in our derivations). In addition to these two most basic operators, the canonical CCG inventory as defined in (Steedman, 2000) contains further operations for English, which are shown in Figure 1.

In our derivations, we furthermore use the Geach Rule, which in standard CCG only occurs wrapped together with functional application in the composition rules. It is denoted as **B**:

$$\textbf{Geach rule: } \ Y/Z \ \Rightarrow_\textbf{B} \ (Y/G)/(Z/G) \quad (1)$$

The Geach rule will allow us to achieve full connectedness of a partial derivation for some configurations for which we cannot achieve fully incremental derivations otherwise, see Section 4 and Figure 3.

CCG assumes the Strict Competence Hypothesis, which suggests (a) that there is a direct correspondence between the rules of the grammar and the operations performed by the human language processor, and (b) that each syntactic rule corresponds to a rule of semantic interpretation. This means that all constituents that can be derived by the grammar have a semantic interpretation, and conversely that only left prefixes of a sentence that can be assigned a semantic interpretation should be derivable as a constituent in CCG.

4 Incremental Derivations in CCG

CCG rules create so-called spurious ambiguity. This means that there are alternative ways and orders of applying these rules, which lead to syntactically distinct but semantically equivalent derivations of a sequence of words. The combination of type-raising and composition can be used to construct *almost* any syntactic tree for a sequence of words. We can thus construct a normal form derivation, which uses the simplest combination of operators, or a more incremental derivation.

For example, the normal form derivation for the sentence "The boy will eat the cake" would not be incremental enough to model the incremental interpretation effect shown in Altmann and Kamide (1999), an English version of the Kamide et al. (2003) experiment, which was discussed in Section 2, Example (1). We could however type-raise the subject NP to type $S/(S\backslash NP)$ to obtain a fully incremental derivation of the sentence, see Fig. 2.

It is however not generally possible to derive grammatical sentences completely incrementally with the standard set of rules and functional categories, and this sets a limit on how incremental a bottom-up CCG parser with these standard rules can actually be.

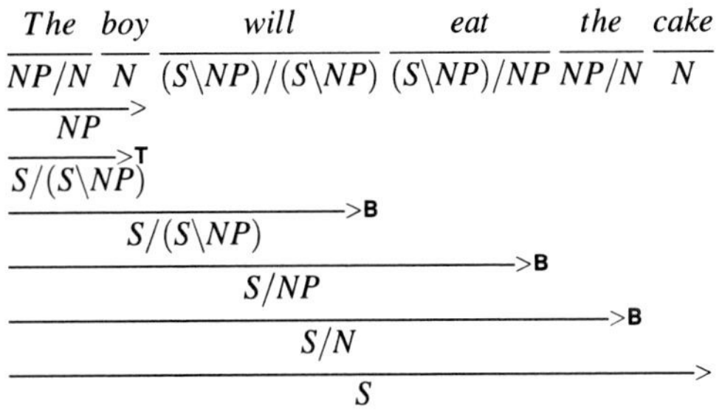

$$
\begin{array}{llllll}
\textit{The} & \textit{boy} & \textit{will} & \textit{eat} & \textit{the} & \textit{cake} \\
\hline
NP/N & N & (S\backslash NP)/(S\backslash NP) & (S\backslash NP)/NP & NP/N & N \\
\end{array}
$$

Figure 2: Incremental derivation of the sentence "The boy will eat the cake".

Post-modification in CCG Even for very simple cases such as incrementally processing post-modification X/Y Y $Y\backslash Y$, it is necessary to type-raise the Y category to $Y/(Y\backslash Y)$. Note that this type-raising would have to happen before having seen any evidence for the post-modifier, thus increasing the amount of ambiguity a parser would have to deal with: When processing Y, the parser would essentially hypothesise that a post-modifier would be coming up and type-raise, as well as maintaining the original category in case no post-modification will happen.

Coordination Coordination is another case which is problematic in terms of strictly incremental processing with CCG. The coordination rule combines two identical categories, which means that the second conjunct must have been combined into a single constituent before the conjunction rule can be applied. As shown by Sturt and Lombardo (2005) (cf. Example (2)), human sentence processing can be shown to be more incremental than the most incremental CCG derivation.

Object Relative Clauses An example where standard CCG rules are insufficient for performing a fully connected derivation are simple object relative clauses like *The woman that Peter saw laughed*. The most incremental parse with the standard rules would involve type-raising *Peter* (from NP to $S/(S\backslash NP)$, and combine that category with *saw* (category $(S\backslash NP)/NP$) using functional composition to yield the category S/NP. This category for *Peter saw* can subsequently combine with the category of the object relative pronoun $(N\backslash N)/(S/NP)$ (using functional application). This derivation is however not strictly incremental. In order to integrate *Peter* directly with the object relative pronoun and only then combine the resulting category with *saw*, we have to use the non-standard Geach rule, see Equation 1. Using the Geach rule, type-raised *Peter* can be geached with category NP, yielding $(S/NP)/((S\backslash NP)/NP)$ as a category for *Peter*. This category can then be combined via forward composition with the relative clause pronoun, and the resulting category can be combined with the category of *saw* using forward application. If we wanted to model with CCG the psycholinguistic results on the experiment by Sturt and Yoshida (2008), see Example (3), we would hence have

to allow the Geach operator, because otherwise, *I ever* (category $S/(S\backslash NP)$) cannot be combined with the previous words before the relative clause verb has been seen.

In object relative clauses where the subject NP contains more than one word (as in *The woman that every man saw laughed*), it is however not possible to achieve full connectedness even with the Geach rule, see Figure 3(c).

In order to make it possible to incrementally derive ORCs without adding more rules, we could change the category of the object relative pronoun from $(N\backslash N)/(S/NP)$ to $((N\backslash N)/((S\backslash NP_i)/NP))/NP_i$, see Figure 4. We here use an encoding for the subject NP which is similar to the one used for the direct object NP in the category of the indirect object relative pronoun: $((N\backslash N)/NP_i)/((S/NP_i)/NP)$[1].

However, there are theoretically motivated reasons for the original object relative pronoun category $(N\backslash N)/(S/NP)$, and for the impossibility of full connectedness within the ORC embedded subject: as any string of words that is connected under a single category is a CCG constituent, deriving a single category for "The woman that every" will mean that coordination of this constituent will be accepted as well by the grammar, i.e. the grammar would accept a sentence like *[the man that every] and [the woman that no] kid saw slept*, which violates an island constraint. The way in which the standard object relative pronoun category prevents such an island violation is by burying the subject NP in the verb category instead of including it in the category of the object relative pronoun: the NP argument in $(N\backslash N)/(S/NP)$ is for the object NP. The subject NP is thus not accessible from outside the relative clause, hence implementing the island constraint. This is a rather fine distinction and one might want to note that similar cases of overgeneration can happen in standard CCG, notably in non-subject relative clauses where the relative pronoun is the indirect object of the verb. For example, standard CCG would accept the sentence *"[girls whom I gave every] and [boys whom you stole no], ball danced"*. See Figure 5 for the complete derivation of this sentence.

---

[1] See Steedman (2000; page 47) for categories of relative pronouns in English.

$$
\begin{array}{ccccccc}
The & woman & that & every & man & saw & laughed \\
\hline
NP/N & N & (N\backslash N)/(S/NP) & NP/N & N & (S\backslash NP)/NP & S\backslash NP
\end{array}
$$

(a) Normal form derivation for an object relative clause.

$$
\begin{array}{ccccccc}
The & woman & that & every & man & saw & laughed \\
\hline
NP/N & N & (N\backslash N)/(S/NP) & NP/N & N & (S\backslash NP)/NP & S\backslash NP
\end{array}
$$

(b) Most incremental derivation of an ORC without Geach rule.

$$
\begin{array}{ccccc}
woman & that & every & man & saw \\
\hline
N & (N\backslash N)/(S/NP) & NP/N & N & (S\backslash NP)/NP
\end{array}
$$

(c) Most incremental derivation of an ORC with Geach rule.

Figure 3: Normal form derivation and most incremental derivation for an object relative clause.

$$
\begin{array}{cccccc}
woman & that & every & man & saw \\
\hline
N & ((N\backslash N)/((S\backslash NP)/NP))/NP & NP/N & N & (S\backslash NP)/NP
\end{array}
$$

Figure 4: Incremental derivation of object relative clause with new object relative pronoun category.

1.	a/b	b/c	c				
2.	$(a/c)/b$	b	c				
3.	a/b	b	$c\backslash a$				
4.	a	$(b/c)\backslash a$	c				
5.	a	$b\backslash a$	$c\backslash b$				
6.	a/c	b	$c\backslash b$	$\Rightarrow_T$	a/c	$c/(c\backslash b)$	$c\backslash b$
7.	a	b	$(c\backslash a)\backslash b$	$\Rightarrow_T$	$c/(c\backslash a)$	$(c\backslash a)/((c\backslash a)\backslash b)$	$(c\backslash a)\backslash b$
8.	a	b/c	$c\backslash a$	$\Rightarrow_{T.B}$	$b/(b\backslash a)$	$(b\backslash a)/(c\backslash a)$	$c\backslash a$

Table 1: Possible category constellations in a sequence of three adjacent constituents that are functors and arguments of one another.

Complement Clauses Similar to object relative clauses, complement clauses like *Ann thinks the man slept* can also not be derived fully incrementally, because the determiner of the subject NP of the complement clause cannot be combined with the sentence prefix *Ann thinks*. The most incremental standard derivation is shown below.

$$
\begin{array}{ccccc}
\textit{Ann} & \textit{thinks} & \textit{the} & \textit{man} & \textit{slept} \\
\hline
NP & (S\backslash NP)/S & NP/N & N & S\backslash NP \\
\end{array}
$$

General patterns of Category Constellations After giving these intuitive examples of constructions which are problematic from the point of view of full connectedness, I want to review more generally for which constellations of CCG categories we can construct fully incremental derivations. Table 1 lists all possible functor-argument relationships between three categories, a, b and c. The first five constellations only use the most standard CCG operations of composition and functional application in order to combine strictly incrementally.

The other tree constellations (6., 7. and 8. in Table 1) require type-raising. The example of postmodifiers in CCG which was discussed at the beginning of this section is an instance of case 6. One important point to note with respect to type-raising is that type-raising is not always allowed in standard CCG, but only when the type-raising rule is parametrically licensed by the specific language (Steedman, 2000). That is, there might be some category constellations where the necessary type-raising for cases 6. – 8. is not allowed (arbitrary type-raising would be very unconstrained and would lead to over-generation). Therefore,

whether a sequence of categories is parsable incrementally depends on the specific instance of cases of the form in 6. or 7. In the eighth case, the functor $c\backslash a$ is not directly adjacent to its argument a. Instead, there is another word in the middle which takes c as its argument. These categories can still be combined incrementally using type-raising and geaching, but, again, the type-raising required for this kind of operation might not be licensed by the language (such a category would subcategorize for its grand-child). Note that the object relative clause case with a subject NP consisting of at least two words, which we discussed above, is not contained in Table 1, as it requires a constellation of four categories.

5 Comparison to other Grammar Formalisms and Discussion

Full connectedness has been implemented with other grammar formalisms: for fully connected PCFG parsing, a top-down (Roark, 2001) or left-corner strategy can be used. Furthermore, there are two variants of tree-adjoining grammar that support full connectedness: the Dynamic Version of TAG (DVTAG, Mazzei, 2005) and Psycholinguistically Motivated TAG (PLTAG Demberg-Winterfors, 2010). A broad-coverage parser exists for PLTAG (Demberg et al., 2012), but not for DVTAG.

All of these approaches incur a larger amount of ambiguity than a non-connected parser would. Regarding the problem of over-generation in CCG given an object relative pronoun which allows for a fully connected derivation of ORCs, current TAG approaches do (to the best of my knowledge) not handle this island constraint case correctly either (regardless of whether they are incremental or not).

Whether CCG "should" be able to strictly incrementally derive object relative clauses and complement clauses is open to discussion from a linguistic / psycholinguistic point of view, as it depends on whether a sentence such as *"[[books that every] and [journals that no]] accordionist liked"* is judged for example as less grammatical than *"[[boys whom I gave every], and [girls whom you gave no]] book"*, which is derivable in CCG; and whether it can be shown that human processing is strictly incremental at the point of the subject NP in an ORC.

6 Conclusions

To summarise, strictly incremental and fully connected derivations are not possible in CCG at points where the left prefix of a sentence is not a constituent in the CCG sense[2]. By changing the category of the involved words to reflect more of the internal structure of a category (in our example, changing the object relative pronoun category such that the subject NP is encoded explicitly in it), we can achieve to derive sentence prefixes in a fully connected way, at the cost of making the grammar overgenerate a bit (here, not observing the island constraint which makes sentences like *The apple that no and the banana that one kid ate were delicious.* bad). For applications which are interested in strict incrementality for psycholinguistical modelling purposes or real-time processing, the options are to either live without full connectedness, accept an overgenerating grammar, or use a top-down or left-corner parsing strategy for CCG instead of the standard bottom-up parsing.

Acknowledgements

I want to thank Mark Steedman and the Edinburgh Incremental Processing reading group for extensive discussion of this topic (a while back in 2007), as well as three anonymous reviewers for their feedback.

References

Altmann, G. and Kamide, Y. (1999). Incremental interpretation at verbs: Restricting the domain of subsequent reference. *Cognition*, 73(3):247–264.

Aoshima, S., Yoshida, M., and Phillips, C. (2007). Incremental processing of coreference and binding in japanese. *Syntax*, page 49pp.

Atterer, M. and Schlangen, D. (2009). Rubisc–a robust unification-based incremental semantic chunker. *Proceedings of SRSL*, pages 66–73.

Baumann, T., Atterer, M., and Schlangen, D. (2009). Assessing and improving the performance of speech recognition for incremental systems. In *Proceedings of Human Language Technologies: The 2009 Annual Conference of the North American Chapter of the Association for Computational Linguistics*, pages 380–388.

Demberg, V. and Keller, F. (2008). A psycholinguistically motivated version of TAG. In *Proceedings of the 9th International Workshop on Tree Adjoining Grammars and Related Formalisms (TAG+9)*, Tübingen, Germany.

Demberg, V., Keller, F., and Koller, A. (2012). Incremental, predictive parsing with psycholinguistically motivated tree-adjoining grammar. *under review*.

Demberg-Winterfors, V. (2010). *A broad-coverage model of prediction in human sentence processing*. PhD thesis, School of Informatics, The University of Edinburgh.

Gibson, E. (2006). The interaction of top-down and bottom-up statistics in the resolution of syntactic category ambiguity. *Journal of Memory and Language*, 54:363–388.

Hassan, H., Sima'an, K., and Way, A. (2008). A syntactic language model based on incremental ccg parsing. In *Spoken Language Technology Workshop, 2008. SLT 2008. IEEE*, pages 205–208. IEEE.

Hefny, A., Hassan, H., and Bahgat, M. (2011). Incremental combinatory categorial grammar and its derivations. *Computational Linguistics and Intelligent Text Processing*, pages 96–108.

Kamide, Y., Scheepers, C., and Altmann, G. (2003). Integration of syntactic and semantic information in predictive processing: Cross-linguistic evidence from german and english. *Journal of Psycholinguistic Research*, 32(1):37–55.

Kato, Y., Matsubara, S., and Inagaki, Y. (2004). Stochastically evaluating the validity of partial parse trees in incremental parsing. In *Proceedings of the Workshop on Incremental Parsing: Bringing Engineering and Cognition Together*, pages 9–15.

---

[2]See definition of constituents in CCG in Steedman (2000), p.12-14.

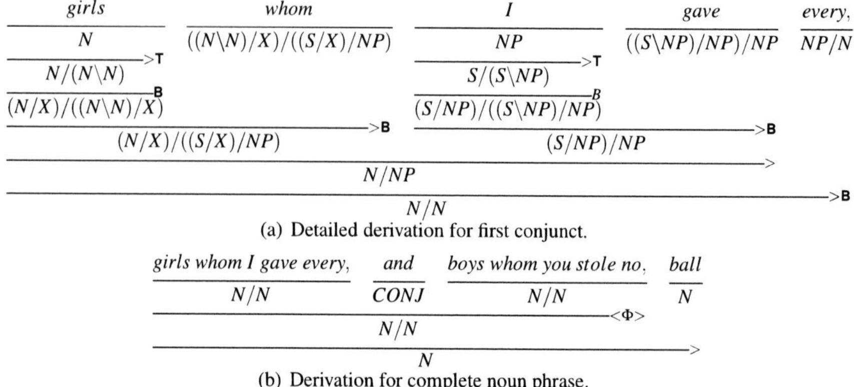

(a) Detailed derivation for first conjunct.

(b) Derivation for complete noun phrase.

Figure 5: Standard CCG derivation of an ungrammatical sentence.

Mazzei, A. (2005). *Formal and empirical issues of applying dynamics to Tree Adjoining Grammars*. PhD thesis, Dipartimento di Informatica, Universita' di Torino.

Mazzei, A., Lombardo, V., and Sturt, P. (2007). Dynamic tag and lexical dependencies. *Research on Language and Computation, Foundations of Natural Language Grammar*, pages 309–332.

Milward, D. (1995). Incremental interpretation of categorial grammar. In *Proceedings of the seventh conference on European chapter of the Association for Computational Linguistics*, pages 119–126. Morgan Kaufmann Publishers Inc.

Morgan, E., Keller, F., and Steedman, M. (2010). A Bottom-Up Parsing Model of Local Coherence Effects. In *Proceedings of the 32nd Annual Meeting of the Cognitive Science Society*, Portland, OR.

Purver, M. and Kempson, R. (2004). Incremental parsing, or incremental grammar? In Keller, F., Clark, S., Crocker, M., and Steedman, M., editors, *Proceedings of the ACL Workshop on Incremental Parsing: Bringing Engineering and Cognition Together*, pages 74–81, Barcelona, Spain.

Reitter, D., Hockenmaier, J., and Keller, F. (2006). Priming effects in combinatory categorial grammar. In *Proceedings of the 2006 conference on empirical methods in natural language processing*, pages 308–316.

Roark, B. (2001). Probabilistic top-down parsing and language modeling. *Computational Linguistics*, 27(2):249–276.

Schlangen, D. and Skantze, G. (2009). A general, abstract model of incremental dialogue processing. In *Proc. of the 12th Conference of the European Chapter of the Association for Computational Linguistics*, pages 710–718.

Schuler, W., Miller, T., AbdelRahman, S., and Schwartz, L. (2008). Toward a psycholinguistically-motivated model of language processing. In *Proceedings of the 22nd International Conference on Computational Linguistics-Volume 1*, pages 785–792.

Skantze, G. and Hjalmarsson, A. (2010). Towards incremental speech generation in dialogue systems. In *Proceedings of the 11th Annual Meeting of the Special Interest Group on Discourse and Dialogue*, pages 1–8.

Skantze, G. and Schlangen, D. (2009). Incremental dialogue processing in a micro-domain. In *Proceedings of the 12th Conference of the European Chapter of the Association for Computational Linguistics*, pages 745–753.

Steedman, M. (1996). *Surface structure and interpretation*. MIT press.

Steedman, M. (2000). *The syntactic process*. The MIT press.

Sturt, P. and Lombardo, V. (2005). Processing coordinate structures: Incrementality and connectedness. *Cognitive Science*, 29:291–305.

Sturt, P. and Yoshida, M. (2008). The speed of relative clause attachment. In *Proc. of the 14th Annual Conference on Architectures and Mechanisms for Language Processing*, Cambridge.

Tabor, W., Galantuccia, B., and Richardson, D. (2004). Effects of merely local syntactic coherence on sentence processing. *Journal of Memory and Language*, 50(4):355–370.

On the Form-Meaning Relations Definable by CoTAGs

Gregory M. Kobele
University of Chicago
Chicago, Illinois
USA

Jens Michaelis
Bielefeld University
Bielefeld
Germany

Abstract

Adding *cosubstitution* to the classical TAG operations of *substitution* and *adjunction*, *coTAGs* have been proposed as an "alternative conceptualization" to resolve the tension between the TAG mantra of locality of syntactic dependencies and the seeming non-locality of quantifier scope. CoTAGs follow the tradition of *synchronous TAGs (STAGs)* in that they derive syntactic and semantic representations simultaneously as pairs. We demonstrate that the mappings definable by coTAGs go beyond those of "simple" STAGs. While with regard to the first component, coTAGs are weakly and strongly equivalent to classical TAGs, the second projection of the synchronously derived representations, can in particular be— up to a homomorphism—the non-tree adjoining language $\mathrm{MIX}(k)$, for any $k \geq 3$.

1 Introduction

Given a classical TAG as, e.g., defined in the handbook article by Joshi and Schabes (1997), the set of derivation trees constitutes a regular set of unordered labeled trees with an additional labeling of the tree edges. The nodes of a derivation tree are labeled with elementary trees, and each edge is labeled with a Gorn address. Such an address indicates the node of the elementary tree (labeling the outgoing node of the corresponding edge in the derivation tree) at which another elementary tree (labeling the incoming node of the corresponding edge in the derivation tree) was adjoined or substituted during the derivation represented by the derivation tree. The representation of a TAG derivation in this way is independent of the derivational order. This is the reason why the set of derivation trees of a classical TAG constitutes a regular tree set.

Work on semantics in the TAG framework often considers the derivation tree as a compact, order independent representation of all derivations yielding the same syntactic tree, but at the same time as a compact representation of different semantics associated with the same syntactic representation. Work in this line, in particular includes the extensive work of Kallmeyer and colleagues as well as Nesson and Shieber.[1]

Suggesting an "alternative conceptualization" to resolve the tension between the TAG mantra of locality of syntactic dependencies and the seeming non-locality of quantifier scope, Barker (2010) proposes to add to the classical TAG operations of *substitution* and *adjunction* as a third operation a modified version of substitution. He calls the resulting operation *cosubstitution* and the version of TAGs incorporating this operation *coTAGs*.

CoTAGs are defined in the spirit of *synchronous TAGs (STAGs)* as introduced by Shieber and Schabes (1990), deriving syntactic and semantic representations simultaneously as pairs. Syntactically, cosubstitution can essentially be understood as substitution, but with reversed roles of functor and argument. Barker notes that for this reason, from a purely syntactic perspective, in the context of simple (i.e. not multicomponent) TAGs, adding cosubstitution affects neither weak nor strong generative capacity (in the sense of derived string and tree languages).

Clearly, however, something is different: after adding the operation of cosubstitution, derivational order matters in the sense that one derived syntactic representation can potentially be associated with more than one simultaneously derived semantic representation. As Barker points out,

---

[1] See, e.g., Kallmeyer and Romero (2004) and Nesson and Shieber (2007), and references cited therein.

Proceedings of the 11th International Workshop on Tree Adjoining Grammars and Related Formalisms (TAG+11), pages 207–213,
Paris, September 2012.

the introduction of the cosubstitution operator allows for a straightforward adaption of the notion of derivation tree such that two derivation trees can be different depending on when a cosubstitution step takes place.

We demonstrate that the form-meaning mappings definable by coTAGs go beyond those of "simple" STAGs (Shieber, 1994; Shieber, 2006).[2] In particular, the set of meanings, the second projection of the synchronously derived syntactic and semantic representations, can be—up to a homomorphism abstracting away from instances of λ and variables—the non-tree adjoining language $\mathrm{MIX}(k)$, for any $k \geq 3$. The complexity of the corresponding set of meanings is a reflex of the complexity of the connected derivation tree set, whose path language—up to a homomorphism— also provides the non-tree adjoining language $\mathrm{MIX}(k)$. The result can already be established when restricting the attention to coTSGs, understood as coTAGs without classical adjunction. From this perspective it could be argued that the additional expressive power is really due to the cosubstitution operation alone.

2 CoTAGs

From the perspective of lexical entries, each coTAG consists of a finite set of pairs of labeled trees. The first component of such a pair $\langle \alpha_{\mathrm{syn}}, \alpha_{\mathrm{sem}} \rangle$ provides a syntactic representation, the second component a semantic representation of the corresponding lexical entry. Nodes in α_{syn} are uniquely linked to nodes in α_{sem}. The label of a node ν_{sem} from α_{sem} linked to a node ν_{syn} from α_{syn} displays the semantic type of the corresponding syntactic subconstituent dominated by ν_{syn}. An operation applying to ν_{syn} must be accompanied by a parallel operation applying to ν_{sem}.

Regarding the syntactic component of the coTAG-relation, coTAGs are identical to classical TAGs except for the following difference: whereas the roots of TAG-initial trees and substitution nodes of arbitrary TAG-elementary trees are labeled with elements from Cat and $Cat{\downarrow}$, respectively,[3] the roots of syntactic coTAG-initial

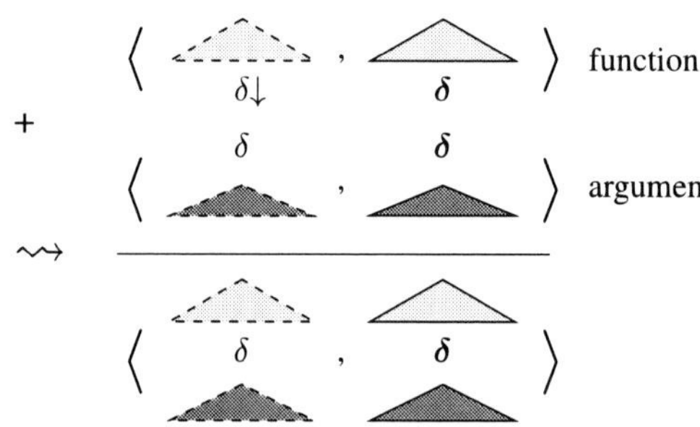

Figure 1: *Substitution* schematically. Syntactically, tree with root-label δ is substituted at leaf labeled $\delta{\downarrow}$; while semantically, the corresponding tree with root-label $\boldsymbol{\delta}$ is substituted at the linked node labeled $\boldsymbol{\delta}$.

trees and substitution nodes of arbitrary syntactic coTAG-elementary trees have labels from the sets $Cat({\uparrow}Cat)^*$ and $Cat({\uparrow}Cat)^*{\downarrow}$, respectively. Expressions of the syntactic component are constructed in very much the same manner as in TAGs, with one important addition: a derived structure β_{syn} with syntactic root-label $\delta{\uparrow}B$ for some $B \in Cat$ and $\delta \in Cat({\uparrow}Cat)^*$ can be cosubstituted into a derived syntactic structure α_{syn} with syntactic root-label B and a leaf labeled $\delta{\downarrow}$ derived structure. The result of applying cosubstitution in this situation is the same as substituting β'_{syn} into α_{syn} at the corresponding leaf labeled $\delta{\downarrow}$, where β'_{syn} results from β_{syn} by replacing the root-label $\delta{\uparrow}B$ of β_{syn} with δ. From this perspective, cosubstitution can be understood as substitution reversing the roles of argument and functor, i.e., α_{syn} is rather cosubstituted onto the root of β_{syn}. As will become immediately clear, the "reversed perspective" of argument and functor chimes in with the operational semantic counterpart of applying cosubstitution.

Regarding the semantic component of the coTAG-relation, the trees derived represent well-typed lambda terms, which can be read off from the yield.[4] The matching semantic operation to applying substitution and adjunction syntactically is also substitution and adjunction, providing us with "functional application" in terms of lambda calculus, cf. Figure 1 for the case of substitution.[5]

[2]While we focus here on coTAGs, the results herein straightforwardly apply as well to *limited delay vector TAGs (LDV-TAGs)* (Nesson, 2009) which would allow for a different implementation of essentially the same mechanism.

[3]Cat denotes the set of categories, i.e. the nonterminals, of the grammar.

[4]Arriving at a concrete lambda term is achieved by replacing each leaf-label which is a semantic type by a variable of corresponding type, when reading off the leaf-labels "from left to right."

[5]For $\delta \in Cat({\uparrow}Cat)^*$ and $B \in Cat$, the boldface versions $\boldsymbol{\delta}$ and $\boldsymbol{\delta{\uparrow}B}$ denote the corresponding semantic types of

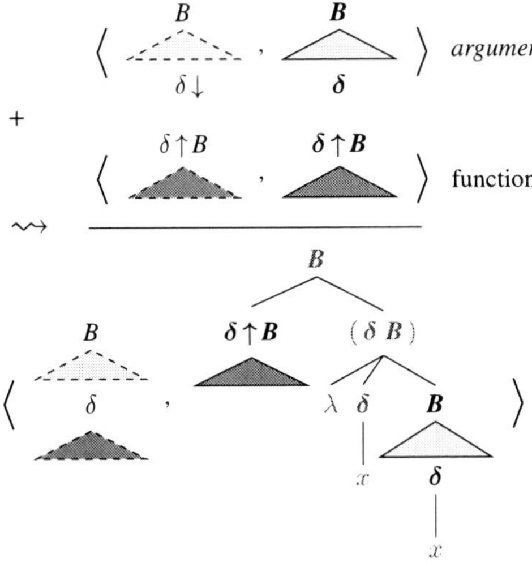

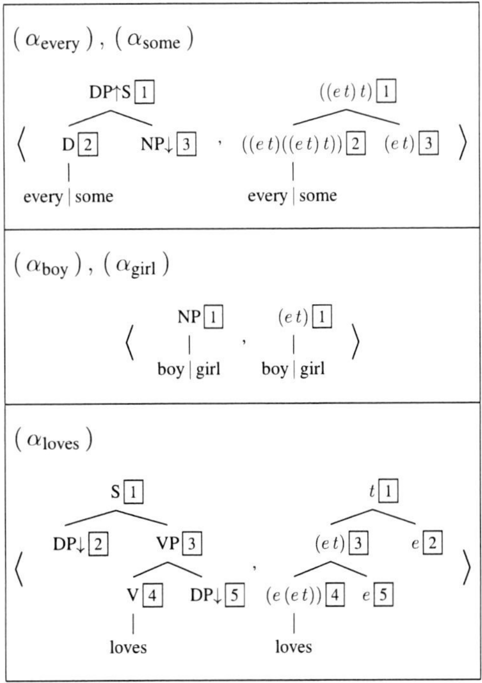

Figure 2: *Cosubstitution* schematically. Syntactically, tree with root-label with root-label $\delta{\uparrow}B$ is cosubstituted into tree with root-label B at leaf labeled $\delta{\downarrow}$; while semantically, the corresponding tree with root-label $\delta{\uparrow}B$ is "quantified in" at the root of the corresponding tree with root-label B.

Figure 3: The example coTAG G_{scope}

The matching semantic operation to applying cosubstitution syntactically consists of a "quantifying in" step as outlined in Figure 2. Note that within the resulting semantic representation, new terminal leaves are introduced labeled by λ and a variable x. The operation is set up such that x is chosen to be "fresh."

As a concrete example, consider the grammar G_{scope} presented in Figure 3.[6] One can start deriving the sentence "every boy loves some girl" either by substituting *boy* into *every*, and then cosubstituting *every boy* into the subject position of *loves* as shown in Figure 4, or by substituting *girl* into *some*, and then cosubstituting *some girl* into the object position of *loves* as shown in Figure 5. Both complete derivations of the sentence are given in Figure 6. The derived syntactic trees are identical, while the semantic trees are different, because of the different order of the derivation steps. Accordingly, we require a novel notion of derivation to represent this "timing" information, which we leave at an intuitive level in this paper

for reasons of space.

Displaying a derivation tree, we use a solid line for drawing an edge in order to indicate an instance of substitution, and the edge label marks the address of the substitution site of the elementary tree into which substitution takes place. We use a dashed line in order to indicate an instance of cosubstitution, and the edge label marks the address of the substitution site of the elementary tree into which cosubstitution takes place. But in contrast to the case of substitution, this elementary tree labels the incoming node of the edge.

3 Expressivity

For $k \geq 1$, we now provide a coTAG G_k generating as its string language the regular language $\{(a_1 \cdots a_k)^m : m \geq 1\}$, while the path language of the set of derivation trees and the set of meanings, up to a homomorphism, provide the language $\mathrm{MIX}(k)$, i.e. the set $\{w \in \{a_1, \ldots, a_k\}^* : |w|_{a_i} = |w|_{a_j}, 1 \leq i, j \leq k\}$.

G_k consists of $k+4$ lexical entries, namely, the entries $\alpha_1, \ldots, \alpha_k, \beta_k, \gamma_k, \tau_k$ and σ_k, and for each entry, we use the (additional) subscripts $_{\mathrm{syn}}$ and $_{\mathrm{sem}}$ in order to refer to the entry's syntactic and semantic component, respectively, cf. Figure 7. S

$\delta{\downarrow}^?$ and $\delta{\uparrow}B$, respectively. $\delta{\uparrow}B$ is the lifted type $((\delta B) B)$.

[6]Links will usually be marked with diacritics of the form $\boxed{n}$ for some $n \geq 1$. We may occasionally avoid explicitly mentioning the links between nodes of the syntactic and the semantic representation, when we think the canonical linking is obvious.

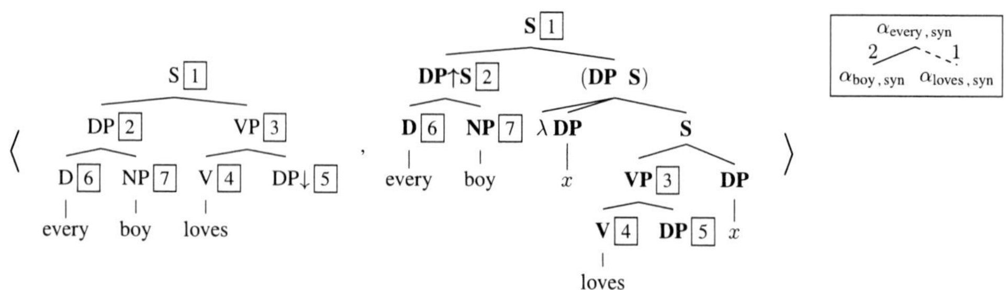

Figure 4: Cosubstituting *every boy* into the subject position before filling the object position of *loves*, derived syntactic tree and semantic tree, and derivation tree.

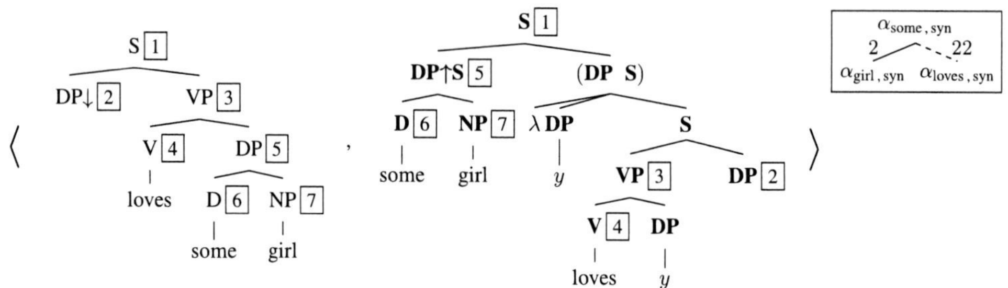

Figure 5: Cosubstituting *some girl* into the object position before filling the subject position of *loves*, derived syntactic and semantic tree, and derivation tree.

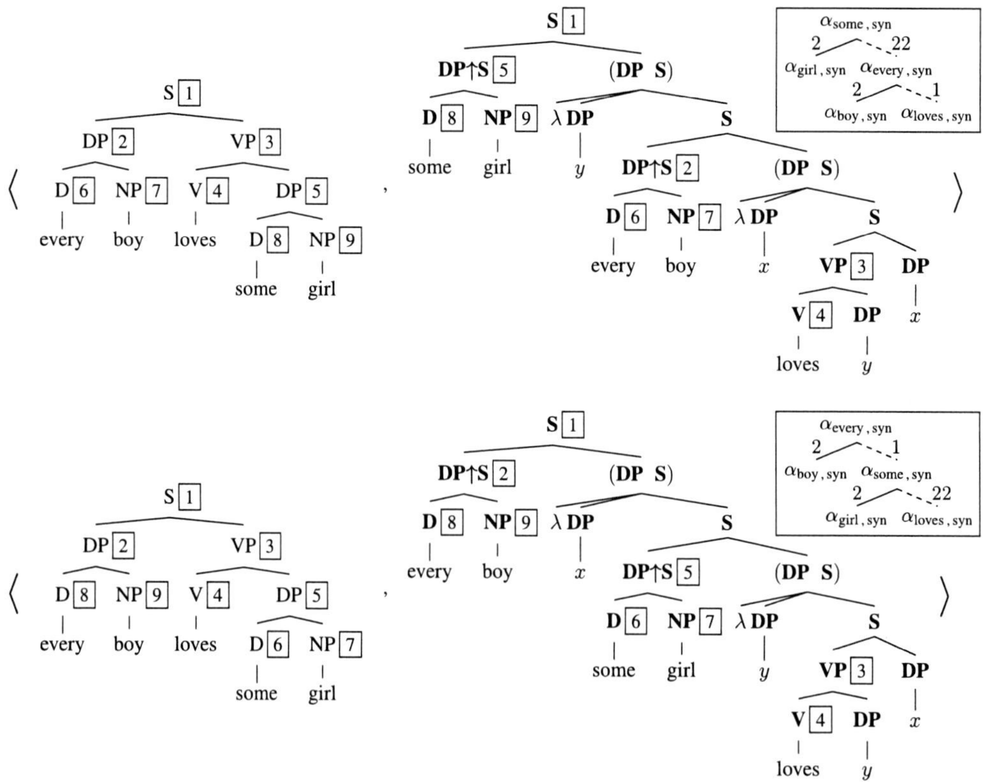

Figure 6: The two complete derived pairs of structures of *every boy loves some girl*, and derivation trees.

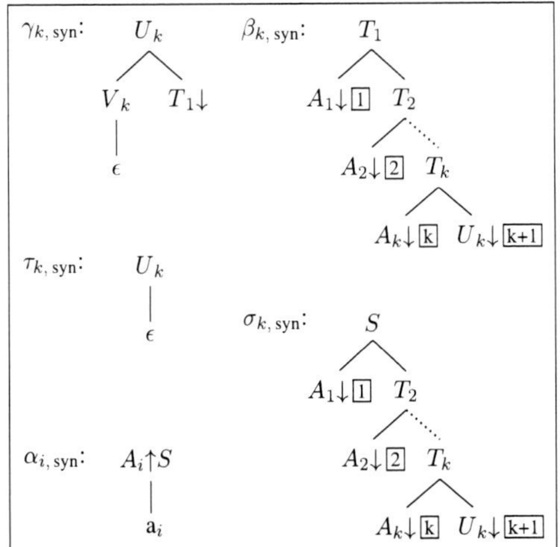
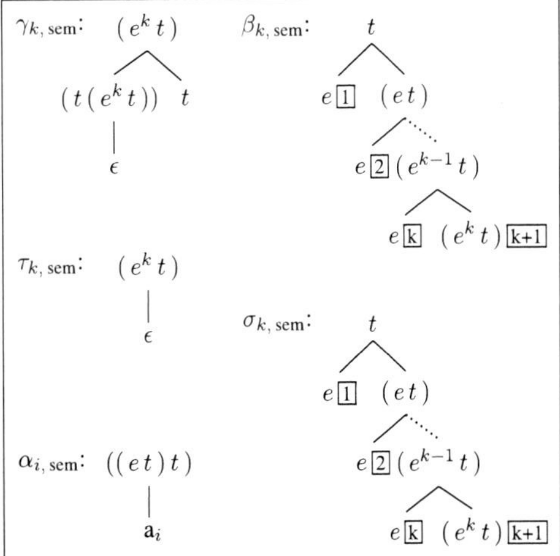

Figure 7: The syntactic and the semantic components of G_k.

is the start symbol of G_k.

For $m \geq 1$, consider $w_{k,m} = (a_1 \ldots a_k)^m$. Each derivation tree for $w_{k,m}$ is a single path. All derivation trees for $w_{k,m}$ share a unique subtree, cf. Figure 8. From a bottom-up perspective, the derivation starts by substituting τ_k directly into σ_k in case $m = 1$, or into β_k otherwise. If $m > 1$, the resulting tree is substituted into γ_k, and the result in its turn is substituted into β_k again. This procedure is repeated $m - 1$ times, before the re-sulting tree is substituted into σ_k. Note that the substitution site in each of these derivation steps is uniquely determined. Note also that we cannot cosubstitute any instance of α_i before we have substituted into σ_k, because cosubstitution of an α_i demands the presence of a root labeled S.

The derived tree described by the derivation tree $D_{k,\mathrm{sub}}$ contains exactly m substitution sites for every A_i. We can now cosubstitute into any of these sites in any order. Thus, for each per-mutation of $(a_1 \ldots a_k)^m$ there is a derivation of $(a_1 \ldots a_k)^m$ such that the permutation is reflected in the corresponding derivation tree in terms of the node labels $\alpha_{i,\mathrm{syn}}$. More precisely, starting at the root following down the unique path, the node la-bels provide a permutation of $(\alpha_{1,\mathrm{syn}} \ldots \alpha_{k,\mathrm{syn}})^m$ before we hit the node label $\sigma_{k,\mathrm{syn}}$.

4 Remarks on ACGs

The formalism of an *abstract categorial gram-mar (ACG)* (de Groote, 2001) has been intro-duced with the idea to provide a general frame-work in terms of linear logic allowing the encod-ing of existing grammatical models. An ACG dis-tinguishes between an abstract language and an object language each of which is a set of linear lambda terms over some signature. Following the presentation by, e.g., Pogodalla (2004b), an ACG $\mathcal{G}$ defines 1) two sets of typed linear lambda terms, namely, a set Λ_1 based on the typed constant set C_1, and a set Λ_2 based on the typed constant set C_2; 2) a morphism $\mathcal{L} : \Lambda_1 \to \Lambda_2$; and 3) and a dis-

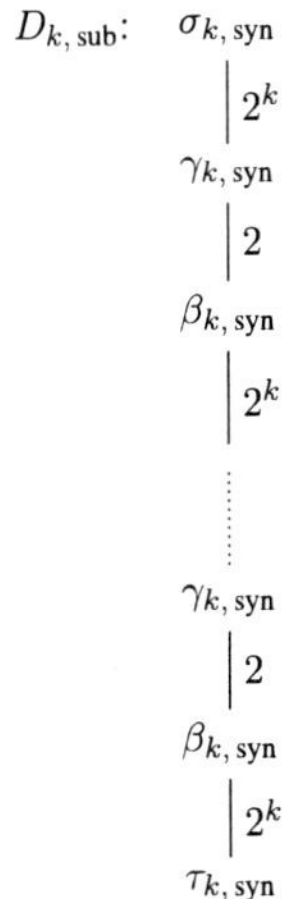

$$\sigma_{k,\mathrm{syn}} \left(\underbrace{\gamma_{k,\mathrm{syn}} \left(\beta_{k,\mathrm{syn}} \left(\ldots \left(\gamma_{k,\mathrm{syn}} \left(\beta_{k,\mathrm{syn}} \left(\tau_{k,\mathrm{syn}} \right) \right) \right) \ldots \right) \right) \right)}_{m - 1 \text{ times}}$$

Figure 8: The unique subtree $D_{k,\mathrm{sub}}$ of any derivation tree for $w_{k,m} = a_1^m \ldots a_k^m$.

tinguished type S. The abstract and the object language of $\mathcal{G}$ are defined as $A(\mathcal{G}) = \{t \in \Lambda_1 \mid t : S\}$ and $O(\mathcal{G}) = \{\mathcal{L}(t) \in \Lambda_2 \mid t \in A(\mathcal{G})\}$, respectively.

In this way the ACG-framework, in particular, provides a logical setting in which an abstract language can be used as a specification of the derivation set of a grammar instantiation of some grammar formalism, and by applying two different morphisms to the abstract language, we can "simultaneously" obtain a syntactic object language and a semantic object language.

The *order* of an ACG is the maximal order of the types assigned to the abstract constants from C_1.[7] As demonstrated by de Groote (2002), each classical TAG can be encoded as second-order ACGs realizing the object language as the set of derived trees, and the set of derived strings can be extracted from that object language by composing the first second-order ACG with a second one. Salvati (2007) has shown more generally, that second-order ACGs, where the object language is realized over a string signature, derive exactly the string languages generated by, e.g., set-local multicomponent TAGs. Kanazawa (2010) has shown, that second-order ACGs, where the object language is realized over a tree signature, derive exactly the string languages generated by, e.g., *context-free graph grammars* (Bauderon and Courcelle, 1987).

Of course, the notion of derivation (trees) and derived trees we have informally presented in the previous sections is essentially one making use of binding and abstraction. Recasting the above notation into the ACG-framework provides one way of analyzing the properties of coTAGs, in particular, from the perspective of an comparison to other formalisms and approaches which fit into the ACG-shape.

Closer inspection reveals Barker's accompanying notion of derivation tree to be in line with the abstract language of the TAG-guided, ACG-based semantic analysis of Pogodalla (2004a; 2007), where the abstract language is a set of lambda terms containing third-order constants.

It is easy to see that, although as far as the syntactic component is concerned, coTAGs are strongly equivalent to TAGs, this is only because the syntactic interpretation of the higher-order derivations "goes through" the second-order derivation trees of TAGs. Once we turn to the domain of meanings, where the higher-order derivation terms are used essentially, we obtain a greater generative capacity. We have exemplified this above with regard to the language $\mathrm{MIX}(k)$, for $k \geq 3$. Note that $\mathrm{MIX}(3)$ is not a tree adjoining language (Kanazawa and Salvati, 2012), and that for $k \geq 4$, $\mathrm{MIX}(k)$ is conjectured to be beyond the scope of set-local multicomponent TAGs.

5 Conclusion

As already mentioned in the introduction, Barker intends to provide an "alternative conceptualization" of TAG semantic computation. An earlier approach to TAG semantics in explicit terms of STAGs has been worked out by Nesson and Shieber (2007, and follow-up work). But in contrast to Barker's presentation, their initial version does not exceed the expressivity of simple STAGs (Shieber, 1994; Shieber, 2006), where also the second component does not exceed the (weak) generative capacity of TAGs.

The difference from coTAGs results from the fact that the semantic component may constitute a tree-local multicomponent TAG, which allows Nesson and Shieber to lexically represent, e.g., a scope-taking quantifier as a pair of an elementary auxiliary tree and an elementary substitution tree. Sticking to the realm of simple STAGs implies that in the context of nested quantifiers and *inverse linking*, when there are more than two quantifiers involved, not all logically possible readings are derivable. Nesson and Shieber discuss this point in the context of the example *two politicians spy on someone from every city*. Their approach delivers four possible readings. A particular fifth reading, namely, the case of scope ordering *every* > *two* > *some* is not available, which some authors, among them Barker, think is a possible reading, albeit hard to process.

Introducing *limited delay vector TAGs (LDV-TAGs)*, Nesson (2009) suggests a modification of the earlier STAG approach which also allows the derivation of the "fifth reading." If for any given LDV-TAG there is no hard upper bound on the degree of delay and on the number of multiple adjunctions that can take place at a single node, our argument for coTAG expressivity can be straightforwardly adapted to LDV-TAGs. That is to say,

---

[7]The order an atomic type is 1. For two types ζ and η, the order of $(\zeta\eta)$ is defined as the maximum of the order of ζ increased by 1 and the order of η.

we can write an LDV-TAG whose set of derivation trees and set of derived meanings is, up to a homomorphism, MIX(k) for arbitrary, but fixed $k \geq 1$.

Arbitrary delay allows for a qualitative increase in the relation-generating power of synchronous TAGs, demonstrated above in terms of coTAGs and the operation of cosubstitution. Recasting this in terms of ACGs allows for a further characterization, which makes clear the increase in derivational generative capacity by moving from second-order abstract constants to third-order ones.

References

Chris Barker. 2010. Cosubstitution, derivational locality, and quantifier scope. In *Proceedings of the Tenth International Workshop on Tree Adjoining Grammars and Related Formalisms (TAG+10)*, New Haven, CT, pages 135–142.

Michel Bauderon and Bruno Courcelle. 1987. Graph expressions and graph rewriting. *Mathematical Systems Theory*, 20:83–127.

Philippe de Groote. 2001. Towards abstract categorial grammars. In *39th Annual Meeting of the Association for Computational Linguistics (ACL 2001)*, Toulouse, pages 252–259. ACL.

Philippe de Groote. 2002. Tree-adjoining grammars as abstract categorial grammars. In *Proceedings of the Sixth International Workshop on Tree Adjoining Grammars and Related Formalisms (TAG+6)*, Venezia, pages 145–150.

Aravind K. Joshi and Yves Schabes. 1997. Tree adjoining grammars. In G. Rozenberg and A. Salomaa, editors, *Handbook of Formal Languages*, volume 3, pages 69–124. Springer, Berlin, Heidelberg.

Laura Kallmeyer and Maribel Romero. 2004. Ltag semantics with semantic unification. In *Proceedings of the Seventh International Workshop on Tree Adjoining Grammars and Related Formalisms (TAG+7)*, Vancouver, BC, pages 155–162.

Makoto Kanazawa and Sylvain Salvati. 2012. MIX is not a tree-adjoining language. In *50th Annual Meeting of the Association for Computational Linguistics (ACL 2012)*, Jeju Island. ACL.

Makoto Kanazawa. 2010. Second-order abstract categorial grammars as hyperedge replacement grammars. *Journal of Logic, Language and Information*, 19:137–161.

Rebecca Nesson and Stuart M. Shieber. 2007. Simpler TAG semantics through synchronization. In Wintner (2007), pages 129–142.

Rebecca Nesson. 2009. *Synchronous and Multicomponent Tree-Adjoining Grammars. Complexity, Algorithms and Linguistic Applications*. Ph.D. thesis, Havard University, Cambridge, MA.

Sylvain Pogodalla. 2004a. Computing semantic representation. Towards ACG abstract terms as derivation trees. In *Proceedings of the Seventh International Workshop on Tree Adjoining Grammars and Related Formalisms (TAG+7)*, Vancouver, BC, pages 64–71.

Sylvain Pogodalla. 2004b. Using and extending ACG technology. Endowing categorial grammars with an underspecified semantic representation. In *Proceedings of Categorial Grammars 2004*, Montpellier, pages 197–209.

Sylvain Pogodalla. 2007. Ambiguïté de portée et approche fonctionnelle des grammaires d'arbres adjoints. In *Traitement Automatique des Langues Naturelles (TALN 2007)*, Toulouse. 10 pages.

Sylvain Salvati. 2007. Encoding second order string ACG with deterministic tree walking transducers. In Wintner (2007), pages 143–156.

Stuart M. Shieber and Yves Schabes. 1990. Synchronous tree-adjoining grammars. In *Proceedings of the 13th International Conference on Computational Linguistics (COLING '90)*, Helsinki, volume 3, pages 253–258.

Stuart M. Shieber. 1994. Restricting the weak-generative capacity of synchronous tree-adjoining grammars. *Computational Intelligence*, 10:371–385.

Stuart M. Shieber. 2006. Unifying synchronous tree adjoining grammars and tree transducers via bimorphisms. In *11th Conference of the European Chapter of the Association for Computational Linguistics (EACL 2006)*, Trento, pages 377–384. ACL.

Shuly Wintner, editor. 2007. *Proceedings of FG 2006: The 11th Conference on Formal Grammar*. CSLI Publications, Stanford, CA.

A Linguistically-motivated 2-stage Tree to Graph Transformation

Corentin Ribeyre[★] **Djamé Seddah**[★,◇] **Eric Villemonte de la Clergerie**[★]

[★]Alpage, INRIA Université Paris Diderot
[◇] Université Paris Sorbonne
`firstname.lastname@inria.fr`

Abstract

We propose a new model for transforming dependency trees into target graphs, relying on two distinct stages. During the first stage, standard local tree transformation rules based on patterns are applied to collect a first set of constrained edges to be added to the target graph. In the second stage, motivated by linguistic considerations, the constraints on edges may be used to displace them or their neighbour edges upwards, or to build new mirror edges. The main advantages of this model is to simplify the design of a transformation scheme, with a smaller set of simpler local rules for the first stage, and good properties of termination and confluence for the second level.

1 Introduction

Tree transformation is emerging as an important and recurring operation in Natural Language Processing, for instance to transform shallow syntactic trees into deeper ones or into semantic graphs (Bonfante et al., 2011a), or to transform syntactic trees from a source language to a target one (in Machine Translation). Another frequent case that initially motivated this work is the transformation from a source dependency scheme to a target one, in order to conduct parsing evaluations or to be used in some post-parsing component based on the target schema.

Two main problems arise when transforming linguistic structures. The first one is related to the diversity of syntactic configurations that have to be identified, knowing that many of these configurations are rare. A large number of rules may have to be provided to cover this diversity. A second problem arises from the non locality of some linguistic constructions, for instance for retrieving the true subject of some controlled verbs at semantic level or in case of coordination. Even when bounding these phenomena, trying to combine them with more canonical cases may lead to an explosion of the number of transformation rules, difficult to create and maintain. And, when not bounding these non local phenomena, it becomes necessary to introduce recursive transformation rules that raise delicate problems of ordering when applying them, as presented in the Grew system (Bonfante et al., 2011b) based on graph rewriting rules.

Many approaches have been proposed for tree or graph transformations, such as Top-Down or Bottom-Up Tree Transducers (Courcelle and Engelfriet, 2012), Tree-Walking Transducers (Bojańczyk, 2008), Synchronous Grammars (Shieber and Schabes, 1990) and (Matsuzaki and Tsujii, 2008) for an application on annotation scheme conversion, or Graph Rewriting Systems based, for instance, on the Single PushOut model (SPO) (Löwe et al., 1993; Geiss et al., 2006). But either they are complex to implement or they suffer from the above mentioned problems (coverage, maintenance, ordering). Moreover, they are not always suited for natural language processing, especially in case of complex phenomena.

Based on a preliminary experiment of scheme to scheme transformation, but motivated by more generic linguistic considerations, we propose a simple new two stage model. The first stage essentially addresses the local syntactic phenomena through local tree transformation rules whose action is to add a set of edges to the target graph being built. By focusing on local phenomena, fewer and simpler rules are needed. Furthermore, it is relatively easy to learn these local rules from a set of example sentences with their syntactic trees, and some partial annotation provided by the transformation designer. These local rules may easily

Proceedings of the 11th International Workshop on Tree Adjoining Grammars and Related Formalisms (TAG+11), pages 214–222,
Paris, September 2012.

be expressed using the SPO model.

The main novelty is the possibility for the first stage rules to decorate the target edges with constraints. During the second stage, the constraints are essentially used to displace edges in the target graph, either the edge carrying a constraint or neighbour edges, in the direction of *"heads"* (*upward direction*). This formulation is clearly in phase with the propagation of information to handle non-local phenomena. It has also the advantage of offering good properties of termination, with no new edge created and the fact that edges can not climb up forever. However, we add a more problematic class of constraints, used to duplicate some edges, for instance to handle sharing phenomena at the semantic level (control, coordination).

The first stage being a rather standard case of SPO-based (Single Push-Out) transformation (Löwe et al., 1993), we will focus, in Section 2, on a preliminary formalization of the second stage constraint-based transformation (Ribeyre, 2012). The expressive power of the approach will be illustrated with a few complex syntactic constructions in Section 3. The conversion experiment that have initially triggered the use of constraint is presented in Section 4.

2 Constraint-based graph transformation

We assume as given a graph domain $\mathcal{G}$ where the transformations take place. A component of $\mathcal{G}$ is a set of edge labels $\mathcal{L}$, partitioned in $\mathcal{L}_1 \cup \cdots \mathcal{L}_n$, the intuition being that each $\mathcal{L}_i$ corresponds to a subset of labels for a specific dimension (for instance, a dimension for the set of labels used as thematic roles and another one for quantifiers or for anaphora as illustrated in Figure 7).

Let e denote an edge $x \xrightarrow{l} y$, with source node x, target node y and label $l \in \mathcal{L}$.

A node y for a graph $G \in \mathcal{G}$ can have several incoming edges $e = x \xrightarrow{l} y$ but only one per dimension (i.e., $\forall e_1 = x_1 \xrightarrow{l_1} y, e_2 = x_2 \xrightarrow{l_2} y, \exists k, l_1 \in \mathcal{L}_k \wedge l_2 \in \mathcal{L}_k \implies e_1 = e_2$). This condition can be a bit restrictive, so we relax it by allowing several incoming edges for the same dimension, but tagging all but one as derived edges of the main one. In other words, the derived edges will be seen as clones of the main one. For a given edge e, we note $\dim(e) = k$ the dimension of e

such that $l \in \mathcal{L}_k$.

Let an extended edge be $e = (x \xrightarrow{l} y, C, H)$, which carries a (possibly) empty set of constraints C to be detailed below and a (possibly empty) history list H formed of node pairs (x', y') retracing the changes of head x' and tail y'.

A configuration (G, Agenda) for the constraint-based transformation includes a graph $G \in \mathcal{G}$ and an agenda of edges to be progressively added to G. The *initial configuration* has an empty graph, while a *terminal configuration* has an empty agenda. The initial agenda provides a list of edges to add returned by the first stage based on local transformation rules.

At each step i, an edge e is selected and removed from the agenda Agenda_i and added to G_i to get $G'_i = G_i \cup \{e\}$. Because of constraints on e or on edges e' in direct contact with e, e or e' may be removed from G'_i to get G_{i+1} and new derived edges with updated history added to the agenda to get Agenda_{i+1}. The process stops with success when reaching a terminal configuration, or with failure when getting a conflict in a graph G'_i, for instance when a node gets two main incoming edges for a same dimension k, or when a cycle is detected in an edge history (i.e., an edge is moved back to a previous place).

We consider four kinds of constraints that may be carried by the edges:

- A **move up** $m\uparrow$ constraint on edge e may be used to move e upwards, as illustrated by Figure 1[1]. The displacement is controlled by an argument pair $(\mathcal{A}, q)$ where $\mathcal{A}$ is a deterministic finite-state automaton (DFA) and q a state for $\mathcal{A}$. The DFA represents all possible transitions for the constraint to move up.[2] We further impose that all transition labels of $\mathcal{A}$ are edge labels in the same $\mathcal{L}_k$ for some dimension k. For an automaton example, see the Figure 8.[3] Intuitively, the constrained edge e can only move upwards along k-paths, and when several k-edges are possible from a node, the main one is chosen.

- A **redirect up** $r\uparrow$ constraint on edge $e =

---

[1]where the green edges are removed from the graph while the red ones are added to the agenda.

[2]This is reminiscent of LFG's functional uncertainty equations (Kaplan and Zaenen, 1995).

[3]Actually, weaker constraints on the automata labels seem to be possible.

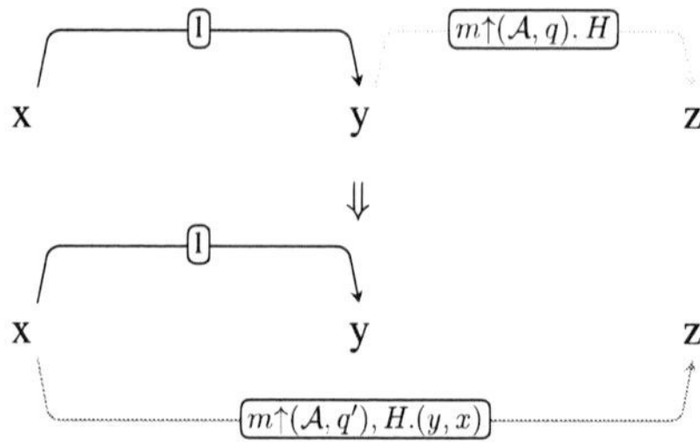

Figure 1: **move up** constraint

$x \xrightarrow{l_e} y$ may be used to move upwards the edges governed by y (the outgoing edges of y), as illustrated by Figure 2. The constraint accepts an argument $\mathbf{L} \subset \mathcal{L}_k$ for $k = \dim(e)$ that restricts the redirection to edges $e' = y \xrightarrow{l} z$ with some label $l \in \mathbf{L}$.

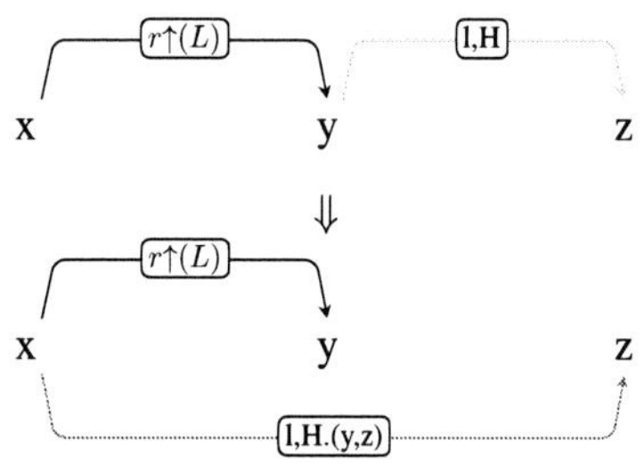

Figure 2: **redirect up** constraint

- A **share up** $s\!\uparrow$ constraint on edge $e = y \xrightarrow{l_e} z$ may be used to duplicate all incoming edges $e' = x \xrightarrow{l} y$ on y as incoming edges on z, as illustrated by Figure 3. Like the $r\!\uparrow$ constraint, the $s\!\uparrow$ constraint accepts an argument $\mathbf{L} \subset \mathcal{L}_{\dim(e)}$ that restricts the duplication to edges e' with label $l \in \mathbf{L}$.

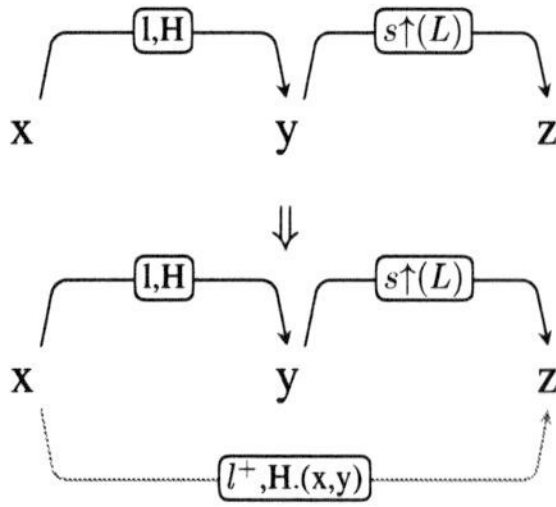

Figure 3: **share up** constraint

- A **share down** $s\!\downarrow$ constraint on edge $e =$

$y \xrightarrow{l_e} z$ may be used to duplicate all outgoing edges of y as outgoing edges of z, as illustrated by Figure 4. The $s\!\downarrow$ constraint accepts an argument $\mathbf{L} \subset \mathcal{L}_{\dim(e)}$ that restricts the duplication to edges e' with label $l \in \mathbf{L}$. Note that the resulting edges have tagged labels l^+, indicating they are secondary edges.

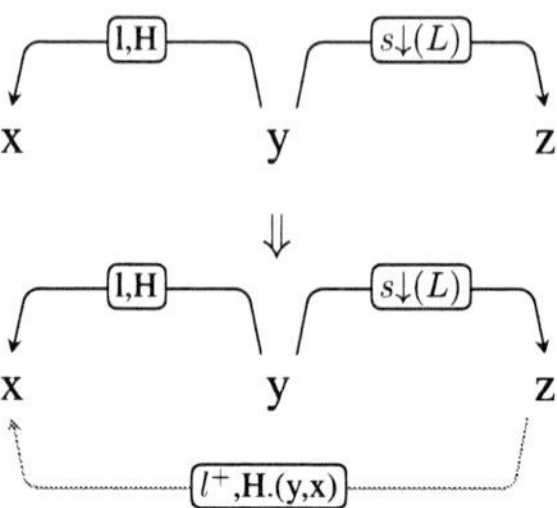

Figure 4: **share down** constraint

We impose further restrictions to handle the interactions between constraints. For instance, the edges with **share** constraints can not be redirected and the edges with **move up** constraints can not be duplicated through the application of a **share down** constraint. The definition of the graph domain and the control provided by the constraint arguments ensure the confluence of the rewriting process. The number of edges can not grow, but through the application of the **share** constraints. By controlling that we do not add an edge twice to the same place (thanks to the history information) and because all movements are oriented upwards, termination may be ensured. Some conflicts may be solved through the use of meta-rules as illustrated in Section 4.

After termination, a cleaning phase may be applied to delete some edges that were added as temporary helping edges, for instance some edges with **share** constraints.

Intuitively, the choice of constraint types is motivated by the idea that movement is driven by heads, with a component moving upward until it finds its place as an head (**move up**) or with components redirected upwards until they attach to the right head (**redirect up**). The **share** constraints are used to deal with coordination (with for instance a subject shared by several verbs), but also but other elliptic constructions as illustrated by control verbs.

In practice, this set of constraints seems to be

sufficient for most interesting situations. However, new kinds of constraints, such as the obvious **move down** and **redirect down**, and the blocking constraints **freeze up** and **freeze down**, should be investigated, in terms of interest and in terms of coherence with the other kinds of constraints (in particular to preserve the confluence).

More interestingly, we are also considering a **transfer** constraint, a generalization of the **share down** constraint that could be used to handle complex cases of edge transfer in repeated elliptic coordination, as illustrated in *Paul wants to eat an apple, Mary a pear, and John an orange.*, where we need some form of copy for *eat* and *want*, and of transfer for the subject and object grammatical functions.

3 A linguistically motivated model

We believe that our approach has a great potential and can be applied to solve in elegant ways various transformations problems. The next section will show how it can be used to handle conversion between dependency schemes, but the current section focuses on its use for transforming shallow syntactic trees into deeper ones or even into shallow semantic graphs as explored in (Ribeyre, 2012). Our motivation is to reach a semantic level with a small set of rules and reduced human cost. A first step in this direction is to induce the triggering patterns of the local transformation rules (based on the SPO approach (Löwe et al., 1993)) by partially annotating some nodes and/or edges in the parse trees of a set of carefully selected sample sentences grouped in sets illustrating the various syntactic phenomena and their configuration.

Given the annotations and the parse trees, the algorithm basically tries to generalize over the selected nodes and edges, through the following steps:

1. Extract a graph from the annotations of the first annotated parse tree

2. Extract a graph from the annotations of the second one

3. Find the maximum common subgraph(s) between these graphs

4. If there is more than one common subgraph, find the most general subgraph by comparing

the features structures attached to the nodes and edges

The algorithm is actually pretty simple, but seems to be powerful enough in most cases.[4] In fact, it provides the possibility of quickly developing a set of rules for a particular application, because most users prefer to select something rather than writing code from scratch. That is the reason why we developed a GUI as part of our Graph Rewriting System. Figure 3 provides a screenshot of the interface, which is divided in three parts:

1. A hierarchical view (left hand panel) where one can manage the set of sentence examples, grouping them by syntactic phenomena;

2. The tree view (right hand panel) where one can select nodes and edges (the red dotted lines);

3. The triggering part (bottom panel) of the induced transformation rule, to be then edited and completed by the transformation part.

The examples described below are annotated with the CoNLL scheme used for the dependency version of the French Treebank (FTB) (Candito et al., 2010a; Abeillé et al., 2003). Our goal is to construct a new version of the FTB with deeper syntactic annotations, as a first step towards a shallow semantic representation for FTB. Hence, in the figures 6, 7 and 9, we illustrate some complex syntactic constructions and try to exhibit simple transformations, using the constraints. In the examples, we use the following color code:

- Red edges for the final edges after all constraint applications,

- Green edges for the initial constrained edges,

- Blue edges for non constrained edges used by constrained ones

- Dotted orange edges for intermediary temporary edges

For instance, in Figure 6, we would like to insert the missing link between a deep subject and

---

[4]but we are aware of its limits: for instance, unless adding negative examples, it is not possible to induce tests on the non existence of an edge.

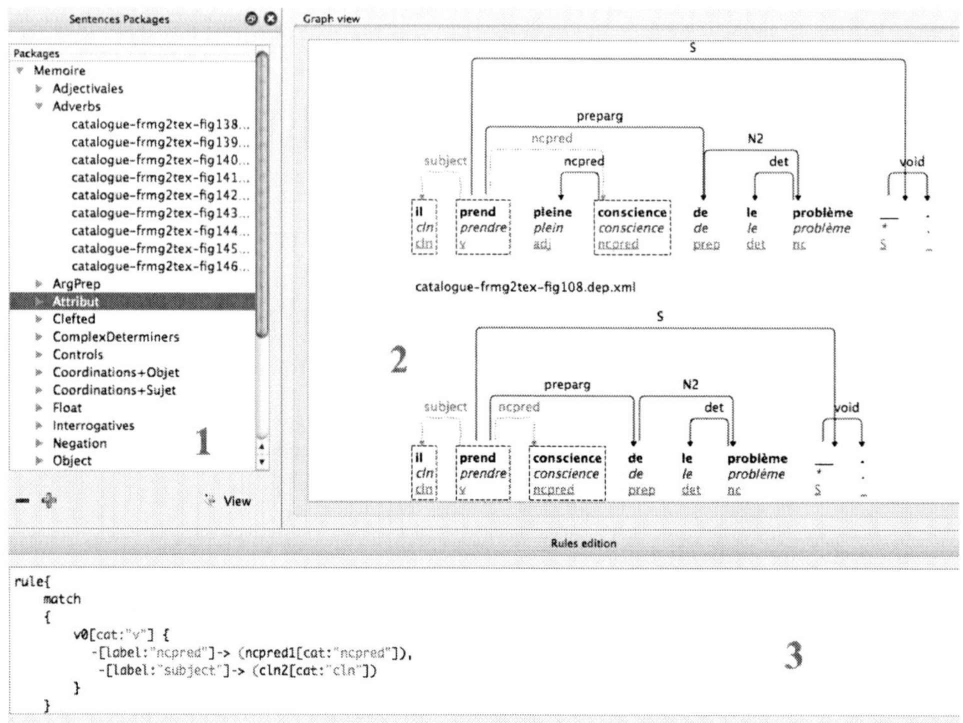

Figure 5: GUI of the Graph Rewriting System

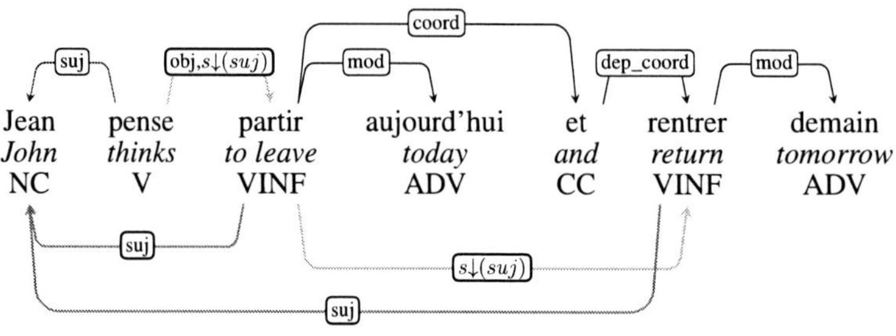

Figure 6: Subject ellipsis + control verb

its verb in the case of subject ellipsis in the sentence: *Jean₁ pense ϵ₁ partir aujourd'hui et ϵ₁ rentrer demain* (*John₁ thinks about ϵ₁ leaving today and ϵ₁ coming back tomorrow*). This example is interesting because of the subject ellipsis and the control verb *penser*. We need to add the following **subject** dependencies, derived from the subject dependency between *Jean* and *pense* :

1. between *Jean* and *partir*, because *Jean* is also subject of *partir*

2. between *Jean* and *rentrer*, because *Jean* is the elliptical subject of *rentrer*

To solve our problem, we simply need to put two **share down** constraints as illustrated in Figure 6. The first constrained edge between *pense* and *partir* results from a rule dealing with subject-controlled verbs. The second constrained edge between *partir* et *renter* results from a rule dealing with coordination between clauses with no subject in the last clause. After applying the constraints, we get the 2 extra subject dependencies (in red). Of course, we can solve these two problems with the two following local rules:

1. One for solving the control verb issue.

2. One for solving the subject ellipsis case.

But, in that case, we may observe that the first rule has to be applied before the second rule, imposing some ordering between the rules. So, the confluence will not be guaranteed by the system.

The system of constraints has been designed to be easy to use but nevertheless expressive enough for powerful transformations. Our second example, in Figure 7, illustrates the use of a **move up** constraint. In this example, we want to retrieve the antecedent "*Jean*" of the relative pronoun "*dont*". We have to follow a potentially unbounded chain of dependencies starting from "*dont*" until we reach a mod_rel dependency. In order to do that, the original de_obj dependency between *dont* and *mère* (*mother*) triggers the addition of an initial ant dependency between the same words (in green) but with a move up constraint built on the automaton $\mathcal{A}$ of Figure 8. The constrained edge will then move up following the obj (green) edges staying in state q_0 of $\mathcal{A}$ (orange ant edges). Finally, the edge moves up through the mod_rel edge, switching to the final state q_1 (red ant edge). One can note that *dont* has several heads, namely the syntactic head *mère* and an head for the **ant** relation. Typically, the **ant** relation will be present in some new dimension for anaphora.

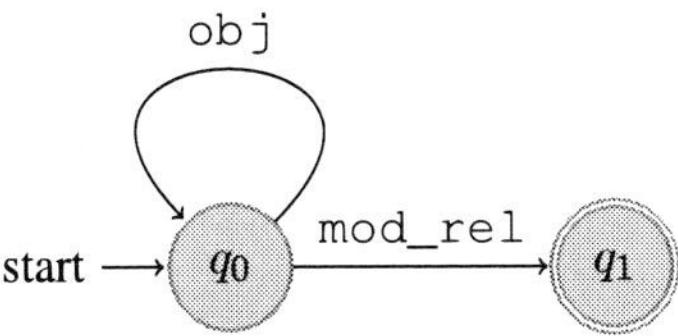

Figure 8: Automaton $\mathcal{A}$ for the **move up** constraint in Figure 7

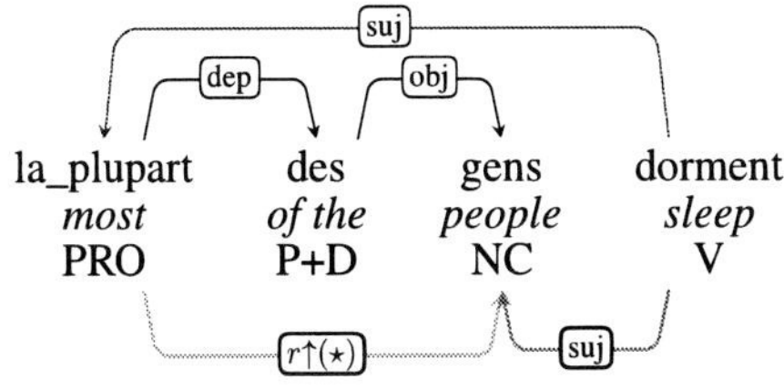

Figure 9: Linguistic application of constraint **redirect**

Finally, Figure 9 illustrates the *redirect up* constraint. In the sentence, "*la plupart*" (*most*) is the shallow syntactic subject of "*dorment*" (*sleep*). However the semantic subject of "*dorment*" is actually "*gens*" (*people*). So we add a redirect edge from *la plupart* to *gens* that can redirect all edges entering *la plupart* towards *gens*, including the subject dependency. The same mechanism would work as well in sentences such as *il parle à la plupart des enfants*. (*he talks to most of the kids*), with a redirection of an a_obj dependency.

4 A use case: a scheme to scheme conversion

The formalization sketched in this paper is a derivative of a preliminary experiment of conversion between two syntactic dependency schemes. The source schema **depFRMG** is a rich and deep dependency schema produced from the output of FRMG, a French wide coverage hybrid TAG/TIG parser resulting from the compilation of a meta-grammar (Villemonte de La Clergerie, 2005). The target schema **depFTB** is the dependency version of the French TreeBank (Candito et al., 2010a; Abeillé et al., 2003), and the choice was initially motivated by evaluation purposes for FRMG.

The **depFRMG** schema, represented using the DepXML format[5], is produced by converting the TAG derivations returned by FRMG, using the elementary tree anchors as heads for lexicalized trees and introducing pseudo anchors for non lexicalized trees (using their root category as label) (Villemonte de la Clergerie, 2010). The resulting dependencies are non necessarily projective, for instance in the case of superlative constructions. The **depFRMG** schema may actually be used to represent a shared forest of dependency trees representing the whole set of analysis returned by FRMG for a sentence. In practice, a phase of disambiguation is applied to return the best dependency tree as illustrated by the above edges[6] in Figure 10 for the following sentence:

---

[5] There are often some confusions, but one should clearly distinguish the notions of *format* such as DepXML or CONLL, *model* to specify the structures and their properties (such as projectivity or shared forests) and, finally, *schema* as an instantiation of a model for a specific resource, associated with a tagset and annotation guidelines. Here, we are really interested by a conversion between two schema.

[6] The edge color indicates the kind of the underlying TAG operation, with blue for substitution, red for adjoining, and purple for co-anchoring and lexical nodes in a tree. The S node corresponds to a case of pseudo-anchor for a non-lexicalized elementary tree.

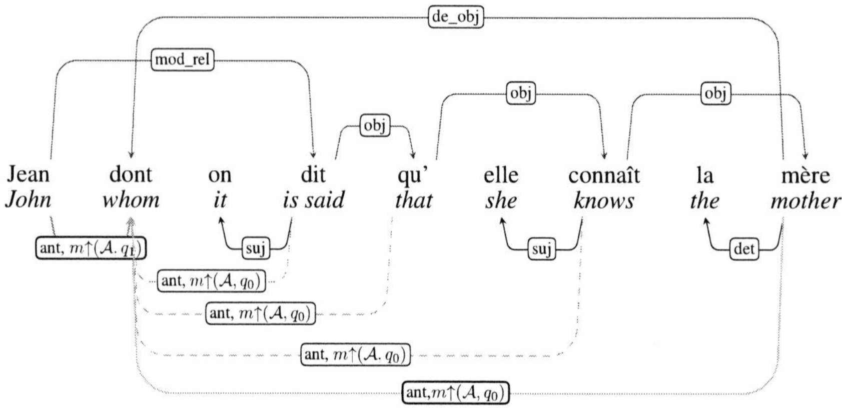

Figure 7: Linguistic application of constraint **move**

par qui   a-t-elle voulu que ces   deux livres
by   whom did-she want that these two books
et   ce   DVD lui   soient rendus   ?
and this DVD to-her be   returned ?

The **depFTB** schema used for the dependency version of the FTB is expressed in CONLL format, a format largely used for training statistical parsers and evaluating them (Nivre et al., 2007). The schema corresponds to projective shallow dependencies using a relatively small numbers of dependency labels. Figure 10 shows a **depFTB** version of our illustrative sentence, as produced by the conversion, with the converted edges below the sentence.

Most cases of conversion are straightforward and may be handled by local rules (for instance for attaching determiners to nouns with det, adjective on nouns with mod, or "object" introduced by prepositions with obj). However, we also already observe non obvious modifications in Figure 10, for instance, the root of the dependency tree is *rendu* for **depFRMG** (because of the argument extraction) while it is *voulu* for **depFTB**. The subject *-t-elle* is attached to the auxiliary *a* in **depFRMG** (because of subject inversion), but to the main verb *voulu* in **depFTB**. These more complex cases may involve potentially non-bounded propagations and changes of heads (with redirection for the dependants). It is also worth noting that our resulting conversion is non projective (because of the attachment of *par* on *rendu*), breaking the expected **depFTB** guidelines that would propose an attachment on *voulu*, but only for projectivization reasons that are considered as more

and more questionable in such situations (so we decided not to do the projectivization).

In practice, we designed 86 local transformation rules, a few of them carrying constraints such as move_up, redirect, frozen (to block displacement), and mirror (a variant of the share constraints). Furthermore, a few meta-rules were added to handle conflicts, for instance when a word gets two distinct governors or when a dependency gets two distinct labels. An example of such mediating rule is given by the following: *if two dependencies d_1 and d_2 share the same target w and if $h(d_1) < h(d_2) < w$, then d_1 is rerooted to have $h(d_2)$ as target* (in other word, the closest preceding potential head wins). A mechanism of log was used to track, on corpus, the most frequent conflicts and check the effectiveness of the mediating rules.

The resulting conversion scheme (coupled with disambiguation tuning learned from the 9881 sentences of the train part ftb6_1 of FTB) allows us to reach (with no prior tagging) a Labelled Attachment Score (LAS) of 85.8% on the test part ftb6_3 of FTB (1235 sentences), not counting the punctuation dependencies (as usually done). This figure may be honorably compared to the 88.2% obtained by the best statistical parser directly trained on the FTB (Candito et al., 2010b). Even if it difficult to measure the impact of the conversion, it seems that the conversion is relatively good. Still, we are aware of some loss coming from the conversion, essentially due to phenomena that can not be directly handled by tree transformation and constraints. More precisely,

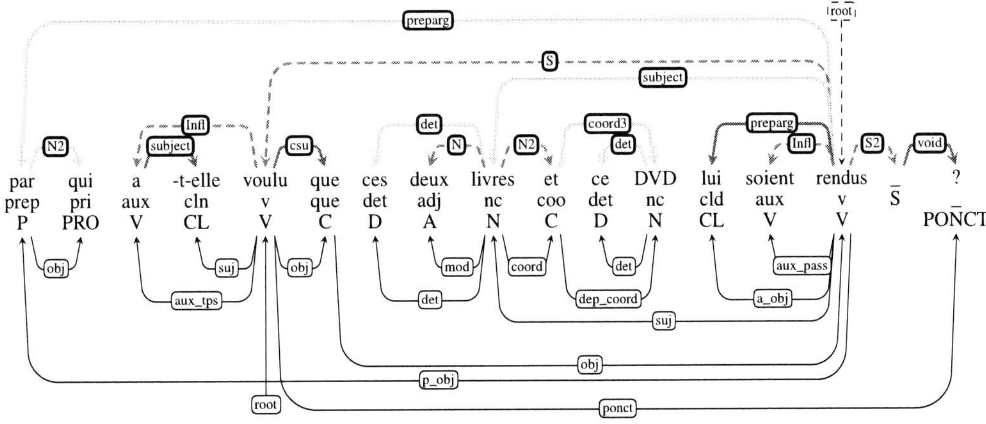

Figure 10: Disambiguated FRMG output, with **depFRMG** edges above and converted **depFTB** edges below

FRMG and FTB do not use the same set of compound words (for instance for complex prepositions, complex adverbs, or named entities) and it is therefore necessary to retrieve the missing **depFTB** dependencies for the FRMG compound words that are not compound in FTB.

If we look more closely at the importance of the constraints in the conversion process, we can observe that their impact is limited but associated with a potentially large number of occasionally rare configurations that would have been difficult to identify.

Only 5 rules out of the 86 rules carry constraints:[7]

- One rule (R_ponct) with a constraint move up, used to attach the final punctuation to the FTB head of the sentence.

- Two rules with a redirect up constraint. Rule R_aux_caus is used to handle the (rare) cases of causative constructions while Rule R_Monsieur is used to handle honorific construction such as *M. Teulade* (*Mr Teulade*) where *Teulade* would be the head for FRMG and *M.* the head for FTB.

- Two rules with a mirror constraint, used to handle enumerations.

---

[7]The small number of constrained rules may be partially explained by the fact that the need for constraints became progressively apparent after some rules were already written. It is possible that the set of 86 rules could be slightly reduced by adding constraints to more of them.

On the 278,083 dependencies present in ftb6_1, we get 5,352 move up resolutions (2%), 1,167 redirect resolutions (0.4%), and 638 mirror resolutions. However, these cases correspond to configurations involving 46 distinct pairs of rules for move up, 27 for redirect, and 24 for mirror. Intuitively, these figures provide a rough estimate of the number of rules (around 97) that should have been found and added to avoid the use of the constraints (uniquely on ftb6_1). It may be noted that this set of potential rules is already greater than the 86 current rules, with no guarantee of being complete.

We also have some indications about the resolution of the conflicts with 5,665 potential head conflicts (2%), 5,320 of them (94%) being handled by the mediating rules.

5 Conclusion

We have sketched a constraint-based graph transformation, motivated by linguistic considerations on the displacement or the sharing of dependencies. This constraint-based transformation may be used as the second stage of a transformation process based on more standard local transformation rules.

We have shown that a very small set of constraint types is sufficient to handle relatively complex syntactic phenomena in elegant ways. A few more types (to be investigated) could prove themselves very valuable to handle complex cases of elliptic coordination.

We believe that the two-stage approach is a

promising one, because of a better division of work and an economy both in terms of number of rules and of development time. The local transformation rules may be relatively easily learned from partially annotated simple examples, the second stage results from a few rules constrained with only a small set of constraint types. The constraints avoid many rule ordering issues related to recursive transformations, providing more stable systems (wrt the addition or modification of rules). Proof of the confluence is also easier.

A preliminary implementation was tried for a conversion process between two dependency schemes, but a cleaner implementation based on the formalization presented in this paper is underway. It will be tested on a larger spectrum of transformations, for instance to build semantic graphs from dependency trees.

References

Anne Abeillé, Lionel Clément, and François Toussenel. 2003. Building a treebank for French. In Anne Abeillé, editor, *Treebanks*. Kluwer, Dordrecht.

M. Bojańczyk. 2008. Tree-walking automata. In *International Conference on Language and Automata Theory and Applications*.

G. Bonfante, B. Guillaume, and M. Morey. 2011a. Modular graph rewriting to compute semantics. In *International Workshop on Computional Semantics 2011*.

G. Bonfante, B. Guillaume, M. Morey, and G. Perrier. 2011b. Enrichissement de structures en dépendances par réécriture de graphes. In *TALN 2011*.

Marie Candito, Benoît Crabbé, and Pascal Denis. 2010a. Statistical french dependency parsing: treebank conversion and first results. In *Proceedings of the 7th Language Resources and Evaluation Conference (LREC'10)*, La Valette, Malte.

Marie Candito, Joakim Nivre, Pascal Denis, and Enrique Henestroza Anguiano. 2010b. Benchmarking of statistical dependency parsers for french. In *Proceedings of COLING'2010 (poster session)*, Beijing, China.

B. Courcelle and J. Engelfriet. 2012. *Graph Structure and Monadic Second-Order Logic, a Language-Theoretic Approach*. Cambridge University Press.

R. Geiss, G. Veit Batz, D. Grund, S. Hack, and A. Szalkowski. 2006. GrGen: A fast SPO-based graph rewriting tool. In *International Conference on Graph Transformation*.

R.M. Kaplan and A. Zaenen. 1995. Long-distance dependencies, constituent structure, and functional uncertainty. *Formal Issues in Lexical-Functional Grammar*, 47:137–165.

M. Löwe, H. Ehrig, R. Heckel, L. Ribeiro, A. Wagner, and A. Corradini. 1993. Algebraic approches to graph transformations. *Theoritical Computer Science*.

T. Matsuzaki and J. Tsujii. 2008. Comparative parser performance analysis across grammar frameworks through automatic tree conversion using synchronous grammars. In *Proceedings of the 22nd International Conference on Computational Linguistics-Volume 1*, pages 545–552. Association for Computational Linguistics.

Joakim Nivre, Johan Hall, Sandra Kuebler, Ryan McDonald, Jens Nilsson, Sebastian Riedel, and Deniz Yuret. 2007. The CoNLL 2007 shared task on dependency parsing. In *The CoNLL 2007 shared task on dependency parsing*.

Corentin Ribeyre. 2012. Mise en place d'un systéme de réécriture de graphes appliqués á l'interface syntaxe-sémantique. M2, Univ. Paris Diderot 7, June.

Stuart M. Shieber and Yves Schabes. 1990. Synchronous tree-adjoining grammars. In *Proceedings of the 13th conference on Computational linguistics - Volume 3*, COLING '90, pages 253–258, Stroudsburg, PA, USA. Association for Computational Linguistics.

Éric Villemonte de La Clergerie. 2005. From metagrammars to factorized TAG/TIG parsers. In *Proceedings of IWPT'05 (poster)*, pages 190–191, Vancouver, Canada.

Éric Villemonte de la Clergerie. 2010. Convertir des dérivations TAG en dépendances. In ATALA, editor, *17e Conférence sur le Traitement Automatique des Langues Naturelles - TALN 2010*, July.

Scope Economy and TAG Locality

Michael Freedman
Yale University
370 Temple Street, Rm 210
New Haven, CT 06511, USA
`michael.freedman@yale.edu`

Abstract

This paper gives an analysis explaining various cases where the scope of two logical operators is non-permutable in a sentence. The explanation depends on a theory of derivational economy couched in the synchronous tree adjoining grammar framework. Locality restrictions made using the STAG formalism allow us to limit the computational complexity of using transderivational constraints and allows us to make interesting empirical predictions.

1 Introduction

Although the relative scope of quantifiers is generally free within a single clause in English, there are a number of cases where the relative scope of quantifiers/operators is non-permutable. We provide here an account for the data below that depends on a theory of derivational economy. It assumes a syntax-semantics interface couched in the synchronous tree adjoining grammar framework (STAG) (Shieber and Schabes, 1990; Han, 2006; Nesson and Shieber, 2007). The intuition underlying the current analysis is a familiar one: that interpretations of a given syntactic derivation are blocked when there is a simpler, competing derivation that can produce the same meaning. However, by couching the intuition in the context of STAG, we derive a number of important limitations on such competition by restricting the comparison class (using the TAG formalism), and maintain a system that is limited in the complexity of the computations it assumes. This allows us to make empirical predictions that other accounts of scope economy couched in other frameworks are unable to make because either they view competition to be global (Grice, 1989; Horn, 1989) or too local (Fox, 1995, 2000).

2 Universals-Negation

Universal quantifiers like *every* and negation are unable to scope freely with respect to one another. When a universal quantifier is in object position, as in (1), it is unable to take scope over negation.

(1)   a. Peter didn't catch every crook. (*$\forall > \neg$, $\neg > \forall$)

        b. Nobody caught every crook. (*$\forall > \neg \exists$, $\neg \exists > \forall$)

Similarly, when a universal is in subject position, it is unable to take scope over negation, as in (2). The pattern breaks down in a number of cases: in (3a), the presence of a raising predicate makes the wide scope universal reading possible; also, in (3b), the presence of an intervening operator allows the universal to scope over negation.

(2)   Everyone didn't meet Peter. (*$\forall > \neg$, $\neg > \forall$)

(3)   a. Everyone didn't seem to meet Peter. ($\forall > \neg$, $\neg > \forall$)

        b. Everyone didn't meet someone. ($\forall > \exists > \neg$)

The goal of the analysis is to explain lack of scope permutability in (1) and (2) while allowing scope permutability in (3).

3 Preliminary assumptions

We assume following Schabes and Shieber (1994) the declarative conception of STAG where quantifier scope is determined in the derivation tree: Here scope can be resolved on the left-to-right order of nodes on a derivations tree; by convention rightmost nodes in the derivation tree correspond with higher scope in the derived tree. In Schabes and Shieber (1994) scope ambiguity is achieved by allowing either ordering in the derivation tree.

Proceedings of the 11th International Workshop on Tree Adjoining Grammars and Related Formalisms (TAG+11), pages 223–231,
Paris, September 2012.

In contrast, we follow the restriction on derivation proposed in Freedman and Frank (2010) which is defined as follows:

> PROMINENCE RESTRICTION ON DERIVATION (PRoD): The children of a node γ (representing elementary tree τ) in a derivation tree must be in an order consistent with both the domination and c-command relations of their corresponding elementary tree's attachment sites on τ.

Figure 1 shows how PRoD works: trees adjoining into δ or ϵ must be ordered before those that adjoin into β or γ which must be ordered before those that adjoin into α.

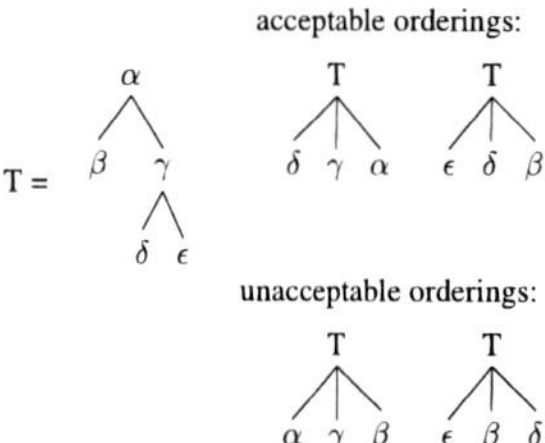

Figure 1: Sample elementary tree T (left) and sample derivation trees that show possible and impossible orderings of attachment following PRoD on derivation tree rooted with a node representing T.

By PRoD, one could not have the subject-tree ordered before the object-tree because the attachment site for the former c-commands the latter. To handle cases of inverse scope, multi-component tree-sets can combine through *split combination (SC)*:

> SPLIT COMBINATION: The node representing a scope-tree within a tree-set may be ordered later than specified by PRoD.

SC allows the scope portion of a quantifier tree set to take scope over a dominating or c-commanding quantifier. The use of split combination adds an extra step in the derivation by separating the scope-tree from the variable tree in the derivation tree. An example is provided in figure 2 for the sentence *a student read every book*; this compares to figure 3 where the tree-set for the quantifier is not split and surface scope is generated. Additionally, SC can be lexically restricted such that only certain quantifiers are able to split.

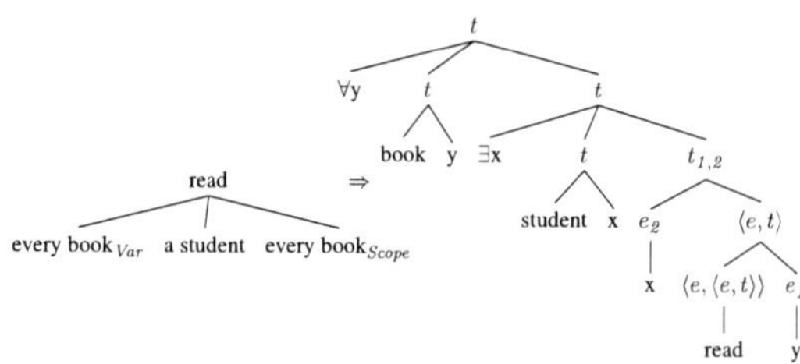

Figure 2: Derived and derivation tree for "A student read every book" with split combination of "every book".

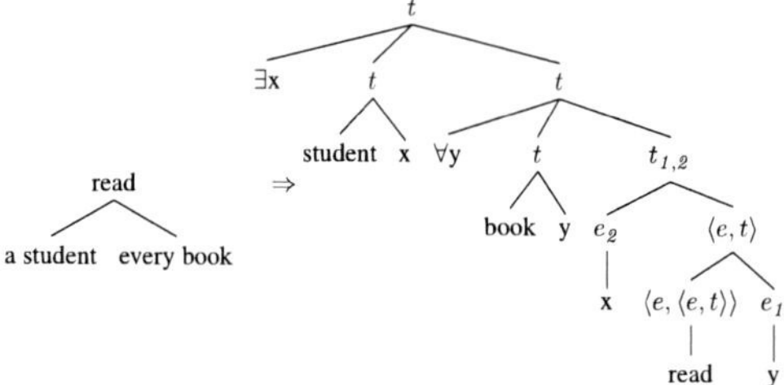

Figure 3: Derived and derivation tree for "A student read every book" without split combination of "every book".

The size of elementary trees follows the Condition on Elementary Tree Minimality (Frank, 2002). For our purposes this dictates that quantificational determiners are in the same elementary tree as the noun that is in their restriction (as depicted in figure 4). In the syntax, clausal negation resides in extended projection of a verb. In the semantics, we assume that negation adjoins in separately from the verb-tree, adding another step in the derivation (as depicted in figure 5).

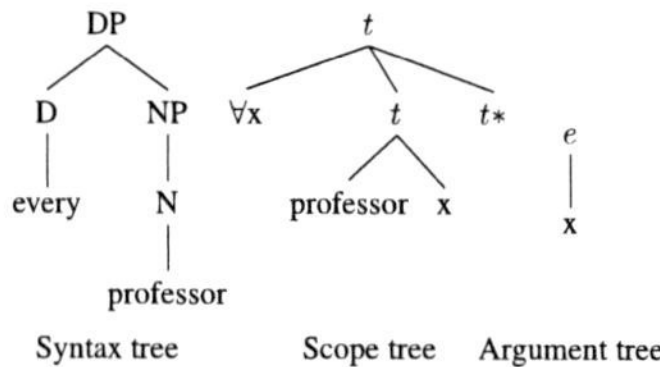

Figure 4: Elementary trees for the Quantifier Phrase "every professor" including the syntax tree and the multi-component semantic tree set consisting of the scope-tree and the argument tree.

4 Analysis

With this general picture in mind, let us proceed to analyse the data in §2: Observe that the unavail-

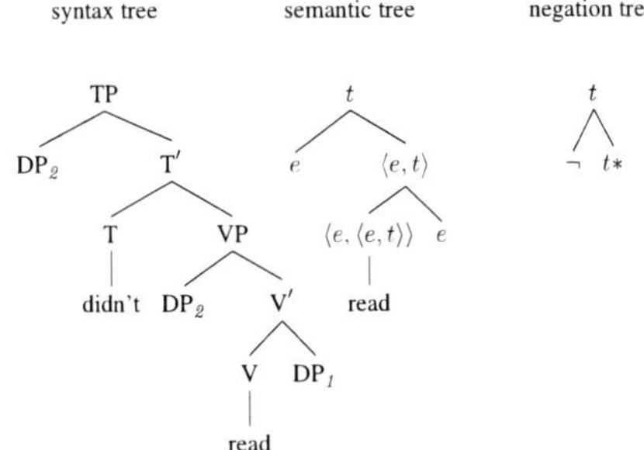

Figure 5: Elementary trees for the verb "read" with negation "didn't" in its extended projection. The semantic tree does not contain the negation; it is a separate tree.

able $\forall\neg$ reading for (1) is available for the example in (4), as $\forall\neg$ and $\neg\exists$ are logically equivalent.

(4)   John didn't read a/any book(s). ($\neg > \exists$)

While the derivation producing this interpretation would require split combination for (1), it does not for (4). Because SC creates an additional step, the derivation for (4) is shorter than the one for (1). An intuitive way of understanding this pattern is to think that (4) blocks (1) on the $\forall\neg/\neg\exists$ reading. A similar line of analysis can explain (2)'s inability to have a $\forall\neg$ reading; it has a competitor (5) that can produce the same meaning ($\neg\exists$) with a shorter derivation.

(5)   No one met Peter. ($\neg > \exists$)

(5) on the relevant reading has a shorter derivation because both quantifiers ($\neg$ and $\exists$) are lexicalized in a single tree; the negative and existential force in (2) must be combined in separately, creating an extra step. This blocking intuition can be formalized in the following manner:

> DERIVATIONAL COMPLEXITY CONSTRAINT ON SEMANTIC INTERPRETATION (DCCSI)
> A derivation d producing meaning m is ruled out if another shorter derivation d' also produces m.

This constraint explains the data in (1) and (2); both have more economical alternatives that block them. Derivation trees for (1) and (4) are provided in figure 6 showing the difference in derivation length. The DCCSI also explains the ability for the universal to take wide scope in (3); because an

operator intervenes, there is no more economical competitor, and no blocking can take place.

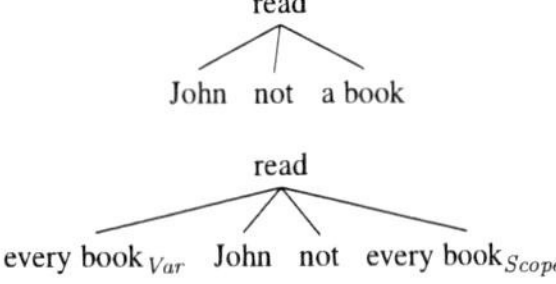

Figure 6: Derivation trees for "John didn't read every book" and "John didn't read a book" on the $\forall > \neg$ reading.

But, as the DCCSI stands, it is unrestricted with respect to comparison class. This causes empirical and computational problems. Computational issues are discussed in §6. Empirically, the unrestricted constraint leads to the puzzle posed by the data in (3a) (repeated as (6a)): why isn't the wide scope universal reading blocked by (6b). Given the definition of the DCCSI, blocking should take place as the relevant derivation for it is shorter than the relevant derivation for (3a).

(6)   a.   Everyone didn't seem to meet Peter. ($\neg > \forall$, $\forall > \neg$)

      b.   No one seemed to meet Peter. ($\neg > \exists$)

To restrict the comparison class we impose a constraint that closely follows TAG intuitions about locality. The TAG-like intuition behind this constraint is that comparison is localized to elements combining into a single elementary tree. The derivation can informally be defined in the following way: A derivation tree D is comparable to derivation tree D' iff D and D' are identical except for the daughters of a single node α. The possible differences between D and D' include D excising or replacing one or more of α's daughters. A more formal definition follows:

> LOCALITY CONSTRAINT ON COMPETITION (LCC) (formal version)
> Derivation tree D' can be compared to derivation tree D (where D and D' are defined as triples consisting of a set of nodes N, a set of labels L and the immediate dominance relation P) iff:
>
> 1. $N' \subseteq N$
> 2. $P' \subseteq P$
> 3. $\exists! n \in N \, s.t.$
>   (a) $P' \supseteq P - \{(n,x)|x \in N\}$

(b) $\forall x \in N, (n, x) \notin P \rightarrow$
$L(x) = L'(x)$

The first two clauses ensure that the derivation trees in the comparison class have no structure that is not present in the original derivation tree D. The third clause ensures that the only change is under a single node of the derivation tree and that daughters can be deleted or labels changed.

The LCC has the benefit of limiting the comparison class in a way that not only makes trans-derivational constraints feasible but also explains the puzzle of the wide scope reading for (3a). The availability of the wide scope universal reading for the example in (3a) can be understood in conjunction with the LCC; while there is a sentence that has a shorter derivation, (6b), it is not able to be compared to (3a) because there are differences under more than one node of the derivation trees (as depicted in (7)): The *didn't*-node is deleted under the *seem*-node and the *everyone* label is changed to the *no one*-label. This finding is possible because of the TAG analysis of raising where raising predicates adjoin into a VP (as shown in figure 8). Since the clausal negation combines into the raising predicate and the nominal quantifier negation combines into the main verb-tree the comparison is non-local, as depicted in figure 7.

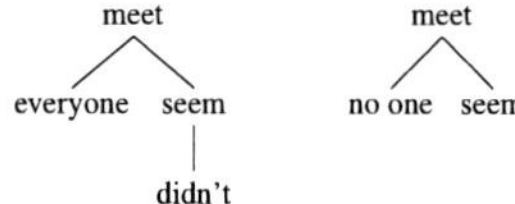

Figure 7: Derivation trees for "John didn't seem to meet everyone" and "No one seemed to meet everyone" on the $\forall > \neg$ reading.

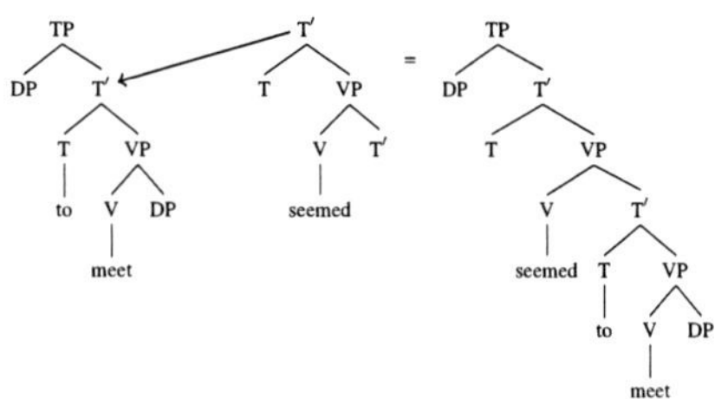

Figure 8: Derivation for a raising construction: the *seem*-tree (the raising predicate) adjoins into the *meet*-tree

Computationally, the DCCSI in conjunction with the LCC can be proven to not exceed the expressive power of TAG. This can be done with a proof by construction where a TAG with the DCCSI can be compiled into a TAG without the DCCSI. In addition, with proper linguistically motivated constraints, it can shown that the size of the grammar does not become unsuitably large with the compilation. This is shown in §7.

5 Double Object Constructions

It has been observed that the relative scope of the internal arguments of double object sentences are only able to have a surface scope reading (Larson, 1988; Bruening, 2001). That is, the sentence in (7a) can have the reading where every photograph was given to one individual but not a reading where the photographs differed in who they were given to. The prepositional dative sentences in (9) differ from those the double object in (7) in that they are scopally ambiguous; both the surface and inverse scopes for the internal arguments are available.

In the double object case, as in (7) and assuming the elementary tree for the double object in figure 9a, inverse scope interpretation can be obtained through the use of split combination which would place the scope of the second object in a higher position than the first object.

(7) a. Peter gave someone every/each photograph. ($*\forall>\exists$, $\exists>\forall$)

    b. Harry told someone every/each plot. ($*\forall>\exists$, $\exists>\forall$)

Note however that the prepositional dative alternative in (8) (and assuming the elementary tree in figure 9b) does not need SC in order to obtain the same reading, making its derivation shorter.

(8) Peter gave every photograph to someone. ($\forall>\exists$)

(9) a. Peter gave every photograph to someone. ($\forall>\exists$, $\exists>\forall$)

    b. Peter put a bagel on every shelf. ($\forall>\exists$, $\exists>\forall$)

Thus, blocking removes the inverse scope structure from the grammar. Why then are the ditransitive sentences in (9) ambiguous? For the prepositional dative cases in (9a,b) the PP argument is able to optionally attach to a higher position than the direct object argument thereby allowing "inverse scope" without SC (the PP can also be under the direct object in a VP-shell), as depicted in figure 9c. Evidence for this structural explanation come from examples like that in (10) where complex existential quantifiers (which have been observed not to take scope over other higher quantifiers (Beghelli and Stowell (1997); Heim (2001))) take scope over a higher quantifier.

(10) John gave an apple to more than three students.

The examples in 11 provide additional evidence for the blocking analysis: In (11a), no blocking occurs if there is an intervening operator that would force the prepositional dative construction to utilize SC to obtain the same scope reading (making the derivation length the same). Likewise, as in (11b), no blocking occurs in constructions that have no prepositional dative construction to compete with.

(11)   a. A teacher gave every student every book. ($\forall_{book} > \exists > \forall_{stu}$)
       b. Peter bet a friend every nickel (he had). ($\forall > \exists$, $\exists > \forall$)

6 Complexity

6.1 TAG with TDC is not a TAL

I show in this section how a TAG with a TDC can generate a language that contains exactly the prime numbers. Since the language that contains only the prime numbers is not in the class of mildly context sensitive languages, the language that is generated by this grammar is not a TAL. This shows that adding a transderivational "economy" constraint can increase the generative capacity of a grammar. We can construct this language in the following way:

Construct a TAG G that composes the natural numbers. Figure 10 shows a TAG G' that generates unary strings that can be interpreted as the natural numbers beginning with 2. The initial tree has an obligatory adjoining constraint; the grammar only generates unary strings of length > 1. Each adjoining operation increases the interpreted value of the string by 1.

An additional tree is added (in figure 11) to the grammar G' (let's call it G) in order to be able to

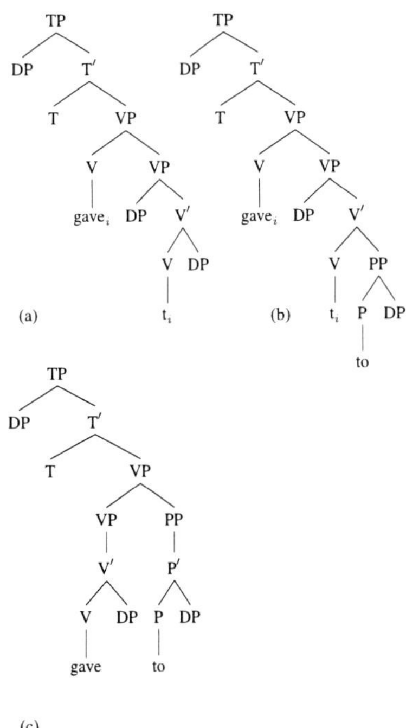

Figure 9: The three elementary trees for ditransitive constructions: (a) double object; (b)dative complement (low attachment); dative complement (high attachment)

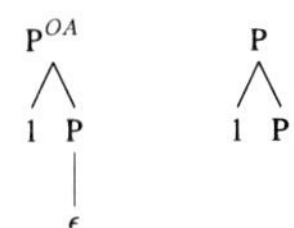

Figure 10: This figure shows TAG G'; it consists of trees that can build up the natural numbers in unary. The left and right trees construct numbers by successively "adding" 1.

represent all of the natural numbers greater than 1 as products of other natural numbers. The tree contains two nodes where adjunction can occur: there is one OA site where at least one 1-tree must obligatorily adjoin and one SA site where a tree may optionally adjoin. Adjoining into this tree can produce any natural number except 1.

The grammar G consisting of the trees in figures 10 and 11 generates the language that consists of the natural numbers in unary and the natural numbers as products of other natural numbers (represented in unary). Now, we introduce a transderivational constraint that will remove from the grammar any derived tree whose value can be

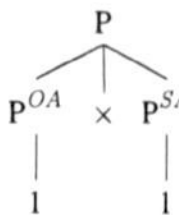

Figure 11: Additional tree for TAG G; this allows natural numbers to be represented by the product of other natural numbers.

more simply derived (fewer derivational steps) by an alternative derivation. We will call the resultant grammar G^c. This constraint is similar to the constraint used in the first half of the paper for grammatical constructions; equivalence in number and equivalence in meaning are both instances of logical equivalence where it is necessary for the truth values to be the same in any possible model (although meaning as defined requires a bit more than logical equivalence). A more formal definition follows:

(12) **TDC on Number Generation** A derivation d taking k steps and generating a string that is interpreted as natural number n is ruled out if a derivation d' takes fewer than k steps and also produces n.

The length of derivation for the purely unary method of combination is equal to the value of the number minus one ($n - 1$). The length of derivation with the product-tree is the sum of the value of each product minus two ($p + m - 2$).

For any prime number no blocking occurs because the length of derivation for both the unary-string and the product-string is the same. The proof by contradiction follows: Suppose that for any prime $n - 1 \neq p + m - 2$. For any prime we know that (1) one of the factors will be 1 ($m = 1$) and that the other factor will be equal to the number ($n = p$). Replacing m with 1 and p with n we get the equation $n - 1 \neq n - 1$. Thus, $n - 1 = p + m - 2$ for any prime number n.

For non-prime numbers there will always be a product-tree derivation that is shorter than the unary-tree derivation. To do this we want to prove that for all n there is a p and an m such that $n - 1 > p + m - 2$ which reduces to $pm > p + m - 1$ when replacing n with pm. This can be proven directly:

First solve for m: $pm > p + m - 1 \Rightarrow pm - m > p - 1 \Rightarrow m(p - 1) > p - 1 \Rightarrow m > 1$.

Then solve for p: $pm > p + m - 1 \Rightarrow pm - p$ $> m - 1 \Rightarrow p(m - 1) > m - 1 \Rightarrow p > 1$.

This shows that the inequality holds as long as $m, p > 1$. Since the problem is defined on non-prime factors, the equality holds in all the relevant cases and the TDC will remove all purely unary representations of non-prime numbers.

Thus with the transderivational constraint all unary representations of non-prime numbers will not be members of G^c.

Next, we will intersect the constructed TAL (U) (from TAG G^c) with the complement of the language that contains the product representation of the natural numbers in unary (L'). L' is a regular language because L is a regular language and regular languages are closed under complementation. Since TALs are closed under intersection with regular languages $U \cap L'$ is a TAL if U is. But, the strings that comprise $U \cap L'$ are only the prime numbers: Since, this language does not have the constant growth property it cannot be a TAL. This result shows that the transderivational constraint takes the grammar out of the class of TAL because the properties of all of the other elements of the construction are known.

6.2 TAG with TDC is beyond NP

This section shows that a TAG grammar with the addition of a TDC is beyond NP. This is shown by generating the language MINIMAL.

The minimization problem for propositional formulas seeks to find a minimum equivalent formula for a given boolean formula; the language MINIMAL consists of all well-formed boolean expression for which there is no shorter equivalent formula (Meyer and Stockmeyer, 1972). Minimality ('shortness') can be defined in a number of ways and for the purposes of this proof it will be defined by the number of connectives in the formula. The complexity class of the minimization problem is unknown but it is known to be beyond NP.

The first step of the proof is to make a TAG that generates the set of propositional formulas. The syntax for PL can be defined in the following manner:

(13) **Syntax of PL**

1. any statement letter α is a well-formed formula (*wff*);

2. if α is a *wff* then $\ulcorner \neg \alpha \urcorner$ is a *wff*;

Figure 12: This figure shows how atomic propositions are constructed. Atomic propositions would be the following: A1, A11, A111, etc.

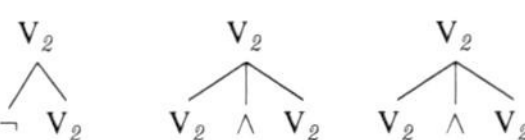

Figure 13: This figure shows trees that with the atomic proposition trees construct (from left to right) negation, conjunction, and disjunction.

3. if α and β are *wff* then $\ulcorner(\alpha \wedge \beta)\urcorner$ is a *wff*;

4. if α and β are *wff* then $\ulcorner(\alpha \vee \beta)\urcorner$ is a *wff*;

5. Nothing else is a *wff*.

A TAG version of (13) follows (which we will call G): The first step creates the atomic propositions in PL. Because of the finite limit to the number of trees in a TAG, the syntax has to recursively construct the atomic propositions. The construction includes an initial tree and an auxiliary tree where the initial tree encodes a single proposition. Each instance of adjunction is a new atomic proposition. The two trees are shown in figure 12. The trees that encode the logical connectives are in figure 13. These trees can combine with one another through substitution to make the full set of possible well-formed formulas for PL.

These trees form G. We can add a transderivational constraint to the grammar (making grammar G^c):

(14) A derivation d taking k steps and producing PL formula m is ruled out if a derivation d' takes fewer than k steps and also produces m.

The addition of the TDC to the grammar would define the language of propositional formulas that do not have alternative semantically equivalent formulas that can be constructed by the TAG in the same or fewer derivational steps. This is equivalent to the minimization problem; if we had an oracle that could determine for any formula ϕ if it was a member of the TAL then we would know the answer to the membership problem for MINIMAL or if we had an oracle that could determine

for any formula ϕ if it was a member of MINIMAL, we would know whether the corresponding tree was in G^c. Since a solution for the minimization problem is beyond NP, the member ship problem for the language generated by G^c is as well.

Given the results that the language generated by a TAG with a TDC is not a TAL and is beyond NP for propositional logic, it is clear that an unrestricted TAG with TDCs is unwanted. I will present a construction in the next section that shows that TAG with the DCCSI and with the addition of the locality constraint (LCC) described in the previous chapter is a TAL.

7 The Expressive Power of the DCCSI

In this section, I will show that the expressive power of TAG is not increased by adding TDCs into the grammar: A TAG with the DCCSI constraint does not exceed the expressive power of a similar TAG variant that does not have the DCCSI. I do this through a compilation: the formalism described in this paper is algorithmically transformed into a standard STAG that is known to be in the mildly-context sensitive class of grammar formalisms. The translation takes three steps: (1) The effects of multiply linked semantic nodes (MLSNs) will be recreated using the formalism outlined in this paper but without having any MLSNs. This step will also make sure that the relevant links are completely ordered with respect to one another. This will allow there to be a single tree for every possible scope configuration. (2) The effects of PRoD and *split combination* will be recreated using the grammar created in step 1 without PRoD and *split combination* and with the overt addition of features to recreate their effects. The addition of features will allow the removal of trees that violate PRoD. (3) The effects of the DCCSI with the grammar created in step 2 will be recreated without the use of the DCCSI. This will be done by eliminating structures that have unwanted scope configurations. Through each step I will show that the increase in the number of trees in the grammar is bounded in a non-problematic way given some restrictions on the properties of natural language grammars. This will show that the grammar created in this paper is no more powerful than a STAG.

This type of proof is possible because the LCC localizes comparison to a single elementary tree.

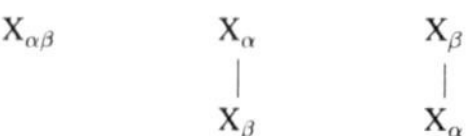

Figure 14: This figure shows the conversion from a multiply linked semantic node to nodes corresponding to the possible orderings of the links. On the left is a node with links α and β. The two trees on the right correspond to the two possible orderings.

It does so by making the compared nodes of the derivation tree necessarily sisters. The comparison can then be represented in a single elementary tree using a finite number of features. The proof goes as follows:

Step 1: Construction of a STAG G' (where there are no MLSNs) from a STAG with MLSNs G: Consider all of the elementary trees in the grammar. In order to convert all trees with MLSNs into trees without them, the following step can be taken: For each node with n links ($n>1$) create a tree for each possible ordering of the links. The ordering is represented by the dominance relation on a single-branching tree. Replace nodes with multiple links with the representations of these ordered trees. This would, for instance take a node $t_{1,2}$ and convert it into two different structures where a t-node dominates another t-node. One tree would have the 1 link dominate the 2 link and another where the 2 link dominates the 1 link. Trees with these structures in them replace the original trees where there are nodes with multiple links.

For n links the number of additional trees is $n!$. For a tree with multiple instances of MLSNs ($m_1...m_n$) the number of additional trees is the product $m_1!... \times ...m_n!$. This, at first glance, is problematic because as n grows, the factorial growth of $n!$ exceeds even the exponential growth rate. This is not problematic for the compilation because of the natural bound of links for a given node. The maximum number of links for a semantic node is the number of nodes in the syntax and since this is finitely bounded, the increase in trees is at worst still manageable. In any actual case, the results will be easier: it is reasonable to think that the maximum number of links for a t node is the number of arguments of the verb plus 1 (for sentence level modifiers.) In conclusion, since there is a finite bound, there is no particular problem with the factorial growth rate.

Step 2: Another necessary step in the conversion is to do the following: Take (scopal) nodes (t-nodes) and make an ordering of their links. If the order is a partial order take the total order extensions of the ordering. Replace the partial ordered trees with their total ordered extensions. For instance, if we have a series of nodes t_1-t_2-t_1, we would end up with t_1-t_2 and t_2-t_1. This step is necessary for future steps where trees are eliminated. Trees where a link is associated with a node that both dominates and is dominated by another link underspecifies the scope relation between different scope taking operators. Since it is necessary to make the scope unambiguous for each elementary tree (in order to remove scope configurations that are unwanted) these trees must be removed from the grammar. At this point, we have constructed separate trees that corresponds to every scope ordering that the linkages allow; in essence this grammar will allow any quantifier to use split combination.

Step 3: Now we have to replicate the effects of the DCCSI. Take the grammar created by step 2 and then remove the tree set types that correspond to the readings that are made unavailable by the DCCSI.

First, we add features that constrain what type of quantifier can adjoin to what DP position of a verbal tree to relevant nodes of trees. In order to get the results described in this paper, for instance, it suffices to only have a +/- quantifier feature, a distributive quantifier feature, and a +/- negative feature. But no matter the actual number of features needed for a complete analysis, it will be finitely bounded.

If the number of features were not stipulated to be finite, the addition of features would exponentially increase the number of trees in the grammar. The addition of trees in general (while also only considering features on arguments) adds $\left(2^n\right)^k$ trees for each tree in the grammar, where n is the number of arguments and k is the number of features.

The nodes of a tree in the worst case would all have the maximal set of features and there would be all of the possible combinations. Since the number of nodes causes exponential growth in the size of the grammar this would be problematic if the number of nodes in the grammar weren't also bounded. Since all trees in TAG are bounded, they must also have a finite number of nodes. Thus,

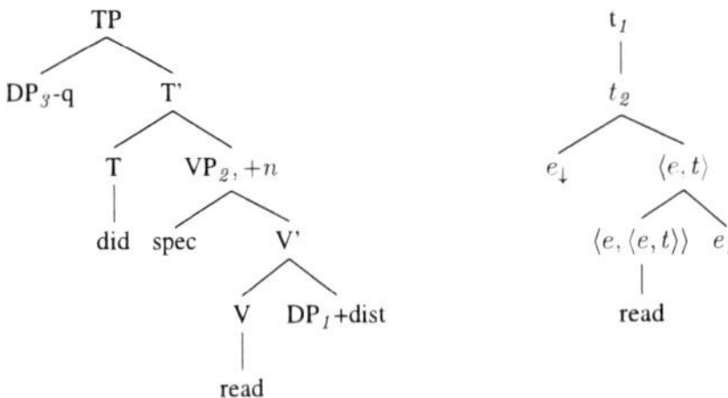

Figure 15: Example of a tree set to be removed to replicate the effects of the DCCSI. This tree-pair would allow a distributive quantifier in object position to take wide scope over clausal negation.

the finite number of features and nodes allows the added number of trees to be manageable.

In figure 15, an example is given; it corresponds to the *not...every* sentences that can not have a wide scope universal reading. Once all of the appropriate tree sets are removed, the resultant grammar is *G'* which is equivalent to G.

This construction has shown how a grammar with a TDC can be a TAL when the comparison class for the transderivational constraint is constrained. Additionally, it was suggested that the growth during the compilation does not increase the number of trees disastrously if some reasonable assumptions are made. For these reasons, it seems that the use of semantic TDCs are not infeasible in grammar when properly constrained.

References

F. Beghelli and T. Stowell. *The Syntax of Each and Every*, pages 71–107. Springer, 1997.

B. Bruening. Qr obeys superiority: Frozen scope and acd. *Linguistic Inquiry*, 32(2):233–273, 2001.

D. Fox. Economy and Scope. *Natural Language Semantics*, 3(3):283–341, 1995. ISSN 0925-854X.

D. Fox. *Economy and Semantic Interpretation*. The MIT Press, 2000. ISBN 0262561212.

R. Frank. *Phrase Structure Composition and Syntactic Dependencies*. The MIT Press, 2002.

M. Freedman and R. Frank. Restricting inverse scope in synchronous tree-adjoining grammar. In *Proceedings of the Tenth International Workshop on Tree Adjoining Grammars and Related Formalisms*, 2010.

P. Grice. *Studies in the Way of Words*. Harvard Univ Pr, 1989.

C.H. Han. Pied-piping in relative clauses: Syntax and compositional semantics based on synchronous tree adjoining grammar. In *Proceedings of the Eighth International Workshop on Tree Adjoining Grammar and Related Formalisms*, pages 41–48. Association for Computational Linguistics, 2006.

I. Heim. Degree operators and scope. *audiatur vox sapientiae. a festschrift for arnim von stechow*, pages 214–239, 2001.

L.R. Horn. *A natural history of negation*. University of Chicago Press, 1989.

R.K. Larson. On the double object construction. *Linguistic inquiry*, 19(3):335–391, 1988.

A.R. Meyer and L.J. Stockmeyer. The equivalence problem for regular expressions with squaring requires exponential space. In *13th Annual Symposium on Switching and Automata Theory*, pages 125–129. IEEE, 1972.

R. Nesson and S. Shieber. Extraction phenomena in synchronous TAG syntax and semantics. In *Proceedings of the NAACL-HLT 2007/AMTA Workshop on Syntax and Structure in Statistical Translation*, pages 9–16. Association for Computational Linguistics, 2007.

Y. Schabes and S. Shieber. An alternative conception of tree adjoining derivation. *Computational Linguistics*, 20:91–124, 1994.

S. Shieber and Y. Schabes. Synchronous Tree-adjoining Grammars. In *Proceedings of the 13th conference on Computational linguistics-Volume 3*, pages 253–258. Association for Computational Linguistics Morristown, NJ, USA, 1990.

The Shape of Elementary Trees and Scope Possibilities in STAG

Robert Frank
Yale University
Department of Linguistics
370 Temple Street
New Haven, CT 06511
robert.frank@yale.edu

Dennis Ryan Storoshenko
Yale University
Department of Linguistics
370 Temple Street
New Haven, CT 06511
dennis.storshenko@yale.edu

Abstract

Work on the syntax-semantics interface in the TAG framework has grappled with the problem of identifying a system with sufficient power to capture semantic dependencies which also imposes formally and linguistically interesting constraint on the kinds of dependencies that can be expressed. The consensus in recent years appears to have shifted to the use of a system that is substantially more expressive than TAG. In this paper, we revisit some of the arguments in favor of more formal power, particularly those from Nesson and Shieber (2008). We show that these arguments can be defused once we adopt a different perspective on predicate-headed semantic elementary trees, namely that they are divided into scope and variable components like their quantificational counterparts. We demonstrate as well that this proposal provides an new perspective on scope rigidity.

1 TAG Semantics and Formal Power

Much of the interest in using Tree Adjoining Grammar as the structure-building component of syntactic theory stems from the combination of its formal and computational restrictiveness and its apparent sufficiency to express the kinds of patterns that are found in natural language. Over the past couple of decades, researchers have attempted to augment TAG models of syntax with mechanisms for assigning semantic interpretations. One line of work in this regard is that of Kallmeyer and Joshi (2003) and Kallmeyer and Romero (2008). In this approach, elementary trees are associated with underspecified semantic descriptions, which are combined using a combinatory mechanism that operates in parallel with TAG derivational steps, essentially a form of feature unification. Though this approach has had considerable empirical success, it does so by sacrificing the restrictiveness of the TAG formal system: unification over unbounded feature structures is Turing complete (Johnson, 1988).[1] An alternative line exploits the TAG combinatory machinery itself to construct semantic interpretations, through a synchronous derivation of syntactic representations and semantic terms (Shieber and Schabes, 1990). Though this Synchronous TAG (STAG) approach is appealing, because it maintains the constrained approach to grammatical combination embraced in TAG, it remains an open question whether it is sufficiently powerful to accomplish the task of assigning compositional interpretations. Indeed, in comparison to the wealth of work on the grammatical complexity of patterns found in natural language syntax, there is precious little work studying the complexity of semantic patterns, or of the syntax-semantics mapping.[2]

Recently, Nesson and Shieber (2008) have argued that there are empirical reasons to move

---

[1] As far as we are aware, Kallmeyer and colleagues have not proposed restrictions on their system which constrains its expressiveness. One interesting avenue to pursue in this connection could follow the work of Feinstein and Wintner (2008) who prove that the class of one-reentrant unification grammars generate exactly the Tree Adjoining Languages. Of course, it remains an open empirical question whether imposing this restriction on this approach would yield a system that is sufficiently expressive to assign meanings in a compositional fashion. We briefly return to this issue in Section 5 below.

[2] See Marsh and Partee (1984) for one notable exceptions, though questions remain about the empirical relevance of this result.

Proceedings of the 11th International Workshop on Tree Adjoining Grammars and Related Formalisms (TAG+11), pages 232–240,
Paris, September 2012.

beyond the tree-local multicomponent version of STAG advocated by Shieber and Schabes (1990) and in Schabes and Shieber (1994), to a system which is greater in power than simple TAG. In this paper, we suggest that Nesson and Shieber were mistaken: the examples that they use to motivate greater expressive power can in fact be dealt with using tree-local MCTAG, but only once we rethink the semantic representations of elementary trees for lexical predicates. We then move beyond English, showing that this new conception of semantic elementary tree set provides a natural way to characterize cross-linguistic variability in scopal flexibility, a variability that is unexpected under the multiple adjunction approach to scope ambiguity. Finally, we briefly discuss a potential analogy between scope and scrambling and the implications that this analogy has for the complexity of the syntax-semantics interface.

2 Puzzles for a Restrictive Semantics

Nesson and Shieber (2008) present a number of sentence types whose semantic derivations they take to require power beyond that possible under tree-local MCTAG. One of these involves "inverse linking", where a quantifier is syntactically embedded within another quantificational NP. Such a case is given in (1):

(1) Mitt courted every person at some fundraiser.
$(\exists > \forall, \forall > \exists)$

To derive an interpretation for this sentence, Nesson and Shieber make use of what has become the standard TAG treatment of quantifiers, given in Figure 1, augmented with dominance links that are crucial only to the inverse linking case. A quantifier's interpretation is assigned two pieces of structure, a scope tree and a variable tree. To derive (1), the quantifier, *some fundraiser*, is combined into the *at*-headed tree set, of which it is

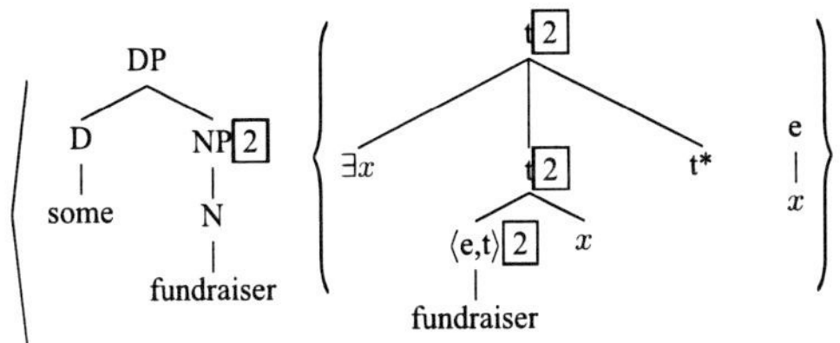

Figure 1: Tree Set for *some fundraiser*

Figure 2: Tree Set for *at* proposed in Nesson and Shieber (2008)

the complement, given in Figure 2: on the semantic side, the variable component of the quantifier substitutes into the $\langle e,t\rangle$-recursive auxiliary tree, following the link in the syntactic tree. However, there is no place in the $\langle e,t\rangle$ recursive auxiliary to host the t-recursive scope component of the quantifier, meaning that tree local combination is impossible. It is only because of the presence of the degenerate t component of this tree set that the combination of the quantifier and preposition is even able to occur set locally. The derivation continues by adjoining the derived tree set into another quantifier tree set, representing *every person*, this time tree-locally, within the set's scope component.

Nesson and Shieber invoke a second kind of example to argue for the inadequacy of even set-local MCTAG. This case involves the interleaving of scopal elements from multiple clauses, of the sort seen in (2).

(2) Some professor remembered to review every paper (that he promised to review).
$(\exists > \forall > \text{remembered})$

In the relevant reading of (2), the universal quantifier that is the object of the lower clause takes scope below the existential matrix subject, but above the matrix verbal predicate. This interpretation cannot be derived even set-locally under standard assumptions.[3] If the tree set associated with

---

[3] In fact, Shieber and Nesson's assumptions about the semantic elementary tree for the control predicate *remember* do not match the ones we are currently making. Instead, they invoke a three-part tree set for the semantics of control predicates like *remember*, including a lambda abstraction over the subject, the lexical predicate and a variable to be inserted into the (controlled) embedded subject position. This move allows them to generate the desired scope for (2), though it does not generalize to slightly more complex cases such as the following, involving a matrix adverbials, as they observe:

(i) Every boy always wants to eat some food.
(always $> \exists > \forall >$ wants)

The proposal we make in the current paper can be seen as

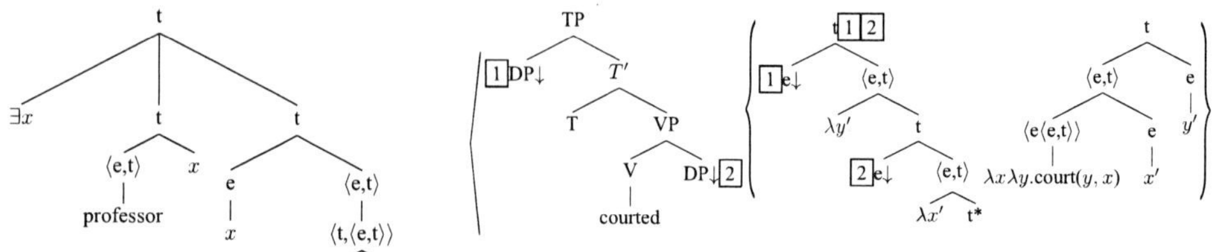

Figure 4: Two-Part Predicate Trees for *courted*

Figure 3: Derived matrix auxiliary tree for *some professor remembered*

the existential quantifier *some professor* adjoins and substitutes into a single-component semantic elementary tree associated with *remembered*, as it must under tree-local or set-local MCTAG, the relative scope of these elements can be fixed (as ∃ >*remembered*), forming a derived auxiliary tree that encapsulates these scopal elements, seen in Figure 3. However, because of the nature of the adjoining operation, there is no way the these two elements can be separated when this derived auxiliary tree into it complement *review*, which will also host the embedded quantifier *every paper*. As a result, this embedded quantifier will be able to take scope above all of the matrix scopal elements or below all of them, but crucially not between them, contrary to fact.

Nesson and Shieber also discuss a third type of example, involving pied-piped relative clauses:

(3) John saw a soccer player whose picture every boy bought.

On the relevant reading, the universal quantifier can take scope outside of the (implicit) existential provided by the pied-piped relative asserting the existence of a picture (i.e., each boy bough a distinct picture of the same soccer player). They argue that neither a tree-local nor a set-local analysis can generate this interpretation. In this case, however, the argument rests on what we take to be an implausible analysis of relative clause syntax and semantics, in which the syntactic head and core semantics of a pied-piped relative clause is provided by the possessive morpheme. Below, we discuss an alternative analysis of such pied-piped relatives in which the relative clause semantics and existential force is provided by a verbally-

headed relative clause tree, and which allows this interpretation to be derived.

3 A Return to Tree-Locality: A New Proposal for Semantic Elementary Trees

Nesson and Shieber's arguments, interesting as they are, rest on assumptions about the nature of the elementary trees that contribute to the relevant derivations. Though the elementary trees they assume are largely in conformity with other proposals in the TAG literature, they provide no underlying theory of what semantic elementary trees should look like. As a result, it is simply unclear whether their arguments hold up if the constituent elementary trees and assumptions about their structure are changed. To get around their arguments and maintain tree-local combination, our proposal in this paper reconceptualizes the semantic elementary trees for predicates as multicomponent sets. These sets will consist of (at least) two pieces: a 'variable part' and 'scope part'. This division is familiar in the TAG semantics literature for quantifiers, and we propose that it be generalized to argument taking elements of all sorts.

Let us be specific about how this works. The semantic elementary tree set for transitive verb, such as *courted*, will contain two pieces. One, which we call the "variable part", will include the lexical predicate with each of its argument positions saturated by variables. The other, which we call the "scope part", contains a lambda operator binding each of the variables in the variable part, with substitution nodes to which each of the lambda operators applies. The resulting tree set is depicted in Figure 4. To use this tree set to derive an example like *Mitt courted some Detroiters*, the subject and object DP arguments will both combine tree-locally in the semantic derivation with the scope portion of the *courted* tree set,

---

a generalization of Nesson and Shieber's multicomponent treatment of control predicates to all lexical predicates. Furthermore, by assuming that temporal arguments license their own semantic component, the scope in (i) can be derived.

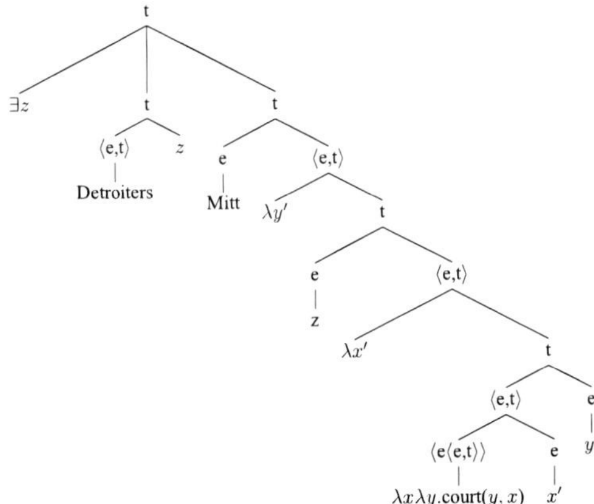

Figure 5: Derived semantic tree for derivation of *Mitt courted some Detroiters*

Mitt through substitution into the higher e node, and *some Detroiters* through substitution into the lower e and adjoining to the root t. When a derivation results with two trees in a single tree set, we assume that they may combine together, with the scope part adjoining to the variable part, resulting in the derived semantic structure in Figure 5. Turn now to the derivation of the putatively problematic inverse linking case (1), repeated here.

(1)   Mitt courted every person at some fundraiser.
$(\exists > \forall, \forall > \exists)$

Note first of all, that our multicomponent approach to the semantics of predicates can be applied to prepositions as well, as seen in Figure 6. Following the derivation tree in Figure 7, the components of *some fundraiser* compose tree-locally into the scope part of *at*, one via substitution and the other via adjoining, just as in the derivation just sketched. Next, both components of *at*'s semantics combine (tree locally) with the scope component of *every person*, via adjoining at either of the $\boxed{2}$-linked t nodes in the quantifier tree set of the same form as the one in Figure 1. If such ad-

joining targets the higher t node, the inverse linking obtains, while surface scope derives from the lower attachment. Now, the derived object quantifier *every person at some fundraiser* can combine with the verbal predicate as we saw, with scope ambiguity with respect to the subject determined by the ordering of the combinations into the verbal scope tree.

Our conception of predicate-headed elementary trees also yields a tree-local treatment of cases of scopal interleaving like (2), repeated here:

(2)   Some professor remembered to review every paper (that he promised to review).
$(\exists > \forall > \text{remembered})$

As before, the tree set representing the object quantifier (tree locally) adjoins and substitutes into the scope component of the (embedded) verb, whose representation will be like the verbal tree in Figure 4. The semantics of the matrix verb *remember* will also involve both scope and variable components, though this time there be an additional variable component corresponding to the controlled argument in the embedded clause. The resulting tree set is given in Figure 8. Interestingly, this tree set is in fact identical to the one adopted by Nesson and Shieber (2008) in their treatment of control. Although they do not explain their motivation for adopting this tree, it is clear that the use of lambda abstraction is driven by the need to have the subject argument of the matrix predicate to bind the variables saturating the external arguments of both the control and embedded predicates. What is less clear is why the lambda operator lies in a separate component from the lexical predicate, and it is this separation that is necessary to derive the scope interleaving. Under the current proposal, the separation of the lambda expression from the lexical predicate into two components is a general property of semantic elementary tree sets. Returning to the deriva-

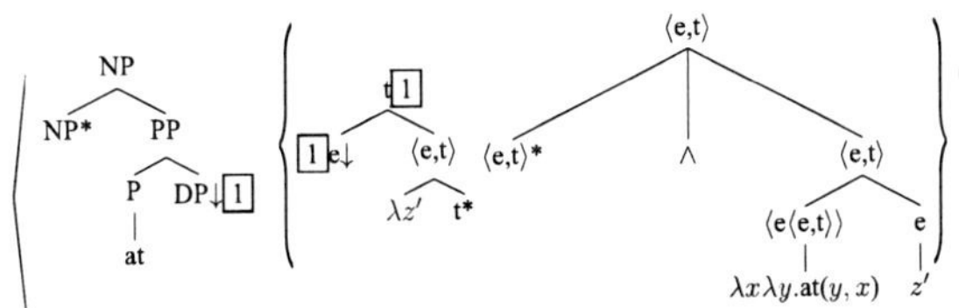

Figure 6: Two-Part Predicate Trees for *at*

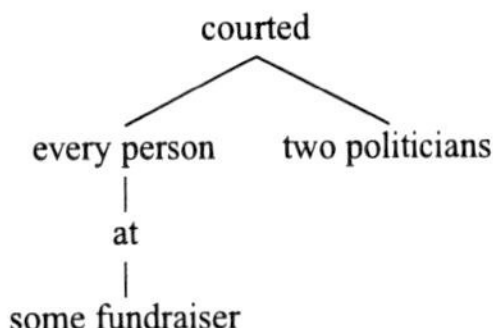

Figure 7: Derivation Tree for (1)

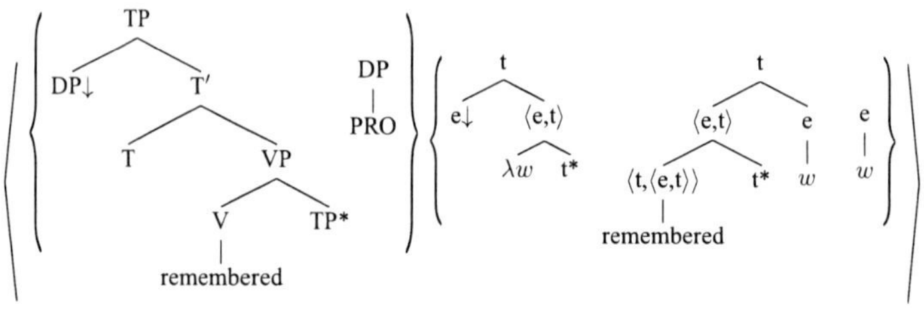

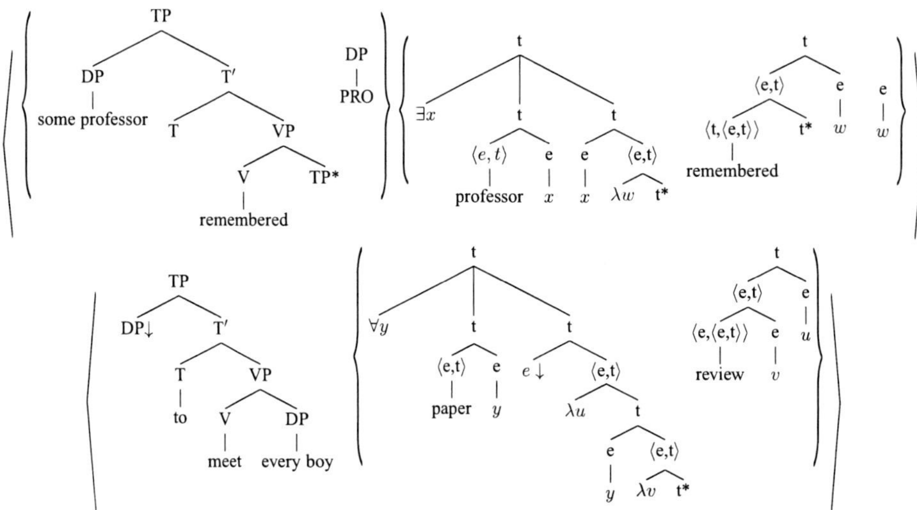

Figure 8: Elementary trees for control predicate *remembered*

Figure 9: Matrix and embedded derived auxiliary trees for interleaving scope in (2)

tion of (2), the matrix quantifier *some professor* will combine tree-locally into the scope component of the *remembered* tree set. The result of these derivational steps is the two derived tree sets in Figure 9. The matrix clause's tree set will now combine tree locally into the scope component of the embedded clause's tree: because of the control relation, it must combine with this tree if we are to be able to substitute the e-type variable (contributed by the control predicate) into the external argument slot of *review*. Now, by adjoining the scope component of the matrix clause at the root of this scope component, and adjoining the predicate+variable component of the matrix at the foot node of this component, we derive the desired relative scopes. As before, we assume that the remaining components are composed to complete the derivation.

Our approach extends to cases discussed by Nesson and Shieber, where additional scopal interleaving arises because of matrix adverbials:

(4) Every boy always wants to eat some food.
(always $> \exists > \forall >$ wants)

The treatment of such cases depends crucially on the incorporation of temporal arguments into semantic elementary trees, about which see Storoshenko and Frank (this volume). We assume that such arguments are lambda bound in the same way as other e-type arguments, in distinct scope components, and this allows us to treat temporal dependencies in a manner similar to control. In the (semantic side of the) derivation of (4), *always* combines with the temporal scope component of *want*, while *every boy* combines with the e-type scope component. The resulting derived tree set then combines, again tree locally, with the scope component of the *eat* elementary tree set. The interleaving interpretation can now be derived if we adopt a version of delayed combination introduced by Freedman and Frank (2010), whereby the different components of a tree set need not be composed into an elementary tree at a single point in the derivation, even if they remain tree local. Specifically, we first adjoin the variable and e-type scope components of the matrix predicate to the scope component of the *eat* tree set. Then, we combine the scope component of *eats* together with its variable component, and finally we adjoin the temporal scope component.

As already noted, Nesson and Shieber argue that tree local derivations cannot generate interpretations for relative clauses with pied-piping, as in (3).

(3) John saw a soccer player whose picture every boy bought.
($\exists$ soccer player $> \forall$ boy $> \exists$ picture)

In fact, we can generate an interpretation for this example by making use of a relative clause tree rather different from the one assumed by Nesson and Shieber. First of all, we apply our split semantics to the verbally-headed relative clause tree set, shown in Figure 10. This tree includes the familiar structure of a t-recursive scope part, and the predicate component. We assume that the existential force associated with pied-piped relatives is in fact associated with this verbally-headed tree set, and is present in the scope part of this set. In addition, this tree set includes a component representing the relative operator, into which the remaining components may substitute. To a degree, this mirrors those accounts that treat the lambda operator associated with the relative as a part of the semantics of the relative pronoun in that the $\langle e, t \rangle$-recursive tree carries only that operator, and takes the remainder of the clause material as an argument via substitution. Though space prevents us form justifying this assumption, we take the semantics of a relativizing DP with a possessive wh-phrase to be of type $\langle e, \langle e, t \rangle \rangle$, so that a wh-phrase like *whose picture* is assigned an interpretation like $\lambda x \lambda y . y$ is a picture of x. The derivation of (3) proceeds by substituting such a relativizing DP and its associated semantics into the $\boxed{1}$-annotated nodes in Figure 10, and combining the universal quantifier at the $\boxed{2}$-annotated nodes. By adjoining the scope part of the quantifier to the higher t node, we can derive the scope indicated in (3), while adjoining at the lower t node will yield a narrow scope interpretation for the universal (where the choice of picture does not vary scope with the boy).

4   Scope Rigidity

In addition to providing a tree-local analysis of certain problematic cases, our proposal for the structure of semantic elementary trees also provides an account of a phenomenon that has received relatively little attention in the TAG literature (but cf. Freedman and Frank (2010), Freedman (2012)). In contrast to English, where subject and object quantifiers often permit both linear and inverse scope, languages like Japanese exhibit scope rigidity, where the scopal relation among quantifiers is fixed by hierarchical order. This is shown in the following example from Hoji (1985).

(5) Dareka-ga   daremo-o   aisiteiru.
someone-NOM everyone-ACC love
'Someone loves everyone.'
($\exists > \forall$, $*\forall > \exists$)

Such scope facts are challenging for any analysis which relies on multiple adjoining at a single t node for all arguments of a given predicate, as scope permutations are predicted to take place freely within a clause so long as the two arguments can combine with verb in either order.

Our analysis as presented thus far does not provide an account of this pattern either: the quantifiers would both combine with the scope part of the verbal elementary tree, in either order, leading to an expectation of scope ambiguity. However, it is straightforward to modify the verbal elementary tree set in Figure 4 to achieve the effect of scope rigidity. In particular, we propose that languages may differ in their representation of scope in predicate elementary trees. In languages like English, lambda operators binding argument variables are collected together in a single scope tree. In contrast, we take canonical clauses in languages like Japanese to be represented by elementary tree sets like the one in Figure 11. Here, the lambda abstraction for each e type argument takes place in its own scope tree. Furthermore, we assume that these scope trees are constrained to adjoin in a way that respects their syntactic hierarchical relation, with the result that the subject lambda abstraction component must be higher in the derived tree than the object lambda abstraction component. As before, we assume that the different components of this tree set, if they remain separate, will compose at the end of the derivation, in a manner that respects the specified hierarchical constraints. Now, if we continue to assume that all

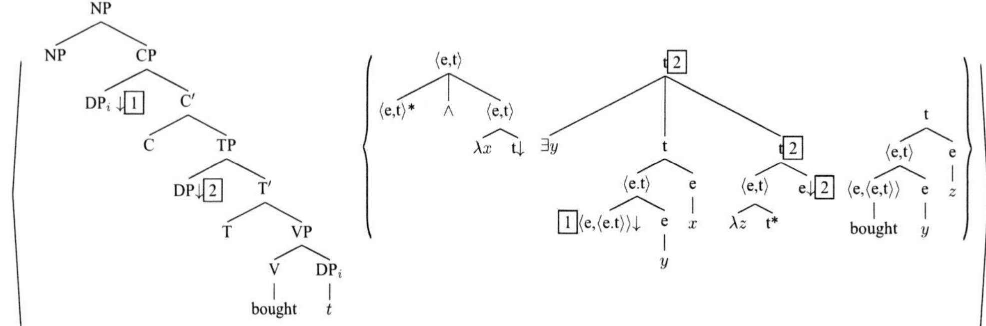

Figure 10: Elementary tree set for pied-piped relative clause in 3

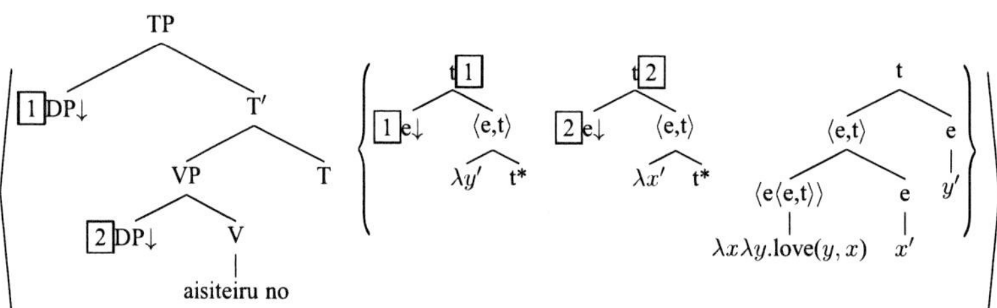

Figure 11: Split scope components for scope rigidity in (5)

combination must take place in a tree-local manner, we derive the unavoidable conclusion that the quantifiers cannot permute with one another: each quantifier tree set substitutes and adjoins to its associated verbal scope tree, with no possibilities for multiple adjoining.

Scope is however not always rigid in Japanese. When an object scrambles past the subject, as in (6), we find the kind of ambiguity familiar from English.

(6) Daremo-o$_i$ dareka-ga t$_i$
someone-NOM everyone-ACC
aisiteiru.
love
'Everyone, someone loves.'
($\exists > \forall, \forall > \exists$)

Such circumvention of canonical scope could of course be modeled by allowing clauses involving scrambling to be derived by an English-like tree set. However, a more intriguing possibility retains the idea of multiple scope trees in Japanese, as in in Figure 11, but removes the hierarchy constraint that we have imposed on the final positions of the scope trees. Scope ambiguity then results because of multiple possibilities for collapsing the

verbal tree set at the end of the derivation. But why would the verbal tree underlying (6) differ in this way from the one underlying (5)? We propose that hierarchy constraints on components of a semantic multicomponent set are the reflection of syntactic hierarchy. In a canonical sentence, the syntax determines a unique hierarchical relation among the arguments, giving rise to a unique possibility for scope. With scrambling, where the object is represented syntactically in both a base and surface position, the hierarchical relation between subject and object is underdetermined, yielding scopal flexibility.

5 A Note on Expressiveness: Scope vs. Scrambling

Though our novel perspective on elementary trees yields a treatment of Nesson and Shieber's problematic cases, one might object that a wealth of other cases await us which cannot be so analyzed. After all, our proposed system for semantic combination remains a tree-local MCTAG, and as such is very limited in the kinds of dependencies that it can capture. Indeed, an anonymous reviewer argues that the kinds of dependencies possible among quantifiers and their variables resembles those between scrambled elements and their associated verbs. The reviewer cites examples of the form in 7, claiming that all scopal orderings of the quantifiers are possible.

(7) Every professor wanted to ask some TA to tell every student to stay at home.

If this is right, the results in Becker et al. (1992) concerning the complexity of scrambling would immediately tell us that scopal dependencies could not be completely captured using tree-local MCTAG.

We see a number of difficulties with this argument. The first of these concerns commutativity of quantifiers. As is well-known, two formulas of first order logic that are distinguished only by the relative order of two quantifiers of the same type (i.e., both universal or both existential) do not have distinct truth conditions. As a result, it is not possible on meaning grounds to distinguish between an ordering of the quantifiers in (7) under which the most embedded universal has scope above the matrix universal or immediately below it. Because of the limited number of quantifier types of natural language, the number of distinguishable scopes will be limited in way that does not parallel the situation with scrambling, where all word orders are easily distinguished. As a result, it remains to be determined whether Becker et al.'s arguments can be adapted to the case of scope, where the set of (semantically distinct) scopes is not equivalent to the set of permutations of the quantifiers.

A second problem for this argument parallels a similar one that has been pointed out for scrambling. As Joshi et al. (2000) note, all word order permutations up to a certain depth of embedding can be generated with tree-local MCTAG using elementary trees of a linguistically plausible sort. To show that a grammar for scrambling requires greater power, we must appeal to more complex cases, whose empirical status is not clear. And although it is not unreasonable to assume that the grammar of scrambling does indeed generalize in way that produces all permutations of arguments over arbitrary levels of embedding including the empirically murky cases (as Rambow (1994) does), Joshi et al. (2000) argue that it is equally sensible to assume that the grammar generates only a subset of the possible cases, because of limits on its generative capacity, so long as this includes all of the cases that are indis-

putably acceptable to speakers. The situation with scope seems to us completely parallel. Although many scopings are imaginable in examples like (7) and more complex cases along the same lines, the empirical situation is far from clear with respect to which interpretations are actually available to speakers. Therefore, the prudent course seems to us to be one which explores the empirical landscape of these cases, in an attempt to find cases that demand additional power.

Acknowledgments

We would like to thank the TAG+11 anonymous reviewers for their helpful comments. This work has been partially funded by SSHRC Postdoc Fellowship 756-2010-0677 to Storoshenko.

References

Tilman Becker, Owen Rambow, and Michael Niv. 1992. The derivational generative power of scrambling is beyond LCFRS. Technical Report IRCS 92-38, Institute for Research in Cognitive Science, University of Pennsylvania.

Daniel Feinstein and Shuly Wintner. 2008. Highly constrained unification grammars. *Journal of Logic, Language and Information*, 17(3):345–381.

Michael Freedman and Robert Frank. 2010. Restricting inverse scope in STAG. In *Proceedings of the 10th International Workshop on Tree Adjoining Grammars and Related Formalisms*. Yale University.

Michael Freedman. 2012. Scope economy and TAG locality. In *Proceedings of the 11th International Workshop on Tree Adjoining Grammars and Related Formalisms*.

Hajime Hoji. 1985. *Logical Form and Configurational Structures in Japanese*. Ph.D. thesis, University of Washington.

Mark Johnson. 1988. *Attribute Value Logic and Theory of Grammar*. CSLI Lecture Notes Series. Chicago: University of Chicago Press.

Aravind K. Joshi, Tilman Becker, and Owen Rambow. 2000. Complexity of scrambling: A new twist on the competence-performance distinction. In Anne Abeillé and Owen Rambow, editors, *Tree Adjoining Grammars: Formalisms, Linguistic Analysis and Processing*, pages 167–181. CSLI Publications, Stanford, CA.

Laura Kallmeyer and Aravind K. Joshi. 2003. Factoring predicate argument and scope semantics: Underspecified semantics with LTAG. *Research on Language and Computation*, 1:3–58.

Laura Kallmeyer and Maribel Romero. 2008. Scope and situation binding in LTAG using semantic unification. *Research on Language and Computation*, 6(3):3–52.

William Marsh and Barbara Partee. 1984. How non-context-free is variable binding? In M. Cobler, S. MacKaye, and M. Wescoat, editors, *Proceedings of the West Coast Conference on Formal Linguistics*, pages 179–190. Stanford University.

Rebecca Nesson and Stuart M. Shieber. 2008. Synchronous vector TAG for syntax and semantics: Control verbs, relative clauses, and inverse linking. In Claire Gardent and Anoop Sarkar, editors, *Proceedings of the 9th International Workshop on Tree Adjoining Grammars and Related Formalisms*.

Owen Rambow. 1994. *Formal and Computational Aspects of Natural Language Syntax*. Ph.D. thesis, University of Pennsylvania, Philadelphia, PA.

Yves Schabes and Stuart M. Shieber. 1994. An alternative conception of tree-adjoining derivation. *Computational Linguistics*, 20(1):91–124.

Stuart M. Shieber and Yves Schabes. 1990. Synchronous Tree Adjoining Grammars. In *Papers Presented to the 13th International Conference on Computational Linguistics*, volume 3, pages 253–258.

Author Index